D1521527

Mark Twain, American Humorist

Mark Twain and His Circle
Tom Quirk and John Bird, Series Editors

Mark Twain
American Humorist

Tracy Wuster

University of Missouri Press
Columbia

ISBN: 978-0-8262-2056-1
Library of Congress Control Number: 2015955238

∞ This paper meets the requirements of the
American National Standard for Permanence of Paper
for Printed Library Materials, Z39.48, 1984.

Interior page design and typesetting: booksbybruce.com
Typefaces: Bodoni and Chaparral

Dedicated with love and laughter to
Jennifer and Josephine

In Memory of
My Dad and Grandparents

Contents

Abbreviations

Budd	*Mark Twain: The Contemporary Reviews*. Cambridge: Cambridge University Press, 1999.
Letters 1	*Mark Twain's Letters, Volume 1: 1853–1866*. Edited by Kenneth M. Sanderson, Edgar M. Branch, and Michael B. Frank. Berkeley: University of California Press, 1987.
Letters 2	*Mark Twain's Letters, Volume 2: 1867–1868*. Edited by Harriet E. Smith, Richard Bucci, and Lin Salamo. Berkeley: University of California Press, 1990.
Letters 3	*Mark Twain's Letters, Volume 3: 1869*. Edited by Victor Fischer and Michael B. Frank. Berkeley: University of California Press, 1992.
Letters 4	*Mark Twain's Letters, Volume 4: 1870–1871*. Edited by Victor Fischer, Michael Frank, Lin Salamo. Berkeley: University of California Press, 1995.
Letters 5	*Mark Twain's Letters, Volume 5: 1872–1873*. Edited by Lin Salamo and Harriet Elinor Smith. Berkeley: University of California Press, 1997.
Letters 6	Twain, Mark. *Mark Twain's Letters, Volume 6: 1874–1875*. Edited by Michael B. Frank and Harriet Elinor Smith. Berkeley: University of California Press, 2002.
MTEB	Hill, Hamlin. *Mark Twain and Elisha Bliss*. Columbia: University of Missouri Press, 1964.
MTHL	*Mark Twain–Howells Letters: The Correspondence of Samuel L. Clemens & William D. Howells, 1869–1910*. Edited by Henry Nash Smith and William Gibson. Cambridge: Belknap Press of Harvard University Press, 1960.

Illustrations

FIGURE INTRO.1 Mark Twain in 1868, San Francisco. Courtesy of Kevin Mac Donnell, Austin, Texas

FIGURE 1.1 Artemus Ward, "An Interview with President Lincoln" from *Artemus Ward, His Book* (New York: Carleton, 1862). Collection of the Author

FIGURE 2.1 Mark Twain Sales Prospectus Poster for *The Innocents Abroad* from *The Innocents Abroad* Sales Prospectus. Courtesy of the Albert and Shirley Small Special Collections Library, University of Virginia

FIGURE 2.2 Mark Twain at the Grave of Adam from *The Innocents Abroad*. Courtesy of Sandra Louise Youngren

FIGURE 2.3 Mark Twain at the Grave of Adam from the *American Publisher* (Hartford, Conn.), July 1872, 8. Courtesy of Hal Bush

FIGURE 2.4 Mark Twain at the Grave of Adam from *Harper's New Monthly Magazine*, May 1875, 849. Collection of the Author

FIGURE 2.5 Mark Twain with Josh Billings and Petroleum V. Nasby, Boston, November, 1869. Courtesy of Kevin Mac Donnell, Austin, Texas

FIGURE 4.1 Mark Twain in the *Galaxy*, August 1870. Courtesy of Kevin Mac Donnell, Austin, Texas

FIGURE 4.2 Mark Twain in the *Aldine*, April 1871. Courtesy of Kevin Mac Donnell, Austin, Texas

FIGURE 4.3 The Lyceum Committeeman's Dream—Some Popular Lecturers in Costume from *Harper's Weekly,* November 15, 1873. Collection of the Author

FIGURE 5.1 Artemus Ward arrives in London—Introduces himself to Mr. Punch. Frontispiece of *Artemus Ward in London* (London: G.W. Carleton & Co., 1867). Collection of the Author

FIGURE 5.2 "Mark Twain" from the *Graphic* (London), October 5, 1872. Courtesy of Kevin Mac Donnell, Austin, Texas

FIGURE 5.3 "American Humour" from *Once a Week*, 259 (December 14, 1872), 521. Courtesy of Kevin Mac Donnell, Austin, Texas

Acknowledgments

Writing a book is a solitary activity that requires a community. It is nice to be able to thank that community here at the start of this book. Any and all mistakes of fact or interpretation are not the fault of that community; they are the fault of my cats—Ada and Rocky. The cats do deserve credit for keeping my feet warm and rearranging stacks of papers in new and unexpected ways.

My dissertation committee helped guide this book from vague idea to completed thesis. Janet Davis chaired my Master's report and dissertation and provided feedback and support throughout my graduate school years. Shelley Fisher Fishkin provided me encouragement to pursue Mark Twain and humor studies, and she introduced me to the field through professional work and personal introductions. Shirley Thompson, Elizabeth Engelhardt, and Phil Barrish provided excellent feedback, astute advice, and key pedagogical models in class and in their feedback on my work. And Brian Bremen mentored, and continues to mentor, me as a scholar and friend.

These scholars were a key part of my academic community at the University of Texas, but many other individuals helped guide me through my experience. Faculty in American Studies—Jeff Meikle, Mark Smith, Steve Hoeschler, and others—and in the English Department—Martin Kevorkian, John Gonzalez, Davida Charney, and Cole Hutchison—provided me with support at various points in my academic and professional development. Cynthia Frese, Ella Schwartz, Brad Humphries, and Valeri Nichols-Keller helped me avoid the pitfalls of bureaucracy and were just plain nice people. Mark Carpenter was both a tremendous boss and a credit to humanity. Bill Fagelson is an excellent friend, boss, and co-teacher.

My experience at UT was largely shaped by the community of students I came into contact with over the years. The key group was my dissertation writing group—Amy Ware, Ben Lisle, and Jason Mellard. Janet Davis's dissertation writing group was also helpful in shaping my research. Tony Fassi, Amy Ware (+Shea), Ben Lisle, David Juarez, Busch, Renee, Pilar, and girlAndi became good friends, which is what graduate school is really all about . . . right? To be clear—I thank Danny Gerling for nothing. I would also like to mention the following friends and colleagues: Allison, Allison, Angie, Anna, Audrey, Axel, Becky, Bill, Brendan, Carly, Croke, Eric, Erin, Gavin, Jackie, Jeannette, Jessie, John, Jonesy, Josh, Katie, Kerry, Kirsten, Kwangjin Kimberly, Laura, Lisa, Marvin, Matt, Mike, Nico, Patty, Phil, Rodney, Rebecca, Rene, Sarah, Sean, Sid, Stephanie, Susan, Vicky, and the members of Machine in the Garden.

Moving outward, my academic career was also shaped by the colleagues and friends I have made in my fields. Judith Yaross Lee mentored me in humor studies, pushed me to get involved in the field, and has continued to support my professional development. Jim Caron has shaped my view of Mark Twain through his scholarship, through his friendship, and through his insightful comments on my book manuscript. Because of Jim, every mention of "Twain" in this book is now a "Mark Twain," which was both a theoretical necessity and a logistical nightmare. Still, I thank Jim heartily. Bruce Michelson has similarly shaped my scholarship and my experience as an academic through smart advice, smart editing, and general smart-ness. Anything dumb in this book, or in my professional development, is not due to the guidance of Judith, Jim, or Bruce. Again, I blame the cats.

Sharon McCoy has provided me with a model of integrity, grit, and passion that all Mark Twain and humor studies scholars have a hard time living up to. That she does so with good humor and grace is both inspiring and humbling. Jeff Melton and Alex Effgen, along with Sharon, have been central to the gratifying work of "Humor in America." I would like to thank the other contributors to that publication: Caroline, Matt, Bonnie, David, Robert, Jan, Tara, Larry, Steven, Matt, Joe, Tom, Jason, Beza, Linda, Amy, Laura, Sam, Carrie, Phil, Don, Alleen, and Ben. I would also like to thank Ann Kiskis, who allowed me to publish a Michael Kiskis piece following his passing, and the family of Michael Giles Purgason, a student of mine who passed away. Writing and editing "Humor in America" has been a gratifying academic and social experience.

The great folks at the American Humor Studies Association welcomed me into the field and put me right to work. Jan McIntire-Strasburg, Ed Piacentino, and Joe Alvarez welcomed me into the organization and en-trusted me with a leadership role. Jennifer Hughes presented with me on many a panel at various conferences and has been a model of dedication. I would also like to thank my academic friends from the overlapping worlds of Twain and Humor Studies: Linda Morris, John Bird, Ann Ryan, David E. E. Sloane, Beck Krefting, Jose Csiscila, Chad Rohman, Larry Howe, Susan

Harris, Jocelyn Chadwick, Tom Inge, Ben Click, Bonnie Applebeet, Joe Slade, Laurie Britt-Smith, Dwayne Eutsey, Kent Rasmussen, Peter Salwen, Horst Kruse, Kerry Driscoll, Hal Bush, Paula Harrington, Phil Nel, Lanita Jacobs, Gillian Johns, Sarah Ingle, Peter Messent, Kevin Mac Donnell, John Pascal, Peter Kaminsky, Mark Dawidziak, and many others.

I would also like to thank the librarians and archivists who made this work possible. The Mark Twain Papers at Berkeley—Neda Salem, Vic Fischer, Benjamin Griffin, and Robert Hirst—helped me with the project both in my visit to the papers and from afar. The staff of the Berg Reading Room and the NYPL and the Harry Ransom Center provided much needed assistance. And Mark Woodhouse of the Mark Twain Archives at Elmira College assisted greatly with my work in Lou Budd's papers. The Center for Mark Twain Studies and its director, Barb Snedecor, provided me with food and shelter for my stay in Elmira, for which I am immensely grateful.

Of course, any good book—make some assumptions there—requires a good publisher. I want to thank Clair Wilcox for taking an interest in this project when it was a tiny baby and for putting up with my delays as I brought it out into the world. Tom Quirk supported the project and gave wise advice. Mary, Jane, and Sara—the excellent editorial staff—shepherded me through the project with grace and patience. The fine scholars and well-wishers of the "Save the University of Missouri Press"—especially Ned and Bruce—deserve praise here for their passion for saving the press from short-sighted bureaucrats. Kevin Mac Donnell graciously provided me with many of the illustrations found herein, as did Martin Zehr, Hal Bush, Dave Thompson, Tom Tryniski, and Sandy Youngren.

Here is as good of place as any: thank you, Steve Martin and Lou Budd.

My friends and family have supported this project and, more importantly, me in ways both big and small. My mom, Sandy Youngren, and dad, Gary Wuster, provided love, guidance, and laughter. Their importance cannot be overstated. If he were alive, my dad may not have read this book all the way through, but he would have been its biggest fan. My stepparents—Judy Wuster, Mike Youngren, and Edna Johnson—helped raise me at various stages of my life, and I owe them each a tremendous debt of gratitude. Growing up, I was lucky in my life to have two father figures. My brother Trent introduced me to so much that shaped my life—key among them, a love of books. Trent showed me that there was more to the world than our small town with its often small mind. The support of Trent and his family—Beckie, Tristan, Tanner, and Nickie—has meant so much to me and my family. That family includes my new parents—Dan and Liz

Jefferson—who welcomed me into their family with love and kindness. They deserve high praise for raising such a terrific daughter.

My love to the members of the extended Mikes Family, the Kinneavy Family, the Rhyne Family, the Subasa Family, and the Jefferson Family. The Nebraska Wusters have always been there for me: Andy and Marvelyn, Sue and Butch, Connie and Mike, Bonnie and Dan, Lindsey and Mike, Dillon and Jennifer, Kelsey and Levi, and Braden, along with the little ones— Macen, Jacen, Liam, Trey, and Andy. I would also like to thank a number of people not related by blood but who are like family. Elaine Ingverstson has long been a family friend. Jody Valentine is the best friend a person could ask for. Amanda McDade, Kevin T. Allen, and Jeff Reading have been friends forever. I would also like to thank Mittie, girlTracy, and Andrea, along with associated husbands and children.

Who knew that the most difficult writing task of this whole project would be thanking Jennifer Jefferson for her contributions to the book and for her overall centrality to everything good in my life. From the initial ideas for this project through each draft to this very set of acknowledg-ments, Jenn has supported me with patience, intelligence, and love. It is no exaggeration to say that this very paragraph may be the only one in this book she did not read and make better. Jennifer has been my untiring supporter, my funniest conspirator, my strongest anchor, and my best friend. She is also the best mom I could imagine for our Josephine, who came along near the end of this project, but joins the cat in shouldering some blame for any recent mistakes. Her knowledge of Mark Twain is scant. Otherwise, she is the best.

Mark Twain, American Humorist

Setting the Scene

Mark Twain, the American Humorist

However, let it go. It is the will of God that we must have critics, and missionaries, and Congressmen, and humorists, and we must bear the burden. Meantime, I seem to have been drifting into criticism myself. But that is nothing. At the worst, criticism is nothing more than a crime, and I am not unused to that.

AUTOBIOGRAPHY OF MARK TWAIN

"Mark Twain" was born on February 3, 1863, in Carson City, Nevada. Some may think he was born earlier, in Missouri somewhere, near the Mississippi River. That is correct, to a degree. "Mark Twain" was not born on that February day, so much as made. Samuel Langhorne Clemens was born in Florida, Missouri, in 1835, the year of Haley's Comet, and he was raised in Hannibal, Missouri, before engaging in a series of careers—itinerant typesetter, Mississippi steamboat pilot, Confederate irregular of very short service, prospector and silver miner, and newspaper reporter. This last job is where Clemens gave birth to "Mark Twain," the last in a long line of pseudonyms, following "Grumbler," "Rambler," "Saverton," "W. Epaminondas Adrastus Blab," "Sergeant Fathom," "Quintus Curtis Snodgrass," "Thomas Jefferson Snodgrass," and "Josh."[1] As a man who lived from 1835 to 1910, Samuel Clemens is a biographical subject—one that includes the forty-plus years during which he was identified with his famous *nom de plume*. Using that name, he created a wide range of cultural performances—newspaper sketches, travel letters and books, articles and stories in periodicals, novels, plays, lectures, speeches, and more—that were all interpreted through the *nom de plume* of "Mark Twain." What meanings attached themselves to that name? How did audiences come to understand the complicated figure of

Mark Twain? And how did Samuel Langhorne Clemens and others work to shape Mark Twain's multiple meanings?

During the first twenty years of Clemens's career as Mark Twain, one label dominated the discussion: humorist. From Clemens's first use of the pseudonym as a reporter through his rise to national and international fame, the description of Mark Twain as a humorist was nearly constant when he was discussed in magazines and newspapers, in reviews of his books or performances, in advertisements and in illustrations, both in America and abroad. Mark Twain was "the famous humorist," "the well-known humorist," or simply "the American humorist." The concept of humorist was central to the making of Mark Twain, along with the related ideas of laughter, joking, irreverence, seriousness, buffoonery, clownishness, satire, and wit. Critics, readers, and Samuel Clemens himself worked to make sense of the meanings of the immensely popular humorist.

The term "humorist" did not signify a low or mass culture position. In fact, the term was often applied to some of the most prominent literary figures of the era: James Russell Lowell, Oliver Wendell Holmes, Nathaniel Hawthorne, and Harriet Beecher Stowe, among others. Building on the model of Washington Irving, humor could be a major component of a well-developed author, who could be a humorist in certain works, and a moralist, a poet, a satirist, or a novelist in other situations. The representatives of quality American humor were closely associated with, and aspired to, English models of humor, tracing a genealogy of humor back to Chaucer and Shakespeare and forward to Thackeray and Dickens. Often, these figures combined their humor with either pathos or satire as an indicator of going beyond the merely entertaining, although both pathos and satire remain undefined in most criticism. Critics saw the role of the humorist in hierarchical terms, as cultural category that included high-culture literary figures, such as James Russell Lowell and Bret Harte; popular humorists, such as "Artemus Ward" and "Petroleum Vesuvius Nasby"; and clowns and minstrels, who were placed at the bottom of the hierarchy. Entering this hierarchy with a splash, Mark Twain muddied the distinctions between class-appropriate leisure and burgeoning forms of mass entertainment, between uplifting humor and debased laughter, and between the literature of high culture and the passing whim of the merely popular.

Mark Twain's reputation as a "humorist" began largely as a story of a supposedly "national humor" found in the works and performances of a small group of humorists who took on a new professional identity as humorists distinct from earlier meanings of the term humorist. The vogue for "American Humor"—which was framed as a distinct subset of the umbrella term it shared—was short-lived, and only Mark Twain emerged into the quality periodical and professional realms that placed him in conversations of canonical American literature. But this was not an easy or clear transition, and it was not fully accomplished in the 1870s or 1880s—if it ever was in Mark Twain's lifetime (or in ours). The hierarchical distinctions that critics used to define humor were clearly linked to ideas of social class. Class-based leisure practices, from reading to lectures to theater, were greatly shifting in this era, as certain forms of leisure were increasingly defined as the province of the educated or refined classes. As Lawrence Levine's examination of cultural hierarchy in the nineteenth century demonstrates, the distinction between high and low cultures was an evolving idea during these years, as once egalitarian entertainments, such as Shakespeare and the opera, evolved into the refuges of various cultural elites.[2] Levine refers to this process as "hierarchicalization," and the question of humor and its relation to class follows a similar pattern as Levine found in other cultural forms. The concepts of humor and the humorist were increasingly coded in class-based language such as quality, refined, coarse, popular, and literary, and the venues where humor was found took on class meanings, as well as racial and gender dimensions.

The hierarchy of humor was not, it should be noted, a simple distinction between "highbrow" and "lowbrow," but instead a dynamic series of debates in which different critics attempted to shape the relative value of humorists through often inconsistent arguments. Examining the responses to Mark Twain's individual books, for instance, shows that some critics found quality in a book that another might dismiss as unworthy of a reader's attention. The efforts of critics and humorists, including Clemens himself, to place "Mark Twain" in this hierarchy of the humorist were never settled, but the multiple attempts to define his cultural freight highlight the myriad meanings of Mark Twain and his milieu. This is a story of widely varying opinions, of friendships and feuds, of promotion and antagonism, of shifting meanings and changing worlds, of debates that crossed oceans as critics debated what "American humor" and "American literature" were and where "Mark Twain, the American humorist" might belong.

In the nineteenth century, defining the role of the humorist in literary and popular culture was not the province of academic literary scholarship—universities were just beginning to recognize American Literature as a subject worth teaching. Instead, influential critics such as William Dean Howells and Josiah Gilbert Holland used their positions as editors of periodicals to shape their readers' understanding of key cultural categories. At the same time, anonymous reviewers from New York City to Central City, Colorado, to San Francisco, from Honolulu to Boston to London (and even the odd French critic), debated Mark Twain's value and the cultural role of the humorist in American culture. Critics varied widely on Mark Twain's meanings in American letters, and they disagreed on the shape and meanings of literary culture more generally. Because the influential critics and journals after the Civil War saw American literature as capable of genuine cultural impact, these discussions also illustrate the ways in which "America," as an idea created and shaped by public discussion, was constructed in various cultures of letters.

The place of Mark Twain in American culture was also shaped in the more concrete literary realm through friendships and antipathies between Samuel Clemens and major figures of American literary culture—both well known and now forgotten: William Dean Howells, Artemus Ward, Bret Harte, James Russell Lowell, Petroleum Vesuvius Nasby, Oliver Wendell Holmes, Thomas Bailey Aldrich (and his wife, Lilian), "Mother" Mary Fairbanks, "Josh Billings," Elisha Bliss, James Redpath, James T. Fields, Harriet Beecher Stowe, Josiah Holland, Charles Dudley Warner, Mathew Arnold, Henry James, James Greenleaf Whittier, and more. Mark Twain strutted on the stage of nineteenth-century culture surrounded by a diverse and wide-ranging cast of characters—and the efforts to make sense of his meaning as he transitioned from minor role to star are central to understanding both Mark Twain and American literary culture in general. In other words, my aim is not to go behind the scenes to meet the real Mark Twain; rather, my aim is to describe the scenes in which Mark Twain came to have meaning.

By discussing the "meanings" of Mark Twain, I am referring to the discussions and debates over what Mark Twain meant to the diverse national and international audiences who encountered him both in print and in person. My aim is to trace how the development of Mark Twain's reputation occurred, not as a simple unveiling of Mark Twain's supposedly true nature as a literary artist, but as a rough critical terrain in which critics varied widely over whether Mark Twain might aspire to literary merit or whether he was merely a passing whim of a debased public. Mark Twain as a cultural figure was shaped by critics and by Samuel Clemens, as that name circulated in American and European literary and popular cultures through newspaper articles, magazine pieces, and books, as well as through platform or lyceum performances and after-dinner speeches.

In each of these cultural locations, Mark Twain came to public attention as a humorist, and the ways in which his works were received—both materially (in terms of books, periodicals, and lectures) and theoretically (in terms of the ways in which people interpreted the idea of Mark Twain)—were distinctly connected with the meanings of this role.

The category of humorist took on whole realms of cultural meaning when words such as quality, popular, genuine, artistic, coarse, professional, profane, or mere were applied to a wide variety of figures—from the performances of clowns and minstrels to the works of elite literary authors. The debates over Mark Twain's meanings as a humorist show the unstable meanings of humor, literature, and related cultural concepts. For instance, the term "quality" might seem to simply refer to the aesthetic qualities of literary works—specifically, the admixture of humor with either pathos or satire—but when one looks closely, the term takes on both commercial and personal resonances. Thus, Mark Twain entered into debates of quality humor when William Dean Howells included him in those debates in the *Atlantic Monthly*—even as other critics denied his "quality." Quality humor, then, was not a category with definite boundaries but a contested territory that critics were continually shaping as new authors and new works entered into the marketplace and as new friendships and enmities formed. Paradoxically, in the effort to settle on a single, stable meaning of Mark Twain, scholars seem to drift further from the most fruitful part of criticism—the tension of debate. This book is an attempt to recover the contested terrain of critical discussion, to understand what it meant for Mark Twain to be a humorist in his own time, and to explore what "humor" signified and encompassed for different audiences of the Gilded Age.

I am engaging Mark Twain as a collection of ideas about a fictional character who circulated in both literary and popular culture, the author of books and sketches, the name of a performer who dazzled and confounded audiences, and the pseudonym of a humorist who would become and remain the most famous humorist in American history. I am not interested in the psychological split between Samuel Clemens, as author, creator, and human being, and his creation Mark Twain.[3] I will refer to "Mark Twain" as a character created by Samuel Clemens—a character who not only appears in stories written by Clemens, but a character who also signs those stories, even the ones in which he never appears, and a character who performs his role on public stages for paying audiences and, it would often seem, for small, semiprivate audiences. I will refer to "Samuel Clemens" when talking about the private man and self-conscious creator of the public persona "Mark Twain," who appeared both in writing and in public. This division is not neat and tidy—from almost the first time the pseudonym appeared in print, critics and readers mixed up and intertwined the names "Sam Clemens" and "Mark Twain," as did the man himself, sometimes signing both names to letters.

In this story, Samuel Clemens shaped Mark Twain both as a character and as a business brand. Clemens's view of Mark Twain's role as humorist was rife with its own ambivalences—between respectability and irreverence, between low and quality humor, between art and commerce, and between literary standing and mass popularity. Samuel Clemens made the Mark Twain *nom de plume* by actively shaping his productions, even if he could not, and did not, control all the meanings of Mark Twain. The fact that Samuel Clemens did not always clearly distinguish between himself and his creation should not keep us from seeing Mark Twain as a character to be interpreted more than as a subject for so many biographies. The overlaps, slippages, and confusions between Mark Twain and Samuel Clemens add to the complexity, fascination, and pleasure of studying Mark Twain.

THE LOCATIONS OF MARK TWAIN

The breadth of Mark Twain's reach during the years 1865 to 1882 was extensive. In order to get at the facets of Mark Twain that I am interested in for this study, my approach focuses on in-depth case studies of specific instances and locations in which Mark Twain appeared on the public stage as both an actor and as the subject of audience interpretation in order to place Mark Twain within larger literary-cultural contexts while also narrating important developments in his career. The goal is not only to understand Mark Twain better, but to show how Mark Twain's position as both a popular humorist and a literary author highlights key transformations of American life: the relationship between increasingly commodified forms of leisure and a literary culture concerned with promoting a national literature that would uplift its readers; the production and circulation of humor and literature and their intertwined critical meanings; the shifting meanings of "laughter" as a cultural expression dependent on class, region, nation, race, and gender; and the circulation of authors and ideas in national and international markets that created a growing culture of celebrity. In the rapidly expanding world of commercial entertainment and the dramatically changing cultures of American letters, public evaluations of Mark Twain were also often discussions of the meaning of American literature, and discussions of American literature were often discussions of the meaning of American culture writ large.

Tracing a history of Mark Twain's transition from Western newspaper humorist to the most famous American humorist of his day requires examining a range of textual, personal, bibliographic, and performative instances across a range of literary locations—newspapers, magazines, lyceum stages, banquets, and books. Mark Twain's reputation was shaped in the print culture of newspapers and magazines and through performances on lyceum stages and after-dinner rostrums, as well as through personal friendships and feuds that took place outside of the public view. While the impressive sales of Mark Twain's books and his sold-out lectures testify to his widespread popularity for mass audiences, the focus of this book is on the ways that critics and authors framed Mark Twain's place in American literature and American culture. Such a methodological approach is partially necessitated by the difficulty in assessing popular readership and the meanings of Mark Twain's mass circulation among a range of readers.[4] But it is also based on my contention that Mark Twain's reputation was mainly shaped by the critical reception of his books, his magazine writings, and his performances, as well as his own framing of his cultural position through his writings, performances, and public life.

Magazines were the major location of critical reputation in mid-nineteenth century American letters. Magazines in both England and America featured discussions of what literature was and should be, if America had any literature worth mentioning, and where humorists fit within a nation's culture. Most notably, a group of American periodicals—modeled on and in conversation with respected British periodicals—helped to shape critical reputation. Designated as "quality" magazines by the editors, readers, and general literary culture, magazines such as the *Atlantic Monthly, Harper's,* the *Galaxy, Scribner's Monthly*, and the *Nation* were a central location of cultural conversation about a range of subjects, from religion and politics to arts and literature. While quality magazines had a smaller circulation than many newspapers and dime periodicals, their influence exerted a central influence over definitions of the "literary" during the Gilded Age. In her book *Reading for Realism*, Nancy Glazener shows how quality periodicals, not the academy, "had the power to confer legitimacy on certain kinds of texts and certain ways of reading them." The critics who wrote about literature in these journals shaped the conversation about what works and authors were part of serious literary conversations. By focusing on the reception of texts in their published contexts, Glazener recasts the way that scholars understand literary cultures and the reputation of individual authors and works: "To begin instead with a sample of canonical works and to invent literary historical categories that account best—or only—for them is to memorialize the values of canon makers, rather than to take up the challenges of valuing works and narrating their historical relations that are presented by any era's range of textual productions by an era's range of textual productions and construction(s) of literariness."[5] Building on Glazener's close attention to periodical contexts, this book's goal is not to understand how Mark Twain fit or did not fit into twentieth- and twenty-first-century definitions of "American Literature" but to understand how specific cultures of letters in the Gilded Age discussed Mark Twain as part of (or excluded from) their criticism—in order to better understand both Mark Twain and the multiple contexts of humor and literature he existed within.

Magazines played a central role in the critical construction of American literature and American humor in the years following the Civil War, but they were not the only venue that shaped readers' experiences. An explosion of daily and weekly newspapers in the mid-nineteenth century increased the amount of reading material available to individual readers, and the "exchanges" through which newspapers shared material meant that news spread across the country, and around the world, more quickly than was possible when printing and communication networks limited circulation. Mark Twain first came to public attention through the newspaper, as a reporter and as a writer of humorous sketches, and then as an object of gossip, used by editors and reporters to fill newspaper columns with writings by and about "Mark Twain," the humorist. This book examines newspaper coverage, but the sheer mass of papers, and the sheer mass of each paper's output, make it impossible to recreate the experience of individual readers or groups of readers. As previous studies of Mark Twain's presence in periodicals have shown, tracing Mark Twain's reputation through individual newspapers produces a mass of conflicting images that might be interesting for larger papers but would require monumental effort beyond the scope of this book if I were to provide a sample of all papers.[6] Instead, newspaper coverage is used to gauge trends and to reconstruct the discourses surrounding individual books and incidents.

Much critical discussion about Mark Twain surrounded the publication of his books—*The Celebrated Jumping Frog of Calaveras County* (1867), *The Innocents Abroad* (1869), *Mark Twain's (Burlesque) Autobiography* (1871),

Roughing It (1872), *The Gilded Age* (1873, in addition to the dramatic version *Col. Sellers* in 1874), *Sketches, New and Old* (1875), *The Adventures of Tom Sawyer* (1876), *Punch, Brothers, Punch!* (1878), *Mark Twain's Scrap Book* (1878), *A Tramp Abroad* (1880), and *The Prince and the Pauper* (1882). Newspapers and magazines greeted each text's publication with critical consideration that attempted to make sense of Mark Twain's place in American humor and American letters. The majority of these books were issued via subscription publishing, which peddled books door-to-door via canvassing agents, rather than being sold in bookstores. This business decision helped Mark Twain reach a mass audience but placed his books at odds with the standard realm of literary circulation and discussion. Subscription books were larger than trade books, often upwards of six hundred pages, and contained numerous illustrations on high-quality paper in order to provide value for customers who paid more for such books. Subscription books were actively marketed by agents who displayed a sales prospectus, or "dummy," that contained sample text, illustrations, and sales puffs that framed the books as products suitable for purchase. These sales dummies are valuable evidence of how Mark Twain's reputation was framed for customers.[7]

The literary reputation of Mark Twain was widely circulated through textual discussions in magazines, newspapers, and books, but his reputation was also shaped by his successes as a public speaker. Beginning in 1866, Samuel Clemens lectured in towns and cities across the country as "Mark Twain," first following the itinerant model of the platform humorist and then as part of the organized lyceum circuit.[8] The lyceum was a key literary activity during these years and a site in which the relationship between humorist and audience was more directly accessible than in a solely textual interchange. After the Civil War, the lyceum began supplementing its educational aim by including humorists as part of the effort to enliven a lecture course (and to sell tickets). Mark Twain lectured on the Sandwich Islands; on his travels to Europe; and on the humorist Artemus Ward across the United States and in England on a number of tours between 1866 and 1873. Mark Twain's successes and failures on the stage highlight the tenuous balance he struggled to maintain between entertainment and edification, the conflicting expectations audiences placed onto the humorist, and the importance of Mark Twain's physical presence as a performer in establishing his identity as a humorist. In these years, Mark Twain was not only the author of humorous texts; he was a living, breathing, joking embodiment of American humor.

Performing his humor both on stage and in everyday interactions, Mark Twain's physical body was a significant aspect of his position as a humorist. Mark Twain took a keen interest in the illustration of his works, which required many images to pad out the required length of subscription books, and his image appeared frequently in his first two books of travel.[9] Illustrations in his books, as well as those in magazines and newspapers, allowed the reading public to visualize Mark Twain. Illustrations spread Mark Twain's public persona beyond a simple pen name by creating a complex mixture of idea and image that readers may have conjured when thinking of Mark Twain. In order to allow readers to picture Mark Twain, the book contains visual images of Mark Twain and related public figures as they would have been popularly available in the time period, as well as personal images where suitable. Mark Twain is such a distinct presence in American culture that almost everyone has an image of Mark Twain in mind. Most often, I would argue, this image is of a white-suited, white-haired man, pictured in black and white and gazing at us from beneath bushy eyebrows. But Mark Twain did not take to wearing the white suit regularly until 1904, and in the 1860s and 1870s, Mark Twain relished creating a spectacle with his wild mane of red hair and his unique Missouri drawl.

The old sage Mark Twain thus must be put out of mind for the remainder of this book. In his place, the reader must imagine the younger Mark Twain, whose physical presence—his dress, his bearing, his speech, and his mannerisms—confused and delighted many, while shocking and dismaying others.

Critics were not the only figures with a vital role in shaping the meanings of Mark Twain. Samuel Clemens was obviously aware of Mark Twain's reputation as a humorist, and he worked to shape those meanings by his choices in publishing, by seeking wider and more respectable audiences, by maintaining friendships with important literary figures, by influencing and reprinting reviews, and by writing about literary concerns in his works. My approach focuses more on those works signed by Mark Twain that relate to his cultural positioning, rather than on the entirety of his works during this era. I look to Samuel Clemens's making of his character's public persona—both in the ways that he privately worked to shape his reputation and the ways in which Mark Twain's writings might have shaped his meanings. I do not, on the other hand, focus on interpreting Mark Twain's major writings. For instance, chapter 2 examines the publication, circulation, and reception of *The Innocents Abroad*, but the chapter focuses almost exclusively on the

FIGURE INTRO.1: Mark Twain in 1868, San Francisco
Courtesy of Kevin Mac Donnell, Austin, Texas

context of the book rather than the *text*. The reader will find analysis of some of Mark Twain's lesser-known works—such as his contributions to the *Galaxy* magazine and the story "A Literary Nightmare"—but only insofar as these works reflect on Mark Twain's position as humorist, author, and public figure in specific contexts.

This book makes use of Samuel Clemens's views—both through the public forum of his writings as Mark Twain and the private views of his letters—to complicate the public image projected by the periodical press. But I have exercised caution, and would advise others to do so as well, not to take Samuel Clemens at his word. The private statements of Clemens and the public pronouncements of Mark Twain are better interpreted as public performances, as his pronouncements are often highly tinted by his skewed interpretations, while sometimes containing patent falsifications. One example: writing to the English critic Andrew Lang in 1890, Mark Twain/Samuel Clemens held that his writing had always had specific class dimensions:

> I have never tried in even one single instance, to help cultivate the cultivated classes. I was not equipped for it, either by native gifts or training. And I never had any ambition in that direction, but always hunted for bigger game—the masses. I have seldom deliberately tried to instruct them, but have done my best to entertain them. . . .
>
> Yes, you see, I have always catered for the Belly and the Members, but have been served like the others—criticised from the culture-standard—to my sorrow and pain; because, honestly, I never cared what became of the cultured classes; they could go to the theatre and the opera, they had no use for me and the melodeon.[10]

This statement, like most of his writings both public and private, must be interpreted as part of a larger reading of his literary and critical reputations. While the quote is highly evocative, evidence throughout Mark Twain's career shows that he aimed for both the approval of the cultured classes and the belly laugh of the masses, along with the pocketbooks of both.[11] The reading of Mark Twain's reputation over time shows that the standards of the elite classes were far from settled, and that the subject of Mark Twain did much to unsettle these further.

Focusing on the development of Mark Twain's reputation requires shifting from strict literary questions to questions about the relationship between literary production and the marketplace. Samuel Clemens was quite aware of the importance of business matters in the development of his career as Mark Twain. Despite the protestations of belles lettres figures—in Mark Twain's time and since—the business of letters was a fundamental consideration in the shaping of critical reputation. As Judith Yaross Lee argues in *Twain's Brand: Humor in Contemporary American Culture,* Samuel Clemens "understood how to exploit Mark Twain as a brand-name commodity of the information economy" in which the circulation of ideas pointed to an emerging postindustrial economy. As Lee notes, the exchange of humor for laughter highlights the commercial nature of Mark Twain's career, in which the brand of "Mark Twain" became both a commercial and aesthetic subject, often in intertwined ways. Samuel Clemens's knowledge of various media, his use of a variety of promotional means, and his decades-long performance as Mark Twain helped establish a durable and influential brand of American humor.[12] And while Clemens was remarkably adept at promoting the Mark Twain brand, he was largely experimenting with a variety of forms during the era under consideration in this book—travel books, periodicals of different quality, almanacs, lectures, commercial products, plays, etc.—that helped make and remake his reputation as he emerged as a national and international celebrity.

Key to understanding Mark Twain's brand was the emergence of the humorist as a professional category in the middle decades of the nineteenth century. Shifts in transportation and communication, especially the railroads and publishing, for the first time allowed humorists to make a living producing sketches, books, and lectures. Daniel Wickberg argues that most scholars of humor in America have viewed humor as a "relatively constant element of national life from the nineteenth century forward." Scholars of humor had largely seen humor as "concerned with the content of humorous texts and schools of writing, rather than the cultural status of humor itself." He writes that only in "the mid- to late-nineteenth century did the term 'humorist' come to refer to the self-conscious creator of a product called 'humor.' Mark Twain, in fact, was probably one of the first humorists in this sense."[13] In fact, Mark Twain followed the model of Artemus Ward to establish his early professional reputation and to spread his *nom de plume* from his western beginnings to the East Coast and Europe. Artemus Ward, the pseudonym of Charles Farrar Browne, combined newspaper writing, book publication, and platform lectures to create an occupation as a professional humorist, and he met with Clemens in 1863 and encouraged him to follow his model. This new class of professional humorist, which is examined in chapter 1, seemed both uniquely American and apart from literary models in which the role of humorist was sub-sumed to that of author. The tension between these two identities is key to understanding the making of Mark Twain as that persona circulated in both mass markets and quality literary markets.

Mark Twain was not the only author of this period affected by market considerations. Authors, editors, critics, and publishers paid close attention to the market, even when they protested to the contrary. The publishers and editors of the *Atlantic Monthly*, for instance, worked to create an *Atlantic* brand that balanced aesthetic aims with commercial necessities. In the 1870s, the magazine offered a portrait of Whittier, Longfellow, or Bryant as an incentive for subscribers. The Whittier birthday dinner, which was framed as a reverent paean to the Quaker poet, was a promotional event used to market the magazine. "Literature" as a subject was not free from the questions of commercialism that helped give meaning to leisure activities from dime novels to minstrelsy, from the circus to newspapers, from opera to Shakespeare. It is crucial to examine the relationships between producers (authors and lecturers), distributors (publishers, periodicals, and the lyceum circuit), and consumers (readers and audiences) in which the meanings of "Mark Twain—the humorist" circulated and took on multiple, and often conflicting, meanings. Quality authors—from Hawthorne to Howells—were never free from the considerations of market, even though they often lamented the fact. From the 1850s through the1870s, the literary marketplace expanded immensely through periodicals, books, and the lyceum, making it possible for authors to circulate their works, their image, and their persons across the nation and across the world. Discussions of cultural production were in many ways theoretical and disembodied, as the "literary" as a subject is an imagined field of thought. But discussions of literary value also took place in material locations: in magazines and in newspapers, in the prefaces of books and in books of criticism, and between individuals, both friends and adversaries—and they often involved questions of money mixed up with questions of literary meaning.

Mark Twain's role as a humorist highlighted the commercial stakes involved in literary production, bringing that which was pushed below the surface into view. When commerce was intentionally repressed, the promotion of Mark Twain's brand could lead to a tension expressed in animosity or disapproval. Samuel Clemens's skill at promoting Mark Twain as both a literary and commercial enterprise discomfited a literary establishment that was struggling with the implications of an expanding information economy. This tension between aesthetic and commercial influenced critical evaluations of Mark Twain's works in his time, and questions about the business of letters have shaped scholarly discussions of Mark Twain.

THE CRITICAL REPUTATION OF "MARK TWAIN"

The roots of Mark Twain's reputation are to be found in the 1860s and 1870s, and the critical categorization of Mark Twain as a humorist affected the ways in which he was understood over the course of his career and after. Academic discourse has largely confined Mark Twain to the category of literary author and in the discipline of English, most often starting from a presumption that Mark Twain should be judged within limited categories of literary study. The goal of this book is to avoid imposing a twentieth- or twenty-first-century vision of Mark Twain—a complex cultural image with its own more than century-long history—onto the Mark Twain that critics and readers may have encountered when he first emerged onto a national stage.[14] The Mark Twain of the late 1860s, the early 1870s, the late 1870s, and so on was not the Mark Twain that we have come to know in retrospect. When he sailed for the East Coast as a newly celebrated humorist and lecturer in 1866, he was not yet the author of *The Innocents Abroad*. When he was reviewed and praised by William Dean Howells in the December 1869 *Atlantic Monthly*, he was not yet the author of *The Adventures of Tom Sawyer* (1876). Even when he began publishing novels and stories, including in the prestigious *Atlantic Monthly*, he was not yet the author of *Adventures of Huckleberry Finn* (1884), which itself was less celebrated at publication than one might expect. And when he became, as Howells claimed in 1882, "the most popular humorist who ever lived," he was not yet accepted by all critics as a part of a canon of American literature who would be taught in schools and discussed at conferences. It is good to remember that Mark Twain's development was not teleological; there is no straight line from the Jumping Frog to Huck Finn or from William Dean Howells to the American canon. Close attention to how Mark Twain was positioned shows that the critical debates over the meanings of Mark Twain are central to understanding him as a subject.

In the late 1860s and early 1870s, many critics held that one particular humorist stood out as a possible genius whose characters and stories belonged in quality publications: Bret Harte. Rising to fame around the same time as Mark Twain, Harte's reputation largely existed separately from the classification of "American humor." He did not perform as a pseudonymous character as many humorists did. He wrote humorous poems and short stories in which humor shaded into pathos, a quality Harte shared with James Russell Lowell and other quality humorists. Moving east in 1870, Harte was welcomed into the circle of the *Atlantic Monthly* and rewarded with a contract to write for the magazine for one year for a $10,000 salary—an unprecedented sum for that time. Harte's early success as a quality humorist, and his later decline as a writer, is a key part of the history of Mark Twain's reputation. As a friend, editor, reviewer, collaborator, and sometime-enemy of Mark Twain's, Bret Harte played a major role in the cultural framing of the category of humorist.

William Dean Howells's promotion of Mark Twain, both in the textual culture of the *Atlantic* and in the personal realm of their budding friendship, is a central aspect of the history of Mark Twain's literary reputation. William Dean Howells first reviewed Mark Twain in 1869, before the two had met, and his praise helped transform the humorist's reputation by placing him in the critical conversation with quality literary humorists, marking a shift into a literary realm that would forever transform his standing. Howells used his editorial platform at the *Atlantic Monthly* to argue that Mark Twain belonged with Bret Harte and Charles Dudley Warner, two humorists Howells promoted as worthy of the company of James Russell Lowell and Oliver Wendell Holmes, the two giants of humor who had both shaped the *Atlantic Monthly* and existed as icons of quality American humor. At times, Howells had to excuse or gloss over instances of Mark Twain's "irreverent" or "coarse" humor, or skip reviewing certain books altogether. But his criticism increasingly argued that Mark Twain's humor was the outward manifestation of a serious moral or artistic purpose—or as Howells put it: "the foamy break of a strong tide of earnestness in him." Mark Twain's humor fit Howells's developing critical ethos at the *Atlantic Monthly*, which modified James Russell Lowell's focus on "humane" and "human" literature into a protorealism that could be found in all genres, from fiction to travel writing and from history to humor. Howells's reframing of Mark Twain's humor as instrumental attempted to elevate him into the more respectable echelons of the hierarchy of humor, although this transformation was neither a smooth road nor a fait accompli.

Howells was not at this point known as "The Dean of American Letters," but he possessed an important platform for shaping American literary tastes. Through encouragement to write for respectable audiences, through publishing his work in the *Atlantic Monthly*, and through critical praise, Howells pushed Twain/Clemens into new realms of literary reputation.

After the critical thrashing of *The Gilded Age* (as Clemens remembered it, at least), Samuel Clemens began to send his books to Howells and a select few critics to set the tone for subsequent reviews—going so far as to send the manuscript of *The Adventures of Tom Sawyer* to Howells for simultaneous editing and review. Clemens, for his part, appreciated the guidance and prestige this friendship brought, and both he and Howells grieved at the perceived disaster of Mark Twain's "failed" speech at the Whittier birthday dinner in 1878.

The centrality of Artemus Ward, Bret Harte, and William Dean Howells in the formation and transformation of Mark Twain's reputation highlights the comparative nature of literary reputations. Too often, scholars frame Mark Twain as a subject unique unto himself, not clearly a part of the era's literary history or of the history of humor of the time. During the 1860s and 1870s, critics discussed Mark Twain in relation to Bret Harte, John Phoenix, and other Californian authors; in relation to the professional humorists, especially Artemus Ward, Josh Billings, and Petroleum V. Nasby; in relation to English authors such as Dickens, Lamb, and Thackeray; and in relation to quality, American humorists such as James Russell Lowell and Oliver Wendell Holmes. As the 1870s progressed, critics began to discuss humorists in relation to Mark Twain, such as the German-dialect poet "Hans Brietman" (Charles Leland) and the humorous essayist Charles Dudley Warner.

The meanings of the cast of characters who performed on the stage of American culture with Mark Twain were the source of critical debates and disagreements over the meanings of American humor and American literature. One major thread of this book is the examination of critical evaluations of Mark Twain's multiple meanings—from the well-known Howells to the then-well-known, but now-forgotten Josiah Holland, who dismissed Mark Twain as a "buffoon" and "trifler," representing the most vocal of critics who sought to diminish his importance or to cast him out of the sacred realm of American Literature. For almost each book or performance between 1865 and 1882, a critic can be found arguing that Mark Twain should be considered a quality humorist for every review considering him a low, ephemeral humorist. Between these poles, critics argued both that he was developing in artistic stature and that he was decreasing in talent; that his humor was of use as a respite from a careworn society or that his humor was a damaging fraud; that his humor was merely entertaining or that it was something more than mere entertainment. These critical debates show that ideas about hierarchy clearly shaped critical discourse, but that Mark Twain did not clearly fit in any one category. In fact, Mark Twain is central to Gilded Age literary and popular cultures both because he muddied these hierarchical categories and because critical evaluations of his meanings highlight key aspects of American literary culture more generally.

Critical debates over the meanings of Mark Twain's works, as they shifted in response to specific books and performances, are another central thread of this book, but these debates can also be seen in the shaping of Mark Twain's scholarly reputation after his death and as he began to be incorporated into academic scholarship in the 1920s. If Mark Twain's popularity had remained confined to that of popular humorist, he may have remained grouped with Artemus Ward, Petroleum Vesuvius Nasby, and Josh Billings—the representatives of American humor with whom he rose to fame. Instead, Mark Twain escaped consignment to a dusty history of American culture and became an icon of American literature, whose works continue to be taught, read, and discussed a century after his death. A large part of this canonization and the broader American culture took place in the aftermath of his death in 1910, through debates within academia and through the complicated work of public memory and memorialization.[15] In the more than a century since Samuel Clemens's death, scholars, authors, and critics have spent innumerable pages trying to define, encapsulate, place, promote, dismiss, redefine, condense, appraise, reconsider, evaluate, re-redefine, examine, analyze, judge, and/or come to terms with the cultural meanings of Mark Twain.

Following Clemens's death and with the increasing presence of American literature in the academy, critics and scholars debated whether and where Mark Twain should be placed in a canon of American literature—a canon that was constantly being shaped and reshaped throughout the twentieth century and into the current century. In Mark Twain scholarship, as during the career of Mark Twain, the meaning of the concept of humorist was a central thread of discussion. But the meanings of humorist in the early twentieth century and on was different than the mid- to late-nineteenth century definitions. The tendency to fix the high-culture, literary world of belles lettres in a binary relationship with the low-culture realms of popular culture creates a puzzle when scholars encounter Mark Twain. One solution, pioneered by Howells, has been to describe a transition from popular to quality, as Mark Twain shifted from early popularity to later literary status. Such an approach necessitates diminishing much of Samuel Clemens's career and the always complicated links between literature and commerce. Another approach has been to lament Samuel Clemens's artistic failures because of Mark Twain's entanglements with popular culture and the marketplace, which are argued to have tainted his artistic development. Neither model is perfect when examining the making of Mark Twain.

Instead, the example of Mark Twain highlights how scholars should not imagine a distinct split between the high culture of belle lettres and the low culture of popular forms. Instead, the literary realm begs to be seen as possessing multiple, often overlapping, yet sometimes conflicting visions of the hierarchy of literature—and of the role of humor in those hierarchies. Literary cultures and popular cultures were not as separate as scholarly disciplines might hold, making it useful to look at literary activities (writing and reading, as well as publishing, performance, and reviews) as leisure activities that should be examined as communal experiences. In this view, literature should be studied not as solitary activity undertaken in a cultural vacuum, but as a social activity in which an imagined community of readers is constructed in different cultures of letters that have important class, gender, race, and national characteristics.

This book's reading of Mark Twain builds on the literary historian Richard Brodhead's concept of "cultures of letters" to examine the multiple ways in which "Mark Twain," as a cultural idea, circulated for multiple publics. In his view, reading is an "acculturated activity," inseparable from the production, distribution, and reception of texts. He writes: "Writing always takes place within some completely concrete cultural situation, a situation that surrounds it with some particular landscape of institutional structures, affiliates it with some particular group from among the array of contemporary groupings, and installs it in some group-based world of understandings, practices, and values."[16] Instead of framing reading as a solitary activity of isolated readers, scholars should see reading as a form of leisure in which individual actors are imagined, and imagine themselves, as part of a group activity of reading various forms of literature. Mark Twain participated in a number of distinct but overlapping cultures of letters in which writing, reading, and laughing took on different and often contested cultural meanings.

Building on Mark Twain and humor studies scholarship, while at the same time preserving the fluid and dynamic nature of Mark Twain's cultural meanings, I argue that there was not one "Mark Twain," but multiple and overlapping images of a complex character in a time of great changes in American literature and American life. Bruce Michelson speculated in

Mark Twain on the Loose (1995) that there has probably been more scholarship devoted to developing plausible theories about what Mark Twain signified than any other American writer of the past two centuries. The urge is toward stabilization, he argues, or the search for "Mark Twain's concealed organizing principles" under a dominant theme or formulation. Michelson writes: "Delving into the affirmation, the grand serious theme, the noble design that lurks (or ought to, as Mark Twain's wisest readers have usually assumed) in the depths of a text or its creator, commentary risks degrading whatever must be dug *through*." The surfeit of Twain scholarship, and of Mark Twain's own writings, calls into question the very processes and goals of such scholarship—eventually any stable "Mark Twain" can be destabilized by another approach or by Clemens/Twain's statements, which often contradicted any stable definition of self or character. By questioning what he sees as "a will to *contain*," Michelson provides a different stance for undertaking scholarship on Mark Twain as an open and flexible field that more closely reflects the complicated performance that was Mark Twain. Michelson's approach to Mark Twain as a subject entails examining and redefining a number of key terms and figures that may have become sedimented in scholarship: "humor" and "literature" to start with, but also "genuine," "coarse," "quality," and "American," as well as the locations one might find these things, such as "subscription books," "the *Atlantic Monthly*," and "the lyceum."[17]

The goal of taking humorist as the central keyword is not to settle on any one definition of that term but to show how the discussions of that term helps us, as scholars, to better understand the figure of Mark Twain and his relationship to American humor and American literature. A first step in reframing the concept of humorist as a fluid and dynamic term necessitates unloosing the term from its fixed meanings in Mark Twain and humor studies scholarship. Central to the founding feud of Twain scholarship is a debate over the role of humorist in Mark Twain's career. Both Van Wyck Brook's *The Ordeal of Mark Twain* (1920) and Bernard DeVoto's *Mark Twain's America* (1932) must be seen within the process by which American literature, as a subject, was coming to be included as a subject worthy of serious study in the academy. Within this context, both scholars sought to diminish the meaning of Mark Twain's role as a humorist, and both critics began with the assumption that Mark Twain should be viewed as an author, an identity separate from, and above, his role as a humorist—a critical legacy that has meant focusing on his novels, with *Adventures of Huckleberry Finn* (1885) as the center of his oeuvre.[18]

For Brooks, Mark Twain's commercial success as a humorist went against Mark Twain's nature and stifled his artistic development. He wrote, "I think we can understand now the prodigious practical success it brought him. And are we not already in a position to see why the role of humorist was foreign to his nature, why he was reluctant to adopt it, why he always rebelled against it, and why it arrested his own development? Obviously, in Mark Twain, the making of the humorist was the undoing of the artist." For DeVoto, Mark Twain was an artist, not primarily a humorist, who was shaped by the frontier and was one of the only important American authors of his period. This argument necessitated rescuing Mark Twain from the charge of being a mere humorist: "However abhorrent the term, he is a humorist before anything else. All other American writers to whom the term is applicable are insignificant compared to him."[19] Both Brooks and DeVoto rest their arguments on their assumptions of what it meant to be a humorist, not how critics and authors in the nineteenth century defined the humorist.

Much of the history of Twain Studies, and of the often overlapping field of humor studies, has been heavily influenced by the basic assumption of this argument—that Mark Twain started out as a humorist but eventually sought to become a literary author. DeVoto went so far as to argue, "So far as any simplification is trustworthy, this one may be ventured upon: the course taken by the literary career of Mark Twain was inevitable . . . nothing very much different from what actually happened could have happened." In opposition to such a teleological vision of Mark Twain, I argue that his transformation from Western newspaper humorist to established literary author was not inevitable nor was it entirely "literary" in the way literary scholarship has often framed that term. In the nineteenth century, the literary and the commercial were not mutually exclusive, nor was the humorist divorced from the "author" in the way in which Brooks and DeVoto assume. While tensions clearly existed between art and its marketplace, these tensions were different in the nineteenth century than twentieth-century scholarship often held.

Subsequent Twain scholarship was forced to account for or defend Mark Twain's position as a humorist. The 1960s saw a shift in focus in Mark Twain studies toward in-depth studies of Mark Twain's humor.[20] In *Mark Twain: The Development of a Writer* (1962), Henry Nash Smith framed the problem of Mark Twain's reputation as a humorist as a matter of the humorist's exclusion from the high-culture realm of belles lettres, largely symbolized in this era by the literary culture of the *Atlantic Monthly*. In discussing his vocation as a humorist, Smith argued that this designation left him in a vexed position: "If he hoped to be accepted as a serious writer, he was apparently obliged to conform to the priestly role of the man of letters. If he devoted himself to humor he must be content with the humble function of providing comic relief from higher concerns." Such a view relies on the binary between high and low, in which high art is viewed primarily as serious and low culture is consigned to matters of popularity and commerce. The perceived distance between high and low, literary and popular, was a creation of the intellectual climate of early academic study of American literature, which privileged the darker, more complicated works of the nineteenth century that reflected the modernist impulses of the times.[21] James Cox, in *Mark Twain: The Fate of Humor* (1966), classified Mark Twain's humor more extensively than previous critics, but to a large extent he relied on the foundation of Brooks and DeVoto. For Cox, Samuel Clemens's decision to adopt and keep the Mark Twain pseudonym "committed him to the fate of a humorist, a fate which Samuel Clemens lived through to the end. Though he came more and more to resent the fate, he never really cast off the identity." The identity of the humorist determined "Mark Twain's" fate to always be humorous. Cox does not deny Mark Twain's role as humorist, but he does start from a view of humor that opposes the humorous and the serious—creating a two-poled theory that precludes the humorist also being a moralist or satirist.[22] While I think Cox is correct to say that attempts to claim that Mark Twain is really "serious" has been a way for some supporters to transform him into the scholarly realm of high art, his argument that "seriousness is . . . the antithesis of humor" leads to an argument that calcifies cultural categories that were (and are) nothing if not fluid and ill-defined.

My examination of the critical reception of Mark Twain shows that the role of the humorist was not an either/or proposition between serious literature and humorous entertainment but a both/and conflict played out in Mark Twain's own cultural position and in critics' views of him. Mark Twain's entry into the respectable literary realm, largely through his tentative acceptance by Howells and the *Atlantic Monthly*, highlighted the tension between the irreverent humor of the frontier and the more restrained humor of New England. Hamlin Hill's statement is indicative: "The Wild Humorist of the Pacific Slope began to edge—sideways, to be sure—into the area of (capital *L*) Literature. It was his special version of the Great Unknown, and Literature never ceased to confuse and frustrate his genius, to be a no-man's-land where he wandered, guided in part by the precepts of his neighbors and in part by the contradictory suggestions of his own magnificent instinct."[23] There were certainly tensions between Mark Twain as a humorist and the New England literary culture, although the tension was not between humorist and serious literature so much as between different hierarchical levels of humor. Rather than the antagonistic relationship between wild frontier humorist and restrained Bostonian, the tension is to be found in close attention to both the varied cultural meanings attached to Mark Twain and the ways in which Clemens made and then remade his character to respond to concerns about both literary standing and fiscal necessity.

The lack of critical attention to the role of the humorist as one who produces humor meant that Mark Twain studies began with a tendency to fix the meanings of Mark Twain's humor into conceptual categories that necessarily elided the complicated, often conflicting, meanings of the classification of Mark Twain as humorist. While there is plentiful and excellent work on the distinctions between individual, regional, and national types of humor as they changed over the course of American history, there is very little that looks at the humorist as a cultural role or as a historical concept. In *American Humor: A Study of the National Character* (1931), Constance Rourke uses the term humorist only four times (twice in a quotation), vacillating between writing about humor as if it just appeared and discussing the works of "authors." Walter Blair, in *Native American Humor* (1960), used the term as if its meaning were self-evident: a humorist was one who produced humor. Very little humor studies scholarship has taken up the shifting meanings of "humorist," or related terms such as comedian, wit, jester, etc. This book represents an initial sounding of these terms in relation to Mark Twain's reputation.

Twain scholarship has increasingly turned toward Mark Twain's complicated place in American cultural history, including increased attention to his ideas of race, class, gender, and nation. Scholars have also demonstrated a renewed interest in the genres and modes in which Clemens made a name for "Mark Twain," such as travel writing, newspaper sketches, lyceum lecturing, playwriting, and a variety of ephemeral forms of performance (occasional speeches, newspaper letters, humor collections, and personal relationships). This cultural turn has opened up new avenues of study for those interested in understanding the role of Mark Twain in the culture of the Gilded Age. My interpretation builds on the work of a number of scholars who have taken Mark Twain as a complex subject whose meaning existed on multiple levels of American culture, starting with Louis Budd's

Our Mark Twain: The Making of His Public Personality (1983), which traces the public image of Mark Twain as a self-creation and a public image that took on its own forms. Budd's focus on Samuel Clemens's creation and adaptation of the public persona of Mark Twain encourages closer attention to the cultural contexts in which various audiences encountered Mark Twain and constructed their own versions of his meaning. But Budd, like many scholars before him, relied on a core definition of humorist that heavily influenced his reading of Mark Twain. He writes: "The function of the humorist centers in resistance, in a liberating aggression that can spin toward tedious venom or anarchy." His role as a subversive humorist allowed Budd to reframe Mark Twain's value and to promote him as a "culture-hero." However much one may or may not agree, this scholarly approach uses a single definition of the humorist to create a new way to classify humor, one that necessarily changes the way Budd approaches Mark Twain's career.[24]

Adding to the complexity of the study of Mark Twain, Leland Krauth argued in *Proper Mark Twain* (1999) that the longstanding critical focus on the subversive Mark Twain has obscured the bounded Mark Twain who "honors conventions, upholds proprieties, believes in commonplaces, and even maintains the order-inducing moralities."[25] Rather than an "outlaw comedian," Krauth finds a tendency to "conventional nineteenth century norms for art," including a link between humor and pathos, compassion, and seriousness. Krauth does not argue that this proper Twain was the only or real Mark Twain, but that ignoring the proper in favor of the subversive misses a key aspect of the Mark Twain persona. I follow this approach to show how Samuel Clemens, especially in his relationships with Mary Mason Fairbanks, Olivia Clemens, and William Dean Howells, increasingly framed Mark Twain in more respectable terms as a quality humorist.

My goal is to avoid hagiography in imposing my own values and definitions onto Mark Twain—making him a star of a different drama than his own (or of a comedy of my own making). For instance, I seek to avoid the tendency in recent humor scholarship to privilege the subversive elements of humor over elements that might reify cultural values or that might simply be fun or may be more conservative than the scholar might like. The aim of my approach is to pay close attention to the shifting evaluations of Mark Twain's critical reputation as shaped by Mark Twain, as well as by critics, friends, and detractors.[26] If the meaning of humor is confined to the cultural subversion of the jester or satirist, then much of the humor of Mark Twain (and others) is written out of cultural importance. Much of Mark Twain's humor falls outside the realm of humorous cultural critique and must be classified as merely pleasurable or even supportive of cultural values that are viewed, in retrospect, as conservative, middle class, Victorian, or some other sobriquet for "old fashioned." The danger is that scholars and readers might judge Mark Twain from our own values, making him either better or worse than one might hope. Instead, the aim of this book is to understand the literary context of his role as humorist within the cultural milieu of his time—not as a hero, nor a villain, but as a key figure in understanding Gilded Age America.

THE AMERICAN HUMORIST: MARK TWAIN'S STAGES

In tracing the development of Mark Twain as a humorist, I have distinguished between three rough stages marked by the dominant critical images of Mark Twain, the main cultural locations in which he was discussed, and Samuel Clemens's efforts to shape his literary reputation. These stages are meant to be useful tools rather than definite demarcations in the meanings of Mark Twain. The first stage runs roughly from the birth of Mark Twain in 1863 through Samuel Clemens's departure from California in late 1866. This ground has been covered quite fully, and I focus mainly on the aftermath of his Western years: the circulation of Mark Twain's reputation outside of the West, the reception of his first book in 1867, and the more general meanings of American humor that helped frame Mark Twain as he became a national and international figure. The move of Samuel Clemens to the East inaugurated the second stage, which was marked by significant personal and professional developments. The influence of "Mother" Mary Fairbanks, and his engagement and marriage to Olivia Langdon, pushed Samuel Clemens to shift Mark Twain's humor to appeal to more respectable audiences, both in his lecture tours and in his first book of travel. During the late 1860s and early 1870s, Mark Twain experimented with a range of more respectable venues for his humor and found a larger and larger audience as he became the most prominent of the popular American humorists. The third stage, I argue, was initiated by William Dean Howells's review praising *The Innocents Abroad* in the *Atlantic Monthly*. While this review did not mark a complete shift in Mark Twain's critical reputation, it did raise the possibility of Mark Twain belonging in the realm of quality humor and, by extension, in the realm of respectable American literature that the magazine promoted. The keynote of this stage was the tension between those who classified

Mark Twain as a quality humorist and those who argued he held little value for American culture.

The first stage was characterized by Mark Twain's birth and development as a newspaper reporter, magazinist, and lecturer in California—with the nicknames of "the Wild Humorist of the Pacific Slope," "the Washoe Giant," and the "Moralist of the Main." During these years, Mark Twain worked for a variety of newspapers and magazines in Nevada and California as he experimented with the possibilities of his humorous persona. James Caron's book, *Mark Twain, Unsanctified Newspaper Reporter*, examines Mark Twain from 1863 through 1867 as a "comic performer" and "literary vehicle," who performed on a public stage in a variety of humorous roles, including the citizen clown, the literary flâneur, and the gentleman roarer.[27] Caron traces Clemens's evolution of the Mark Twain character who left behind regional attitudes and adopted an urbane stance as a cultural critic—a move that included the desire to reach national audiences. My book attempts to pick up the story from there: to examine Mark Twain's reputation as it moved beyond the Pacific Slope to become national and international and to understand how Samuel Clemens made and remade the image of Mark Twain as he shifted from western bachelor to respectable eastern family man.

The second stage was distinguished by Mark Twain's classification with a new school of humorists who were defined as the uniquely national phenomenon of "American Humor." Critics writing in British and American periodicals perceived a new type of humor growing from the American soil—a humor that was seen as a first truly national expression, distinct from the regional traditions of the antebellum period. Coming to prominence during and after the Civil War, critics sometimes referred to this school of humorists as "American Humor," a category that defined the national humor of the country as outside of the sectional conflicts of the decade, as well as separate from women's humor and the humor of African Americans, among other groups. This "American Humor" was unique not for its aesthetic features—although its reliance on chronic misspelling and dialect are important—but for its professional and national meanings. The expanded national and international market for humor enabled these humorists to pursue humor as a professional career. Following the release of his first book, *The Celebrated Jumping Frog of Calaveras County* in 1867, Mark Twain became a subject of critical attention in relation to "American humorists," most notably Artemus Ward, Josh Billings, and Petroleum Vesuvius Nasby. For his part, Samuel Clemens experimented with a variety of subjects and venues for his humor: newspaper letters and lectures on his travels, sketches in higher quality magazines, and the subscription book—all of which helped spread his fame as a humorist across the country and around the globe.

Chapter 1 explores Mark Twain's entry into the national and international discussions of "American Humor." In the 1850s and 1860s, English and American critics developed a critical framework in which humor was judged hierarchically, from a standard of quality, literary humor down to the humor of clowns and minstrels.[28] Critics privileged those who produced literary humor—Washington Irving, James Russell Lowell, Oliver Wendell Holmes, Nathaniel Hawthorne, and Harriet Beecher Stowe most often, along with Dickens, Thackeray, and other English humorists. The transatlantic concept of hierarchy provided critical language by which individual humorists, and groups of humorists, were discussed and classified. The popularity of Artemus Ward, Mark Twain, and other "American humorists" placed them in a new middling position existing between belle lettres and the entertaining but undignified humor of popular culture. While no critics at this time found Mark Twain to be at the highest level of quality, at least one prominent magazine found Mark Twain to be "the best of our second-rate humorists."

Heeding "a 'call' to literarture [sic], of a low order—i.e. humorous," Clemens sought to make a career as a humorist pay as Mark Twain's fame spread across the continent through his periodical writings, which were widely copied into eastern journals before and after his move east. Clemens followed the model of his friend Charles Farrar Browne—better known as the comic writer and performer "Artemus Ward"—in order to take Mark Twain to a national audience. Although other works had circulated on the East Coast, the publication of "Jim Smiley's Jumping Frog" in a prominent New York periodical in 1865 came to symbolize Mark Twain's "leap" into national and international prominence. At the end of his time in the West, Mark Twain also discovered a new forum for delivering his humor: the platform lecture. Leaving California and Nevada behind, Samuel Clemens was prepared to capitalize on the opportunities Mark Twain's success might afford. The critical reactions to his first book, *The Celebrated Jumping Frog of Calaveras County* (1867), and to his new role as a humorous lecturer established Mark Twain as a humorist on a national scale.

Chapter 2 examines Mark Twain's rise to national and international fame through the mass success of his travel humor in the form of letters, lectures, and his second book—*The Innocents Abroad* (1869). Samuel

Clemens's reportage on a prominent tourist trip to the Middle East and Europe provided him with the material to capitalize on his growing reputation as a humorist. Some critics questioned the reverence of Mark Twain's travel descriptions—a worry that Clemens shared, especially as it related to book sales and audience response to his lectures. In editing the material, Clemens looked to specific, respectable readers to help tame his wilder impulses in order to sell his books to a wider audience. Issued by subscription, the book was sold door-to-door by agents who sold Mark Twain as a humorist fit for the family table.

Both before and after the appearance of the book, Mark Twain toured as a lecturer as a means of both financial support and publicity. Moving from the itinerant model of the comic platform lecture to the more respectable lyceum circuit, Mark Twain found himself in direct contact with his audience—a situation that highlighted the expectations of both performer and audience. The increased respectability of both subscription and lyceum audiences caused Samuel Clemens to adjust his humor and critics to question the meanings of Mark Twain as an increasingly popular product in American culture. The success of *The Innocents Abroad*, critically and commercially, made Mark Twain the most prominent of the "American humorists." Many critics praised Mark Twain, some questioned his value, and a few argued that he might be something more than a mere popular humorist.

The third stage of Mark Twain's reputation was highlighted by the tension between his mass success and the possibility of literary respectability. In the 1870s, the distinct category of "American Humor" faded as a means of classifying certain types of humorists. Mark Twain's reputation shifted as he came to be discussed in, and write for, a new culture of letters—the quality periodical. The promotion of his work by key critics pushed him out of the position of a merely popular favorite into the realm of quality humorist, where he would be discussed in the company of the best authors of the country, even if this company did not always feel comfortable with the affiliation. The business success of Mark Twain's books and other literary ventures, as well as the personal eccentricities of Samuel Clemens, mitigated against his full acceptance, and many of his works during this period betray an anxiety about his position as a humorist.

Chapter 3 explores the impact of one significant review of *The Innocents Abroad*. In December 1869, William Dean Howells argued that Mark Twain was a humorist who was "quite worthy of the company of the best" in the pages of the *Atlantic Monthly,* the major American venue for determining literary value. Reviewing the book before he had met Samuel Clemens, Howells included Mark Twain in the literary tradition of the *Atlantic Monthly*, not by downplaying or diminishing Mark Twain's humor, but by reframing it within the traditions of the magazine. Reading reviews of Mark Twain's books—especially *The Innocents Abroad* and *Roughing It* (1872)—within the context of the magazine's editorial ethos, this chapter argues that Howells elevated Mark Twain's critical reputation into the realm of respectable humor and canonical literature by placing him into conversation with James Russell Lowell and Oliver Wendell Holmes, as well as newer authors like Charles Dudley Warner, Henry James, and Bret Harte. Mark Twain's inclusion in the *Atlantic Monthly* illustrates Howells's developing ideas of realistic literature, which focused on "real" and "humane" characters in a variety of genres: the novel, the romance, travel writing, poetry, and humor. In the late 1860s, the *Atlantic Monthly* was one central periodical in shaping ideas of American literature, and its competitors—notably the *Galaxy* and *Scribner's*,—reacted to, and sometimes against, the magazine's view of American literature and its leading figures. Mark Twain's elevation into the company of the *Atlantic*'s authors was thus a seismic shift in the ways in which his reputation could be perceived.

Chapter 4 examines the early 1870s as a key period in which Mark Twain's work as editor, magazine columnist, and lyceum speaker made him the most prominent and widely circulated American humorist. From 1870 to 1871, Mark Twain authored a monthly column in the *Galaxy*, which led to a larger circulation for the humorist's sketches than his previous productions. Unable to fully control the meanings of his humor or his reputation, Mark Twain's work showed a keen anxiety about his cultural position as a humorist, sometimes causing him to lose his sense of humor, especially in response to a hoax review he wrote of *The Innocents Abroad*. As Clemens moved up the scale of respectability and into a life of literary pursuits in Hartford, Connecticut, the reputation of Mark Twain shifted to include discussions of literary quality, which included detractors questioning his place in American literature. The division between the popular and the uplifting frames how different audiences, and Samuel Clemens himself, understood the cultural freight of the humorist. Mark Twain's presence in quality venues—magazines and the lyceum—highlights the difficult position of the humorist who was faced with audiences who held diverse, and occasionally divided, expectations.

Quitting both magazine and newspaper editing in 1871, Mark Twain embarked on a lecture tour speaking on "Artemus Ward"—a tour in which he struggled to balance humor with eloquence and information. Mark Twain experienced a split between audiences who enjoyed his humor as an entertaining cure for the blues and those who saw no place for humor in the educational realm of the lecture hall. Reading the audience reactions to this lecture tour highlights the meanings of laughter in the context of the lyceum performance, a space in which different audiences demonstrated the contested meanings of humor. During this tour, Josiah Gilbert Holland, a highly popular author and the influential editor of *Scribner's Magazine*, attacked Mark Twain and other "triflers" and "buffoons" as examples of a debased popular culture. Holland used his editorship of *Scribner's Monthly* to subtly attack both Mark Twain and Howells, questioning the value of Mark Twain on the lyceum stage and in quality literature. In response to Holland, Mark Twain again lost his sense of humor and defended himself in an unpublished article that illustrates his anxieties about his cultural role.

Chapter 5 examines Mark Twain's reception in England, where he was fêted during his visits in 1872 and 1873, as Artemus Ward had been before him. Mark Twain's books were widely pirated in England and its colonies, and his lectures in 1873 helped establish him as a literary celebrity. British criticism framed Mark Twain and "American Humour" differently than did American criticism. For many British critics, American letters had largely failed to transcend European models and develop a truly national literature. In this critical view, the humor of James Russell Lowell, Artemus Ward, Bret Harte, and Mark Twain represented the first fruits of a new national literature that was highly valued in England because it "smacked of the soil" as an expression of American character. His warm welcome as the "Lion of London," and the success of his lectures in London in those same years, further elevated his literary status—in the United States more than in England. This chapter includes a brief foray into French criticism, which Mark Twain mocked even as he valued British praise. Mark Twain's transatlantic value created a situation in which his warm reception caused some English critics to devalue "American humour" and some American critics to elevate that same commodity. While Samuel Clemens (and American critics) took the laughter of his English audiences and the kindness of English literary society as a sign of his elevated reputation, the larger discussion of Mark Twain's reputation shows a much more ambivalent picture, especially in relation to Bret Harte's and Artemus Ward's.

Chapter 6 examines the tensions that Mark Twain experienced as an increasingly respectable humorist who challenged the common view that artistic pursuits and business interests were ideally separate concerns.

In 1873, Samuel Clemens and Charles Dudley Warner, his neighbor and fellow humorist, co-wrote *The Gilded Age,* a satirical novel on the fever of speculation, expansion, and corruption endemic to the age of Grant. This book partook in the speculative conditions it satirized, as Clemens and Warner sought publicity and solicited favorable reviews to help the book sell. The marketing of the book, and the subsequent reviews, highlighted literature's role as a commodity in American culture—a fine line that tipped between satire and sales fraud. The reactions of reviewers to the novel split between those who liked the satire of the book, even if it did not live up to the humor of either author, and those who felt the public had been "sold" by an inferior product designed to make money on the reputation of its authors.

Negative criticism often rankled Mark Twain, and Clemens attempted to control the reception and sales of his books by controlling publicity through working closely with his publisher, soliciting favorable reviews, and by creating publicity through coverage in newspapers, which eagerly printed news about the celebrated Mark Twain. Released at the beginning of the Panic of 1873, the novel did not sell as well as hoped. The following year, Mark Twain extended the value of the book by adapting his portions as the play "Colonel Sellers," which was a tremendous success in New York and was thought by some critics to represent the beginning of a uniquely American theater. The profits of the book and the play helped Clemens recoup losses he suffered from his own failed speculations and were a significant moment in the development of Mark Twain's brand of humorist. Mark Twain's financial success as a subscription author, playwright, and businessman, combined with Samuel Clemens's failed business and literary speculations, highlight the importance of the connection between business and letters in the shaping of literary reputation.

Chapter 7 examines Mark Twain's increased presence in the culture of letters surrounding Howells and the *Atlantic Monthly* in the 1870s. Starting in 1874, Mark Twain began contributing to the magazine. Some of the work published in the magazine marked promising new directions in Mark Twain's literary development, especially "A True Story" and "Old Times on the Mississippi." Other pieces, such as "A Literary Nightmare," pointed to an anxiety about his position in the magazine, even as he claimed to enjoy an audience who did not expect him to paint himself in stripes and stand on his head for their enjoyment, as he put it to Howells. With the publication of *Sketches, New and Old* (1875) and *The Adventures of Tom Sawyer* (1876), critics attempted to make sense of the possibility of a professional humorist as a quality author and novelist. Samuel Clemens reacted with a continued anxiety about his role as a humorist, both through his *Atlantic* contributions and his personal interactions with the "littery atmosphere," as he famously called it.

Samuel Clemens, and his character of Mark Twain, found a tenuous acceptance into the elite literary culture of Boston, which was dramatized through several performances at after-dinner banquets in honor of the magazine and of specific contributors. Mark Twain's presence in the *Atlantic Monthly* as a contributor, and his speeches at its banquets celebrating its version of American letters, illustrate that Mark Twain had not made a simple transition to quality literary standing, but rather remained a contested figure within a hierarchy of humor. Mark Twain's tentative acceptance in the culture of the *Atlantic* was dramatized at the celebratory Whittier Birthday Dinner, where Mark Twain's speech highlighted the hierarchical tensions between literary respectability and mass success, between quality humor and entertaining or possibly dangerous humor, and between authors-as-ideas and authors-as-people. Mark Twain's "hideous mistake" at the Whittier birthday dinner resonated in Boston's literary culture and in newspapers across the country. The explosion of criticism, even if the criticism was exaggerated in Clemens and Howells's memories (and in scholarly appraisals of the dinner), following this event has made the speech central to understanding Mark Twain's reputation and how humor, celebrity, and reverence intersected as people defined American literature and its meanings. After several years in Europe, Clemens returned to the banquet in speeches on Ulysses S. Grant and Oliver Wendell Holmes that reintegrated him into respectable letters.

Finally, the conclusion examines the ways that Mark Twain's reputation would continue to transform during the 1880s when he entered a fourth stage as the major American humorist to whom other humorists would be compared. By the end of the 1870s, Mark Twain was an established literary figure whose popularity and sales gave him a central importance in American culture and whose reputation was an established topic of critical conversation, even if no consensus as to his value had emerged. Even the works focused on the subject of the Mississippi River, which are now considered his primary works, were both praised and damned by the critics during his lifetime. After the Whittier banquet, Mark Twain spent almost two years in Europe. Mark Twain returned in 1879 and published *A Tramp Abroad* (1880), a book that returned him to the financial success of his first two books of travel. Returning to the form that brought him public acclaim,

A Tramp Abroad capped Mark Twain's ascension to international fame and pointed to new directions of literary reception, as critics no longer compared Mark Twain's works to those of other humorists but rather to his previous works.

Both the so-called "American Humorists" and Bret Harte had faded during the 1870s, and no new humorist emerged to compete with Mark Twain in either sales or reputation. The release of *The Prince and the Pauper* (1882) signaled a "new departure" in topic, artistic quality, and overall reputation. By the 1880s, Mark Twain was in many ways *the* American humorist as he took the position of, in Howells's words, "the most popular humorist who ever lived." Throughout these stages, critics placed Mark Twain in a variety of hierarchical positions as a humorist—from arguing for his position in an American canon to claiming that his value was ephemeral and that he was soon to disappear. This debate over the role of the humorist in American literature became, in many ways, the keynote of criticism about Mark Twain—in his time and through Mark Twain scholarship.

CHAPTER ONE

"Of a low order—i.e. humorous"

American Humor and the Meanings of Mark Twain

I n a letter to his brother, Orion, and his sister, Mollie, in October 1865, Samuel Clemens discussed the process of choosing one's profession. The thrust of the letter was to convince Orion, then struggling to make a living in Carson City, Nevada, to take up a career as a preacher. Clemens, for his part, offers to preach a "sermon" to his brother. In his life, he wrote, he had had only two powerful ambitions for an occupation: a steamboat pilot and a preacher of the gospel. He continues:

> *I accomplished the one & failed in the other, because I could not supply myself with the necessary stock in trade—i.e. religion. I have given it up forever. I never had a "call" in that direction, anyhow, & my aspirations were the very ecstasy of presumption. I have had a "call" to literarture [sic], of a low order—i.e. humorous. It is nothing to be proud of, but it is my strongest suit, & if I were to listen to that maxim of stern duty which says [that] to do right you must [multiply] the one or the two or the three talents which the Almighty entrusts to your keeping, I would long ago have ceased to meddle with things for which I was by nature unfitted & turned my attention to seriously scribbling to excite the laughter of God's creatures. Poor, pitiful business!*[1]

This "call" to humorous literature was a religious call insofar as Clemens is arguing that one's true profession is preordained, but he was forwarding this argument to convince Orion to follow his call to preaching instead of the law or any one of the myriad of occupations for which Orion would prove himself unfit. As a call, Mark Twain's effort to "excite the laughter of God's creatures" through his scribbling is not equating humorous writing with a form of preaching, although he would later do so. At this stage in his new career, Mark Twain was not a "sage" or "philosopher" aiming his message at the masses through a low form—he was a humorist who, at this moment at least, consciously placed himself near the bottom of a hierarchy of humor.

Resigning himself to a low form of literature, Mark Twain acknowledged that not all humorists were of the same class. He writes: "Though the Almighty did His part by me—for the talent is a mighty engine when supplied with the steam of education—which I have not got, & so its pistons & cylinders & shafts move feebly & for a holiday show & are useless for any good purpose." If humor is a machine-like talent given by God, the sermon infers, then Mark Twain lacked the education to make his humor into a finely tuned machine.

In an addendum directed at his sister, Clemens ended his letter by adding a more specific dimension to his calling as a humorist being a "poor, pitiful business!": "You are in trouble, & in debt—so am I. I am utterly miserable—so are you. Perhaps your religion will sustain you, will feed you—I place no dependence in mine. Our religions are alike, though, in one respect—neither can make a man happy when he is out of luck. If I do not get out of debt in 3 months,—pistols or poison for one—exit *me*. {There's a text for a sermon on Self-Murder—Proceed.}" To his brother, he remarked that if Orion would take up the call to preaching, he would take up his call to humor and "strive for a fame—unworthy & evanescent though it must of necessity be." The attention of others to his writing had convinced him that his call might eventually pay: "*You* see in me a talent for humorous writing, & urge me to cultivate it. But I always regarded it as brotherly partiality, on your part, & attached no value to it. It is only now, when editors of standard literary papers in the distant east give me high praise, & who do not know me & cannot of course be blinded by the glamour of partiality, that I really begin to believe there must be something in it." As Mark Twain, Samuel Clemens stood between two possibilities: the despair of debt and the glimmer of fame. The road forward was neither clear nor preordained—depending on one's theology, of course.

This chapter traces Mark Twain's emergence into national popular culture as part of a "school" of humorists that critics increasingly defined as uniquely American. In both British and American periodicals, Mark Twain was linked with Artemus Ward, Josh Billings, Petroleum V. Nasby, and Bret Harte, among others, as examples of a new strand of American humor that captured the unique flavor of the American nation. These new humorists were distinctly popular—their works sold well, both in print and in person, enabling a select few to pursue a career as full-time humorists. The popularity of this new, "racy" humor created a distinct middle ground between the quality literary humor that defined the height of the hierarchy of humor and the low humor that defined its base. "American humor" drew on a variety of regional sources but was imagined as both national and "Western," which was largely meant to be outside of sectional classifications (and conflicts), imagined on a frontier that could mean California, Maine, or Cleveland. Emerging just before and during the Civil War, the national humor was embodied in a small group of white, male figures who portrayed their pseudonymous characters not only in print but also on the stage. The national and professional dimensions of these humorists—more than aesthetic or ethical similarities—explain the linkages between the diverse group of humorists who came to be defined by some as "American humor." This category imagined a white frontier masculinity as the humor of the national character, excluding most women and ethnic humorists from critical consideration as distinctly American.

The critical meanings of this new class of humorist were greatly influenced by British criticism that created a hierarchy of humor in which quality humor reflected an early growth of a national literature. At a time when American authors and others were anxious about the lack of a truly national literature, British critics defined "American Humour" as the first fruits of the national soil—a literature not refined but reflective of the American character. And because of the lack of international copyright, the products of the American humorists sold well in England, just as English authors dominated the American marketplace. This transatlantic trade helped make American humorists and "American Humour" the subject of critical consideration and appreciation in America only after British approval. British critics praised Artemus Ward and Bret Harte for their distinctly American humor, causing American critics to reconsider their consignment of popular humor to a middling hierarchical position.

While the humorists who emerged in the 1860s were influenced by a range of humorists and traditions, the major model for the career of a professional funny man was that of Charles Farrar Browne, who rose to prominence through his character of "Artemus Ward" in newspapers, magazines, and on the lecture platform in the late 1850s and early 1860s. Browne and Clemens met in Nevada in 1863 when the former was touring the country, and Browne encouraged Clemens to take Mark Twain east. With the help of Browne and others, Mark Twain's reputation circulated across the country through the publication of his magazine writings in eastern magazines and newspapers. Especially important was the publication of "Jim Smiley and His Jumping Frog" in the prestigious Bohemian journal, the *Saturday Press*, in November 1865, a month after he wrote the letter to his siblings proposing either monetary success or self-murder. The *Saturday Press* was famous for paying its contributors with the promise to pay. But the circulation of the jumping frog story, as it was reprinted in newspaper exchanges and in ephemeral humor collections, paid Mark Twain in the praise of "standard literary papers" and the capital of an emerging literary reputation. "The Jumping Frog," published under a number of different names, was not the only Mark Twain sketch that circulated widely through the American press, but it was clearly the best known and came to be the primary symbol of his fame.

As Mark Twain rose to national prominence, Samuel Clemens sought new ways to capitalize on the increased reputation of his character. Travel writing—whether about the Sandwich Islands or about his voyage from California to New York—helped further solidify Mark Twain's reputation by creating a distinct voice of Mark Twain as traveler, a voice that would be especially important in the success of his second book in 1869. For his first book, Mark Twain contracted in 1867 with Charles Henry Webb, a humorist and publisher, to put out *The Celebrated Jumping Frog of Calaveras County, And other Sketches*—which collected a selection of sketches mostly from the *Californian*, of which Webb had been the publisher. While the book sold worse than either man hoped, it worked as an advertisement for Mark Twain's move from "the Wild Humorist of the Pacific Slope" to "the best of our second-rate humorists." The move from western humorist to national figure was also accomplished by Samuel Clemens's literal move from the West to the East in 1867. A major impetus for this move was Clemens's new role as a performer on the lecture stage, which he undertook after his return from the Kingdom of Hawaii. Mark Twain's performance as a lecturer, first on the West Coast and then moving to eastern venues, helped propel his reputation across the nation. As a lecturer, Samuel Clemens embodied the character of "Mark Twain," making him real to audiences who paid to see the living, breathing, joking American humorist.

"IT SMELLS OF THE SOIL": THE HIERARCHY OF AMERICAN HUMOR (OR "HUMOUR")

Mark Twain entered onto the stage of popular culture already well populated with a cast of humorists. Critics attempted to classify these humorists largely according to ideas of quality and of nationality, with the point of humor varying from entertainment to edification, while also reflecting the national character of a people. Critics writing in magazines and newspapers debated and discussed virtually all of the appearances of Mark Twain across a wide literary and popular culture landscape. British critics did much to establish the figure of the humorist in hierarchical terms. As James Caron has shown, the idea of hierarchy shaped both the artistic and commercial prospects of comic authors both before and after the Civil War. The "high-culture norm" often defined quality humorists in terms of being "genial," mixing humor with pathos, sentiment, and/or morality. On the other end of the spectrum, comic writers were excluded for being "low," "broad," "coarse," "vulgar," or for soliciting the "horse-laugh."[2] The meaning of Mark Twain, like the meanings of other humorists, was defined within ideas of hierarchy and its vocabulary.

As with most concepts based on ranking or rating—from the "canon" to the "best-of" list—the concept of hierarchy was not ordained from above but contested in its creation. No single critic or author had the power to define what the hierarchy was or who was placed where. Instead, hierarchical definitions were unstable: how hierarchy was defined depended on how the critic viewed the subject of American Literature, which was influenced most keenly by whether the critic was American or European, as well as by the editorial ethos of the author's publication. Some English critics, for instance, tended to view American humor as a major development in the creation of a uniquely American literature, more important than the work of more serious writers such as Emerson. The popularity of American humor and humorists in England was key for the development of Mark Twain's reputation on both sides of the Atlantic. American critics, on the other hand, were more varied in their views of new developments in American humor, reflecting the influence of British criticism but assigning it a variety of ranks and meanings.

The most sustained critical discussion of humor, and clearly the most influential in setting the terms of discussion, was not in American periodicals but that of critics who wrote on the subject of "American Humour" in British periodicals. The main critical thread of British criticism viewed American humor as an indigenous growth of a people and one of the first expressions of a national literature that was initially highly praised in the works of Lowell and other genial humorists, and later in the work of Artemus Ward, Bret Harte, and Mark Twain. British critics held a broad critical perspective that great literature was distinctively national and that Americans had not yet fully developed such a national literature, which became the framework in which almost all American writing was discussed in British periodicals. Whereas American literature, philosophy, and theology had largely been imitative of European models, British critics consistently saw American "humour" as a new development that expressed important aspects of American life: the scale and grandness of the land through exaggeration, the democratic variety of people through its diversity, and the immaturity of the country and its people through its exuberance and occasional profanity.

Over the first half of the nineteenth century, British critical interest in American literature gradually increased, with strong interest developing in the 1850s and 1860s. During the 1850s, critics focused on the work of Harriet Beecher Stowe and Henry Wadsworth Longfellow, both immensely popular in America and England, as well as on the figures of Poe, Hawthorne, Emerson, Melville, Lowell, and Holmes. In the 1860s and 1870s, critics continued to focus on established New England authors, with increased attention to humorists and other new authors, including Artemus Ward, Bret Harte, Mark Twain, William Dean Howells, Walt Whitman, and Henry James.[3]

A large portion of this interest fell on American humor as both a uniquely American form of literature and a highly popular imported product. In writing on American humor, British critics often spoke in terms of growth—roots and soil, fertility and fruit—in a manner that linked the prominent national meaning of "race" with its older roots in agriculture—meaning "of the soil." A consistent critical term of praise when discussing humor was "racy"—i.e., Lowell's poems were "racy in hilarious hyperbole"—which is an adaptation of a winemaking term that was adapted to refer to that which is strongly characteristic of a people or nation, especially in the term "racy of the soil." In this critical view, American humor was more praiseworthy than other products of American letters because it was in the production of humor that the Americans were developing the first fruits of an American literature distinctive in its exaggeration, in its use of language, and in its "raciness." The British saw humor as a national growth of a young nation, the first literary fruits of the national soil. Generally, critics consistently linked the representatives of quality American humor who existed at the top of the literary hierarchy with English models of humor, tracing a genealogy from Chaucer and Shakespeare to Thackeray and Dickens.

As far back as 1838, a British critic writing about the humor of Sam Slick, Davy Crockett, and Major Downing struck this keynote of criticism:

> instead of being European and English in their styles of thought and diction, [these writers] are American—who, therefore, produce original sounds of far-off echoes,—fresh and vigorous pictures instead of comparatively idealess copies. A portion of American literature has become national and original, and, naturally enough, this portion of it is that which in all countries is always most national and original—because made more than any other by the collective mind of the nation—the humorous.[4]

This argument was based on the critical assumption that humor as a genre was national in expression, that "it is impregnated with the convictions, customs, and associations of a nation." American humor expressed the conditions of the people, a list that included: institutions, laws, customs, characters, scenery, Democracy, forests, freedom, universal suffrage, bear-hunts, Puritans, the American revolution, and the "influence of the soil and the social manners of the time."[5] Such peculiar characteristics of a nation infused themselves into men, who expressed the national character through their literature—starting with humor.

The English poet and critic Gerald Massey, writing on "American Humour" in 1860, argued that American literature lacked the "humanized soil of the historic past, which has for ages been enriched by the ripe droppings of a fertile national life" and had not developed the "crust of richness that comes with maturity," which one finds in old-world wines.[6] The lack of a past meant that Americans needed to look to the future, past the "imitative phases," and rely on a "future full of promise" in the development of a national literature. Humor was the first crop of such a national literature. English humour was, unsurprisingly for Massey and most British critics, the most mature and developed of national humors, stretching from Chaucer and Shakespeare to Dickens, Thackeray, Jerrold, and Lamb, but American humor, growing from the same root in different soil, showed promise of developing into a quality expression of its national life.

Creating abstract classes of humorists was relatively easy, but placing individual humorists in those categories proved more difficult. Massey noted: "America has produced four . . . genuine and genial humorists in Hawthorne, Mrs Stowe, Holmes, and Lowell. These have given to American literature a better right of challenging a comparison with other literatures, in the department of humour, than perhaps in any other." In this definition of "humorist," the aims and meanings of humor went beyond laughter, entertainment, or fun. The use of humorous characters—as in Stowe's use of comic African American characters in *Uncle Tom's Cabin*—or of humorous language—as in the satiric verse of Lowell's *The Biglow Papers*—was not the aim but a means toward a serious purpose.[7] The end goal was not laughter, but thought, feeling, or action. Genial humorists used humor as a tool; it was instrumental. In this case, "humorist" became an adjective that joined a list of generic approaches that authors used to engage in meaningful writing on society: novelist, moralist, dramatist, satirist, poet, essayist, humorist. Such humor would be of lasting value—aesthetically or culturally—distinct from popular humor that was of temporary value, if of any value at all.

Massey's categorizations flounder when attempting to classify actual humorists via his metaphorical and philosophical descriptions of humor. Washington Irving, for instance, is high quality, but he is purposely excluded from consideration, as his humor was of a "fine-old-English-gentlemanliness," and does not, Massey argues, "smack strongly of the American soil."[8] The humor of Sam Slick and other Down East humorists represents an early Americanism, especially in its exaggeration, which "consists of fattening up a joke until it is rotund and rubicund, unctuous, and irresistible." He argues that only in recent years had America produced the "genuine and genial humorists" whose humor could compare to other national literatures and national humors.

The general consensus, according to Massey, is that the highest quality American humor is that of James Russell Lowell, especially that of the *Biglow Papers*. Reminiscent of the "lusty strength and boundless humour" of Elizabethan writers, Lowell's humor is "an indigenous growth" that exists independently of European literature. Massey writes:

> *The book is a national birth, and it possesses that element of nationality which has been the most enduring part of all the best and greatest births in literature and art. In the instance of all the greatest poets and painters, they are the most enduring and universal who have drawn most on the national life. The life of art, poetry, humour, must be found at home or nowhere. And the crowning quality of Lowell's book is, that it was found at home. It could not have been written in any other country than America.*[9]

Such a critical view reflected Lowell's own promotion of American literature through his role as editor of the *Atlantic Monthly*—linking the literature of a nation to its local conditions without reliance on outside models.

The other major humorist Massey discussed as a genuine American product was Oliver Wendell Holmes, who more than any other American author relied on wit in his writing. Massey spends the first portion of his essay distinguishing between "wit"—as an intellectual, verbal form—and "humour" as a deeper, physical product. Wit, he writes, is based in thought rather than character; it is "artificial, and a thing of culture; humour lies nearer to nature." He continues:

> Wit is thinner; it has a subtler spark of light in its eye, and a less carnal gush of jollity in its laugh. It is, as we often say, very dry. But Humour rejoices in ample physical health; it has a strong ruddy nature, a glow and glory of sensuous life, a playful overflow of animal spirits. As the word indicates, Humour has more moisture of the bodily temperament. Its words drop fatness, its face oozes with unctuousness, its eyes swim with dews of mirth. As stout people often make the best dancers and swimmers, so Humour relies on size. It must have "body," like good old wine.[10]

Humor, he writes, comes before wit in the development of society. A younger people (as with younger human beings) are "most fruitful in humour." Holmes represents an important development in American literature as a native wit whose writing, while not as racy as Lowell's, displays a "quiet nationality": "The writer has made no straining and gasping efforts after that which is striking and peculiar; which has always been the bane of youth, whether in nations or individuals."[11] Massey frames both humor and wit as indicators of the development of national character, with humor and its connection to the soil and the body being the initial indicators of a developing national literature, while wit is evidence of an evolving national literature.

While Lowell and Holmes were the most cited representatives of genial, literary humor, Massey also discussed Hawthorne and Stowe as exponents of a type of humor seemingly more refined than would hold for such a new country. Hawthorne is a humorist for "the fastidious few, not for the multitude," whose humor is most often linked with a deep pathos more closely linked with English authors than with anything distinctly American. Stowe's humor is also of the "depth . . . where it passes into pathos," although her best humor is used to delineate her African American characters, highlighting the complicated place of representations of race in the hierarchies of American humor. Both Hawthorne and Stowe, like Irving, fit only tenuously into Massey's definition of American humor. Stowe is unique in this critical conversation, as she was the only female author discussed in critical evaluations of humor and the most cited instance of humor in her work is the dialect speech of slaves in *Uncle Tom's Cabin* and her other antislavery novels. Massey wrote:

> It is noticeable that Mrs Stowe's richest and most affecting humour should be Negro humour. Is this intentional—her wilier way of pleading their cause? or is it a confession that the dark people have lighter hearts and merrier natures, in spite of slavery, than her Yankee white friends have, with all their freedom? We consider her power of differenciating [sic] the Negro character, by means of the individual humour, to be one of her most remarkable gifts as a novelist.[12]

As Mimosa Stephenson has traced, the humor of *Uncle Tom's Cabin* was central to its critical reception in the nineteenth century, but the characterization of the humorous black characters based on the minstrel tradition makes them ambivalent—part Sambo, part trickster.[13] The categorization of Harriet Beecher Stowe as humorist highlights the omission of other female authors and the marginalization of African American traditions of humor from the majority of hierarchical discussions of American humor.

In discussing American humor, critics would occasionally discuss the tradition of African American oral humor, most often praising it above its bastardization in black-face minstrelsy but placing it outside of the hierarchy of "American humor." Critics between 1865 and 1880 did not recognize any influence of black voices on Mark Twain's writings, even though African American voices were central to shaping Mark Twain's creative imagination and the very language of American humor, as Shelley Fisher Fishkin has argued.[14] The role of African American humor and female humorists in American culture calls for more attention, but critical discussions of American humor and Mark Twain in his time show that such connections were almost wholly elided, with "national" humor being found almost exclusively in the work of white male humorists. The histories of African American and women's humor were largely erased in critical discourses of so-called "American humor" and in the quality humor of literary culture. These traditions existed in mostly separate cultures of letters with their own meanings.

The cultural position of Marietta Holley is an example of the linkages and disjunctures of humor traditions. Like Mark Twain, Holley wrote in the American vernacular tradition and was brought to widespread fame through the promotion of Elisha Bliss and the American Publishing Company, which published her first book, *My Opinions and Betsy Bobbet's,* in 1873. Writing as "Josiah Allen's Wife," Holley published five books with the American Publishing Company and twenty-one books overall, combining humor with feminist concerns that made her a favorite of feminist leaders. Her popularity was such that an article in 1905 in the *Critic* magazine wrote that "she has entertained as large an audience, I should say, as has been entertained by the humor of Mark Twain."[15] But despite their shared publisher and shared humor tradition, critics made no connection between Mark Twain and Holley, and their personal connection seems to be confined to Mark Twain's inclusion of one story of Holley's in his *Library of Humor* (1888).

Holley and Stowe are examples that point out the absence of women in critical evaluations of American humor. Hierarchical classifications of humor, especially longer articles, are noteworthy as much for the absences and inconsistencies as for the coherence of their definitions and classifications. The introduction of the new class of popular humorists in the 1860s further muddied such evaluations by asking critics to take account of a humor that seemed distinctly American and quickly became popular in England. The popularity of Charles Farrar Browne's Artemus Ward character—both in print and in person—exemplified this new and more complicated attention to American humour in British culture and criticism.

Writing in 1866, the critic Leslie Stephen largely followed Massey's arguments in an essay also entitled "American Humour." While America had developed a distinct national character, he argues, it had not developed a national literature to express its transition out of the "hobbledehoy stage" (we might say "adolescence") into maturity. Emerson, Hawthorne, Longfellow, and others had ability, but they remained a "second rank" whose efforts "remind us rather of extremely clever essays by undergraduates." American humor, on the other hand, is the one distinctly American product of the country: "American humour has a flavour peculiar to itself. It smells of the soil. It is an indigenous home growth. Like the native wines of a country, it has an aroma of its own, and is not made up to imitate the Champagnes and Burgundies of a different climate. And if its qualities have not yet been fully developed, there is hope that with careful cultivation, it may be brought to future excellence." For Stephen, national humors reflected national character; for instance, the French had little appreciation for humor, although they were skilled at verbal wit; the Scottish had little propensity for humor; and the Germans were "about as sensitive to humour as so many apple dumplings" (possibly due to the "effectual prophylactics" of sauerkraut and Bavarian beer).[16] Being an off-shoot of the superior English stock, and sharing its language, American humor might develop into greatness. British critics can thus be seen as patronizing American literature, both in the sense of condescending to notice an inferior rank and in the sense of promoting the development of an artistic vision. But the promotion of American humor as the stalk of a truly American literature was not the product that most American critics and authors wanted to represent as the first crop of a national character.

The major development in both Stephen's article, and in Massey's revision of his earlier article published the following year as "Yankee Humour" (1867), was the advent of Artemus Ward and other popular humorists into the British literary-critical consciousness. Both articles overlap considerably, and, taken together, they provide a clear picture of the critical hierarchies of American humor presented in British periodicals leading up to Mark Twain's rise to international prominence. For Massey and Stephen, Artemus Ward was the "best specimen of the last crop of humourists," mentioning Orpheus Kerr, Major Downing, Josh Billings, and George William Curtis as the other fruits of the season. But Artemus Ward and his fellow humorists were of a "lower mental range," which "hardly attains the dignity of literature" due to their reliance on tricks of spelling, rather than in the genuine use of dialect, as in Lowell and Burns. The minstrel tradition, distinct from a native black humor that Massey praises, occupies the lowest rung of humor, while Artemus Ward and his ilk occupy a middle ground. William Dean Howells reviewed Lowell's second series of *The Biglow Papers* one year after Stephen's article and in the same month as Massey's, making an argument for Lowell's value based on similar hierarchical arguments, a review that will be discussed in detail in chapter 3.[17]

Massey and Stephen held Lowell's *Biglow Papers* to be the height of American humor; only Lowell had mastered the "applied humour" of expressing the "racy" and "genuine American flavour" of the people. Irving and Hawthorne, while showing "delicate humour," were not distinctly American. Holmes was American, but his humor was more refined than most, falling into a category Stephen termed "pure humour," being humor for its own sake stemming from a leisure class who can appreciate intellectual exercises. Still, Artemus Ward's humor, while not artistically brilliant, best represented "the average popular sentiment" of American humor that was becoming increasingly popular in America and England. In generalizing this humor, both critics focused on the use of exaggeration—of bombast, buffoonery, buncombe, boasting, and tall talk in the form of either overstatement (hyperbole) or understatement (meiosis). Stephen uses the example of the American who, when asked if he had crossed the Alps while in Europe, replied "Well, . . . I guess I passed some risin' ground." Exaggeration was used to satirize "high-falutin' sentiment" in the form of the abstract principles of religion, nation, or party. Importantly, the American humorists presented their humor in a general deadpan style, which was described as "dry," "droll," and as a type of "knowing unconsciousness." This type of humorist "has a knack of splitting his sides silently and making no outward sign. He does not laugh, he only chuckles internally."[18]

While exaggeration, a contempt of "highfalutin' sentiment" and other types of humbug, and a dry, deadpan delivery characterized the major aspects of the new crop of American humor, both critics noted a tendency toward coarseness or profanity in the humor that they hoped was fading. Stephen critiques an occasional lack of reverence toward the higher aspects of religion and politics that strikes Englishmen as profane, while Massey finds that American humor, while given to profane language, is "morally healthy and sound" with no tendency of "dalliance with the devil in playing with forbidden things," as with French humor. On the whole, Massey notes that the development of a national American humor had created "a fine opening for the great humourist with genuine insight and a sure touch; a nature that can 'coin the heart for jests,' use the scalpel smilingly, apply the caustic genially, and give the bitter drink blandly. Would the Americans welcome such a writer? There was a time when they would not: we think there are signs that they now would."[19] The critical tendency might be to see Mark Twain as the logical candidate for the position Massey describes, but in 1867, Mark Twain's works were just beginning to reach the national stage from which they would influence the critical conversations taking place on both sides of the Atlantic.

"NOT ONLY HUMORISTS IN THE ORDINARY SENSE OF THE TERM": MARK TWAIN, THE AMERICAN HUMORIST

Understanding Mark Twain's cultural position requires examining how critics defined him in relation to ideas of hierarchy and in relation to other humorists. During the 1860s, critics noted that a new type of humorist had entered the scene—pseudonymous characters who found unprecedented success with characters they performed in periodicals, in books, and on the stage. As the *Nation* put it in an 1870 article on "The 'Comic Paper' Question":

> [T]he United States possesses, what no other nation does, several professed jesters—that is, men who are not only humorists in the ordinary sense of the term, but make a business of cracking jokes, and are recognized as persons whose duty it is to take a jocose view of things. Artemus Ward, Josh Billings, Mark Twain, and the Rev. P.V. Nasby, and one or two others of less note, are a kind of personages whom no other society has produced, and who certainly could in no other society attain equal celebrity.[20]

Following the first stage of his career, in which he developed the "Mark Twain" personae in Nevada, California, and in the Kingdom of Hawaii, Samuel Clemens embarked on a second stage of national and international acclaim, during which he transitioned from California humorist to "American humorist."

Publishing in periodicals, such as the *Saturday Press* and the New York *Tribune*, helped spread Mark Twain's reputation nationally. He experimented with popular forms—the tall tale of Southwestern humor, comic raillery, the hoax, the burlesque sketch, and travel writing. In his early career, he was associated with a group of humorists, all of whom had come to California and Nevada from elsewhere and who had established their humorous voice writing about the picturesque life of the Pacific Coast, among them Bret Harte, Charles Warren Stoddard, "Dan DeQuille" (William Wright), Ralph Keeling, "John Paul" (Charles Henry Webb), and Henry Prentice Mulford. Following Webb and trailed by Harte, Samuel Clemens left the West in 1866 to pursue the career of humorist full time.

Following the publication of his first book in 1867, Mark Twain entered into the national and international discussion of American humor as a member of a particular school, most often referred to in scholarship as "literary comedians," although that usage is a largely twentieth-century categorization.[21] At the time, these men were sometimes referred to as "phunny phellows," but I would argue that more importantly, although more confusingly, these figures were often classed as representing "American humor," a category that imagined a distinctly national humor contained in the productions of white, male humorists whose popularity placed them somewhere between the high humor of American belles lettres and the low humor of the clowns and minstrels.

The new American humor largely emerged from the antebellum periodical humor of regionally based vernacular humor. As Walter Blair noted, newspapers had been employing humorous writers since the 1830s to write columns with names such as "Nuts to Crack," "Flashes of Fun," and "Jottings." Due to the practice of newspaper exchanges, which allowed newspapers to mail copies to other editors for free and to use the material freely, newspaper humorists were widely copied, making humorous characters such as Seba Smith's "Jack Downing" and B. P. Shillaber's "Mrs. Partington" household names in antebellum America. When particularly popular, newspaper humorists found success in collections of their works into books or almanacs, such as Shillaber's *Life and Sayings of Mrs. Partington* (1854), which may have sold as many as 50,000 copies, and Miriam Berry Withcher's *Widow Bedott Papers* (1855), which sold over 100,000 copies. Regional newspaper humorists created vibrant traditions of vernacular humor that influenced Mark Twain, especially the Old Southwest humor of "Sut Lovingood," the Yankee humor of "Sam Slick, of Slickville," the New York humor of "Q.K. Philander Doesticks, P.B," and the Down East humor of "Jack Downing of Downingville." The career of George Horatio Derby—who wrote under the pseudonyms "Squibob," "Dr. Herman Ellenbogen," "John Pea Tarbox," and most famously "John Phoenix"—helped establish humorous newspaper sketches in California and influenced both Mark Twain and American humor through the collection *Phoenixiana* (1856).[22]

Mark Twain was born into this family of humorists, but the figures with whom Mark Twain was classed when he entered onto the national stage performed a different role than their predecessors. Periodical humorists in the antebellum era had largely been humorists as a second career, not as a professional identity. In the 1860s, humorists were increasingly able to pursue humor as a full-time career that involved the performance of their personae on multiple public stages: newspapers, magazines, books, and the lecture platform. Combining the older tradition of newspaper and periodical sketches with the newer career of platform lecturer, these funny fellows became nationally known as their humorous characters, and their humor came to the notice of critics and authors of a literary bent, who had previously largely ignored the realm of newspaper humor. Most importantly, critics defined these humorists as uniquely "American," a designation that erased regional differences at a time when sectional strife was central to the American polity, erasing the divisions of the era by imagining the white, male humorist as the expression of the nation's character. The emergence of the "American humorist" thus took place at a time when the career of the humorist was changing to allow for a funny man to perform his identity full time as a lucrative professional career in print and on the platform.

The category of "American humor" became critical shorthand for the humorists who built on previous regional humor traditions—including Yankee humor, Down East humor, and Old Southwest humor.[23] But there was something different here. The difference, in this case, was not as much in the humor as in the humorist. The major shift was the professional climate in which these new humorists emerged, in the new cultural role the humorist was playing in America and abroad. Starting in the 1860s, a certain class of humorist was able to use the payments from periodical writing and platform performances to support a full-time career as a humorist, largely due to the ability to circulate more easily across the nation and to Europe both in print and in person. The success of Charles Farrar Browne in his character of "Artemus Ward" in newspapers, magazines, and as a comic lecturer was the model for a group of pseudonymous humorists who would be grouped under the school of "American humor": most frequently, "Josh Billings," "Orpheus C. Kerr," "Petroleum Vesuvius Nasby," and, as his reputation spread nationally and internationally, "Mark Twain." The popularity of these humorists positioned them as uniquely American examples of humor—figures that built on previous traditions but seemed somehow different because of their new cultural positioning.

In the 1860s, the new class of humorists became nationally and internationally known by pursuing humor as a full-time career, performing their comic personae in both print and in person.[24] The commercial success of these new humorists allowed them to make a living, and often a decent living, from their humor. The national and international stages available for humorists like Mark Twain in the middle decades of the nineteenth century marked this class of humorists as something new and noteworthy, and critics worked to make sense of the success of these humorists within ideas of hierarchy. This new class of humorist was not only professionally unique but also seemed to represent something new in terms of the national meanings of humor. Critical evaluations were often framed in national terms via a transnational circulation of critical ideas. The major formulations of this new revision of the concept of a humorous hierarchy came from British critics, who continued to fit popular humorists into a discussion of the development of American Literature more generally.

Mark Twain was initially classified as a member of a unique school of humorists based not so much on aesthetic or ethical factors but on professional and cultural meanings. These humorists largely occupied a nebulous middle position in the hierarchy of humor, of note as an expression of national character but of questionable literary value. The new type of American humor was viewed as a separate development from previous popular humorous traditions, which were largely seen as regional growths. The name "American humor," as a time-specific subset of humor produced in America, leads to obvious conceptual difficulties, which may be why the designation has not been discussed extensively. This category might also be less prominent in scholarship because the distinction makes little sense in terms of conventional scholarly methods of grouping literary figures. Aesthetically, the category might cohere without the presence of Mark Twain and a few other authors who did not practice the chronic misspelling of "cacography." The prominent use of exaggeration, a dislike of "high-falutin'" sentiments, a tendency for "dry," "droll," or deadpan delivery—these aesthetic features link these humorists but also could incorporate a large number of other humorists. Instead, the linkage between these figures is in their cultural position as a new type of humorist than in similarities to be found in their humor.

A longstanding source of confusion has been the scholarly association of Mark Twain with the Old Southwestern school of humorists (also called the "Southern Frontier Humorists"). Kenneth Lynn's *Mark Twain and Southwestern Humor* (1959) solidified a thread of scholarship that saw Mark Twain as the "culmination" of Southwestern humor. Other scholars have argued that the influence or importance of Southern Frontier literature has been overstated or misconstrued by focusing on the influence of other comic traditions on Mark Twain, as well as on refining the ways in which Southwestern humor links to his work (or does not). Especially important in questioning the genealogy of Mark Twain's humor has been the introduction of the influence of the "literary comedians" by David E. E. Sloane in *Mark Twain as a Literary Comedian* (1979). Sloane found the Southwestern influence on Mark Twain to be overstated and instead argues for the influence of those humorists he termed the "literary comedians"— especially Artemus Ward—in terms of the development of Mark Twain's ethical viewpoint. Sloane's book pointed out key linkages between Mark Twain and other American humorists, and it was with those humorists that he was most often associated during his time, as opposed to the Southwestern humorists with whom he was seldom linked.[25]

By far the most frequent humorist to whom Mark Twain was compared was Artemus Ward, whose success as a professional humorist helped establish a model for Clemens and other humorists to follow. With "Artemus Ward," Charles Farrar Browne innovated the model of the professional humorist. Browne began his career as a writer in 1851 at the Boston weekly *The Carpet-Bag*, edited by B. P. Shillaber, where he published seven stories under the name "Lt. Chubb."[26] In May 1852, Samuel Clemens published his first known piece of writing in *The Carpet-Bag*. In 1858, Browne invented the character of "Artemus Ward" while an editor of the Cleveland *Plain Dealer*, and the twenty Artemus Ward letters he wrote between 1858 and 1860 found widespread success through the newspaper exchanges.

In 1860, Browne left Cleveland for New York and became a contributor and then editor of *Vanity Fair*, one of the many humorous magazines of the period. Browne made a name for "Artemus Ward" as the "genial showman," an itinerant performer who wrote letters about his menagerie of "snaix" and "wax figgers" and lectured on his travels. Browne based much of his written humor on the orthographic torturing of the English language. In a piece for the Virginia City *Territorial Enterprise* in November 1863, Mark Twain wrote of Artemus Ward's imminent visit in a selection that contrasts the authors' styles:

> We understand that Artemus Ward contemplates visiting this region to deliver his lectures, and perhaps make some additions to his big "sho." In his last letter to us he appeared particularly anxious to "sekure a kupple ov horned todes; alsowe, a lizard which it may be persessed of 2 tales, or any comical snaix, and enny sich little unconsidered trifles, as the poets say, which they do not interest the kommun mind. . . . I was roominatin' on gittin' a bust of Mark Twain, but I've kwit kontemplatin' the work. They tell me down heer to the Bay that the busts air so kommun it wood only bee an waist of wax too git us kounterfit presentiment." We shall assist Mr. Ward in every possible way about making his Washoe collection and have no doubt but he will pick up many curious things during his sojourn.[27]

Artemus Ward's sketches, most of which featured such chronic misspelling, were printed in magazines and newspaper exchanges, establishing his national popularity.

His sketches were collected into *Artemus Ward, His Book* (1862), which sold 40,000 copies almost immediately and established him financially.

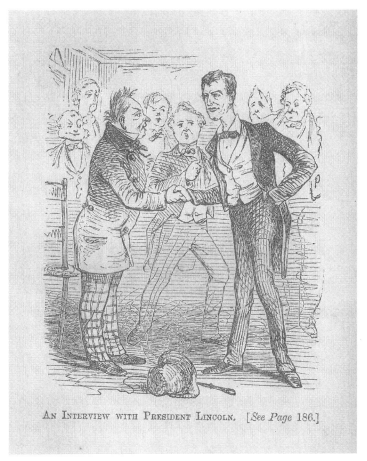

AN INTERVIEW WITH PRESIDENT LINCOLN. [*See Page* 186.]

FIGURE 1.1: Artemus Ward, "An Interview with President Lincoln"
From *Artemus Ward, His Book* (New York: Carleton, 1862)
Collection of the Author

From 1860 to his death in 1867, Browne lectured as Artemus Ward across the United States, in Canada, and then in England, where he experienced his greatest success. Artemus Ward's deadpan lecture style influenced Mark Twain and other comic lecturers who came after. *Artemus Ward; His Travels* (1865) combined sketches based on chronic misspellings with a section of travel writing composed in normal prose but containing an extravagant account of his travels across the United States.

Mark Twain met Artemus Ward (and Clemens met Browne) in Virginia City, Nevada, in December 1863. In addition to a Christmas Eve feast, in which the drunken humorists were almost shot by a police officer while clambering along the town's rooftops, the two struck up a personal and professional relationship that provided Clemens with the model and encouragement to pursue the career of professional humorist. Browne encouraged Clemens to seek his status in the East. The author Fitz Hugh Ludlow, who was also visiting San Francisco, wrote that "In funny literature, that Irresistible Washoe Giant, Mark Twain, takes quite a unique position. He makes me laugh more than any Californian since poor Derby died. He imitates nobody. He is a school by himself." To his mother, Clemens crowed of his connections to both authors: "Artemus Ward said that when my gorgeous talents were publicly acknowledged by such high authority, I ought to appreciate them myself—leave sage-brush obscurity, & journey to New York with him, as he wanted me to do. But I preferred not to burst upon the New York public too suddenly & brilliantly, & so I concluded to remain here."[28] Artemus Ward's tour connected the western humorists with whom Mark Twain was associated at that point with the humorists who were rising in celebrity in the East and who would soon be known for exporting "American humour" to England. Even at this point, criticism of Artemus Ward reflected a hierarchical view of literature that distinguished between literary quality and national importance. Writing in December 1863, Bret Harte noted:

> Artemus Ward is not the greatest American humorist, nor does he himself profess to be, but he deserves the credit of combining qualities which make him the representative of a kind of humor that has more of a national characteristic than the higher and more artistic standard. His strength does not lie simply in grotesque spelling . . . but it is the humor of audacious exaggeration—of perfect lawlessness; a humor that belongs to a country of boundless prairies, limitless rivers, and stupendous cataracts. In this respect Mr. Ward is the American humorist par excellence, and His Book is the essence of that fun which overlies the surface of our national life, which is met in the stage, rail-car, canal- and flat-board, which bursts out over our camp-fires and around barroom stoves—a humor that has more or less local coloring, that takes kindly to, and half elevates, slang, that is of to-day and full of present application.[29]

Harte's view expressed a hierarchical view that distinguished artistic humor from popular humor that expressed something unique about the national character.

It should be noted that this version of the national character ignored the ongoing presence of the Civil War—as well as the experience of women, people of color, immigrants, and city dwellers—and posited "American humor" as a frontier humor outside of the massive social and cultural upheavals of the era. The humor of boats, barrooms, and campfires was only "local" to a small portion of Americans, and the experience of campfires for soldiers surely had different connotations than for Harte.[30] The persistence of the dominance of American humor with its frontier aspect as the dominant theme helps account for the privileging of this thread of American humor in the scholarship of foundational humor studies from Constance Rourke to Walter Blair. The privileging of the frontier as the keynote of "American humor" helped link Mark Twain to Southern Frontier humor, just as it had earlier elevated Artemus Ward, then Bret Harte, then Mark Twain to the role of American humorist par excellence.

Samuel Clemens would not head east until 1866, but in the mid-1860s Mark Twain's reputation circulated in eastern periodical exchanges in relation to Artemus Ward and other American humorists. Seeking to expand his audience, Samuel Clemens sent Browne a story in 1865 for possible inclusion in the next Artemus Ward book. While the story arrived too late to be included in the book, the first published version in *The Saturday Press* sought to capitalize on the popularity of Artemus Ward by addressing the story to "Mr. A. Ward," beginning, in part:

> *Dear Sir: — Well, I called on good-natured, garrulous old Simon Wheeler, and inquired after your friend, Leonidas W. Smiley, as you requested me to do, and I hereunto append the result. If you can get any information out of it you are cordially welcome to it. I have a lurking suspicion that your Leonidas W. Smiley is a myth — that you never knew such a personage, and that you only conjectured that if I asked old Wheeler about him it would remind him of his infamous Jim Smiley, and he would go to work and bore me nearly to death with some infernal reminiscence of him as long and tedious as it should be useless to me. If that was your design, Mr. Ward, it will gratify you to know that it succeeded.*

The Saturday Press highlighted Mark Twain as a rising humorist—whose works from San Francisco had been copied so extensively "as to make him nearly as well known as Artemus Ward."[31] The publication of "Jim Smiley and His Jumping Frog" helped solidify Mark Twain's reputation as a humorist whose work would be included in conversations on the state of American humor. The influence of Artemus Ward on Mark Twain's professional development is key to understanding Clemens's move to a broader audience for his humor.

Soon after his departure from the West, which included a sojourn in the Kingdom of Hawaii, Samuel Clemens took up "Mark Twain's" full-time call to low literature by moving east and expanding his career as a full-time humorist. The success of the jumping frog story, along with the circulation of other articles, proved the time right for Mark Twain to follow in the footsteps of Artemus Ward.

"THE BEST OF OUR SECOND-RATE HUMORISTS"
MARK TWAIN AS AN "AMERICAN HUMORIST"

Mark Twain's move to a national audience was not an accidental leap across the continent but a planned career move based on a calculated desire to appeal to a more select magazine audience. Scholars have long argued that the main factor in Mark Twain's rise to prominence was the publication of "Jim Smiley and His Jumping Frog" in the *Saturday Press* on November 18, 1865. The reputation of this magazine as a major New York periodical—one of the main literary periodicals of its time, along with the Boston-based *Atlantic Monthly*—certainly buoyed Mark Twain's East Coast reputation. But as James Caron has argued, the importance of the jumping frog story in establishing Mark Twain's reputation may be overstated. Instead of a sudden burst into public consciousness, the piece represents the culmination of more than a year of success on both coasts, where newspapers had reprinted Mark Twain's writings for the *Californian*, a magazine aimed at national and international, rather than regional, audiences.[32]

Indeed, the first critical notice of Mark Twain in an East Coast periodical had appeared shortly before the publication of "The Jumping Frog" in the *Round Table*, a New York–based weekly. More than any other magazine of the time, the *Round Table* sought to define the new type of American humor that had captured "a national feeling for exaggeration and burlesque." In an article from September 9, 1865, entitled "American Humor and Humorists," an unnamed critic wrote that American humor was distinct from other humor, specifically that of the English and French "jokers," in its extreme exaggeration: "There is no attempt at subtlety, at playing upon words, or any of the refinements of polished wit; but it is a plain, square exaggeration carried to the utmost confines, and generally calling up some irresistibly laughable figure." This article traces a lineage of this uniquely American humor through David Crockett, John Phoenix, Philander Doesticks, Artemus Ward, Orpheus C. Kerr, and George

Arnold—humorists Mark Twain was most often associated with in the criticism of the era, excepting Crockett and Arnold.[33] In this article, as in many, Artemus Ward was seen as "the most thoroughly American humorist now actively before the public," although the article then follows the common tack of complaining about Browne's use of cacography.

While the listed authors were more or less well known, the humor of California had just begun to reach the East. Mark Twain's reputation was still fresh:

> The foremost among the merry gentlemen of the California press, so far as we have been able to judge, is one who signs himself "Mark Twain." Of his real name we are ignorant, but his style resembles that of "John Phoenix" more nearly than any other, and some things we have seen from his pen would do honor to the memory of even that chieftain among humorists. He is, we believe, quite a young man, and has not written a great deal. Perhaps, if he will husband his resources and not kill with overwork the mental goose that has given us these golden eggs, he may one day rank among the brightest of our wits.

Mark Twain's reputation was beginning to circulate in the eastern press even before the success of the jumping frog story. Nevertheless, the success of the jumping frog story was often cited by critics of the time as the major factor in the elevation of his reputation to a national and international circulation.

The *Round Table* article highlights many of the themes and humorists that would be used to define "American Humor" as a distinctly national genre. First, the article holds that the main thematic thrust of the humor was exaggeration to the point of absurdity. As a corollary, the author notes a tendency toward "coarseness and a tendency to make light of those sentiments which most persons hold sacred." Both "coarseness" and "profanity," in the older sense of mocking sacred objects or ideas, were common means of judging American humor, often in conjunction with the ideas of "reverence" and "irreverence." Second, the article critiques the technical use of cacography, that is, "the rather cheap and very hackneyed peculiarity of orthography," especially in the work of Artemus Ward. The distinction between dialect and misspelling for effect would be a consistent source of distinction in humor hierarchies, one that reflected well on Mark Twain for most critics. Third, the article points to the belief that humorists risked overexposure and the decline of their humor by producing too much work, a fear that Mark Twain expressed several times over the course of his career. Finally, the article frames popular American humor in terms of its entertainment value, rather than its literary standing. In discussing the success of Ward, the critic notes that his humor had "been the source of much pleasure, of a rollicking and unthinking sort, to many thousands of persons of all classes and conditions, between Maine and California." The hierarchical distinction between literary humor and popular—between lasting quality and the ephemeral fun—would be the keynote of Mark Twain's literary reputation for the next two decades and beyond.

This article is noteworthy for previewing many of the major critical tropes of subsequent critical discussion of American humor and for introducing Mark Twain's reputation into this discussion. Mark Twain was not the only humorist to be considered a contender for acclaim in the mold of Artemus Ward. In reviewing Bret Harte's *Condensed Novels* in 1867, the *Round Table* specifically compared Harte to John Phoenix and Mark Twain, his fellow California humorists. Harte was "in some respects superior to either. Not, perhaps, as a humorist; but Mr. Harte is something more, and his miscellaneous papers show traces of scholarly tastes and such graceful fancy as should win a higher reputation than that of a merely funny writer."[34] Through much of this period, Bret Harte's reputation was linked to Mark Twain, with Harte as the author whose position as a humorist might aspire to that of Lowell or Thackeray.[35] The distinction between humorous works that were entertaining sketches of local color and works that were of higher quality, either through their moral quality or some other "serious" indicator, is central to understanding Mark Twain's shifting positions within the hierarchy of humorists. As Mark Twain's work circulated both more widely and in higher quality venues, critics increasingly debated whether Mark Twain might be classed—in both literary and social terms—with the quality humorists whose work transcended the taint of the merely funny. The history of this critical contest—a debate which was never won or lost—is the history of Mark Twain's reputation as a humorist.

The popularity of "American humor" as a peculiarly American growth, both in the United States and in England, encouraged more and more critics to come to terms with the school of humor and its meanings. During its existence from 1863 to 1869, the *Round Table* continued to show an interest in the development of American humor as a popular expression of American life. Despite being disappointed in the book overall, the magazine touted *Artemus Ward; His Travels* (1865) as "perhaps, the best expression of that somewhat intangible national property known as American humor." In discussing "American Humor in England" in 1866, the magazine noted that English humor had faded and that English critics and authors had turned to Artemus Ward and his school of "wild humorists of the plains," whose "fresh and vigorous humor" was becoming recognized as "being peculiar to America." In reviewing Petroleum Nasby in 1867, the magazine notes that Nasby's "style of fun . . . is, whether we like it or not, that which is becoming universally recognized abroad as 'American humor,' and the enthusiasm with which it is received at home makes it difficult to deny that it is so." The review makes the hierarchical position of this type of humor clear by stating that "the entire Nasby order of literature, we need scarcely say, is one for which we have little respect; it is, nevertheless, that which is found to gain the most readers." Humor of this national type was ranked as less than quality, but of an unsettled hierarchical place, as when a notice of a British edition of Josh Billings's works sardonically noted that the English preference for American humor gave English readers an advantage over American readers, "who prefer the antics of a clown in the ring rather than in letters."[36] If the American humorist was a clown, he was at least a clown above the circus clown.

Heading east in late 1866, Samuel Clemens was positioned to capitalize on the vogue for American humor and the success of the jumping frog and other of Mark Twain's stories. In the period between "The Jumping Frog" and his move to the East Coast, Samuel Clemens had decided against self-murder, instead spending six months in the Kingdom of Hawaii, where he wrote a series of successful travel letters on the islands. His discovery of humorous travel writing—and of humorous lectures on his travels—helped him capitalize on the popularity of works on travel and to refine the voice of "Mark Twain."[37]

In the short time he was on the East Coast before heading on another travel assignment, this time to the Middle East and Europe, Samuel Clemens reached an agreement with Charles Henry Webb to publish a book of sketches, which was issued as *The Celebrated Jumping Frog of Calaveras County, And other Sketches* in late April 1867. Webb had been the publisher of the *Californian*, which had printed the early magazine sketches that had helped establish Mark Twain's reputation as a humorist through their reprinting in eastern journals. Webb also wrote humorous works under the pseudonym "John Paul," under which name he wrote the introduction to the book. In the piece, "John Paul" introduced Mark Twain by focusing on both the popularity and the morality of his works:

"Mark Twain" is too well known to the public to require a formal introduction at my hands. By his story of the Frog, he scaled the heights of popularity at a single jump, and won for himself the sobriquet of The Wild Humorist of the Pacific Slope. He is also known to fame as The Moralist of the Main: and it is not unlikely that as such he will go down to posterity. It is in his secondary character, as humorist, however, rather than in his primal one of moralist, that I aim to present him in the present volume.[38]

If Webb was indeed being serious, his introduction of Mark Twain as primarily a moralist, rather than a humorist, was the most forceful argument in favor of his underlying serious purpose during the early years of his career. Few critics took up the framing of Mark Twain as moralist, and both nicknames applied here did not gain currency as references to Mark Twain in critical writings of the time.

Samuel Clemens was disappointed by the sales of the book, which he had hoped would reach 50,000, but which only sold approximately 4,000 copies. To his family in June he wrote stoically: "As for the Frog book, I don't believe that will ever pay anything worth a cent. I published it simply to advertise myself & not with the hope of making anything out of it." If he had really not expected to make money, which is to be highly doubted, he was at least correct in seeing the book as advertising for the brand he was establishing—"Mark Twain." As Judith Yaross Lee points out, the association of Mark Twain's brand with the jumping frog was well established early in his career, and these associations soon took on international dimensions as representatives of "American Humour."[39]

Reviews of the book represent the initial efforts of critics to define Mark Twain's reputation, although several papers showed their lack of familiarity with Mark Twain by referring to him as "Mr. Clements [*sic*]." Of course, no one reader or critic would have had access to all the opinions of book reviewers in newspapers and magazines spread across the country, as well as in England and other countries. As Budd notes, a full survey of Mark Twain's literary reputation awaits "a utopian day [when] some brave scholar-critic" has access to all the reviews and information on the slant of the mostly anonymous reviewers, as well as the highly political and/or religious slants of most newspapers.[40] That day may remain utopian, but a reading of the existing archive shows consistent themes that run across reviews of individual books and across Samuel Clemens's career, with intriguing variations across time, geography, and nation and with crucial insights into American culture when attention is paid to the details of the critical discourse on Mark Twain and humor.

Reviews of Mark Twain's first book touched on a number of the prominent themes that would run through evaluations of Mark Twain's reputation over the course of the next decade and beyond: his wise choice not to resort to cacography, his relationship to Artemus Ward and related humorists, the regional and national meanings of humor, and the different roles humor might play in American culture—both in its alleviating cares through entertainment and in the edification of quality humor.

Despite the fact that several of the sketches from the *Californian* had circulated widely, reviews of the book testified to the centrality of the jumping frog story in establishing Mark Twain's reputation. The New York *Times* approved of the story providing the collection's title, as "it has done more than any other single paper to secure for the writer whatever reputation he may have." The New York *Citizen* argued that the story was well known across the country, writing: "It is altogether the jolliest story that we have ever been fortunate enough to laugh over. 'Humorous,' or 'comic,' does not begin to express its peculiar character. It is thoroughly, perfectly, inexpressibly jolly, and is entirely unrivaled in its peculiar style of excellence." Many reviews ranked the Jumping Frog story as the best story in the collection, but most cited other stories as of high quality, especially "The Story of the Bad Little Boy Who Didn't Come to Grief," "The Killing of Julius Caesar 'Localized,'" and "Lucretia Smith's Soldier." Only one notice, in the New York *Evening Post*, disparaged the collection, stating that it was a mistake: "The story of the 'Jumping Frog' is one of the best of its kinds that we remember; but the remainder of the little book, with one or two exceptions, is dreary, and often worse. It is not suited to this longitude."

While several of the reviews critiqued Mark Twain for being occasionally "coarse," reviews more frequently used the terms "genial" and "genuine," terms of praise for humorists often applied to the quality humor of James Russell Lowell and Oliver Wendell Holmes. These qualities seem to have lifted Mark Twain to the top of the school of "American humorist." The New York *Citizen* wrote: "Mark Twain is a genuine humorist. He does not depend on misspelling, or on punning, for the comic effect of his sketches, but on legitimate wit and humor. Perhaps his chief characteristic is his habit of bringing two utterly incongruous things in close juxtaposition. He imitates no one, but his humor is thoroughly and entirely his own."[41]

How original Mark Twain's humor was remained a central question as critics attempted to define his place in the hierarchy of American humor. The San Francisco *Daily Evening Bulletin* made this relational positioning clear, along with the reasons for elevating Mark Twain over other humorists, writing: "We regard him as by far the best of our second-rate humorists. He is superior to Artemus Ward, for his fun has a purpose to it, and is worth a hundred Petroleum V. Nasbys and Josh Billingses. He is something more than a mere writer of funny sayings. Beneath the surface of his pleasantry lies a rich vein of serious thought. He instructs as well as amuses and even his broadest jokes have a moral more or less obvious."[42] The classification of humor, both in the relational critical reputations of its main figures and in terms of a hierarchy predicated on an underlying moral seriousness, were the key frames through which Mark Twain's reputation was contested within critical discourses.

As the periodical that paid closest attention to the "peculiar" field of "American humor," the review from the *Round Table* is notable for the way it placed Mark Twain in the conversation by stating that "Mark Twain has succeeded to the vacant chair of the lamented Artemus Ward." In both his lectures and books, the review continued, "there is a strongly marked nationality, a keen appreciation of the ridiculous, and a love of fun untinged with cynicism." According to the reviewer, the main benefit of this fun is to "unbend the thoughts which may be too much stretched by care," concluding that: "We commend this little volume to all who seek a few moments' relaxation from the serious cares of life, and who concur in believing that

> "Care to our coffin adds a nail, no doubt;
> And ev'ry grin so merry draws one out."[43]

The role of humor in alleviating everyday cares was a common theme in reviews of Mark Twain's works, often in terms of the "fun" that the pieces provided.

In general, reviews of Mark Twain's first book placed him squarely at the head of the second-rate humorists, an improvement over Artemus Ward and Petroleum Nasby because he worked "without resorting to tricks of spelling or any other buffoonery." Several papers predicted success for Mark Twain based on his "originality." The Sacramento *Union* noted certain literary and satirical powers that placed him above Ward and Orpheus C. Kerr and presaged a "more enduring fame" for "our Pacific humorist." The Chicago *Sunday Times* took up Mark Twain's difference by noting that many current humorists took satirical aim at one topic, but that Mark Twain's sketches had offered a unique approach to a variety of subjects.[44] This review is unique in comparing humorists to "comedians"—meaning those actors who performed comic roles on stage—a comparison that is quite rare in this era. Both, the critic avers, are subject to criticism and both must not offend certain sensibilities in order to be successful, stating: "The humorist who is most generally successful, is he who thrusts with foils, not he who cuts and slashes with broadswords. He may step on toes, but he should avoid the corns. It is very jolly on certain occasions to be punched in the ribs with the fore-finger, but not at all pleasant to be knocked down." Mark Twain's writings are judged to be "good, hearty enjoyment" without satiric intent that might offend. "One can read Mark Twain," the critic notes, "with the simple object of laughing."

However, "the simple object of laughing" was never all that simple, when reviews of a book or performance of Mark Twain's are concerned. Critical evaluations of each work varied widely, ranging from fulsome praise to gleeful contempt. Evaluations of the Jumping Frog book both previewed later critical trends and offered some unique exceptions. Reviews tended to focus on the future of Mark Twain as a humorist. As the *Wilkes Spirit of the Times* noted, the "Wild Humorist" of the Pacific was now in "the color-guard of American humorists."[45] And while many of the sketches had circulated widely in periodicals, Mark Twain was still "comparatively unknown" to many Americans, especially in the East. A confluence of events—the release of the book, Mark Twain's debut as a lecturer in New York, and the death of Charles Farrar Browne ("Artemus Ward") in March—made the spring and summer of 1867 a crucial time for the development of Mark Twain's reputation.

Reviews of *The Celebrated Jumping Frog of Calaveras County, And other Sketches* anticipated later discussions of Mark Twain's works by focusing on the regional and national dimensions of his reputation. More than subsequent productions—where Mark Twain was most often framed as distinctly "American"—the Jumping Frog book was framed as a product of the West. Most reviews mention Mark Twain's connection to California or "the Pacific slope," with sketches that were "apparently suggested by the exhilarating atmosphere of California." The Chicago *Sunday Times* argued that "Mark Twain's may be justly pronounced a western humor, as distinguished from that of other writers" to whom he was compared, with the exception of Bret Harte.[46]

The regional dynamic created a brief spat in the press when the *Californian*, where many of the pieces from the book had first been published, noted that the author was too well known to need Webb's introductory note.

The New York *Citizen*, which had praised both Webb and Mark Twain in a review, took exception by noting that Mark Twain may not have needed introduction to a *Californian* public, but he did need introduction to an *American* public, to which he was "very little known."[47] The paper faults the *Californian* for assuming Mark Twain's national reputation and for slighting Webb, whom they note, incurred the cost for a book that had not paid. Further, the article argues that "John Paul" had stretched the truth by saying that Mark Twain was never coarse, "when the reverse is essentially true." The *Californian* took exception not to the "fair hit" but to the question of the coarseness of "the Californian humorist,"

> . . . the decision of which would depend a great deal upon definitions, and might ultimately resolve itself into a question of taste. The canons by which it is to be decided, are . . . unsettled and confused. . . . We know of no satisfactory dogmas by which questions of this kind can be set at rest. So far as our own taste is concerned, while recognizing that "Mark Twain's" humor is of quite a different strain from Frank Bret Harte's for instance, we think we could find a better and more accurate term than "coarse" by which to characterize it.

The questions of "taste" by which canons of literary value were determined is here dramatized in a critical skirmish that spanned the country. While such literary conflicts over taste and value were usually not so direct or clear, the contested nature of Mark Twain's reputation was shaped through just such critical concerns.

Literary value was not solely determined in American circles, of course. The success of Mark Twain and his books in England—in terms of both sales and criticism—helped elevate Mark Twain's reputation in both Europe and in America. While Mark Twain's reputation in England will be discussed in chapter 5, the two reviews of the pirated version of *The Celebrated Jumping Frog* from English journals are worth noting here. In September, the *London Review* compared Mark Twain's work with that of Artemus Ward. The English had raised Artemus Ward far above his American reputation, especially following his death in London earlier in 1867. Thus, Mark Twain's decision not to use cacography was not a better choice, just a different tack that he managed to succeed with. "Not that we would place him before Artemus in all things," the review noted, "but in two or three touches of tickling fun he proves himself almost as much a master of the art of joking." Part of this mastery included touches of "pathetic jocoseness" that combined sentiment and fun to prove "Mark Twain to be something much better than a clown or jester." Similarly, the comic journal *Fun* praised the book's "genuine" and "genial fun" above the many other humorous books sent across the Atlantic.[48] Mark Twain's transatlantic reputation would become increasingly important as both American and British critics considered his works as examples of "American humo(u)r."

THE TROUBLE BEGINS AT EIGHT
PERFORMING "MARK TWAIN"

In 1866, as the success of the Jumping Frog story was still reverberating across the country, Samuel Clemens sailed to the Hawaiian Islands as a reporter for the Sacramento *Daily Union*, for which he wrote twenty-five letters during his more than four-month stay in the islands. Referring to them as the "Sandwich Islands," Clemens found a rich vein of topics in his first foreign journey—and he would return to the topic of the islands at various points for the next 30 years.[49] Equally important, for the development of his career and reputation, was a discovery upon his return to San Francisco: the lecture. On stage, Mark Twain entered into a culture of performance in which the comic platform lecture helped the new class of humorist maintain a career as a professional humorist. Following the model of Artemus Ward, both professionally and in his deadpan style, Samuel Clemens found a widespread success that helped spread "Mark Twain's" reputation across the nation. Before the success of his next book, *The Innocents Abroad*, cemented his reputation as one of the most popular and most discussed American humorists, Mark Twain's lectures had helped spread his reputation across the nation and solidify his place at the forefront of American humorists. Finding both financial success and public approbation, Mark Twain lectured professionally on an intermittent basis from 1866 to 1873, first following the model of humorous platform lecturer pioneered by Artemus Ward and then on the lyceum circuit—a more respectable venue in which Mark Twain's lectures were included in a series of lectures by prominent figures of the day.

On October 2, 1866, the 31-year-old Samuel Clemens—performing as Mark Twain—found himself onstage at the San Francisco Academy of Music, giving a "serio-comic" lecture on the subject of the Sandwich Islands. Mark Twain would tell the story of the speech in his second travel book, *Roughing It*, with his usual propensity for sacrificing facts for the sake of a story that might expose a deeper truth. In this case, he tells of returning from the Kingdom of Hawaii penniless and deciding upon a lecture as a means of making money. While many friends discouraged him, one unnamed editor encouraged him to take the largest house in town and to charge $1 a ticket, in hopes of creating a sensation that would sell. Advertisements promised:

Doors open at 7 ½. The trouble begins at 8.

Doubtful of his success, Mark Twain tells of how he sought out a group of friends, a prominent lady, and a good-natured drunk and planted them in different parts of the audience to laugh when prompted in order to incite the audience to laughter. The day of the performance, Mark Twain was struck with terror, and, finding the box office closed when he thought it should be serving customers, he resigned himself to his fate of failure, or so he recounts. Instead, he found the house sold out and filled to bursting. His allies in the audience led the audience in laughter, although one bit of serious pathos was ruined when he accidentally gave the signal for laughter: a smile.[50]

Despite his possible misgivings and initial stage fright, the lecture launched Mark Twain into a successful new career as a lecturer. As Walter Francis Frear writes: "The feat was accomplished, and with undreamed of success. The Sandwich Islands had given Mark Twain a new, then and times afterwards, sorely needed, lucrative profession, that of lecturer— later expanded to include author's readings and after-dinner speaking." Following the success in San Francisco, Clemens toured as Mark Twain through California and Nevada, giving the lecture fifteen times before traveling eastward while giving the lecture through the Midwest and East before heading out on another traveling excursion, this time to the Middle East and Europe, a trip that would result in *The Innocents Abroad* and another popular lecture topic. The Sandwich Islands lecture not only represented Clemens's move into a new profession, but an advance in his creative development that he himself considered "one of the turning points of his career." His biographer, Albert Bigelow Paine, comments that the lectures possessed a quality the letters had not: "His Sandwich Island letters to the Sacramento Union had been nothing remarkable, but the lecture he was persuaded to deliver a few months after his return indicates a mental awakening, a growth in vigor and poetic utterance that cannot be measured by comparison with his earlier writings, because it is not of the same realm."[51] Coming at roughly the same time as the publication of the jumping frog book, Clemens's lectures introduced Mark Twain to the public in a new manner and provided a stage from which to embody the character as a representative of American humor.

Key to Mark Twain's popularity was his stage presence as a lecturer. Much has been written about Mark Twain's manner as a public speaker, which remains somewhat of a mystery because no audio recording of Mark Twain speaking exists and the texts of the speeches mostly exist as composites based on newspaper reports and fragmentary notes.[52] Nonetheless, much is known about Mark Twain's manner as a speaker. As Brander Matthews pointed out in a 1924 article, Mark Twain was "a born actor, a born speech maker, as he was a born storyteller;" but that this naturalness was supplemented by hard work on his part: "However spontaneous, unpremeditated, offhand one of his successful speeches might seem, it was the result of skilful preparation. It had been thought out; and it was often written out. It had been rehearsed until every word, every pause, every gesture was exactly right. He left nothing to chance." His presence on stage was almost as much of an attraction as the content of his speeches. Frear describes the effect: "He was striking in appearance, with his shock of reddish-brown hair and mustache, and his keen and sparkling eyes, and his easy, though slightly awkward, carriage on the stage. He made no attempt at elocution. He was noted for his drawl, somewhat monotonous, at first perhaps a little disconcerting to his audience, and then an added fascination."[53] As with Artemus Ward, the lecture platform was a significant stage for the development and performance of Mark Twain's role as a humorist.

Mark Twain lectured in front of a variety of audiences—from Red Dog, Nevada, to New York City to—several years later—the most fashionable hall in London. The lectures were events to be promoted, viewed, and discussed. On a basic level, lecturing provided Clemens a means of supporting himself as a humorist, which was a central concern not only of humorists but of literary figures more generally. The lecture tour also worked to spread Mark Twain's reputation by literally placing Mark Twain in front of his audiences. The performative nature of Samuel Clemens's career lecturing as Mark Twain frames that activity as different from the textual nature of the books, reviews, and articles that surround Mark Twain's written works. But these performances are not separate from the larger questions under consideration in this book—the meaning of humor and the humorist.

In a lecture, Mark Twain was transformed from a humorist-as-author to a humorist-as-speaker, and he thus came to embody this character

through his physical presence and his unique voice. At a time when illustrations were just coming to provide audiences an image of authors,
Mark Twain was first seen by large portions of his audience through
his lectures. As a performance, a lecture by Mark Twain dramatized the
role of the humorist in relation to his audience. Reports of lectures give
more direct evidence of the expectations of audiences when encountering
Mark Twain and of their reactions, helping to flesh out key questions
about the changing role of the humorist, the question of reputation,
and the meanings of Mark Twain as he shifted from western humorist
to international fame. Mark Twain's successes and failures on the lecture
platform highlight the tenuous balance he struggled to maintain between
entertainment and edification, the conflicting expectations audiences
held for the humorist, and the importance of Mark Twain's physical
presence as a performer. In these years, "Mark Twain" was not only the
author of a set of texts; he was a living, breathing, joking embodiment
of American humor.

Throughout his career, Samuel Clemens was a believer in the importance
of the press in setting the tone for the reception of his products, both his
books and his lectures, and he often sought friends to write early reviews
in order to influence critical discourse. For his first lecture, Clemens could
rely on his friends in the San Francisco press to help ensure a positive start
to his lecture career. The San Francisco *Evening Bulletin* noted that "the
greatest good feeling existed" throughout "one of the most interesting
and amusing lectures ever delivered in this city."[54] While Mark Twain's
reputation as a humorist was expected, the review noted with surprise
the elements of eloquent description, especially his "word-painting" of
the volcano of Kilauea, and the factual material on the islands that was
interspersed with the "side-splitting jokes," although the contents of the
jokes were seldom described. His ability of "mixing (so to speak) as with a
blender the pathetic with the humorous" was central to his successes as a
lecturer, and his failures as a performer and author were often attributed
to an imbalance of humorous and more serious material. Still, several
newspapers in San Francisco questioned the "coarseness" of jokes that
"could not be heartily laughed at by ladies."[55]

In addition to commenting on the manner of his delivery and his
mixture of "fact, fun, and fancy," reviews of Mark Twain's performances
throughout his career often compared him to other humorous lecturers,
especially to Artemus Ward. As with his writings, this relational figur-
ing linked Mark Twain to other humorists, as when the *Daily Bulletin*

compared him favorably to Ward: "The lecture was superior to Artemus Ward's 'Babes in the Woods' in point of humor. It evinced none of that straining after effect that was manifested in the great showman, and possessed some solid qualities to which Ward can make no pretensions. As a humorous writer Mark Twain stands in the foremost rank, while his effort of last evening affords reason for the belief that he can establish an equal reputation as a humorous and original lecturer." The *Alta California* compared him to John Phoenix, while the *Golden Era* stated, "Quote Artemus Ward no more; our Pacific slopes can discount him."[56]

Following his debut, Mark Twain lectured in California and Nevada before his move east, where he performed the lecture on a trip to the Midwest, including St. Louis and his hometown of Hannibal in the spring of 1867. His first performance in New York City, on May 6, 1867, was booked into the Cooper Union, one of the largest and most intimidating theaters in the city. Most likely unknown to Samuel Clemens, or his audience, was the death of Charles Farrar Browne that same day in England, where he had gone to perform as Artemus Ward. Mark Twain would continue to follow Artemus Ward's model, including a successful reception in England.

A number of the reviews of *The Celebrated Jumping Frog of Calaveras County*, released that spring, mentioned the lecture as central to Mark Twain's further rise to fame as a humorist. The success of the lecture, along with the publicity from the book, helped establish Mark Twain as a major exponent of American humor in the mold of Artemus Ward—popular in print as well as on the platform. The success of Clemens's career as a humorous performer helped further construct the persona through which he transformed himself from western newspaperman into a national and international celebrity.

The advertisements for the New York performance illustrate both Mark Twain's concern for launching a new venture with fanfare and the varied and vibrant entertainment options available to his potential audiences. Mark Twain advertised the lecture with a letter to the New York *Tribune* in the form of a letter from a list of prominent gentlemen from California, as well as Senator James Nye of Nevada, vouching for the "entertaining, instructive, and amusing" nature of the entertainment. An advertisement in the New York *Times* on May 6 grouped the lecture with Barnum's Museum and Menagerie, minstrel companies, a troupe of Japanese acrobats, and various theater productions under the heading "Amusements." Under the separate heading of "Lectures" was advertised a lecture by Schuyler Colfax, the Speaker of the House of Representatives, entitled "Across the Continent."[57]

Facing such diverse competition, Mark Twain's New York debut failed to sell many tickets, but an enthusiastic crowd, drawn in with free tickets, helped make the evening a success as a performance, if not financially. According to Mark Twain's memory of the event, the promoter Frank Fuller had advertisements printed and hung on strings in bunches of fifty on the city's omnibuses. In an autobiographical dictation resonant in meaning, if questionable in veracity, Mark Twain wrote that:

> My anxiety forced me to haunt those omnibuses. I did nothing for one or two days but sit in buses and travel from one end of New York to the other and watch those things dangle and wait to catch somebody pulling one loose to read it. It never happened—at least it happened only once. A man reached up and pulled one of those things loose, said to his friend, "Lecture on the Sandwich Islands by Mark Twain. Who can that be, I wonder"—and he threw it away and changed the subject.[58]

As would be the case with future lecture tours, the advertisement for the lecture blurred the lines between funny and serious discourse, both burlesquing the conventions of lecturing and reassuring audiences that humor would be supplemented by information, instruction, and eloquence. The advertisement promised a "SERIO-HUMOROUS LECTURE" covering thirty-eight subjects, some promising details on Hawaiian customs and other promising fun, such as:

> 38. The performance to conclude
> with a joke which cannot fail to
> amuse such persons as may
> chance to be amused by it.

The advertisement concluded with a statement linking humor with information and pathos:

> CAREFULLY ELABORATED JOKES
> will be attached to each of these thirty-eight subjects—some of them
> being fearfully and wonderfully made; but everything in the discourse
> except those jokes, can be relied upon as useful and accurate information.
> Some little pathos will be infused into this lecture, and persons who are

overcome by it, may go out for a few minutes; but no weeping
will be allowed on the premises.[59]

While the promises of accurate information and pathos are promised in a joking fashion, possibly undercutting their presence, the advertisement speaks to the complicated expectations that lecture audiences may have brought to a comic lecture. Mark Twain "made fun" of pathos, both by mocking it and by using his own skill with sentiment to play the issue both ways.

The reviews of this performance, and a subsequent performance in Brooklyn, illustrate several main dimensions of Mark Twain's reputation that were unique to, or at least uniquely highlighted by, the immediate presence of an audience. Reviews held that audience members largely expected to be entertained by the humor of the lecture. The New York *Times* wrote that "nearly every one present came prepared for considerable provocation for enjoyable laughter, and from the appearance of the mirthful faces leaving the hall at the conclusion of the lecture, but few were disappointed."[60] Mark Twain's reputation as a humorist preceded him, even at this early date, and since the audience was "frequently convulsed with hearty laughter," the evening was pronounced a success. Both the manner and the matter of Mark Twain's lectures were important to audience enjoyment, with his slow, drawling style being declared "peculiar and original."[61] Finally, audiences and critics were often pleasantly surprised that Mark Twain's lectures contained eloquent descriptions and accurate facts, in addition to amusing anecdotes.

Most reviews of the New York lectures, and of subsequent lectures, focused on his manner of speaking and his reputation as a humorist, largely ignoring the subject matter of his speech. The humor of the performance relied on burlesquing the conventions of lecturing, specifically of travel lectures. As burlesques, Mark Twain's lectures gently mocked the American exceptionalism on which writing and lecturing on travel were based. Few of the reviews of Mark Twain's early lectures noted a tendency toward irreverence or took offense at the presence of a humorist on the platform stage. But as he moved into more respectable venues, especially through the booking agency of the lyceum bureau in 1868, reviews of Mark Twain's lectures increasingly were split between critics who enjoyed the performance with hearty laughter and those who frowned their disapproval at the presence of a clown in the serious realm of the public lecture.

The subject of these speeches—the Sandwich Islands—was a major symbolic location through which Mark Twain explored the meaning of American expansion.[62] In an age of European imperial expansion, American interest in the Kingdom of Hawaii on the part of American businessmen and politicians made the islands an important site of nascent American imperialism. Samuel Clemens had been sent to the islands, in part, to examine the prospects of American business in the islands. Mark Twain would use a version of the speech, most often titled "Our Fellow Savages of the Sandwich Islands," on his lyceum tour in 1869–1870 and in his lectures in England in 1873.

Mark Twain's debut in New York helped further establish him as a humorist of national renown. The Brooklyn *Eagle* wrote that, "In California Mr. Twain is well known, and draws like a poultice, but among us he is a stranger. Notwithstanding this he will soon win his way to public favor. . . . He should be heard by every person who appreciates humor in its very drollest features." The drama critic Edward "Ned" House wrote an extensive review of the lecture, commenting on his rise to fame and comparing him to Artemus Ward, with whom House had been friends and with whom he had traveled in England. In the unsigned review, House wrote that "Joe Smiley and his Jumping Frog"—the story went by many names (some that Mark Twain used, some not)—had taken an unknown author and attracted "prompt and universal attention among readers of light humorous literature."[63] Mark Twain was immediately regarded "as a candidate for high position among writers of his class, and passages from his first contribution to the metropolitan press became proverbs in the mouths of his admirers." House continued to note that Mark Twain's rapidly won reputation was supplemented by subsequent reprintings of sketches from California periodicals, but it was unclear whether his new position would draw a crowd. Either unaware that the house had been filled largely through free tickets, or kindly choosing to ignore this fact, House heralded the full house as a sign of the humorist's reputation:

> The chance offering of "The Jumping Frog," carelessly cast, eighteen months
> ago, upon the Atlantic waters, returned to him in the most agreeable form
> which a young aspirant for public fame could desire. The wind that was sowed
> with probably very little calculation as to its effect upon its future prospects,
> now enables him to reap quite a respectable tempest of encouragement and

cordiality. . . . No other lecturer, of course excepting Artemus Ward, has so thoroughly succeeded in exciting the mirthful curiosity, and compelling the laughter of his hearers.

The critical consensus was that the combination of the "Jumping Frog"—the story and the book—and the Sandwich Islands lecture cemented Mark Twain's reputation as an aspirant to the position of "American humorist." Overall, the success of the lecture, along with the reviews of the jumping frog book, helped spread his reputation nationally. As the San Francisco *Daily Dramatic Chronicle* noted: "'Mark Twain' made a successful *debut* in the character of a lecturer at New York, a few days since. He has become a man of sufficient mark to have his movements telegraphed across the continent."[64] Samuel Clemens's "calling" as a humorist had proved to draw a crowd, and he sought to make Mark Twain's position as humorist pay. Positioned at the head of the second-rate humorists, below the quality of literary humorists, but notable because of his racy humor, Mark Twain was uniquely positioned to capitalize on new opportunities as the preeminent American humorist.

CHAPTER TWO

An American Birth Abroad

The Innocents Abroad and American Humor

On June 8, 1867, just over a month after his lecture debut in New York, Samuel Clemens sailed on the streamer *Quaker City* for a trip to Europe and the Middle East. The trip was billed as the first purely pleasure excursion to the Old World, and the organizers had hoped that a number of well-known passengers would help sell tickets for the tour that featured France, Italy, Greece, Russia, Turkey, Syria, Palestine, Egypt, and Spain. As such, the *Quaker City* excursion was among the first commercial versions of Old World tourism, combining parts of the Grand Tour of Europe with a pilgrimage to the Holy Land. Henry Ward Beecher and General Sherman, along with several other notables, had been advertised as possible passengers, but both pulled out of the journey, leaving the humorist Mark Twain as the most famous member of the party.[1] Samuel Clemens, as "Mark Twain," had written travel letters to various newspapers about his trip to the Kingdom of Hawaii in 1866 and about his travels through the United States, and he was well aware of the popularity of travel writing. Mark Twain convinced the San Francisco *Alta California* to pay his $1,250 fare in exchange for fifty travel letters and also contracted with the New York *Tribune* and New York *Herald* to write additional letters. Mark Twain's travel letters, published in California and New York papers (and quoted widely), helped solidify his reputation as one of the most popular humorists of the nation. The success of his travel writing, especially as it was revised and published in *The Innocents Abroad*, helped transform Mark Twain into both the most notable American humorist and, according to some critics, pushed him into a new realm of quality that distinguished him from the mere popular humorist.

The cruise lasted for five months, returning November 19, 1867. Clemens stayed in New York for a brief time, writing a scathing letter about the trip for the *Tribune*, seething that "the pleasure trip was a funeral excursion without a corpse." Soon thereafter, Clemens moved to Washington, D.C., for a job as the private secretary to Nevada senator W. M. Steward, while at the same time writing letters for the New York *Herald* and considering options for transforming his *Quaker City* travel letters into a book. On the same day he left for Washington, the New York *Herald* wrote a brief notice predicting success if he chose to write a book: "We are not aware whether Mr. Mark Twain intends giving us a book on this pilgrimage, but we do know that a book written from his own peculiar standpoint, giving an account of the characters and events on board ship and of the scenes which the pilgrims witnessed, would command an almost unprecedented sale." On the same day, November 21, Elisha Bliss of the American Publishing Company of Hartford, Connecticut, wrote to Clemens suggesting that he publish a book with the firm based on his travel letters. The letter stated that the firm was "perhaps the oldest subscription house in the country, and have never failed to give a book an immense circulation" and trumpeted the large printings of A. D. Richardson's books, the first of which had sold almost 100,000 copies.[2]

While his book was in process, Mark Twain lectured on the platform in California and Nevada and as part of the lyceum circuit in the East and Midwest. Moving into the lyceum, which promoted a lecture series to instruct and edify, shifted the audience expectations Mark Twain faced as a performer, which highlighted significant factors of his reputation and the meanings of his humor as a product. This chapter examines the reception of Mark Twain's first book and the lecture performances it engendered. These productions changed Mark Twain's reputation in crucial ways, placing him at the forefront of American newspaper humorists and, in the view of some critics, elevating him into the realm of literary humor. Mark Twain's lectures on the lyceum stage placed him in conversation with literary men in a venue that was expanding after the Civil War as a public space that balanced entertainment and edification. Audience reactions highlight the shifting expectations critics placed on the humorist in the public sphere. Published via the subliterary form of the subscription press, the popularity of *The Innocents Abroad* would have mitigated his reputation in serious literary realms. But through the work of the publisher and author—as well as the arguments of certain critics—the reception of his book pushed him out of the merely humorous into discussions of quality humor and into the possibility that Mark Twain should be thought a humorist of quality. Especially important for Mark Twain's lecture and his first subscription book—*The*

Innocents Abroad (1869)—was the question of his humorous attitude toward the sacred sights of the Holy Land, especially the question of irreverence.

Critical evaluations of *The Innocents Abroad* generally held that the book was one that should be purchased and read, despite some tendency toward coarseness, and that the book would improve his standing as a humorist. These reviews are key moments in which the reputation of "Mark Twain" was raised, discussed, and contested. No critical consensus emerged as to his standing as a humorist. Some critics held that his work was at or near the head of the school of American humor; some critics held that he had moved beyond this categorization, approaching something of the lasting humor of quality humorists; some dismissed this group of humorists as degrading to literary life, while others simply ignored Mark Twain and American humor altogether. But the success of *The Innocents Abroad* marked a transition from "Wild Humorist of the Pacific Slope," as he was sometimes called, to a central figure in the critical debate over the meaning of American humor.

"HE LOOKS AS IF HE WOULD MAKE A GOOD HUSBAND AND A JOLLY FATHER": THE LIBERALIZATION AND PROFESSIONALIZATION OF THE WESTERN VANDAL

The preparation and publication of *The Innocents Abroad* occurred in the context of major changes in Samuel Clemens's material life, especially his courtship and engagement to Olivia Langdon. The pressures of respectability—both personal and professional—worked to shift Clemens's world from that of a western rowdy to eastern family man and Mark Twain's work from "wild humorist of the Pacific Slope" to the forefront of American humorists. The choice to pursue a woman from a respectable family, as well as the influence of respectable literary advisors, helped Clemens shift Mark Twain's works toward more respectable—and larger—audiences. The mixture of personal and business concerns resulted in a book and lecture tour in which the relationship of humorist and audience was central, both artistically and financially. In his lecture tour on the *Quaker City* excursion, which occurred while the book was in process, Mark Twain framed himself as one of the American "Vandals" who had plundered the Old World. But in his career and personal life, Samuel Clemens was transforming from vandal into a humorist fit for family reading.

The most consequential decision Clemens made upon his return may have been his choice to publish his second book via subscription. Unclear on the details of subscription publishing, he responded to a proposal by Elisha Bliss, of the American Publishing Company of Hartford, in December 1867, making his primary interest clear when he asked "what amount of money I might possibly make out of it. The latter clause has a degree of importance for me which is almost beyond my own comprehension. But you understand that of course." For an author disappointed in the poor sales of his first book, the prospect of higher sales was met with excitement. Over the next two years, as Clemens prepared the manuscript and Bliss prepared the publication, the letters to his publisher show a keen interest in the material business of publication, from a discussion of royalties (5 percent of the subscription price) to an angry letter protesting the delay of publication to fit the publisher's schedule.[3] Clemens's eyes were keenly on the publication, promotion, and sales of the book. When the book was finished and awaiting release in the fall of 1869, his position had shifted tremendously professionally and personally; he had gone from newspaper humorist to successful lyceum performer and editor/part-owner of the Buffalo *Express*, and he was preparing to marry Olivia Langdon, a woman from a respectable and wealthy family.

While on the *Quaker City* excursion, Clemens had come under the influence of Mrs. Mary Fairbanks, the wife of the owner and editor of the Cleveland *Herald*, who traveled on the trip alone, writing twenty-seven travel letters for her husband's paper under the name "Myra." He referred to her affectionately as "Mother Fairbanks" and experienced a measure of reformation from his posture as western rowdy under her supervision. While scholars disagree about the extent of her editing, Clemens willingly claimed that she helped to refine both his writings and his personal manners. As Jeffrey Steinbrink has examined, Mark Twain sought to refine his professional image and his personal life as Samuel Clemens after the *Quaker City* excursion. Mark Twain did not become fully "respectable," and the domestication of Samuel Clemens is out of the scope of our concern, but in the revisions of his travel letters into the book that would become *The Innocents Abroad*, Mark Twain showed an effort to prune slang, indelicacies, and other vulgarisms, largely to cater to an audience that was comically dramatized in his relationship to Mother Fairbanks.[4]

Clemens's playful relationship with Fairbanks touched on one topic of concern intimately connected with his revisions to his travel letters, which he began in the winter of 1868 and continued in California that spring. This was the topic of reverence—and of irreverence. In reviewing American humorists, critics frequently brought up the topic of reverence, sometimes faulting humorists of the type with which Mark Twain was classed, for their coarseness in regard to sentiments many held sacred. With Mark Twain's travel letters, especially the ones written in frustration close after the end of the trip, a lack of reverence for both his fellow passengers and for certain subjects, especially that of religious sites, was called into question. Clemens apologized to "My Dear Forgiving Mother" on December 2, 1867, claiming that he had been rightfully angry with some of the trip's participants. As if to make up for his transgression, in the same letter he bragged that she had cured him of his habit of swearing—his skill at which had put most people to shame, he boasted—and that the American Publishing Company had contacted him about publishing a book.[5] Mary Fairbanks, and then Olivia, served as the idealized polite audiences whom Clemens sought to amuse, constructing them not so much as genteel censors but rather as representative customers.

While on the West Coast, Mark Twain lectured over eleven nights in San Francisco, Sacramento, Virginia City, and several other cities. He performed portions of his forthcoming book—the Holy Land, Venice, and his fellow tourists. Reviews covered familiar subjects: Mark Twain's manner of lecturing, the mixture of funny and eloquent passages, his similarities to and differences from Artemus Ward, and the widespread enjoyment of the large audiences. For the first appearance, Mark Twain asked the local press not to publish the contents of his lecture, so as not to ruin the effect of the subsequent performances. This became a repeated tactic, as he felt that shoddy reports of his speeches ruined his audiences. In his history of Mark Twain's lectures, Fred Lorch wrote that his objections went beyond the damage such a report did to the humor; Mark Twain believed that his lectures were his literary property and that reprinting them did monetary damage to his livelihood.[6]

As he was discovering while editing his book, a major question for lecture audiences was the question of reverence. In his lectures drawn from his travels, Mark Twain learned that certain subjects—especially the Holy Land—immediately raised the question of how far the humorist could make fun of certain subjects without being considered profane. The San Francisco *Daily Morning Call* described the lecture in these terms: "His journey to the Holy Land has been called a pilgrimage. It was more properly a *crusade*—a humorous tilting against shams and sentiment. He battered the casques of friends and foes, perhaps not always fairly, but always effectively. He was a crusader on his own hook—a kind of free lance, working himself into a grotesque rage over dullness, carving the sconces of proper folk, and making it lively for infinite respectability."[7] Mark Twain's rage over the shams and sentiment of "infinite respectability" would be a common theme of later discussions about the quality of his humor. The Sacramento *Daily Union* also described his irreverence in positive terms, relating his stance to one of the major figures of quality humor: Voltaire. Writing of his viewpoint on the Holy Land, the reviewer writes:

> *He saw them only with the eyes of a practical American, keenly alive to progress and the present, and prepared for ridicule in spite of the gloss of romance and the eld of history. Yet they are mistaken who deem that he has no fancy or poetic feeling. Voltaire had this none the less because he ridiculed time-honored custom and things held sacred by great names. We confess to a partiality for this California humorist. At the bottom of his intellectual character there seems to us to lie a vast deal of good sense, which his humor is only used to dress up in such presentable style as will hardly fail to please any audience.*[8]

On the West Coast, Mark Twain's irreverence was largely viewed positively as a type of satire, at least in the press. So-called sacred subjects—transformed into shams by respectable sentiment—required a humorist with good sense to pierce the hypocrisies of "common folk." Mark Twain's respectability was precisely the issue as he moved east, both physically, as a lecturer and to settle down, and commercially, as he published with an eastern press focused on selling to respectable customers.

On July 2, 1868, Mark Twain gave his lecture on "Venice, Past and Present" in San Francisco. Four days later, he left California for New York, never to return to the state with which he was most closely associated at that point in his career. From August 1868 to February 1869, Clemens did or heard little on the book, as Bliss presumably read the proofs to offer his own suggestions but more likely was concentrated on the promotion of a biography of Grant. In March 1869, Clemens and Olivia Langdon, now engaged, read the proofs of the book together. During that winter and spring, Mark Twain lectured using a revised version of his western lecture on the trip under the new title, "The American Vandal Abroad." From November to March, he lectured in forty cities, largely smaller towns in the Midwest and upstate New York.[9] Mark Twain's lecture tours did much to establish his fame and increase his audience, and the consideration of their importance cannot be separated from the consideration of his written works in delineating his critical and popular reputation.

With this lecture tour, Mark Twain transitioned to professional lyceum humorist under the representation of the Redpath Boston Lyceum Bureau. In the years following the Civil War, the lyceum was transformed from a local and regional system dedicated to serious lectures to an increasingly national system of lecturers booked by agencies and populated by new types of speakers, notably the inclusion of humorists as occasional lecturers to lighten the tone of a season's series. This professionalization, argues Robert T. Oliver, changed the expectations of the audiences, who no longer came to listen to impassioned amateurs but instead rewarded polished speakers with palatable messages and impressive speaking skills. Lyceum committees faced a split between those who saw the lecture course's purpose as educational and those who appreciated some entertainment with their uplift. The commercialization of the institution was summarized by Josh Billings, himself a successful platform humorist, who wrote in his "Advice Tew Lectur Kommittys": "Don't hire enny man tew lectur for yu (never mind how moral he iz) unless you kan make munny on him." The professionalization of the lecture bureau meant that committees paid higher rates in advance to acquire talent and had to pick lectures that would sell.[10] Mark Twain quickly became the most sought-after humorist by lyceum committees looking to leaven the educational seriousness of their lecture season. Like the circus and other forms of mass culture, but also like the quality magazines and other forms of respectable culture, the lyceum relied on a rhetoric of respectability and uplift through leisure while catering to as large an audience as possible to fill seats or buy subscriptions.

The direct reactions of audiences to Mark Twain's lecture performances provide crucial insight into the reception of humor and his reputation as a humorist as these shifted in the late 1860s and early 1870s. Mark Twain began his vandal tour on the lyceum circuit in Cleveland, where the beneficent presence of Mother Mary Fairbanks helped set the tone for the reception of the lecture. As he composed the lecture, he sent updates to Fairbanks seeking to reassure her that the lecture would be "a creditable one. If diligent effort will do this I shall accomplish it." Nevertheless, Clemens sought to strike a balance between serious description and humor for his new role as lyceum lecturer: "Of course, scattered all through, are the most preposterous yarns, & all that sort of thing. But I *think* it will *entertain* an audience, this lecture. I *must not* preach to a select few in my audience, lest I have only a select few to listen, next time, & so be required to preach no more. What the societies *ask* of me is to *relieve* the heaviness of their didactic courses—& in accepting the contract I am just the same as *giving my word* that I will do as they ask." Despite his joking, Clemens traveled to Cleveland several days before the lecture, "so you can get ready to scratch. I'll expunge every word you want scratched out, cheerfully."[11]

Eschewing almost any discussion of the Holy Land, and only briefly touching on the art of the Old Masters, topics that had raised his ire in the travel letters, Mark Twain focused on European scenes, with large portions of description interspersed with humor. In his "American Vandal" lectures, humor was largely complimentary to the ideas of American superiority that underwrote much travel writing of the era, a sentiment that he had attacked through his satires of the "pilgrims" of the tour. Here, Mark Twain followed the "vandal" through Europe (and to see the Sphinx), but he was careful not to define the vandal "in derision or apply it as a reproach," but to use it to mean "the roving, independent, free and easy character of that class of traveling Americans who are *not* elaborately educated, cultivated and refined, and gilded and filigreed with the ineffable graces of the first society."[12] Undoubtedly playing to his audience's sentiment, Mark Twain praised American women: "We saw no ladies anywhere that were as beautiful as our own ladies here at home & especially in this audience." He ended with a lengthy passage that was not undercut by facetiousness, but spoke to a serious moral, although he had written Mrs. Fairbanks that "the moral is an entirely gratuitous contribution & will be a clear gain to the societies employing me, for it isn't deduced from anything there is in the lecture."[13] It went, in part:

> *If there is a moral to this lecture it is an injunction to all Vandals to travel. I am glad the American Vandal goes abroad. It does him good. It makes a better man of him. It rubs out a multitude of his old unworthy biases and prejudices. It aids in his religion, for it enlarges his charity and his benevolence, it broadens his views of men and things. . . . It liberalizes the Vandal to travel. You never saw a bigoted, opinionated, stubborn, narrow-minded, self-conceited, almighty mean man in your life but he had stuck in one place ever since he was born and though God made the world and dyspepsia and bile for his especial comfort and satisfaction. So I say, by all means let the American Vandal go on traveling, and let no man discourage him.*[14]

The speech contained little that could be called irreverence, and apart from some slight deflating of the romance of Venice and other European cities, it reads mostly as a paean to travel by a man who was becoming something of a *liberalized* vandal himself.

Reviewers found much of the humor in Mark Twain's lectures in his peculiar delivery and in his unique physical presence—in Mark Twain's later description: the *manner* of telling rather than the *matter*. The Chicago *Tribune* provided a lengthy description of the "well-known humorist" following his performance, which read, in part:

> *Blessed with long legs, he is tall, reaching five feet ten inches in his boots; weight, 167 pounds; body lithe and muscular; head round and well set on considerable neck, and feet of no size within the ken of a shoemaker, so he gets his boots and stockings always made to order. . . . He smokes tobacco. Drink never crosses the threshold of his humorous mouth. Fun lurks in the corners of it. The eyes are deep set and twinkle like stars in a dark night. The brow overhangs the eyes, and the head is protected from the weather by dark and curling locks. The face is eminently a good one, a laughing face, beaming with humor and genuine good nature. He looks as if he would make a good husband and a jolly father. . . . His manner is peculiar; he hangs round loose, leaning on the desk, or flirting round the corners of it; then marching and counter-marching in the rear of it, marking off ground by the yard with his tremendous boots. . . . His voice is a long monotonous drawl, well adapted to his style of speaking. The fun invariably comes in at the end of a sentence, after a pause. When the audience least expects it, some dry remark drops and tickles the ribs, and endangers the waist buttons of the "laughists."[15]*

In a letter to Olivia Langdon, Clemens told of a reporter who had wanted to print a synopsis of his lecture, to which he replied:

> *And I said to take the points out of a humorous lecture was the same as taking the raisins out of a fruit cake—it left it but a pretense of a something it was not, for such as came after.*
>
> *And further, the charm of a humorous remark or still more, an elaborate succession of humorous remarks, cannot be put upon paper—& whosoever reports a humorous lecture verbatim, & necessarily leaves the soul out of it, & no more presents that lecture to the reader than a person presents a man to you when he ships you a corpse.*

> *I said synopses injure—they do harm, because they'd travel ahead of*
> *the lecturer & give people a despicable opinion of him & his production.*[16]

Samuel Clemens's embodiment of Mark Twain's humor through his body, voice, and speech were commented upon more often than the content of his lectures over the course of his lyceum career, and the reviews that attempted to transcribe or paraphrase his speeches were distinctly lifeless.

Following Mark Twain's performance in Cleveland on November 17, 1868, Mrs. Fairbanks wrote a review in her husband's paper, the *Herald*. As would be expected, the review was glowing. But the terms of the approbation are highly telling as expressions of hopeful praise meant to convince other audiences, including the members of lyceum committees, that the humorist "Mark Twain" was respectable entertainment. The audience was ready to "criticize closely this new candidate for their favor," but he quickly won his judges' favor and held their attention "by the magnetism of his varied talent."[17] Undoubtedly at Clemens's request, the review did not provide any transcript of the lecture and claims not to want to damage the beauty of the lecture—"for beauty and poetry it certainly possessed, though the production of a profound humorist." The praise continued: for the amusing stories, for the gem-like descriptions, for the word painting, and for the "good-natured recital of the characteristics of the harmless 'Vandal'." Fairbanks found no hint of irreverence, concluding:

> *We congratulate Mr. Mark Twain upon having taken the tide of public*
> *favor "at the flood" in the lecture field, and having conclusively proved*
> *that a man may be a humorist without being a clown. He has elevated*
> *his profession by his graceful delivery and by recognizing in his audience*
> *something higher than merely a desire to laugh. We can assure the cities*
> *who await his coming that a rich feast is in store for them and Cleveland*
> *is proud to offer him the first laurel leaf, in his role as lecturer this side*
> *of the "Rocky-slope."*

The review gave official sanction to Mark Twain's increasing respectability and the consequent shedding of his irreverence. Unlike the reviews of his lectures in California, none of the extant reviews of the lyceum tour discuss his attitude toward the sacred.

One review was highly critical of Mark Twain. Several days before his lecture, the Iowa City *Republican* declared that, although they had not heard "the celebrated humorist" lecture, he had earned a reputation as a speaker "that he could not have made without merit."[18] The reviewer was later disappointed. "As a lecture it was a humbug," the review stated:

> As an occasion for laughter on very small capital of wit or ideas it was a success. There were one or two passages of some merit. His apostrophe to the Sphinx was decidedly good, as was also his description of the ruins of the Parthenon, and of Athens by moonlight. Some touches of Venice did very well, but it was impossible to know when he was talking in earnest and when in burlesque. It was amusing and interesting to see such a crowd of people laughing together, even though we knew half of them were ashamed that they were laughing at such very small witticisms. We were very much disappointed that there was so little substance to his lecture. We would not give two cents to hear him again.[19]

The distinction between earnest substance and humorous burlesque was the pivot on which much of Mark Twain's humor turned, with passages of "word painting" alternating with moments of levity. For example, the vivid description of Athens and the Parthenon by moonlight mentioned in the review ends with Mark Twain apostrophizing about walking in the same steps as Plato, Aristotle, and Herodotus until he and his comrades get to stealing grapes and are marched back to the ship by a military escort. He concluded: "[A]h, I never traveled in so much state in all my life."[20]

At this date, the inclusion of a humorist as an official part of a lyceum course was still a novelty, but few reviews questioned Mark Twain's role on the lecture stage. The above review presages a split that would grow between reviewers who found Mark Twain's fun to be worthwhile, as evidenced by the audience's laughter, and those who found fault with his humor as being of poor quality and out of place in the lyceum. For these reviewers, the respectable portions of the audience laughed, if they did so at all, because others did and with a certain shame. Reviews of Mark Twain's lectures increasingly split between those who found pleasure in laughter and those who reacted in disgust to the type of laughter that Mark Twain inspired.

"BOOKS WERE BOUGHT BY THE POUND"
WRITING FOR THE SUBSCRIPTION AUDIENCE

The possibility of Mark Twain's humor striking audiences as profane or shameful was clearly on Clemens's mind as *The Innocents Abroad* was prepared for publication in 1869. Mark Twain's lectures had shown an awareness of the problem of reverence, especially in relation to discussions of the Holy Land, which he had merely avoided in his later "American Vandal" lecture. For the book, this issue could not be avoided, as Clemens had to include his observations on the Holy Land, as this was a central part of the tour, and he needed a large amount of material to fill out the book's necessary length of 600 or so pages.

As would often be the case during his career, Clemens pruned portions of his works based on objections from outside readers: Bret Harte, "Mother" Fairbanks, William Dean Howells, and Olivia Langdon. Called Livy Langdon, she was the sister of Charley Langdon, who had been a fellow traveler on the *Quaker City* voyage. She would act as an editor and literary conscience in the mold of Mother Fairbanks, and scholars have debated the extent to which her influence acted as censorship representing the voice of Victorian propriety or acted as a sometimes necessary bulwark against Mark Twain's wilder urges.[21] But in the spring of 1868, it was Bret Harte who acted as Clemens's literary conscience. Editing the manuscript, Harte advised cutting several irreverent or improper passages, and in return, Harte published extracts from the book in his new magazine, the *Overland Monthly*, which billed itself as the *Atlantic Monthly* of California. Writing to Thomas Bailey Aldrich in 1871, Clemens credited Harte with a considerable role in helping to elevate his writing. He wrote that Harte had "trimmed & trained & schooled me patiently until he changed me from an awkward utterer of coarse grotesquenesses to a writer of paragraphs & chapters that have found a certain favor in the eyes of even some of the very decentest people in the land."[22] Clemens delivered the manuscript to Bliss in August 1868, presumably trimmed of coarse grotesqueness, after adding a considerable amount of material to fill out the pages of a subscription-length book.

The exact audience for subscription books escapes classification. On a basic level, subscription books were not sold in bookstores and were only available for purchase from canvassing agents. The average subscription book cost roughly three times the cost of a trade book, depending on the binding chosen (between $3.50 and $5.00 for *The Innocents Abroad*).

Subscription books were longer than average trade books, featured more illustrations, and were printed on higher quality paper. These traits led to a common view that the books were objects of display, not actually for reading. George Ade, a realist author and humorist of the late nineteenth and early twentieth centuries, wrote of the subscription trade following Samuel Clemens's death:

> The new books came a year apart, and each was meant for the center table, and it had to be so thick and heavy and emblazoned with gold that it could keep company with the bulky and high-priced Bible.
>
> Books were bought by the pound. Sometimes the agent was a ministerial person in black clothes and a stove-pipe hat. Maiden ladies and widows, who supplemented their specious arguments with private tales of woe, moved from one small town to another feeding upon prominent citizens. Occasionally the prospectus was unfurled by an undergraduate of a freshwater college working for the money to carry him another year.
>
> The book agents varied, but the book was always the same,—many pages, numerous steel engravings, curly-cue tail-pieces, platitudes, patriotism, poetry, sentimental mush. One of the most popular, still resting in many a dim sanctuary, was known as "Mother, Home, and Heaven." A ponderous collection of "Poetical Gems" did not involve the publishers in any royalty entanglements. . . .
>
> Nobody really wanted these books. They were purchased because the agents knew how to sell them, and they seemed large for the price, and, besides, every well-furnished home had to keep something on the center table.[23]

The boys of the seventies, Ade writes, discovered Mark Twain when they were expecting Tupper and were delivered from a "Mausoleum into a Temple of Mirth." The majority of subscription books were travel books, books of history or what was called "ethnology," or bland collections of wit and wisdom. Mark Twain's books stand out both as some of the best-selling subscription books and as the main subscription offerings discussed in larger cultures of letters as aspiring to "literature."

Key to the revisions of *The Innocents Abroad* from newspaper humor to subscription book was a perceived difference in audience. As Hamlin Hill has argued, the subscription audience sought a mixture of information and anecdote, entertainment and edification, and topics of general interest rather than literary works.[24] The audience was marked as distinctively domestic, in that the books were purchased in the reader's home and meant to be displayed in the home. Unlike his newspaper work, which was by its nature ephemeral and often masculine, the subscription book was aimed at an audience comprised of men, women, and children, whose sentiments had to be taken into account. As Nancy Cook has argued, by publishing via subscription, Mark Twain became not only the author of his books, but their "*maker*" in a way different from the romanticized literary productions associated with trade publishers like Ticknor and Fields.[25] The audience of subscription books was similar to the audience of literary publishers in that both sought a respectable reader with a certain level of developed taste. And while the tastes of literary periodicals, trade books, and subscription readers possessed major differences, the concept of "respectability" shaped each and allowed Mark Twain's newer, less profane, role as a humorist to place his book in the realm of literary respectability.

Published and sold by subscription, *The Innocents Abroad* was issued in July 1869 in the midst of a slump in the book industry that had depressed trade sales. Hamlin Hill notes that Clemens held subscription publishing in high regard, as long as the books were selling to his satisfaction, but when sales flagged or missed expectations, he blasted his publishers with his most fiery wrath. Hill finds in Samuel Clemens's dealings with his publishers an ambivalence between commercial success and literary respectability. He writes: "One of Mark Twain's aquiline eyes was on the cash box, while the other focused on the almost ascetically high-minded world of the New England literary Brahmins."[26] This generalization is true of Mark Twain in the 1870s, but in the late 1860s the question was not literature but lucre.

The promotion of *The Innocents Abroad* took two major forms: the subscription prospectus, or "sales dummy," and newspaper reviews. In issuing a sales prospectus for agents to present to potential customers, Bliss selected approximately ten percent of *The Innocents Abroad* for presentation. Two versions of the prospectus were issued. Hill notes that the first version focused on passages of "fairly low humor and burlesques of sentimentality, highfalutin airs, and erudition." The second version replaced a passage of broad burlesque with the description of the Sphinx, which had been a highlight of reviews of Mark Twain's lectures as a quality piece of "word painting." Hill speculates that this change reflects Bliss's growing awareness of Mark Twain's more literary values and the value of selling Mark Twain's quality writing "to an audience who wanted at least a tiny taste of the merits of accepted, cultivated literature."[27]

The major thrust of the prospectus was its presentation of Mark Twain's position as an "original" and "unique" observer, one who saw well-known sights differently than writers before him had. Each version reprinted the preface to the book, in which Mark Twain framed the book not as a scientific record or conventional travel book, but as a "pleasure trip" and a "record of a pic-nic." His purpose, he wrote, was "to suggest to the reader how *he* would be likely to see Europe and the East if he looked at them with his own eyes instead of the eyes of those who traveled in those countries before him."[28] In the prospectus and the finished book, Mark Twain was the central character, and many of the illustrations show him in various poses and adventures. A promotional description, placed at the end of both versions of the prospectus, emphasized the author's "new and entirely original view of persons, place and things abroad, describing them as they appeared to him." Echoing the positive critiques of his lectures, the blurb trumpeted "humorous and witty delineations," "vivid and sparkling descriptions," and "fresh and amusing anecdotes." The description ends with a fascinating statement:

> *While running over with wit and humor, and sharp with satire upon many of the customs and follies of the age, it still teams with glowing descriptions, and with elegant and classical allusions. The scholar will find pleasure in its perusal as well as others. No one will rise from its reading without having a better and clearer knowledge of the countries it describes than ever before, and more ability to judge between truth and fiction in what he may read respecting them in the future.*

Linking humor, satire, description, classical allusions, and more, the prospectus aimed for the widest possible audience by trying to convince every reader that the book was "unique" and would provide the reader with a sense of just how *he* would see the same sights, flattering the reader that he also had a keen sense of humor. In the prospectus, this blurb was located after the book selections facing a full-page poster with an illustration of Mark Twain as a traveler, wearing a suit coat over a mixture of pioneer and American Indian garb, with a travel case in one hand and a tomahawk in the other—the image of a western savage abroad.

Reflecting a concern with how Mark Twain was framed as a humorist and writer within the larger culture of American letters, the second version of the sales dummy reprinted four pages of "Paragraphs from Notices of this Book" and a one-page "Opinions of the Press." The notices were drawn

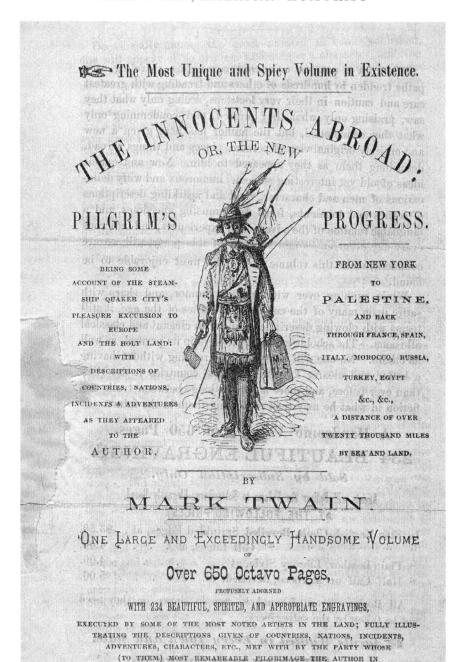

FIGURE 2.1: Mark Twain Sales Prospectus Poster for *The Innocents Abroad* From *The Innocents Abroad* Sales Prospectus. **Courtesy of the Albert and Shirley Small Special Collections Library, University of Virginia**

from a four-page advertising circular that Bliss had printed, which included the notices, a version of the poster above, the advertising puff discussed above, and a page of price listings.[29] The page of "Opinions of the Press" consisted of four reviews of Mark Twain's "American Vandals" lecture, with Mary Fairbanks's review from the Cleveland *Herald* as the first on the page. Additionally, two pre-publication notices of Mark Twain's book were printed, including one from the Elmira *Daily Gazette* that was based on advance sheets it had received, presumably from Clemens on a visit to Olivia Langdon. This notice contained a description of Mark Twain's book that argued for his elevation beyond his place as a mere funny man. The book's scenes, it read:

> are treated in that peculiarly attractive vein of power and genuine humor, which has made him widely famous, and placed him at the head of the witty writers of America. Mr. Clemens, however, is something besides a literary humorist. There occurs in his writing a blending of sentiment and thought as fine and striking as they are beautiful and sparkling—ideas as clear and penetrating as his humor is fresh. From what we have seen of his new book we are led to believe that it will do much towards advancing his reputation, and establish it on an enduring basis. That it will be a success is already assured.

This paragraph frames the key questions of the reviews of the books that would follow: was the book something more than mere humor and, if so, what did the quality of the book mean for Mark Twain's reputation?

Mark Twain had varying views on the value of newspaper promotion, asking Bliss not to send copies of *The Innocents Abroad* for review but also blaming lower sales of his next book on a lack of newspaper attention. Hamlin Hill notes that Samuel Clemens blamed Bliss no matter what he did, so Bliss largely did what he thought was best in promoting the book through the content of the prospectus and through newspaper reviews.[30] Clemens and Bliss paid close attention to reviews, and they each collected early reviews for advertising use and timed later reviews to coordinate with the presence of canvassers in particular cities. On September 2, 1869, Clemens wrote Bliss about his idea to print a selection of "Notices of the Press" to distribute with the book's canvassers. In this letter, Clemens asked when an agent would be in Buffalo to canvass for the book, so that Bliss could solicit reviews at that time, which helps to explain the wide range of review dates for the book. On October 9, the Buffalo *Express* printed an advertising supplement with thirty-nine press notices of Clemens's new job as editor of the paper and forty-six selected from reviews of *The Innocents Abroad*. For these reviews, Clemens relied on a selection of notices printed in the new version of the sales prospectus, which had been issued sometime in September and contained selections from twenty-eight reviews.[31] In both this circular and in the revised prospectus, Samuel Clemens and/or Bliss edited the reviews to lessen criticisms and highlight praise.

Following the issue of the new sales dummy and the Buffalo *Express*'s advertising supplement in the fall of 1869, Clemens's concern over sales and promotion continued, and throughout the fall, he discussed promotion with Bliss.[32] In January, he praised Bliss's promotion of the book, writing: "Yes, I *am* satisfied with the way you are running the book. You are running it in staving, tip-top, first-class style. I never wander into any corner of the country but I find that an agent has been there before me, and many of that community have read the book. And on an average about ten people a day come and hunt me up to thank me and tell me I'm a benefactor!! I guess that is a part of the programme we didn't expect, in the first place."[33] Clemens then noted that sales in December had been much higher than in November or January, but that he couldn't complain about the $4,309.42 royalty check Bliss had sent, representing profits on a quarterly sale of approximately 23,500 copies, bringing the sale to upwards of 39,000 and over $7,000 in payments. The book maintained an average of 9,000 copies per month during the first three months of 1870 before reducing to approximately 3,000 per month. At the end of one year, just over 77,800 copies had been bound for sale,[34] with approximately 12,000 more bound by the end of the next year, and 125,749 copies bound at the end of 1879. By the standards of trade publishing, this was an astonishing success given the fact that the average book sold approximately 2,000 copies during this period. By the standards of humorous publishing, in which sales were often higher, Mark Twain's book qualified as a distinct success. For the American Publishing Company, the success of *The Innocents Abroad* was also unprecedented, allowing the company to expand with more authors and productions, which would please Samuel Clemens as stockholder and member of the board of directors from 1873 to 1881.

"JUST THE THING FOR FIRE-SIDE READING"
CRITICAL EVALUATIONS OF *THE INNOCENTS ABROAD*

Criticism of the work is almost impossible; as sufficient gravity of
countenance for the purpose, can hardly be maintained over the
volume. To think of, or look at it, is to smile, but to read it is to over-
whelm all criticism with uncontrolable [sic] laughter. It is truly an
original affair, and does credit to its author. . . . Altogether the book is
a good one; one we can heartily recommend to our readers. It is pure
in morals, and just the thing for fire-side reading. Buy this Book, say
we, and, our word for it, you will not regret the outlay.

—From the New Jersey *Journal,*
reprinted in "Paragraphs from Notices of This Book"
in the Buffalo *Express* and sales dummy of *The Innocents Abroad*

Reviews of *The Innocents Abroad* were extensive. The Buffalo *Express* claimed that over 1,200 newspapers had reviewed the book. Louis Budd, in his collection of reviews, lists 93 total reviews, including English notices, between July 28, 1869 and April 1871. Whether numbering over a thousand or closer to one hundred, the book was reviewed more than any of Mark Twain's books between 1865 and 1882. The reviews covered a range of topics: the quality of the book and its prospects for sales; the laughter the book inspired and its effect; the question of irreverence and how it mattered; and Mark Twain's reputation as a humorist and the effect of the book thereupon. While Samuel Clemens and his publisher were clearly concerned about the book's perceived irreverence affecting its sales, the reviews were almost uniformly positive, even when they wished Mark Twain had left out some passages that others might consider irreverent. Reviews of the book largely framed Mark Twain as a humorist—he was "that rollicking humorist," the "inimitable humorist," "the American humorist," "one of the best of American humorists," "that comic genius," "the greatest and purest humorist of the day," "the distinguished humorist," "a humorist of the highest order," or, more prosaically, "Mark the playful man." For the *Saturday Evening Review* of Elmira, Mark Twain was "the prince of American humorists," and the Toledo *Commercial* opined that "Mr. Clemens is the most elegant of the popular humorists of his day, and he deserves the reputation he has gained." Many reviews simply refer to him as a "humorist," although the magazine *Flags of Our Father* saw fit to formalize this title by noting that: "Mark Twain, the Humorist, has won a warm place in the popular heart."[35]

In introducing the book to its readers, many reviews assumed that the audience would know who Mark Twain was and may have already read many of his works. Highlighting the tendency to use both "Clemens" and "Mark Twain" in reference to the author, and the critical confusion this could engender, the Albany *Journal* began its review by noting that "Mr. Samuel L. Clemens—the Mark Twain of 'Mark Twain' of current literature—is deservedly one of our most popular humorists." Reviews consistently noted that Mark Twain's stories and travel letters had already circulated widely in newspapers, especially singling out "The Jumping Frog" as central to establishing his reputation as a humorist. The Cleveland *Leader*, for instance, observed that "the inimitable drolleries of Mark Twain had become current coin in the newspapers," and that many had judged the jumping frog story to be "the best piece of humor in American literature."[36] Reviews of *The Innocents Abroad* helped set the stage for a new dominant critical debate about Mark Twain's reputation, in which he was either at the head of the school of "American Humor" or in which he had surpassed that school to be classified, in the phrase of William Dean Howells, "in the company of the best." Mark Twain as a humorist improved hierarchically with *The Innocents Abroad* and used these evaluations—often in modified form—to sell himself as a new type of humorist: one who was both unique and fun, respectable and laugh inducing, and most importantly, a humorist whose book you would not regret buying.

The fact that the book was a subscription book did not seem to affect the number of reviews, as some scholars have argued, but it did affect the timing of reviews, and many of the reviews commented on the extra padding required to make it subscription length.[37] The New York *Evening Post* concluded its review with a line of praise, tempered by a critique of the length. The praise (italicized in the quotation) was included in the Buffalo *Express* collection of reviews and sales prospectuses, without the concluding point: "*The* Innocents Abroad *contains many scenes of real merriment that few can read without laughter; the cleverness, frankness and catholic spirit of the writer are everywhere apparent;* but the volume is much too ponderous, and would have been more acceptable to the public, and more creditable to the author's well-established reputation, had it been less by two-thirds." While a number of reviews echoed the point about length, several others held that the book could very well have been longer. The Paterson *Guardian*, in another instance excerpted in the prospectus (in italics), stated: "*It is a large book*—a very large book—*but* then *a reading of a few pages is sufficient to convince the reader that Mark is equal to it, and could stand a good deal longer one. The public could also.*"[38]

Echoing the critical praise for his lectures, numerous reviews discussed Mark Twain's abilities in the realms of description and eloquence, as well as with humor, such as the New York *Sun*'s view that "Aside from its mirth, the book abounds in clear and graphic description, and now and then the author indulges in sentimental writing and bursts of eloquence quite in contrast with his levity on other pages. Altogether the book is both instructive and entertaining. . . ." The Newark *Morning Register* praised the book for its "pages of real humor, sparkling narrative, and graphic descriptive writings," continuing to say that "it is a rare and wonderful combination. The humor is natural, never forced; the narrative is instructive, and the descriptive passages are some of the finest in the English language, abounding in choice expressions and beautiful metaphor."[39] As evidence of the quality of eloquence, the reviews occasionally quoted Mark Twain's description of the Sphinx, while more often citing his tears at finding the grave of a relative at the Tomb of Adam as the height of levity. An illustration of the Sphinx was included in the sales dummy, but the illustration of the Tomb of Adam was not; however, the association of Mark Twain and Adam would become a popular trope when illustrating his image, as would his association with jumping frogs. Reviews held that the quality of Mark Twain's humor was enhanced by the mixture of fun and fact, of eloquence and clear description, of sentiment and the occasional pathos.

Reviews of the book contained one theme that would have been gratifying to both Mark Twain's interests as an author and Samuel Clemens's interests as a man engaged to be married: sales. Reviews often noted the presence of a canvasser selling the book in town, as canvassers or the publisher supplied books for review to prime the public for sales. For instance, the city of Cleveland was targeted for canvassing in late September, and three local papers reviewed the book between the 23rd and 29th. The Cleveland *Plain Dealer* stated that "the mere announcement of publication will create a demand that the publishers will do well if they can supply," while the Cleveland *Leader* held that "It is hardly too much to say that no book published in this country for years has been awaited

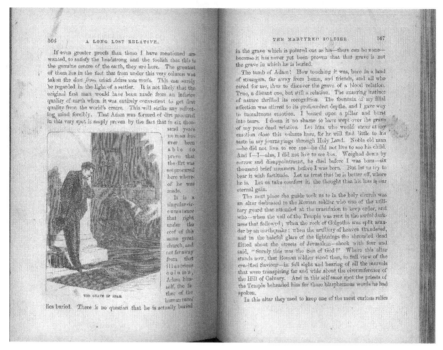

FIGURE 2.2: Mark Twain at the Grave of Adam. From *The Innocents Abroad*.
Courtesy of Sandra Louise Youngren

with more feverish anxiety." The newspaper where "Mark Twain" was born as a contributor, the Virginia City *Territorial Enterprise*, did not so much review the book as announce its sale to his "thousand friends and admirers" who would be sure to order from the "lady [who] arrived in town yesterday," concluding: "But it is unnecessary for us to speak of its merits or demerits, as everybody will buy it and all that could be said would pass unheeded in the enjoyment of the work itself." The *Saturday Evening Review* of Elmira brought together many of the thread of reviews in a manner that would have surely made Clemens and Bliss hopeful for continued sales, writing: "There is a health about it, and it beams with a cheerful, hopeful, religious vein—is adapted to all classes, and will undoubtedly become a welcome visitant to most of the reading firesides scattered throughout the land." As the Pittsburgh *Gazette* noted: "As we don't suppose there is one person out of ten who wouldn't read Mark Twain's books if he could, there is hardly any necessity for doing more here than merely to announce that this new work is in the hands of agents now, and will shortly be brought before the people."[40]

FIGURE 2.3: Mark Twain at the Grave of Adam. From the *American Publisher* (Hartford, Conn.), July 1872, 8. **Courtesy of Hal Bush**

The major factor by which the book was judged was its ability to incite laughter. As Jennifer Hughes has pointed out, one major historical meaning of laughter in the nineteenth century was in its use as a medicinal panacea,

MARK TWAIN AT THE TOMB OF ADAM.

FIGURE 2.4: Mark Twain at the Grave of Adam. From *Harper's New Monthly Magazine*, May 1875, 849. **Collection of the Author**

a view that held that laughter was a medical benefit, no matter the cause.[41] Several of the reviews recommended the book as a cure for "dyspepsia" and other diseases. One such review in the *Saturday Evening Review* held:

> It is not only a readable, but an enjoyable book, good for the blues, lively for dyspepsia, a damper on melancholy, a solace for many woes, an enlivener for anybody who has been lately dabbling in gold stocks. . . . [T]he verriest old blue stocking cannot read it without laughing at its rare and strange combinations of facts and incidents.—It is probably one of the best specimens of quaint and characteristic American humor, and too liberal effects can be avoided by imbibing in interrupted doses—not swallowing the whole at once.[42]

In a passage quoted in the sales prospectus, the Newark *Advertiser* also warned its readers to "rest your ribs" because Mark Twain's passages of eloquence and sentiment fail to provide enough relief—"There is more fun in it than it is safe to swallow at once."[43] The Fort Plain (N.Y.) *Mohawk Valley Register*, seems to have been swept away with the book's spirit in writing:

> *It will cause the lean to grow fat, the weak to wax strong, the blind to open their eyes, and the dolefully delirious to dance with joy! Buy it, by all means! . . . Buy it, and you will bless "Mark Twain" to the end of your existence. Its mirthful memories will shed a halo of the happiness around your pathway and over your declining years, like the mellow hues of a holden sunset around the rock-ribbed, snow capped, cloud-enveloped Sierras of the West!*[44]

The *Saturday Evening Post* of Philadelphia was even more direct: "Buy the book, laugh, and grow fat."[45]

Some references to the book's fun did mention the moral dimensions of such entertainment. The review in the Hartford *Courant* pointed out the moral dimensions of laughter in a quote that was only partially included in the sales prospectus (highlighted in italics): "With a dislike for a good many things in it that are not refined, and with the best intention to frown down on the book, *very few will be able to read it without laughing at least half the time. It may be absurd, but it certainly is funny*." For certain perceived audiences, Mark Twain's humor was not refined, but it caused people to smile who might wish to frown. The review from the Fairbanks's Cleveland *Herald*, while probably not written by "Mother," promoted Mark Twain's book as more than a "funny book," holding that Mark Twain was superior to most humorists of his kind and that the reader's response would reflect this fact: "It is sufficient to say that Mark Twain manages to tickle the risibilities of his readers, and that the readers are not ashamed of being provoked to laughter on such slight occasion."[46] As reviewers of Mark Twain's books and lectures would occasionally point out, there was laughter that one should be ashamed of and which the humorist should be ashamed of producing. No such shameful laughter was found in this review, although the reviewer had to justify Mark Twain as something more than "a mere buffoon or professional joke maker" and to address the big question of the reviews—the issue of Mark Twain's reverence.

A majority of the reviews discuss the question of reverence in the book, especially in relation to Mark Twain's treatment of the Holy Land and religious subjects, but also in relation to a general tone of approaching all subjects in a humorous manner. Critics often used the terms "flippant," "profane," "sacred," "reverent," and especially "coarse" when discussing this question. A reviewer in the *Saturday Evening Review* of Elmira, writing under the name "Ishmael," argued that the book was of high quality but that it faced one major problem: "To many minds, alas! for what human work can be perfect, this book has one blot that I fear will mar its sale—its apparent irreverence, its playful allusions to matters that a large portion of mankind have been taught to regard as sacred. It is dangerous in the extreme for one depending on the people of Christian lands for his success in life, to rub up violently or pleasantly, against religious prejudices."[47] Based on Bliss and Clemens's editing of the selected reviews for the revised sales prospectus, they were keenly aware of the charge of irreverence and were eager to erase this question from the sales pitch for the book. However, few reviews saw Mark Twain's treatment of such subjects as an impediment to sales. The majority of reviewers either argued that the book was not actually irreverent, despite what people might say, or that the incidents of irreverence might have been better left out but that Mark Twain was in fact "earnest" in his humor.

Reviews that charge Mark Twain with irreverence largely noted the presence of some questionable material, while also promoting the book as worth reading. The San Francisco *Evening Bulletin*, for instance, held that Mark Twain was "occasionally coarse, but never ill natured." The review then excoriated him for "offenses against good taste" by holding nothing to be sacred and wished that he had treated the Holy Land "less flippantly, with less levity, and a greater deference to the feelings of those more reverent and strong of faith."[48] But despite focusing almost entirely on incidents of Mark Twain's irreverence, the review ends by stating: "But barring these minor blemishes, the book is one of the most fresh, breezy, stimulating, and delightful we have read in many a day." No review recommended the reader avoid the book, and the vast majority recommended it to readers.

The review from the New York *Tribune* leveled some of the strongest critiques of the book's lack of reverence, while still recommending the book for most readers. In mid-August, Mark Twain requested a review from Whitelaw Reid, editor of the *Tribune*, where he had published several *Quaker City* letters and other pieces.[49] The review appeared on August 27 and clearly took exception with Mark Twain's irreverence, noting:

> *Mr. Clemens has an abominable irreverence for tradition and authority,—which sometimes unfortunately degenerates into an offensive irreverence for things which other men hold sacred,—and makes not the slightest hesitation at expressing his opinions in the very plainest possible language,*

no matter how unorthodox they may be. There is nothing which he fears to laugh at, and though some people may wish that he had been a little more tender of the romance of travel, it is certainly refreshing to find a tourist who does not care. . . .[50]

Mark Twain ignored the *Tribune*'s criticism in his subsequent use of it in the book's sales dummy. Eliding the critical sting, the notice from the *Tribune* was quoted as follows, beginning where the above quote ends: "It is refreshing to find a tourist who does not care what other tourists have said before him. Mark Twain must be rated as the chief representative of that peculiar kind of humor whose principal elements are not bad spelling and verbal burlesque, for he does not practice these arts. The greater part of his book is pure fun, and its freshness is wonderfully well sustained."[51] Clemens viewed the *Tribune* as the most important newspaper in setting the critical tone for a book (and its sales), and he focused on the positive portions of the review. On September 7, he wrote to thank Reid for the review: "Certainly & surely it isn't every adventurer's maiden experiment that fares so kindly at the hands of the press as mine has, & so if it don't sell a prodigious edition, after all the compliments & the publicity it has received, the fault will lie elsewhere than with the press."[52] An excerpt of the review cited in the advertising prospectus was transformed from: "But aside from religious traditions and the light treatment of them, this is a book which must be read to be thoroughly enjoyed" to "The 'Innocents Abroad' must be read to be thoroughly enjoyed."

Throughout the notices of the book reprinted in the prospectus and in the Buffalo *Express*, criticisms of the book's irreverence were cut in favor of the portions of the reviews that praise Mark Twain's humor and the book's value. Writing to Bliss, Clemens displayed an evident concern over the question of irreverence and the censorship of the issue for advertising purposes. On September 3, he wrote of the New York *Herald*'s review: "Yes the Herald's is a good notice & will help the book along. The irreverence of the volume appears to be a tip-top good feature of it, ~~financially~~ diplomatically speaking, though I wish with all my heart there wasn't an irreverent passage in it."[53] A certain amount of irreverence sold. In the Buffalo *Express* article that accompanied the notices, the unsigned reviewer noted that "what is to be told soberly he tells soberly, and with all the admiration or reverence that is due the subject." On the other hand, the review noted that Mark Twain was also fond of sticking a pin in "venerable moss grown shams"—and the distinction between subjects deserving reverence and those deserving satire was thus a key critical question in reviews of Mark Twain's works.[54]

Reviewers attempted to make such a distinction between the truly sacred and those "humbugs" or "shams" that are claimed to be holy but are not, such as the large quantities of relics passed off as real. The Elmira *Advertiser* expressed a somewhat common sentiment in writing that "an occasional allusion, which borders on irreverence, we could well wish omitted, but his wholesome satirical attacks upon everything in the way of hypocrisy, sham and cant, we sincerely thank him for." A more frequent tack was to acknowledge the occasional profane sentiment but to argue for a deeper reverence underlying Mark Twain's fun. The Cleveland *Herald*, in its prominent role as Mark Twain defender, argued that his role as "the laughing philosopher" forced him to counter the reverence of the travel party by making fun of what others held sacred. In reality, the reviewer argues, Mark Twain's "antic disposition" belies an earnest appreciation of the sublime and beautiful.[55] In causing his readers to laugh, Mark Twain was forced to balance between satirical jabs at false pieties and a certain reverence toward serious subjects. In both his books and his lectures, this balance was key to satisfying the multiple audiences who looked to the humorist for fun but not always for pointed satire.

The idea that the book might be hurt by its attitude toward the Holy Land and other sacred subjects may have simply been a critical shibboleth critics used to argue that they got the joke that other critics, more staid and less joyful, had missed. The New York *Herald* averred that their reading of the book's humor saw the real point of Mark Twain's seemingly irreverent approach to the Holy Land: "This part of the work some over-pious and fastidious critics have condemned because, as they urge, of its levity. We cannot find anything so very irreverent in his account. He merely insists upon taking a comical view of the situation."[56] The Syracuse *Standard* similarly took up Mark Twain's cause against "critics of the ultra refined order" who had criticized the book. In an unusual stance, the reviewer took the irreverence of the book to be its main selling point, writing that "if we had written just such a book . . . , we would consider it the highest praise if we were told that we were not a bit reverent in it. Its lack of reverence is to us the chiefest charm of *The Innocents*." Taking up the main point of the book's preface, the review notes that Mark Twain saw "just what all of us would see under the same circumstances" and told the truth, rather than what he thought he should say based on outdated authorities, which is their definition of reverence.[57] These reviews highlight the debates over the status of humor and laughter in a nation whose character was thought to be jolly.

While irreverence was a major critical concern, a number of reviews mentioned nothing about the subject, instead focusing on the relational position of Mark Twain to other humorists. Critics speculated on whether the book had solidified his position as heir to Artemus Ward's school of "American humor," or whether Mark Twain might be something more as a humorist. The quality of his humor, in its mixture of humor with artistic writing and in its (mostly) solid moral outlook, recast his position in relation to the other humorists with whom he was associated at the time.

Apart from his designation as a "humorist," no clear critical consensus emerged from the reviews, and not every review took up the question of Mark Twain's position in the hierarchy of American humor. Some reviews held that the success of *The Innocents Abroad* had elevated Mark Twain's role as an "American humorist," as when the New York *Leader* stated that "Mark Twain is now at the head of American humorists. His keen satire, his glowing wit, his quaint humor, are as much a part of American literature as the best productions of John Phoenix and Artemus Ward." The Philadelphia *Inquirer* stated that "Mark Twain is, of course, known to all of our readers as a humorist, and one fit to wear the mantle of the late Artemus Ward," noting that the book backed up his claim "to be considered the first of living American wits." Not all reviewers found Mark Twain's position as humorist to be as impressive. The Springfield *New England Homestead* praised the humor of the book as "fresh and vigorous" but gave a tempered praise to the author: "To 'Mark Twain,' (Mr. Samuel S. [*sic*] Clemens,) undoubtedly belongs the distinction, whatever it may be worth, of the American humorist of the period." The *Independent*, which would often be less than impressed with Mark Twain over the years, did not doubt the work would find readers but questioned the literary value of the work and its author's position as humorist. "We do not mean to say that Mark Twain is the best of American humorists," the notice read "for we do not think so, although the list is not very long."[58] The relative place of Mark Twain as an American humorist and the value of that position within larger literary realms of quality were central for evaluations of this book and subsequent books as he solidified his position as the most popular and prominent humorist in America.

While Mark Twain's position in the foremost ranks of the American humorists might have been an enviable place, other reviews reminded readers of the distinction between merely entertaining humor and quality humor of a higher sort:

> *America has, within the past few years, developed a new type of humor. If it is not very elevating, it is unique, and if it does not satisfy the wants of the more critical, it ministers to the pleasure of "the million." People who cannot relish Thackeray will go into ecstasies over Orpheus Kerr; people to whom Dickens is dully and dreary, will split their sides over Josh Billings. And the fact that this style of humor is as popular in England as it is with us, may be accepted as evidence of its genuineness.*[59]

The reviewer argues for a humor that is more refined, one that finds a home with both British and American audiences, thereby elevating American works and, implicitly, American audiences. While the popular American humor "of 'the million'" lacks the quality of English humor, the popularity of the American humorists in England elevated their works in the eyes of their countrymen. In the context of these "fun-creating worthies," Mark Twain possessed the best traits of this American fun: "He is something more than a literary harlequin—something more than a dislocator of parts of speech." As the review then focused on multiple instances of his irreverence while praising his work as "fresh, breezy, stimulating, and delightful," the review, like many reviews of the book, reads not so much as a critical conclusion on Mark Twain's value as a humorist as it does a telling incident of the critical consternation many reviewers exhibited as they tried to make sense of his reputation.

Almost every review discussed the qualities of Mark Twain's humor, often repeating a number of keywords that were in common critical usage as terms of approval for humor: droll, honest, genial, genuine, original, quaint, and racy.[60] Multiple reviews praised Mark Twain for his use of proper English grammar, rather than "resorting to the trick of misspelling words, which even Lowell was not ashamed to pursue, and which has been adopted by a brigade of adventurers."[61] *Packard's Monthly* praised Mark Twain for not resorting to bad spelling and for introducing a new style into American humor:

> *Mark Twain is a born journalist, besides being at the present time first among American humorists. It is, indeed, doubtful if he has ever had an*

*equal; he certainly has not had in his line—that of dry, self-contained,
unobtrusive and pervading fun. There is no glare in his emanations—no
blinding coruscations of wit, which, flashing suddenly upon you, as suddenly
go out, leaving you in darkness and uncertainty; no apparent striving after
sharp effects; no digging in poor soil for poorer puns.*[62]

As with many discussions of "American Humor," these critics did not
come to a consensus so much as they demonstrated continued questions
about the meaning of American humor and the humorist.

Displaying a central critical confusion, reviewers sought to define what
"American humor" consisted of if its newest star did not incorporate
cacography, what many found to be its most obvious characteristic. One
paper noted, "As humorist Mr. Clemens has all the audacity, the extravagant exaggeration, and the adroitness in bringing together ludicrously
ill-fitting ideas that characterize the American school. His humor is pure
and legitimate—unlike Nasby, Ward, Billings and the rest he derives no
support from bad spelling of ungrammatical composition." The New York
Tribune sought to redefine this school of humor to include Mark Twain by
writing: "Mr. Clemens, since the death of Charles F. Browne, must be rated
as the chief representative of that peculiar kind of humor in which Artemus
Ward was without parallel. It is a humor whose principal elements are not
bad spelling and verbal burlesque, for Mark Twain does not practice those
arts, but a sort of solemn audacity and a wild commingling of the most
incongruous ideas." This passage is the only excerpt selected for the sales
prospectus that discusses Mark Twain's reputation as a humorist, although
the passage was edited to read: "Mark Twain must be rated as the chief
representative of that peculiar kind of humor whose principal elements are
not bad spelling and verbal burlesque, for he does not practice these arts.
The greater part of his book is pure fun, and its freshness is wonderfully
well sustained."[63] This editing dislocates the review's meaning by moving
Mark Twain from the center of a school of humorists to something outside, and above, those humorists who are mere bad spellers. Clemens and
Bliss seem to have been eager to disassociate Mark Twain from his fellow
humorists in order to make him a unique product.

As a means to elevate Mark Twain's reputation, a few reviewers took
the further step of positioning his reputation by relating him to quality
humorists from England. The Toledo *Commercial* held that "Mr. Clemens is
the most elegant of the popular humorists of the day, and he deserves the
reputation he has gained. But, as in the case of Hood and as must always

be the case where there is true humor, there is a deeper vein of sense and of feeling." The Albany *Journal* also elevated Mark Twain's reputation as a humorist through comparison to English humorists but argued that the change was one of type, not just degree. Even Lowell had resorted to the trick of poor spelling, the review held, but Mark Twain's book "has very much increased our respect for 'Mark Twain's' abilities. We shall not longer be willing to assign him to the school of caricature in which 'Nasby' and 'Artemus Ward' are bright and shining lights. His genius belongs rather to the refined and scholarly class of which Charles Lamb and Theodore Hook were the brightest specimens."[64] As Clemens would learn on his visits to England in 1872 and 1873, the comparison to English authors, and the approval of the English in general, greatly improved one's reputation in America. English reviews of *The Innocents Abroad* will be discussed further in later chapters.

One final review, from the Unitarian weekly *Liberal Christian*, argued for a new way of looking at Mark Twain as an author and social figure. Instead of addressing the question directly, the review praised Mark Twain's work on an entirely different level, which the sales prospectus of the book quoted at length. The passage read, in part:

> Here are no homilies; no essays on politics, no discussion of philosophies, or art, or archaeology; yet the book preaches nevertheless, and is full of health and aglow with that cheerful, hopeful, wholesome religion which has so much faith that it does not fear to crack a joke or to make one. It tells a great deal that other and more serious writers consider it beneath their dignity to tell, and it keeps striking the spear-point of its shrewd Yankee common sense into the cracks and crevices of antique customs and institutions until we half expect a general tumbling down of European civilization upon the Pilgrims' heads.[65]

Elevating Mark Twain above both the low buffoon and the merely entertaining humorist, the review makes the humorist a type of preacher, but a preacher in a different sense than Clemens had meant when he discussed his "calling" to humor with his siblings in 1865. This manner of equation of humor with a serious purpose signified a new level of meaning for Mark Twain's humor, although the review qualifies its praise by noting that the main value of the book would be to interest larger numbers of people in its topics than a more "serious" volume would, leading them to read more and better books than Mark Twain's.

In the December 1869 *Atlantic Monthly*, an unsigned review would further elevate Mark Twain out of the realm of the popular humorist into the "company of the best." The power of the *Atlantic* to influence critical reputation was key during this period, and the approval of Mark Twain in its pages shifted his reputation in ways that demand significant attention. Samuel Clemens's friendship with the review's author—William Dean Howells—would come about directly from this review, and the Howells–Clemens/Mark Twain relationship would be central to the major shifts in Mark Twain's meanings in the 1870s and beyond. While the next chapter will trace the influence of Howells and the *Atlantic* in depth, the remainder of this chapter will focus on the lyceum tour of 1869 and 1870 during which Mark Twain was first introduced to Boston audiences.

INTRODUCING "MARK TWAIN"
OUR FELLOW SAVAGE ON THE LYCEUM CIRCUIT

> *Ladies and Gentlemen.—The next lecture of the course will be delivered this evening by Samuel L. Clemens, otherwise Mark Twain, a gentleman whose high character and unimpeachable integrity are only equalled by his comeliness of person and grace of manner. And I am the man. You will excuse me for introducing myself, for I have just excused the chairman from introducing me. I know it's not the ordinary way, but the fact is I never yet have found a chairman of a lecture committee who was equal to the task of introducing me as I ought to be introduced.*
>
> —"MARK TWAIN'S LECTURE,"
> OSWEGO *COMMERCIAL ADVERTISER AND TIMES*, JANUARY 17, 1870

Samuel Clemens's life was changing rapidly in late 1869. He was engaged to be married in February, and he had purchased a stake in the Buffalo *Express*, in which city he was to settle with his new wife. "Mark Twain," as his public face, was slated to begin publishing a regular humor column in the *Galaxy*, a respectable New York based magazine, and *The Innocents Abroad* was proving to be a critical and financial success. After initially agreeing to lecture that season, he attempted to cancel his obligations but ended up lecturing largely in New York and New England from November 1 to January 21. He had originally planned to use a new lecture called

"Curiosities of California," but instead chose to return to "Our Fellow Savages of the Sandwich Islands." The lecture tour paid $100 per night, a high rate that reflected Mark Twain's strong appeal.

Reviews of the lecture reflect Mark Twain's new success as an American humorist who was rapidly gaining notice both in America and in England. The review of the first night's performance, in the Providence *Herald*, noted the "intelligent and appreciative audience, all of whom had heard of the celebrated Mark Twain, and were anxious to see what he was like, and whether his tongue held pace with his pen." Clemens included this review in a letter to Olivia.[66] The Boston *Daily Advertiser* noted the surprise Boston had received in the form of "Mr. Samuel L. Clemens, who is known to fame as the humorist Mark Twain. Known to fame, we say, for who that breathes the vital air in America has not heard of the jumping frog of Calaveras County, California?" Writing to his sister, Clemens noted that Boston audiences played a large role in determining the success of a lecture: "To-morrow night I appear for the first time before a Boston audience—4,000 critics—& on the success of this matter depends my future success in New England. . . ." To Livy, he wrote that "But tonight, my darling—tonight is the rub. Can't possibly tell how I shall come out."[67] Mark Twain's success in Boston was surely satisfying, as he wrote to Livy: "Darling, it is midnight. House full—I made a handsome success—*I* know that, no matter whether the papers say so in the morning or not." Enclosed with the letter was the *Advertiser* review, with the synopsis torn out, noting "I like this notice first-rate—it is all namby-pamby praise."[68]

Clemens's appreciation of the Boston paper's affectionate praise was clear, and his belief that the success in Boston would augur well for the reception of the rest of his tour was largely correct. The extensive review in the *Advertiser* rehearsed many of the main points of subsequent reviews—the eager anticipation of the audiences, his strange manner of delivering his lecture, the audience's reactions, and Mark Twain's growing role as both a "genuine" and "original" humorist. Only later in the tour did newspapers question whether Mark Twain's performance would or should satisfy the lyceum audience.

As the *Advertiser* had noted, many papers discussed the large and expectant audiences that awaited the "mirth-provoking" and "celebrated" humorist. Like many reviews, this one pointed out the centrality of Mark Twain's performance of his material and argued that "there is little use in trying to write a sketch of the discourse"—but they then proceeded to try, to Mark Twain's evident dismay. Simply reading Mark Twain's lectures, as

William Dean Howell's pointed out in an introduction to a 1910 collection of speeches, does not affect the reader in the same way as when delivered by the great author and actor. Howells attempted to give some feel for Mark Twain's delivery: "He studied every tone and every gesture, and he forecast the result with the real audience from the result with that imagined audience. Therefore, it was beautiful to see him and to hear him; he rejoiced in the pleasure he gave and the blows of surprise which he dealt; and because he had his end in mind, he knew when to stop."[69] In the essay "How to Tell a Story," from 1895, Mark Twain delineated the difference between the humorous story—an American invention—the comic story (English) and the witty story (French). The comic and witty stories focus on the *matter* of the subject, whereas the American humorous story relies on the *manner* of telling. Mark Twain wrote of the difference:

> The humorous story may be spun out to great length, and may wander around as much as it pleases, and arrive nowhere in particular; but the comic and witty stories must be brief and end with a point. The humorous story bubbles gently along, the others burst.
>
> The humorous story is strictly a work of art—high and delicate art—and only an artist can tell it; but no art is necessary in telling the comic and the witty story; anybody can do it. The art of telling a humorous story—understand, I mean by word of mouth, not print—was created in America, and has remained at home.[70]

While many of Mark Twain's best-known works follow this model, the speeches are most clearly related to this model of deadpan storytelling that depended on the performance of the material as much as, if not more than, the material itself. Mark Twain's success as a humorous lecturer depended on his presence as the American humorist on stage, telling funny stories while not acknowledging their humor.

The *Advertiser* review focuses largely on the manner of Mark Twain's speech, starting with a description and moving on to his facial expression, vocal delivery, and style of delivery:

> Mark Twain is a very good looking man. He is of medium height and moderately slender build, has light brown hair, a reddish brown moustache, regular features and a fresh complexion; and he has a queer way of wrinkling up his nose and half closing his eyes when he speaks. The expression of his face is as calm and imperturbable as that of the sphinx. Looking at him

you feel it to be an impossibility that he should ever hurry or ever be out of temper, and you might suppose him to be incapable of a joke, if it were not for the peculiar twinkle in his merry eyes. His voice is remarkably light and remarkably dry—like some German wines—and it seems to be modulated to only two keys. His style of speaking is unique to the last degree. It is all of a piece with the quality of his humor, and fits him like a glove. He delivers his sentences without haste, and in a tone of utter indifference, marking the highest waves of his thought only by a strong flavor of nasality, and knowing for the most part only the rising inflection at the beginning, middle and end of his sentences.[71]

But the reviewer did not divorce his manner from his matter, instead noting that the two complement and reinforce each other.

While some reviewers simply noted that the audience enjoyed the lecture, the Boston paper went further to describe the strange effect Mark Twain's performance had on the auditors:

In short, the platform manner of Mr. Clemens is the exact reflection in speech of his peculiar style of composition. The fun of both is genuine enough; but the perception of the fun is unmeasurably heightened by the apparently serious intention of the general discourse, and at times by an air of half seriousness in the joke itself. The audience gets into a queer state after a while. It knows not what to trust; for while much is meant to be seriously taken, the fun is felt to be the real life of the thing; and yet they never know where the fun will come in. Even when Mr. Clemens has made a really fine period, or introduced a brilliant descriptive passage, he takes pains to turn the affair into a joke at the end.

As Mark Twain was perfecting his humorous storytelling, he noted the impact of his style on audiences and worked to perfect his delivery. To Livy, Clemens wrote, "The other night at Meriden I struck upon an entirely new *manner* of telling a favorite anecdote of mine,—& now, without altering a single word, it shortly becomes so absurd that I have to laugh, myself." Reviewers noted that Mark Twain's style had "literally jumbled us all up," or had disappointed the audience "quite agreeably" with his "queer, quaint, and quizzical remarks."[72]

Compared to his previous lecture tours, reviews now pointed to "Mark Twain" as a humorist well known to the majority of his audience, who sought in his lectures entertainment similar to that they found in his works. The reviews also pointed to something of a new status of Mark Twain as a humorist in comparison to other humorists. The *Boston Daily Advertiser* noted: "Perhaps he is not a great humorist, but he is a genuine humorist. The man who can say that the Islanders' dish of plain dog 'is only our cherished American sausage Boston *Daily Advertiser* with the mystery removed' is one whose reputation fame will not suffer to die; and if Mr. Clemens can please everywhere as he pleased in Boston last night, he will be sure to make his fortune if he does not become a standard author." Other papers were even more effusive in their praise of Mark Twain. The Philadelphia *Daily Evening Bulletin* wrote of him as "the best of the humorists of his class" and compared him favorably to John Phoenix, Artemus Ward, and Josh Billings. In Mark Twain, the reviewer found something more than mere humor—a "hearty hatred of sham, hypocrisy and cant" that showed how he could use his ridicule as a weapon of reform. While the review doubted his desire to become a reformer, it held him as furnishing some of "the purest and best entertainment," which has its own dignity: "There may be some who will regard his calling as of smaller dignity than that of other men. Perhaps this is the class with which he is at war. The mass of intelligent people will agree with us that genuine humor is as rare and excellent a quality as any other, and that it is as respectable to amuse mankind as to stupefy them. The number of persons engaged in the former work is small; those who attempt the latter abound in quantities." The Hartford *Courant* similarly praised the "genuine humorist" who could provide "an hour of hearty laughter" as a public benefactor that should not be expected to expound on political economy or Kant, summing up with: "Humor has its office."[73]

While most of the reviews of the tour were positive, two incidents pointed to a portion of the audience that did not fully enjoy or appreciate the elevation of the humorist onto the lyceum stage. The New Haven *Daily Palladium* wrote that everyone is familiar with "Mark Twain," but few had had the chance to see "Mr. Samuel H. Clemens [sic]." And once most people saw him once, his success as a lecturer would "end when the curiosity of his thousands of readers shall have been satisfied by a good square look at him." His lecture, they wrote, was: "a tissue of nonsense from beginning to end, and his delivery is as disgusting as the lecture is foolish. Still, people clamor for a look, and we are inclined to think one dose will be enough for the most admiring. The audience last evening enjoyed, not the hearty laugh they anticipated, but a protracted, vexatious titter, and felt relieved when the end came."[74] This description of an audience that came to see

Mark Twain and experienced an unsatisfying laughter would resonate with later critiques of Mark Twain's performances, as well as with critiques that found that humor had too prominent of a place in American culture.

While Samuel Clemens's financial success as a lecturer demonstrates the fact that a majority of his audience found his performances funny, his final performance of the 1869–1870 tour demonstrated the conflicting values of some lyceum audiences and the possibility that the lecture could be seen as a critique of American values. On January 21, 1870, Mark Twain ended his tour in Jamestown, N.Y.—where he unknowingly stepped onto the stage in the midst of a feud between local newspapers over the tone and direction of the lyceum. The Jamestown *Journal* printed three separate items after Mark Twain's lecture. The first was a sarcastic review written for the rival paper, in which extreme pains are taken not to offend anyone. The second was a more serious review of the lecture, defending Mark Twain and mocking those who expected information, history, or reform from his lecture. Instead, the author claimed that the lecture was the work of "an honest jokist" who was "to the comic world what Wendell Phillips is to the serious and philosophic."[75] The editor continued:

> . . . we feel sorry for the disappointment of the people who expected sense last night and only realized nonsense. They naturally feel defrauded and imposed upon. The Y.M.C.A. really out to tell the folks in advance when a comic lecturer is coming.
>
> We went to hear a little nonsense and got a good laugh and were not disappointed. Looking at the lecture seriously it was a lamentable failure; viewed from the humorous side it was capital.

A portion of Mark Twain's audiences may thus have viewed his work as merely entertaining, as being "nothing *but* a joker," which had its own value for some. But Mark Twain's literary status made him something more than a mere joker in a culture where the "humorous" and the "serious" were not always so easily divided as this review would hold—a fact that engendered debate about the meanings of humor, laughter, and propriety.

In the same issue of the *Journal*, a letter to the editor from "An Indignant Spectator" took up the argument that Mark Twain's lecture was in bad taste and inappropriate for the venue. While it is tempting to consider this article as a satire on the overly serious interpretation of the lecture, Mark Twain seemed to think it was written by a separate party than the other pieces. The reviewer held that the lecture had offered no new or valuable information about the islands but had been silly and in poor taste. The "victim" of the lecture claimed that Mark Twain insulted America with his comparison of America with cannibals, and that "his intimation that *civilization* was responsible for the decrease in population there is another insult to America."[76] Unlike his Vandal lecture, the Sandwich Islands speech contained a satire of American exceptionalism that some audience members seemed to find irreverent. The humorous critique of America's imperial pretensions is evident in his use of the exaggerative style of "American humor" to make fun, in both senses, of the ideas of "civilized" and "savage" that underwrote American superiority. While Mark Twain's lecture audiences laughed at his unique performance style, or at the verbal humor of his descriptions, they also laughed at Mark Twain's deflation of cherished cultural concepts. For instance, he turned the role of civilization in the decline of native population into a joke:

> When these islands were discovered the population was about 400,000, but the white man came and brought various complicated diseases, and education, and civilization, and all sorts of calamities, and consequently the population began to drop off with commendable activity. Forty years ago they were reduced to 200,000, and the educational and civilizing facilities being increased they dwindled down to 55,000, and it is proposed to send a few more missionaries and finish them off.[77]

By placing civilization and education in the same conceptual category as calamity, Mark Twain mocked the efforts of missionaries and others who aimed to improve a foreign society but ended up as agents of disaster.

At one point in his lecture, namely, in the midst of a discussion of cannibalism, Mark Twain paused and said with an indescribable look: "At this point I usually illustrate cannibalism before the audience: but I am a stranger here, and feel diffident about asking favors. However, he said, if there is any one present who is willing to contribute a baby for the purposes of the lecture, I should be glad to know it now. I am aware, though, that children have become scarce and high of late, having been thinned out by neglect and ill treatment since the woman movement began."[78] The indignant spectator was especially incensed by the descriptions of cannibalism, writing:

> In equally bad taste was his reference to cannibalism. That incident about the poor old sea-captain who was so barbarously devoured was of course affecting, but why need he to introduce it without giving the moral to it—

especially as he said he told it only for the moral that was in it? Is it not an
evidence to Mark Twain's excessive stupidity that he could tell that story
as he confessed, forty or fifty times without once giving the moral to it.[79]

By so obviously missing the joke, the reviewer decried the inclusion
of comic lecturers in lyceum programs. Expecting a serious and infor-
mative lecture, this auditor experienced "shame, disgust, annoyance,
chagrin, and mortification" rather than the laughter of the "silly young
people" who enjoyed the performance.[80] It could be argued that such
sanctimonious "victims" were the true targets of Mark Twain's satire,
although Mark Twain preferred his audience to laugh rather than to
cringe in shame and disgust.

The office of humor, and of the humorist delivering it to the public,
were central questions when the public encountered Mark Twain—either
through his writings or through his lectures. Personally, Clemens disliked
the rigors and rituals of touring, and his tour the next year was fraught
with difficulties, as will be explored in chapter 4. Even more personally, the
end of the tour was followed by Samuel Langhorne Clemens's wedding to
Olivia Langdon on February 2, 1870. Professionally, the tour established
"Mark Twain" as a name that could successfully draw large crowds for
well-received lectures, even in Boston.

Reviews of Mark Twain's lyceum lecture pointed to continued questions
of audience reception and the role of humor in the realm of the public
lecture—questions that would be even more important the following
year when Mark Twain's lecture contained more humor and less serious
material. Mark Twain's performances also highlight many of the same
questions raised by the release of *The Innocents Abroad*—the place of humor
in American society, the relative quality of his productions in relation to
other humorists and authors, the question of reverence, and the shifting
critical reputation of Mark Twain as he entered new venues in which his
"quality" was open for debate.

ABSURD LITERARY REMAINS
THE HUMORIST "MARK TWAIN"

At the close of the letter to his siblings in October of 1865—in which he
spoke of his calling as a "low" humorist—Samuel Clemens added a brief
postscript, writing: "P. S. You had better shove this in the stove—for if we
strike a bargain I don't want any absurd 'literary remains' & 'unpublished

letters of Mark Twain' published after I am planted."[81] Of course, in the more than one hundred years since Clemens was "planted," an absurd amount of remains have been published, picked over, and analyzed by the reading public and by scholars, who have found Mark Twain's calling to "low literature—i.e. humorous" to contain a deeper vein of quality.

Examining the literary and cultural remains of "Mark Twain" does not prove that that quality was there all along, which may very well be a judgment always contingent on historical meanings of "literature." But it does clearly show that the debate over Mark Twain's reputation was always present. As Mark Twain rose to fame in the late 1860s and solidified his place as the foremost American humorist of the era, numerous articles discussed Mark Twain and his relation to other humorists and to the ideas of American humor, American literature, and American culture. Some of these articles, such as groups of reviews about individual books or lecture tours, can be interpreted together. Others came into the public sphere individually and do not fit easily into a chronological or thematic narrative of Mark Twain's development. Nevertheless, a number of these pieces are worth noting as indicators of the wide range of places where "Mark Twain" was discussed and the range of interpretations of his cultural freight. These fugitive pieces on Mark Twain do not add up to anything more than their individual reflections on his reputation, but they are valuable as evidence of his circulation.

The case of William Ward is intriguing, as an example. Ward was a minor poet and editor of the small newspaper the Macon *Beacon* of Macon, Mississippi. In Albert Bigelow Paine's *Biography* of Mark Twain, Ward is mentioned as an exception to the American critics who held Mark Twain to be merely a humorist. Paine writes: "Ward did not hold a place with the great magazine arbiters of literary rank. He was only an obscure country editor, but he wrote like a prophet."[82] In 1870, Ward published an extended review of American humor in prose from Irving through Southern humorists like "Sut Lovingood" to Billings, Ward, Nasby, and Mark Twain. Of the twelve humorists he discussed, he argued that only the popularity of Irving and Mark Twain would last, writing:

> *They have all had, or will have their day. Some of them are resting beneath the sod, and others still live whose work will scarcely survive them. Since Irving no humorist in prose has held the foundation of a permanent fame except it be Mark Twain, and this, as is the case of Irving, is because he is a pure writer. Aside from any subtle mirth that lurks through his composition,*

the grace and finish of his more didactic descriptive sentences indicate more
than mediocrity.[83]

The review may have been prophetic, for those scholars who would canonize Mark Twain, but it is not clear that it had any influence on his reputation during his lifetime.[84]

The question of Mark Twain's role as a humorist circulated in other periodical cultures separate from the magazines focused on the relationship between literature and culture. Mentions of "Mark Twain" popped up occasionally in women's magazines, church magazines, and farming magazines, and as he became more famous, his quotes could be found in almost any kind of periodical. *The Phrenological Journal of Science and Health* occasionally mentioned Mark Twain and humor in general as part of its scientific explorations. In August 1870, an editorial discussed a group portrait labeled "American Humorists" of "Josh Billings," "Petroleum V. Nasby," and "Mark Twain." The editorial examined the photograph (printed in Figure 2.5 below, but not in the magazine) for the hints as to the humor of the men, although their miens show that "there is certainly very little, in form or expression, to suggest the presence of irrestrainable jollity."[85] In a critical trope so common that one wonders why any humorist dared to misspell a word, the article critiqued Billings's "vile orthography" and stated that "as we look into his great innocent face, and think how much his manners, if not his morals, might be improved by a little attention to the rudiments of English education, we can not resist the schoolmasterly instinct to tell him so." Mark Twain was praised for his decision not to follow the example of his fellow humorists, which made his humor of a higher quality. Unique to this evaluation is the consideration of the humorists' physical features in connection with the subject of the magazine:

> *Mark Twain is a quiet, unostentatious, modest-looking genius. He is per-*
> *mitted to stand in the group, to show—as we presume—that he is head*
> *and shoulders above his co-humorists, which we honestly believe him to*
> *be. There is very little in Mark's personal presence that would stamp him a*
> *funny fellow, and the fact that he really is funny . . . is as much a continual*
> *surprise to him as it can be to anybody. In fact, so contradictory are his*
> *characteristics of appearance, speech, and action, that we never think of*
> *doubting anything strange which may be said of him—not even what he*
> *may say of himself, which is the strangest of all.*[86]

Josh Billings.   Mark Twain.   Petroleum V. Nasby.
THE AMERICAN HUMORISTS.
Published by G. M. Baker. 149 Washington St., Boston.

FIGURE 2.5: Mark Twain with Josh Billings and Petroleum V. Nasby, Boston November, 1869. **Courtesy of Kevin Mac Donnell, Austin, Texas**

Being outside of literary realms, this evaluation is nonetheless interesting as evidence of how far Mark Twain's reputation would travel and how wide was the interest in the subject of humor.

One further literary remain from 1870 is worth considering—a biography of Mark Twain written by Josh Billings and printed in the New York *Weekly* in October 1870, which provides a sample of the cacography that seems to have been the almost universal bane of critics and well-liked by the public, if judged by its sales. Several of the descriptions of Mark Twain touch on the question of the role of the humorist in American culture:

> He lives in Buffalo, and what iz most wonderful, and the hardest to understand, iz sed tew be rich. Wealthy humorists are scarce tew be had, they generally invest all ov their money as they go along, in the common occurrences of the day.
>
> Report sez he wont lektur no more. I hope report lies (for once in its life), for Mark Twain, before an audiance, iz az easy tew understand az strawberries and cream.
>
> Hiz late book, called "Innocence Abroad," iz the most delishus history i ever perused. It haz all the integrity ov the mutliplacashun table, and, at the same time, iz az full of divitry as "Gulliver's travels." ...
>
> All genuine humorists (altho fun iz their game, and altho they beleave that even virtew haz a ridickilus side to her) have in their bottom natur menny places where they kneell down (in private) and say good things in a low tone.[87]

Mark Twain's position as a humorist who "iz sed tew be rich" touched on a major concern of both Samuel Clemens and of the press in discussing him. The question of Mark Twain's money, and of the relationship of commerce to art more generally, was a frequent subject of fugitive pieces in newspapers and magazines as the humorist rose to new heights of fame.

Attempting to capitalize on the success of *The Innocents Abroad* and for both the success and obligations of his marriage to Olivia Langdon on February 2, 1870, Samuel Clemens was undertaking a number of projects in the early 1870s: his role as editor and contributor to the Buffalo *Express*, his lyceum lecture tour in the winter of 1869–70, a monthly column called "Memoranda" for the *Galaxy* magazine starting in April 1870, and a sequel to his travel book, which would become *Roughing It* (1872). In 1870 he also contracted with the publishers of the *Galaxy* to release a pamphlet consisting of several of his sketches (cost: 40 cents for cloth, 75 for muslin). Publication problems pushed its release to February 1871, past the Christmas market that Clemens had originally aimed for. The main feature of this collection was "Mark Twain's (Burlesque) Autobiography," by which he sought, as he said in the introduction to the piece, to satiate a public demand for his history: "Two or three persons having at different times intimated that if I would write an autobiography they would read it, when they got leisure, I yield at last to this frenzied public demand, and herewith tender my history."[88] The history of Mark Twain's line is then traced through a series of brigands, forgers, "reformers" of the Indians, pirates, missionaries, and other villains of history, all described through deadpan euphemisms, such as:

> *Augustus Twain, seems to have made something of a stir about the year 1160. He was as full of fun as he could be, and used to take his old sabre and sharpen it up, and get in a convenient place on a dark night, and stick it through people as they went by, to see them jump. He was a born humorist. But he got to going too far with it; and the first time he was found stripping one of these parties, the authorities removed one end of him, and put it up on a nice high place on Temple Bar, where it could contemplate the people and have a good time. He never liked any situation so much or stuck to it so long.*

At the end of the piece, Mark Twain demurs from telling his own history, at least until he is hanged or meets some other notable death like his ancestors.

Mark Twain soon feared that this book would hurt his reputation and purchased the plates.[89] The cheap, largely ephemeral forms of the pamphlet and comic almanac had appealed to Mark Twain, who had seen Josh Billings make large profits on the comic almanac, but his shifting literary reputation made such works less appealing as he increasingly improved the standing of his literary productions, as with his monthly column in the *Galaxy*, a higher class of magazine out of New York. That column will be examined in chapter 4 as a key barometer of his anxiety about his position as a humorist. First, the next chapter will examine his move into the most highly respectable of American periodicals, the *Atlantic Monthly*, whose positive review of *The Innocents Abroad* elevated him into a new realm of respectability.

CHAPTER THREE

"The Company of the Best"
Phunny Phellow in the *Atlantic Monthly*

In late November 1869, while in Boston to give his "Our Fellow Savages" lecture, Samuel Clemens visited the offices of the *Atlantic Monthly* to thank James T. Fields, then the editor of the magazine, for the unsigned review of *The Innocents Abroad* that had recently appeared. Fields introduced Clemens to William Dean Howells, the assistant editor who had written the review. The two men would eventually become friends, collaborators, and major American authors, but at the time, both were new figures within American letters and both were developing vastly different reputations. During these years, Howells was establishing himself as a critical presence, first as an assistant editor (1866–1871) and then as editor (1871–1881) of the *Atlantic Monthly*. Just as Mark Twain's reputation was much different at this point in his career from that of the white-suited, white-haired author who colors so much current public perception, Howells was not, in the late 1860s, yet known as "the Dean of American Letters," promoter of literary realism and arbiter of literary taste. Instead, he was an author developing a new view of fiction and a sometimes insecure editor worrying about both circulation and canonization. In the development of the *Atlantic Monthly* under his editorship and of his ideas of realistic fiction, he promoted Mark Twain as a quality author to be considered as a part of a developing national literature.

The *Atlantic Monthly*'s promotion of Mark Twain, and Howells's personal and professional relationship with Samuel Clemens, make the magazine and its editor central to understanding the remaking of Mark Twain into a quality humorist. The humorists with whom Mark Twain was largely associated had gained very little notice in the *Atlantic Monthly*, with the exception of Bret Harte. In September 1869, Howells had written one of the few notices discussing the professional humorist in the magazine, writing: "It is the humorist like Artemus Ward, and the humorists of his school, who perplex and mystify the judgment-seat. The rogues make you laugh, in defiance of every good principle of taste and art." Three months later, Howells reviewed *The Innocents Abroad*, a book that most critics had largely classed near or at the head of the humorists of Artemus Ward's school. Shifting Mark Twain's critical reputation from Artemus Ward's rogue's gallery of humorists to the status of *Atlantic* humorist, Howells concluded the review with the judgment: "Under his nom de plume of Mark Twain, Mr. Clements [*sic*] is well known to the very large world of newspaper-readers; and this book ought to secure him something better than the uncertain standing of a popular favorite. It is no business of ours to fix his rank among the humorists California has given us, but we think he is, in an entirely different way from all the others, quite worthy of the company of the best."[1] Whereas most critics had grouped Mark Twain with the peculiar school of "American humor," Howells made the argument, surprising for its time and circumstance, that his humor may have belonged with that of Oliver Wendell Holmes and James Russell Lowell, rather than with the rogues who inspired laughs of questionable taste.

A review of Mark Twain's book in this venue was more incongruous at the time than it may seem in retrospect. Finding a review of a book of humor issued by subscription may very well have shocked the sophisticated readers of the *Atlantic*, and the review's praise may have been unexpected to readers accustomed to dismissive notices of popular books in the magazine. The only other quality magazine to review Mark Twain's book was the *Nation*, which directly defined him as the successor to the Artemus Ward school of "American humor," writing: "All the prominent characteristics of our peculiar school of humorists—their audacity, their extravagance and exaggeration—Mr. Clemens displays in the course of his ramblings."[2] By framing Mark Twain as a praiseworthy humorist, even before the advent of their personal friendship, Howells took an early step toward transforming the public perception of "Mark Twain" from a merely popular humorist to a quality humorist worthy of consideration in American letters as constructed in the pages of the *Atlantic Monthly*. Howells's review of *The Innocents Abroad* had a different importance than other reviews because of the centrality of the magazine in defining American literary culture in the 1860s and 1870s, an era in which magazines were the key location for critical discussion of literary and other cultural matters in America. Howells put Mark Twain on a new stage in American culture—a platform of respectable literary and cultural discussion that had the power to confer literary distinction on its subjects.

In the magazine's culture of letters, the role of humor was dramatized by James Russell Lowell and Oliver Wendell Holmes, whose works modeled the two aims of quality humor: quality entertainment and the artistic expression of moral thought. The *Atlantic Monthly* was founded in 1857 by a group of authors that included Lowell, who was the founding editor and published his second series of *The Biglow Papers* in the magazine, and Holmes, who provided the name for the magazine and published in its pages almost continuously, including his popular "Autocrat of the Breakfast Table" series. The *Atlantic Monthly* was the major American culture of letters that promoted a hierarchy of humor in which artistic and ethical quality humor undertook the same goal as all other arts—the improvement of American society through the creation of a quality American canon of letters. The definition of humor in the magazine as a type of artistic expression, rather than a professional category, was highly influential in creating and maintaining the idea of a hierarchy of humor. As the main organ of creating and circulating ideas of American belles lettres during the 1860s and 1870s, the *Atlantic* was the most influential periodical in defining a quality humor distinct from the merely popular humor of other newspapers, magazines, and the platform.

The editorial ethos of the *Atlantic Monthly* developed under James Russell Lowell, who linked a liberal view of intellectual discussion with an ethical thrust that viewed artistic and cultural expression as agents of cultural uplift. In doing so, Lowell promoted an American literary nationalism that placed realistic works at the center of an American canon. Writers in the pages of the *Atlantic* were frequently praised for the breadth of their endeavors, often by way of a string of descriptive epithets: novelist, moralist, poet, dramatist, humorist, and artist. "Humorist," in this sense, was an aspect of an author's production, not a professional identity. As a category of literary skill, "humorist" was applied to a certain canon of figures, delineated in one article as "Aristophanes, or Lucian, or Rabelais, or Swift, or Sterne, or Fielding, or Dickens, or Thackeray."[3] Placing Mark Twain in this company shifted the terms of literary discussion and raised the possibility that his humor might be put to use for artistic and ethical purposes that went beyond entertainment or laughs. While a few newspaper reviews had raised similar arguments, the scope and influence of the *Atlantic Monthly* made the question of Mark Twain's quality a topic that could not be ignored in future criticism.

By reviewing Mark Twain's books in the magazine, and in eventually bringing him to the magazine as a contributor, Howells elevated the debate about his literary reputation into an entirely different realm of critical and cultural discussion. The possibility of Mark Twain's writing being of a quality that placed him in the realm of the *Atlantic* authors is a central transition point in his development from "the best of our second-rate humorists" to humorous author who could be included in discussions of American literature writ large. As the author of many of the book reviews in the *Atlantic* during the 1860s and 1870s, Howells helped shape a critical conversation about the meaning of literature while also modifying the magazine's scope as he moved toward his more distinct promotion of "realism" in the 1880s. Howells selected, edited, and promoted work by a large portion of the prominent authors of the period. When Howells argued for Mark Twain's inclusion with the company of the best, he argued for more than his inclusion within an ephemeral magazine. Instead, Mark Twain's presence in the *Atlantic* was implicitly an elevation to a certain cultural canon—a theory of American literature with specific aesthetic and ethical dimensions and one that viewed certain types of literature and humor as central to the development of American culture and character.

Howells's inclusion of Mark Twain as an *Atlantic* author illustrates a vision of American literature that imagined it to be a national product made up of distinctly regional authors, whose accurate portrayal of their own experiences paradoxically elevated them to the status of "American authors." Through the book reviews, articles, and the literature that it chose to publish, the magazine aimed to shape the reading habits of its audience—not only the *what*, but the *how* and *why* as well. Part of this goal was to create the *Atlantic* as a culture of letters largely dedicated to discussing American literature as worthy of inclusion in the company of European literature. Despite its relatively low circulation and later decline in the face of a raft of competing magazines, the *Atlantic Monthly* under Lowell and his successors established a model of literary production that played a prominent role in shaping literary culture for the remainder of the century.

In his *Atlantic* reviews, Howells built on the critical work of Lowell, which privileged "real" and "humane" literary forms over the sentimental and didactic, all terms with loaded artistic and cultural meanings that will be explicated further in this chapter. Expanding on this critical tradition, Howells framed "realistic" writing as something that readers could find not only in fiction, but in romance, travel writing, nonfiction, and, key for our purposes, humor. Howells's criticism framed realistic writing not as a genre of fiction, as it is largely understood, but as a practice of reading texts in specific ways that pointed to their relation to questions of American literature. Reading Howells's discussions of Mark Twain within the context of his 200-plus reviews from the *Atlantic*—and in relation to specific authors, such as Bret Harte, James Russell Lowell, Henry James, Oliver Wendell Holmes, Charles Dudley Warner, and James DeForest—offers an important prehistory of Howells's later theory of realism and helps to make sense of his inclusion of Mark Twain in his own pantheon of American letters. Howells's argument for including Mark Twain in the company of the *Atlantic*'s best was not simply the by-product of their friendship, nor was it an outlier in the development of Howells's own variation of the *Atlantic*'s critical ethos. Instead, Howells's promotion of Mark Twain was part of a larger effort by Howells to define a type of "realistic" writing that could be placed at the center of American Literature.

"THE AMERICAN IDEAL": HUMOR, NATIONALISM AND LITERATURE IN THE *ATLANTIC MONTHLY*

> *In politics the **Atlantic** will be the organ of no party or clique, but will honestly endeavor to be the exponent of what its conductors believe to be the American idea. . . . In Literature, to leave no province unrepresented, so that while each number will contain articles of an abstract and permanent value, it will also be found that the healthy appetite of the mind for entertainment in its various forms of Narrative, Wit and Humor, will not go uncared for. . . .*
> —PUBLISHER'S STATEMENT, INSIDE COVER OF THE FIRST ISSUE OF THE *ATLANTIC MONTHLY*, NOVEMBER 1857[4]

When William Dean Howells categorized Mark Twain in the "company of the best," he included him in a critical conversation on the types and aims of humor, the proper genres and approaches to literary production, and the link between American humor, American literature, and American culture. This was not a simple conversation. The magazine's vision of American culture, and of the roles of literature and of humor in that culture, is thus centrally important to understanding the literary world of the 1860s and 1870s as Mark Twain moved from the realm of the popular humorist into the discussion of quality humor. By bringing "Mark Twain, Mr. Clements" into the magazine as a subject of lasting significance, rather than of passing interest, Howells helped establish Mark Twain in a conversation of profound significance for the making of Mark Twain's reputation.

Every periodical imagines an audience of readers distinguished by factors of class, race, gender, region, and/or nation; by political or religious persuasion; and by intellectual interests and skills. This imagined audience is constructed by editorial framing, book reviews, and the types of pieces published. The *Atlantic Monthly* was a periodical culture with a distinct yet dynamic editorial ethos—a set of beliefs, practices, and ideals that shaped both the content of the magazine and its perception by its audience. Neither static nor deterministic, "editorial ethos" is an important concept for imagining how a magazine shapes meaning for its authors and readers. Within the *Atlantic*, a consistent yet evolving editorial stance structured the contents, reviews, and overall intellectual and cultural orientation of the magazine and its readers. In other words, *who* and *what* the magazine chose to publish, review, and discuss went a long way in determining *who* and *what* were defined as "literary," especially during the height of the *Atlantic's* influence in the 1860s and 1870s.

The *Atlantic's* audience was imagined as being broadly educated, although not necessarily schooled, and widely interested in subjects ranging from classical and European literature to the social problems of the day. Both men and women were among the expected audience, with the unwritten expectation that the readers were of a certain class socially (from the newly emerging middle class to more established wealth) and were of European descent (or actually European). The audience was also framed as continuous readers, that is, longtime subscribers aware of the traditions of the magazine. For instance, many book reviews assumed that readers would have already read a novel that had been serialized in the magazine. The magazine's relatively stable base of subscribers seems to have exerted a conservative force on the editors, who were slow in introducing new developments that might alienate those used to the magazine's traditions.

Founded as an antislavery journal and as a venue for the dissemination of serious cultural thought, the *Atlantic Monthly* quickly became the most significant culture of letters in which well-known authors, critics, and public figures debated ideas of American literature and culture. The *Atlantic's* success cemented Boston's place at the center of literary activity for a generation, challenging Philadelphia and New York City's earlier dominance in publishing before fading in importance as publishing centralized in New York once again in the 1880s.[5] Van Wyck Brooks, a later chronicler of the New England Renaissance, would write: "The founding of the *Atlantic Monthly*, in 1857, marked [the] high tide of the Boston mind."[6] The magazine was undertaken with both idealistic and commercial hopes, with some mainly promoting intellectual goals and others hoping for economic success. The intellectual coterie involved in the founding of the *Atlantic Monthly* were not a narrow, conservative class intent on maintaining a rigid class status, but a relatively tolerant array of intellectuals dedicated to the publication and dissemination of aesthetic and ethical work that would uplift the larger American culture, which they saw as in danger of fragmenting in the face of the waning influence of religion, the sectarian debates over slavery, and the expansion of American culture geographically, intellectually, and culturally.[7] The *Atlantic* promoted a culture of letters based on intellectual openness and tolerant discussion of politics, religion, science, and literature.

While the magazine's openness was limited by its staunchly Republican base and antislavery views, as well as its tendency to rely on established New England authors, it did provide a relatively liberal space free of dogmatic religious or philosophical constricts in which serious, and often controversial, social criticism was promoted. Ellery Sedgwick, in his history of the magazine's first half century, defines the magazine's intellectual stance as a "tolerant liberalism" based on intellectual independence and engaged social criticism. Sedgwick argues that the so-called "American Renaissance" in publishing and in the *Atlantic Monthly* has been wrongly flattened as a literary-historical era. Shaped largely by Vernon Parrington's classification of the literary culture of mid-century New England as essentially conservative, the designation makes sense only if one ignores the context of the actual historical actors.[8] The constellation of authors and intellectuals in the *Atlantic*'s orbit was more varied in geographical, educational, and intellectual origins than the social and economic elite of Boston. While Holmes and Lowell were from established Bostonian families, many of the other *Atlantic* contributors, including Fields and Howells, came from outside the New England elite. Inclusion in the *Atlantic Monthly* was based not on class status but on meritocracy, albeit a meritocracy based on adherence to a specific ethos. And while this intellectual egalitarianism was predicated on certain intellectual positions, especially antislavery beliefs before and during the Civil War, the magazine was open to more intellectual variety than the caricature would hold. Within its historical context, the magazine's intellectual position was more open, its humor more subversive, and its politics more liberal than dominant views of literary history may hold.[9]

The role of the *Atlantic Monthly* as a cultural force was based on the vision of a magazine that would model the appropriate uses of culture and leisure by precept and example. Along with the lyceum lecture course, the museum, the free library, and other forms of intellectual leisure, quality periodicals aimed to provide educational leisure, a kind of enjoyable training not available widely through colleges or public schools.[10] Such institutions were by definition hierarchical in their desire to educate a wide public to the intellectual standards of community leaders, public speakers, or other educated individuals. In its early years, the *Atlantic Monthly* imagined its role in more egalitarian terms of influencing, as well as training, the public taste to the proper uses and enjoyments of leisure time. Instead of viewing serious cultural production as a marker and enforcer of social distinction, the Yankee humanists viewed cultural production as a moral obligation in which the production and dissemination of work with high standards would uplift the masses.[11]

The *Atlantic Monthly*'s critical ethos portrayed the magazine as an alternative to the reading habits of both the mass fiction of dime novels and of popular didactic and sentimental fiction. It envisioned an educated class of readers distinct from both working-class readers and wealthy, elite readers, but this model of reading was available to all who would subscribe to the magazine, both philosophically and physically. Numerous anecdotes testify to the cherished place the magazine held in its subscribers' homes—largely in New England but stretching into the Midwest and beyond. The arrival of the magazine was an event in small communities, where it connected readers to the larger world of intellectual and social discussion in a way similar to lyceum societies.[12] For aspiring authors, the magazine provided a model of culture that was viewed with veneration: Emily Dickinson viewed it as "a temple" and sought the advice of Thomas Wentworth Higginson, one of its main critical voices; Louisa May Alcott saved her best work for the magazine; and a young William Dean Howells visited Lowell and other contributors in Boston as if on a spiritual quest, which will be discussed in the next section.

The *Atlantic Monthly*'s intertwined goals of promoting intellectually open social critique and working as a model of cultural uplift were also linked with the specifically American context of the magazine. Modeled on respected British magazines that promoted British cultural and literary nationalism, the *Atlantic* aimed to foster an American intellectual tradition similar to, and the equal of, European literatures. The *Atlantic* relied largely on American authors, especially after its first few years, and aimed to promote American literature as part of a transatlantic conversation about the value of American literature in a larger critical canon. Sedgwick traces a "cultural nationalism" through the magazine's early years in which its selections promoted "intellectual independence and encouraged America to see itself as culturally distinct, particularly in its democratic individualism, freedom from tradition and authority, moral conscience, and broader social tolerance."[13] In this view, American literature would be a reflection of the growth of American culture, a product of its rapid progress as a nation to the status of international player. The *Atlantic* was intended to increase the circulation of the works of certain American authors who had not reached a wider audience—a goal that linked commercial and ethical purposes.[14] Many of the major contributors to the *Atlantic*, Harriet Beecher Stowe excepted, experienced low circulation of their books and looked for ways to get their works to a larger public, a goal they viewed as important for the nation's progress. In creating a venue for quality literary work to be published and discussed, the *Atlantic* aimed to create and promote an American canon that placed Hawthorne, Emerson, and other American authors in conversation with English, French, German, and Russian authors, as well as providing a model to which young authors should aspire.

As both editor and exemplar, Lowell promoted a critical view of literature that eschewed sentimental and didactic writing in favor of works based in the everyday life of people—an early promotion of realistic writing that would be crucially important in shaping Howells's criticism. The magazine promoted work that grew from a close attention to local conditions—a critical view that promoted local color fiction and regional writing, often by female authors, such as Elizabeth Phelps, Celia Thaxter, and Sarah Orne Jewett—as well as nonfiction genres such as travel writing and early investigative journalism. By promoting regional writing as a central genre of the *Atlantic*'s literary expression, Lowell linked a literary classicism with a literary nationalism that modeled for his readers a theory in which literary greatness sprang from and reflected national character.[15] In this view, a national literature would come from national subjects, rather than in the aping of styles or genres borrowed from established national canons. In other words, Lowell took from his European models the belief that an American literature worthy of classical status would only come from American authors writing about American subjects—just as great authors from Shakespeare to Goethe transformed their British and German experiences into great art.

The promotion of an early form of realistic writing was combined, in Lowell's *Atlantic*, with a distinct tendency toward ethical concerns. The ethos of intellectual discussion and social uplift envisioned by the magazine was implicitly linked to a vision of an improving American society. But this was not a simplistic moralism; Lowell promoted writing in which an ethical impulse was distinct from a sentimental or didactic approach. In the first issue of the magazine, he made this point through the poem, "The Origin of Didactic Poetry." In the poem, the goddess Minerva reads didactic verses to the gods, who in turn invent excuses to take leave of her tired moralizing. Discarded from Olympus onto the Earth, the verses sprang up as "two strong narcotics": poppies and didactic bards. Minerva concludes:

> "Discriminate," she said, "betimes;
>   The Muse is unforgiving;
> Put all your beauty in your rhymes,
>   Your morals in your living."[16]

In this poem, Lowell both previews the importance of humorous contributions to the new magazine and makes a critical statement on the role of didactic work in the magazine—which promoted strong opinions in nonfiction but promoted a literature focused on everyday life without direct moralizing. Through his editing, Lowell established the *Atlantic*'s dedication to an early realism that saw ethical concerns as being rooted in the portrayal of experience rather than sentimental or didactic approaches—morals through one's living characters.

Following the magazine's aim, stated in the first issue, of printing both works of "abstract and permanent value" and those catering to "the healthy appetite of the mind for entertainment in its various forms of Narrative, Wit and Humor," Lowell did not publish and review only works of permanent artistic value in the magazine. Lowell took the job as editor on the condition that his friend, Oliver Wendell Holmes, would be a regular contributor. Holmes published occasional poems and sketches in the magazine, as well as four serialized books of "table-talk," including *The Autocrat of the Breakfast Table*, which established him as one of the most popular *Atlantic* authors and one of the most popular writers and thinkers of the era.[17] Holmes's contributions, along with the works of Harriet Beecher Stowe and Longfellow, helped establish the magazine's subscription list, just as Emerson and Lowell (in his serious modes) helped establish its intellectual heft.

The *Atlantic* found room within the magazine for both serious works and lighter fare, often within the same magazine and often by the same authors. For instance, the January 1861 issue contained a sketch by Oliver Wendell Holmes entitled "A Visit to an Asylum for Aged and Decayed Punsters," which was framed as a first-person account of the author's visit to an asylum for men afflicted with the disease of punning.[18] This lighthearted piece of humor was immediately followed by an editorial by Lowell excoriating the outgoing Buchanan administration and outlining the question of slavery and secession philosophically, practically, and historically. While the second of these pieces was instrumental in establishing the *Atlantic*'s position on the South for the remainder of the war, it is also interesting in its juxtaposition with the humorous piece that preceded it, which shows that the readers of the magazine, along with the regular contributors, were used to abrupt shifts in tone and subject matter in the magazine. Both the intellectual wit of Holmes and the scathing satire of Lowell were promoted as worthy of the *Atlantic*'s readers' leisure time, and each humorist was framed as artistically and ethically excellent.

Reflecting ideas of hierarchy most likely borrowed from English criticism, the *Atlantic* distinguished between quality humor and other forms of temporary fun. Several articles on British humor periodicals appeared, and the first American version of *Vanity Fair*, edited by Artemus Ward, received several positive notices in the early 1860s. In one of these, the reviewer notes that such ephemeral humor is valuable as an indicator of an epoch's "tendency of thought" and that such a magazine might function as an "exponent of our national spirit of mirthfulness."[19] The review ends by advising the *Atlantic*'s readers that, despite slight offense to good taste, the humor magazine "deserves admission to the library and the drawing room." In defining a hierarchy of humor, the *Atlantic* distinguished between multiple levels: quality literary humor, entertaining magazine humor (if it avoided coarseness), and low forms of mass spectacle, most often in comparison with the clown or minstrel.[20] In an 1860 article on the English humorist Thomas Hood, the distinction between merely amusing joking and a deeper form of humor is discussed in order to elevate the humorist: "In much of his that seems burlesque, the most audacious, there are hidden springs of thought and tears. Often, when most he seems as the grimed and grinning clown in a circus girded by gaping spectators, he stops to pour out satire as passionate as that of Juvenal, or morality as eloquent and pure as that of Pascal. And this he does without lengthening his face or taking off his paint." In an 1865 article on "The Popular Lecture," the author and lecturer Josiah Holland used a hierarchical definition to distinguish between "triflers" on the platform and quality speakers, stating that humorous lecturers had "no better motive and no higher mission than the stage-clown and the negro-minstrel."[21] Holland later extended this distinction to exclude Mark Twain from the respectable ethos of his own magazine, *Scribner's Monthly*, a culture of letters that will be examined in the next chapter.

Humor functioned in the *Atlantic* as a counterweight to heavier pieces, as an enticement to readers who desired lighter leisure from their reading, as an indicator of social and cultural trends, and, in its more serious moments, as an ethical and political tool. This last use is demonstrated through the magazine's best-known satire—Lowell's second series of *The Biglow Papers*, which ran intermittently from 1862 to 1865. These papers revived Lowell's successful humorous productions—poems and letters written in dialect—which had been introduced in 1846 as a satire on the war with Mexico.[22] In these books, Lowell wrote in the voice of three characters from the same fictional town of "Jaalam" Massachusetts: Hosea Biglow, the shrewd Yankee; Parson Homer Wilbur, the pompously educated villager; and Birdofredum Sawin, a fool who had rushed off to fight in the Mexican War.

Biglow and Sawin write letters in verse to Parson Wilbur, who forwards them to the *Atlantic*, complete with a pompous introduction. In the first "Biglow letter" of the second series, from January 1862, Birdofredum Sawin describes the years since he went to Mexico: he lost his leg in the war; escaped through swamps; was accused of theft, tarred, feathered, and ridden on a rail; imprisoned and then released; forced to pay for the feathers used for his punishment; and married to the widow whose feather bed was used when he could not pay. The letter satirized Southern institutions and logic through the character of the ignorant Yankee who claimed to be better educated than his Southern peers and who could explain Southern life to the Parson, as when he explained the region's "p'liticle econ'my" that necessitated trading in cotton and slaves when gold and silver were scarce:

> Ner't ain't quite hendy to pass off one o' your six-foot Guineas
>   An' git your halves an' quarters back in gals an' pickaninnies:
> Wal, t' ain't quite all a feller'd ax, but then ther' 's this to say,
>   It's on'y jest among ourselves thet we expec' to pay;
>   . . .

For Jacob warn't a suckemstance to Jeff at financierin';
  He never'd thought o'borryin' from Esau like all nater
An' then cornfiscatin' all debts to sech a small pertater;
  There's p'liticle econ'my, now, combined 'ith morril beauty
They saycrifices privit eends (your in'my's, tu) to dooty!

Mr. Sawin's main purpose in writing is to solicit help in getting out of his first marriage, which he reasons has been dissolved by secession:

Nex' place, my State's secedin' out hez leg'lly lef' me free
  To merry any one I please, pervidin' it's a shee;[23]

Lowell linked his humor with the moral dimension of satire, attacking the underpinnings of slavery and its defenses.

While he used the pages of the *Atlantic Monthly* to attack slavery with direct editorials, his dialect humor proved to be more popular and longer lasting. In the introduction to the book version of the Second Series, he wrote that he found, upon first publishing the papers in 1848, that his new creation was popular, indeed more well known than his serious writing and that, "I held in my hand a weapon instead of the mere fencing-stick I had supposed." His description of humor's value as a weapon demonstrates both his ethical purpose and his goal of lasting artistic accomplishment beyond the immediate aims of satire:

> If I put on the cap and bells and made myself one of the court-fools of King Demos, it was less to make his majesty laugh than to win a passage into his royal ears for certain serious things which I had deeply at heart. I say this because there is no imputation that could be more galling to any man's self-respect than that of being a mere jester. I endeavored, by generalizing my satire, to give it what value I could beyond the passing moment and the immediate application.[24]

This model of humor—not necessarily as a genre, but as a cultural weapon with ethical aims—envisioned humor as a form of serious artistic production, while at the same time justifying humor as having a value beyond the "mere jester."

Lowell took up the hierarchical classification of humor in his review of Holmes's first novel, *Elsie Venner* (April 1861). In arguing for the quality of Holmes's work as lasting art, Lowell introduced two critical tropes that were central to the delineation of quality humor: the false devaluation of humor and the difference between surface and depth. "People in general" he writes "have a great respect for those who scare them or make them cry, but are apt to weigh lightly one who amuses them. They like to be tickled, but they would hardly take the advice of their tickler on any question they thought serious."[25] This diminishment of humor as of lesser value than "serious" forms—what later critics would call "the penalty of humor"—stemmed from the failure to distinguish between real wit—"it is generalization in a flash, logic by the electric telegraph, the sense of likeness in unlikeness, that lies at the root of all discoveries"—and a "surface-wit," which is "the sign of a light and shallow nature." The focus on the surface-wit, he continued, "has made men distrustful of all laughers; and they are apt to confound in one sweeping condemnation with this that humor whose base is seriousness, and which is generally the rebound of the mind from over-sad contemplation. They do not see that the same qualities that make Shakespeare the greatest of the tragic poets make him also the deepest of humorists."

As his biographer Martin Duberman points out, Lowell was concerned with being thought of as a "mere" humorist, even as most critics held that his humorous work surpassed his serious, both artistically and ethically.

Lowell's great contribution to American literature may have been the introduction of dialect as a serious component of American writing. The lasting artistic accomplishment of *The Biglow Papers*, according to Lowell, was the use of dialect to portray "the life, invention, and vigor shown by our popular speech." Lowell argued that in dialect and patois are the living life of the American language and the sources of both poetry and humor, which spring from the same source.[26] Humor, in this sense, is different in extent, not in kind, from the true sources of poetic expression, and both are based in local particularities of expression. American humor is not mere exaggeration, Lowell argued, but the apprehension and expression of incongruities. For instance, he writes:

> I heard a man, in order to give a notion of some very cold weather, say to another that a certain Joe, who had been taking mercury, found a lump of quicksilver in each boot, when he went home to dinner. This power of rapidly dramatizing a dry fact into flesh and blood and the vivid conception of Joe as a human thermometer strike me as showing a poetic sense that may be refined into faculty. At any rate there is humor here, and not mere

> *quickness of wit,—the deeper and not the shallower quality. The tendency of humor is always towards overplus of expression, while the very essence of wit is its logical precision.*[27]

In framing his most popular work, Lowell connected the humorist's use of dialect with the dynamic language of true art. Dialect, in Lowell's sense, was distinct from slang and other tricks of speech and writing that other humorists relied on.[28]

Holmes and Lowell were the main representatives of quality humor for the readers of the *Atlantic Monthly*, and their works were widely popular well into the Gilded Age. But their reputation faded in the twentieth century as literary historians enshrined Emerson, Thoreau, Hawthorne, Melville, and Whitman as the major authors of "the American Renaissance." As Vernon Parrington notes, Holmes was the center of Boston's literary life, "the autocrat of her social gatherings, the acknowledged head of her mutual admiration society." But in Matthieson's foundational text, Holmes only warrants three mentions.[29] Holmes has been marginalized from literary history, along with Lowell, Whittier, Bryant, and the extremely popular Longfellow, due to the privileging of modernist criteria of genre, style, and subject matter, rather than an evaluation of the roles they played in the literary world of their day.[30] Literary history has also marginalized Holmes, it would seem, largely based on the perceived conservative nature of his politics. Holmes's beliefs tended toward hierarchical views of democracy, social progress, and the civilizing value of high culture, placing him squarely within the intellectual tradition of the *Atlantic Monthly*, while diminishing his historical standing with scholars who privilege subversive and radical traditions of literature. While relatively conservative in some areas—women's rights and racial views most clearly—Holmes prided himself on the promotion of free intellectual development, especially in his satires of religion and other dogmas. Parrington wrote: "In his own special way, then, as a Brahmin of the Brahmins, Holmes was a rebel, a puller-down of worm-eaten structures, a freethinker rejoicing when free thought tossed a cargo of obsolete dogma into Boston Bay, or drew out a linchpin of some respectable social coach. He loved Boston the more because he believed Boston was the home of free thought and free speech, the capital of American brains, the intellectual rebel of the continent."[31] Holmes reserved his most stinging wit for the Calvinist orthodoxy of Boston and the Puritanical cast of mind he found limiting to intellectual and social growth. This criticism consistently rankled orthodox aspects of the

New England elite, who criticized Holmes and the *Atlantic* for years at the pulpit and in the press.[32] Holmes's use of humor as a weapon aimed at the conservative religious elite of New England demonstrates the magazine's willingness to push against the orthodoxies of the era, acknowledging that those orthodoxies are not our orthodoxies and that the humor of one era works differently than the humor of others.

The place of Lowell and Holmes within the history of humor has been largely flattened into a caricature. For instance, Walter Blair and Hamlin Hill's survey of the history of American humor classifies the two under the title "The Reputables" and places them within a tradition of humor stemming from the Puritans that "supported conventional notions about propriety, decorum, restraint, and morality."[33] Blair and Hill clearly trace the foundations of New England humor: a focus on morality, the dignified position of the humorist-author, and the major forms that focus on wit (poems, letters, essays) rather than humorous stories or tall tales. And while this tradition clearly influenced Lowell and Holmes, it does not follow that their humorous works supported a simple Bostonian status quo, despite the dignified bearing of the authors and the moral outlook of their humor. The confusion of classification is further illustrated in Hill and Blair's classification of Lowell as "pro-Establishment," except for the antislavery *The Biglow Papers*, for which he is classified with the "Down East" humorists and praised for the subversive quality of the work. While they were certainly of the "Brahmin caste" of Boston—Holmes coined the term "Brahmin," in fact—their humor should not thus be lumped as merely "pro-Establishment humor."

Holmes and Lowell played central roles in establishing the *Atlantic* as a magazine that valued both light, entertaining humor and more serious artistic and moral humor. As editor from 1857 to 1861, Lowell established the basic traditions that the magazine would maintain, with slight alterations by successive editors, for at least the remainder of the century. The two subsequent editors—James T. Fields and Howells—built upon Lowell's traditions while modifying the magazine's stance to reflect their own views of literature and society. In the *Atlantic*'s critical ethos, the editors intertwined the goals of creating an open intellectual space in which cultural and literary productions would uplift American culture and act as a model for intellectual endeavor and respectable leisure. As the foremost of the so-called "quality magazines" of the era, the *Atlantic* played a central role in shaping discussions of American Literature as a subject and of humor's place within the literary hierarchy.

FROM BOSTON CRITICISM, BOSTON THEORIES TO AN AMERICAN CRITICISM: WILLIAM DEAN HOWELLS AND THE DEVELOPMENT OF THE *ATLANTIC MONTHLY*

While William Dean Howells has come to be known as "the Dean of American Letters"—the key critic of the Gilded Age and the promoter of the genre of realism—when he arrived in Boston as the assistant editor of the *Atlantic Monthly* in 1866, he was not known as much of anything. He had published several poems in the *Atlantic* and other magazines, he had written a biography of Lincoln that had resulted in a consulship in Venice, and he worked for a short time under E. L. Godkin at the newly formed *Nation*. As aspiring literary man and as editor, Howells was shaped by and built on the editorial ethos of the *Atlantic Monthly*, especially the views of literature and criticism developed by James Russell Lowell, whom he viewed as his true mentor. As the assistant editor from 1866 to 1871 and as editor from 1871 to 1881, Howells developed a theory of American letters that pushed the *Atlantic*'s intellectual foundations in new directions through his writings, through his editorial selections, and through his promotion of realistic approaches to fiction, humor, and other genres.

While scholarly discussions of Howellsian realism might seem to place the question of humor and the category of "realism" as separate concerns, the development of his nascent views of realism were crucial for his promotion of Mark Twain as a quality humorist. In his years at the *Atlantic Monthly*, Howells promoted Mark Twain as part of a vision of American letters that incorporated humor, travel writing, and different types of fiction into a vision of "realistic" art based on a fidelity of plot, language, and especially character. While not defined as "realism" per se, Howells's early criticism provides a pre-history of American literary realism that helps us understand the elite culture of New England letters and Mark Twain's place within it.

There is perhaps no better example of the literary influence of the *Atlantic Monthly* in shaping the ideas of American letters than that of William Dean Howells. Exemplary if not typical, the influence of the magazine on Howells testifies to the importance of its vision of American letters. As an aspiring literary man in Ohio, Howells was influenced strongly by the culture of letters of the magazine, attempting to shape himself as a writer in its image. In "My First Visit to New England" (1894), he tells the story of his development as a young litterateur who looked to New England and Europe for his literary models—specifically citing George Eliot, Charles

Reade, Heinrich Heine, and W. M. Thackeray, along with Hawthorne, Emerson, and Longfellow. These figures mainly circulated to Columbus, Ohio, Howells notes, by magazine:

> We looked to England and the East largely for our literary opinions; we accepted the Saturday Review as law if we could not quite receive it as gospel. One of us took the Cornhill magazine, because Thackeray was the editor; the Atlantic Monthly counted many readers among us; and a visiting young lady from New England, who screamed at sight of the periodical in one of our houses, "why, have you got the Atlantic Monthly out here?" could be answered, with cold superiority, "There are several contributors to the Atlantic in Columbus."[34]

Howells romanticized the "vigorous intellectual life" found among the New England writers associated with the *Atlantic*. Framing literary culture in terms of publishing prestige, Howells wrote that Boston was the literary center of the United States in 1860, and every young author "was ambitious to join his name with theirs in the *Atlantic Monthly*, and in the lists of Ticknor and Fields."[35]

Encouraged by the *Atlantic*'s acceptance of several poems, a positive review of his first book of poems, and a letter of recognition from Lowell, the twenty-three-year-old Howells traveled to New England in 1860. The "devout young pilgrim from the West" saw literature in everything, composing lines of poetry constantly and looking for literary associations in every city, and he sought out the New England luminaries in hopes of establishing himself in the literary profession. Howells's account of his visit focuses not on the rarified air of literary Boston, but on the air of conviviality between the authors he met. The physical dimensions of friendship were highlighted by the motto Lowell used when ideas veered toward the transcendental—"Remember the dinner-bell." Indeed, Howells's introduction to New England's literary culture was marked by personal interactions—long talks with Lowell on literature and the profession of authorship; breakfast with Fields, who expressed burlesqued grief that Howells had never eaten blueberry cake; tea with Holmes, whose talk Howells saw to be much like that of his most famous character; a long talk with Hawthorne on a hill overlooking Concord, who then sent a letter of introduction to Emerson containing the line: "I find this young man worthy."[36] Most famously, Howells attended a dinner with James T.

Fields, Holmes, and Lowell—who referred to each other as "James" and "Wendell," to Howells's delight—at which Holmes famously quipped, "Well, James, this is something like the apostolic succession; this is the laying on of the hands."[37]

The Boston of the *Atlantic Monthly* provided Howells with a model of literary production, much more than the Bohemian culture of letters of New York. Immediately after visiting Boston, Howells traveled to New York City, where he visited the offices of the *Saturday Press*, a weekly literary magazine founded in 1858 that had published a number of his poems. Of the magazine, Howells spoke favorably, writing: "The young writers throughout the country were ambitious to be seen in it, and they gave their best to it; they gave literally, for the *Saturday Press* never paid in anything but hopes of paying, vaguer even than promises. It is not too much to say that it was very nearly as well for one to be accepted by the Press as to be accepted by the *Atlantic*, and for the time there was no other literary comparison."[38] But Howells found the posturing of the Bohemians to be tiring, especially their dogmatic desire to counter all respectability and shock all proprieties for the sake of the pose, which he considered to be rather more French than American. The culture of letters surrounding the *Press* offered an alternative of literary production to that of the *Atlantic*, although the magazine ceased publication in 1860, to be reborn in August 1865, just before it published Mark Twain's "Jumping Frog." Howells chose to follow the model of Boston.

Narrating his arrival in Boston in retrospect, he noted that the bulk of quality writers were either in New England, or of New England birth and the "New England race," although the *Atlantic* had "been characterized by what was more national, what was more universal, in the New England temperament."[39] The South and the West had done little to establish literary culture, he held, and the writers who had come from these areas, like himself, based their ideas of literature on the "New England ideals and examples": "I am very sure that in my early day we were characterized by them, and wished to be so; we even felt that we failed in so far as we expressed something native quite in our own way. The literary theories we accepted were New England theories, the criticism we valued was New England criticism, or, more strictly speaking, Boston theories, Boston criticism."[40] William Dean Howells was shaped as a literary man by the vision of literary life that the *Atlantic* promoted. His introduction to the *Atlantic*'s culture points to the dual nature of the magazine's culture of letters—the abstract reverence readers held for the idea of the magazine and the personal dimension embodied in the relationships between its figures.

While the major expression of a periodical exists in its pages, the personal dimension of a culture of letters should be noted as a vital aspect of its ethos. Ideas about literature and culture are embedded in friendships and equally personal feuds, in meetings and meals, and within the social and intellectual circle a magazine creates. The young author from Ohio joined the *Atlantic*'s culture of letters as an outsider, but the influence of the magazine's ethos on his intellectual development may have made him a stronger promoter of its ideals than its previous editors as he came to the editorship already shaped by the magazine's goals. But he was also quite aware of the ways in which it fell short of its aims. In his role at the *Atlantic Monthly*, Howells worked to expand the magazine's scope to a truly national representation of American letters, transforming Boston theories into an American criticism.

With the departure of Lowell in 1861, the magazine changed relatively little in format or substance. James T. Fields, a self-educated business-man from New Hampshire, had worked his way from bookstore clerk to co-owner of a leading publisher, which purchased the magazine. Demon-strating the openness of the *Atlantic*'s culture of letters, Fields was not an intellectual heir to Lowell, but he did recognize and promote the major traditions of the magazine, out of both business acumen and idealism. The changes in tone and content that occurred under Fields occurred slowly, most importantly the increased promotion of so-called *Atlantic* authors, the scouting of new authors for the magazine and the publishing house, and a gradual lightening of tone. To promote the magazine through its associations, Fields ended Lowell's practice, adopted from the general pe-riodical practice, of publishing all articles in the magazine anonymously. Fields solicited younger and less established writers, hoping to fill out his firm's publication list. Howells rose to influence at the *Atlantic Monthly*, at least in part, due to his perceived ability to move the magazine into an era of mass publishing because Fields supposed him to be "alert to new developments in literature."[41]

From 1866 to 1871, Fields and Howells promoted new types of con-tributions, such as first-person and investigative journalism, domestic subjects, and travel writing, while continuing the traditional focus on intellectual subjects and realistic fiction.[42] One suggestion to promote the magazine that Fields did not take was from James Parton, a popular journalist whom Fields had hired to write contemporary pieces for the *Atlantic*. Parton recommended the magazine would sell better with less Emersonian writing and more modern subjects and if "a writer named Mark Twain [were] engaged. . . ."[43] Howells encouraged new authors, such as Thomas Bailey Aldrich, Sarah Orne Jewett, William De Forest, Clarence Stedman, Bret Harte, and Henry James, Jr., to submit to the magazine. It was also during his time as assistant editor that Howells first brought Mark Twain into the *Atlantic* through his review of *The Innocents Abroad*.

From the critical tradition established by James Russell Lowell, Howells developed central ideas of realistic literature that would influence his later theories, while shifting from what he saw as the magazine's focus on ethics toward an aesthetic theory of American literature. From the editorial work of James T. Fields, Howells inherited a view of the *Atlantic* author as the center of the American literary canon, along with the necessity of the magazine to expand its reach to new authors in order to sustain the magazine and expand its national scope. Under Lowell, the *Atlantic* had been known as a place for relatively honest critical reviews that largely focused on the positive aspects of books, especially if those books were by contributors to the magazine or were reviewed by the author's friends. During his years as editor, Fields continued to employ the same major critical voices that had helped establish its editorial ethos—including, Lowell, T. W. Higginson, and Horace Scudder—and brought in Howells as a new critical voice. Fields solicited positive reviews as promotional material and censored harsh criticism from reviews, using his position as editor to promote the reputation and sales of the magazine's and his firm's writers, in many cases to the detriment of the quality of the reviews. At one point, Fields wrote a friend: "All is well, the pills are puffed, and pills thus puffed will sell."[44] Fields's major skill as editor and publisher was in developing and promoting authors through encouragement and friendship, which was a skill Howells adopted.

As assistant editor from 1866 to 1871, Howells reframed the *Atlantic*'s critical tradition from the ethical focus of New England romance to an aesthetic promotion of writing in which ethical concerns were embodied in realistic characters. In doing so, he pushed the magazine beyond the safe confines of New England, publishing and reviewing a good number of midwestern, western, and a few southern authors, as well as a number of New Yorkers who had been critical of the magazine under Lowell and Fields.[45] He introduced into the magazine a significant cohort of authors who would shape literary production for much of the remainder of the century, including Bret Harte, Henry James, Jr., John DeForest, Charles Dudley Warner, and Mark Twain. The book review section of the magazine provided him a platform to prepare readers for new meanings of "realistic" literary production and new authors who might enter into American literature. In this role, Howells expanded on Lowell's main goals of promoting open discussion, encouraging cultural uplift, and establishing a national literature. Reviews created a continuity within the magazine's critical tradition, from Lowell through Fields to Howells, all of whom envisioned an educated readership shaped by the magazine's articles, stories, and criticism.

Although Howells felt some trepidation at his position as an outsider in the center of literary America, his role was significant, especially in the book review section, which he took over almost immediately. The bulk of Howells's critical views were confined to the "Reviews and Literary Notices" section in the back of each issue, which he gradually expanded over the years as part of his increasing focus on literary topics. Whereas Fields had reviewed approximately five major works of fiction per year, Howells increased this number to thirty-two by 1870 and seventy-one in 1880. Howells's reviews during these years often focused on broad topics: the role of the critic as a reviewer, a shift from ethical to aesthetic criticism of fiction, and the importance of developing a realistic American literature and criticism, in both fiction and humor.[46]

Shortly before arriving in Boston in 1866, Howells published an anonymous piece in the *Round Table* under the title "Literary Criticism." The article reads as a critical manifesto, decrying the tendency of reviewers to base their views on "spleen, personal liking or animosity, a bad temper, a bad digestion, a chronic tendency to fault-finding" rather than "the love of truth and justice and an honest devotion to the cause of pure literature" that inspires "fearless criticism."[47] Rather than criticism debased by "alien purpose," whether animosity, partisan feeling, or anxiety "not to hurt the author's feelings or the publisher's profits," Howells argued that:

> *True criticism, indeed, is the function and natural habit of every intelligent and candid mind—which, accordingly, is probably the reason why the ignorant and dishonest always feel annoyed and alarmed at its appearance. Criticism implies in its very derivation and significant judgment, discernment, sifting, separating good from bad, the wheat from the chaff. True criticism, therefore, consists of a calm, just, and fearless handling of its subject, and*

in pointing out in all honesty whatever there is hitherto undiscovered of merit, and . . . whatever there has been concealed of defect.

Howells framed criticism as the act of distinguishing good from bad, in which the professional reviewer acts as a more experienced guide in reading, training readers in the literary instincts that should guide their taste.[48] "Honest criticism," he argued, is "the indication of an educated and refined literary taste. It is the impulsive act of an accomplished mind." Howells brought this view of criticism as the act of reading well to the *Atlantic*, where it found a natural home.

Following general editorial practice, Howells wrote reviews in the editorial voice—using "we," "us," and "our" and publishing all reviews anonymously. In an August 1870 review of an updated volume of a critical dictionary, reviewed in the *Atlantic* a decade earlier, Howells joked: "Recurring to the notice which we (editors pass, but the editorial pronoun endures) made . . . when it appeared some eleven years ago, we find that we can say little of his second which would not appear stale to our readers; for we take it that none of them can have forgotten any past criticism in these pages."[49] Sometimes this voice included all readers, although it was occasionally limited to readers of the *Atlantic*, such as when the book under review was previously published in the magazine. In a review of Thomas Wentworth Higginson's collection, *Atlantic Essays*, Howells specifically addressed "the constant reader" of the magazine—or "all lovers of good literature, be they lay or cleric"—who made up the imagined audience of the magazine.[50] Rereading Higginson, who had written many of the literary essays in the early years of the *Atlantic*, would remind these readers of the value of good literature and good criticism, while also pointing to a division between readers based on perceptions of literary value. He writes: "Still, though these things cannot teach those to whom reading and writing have not come by nature the virtues that they praise, they ought to have a tonic and heartening effect upon others, and keep them from yielding to the temptations of a public that buys and pays [for] trash as if it loved it." Howells's editorial voice framed the aim of criticism in the *Atlantic* as an act of uplift by teaching discernment to readers, who would then pay for the proper types of reading, which would include the magazine and the books it promoted. The hierarchical considerations here contain a distinct class difference between the *Atlantic*'s readers and the "public" of mass consumption.

Howells's early reviews show a willingness to criticize books and authors for artistic or moral failings, even in works published by his employer's firm. Howells's critical stance and the efficiency of Fields's publishing integration collided in the case of Charles Reade's *Griffith Gaunt*, which was serialized in the *Atlantic* from December 1865 to November 1866, published by Ticknor and Fields in December, and reviewed by Howells (anonymously) in that month's issue. Howells addressed his review to the magazine's readers, assuming they had all read the serialization and found—as he had—the novel lacking in "moralities and proprieties." He reframes the question of morality in fiction as a question of aesthetics. "It is not as a moralist that we have primarily to find fault with Mr. Reade," he writes, "but as an artist, for his moral would have been good if his art had been true."[51] Despite the failings of Reade's artistic conception in the book's ending, Howells also focuses on the artistic strength of its characters: "The management of the plot was so masterly, that the story proceeded without a pause or an improbability until the long fast of a month between the feasts of its publication became almost insupportable. It was a plot that grew naturally out of the characters, for humanity is prolific of events, and these characters are all human beings. They are not in the least anachronistic." In this review and others, Howells forwarded a criticism that privileged aesthetic reality over didactic sentiment: art needed to be true to life, first, and could then convey a moral content more clearly.

This review was immediately followed in the magazine by a puff of Ticknor and Fields brand pills in a review of four of the firm's books by key authors—three reprints of works by Longfellow, Whittier, Lowell, and a new book by Longfellow. Not so much a review as a sales pitch, the piece focuses on the canonical status of the authors and on American letters in relation to European:

> Of these volumes three have long since taken their place in the letters of America, and in the hearts of all who know and love the purest, the truest, and the best that poesy can offer. . . .
>
> But it is not our purpose to pause in criticism over works that may fairly be said to have passed beyond the province of contemporary criticism. Rather is it our desire to welcome them as they are tendered to us in a new form, and to commend the artistic character of their presentation.[52]

The review attempts to canonize the "*Atlantic* authors" as an American literature commensurate with an English model. An alert reader would have been aware, of course, that the books under consideration in both reviews were published by the same company as the magazine they were reading, but readers would not have known that the first was written by William Dean Howells, who was developing into the most important critic of the Gilded Age, while the second was written by Albert Stuart Evans, who only wrote this single piece for the *Atlantic*.[53]

Howells tended toward sympathetic reviews of most works, especially those by contributors, and he occasionally skipped reviewing a book by a colleague when the review might be untoward. But Howells also sought to educate his readers by dismissing certain works as not worth the reader's time. An 1869 review of nine works, lumped together as "A Poetical Lot," provides a humorous window into Howells's willingness to dismiss literary endeavors. The older, "inhuman" critic, he began, would have feasted in public upon the books considered. But the more refined critic, the sort the *Atlantic* now employed, took a different approach:

> . . . *nothing is allowed to appear that would shock the nerves of the most delicate female. It is understood, of course, that a rhymester, now and then, has to die; but the reader shall see nothing but what is perfectly decorous and kind. At the most he shall hear a confused shuffling behind the scenes, a blow perhaps, a faint cry; but the critic will immediately come forward again with a pleasant, reassuring smile, and go on with his general remarks upon the science of aesthetics.*[54]

Howells proceeded to dismiss most of the books in a very public manner, using the exercise as an occasion to discourse on literary subjects, such as the difference between fake sentiment and "real feeling."[55] Like Lowell, Howells himself wrote relatively few longer critical articles on literary subjects during his years at the *Atlantic*, but he used his role as reviewer to hold forth on literary subjects, often forgetting the book at hand until the end of a review, where it could be summarily praised or dispatched.[56]

In the *Atlantic Monthly*'s editorial ethos, authors were encouraged to portray their subjects realistically, although this concept was never clearly defined. Helen McMahon, in her study of trends of criticism in the *Atlantic*, points out that book reviews, beginning in the early years of the magazine, praised literature in terms that were linked to ideas of realism—such as realistic, pure, humane, natural, truthful, fidelity, and faithful representation.[57] For Lowell, this form of reality in literature was not a matter of genre, style, or subject—rather it was a matter of the proper relation between author and subject. Even poetry that idealized experience could be praised as realistic if it portrayed the right kind of

American scene.[58] In the *Atlantic*, the positive literary judgments implicit in terms like *reality*, *truth*, and *natural* were applied to almost any literary genre and in reference to both moral and aesthetic realities. In a letter to Harriet Beecher Stowe in 1859, Lowell wrote:

> *A moral aim is a fine thing, but in making a story an artist is a traitor who does not sacrifice everything to art. . . . My advice is to follow your own instincts,—to stick to nature, and to avoid what people commonly call the "Ideal." for that, and beauty, and pathos, and success, all lie in the simply natural. . . . Don't I feel it every day in this weary editorial mill of mine, that there are ten thousand people who can write ideal things for one who can see, feel, and reproduce nature and character.*[59]

In portraying the realities of everyday life, Lowell held that the author would follow the model of Shakespeare whose "breadth of nature" made him "incapable of alienation from common human nature and actual life."[60] In other words, to write realistically was to write about what one knows, which was what all great writers had done.

Howells reworked the meanings of terms such as "reality," "humane," and "true" to refocus the magazine's critical ethos on aesthetic, rather than ethical, criticism. Howells focused on the categories of style, plot, subject, and, most extensively, character. While brief mention was made of the French school of "realism" in 1862, neither Lowell nor the other major critics of the magazine developed a unified theory of literary realism, nor would Howells during his tenure at the magazine. Like Lowell, Howells did not frame realism only in relation to fiction, separate from other genres. Instead, he judged all genres in terms of fidelity to the aesthetic and ethical truth of a situation—an often maddeningly vague application of the possible meanings of "realistic" writing. For instance, in a critical move that undercuts the logic usually associated with ideas of realism, Howells argued that the romance of the New England tradition was, in fact, the most realistic form of portraying certain aspects of the New England character, and works of romance could and did fit into the larger cultural logic of the *Atlantic*'s critical approach. The romance, he wrote, "is always an allegory, and the novel is a picture in which the truth to life is suffered to do its unsermonized office for conduct; and New England yet lacks her novelist, because it was her instinct and her conscience to be true to an ideal of life rather than to life itself." Howells consistently praised Hawthorne as a master of the form, and he called *Uncle Tom's*

Cabin "the greatest work of imagination that we have produced in prose," but argued that it may or may not be properly termed a "novel," since its virtue is its appeal to "conscience" rather than "taste," to "ethical sense, not the aesthetical sense."[61]

While Howells's critical ethos was flexible enough to incorporate humor, romance, and other genres of writing into his promotion of realistic literature, increasingly he promoted fiction, both the novel and short stories, as the main genres of American literary endeavor. As editor, Howells continued and extended Lowell's promotion of locally based fiction that sublimated the moral purpose to the realism of the characters. In one of his first reviews as editor in 1871, Howells gingerly made this point, while showing deference to Harriet Beecher Stowe as one of the *Atlantic* giants. Of Stowe's new novel, he wrote: "Mrs. Stowe fairly warns her readers at the outset that her story is but a sermon in disguise; and no one has the right to complain if it falls below her other novels in the proper interest of fiction. Of course one may doubt if a little more lifelikeness in some of the people . . . might not have helped the effect of the discourse; and for our own part, we feel that the declared moral is rather forced out of it than naturally evolved."[62] In this tendency to "helplessly" point to the moral in all their writing, what he later termed sacrificing "the song to the sermon," Howells believed that most novels in the romance tradition expressed their vision of society in ways "marred by the intense ethicism that pervaded the New England mind."[63] This is not to say that Howells devalued morality in literature; in fact, his criticism always viewed literature as distinctly ethical, although his views on the subject were scattered through reviews and articles much like his views of literature. But the morality that he had imbibed from the formative exposure to the *Atlantic Monthly*—a focus on social uplift through liberal cultural production with a background of religious, but not orthodox, beliefs—was gradually placed into aesthetic terms, holding that literature was ethical because it was true to certain aesthetic goals.

The picture of "realistic" writing that Howells developed was not a unified theory or genre but a general approach to both writing and reading that privileged works that connected to "real" American life, while the specifics of what that meant remained consistently unspecified. This lack of critical centering may be frustrating to the scholar searching for a definition of "Howellsian realism," but it reflected the critical tradition of the magazine's editorial ethos, which was more concerned with defining quality broadly than within a single prescribed genre. As Howells argued in 1867, the job of the critic was not to base reviews on an established critical principle or a "supposed law of aesthetics," but to form opinions based on cultivated tastes and experience. Arguing that criticism was an art, Howells quipped: "In fact, criticism is almost purely a matter of taste and experience, and there is hardly any law established for criticism which has not been overthrown as often as the French government."[64] Howells's inclusion of Mark Twain in the company of realistic writers in the *Atlantic* can thus be read as a crucial part of an evolving critical argument that viewed humor as a possibly realistic genre, capable of being categorized within an American canon.

"HUMOR, WITH THE LARGE H": HOWELLS ON HUMOR AND OTHER REALISTIC GENRES

While the Twain-Howells friendship is one of the most written about in American literary history, surprisingly little attention has been paid to Howells's critical writings in the *Atlantic Monthly* on Mark Twain's early works, or about Howells's early criticism more generally. The standard critical approach has been to read Howells's *Atlantic* reviews of Mark Twain's early works as part of the forty-plus years of criticism that Howells wrote on the subject Mark Twain. Similarly, the critical writings of William Dean Howells are often examined in relation to the development of his theories of realism, often beginning after he had left the *Atlantic*, focusing on his criticism for the *Century* magazine and on his editorship of *Harper's*, which he began in 1886.[65] It was in the pages of *Harper's*, and in his critical manifesto *Criticism and Fiction* (1891), that Howells forwarded a developed theory of realism (and started the so-called Realism War), focusing on the production of fiction opposed to the traditions of "Romance" and sentimental literature. It is this version of realism that scholars generally have referred to when examining Howells's critical view of Mark Twain.[66] While these approaches have produced important insights, they elide many of the works that established Mark Twain's reputation and minimize Howells's critical development at the *Atlantic Monthly*. And while critics have found that Howells's later theories of literary realism fit poorly with Mark Twain's written works, adoption and extension of the *Atlantic*'s critical approach points toward a theory of "realistic" writing in multiple genres—including humor—that better accounts for Mark Twain's role in Howells's literary ethos.

Reading Howells's early reviews of Mark Twain in the context of the more than 200 reviews and articles that he wrote for the *Atlantic* shows how Mark Twain's inclusion in the company of the best placed him in a new professional realm that raised new questions about his place in the hierarchy of American humor.[67] Rather than straining to fit Mark Twain into a narrow definition of "realism," Howells's reviews relied on a theory of realistic writing critically flexible enough to contain humor. Howells's criticism of humor linked the aesthetic synthesis of character, approach, and embodied ethics in order to integrate quality humor into his developing conception of realistic American literature.[68] While all humor could be funny—that is, it might make one laugh—the value of humor needed to be delineated into quality literature, entertaining leisure, or funny trash in order to distinguish certain humorists from others. In this context, Howells's critical transformation of Mark Twain into a humorist who could share space with Holmes and Lowell was part of the development of a critical ethos that built on the *Atlantic Monthly*'s intellectual and cultural goals while expanding the magazine's reach—geographically and aesthetically.

In his first review of a humorous work as assistant editor of the *Atlantic*, Howells wrote an extensive review of Lowell's second series of *The Biglow Papers* in the January 1867 issue. More a discourse on humor than a review of the book per se, Howells used the space to set up a hierarchy of humorous writing by distinguishing between Lowell and newspaper humorists. In Lowell, Howells found "everything to admire, and nothing to blame." He found: "Quick, sharp wit, pervading humor, trenchant logic, sustained feeling,—well, we come to the poverty of critical good-nature in spite of ourselves, and it is a satisfaction to know that the reviewed can suffer nothing from it, but will remain as honestly fresh, original, and great as if we had not sought to label his fine qualities."[69] Howells praised the reality of the character of Hosea Biglow, who "is the type of a civilization, and who expresses, in a genuine vernacular, the true feeling, the racy humor, and the mother-wit of Yankee-land." In establishing his critical ethos on humor, Howells borrowed heavily from English critics and the hierarchical division of humor.

While Howells privileged the aesthetic over the ethical in his criticism, this never meant a disregard for the ethical in writing—a fact that later critics used to dismiss Howells and his literary values.[70] The satire of the papers reflected the central moral purpose of Lowell's humor. In "confronting us with their errors," Lowell did not degrade his characters with satire. Instead, Howells argues that "there never was political satire so thoroughly humane as Hosea Biglow's; there never was a satire so noble before." His reframing of quality satire as humane and noble, as mildly corrective rather than harshly critical, fits with his early preference for literature that reflected the "smiling aspects of American life."[71] But Howells focused on both the moralistic position of the humorist and the artistic excellence of his productions, writing: "[Nasby] is wittier and bet-ter-hearted than Artemus Ward, and he has a generosity of purpose and elevation of aim, but he is only a moralized merry-andrew; whereas one may lift his glance from the smiling lips of the Yankee minstrel, and behold his honest eyes full of self-respectful thought, and that complement of humor, pathos,—without which your jester is but a sorry antic."[72] In these early reviews, Howells established a series of critical concerns that would influence his future reviews of humor: the aesthetic aims of humor, the distinction between dialect and misspelling, and the connection between the humorist and morality.

In this review, Howells theorized the major factors that defined his hierarchy of American humor as a combination of real characters whose humor—whether in satire or characterization—was both kind and realis-tic to human nature. By comparison, Howells distinguishes the humor of Lowell from that of Artemus Ward and other humorists by noting that the character of Biglow states that he spells however he wants, with the main aim to "squeeze the cents out of 'em, it's the main thing, and wut they wuz made for." Howells fears that this will lead readers to confuse true dialect for intentional misspelling, which has already led "feeble critic-folk" to hold Lowell "responsible for the clownish tricks in orthography of Artemus Ward, Josh Billings, and the like." He then goes to pains to distinguish between Lowell's "perfect art and lawful nature of . . . quaintest and most daring drollery" and the "merry monsters" distinguished by "laboriously fantastic orthography"—and he charges Thackeray with the bastardry of "the showman and the confederate gospeller."[73] While Ward and Nasby create a type of local humor, which makes "us" laugh and is not without wit, Howells dismisses them. "For the present they have a sort of reality," he writes, but Lowell's humor would be valued by future generations, who would read him "for the imperishable qualities of his humor and sentiment," while being "somewhat puzzled to recall the immortal name of Petroleum V. Nasby." In distinguishing between two types of American humor—Lowell's artistic and quaint drollery and the merry monsters of misspelling—Howells created a theoretical distinction between popular humorists who relied on cheap effects, which might be entertaining yet ephemeral, and quality humor that would stand the test of time.

Howells's hierarchical view of American humor required an experienced and honest critic to teach the reader to distinguish between quality humor and the merely funny—a task he admitted was not easy. In a review from 1869 of the German-American dialect poetry of Charles Leland, writing under the pseudonym "Hans Brietmann," Howells defines a central problem for the critic—that an author is a humorist if he makes one laugh, no matter the quality. "If a man does not make you smile," Howells writes, "it is pretty certain that he is no humorist—for you; and if he does, there is no arguing him down: funny he is, beyond all cavil. The quality of his fun is another matter."[74] Then, he delineated several examples of humorists who make people smile, but who lack a certain type of quality: most prominently, the circus and minstrel performer Daniel Rice (who billed himself as "The Great American Humorist") and Artemus Ward "and the humorists of his school." Howells easily dismissed Rice, saying that his popularity to great numbers of Americans "did not so much honor him as it dispraised them." On the other hand, Artemus Ward and his ilk "mystify the judgment-seat": "The rogues make you laugh, in defiance of every good principle of taste and art." The dialect poems of Brietmann presented an interesting case. Howells, using his critical "we," was unsure whether the poems, although fun, would be judged well in the future. Humorous effects, he noted, depend "ever so much on temporary conditions and circumstances," so it was hard to tell whether a work was artistically excellent, as he had judged Lowell, or temporarily fun, as he had judged Ward, Rice, and Nasby. Howells writes of a sample poem: "This is laughable, we say; but is it—will it always be—humor,—Humour with its mystical H, its archaic small u in the last syllable, its inscrutable difference from Wit, its secret depth of Pathos?"[75] Here we find a key formulation of Howells's hierarchical view of humor, one that sought to distinguish quality humor from the merely funny through its artistic value and its connection to ethics via the concept of "pathos."

Two other main arguments allowed Howells to fit humor within his developing critical view of realistic writing: humorous character and national character. Even though exaggeration created much of the fun of humor, he argued, quality humor did not exaggerate beyond the realms of the probable. The humor of Edward Hale, for instance, belongs "to the range of fact, but not to that of probability." Howells writes that the "charm" of

Hale's characters lies in this realm of "the improbable": "the characters, in no matter what absurdity of attitude or situation they find themselves, always act in the most probable manner; the plot is as bizarre or grotesque as you like, but the people are all true to nature, and are exactly our friends and neighbors, or what our friends and neighbors would be if they were a little livelier."[76] Such a formulation gave Howells the ability to judge humor "realistic" as long as the characters seemed real, no matter how absurd or exaggerated the plot.

Extending the *Atlantic*'s cultural nationalism to critical judgments of humor, Howells argued that the critical faculty necessary for judging humor was nationally based. With tongue partially in cheek, Howells admitted a new theory about English criticism, writing:

> *Time was when the good opinion of the London press would have settled the matter for us; but of late—the confession is wrung from us—we are beginning to be very shy of the Englishman 'who reads an American book' and praises it. We suspect . . . that there is a conspiracy among the English critics to lure our authors to their ruin,—to make them write worse and worse, till they become absolutely intolerable . . . when our hereditary enemies will have the whole literary field to themselves.*

Writing about *The Biglow Papers*, he had pointed out that Lowell's definition of American humor as a matter of "perception rather than expression,—might teach something to our Transatlantic friends, who suppose it to be merely a quality of exaggeration."[77] More so than in other types of literature, Howells connected humor with national character and used this link to distinguish American writing and criticism from English. Howells used the argument to declare a measure of independence from British criticism, on which he had largely based his views of humor as hierarchy and humor as distinctly national. As chapter 5 explores in more depth, American authors during the nineteenth century both looked to British critical standards and attempted to resist them by insisting on a uniquely American literature. In these transnational critical skirmishes, humor played a significant role in defining American humor, and Mark Twain increasingly became—for critics on both sides of the *Atlantic*—the primary example of American humor.

In his reviews of Mark Twain, Howells placed Mark Twain in the company of Lowell, Holmes, and other quality humorists, rather than categorizing him with the merely entertaining humorists, by linking his "true" or "real" portrayals of human nature to a "humane" ethicism. In bringing Mark Twain into this company, Howells transformed his reputation by arguing for his Americanism, his combined aesthetic and ethical quality, and his place in an evolving vision of the *Atlantic*'s role in American literary culture.

Howells's review of *The Innocents Abroad* set the tone for much of what Howells would discuss in his criticism of Mark Twain for the next decade and a half. Howells began the review by discussing the idea of "American humor," stating: "The character of American humor, and its want of resemblance to the humor of Kamatschatka or Patagonia,—will the reader forgive us if we fail to set down here the thoughts suggested by these fresh and apposite topics? Will he credit us with a self-denial proportioned to the vastness of Mr. Clement's (*sic*) very amusing book, if we spare to state why he is so droll, or—which is as much to the purpose—why we do not know?" And while Howells says this starting point left him little to analyze of the book, he proceeded with several columns of analysis. Howells described Mark Twain's humor as an "always good-humored humor," charming even in its impudence: "[W]e do not remember where it is indulged at the cost of the weak or helpless side, or where it is insolent, with all its sauciness and irreverence."[78] Reframing the critical discussion of the book's "irreverence," Howells created two categories of irreverence: the insolent and the impudent. Thus, while Mark Twain's humor might be occasionally impudent or "saucy," its ethical impulse was humane not cruel—an evaluation that was summed up in Howells's phrase "good-humored humor."

Ethically, then, Mark Twain's work was in line with Lowell's in avoiding cruelty, even if Howells did not yet argue for a high moral purpose in Mark Twain's humor. Aesthetically, the book met Howells's literary standards. The characters are "carefully and exactly done," if occasionally caricatured, and Mark Twain's style of "colloquial drolling" is highly enjoyable and fitting for the book.[79] While the book did not fulfill the goal of serious travel writing—which is, as Howells states, to provide information about "the population of the cities and the character of the rocks in certain localities"—it did provide a level of instructional value through Mark Twain's grasp of human nature: "[T]he man who can be honest enough to let himself see the realities of human life everywhere . . . is far from a useless guide." In a further extension of this praise, Howells writes that "there is an amount of pure human nature in the book, that rarely gets into literature."[80] In this first review, before the beginning of their personal relationship, the reader saw the outline of the themes that Howells would use to shape how one should read Mark Twain—the proper types and goals of humor (and a stated reluctance to explain humor), the presence of realist content in the book through its humorous characters, and the transformation of Mark Twain into an American author worthy of critical consideration.

In judging the work of a humorist to be permanent art, entertaining fun, or low humor, Howells increasingly turned to an aesthetics of realistic literature as the distinguishing factor used to convince the reader of a work's excellence, as with "the amount of pure human nature" he found in Mark Twain's first travel book. In his review of *Roughing It*, Howells framed Mark Twain's reputation as that of the western humorist, but one whose humor was close to life as it was lived in the West, writing: "The grotesque exaggeration and broad irony with which the life is described are conjecturably the truest colors that could have been used, for all existence there must have looked like an extravagant joke." Howells here redefined the purpose of travel writing/memoir—from presenting the reader with facts fit for an encyclopedia to a realistic representation of the mood of the subject, much as the Romance had fit the mood of New England in an earlier period. In other words, for Howells some subjects were uniquely suited to a humorous treatment. Still, Howells had a hard time praising the book fully, as it undoubtedly stretched his sense of propriety at points. He ended the review with somewhat ambivalent praise: "[T]he work of a human being, it is not unbrokenly nor infallibly funny; nor is it to be always praised for all the literary virtues; but it is singularly entertaining, and its humor is always amiable, manly, and generous." Howells's praise of Mark Twain's first two books placed the humorist in the tradition of entertaining and amiable humor better represented by Oliver Wendell Holmes than by Lowell's artistic humor.[81]

Mark Twain was not the only humorist to be elevated into the *Atlantic* through Howells's promotion. Charles Dudley Warner, who would later become Samuel Clemens's neighbor and collaborator, was in many ways more to Howells's liking as a humorist. Writing in the conversational style of Oliver Wendell Holmes, Warner's humor was enjoyable without being crude, coarse, or controversial, a claim that could not be made for Mark Twain's first books. Howells had befriended both Warner and Clemens, and he frequently visited the two men at Nook Farm, on the outskirts of Hartford after 1872. Howells praised Warner's books in the *Atlantic* for their light humor and for "their delicate little pictures of nature and human nature." Howells wrote of Warner's third book, *Backlog Studies*: "It is shrewd, and has its edge of satire, but it leaves particular matters pretty much where it found them, only teaching, as all true humor does, quite as much modesty and mercifulness generally as human nature is capable of learning." Reviewing Warner's fourth book, Howells wrote of Warner's "gentler sort of humorous literature," one that did not "thrust you in the ribs" and was thus considered by some to be "thin." Defending Warner against critics who liked their humor "thick," Howells wrote that both sorts could be funny, although his personal preference was clearly with Warner, whose good-natured humor more closely reflected Howells's own use of humor.[82] Mark Twain, on the other hand, kept Howells on edge, both with his published humor that pushed the bounds of the *Atlantic*'s respectability and in his personal eccentricity that sometimes embarrassed the proper editor.

Howells chose not to review *The Gilded Age* (1873), the collaborative novel of Mark Twain and Warner, a book that will be discussed in more detail in chapter 6. But around the time of that novel, he did discuss the humorous literature of California in a review of Charles Warren Stoddard's *South Sea Idylls*. Here, as in his review of *Roughing It*, Howells discussed the humor of "Mr. Mark Twain Clemens" as uniquely suited to the humorous reality of California (of which Nevada, where Clemens spent most of his time, seems to be included as a suburb). But the California humor is not only a local variation but had become a national humor: "[T]his sense of one's own grotesqueness in the midst of grotesqueness is Humor, with the large H, which we have been gradually coming at. . . . [T]he conditions being exaggerated in the case of the Californian *litterateurs*, we can readily account for the greater irreverence and abandon in their humor, which has now become the type of American humor, so that no merry person can hope to please the public unless he approaches it."[83] Along with a number of other "Californians of occasion," who had lived temporarily in the state but had all moved on, Howells argued that the Californian humor of Mark Twain, Bret Harte, and Stoddard had become the main form of American Humor.[84] This ran counter to the view of the *Round Table*, which had classed Mark Twain with Ward, Nasby, and Billings as the representatives of an "American Humor." That magazine had ceased publication in 1869.

Howells framed Mark Twain as "the greatest humorist of the three, strictly speaking . . . who has, perhaps, also the most thoroughly original expression." Howells complimented him for not having a literary or poetic style like Harte or Stoddard: "[W]e read Mr. Clemens solely for the humor of Mark Twain. He is . . . present in all he writes . . . and this perpetual personal companionship with his reader is as characteristic of the pure humorist, as distinguished from the humorous dramatist or novelist." Mark Twain's reputation as a humorist, based on his magnetic presence, here placed him as a representative American humorist and limited his humor to nonfiction and short sketches, implicitly critiquing *The Gilded Age* as his first attempt at sustained fiction. While Howells placed him in new company, his early focus on the character of "Mark Twain" prevented the author from being considered in the realm of fiction.

Howells's promotion of Mark Twain as a "realistic" humorist, rather than as a newspaper humorist, shifted his positional relationships to other authors. Instead of Artemus Ward and Petroleum Vesuvius Nasby, Mark Twain was placed into critical conversation with two authors Howells similarly promoted as part of the *Atlantic*'s company: Henry James and Bret Harte. Scholars have taken the existence of Mark Twain and Henry James under a banner of Howells's literary theories as a symbol of the critical difficulties of defining a Howellsian realism that can include both writers.[85] The two authors shared a remarkably similar position in regard to Howells, who promoted their reputations as American authors in the *Atlantic Monthly*, and thereafter, through reviews, publishing opportunities, and personal friendship. On the other hand, the two came from vastly different backgrounds, represented vastly different approaches to writing, and developed vastly different critical reputations. And they thought little of each other as writers.[86]

Both authors represented a challenge to traditional expectations of *Atlantic* readers, and Howells promoted both through reviews that focused on their realistic content. Although James first published before Howells joined the magazine, Howells increased James's presence in the magazine and used reviews to promote James as an exemplar of writing and reading fiction. During Howells's time at the *Atlantic*, James published numerous reviews, seventeen short pieces, two novellas, and his first three novels—*Roderick Hudson* (1875), *The American* (1876–1877), and *The Portrait of the Lady* (1880–1881). In the April 1875 issue, Howells wrote an extensive review of James's first collection of stories, most of which had appeared in the magazine. Howells began by admitting that James was an acquired taste to some readers. Using the *Atlantic*'s critical "we," Howells gave little doubt as to the reputation James should have: "To ourselves it has been a very great pleasure, the highest pleasure that a new, decided, and earnest talent can give; . . . In richness of expression and splendor of literary performance, we may compare him with the greatest, and find none greater than he." Following his critical ethos, Howells praised the realistic nature of the characters, but he also praised the stories he found to be of a "romantic conception" for being more real than the "realistic subjects which we find less real than the author's romantic inspirations."[87] Extending the tradition of Hawthorne, Henry James was, for Howells, the great realistic Romancer, placing him in the same realistic realm as Mark Twain, but in an entirely different genre of writing.

Bret Harte, on the other hand, raised the possibility of an American humorist whose realism might be elevated to the level of artistic excellence and provide a model for American fiction. Harte had left California, like most of the California humorists of the 1860s, looking to establish himself artistically and financially as a man of letters. In early 1871, he had resigned his editorship of the *Overland Monthly* and headed east, preceded by a constant barrage of telegraph and newspaper reports of his progress. Arriving in February 1871, Harte was celebrated by the literary elite of Boston—Emerson, Holmes, Longfellow, Lowell—and accepted the unprecedented offer to publish one piece a month in the *Atlantic* for the sum of $10,000 for one year. Unlike the reverence of Howells in the presence of the Boston elite, Harte acted as conquering hero, remarking of Boston with typically western flair: "Why, you couldn't stand on your front porch and fire off your revolver without bringing down a two-volumer." For his part, Clemens could barely hide his mix of admiration and jealousy, writing in a letter: "Do you know who is the most celebrated man in America to-day?—the man whose name is on every single tongue from one end of the continent to the other? It is Bret Harte. And the poem called the "Heathen Chinee" did it for him. His journey east to Boston was a perfect torchlight procession of éclat & homage. All the cities are fussing about which shall secure him for a citizen."[88] As the "Jumping Frog" had helped establish Mark Twain's name nationally, the poem "Plain Language from Truthful James" (better known as "The Heathen Chinee") had boosted Harte from an editor and author in California to a national and international literary figure, transforming his first book, *The Luck of Roaring Camp* (1870), to bestseller status and securing him a number of lucrative literary offers.

In 1871, it was Harte, not Mark Twain, who was the gifted humorist from California who had been taken in by the New England establishment. The possible reasons may be simple—Harte had produced a series of short stories and poems that had caught the attention of the literary

elite for their formal excellence and their strong local color, while Mark
Twain's main literary output at that point was in the more marginal genres
of travel writing, humorous sketches, and lectures. Most importantly,
Harte's stories contained a strong measure of "pathos," the quality that
raised humor to artistic and ethical quality in the eyes of many critics at
the time, including Howells.[89]

Reviewing Harte's book in 1870, Howells praised the writer for deal-
ing "simply, directly, and briefly with his reader" in writing the stories
of the wild California life of the Gold Rush. Harte does not "overpaint,"
but instead shows his subjects in "all their natural colors and textures,
and all their wildness and strangeness of place." Howells found the plots
to be weak at points, but the key was in Harte's characters as realistic
representations of human nature. Directly seeking to shape the readers'
view of fiction, Howells argued that evolved readers would know the
relative importance of plot and character, writing, "People are growing,
we hope,—and if they are not, so much the worse for people,—to prefer
character to situations, and to enjoy the author's revelations of the former rather than his invention of the latter." Harte's characters in various
stories are described as "probable," "natural," and "full of the true color of
life in the diggings." Howells summed up by stating that ". . . the strength
and freshness are in the manners and character, and the weakness is in
the sentimentality which . . . does not seem to be quite his own. His real
feeling is always as good as his humor is fresh."[90] By instructing his readers
to focus on the realism of character, Howells was able to transform Harte's
sentimental plots into something less important than the "real feeling"
of his human, and humane, characters, although a tendency toward false
sentimentality would increasingly mar Harte's writings.

Both Harte and James became the early models of fiction for Howells
as his reviews more and more focused on the aesthetics of realism. Mark
Twain was less important in this genre than other writers, but his move
into the *Atlantic* as an author, with "A True Story" (1874) and other
pieces, further enhanced his literary reputation. With the publication
of *The Adventures of Tom Sawyer* in 1876, which Howells helped birth as
editor and friend, Mark Twain's position as an author was truly worthy
of inclusion in Howells's definition of quality American literature. But
these texts came to the attention of the public and the critic after a
number of central developments in Mark Twain's career and life that will
be discussed before we return to the subject of the *Atlantic Monthly* as a
culture of letters in chapter 7.

THE DREAM OF MARK'S LIFE

On November 2, 1871, Samuel Clemens was invited to a lunch in Boston in honor of his friend, occasional collaborator, and later enemy, Bret Harte. Given by Ralph Keeler, a fellow Californian and the *Atlantic*'s proofreader, Clemens joined Harte, Howells, Thomas Bailey Aldrich, and James T. Fields, who had just retired from the publishing business. Howells later recalled the afternoon as being filled with "joyful talk-play" and "eager laughter." Over the steak and mushrooms, and witty and blasphemous stories, Howells recalled a moment of telling significance: "Bret Harte's fleeting dramatization of Clemens's mental attitude toward a symposium of Boston illuminates. 'Why, fellows,' he spluttered, 'this is the dream of Mark's life,' and I remember the glance from under Clemens's feathery eyebrows which betrayed his enjoyment of the fun." Clemens, still an outsider to the Boston "illuminates" despite Howells's positive review of *The Innocents Abroad*, may have both enjoyed the joke and felt it as a jab at his uncertain status, especially in relation to Harte, with whom this lunch seems to have been a reconciliation after a year of private feuding.[91]

At this point in his career, Samuel Clemens was as yet unsure of his acceptance—or that of "Mark Twain"—into the literary culture into which Bret Harte had been welcomed as a literary star and as the highest-paid and most-discussed author of 1871. Harte's comment may have stung more coming from a man whom Howells had introduced to the major *Atlantic* authors. Howells had not done the same for Clemens, later writing that he had guarded him from "the critical edge of Cambridge acquaintance," who might not have appreciated him in the way the masses did in America or the classes did in England. "In proportion as people thought themselves refined," Howells would write, "they questioned that quality which all recognize in him now, but which was then the inspired knowledge of the simple-hearted multitude."[92] Howells was beginning to shape the literary taste of his readers to include Mark Twain's writing, as well as shaping Mark Twain's writing to move in the direction Howells saw fit for him. While influential, Howells did not have the literary heft to single-handedly lift Mark Twain into the canon of American letters, even within the circle of authors surrounding the *Atlantic Monthly*

The "dream of Mark's life" seems to have pushed him to imagine a cultural position beyond his calling in low humor. But this transition from popular to quality humorist was not easily accomplished, nor was it a linear path. Throughout his career, Clemens vacillated between the desire for literary acceptance and the desire for popularity, and the financial benefits accrued thereof. His reactions to his position as the most popular American humorist of his day show his anxiety at how others interpreted his humor, and how people viewed the figure of the humorist in general. As Mark Twain became a part of the eastern literary world—through his increased presence in quality magazines and through his presence on the lyceum circuit—he seemed to experience a measure of anxiety at his status as "mere" humorist, and his writings and lectures show that he was aware of, and defensive toward, the criticisms that some in the literary establishment felt toward triflers and buffoons. That anxiety might have been heightened for this lunch, which came the day after Mark Twain had lectured on Artemus Ward. The difficulties of this lyceum tour, and the mixed critical reactions to Mark Twain's lecture, brought Mark Twain's worries about his position to the surface, as will be discussed in depth in the next chapter.

In the early 1870s, the public saw a dual transformation of the figure of Mark Twain: the grounding of Samuel Clemens as a well-off family man and the shift of Mark Twain's reputation from popular favorite to quality humorist found in a variety of so-called "quality magazines." Just a few months after first meeting Howells, the 35-year-old Samuel Clemens married Olivia Langdon and settled in Buffalo as part-owner, editor, and writer for the Buffalo *Express*. Livy and her family provided Clemens with a new level of personal respectability. Jervis Langdon, Clemens's father-on-law, had made his money during the Civil War through iron and coal. Combining business avarice with social activism, Langdon was an abolitionist, a supporter of the freedmen, and a friend of Frederick Douglass. He accepted Clemens as a son-in-law, despite several letters of reference that Samuel Clemens had that questioned his character; one clergyman wrote: "Twain is a humbug . . . a man who has talent, no doubt, but will make trivial use of it." Livy, for her part, joined with Mrs. Fairbanks in promoting Mark Twain as something more than a humorist. In a letter from December 1868, while Clemens's suit was being heard, she wrote Mrs. Fairbanks thanking her for a kindly letter, which had apparently praised him, writing, "I want the public, who know him now, only as 'the wild humorist of the Pacific slope', to know something of his deeper, larger nature—I remember being quite incensed by a ladys asking, 'Is there any thing of Mr Clemens, except his humour', yet as she knew of him it was not an unnatural question—"[93]

Twain and Livy were engaged on February 4, 1869, and married almost one year later, on February 2.

Olivia Clemens and Howells would find common cause for decades in the promotion of Mark Twain as something more than a mere humorist. Howells's argument that Mark Twain belonged among the *Atlantic* authors was not fully accepted by critics, authors, and readers, who chose to situate him differently within their own views of the relationship between humor and culture. Socially, Samuel Clemens was only ambivalently accepted into the literary culture of Boston. While he enjoyed many dinners with Howells, Aldrich, and other men of the magazine's circle, he had not yet been introduced to the *Atlantic* greats, as Bret Harte had been.

One story helps illustrate his ambivalent position through the introduction of a woman who would symbolize for Mark Twain the stodgy and judgmental side of literary Boston: Lilian Aldrich, the wife of Thomas Bailey. In her memoir, Mrs. Aldrich described her first impressions of meeting Mark Twain, although she did not know who he was:

> . . . Mr. Aldrich came home bringing with him a most unusual guest, clothed in a coat of sealskin, the fur won outward; a sealskin cap well down over his ears; the cap half revealing and half concealing the mass of reddish hair underneath; the heavy mustache having the same red tint. The trousers came well below the coat, and were of a yellowish-brown color; stockings of the same tawny hue, which the low black shoe emphasized. . . . But when the wearer spoke it was not difficult for the listener to believe that he was not entirely accountable for the strange gear. It was but too evident that he had looked upon the cup when it was red, for seemingly it had both cheered and inebriated, as the gentleman showed marked inability to stand perpendicular, but swayed from side to side. . . .[94]

Taking off his coat, the unnamed guest unveiled a neck-knot of violet. While Mr. Aldrich and Clemens laughed, Mrs. Aldrich stared coldly, shocked by the seemingly drunken jester. As the dinner hour passed with no hint of inviting the guest, Clemens left and Mrs. Aldrich broke into hysterical tears and demanded why her husband had brought home an intoxicated man. Mr. Aldrich responded: "Why, dear, did you not know who he was? What you thought wine was but his mannerisms and idiosyncrasies, characteristics of himself, and born with Mark Twain."[95]

This domestic scene dramatizes the uncertainty with which polite Boston met the odd congruence of Samuel Clemens and Mark Twain, whose eccentricities, born of his position as a humorist, presented something of a puzzle. Upon first meeting him, Thomas Wentworth Higginson—the Unitarian minister, Civil War colonel, and *Atlantic* contributor—described him as "'something of a buffoon, though with earnestness underneath; and when afterwards at his own house in Hartford, I heard him say grace at table, it was like asking a blessing over Ethiopian minstrels."[96] The culture of letters of the *Atlantic Monthly* existed both on the textual level and the personal, and Mark Twain's presence in each of these was never fully accepted by everyone within those circles. Having settled into a respectable life, with all the implications of social class that such a move implied, Samuel Clemens struggled to recast his "Mark Twain" as both respectable and marketable, as quality humorist and as celebrity. The tension between his role as a humorist, rather than being eased by his new company and his dreams of quality, increased as he experimented with new venues for his humor, while seeking an increasing monetary reward to support his new life as a family man.

CHAPTER FOUR

A Worried Mother

Mark Twain and the Circulation of the Humorist

William Dean Howells's discussion of Mark Twain within the context of the *Atlantic Monthly*'s critical ethos, and within his own developing ideas of realistic writing, is crucially important for understanding the development of Mark Twain's reputation as a humorist. But Howells's promotion of Mark Twain did not settle the question of his cultural position, nor did the imprimatur of the *Atlantic Monthly* immediately elevate him to a lasting level of cultural respectability. Mark Twain continued to circulate as a popular humorist—through his continued insistence on subscription publishing, through humorous lectures on the lyceum circuit, and through his appearances in magazines, newspapers, comic papers, and other forms of mass-circulated humor. If anything, the critical attention and personal friendship of William Dean Howells inaugurated and heightened the tension between the high-culture and mass-culture meanings of "Mark Twain," tensions that lasted throughout Mark Twain's career and into Mark Twain scholarship. Other magazines built on and competed with the *Atlantic*'s view of literature and culture, and Mark Twain played a variety of important roles in those magazines.

Samuel Clemens was aware of the ambivalent cultural position of his character. He demonstrated a clear anxiety about the unexpected elevation of Mark Twain to a new level of respectability. In May 1872, shortly after Howells's review of *Roughing It* appeared in the *Atlantic*, Clemens wrote a letter expressing his gratitude, as well as some reservations: "Since penning the foregoing the 'Atlantic' has come to hand with that most thoroughly & entirely satisfactory notice of 'Roughing it,' & I am as uplifted & reassured by it as a mother who has given birth to a white baby when she was awfully afraid it was going to be a mulatto. I have been afraid & shaky all along, but now unless the [N.Y.] 'Tribune' gives the book a black eye, I am all right."[1] This response shows an awareness of the power of book reviews to influence public opinion and a keen anxiety at his new position in American letters through the equation of racial mixing with the mixing of literary levels. The metaphor of miscegenation echoes critical hierarchies of American humor, in which the lowest forms of humor were often compared with black-face minstrelsy. The shock of the racial metaphor raises questions about the relationship between Mark Twain's humor and that of African Americans, although no critics took up this connection until Shelley Fisher Fishkin did so much later. Howells, for his part, was shocked enough by Clemens's metaphor that he referred to it in general terms, even after Clemens's death—as "a story wonderfully allegorizing the situation, which the mock modesty of print forbids my repeating here."[2]

Written by Louise Chandler Moulton, a frequent contributor of verse to the *Atlantic* during the 1870s, the review in the New York *Tribune* also praised the book:

> For pure fun, I know of nothing which has been published this year to compare with "Roughing It," by Mark Twain (Samuel S. [sic] Clemens), a New-England, though not a Boston, issue. . . . In his preface the author penitently deplores the fact that there is information in the volume, concerning an interesting episode in the history of the Far West. . . . Having thus deprecated censure for any misplaced wisdom which may be gleaned from his pages, the author commences his irresistible tale. It is funny everywhere.[3]

Clemens responded to this review with a similar sentiment as he had with Howells, but with a more proper tone, writing to Moulton: "I am *content*, now that the book has been praised in the Tribune—& so I thank you with all that honest glow of gratitude that comes into a mother's eyes when a stranger praises her child."[4] Samuel Clemens's figuration of Mark Twain's writings as children, but children of which the parent has doubts, betrays an anxiety with his work's cultural position. The fact that Howells found the book to be metaphorically "white" did not necessarily settle the issue; as with other narratives of passing, the fear of discovery, despite ostensible appearances, did not disappear but remained just under the surface, recurring in different guises when Mark Twain's anxieties rose into view.

This anxiety about his role of humorist would continue to be a central issue for Mark Twain, as well as editors, readers, and other audiences, as he increasingly circulated in national and international cultures of letters. As Mark Twain became more well known and more widely considered,

discussions about his cultural position as a humorist were increasingly
dramatized in the 1870s in magazines and newspapers, in dining rooms
and editor's offices, and on the platform stage and the after-dinner rostrum.
The meanings of the humorist as a cultural figure continued to evolve,
illuminating Mark Twain's career in relation to the evolving meanings of
American literature, American humor, and American culture.

The years between 1870 and 1873 saw Mark Twain reach an apex of his
career as a professional humorist, taking the model of Artemus Ward to
new levels of celebrity and success. Through the success of *The Innocents
Abroad*, his periodical writing, and his lyceum tours, Mark Twain circulated
throughout American culture, in print and in person, as the most successful
humorist of the day. In these years, Samuel Clemens settled down into
what may have seemed a sustainable career—newspaper editor and magazine contributor, occasional lecturer on the lucrative lyceum circuit, and
author of humorous travel books that seemed to sell and sell. The model
of the popular humorist may have been enough for some, but Clemens/
Mark Twain had also made connections to the Boston literary world of
Howells and the *Atlantic*, a culture of letters that had accepted Bret Harte
and had made overtures toward Mark Twain.

The culture of letters of the *Atlantic Monthly* may have been the most
influential American periodical culture of letters of the era, at least in
literary matters. But it was not the most widely circulated nor was it the
only magazine that offered a vision of American letters in relation to
American culture. The position of the magazine as a major cultural force
was gradually eroded as the circulation of the magazine decreased in the
face of new competition. Following the Civil War, a new generation of New
York-based magazines— especially the *Nation* (est. 1865), the *Galaxy* (est.
1866), *Scribner's Monthly* (est. 1870), and *Harper's Monthly*—competed
for prestige, for authors, and for subscribers in ways that both implicitly
and explicitly challenged the vision of American culture promoted by
the *Atlantic*. By paying at higher rates, these new magazines attracted
both traditional "*Atlantic*-authors" and less-established popular authors.
They were popular for the quality of their contents—both writing and
illustrations—but also for the editorial ethos they presented on questions of American culture and literature. Whereas Lowell and Howells
are now the best known of American magazine editors of the era, other
editors carved out their own influence on the literary culture of the era,
often speaking to, and presumably for, larger numbers of readers than
the *Atlantic* ever reached.

In 1870, Mark Twain joined the ranks of the quality periodical as an author, writing a monthly column of "Memoranda" in the *Galaxy*. Mark Twain viewed his column as a step up in prestige for his writing, but he ended up creating a column that burlesqued the print culture of magazines and newspapers by making fun of both the authority of the written word and the ability of readers to interpret it. Most significantly, Mark Twain published a hoax review of his *The Innocents Abroad*, purportedly written by the London *Saturday Review*, in which the reviewer took the book as a serious travelogue, creating a conceptual puzzle about the meaning of Mark Twain's humor. This hoax, or "put-on" as I will theorize it, eventually slipped out of his control, as newspapers questioned who was "sold" by the joke, with some insisting that the joke was on Mark Twain himself. As his humor circulated in more contexts, Samuel Clemens's inability to control its meanings frustrated the humorist and, in this case, caused him to lose his sense of humor through the character of Mark Twain.

Following his departure from his monthly column after almost a year, Mark Twain struck out on another lyceum tour. For this tour, he struggled to find a suitable topic and spent the first part of the tour lecturing on his fellow humorist, the late Artemus Ward. Praising his friend and model as the great American humorist, the lecture created the ironic situation of Mark Twain being too funny to fulfill the expectations his audience had for humorous lecturers. By taking a humorist as its subject, the lecture contained neither the artistic "word painting" nor the instructive sections that had balanced his previous travel lectures between the entertaining and the instructive. Mark Twain burlesqued audience expectations of physical deportment, eloquent speech, and serious discourse in his lectures, but this tour, which he came to call his "detestable campaign," showed the limits of his performance as a humorist in an era in which the purposes of the lyceum were increasingly contested. Many audiences did find Mark Twain's performances to be funny, and reports focus on the laughter as one of the central expectations of his audiences. Laughter had multiple historical meanings shaped by commercial, political, and aesthetic factors. When audiences laughed at Mark Twain's lecture, they expressed a range of responses to the performance of a humorist trespassing where the serious lecture was generally held. In positive reviews, laughter was seen as an innocent form of enjoyment, creating cheer, and driving away "the blues"—an effect that large portions of the audiences sought out and willingly paid for. Other people laughed, but did so despite it being "undignified" and stopped when discovered. These reluctant laughers had their views expressed by reviewers who held Mark Twain's performance to be no laughing matter and chided him for his poor performance style, his lecture's lack of substance, and the folly of having him perform on the lyceum stage. The ambivalent reception illustrates a growing divide between those audiences who sought out popular entertainment, especially in Mark Twain and other humorists, and those audiences who thought such performers had no place in what should be a moral and uplifting leisure culture.

Giving voice to these worries, Dr. Josiah Gilbert Holland expressed his concern with "triflers of the platform" shortly after the end of Mark Twain's lyceum tour. As editor of the influential *Scribner's Monthly*, a quality magazine that competed with the *Galaxy* and the *Atlantic Monthly* to define and shape literary and popular cultures, Holland spent much of his tenure at the magazine defining a Christian popular culture that would help lead the country in a moral direction. Holland consistently used his editorial column to promote a vision of American culture that included a moral mass culture in which popularity would, or at least should, be a measure of the Christian value of a literary artwork. Mark Twain's success challenged this model, and Holland consistently instructed his readers to avoid "triflers," "dandies," "buffoons," and "dilettantes"—and these categories clearly included Mark Twain. Holland's attacks hit Samuel Clemens at a point in which he was anxious about his own position in the popular culture of his time. He responded in the summer of 1872 with a withering attack on Holland as a "remorseless intellectual cholera" who had killed lyceum committees through his moral instruction. The article was never published, but it demonstrates an instance in which his anxiety came tenuously close to causing him to lose his temper. While Clemens's passion about the incident was short-lived, Holland's continued critical attacks on both Mark Twain and the literary ethos of Howells's *Atlantic Monthly* provide a central instance of an influential critic who questioned the value of Mark Twain's inclusion in the company of the best.

Mark Twain's sometimes less-than-successful ventures into the respectable literary venues of the quality magazine and the lyceum stage, along with his personal friendships with prominent literary figures, increasingly raised the question of his role in American literary culture. On these multiple stages, the question of his literary reputation became a topic of conversation, consternation, or concern as his role in American literary and popular cultures was dramatized and debated. While Mark Twain circulated more widely as a humorist—through his writings, his performances, and his role as celebrity—a distinct strain of criticism argued for a more serious version of American popular culture dedicated to reverence for certain values and used the figure of Mark Twain as their example when encouraging their readers to take their leisure more seriously.

ON BEING SOLD: MARK TWAIN'S *GALAXY* WRITINGS AND THE CIRCULATION OF HUMOR

From May 1870 to April 1871, Mark Twain contributed a column entitled "Memoranda" to the *Galaxy* magazine. Founded in 1866, and named by Oliver Wendell Holmes, the *Galaxy* shared the aim of the *Atlantic* to be the premier and central expression of American life and culture. The magazine was viewed by many of its contributors as an alternative to the perceived New England bias of the *Atlantic*, although the two magazines shared many prominent contributors. The *Nation*, in reviewing the first issue in April 1866, saw the magazine as a response to "a 'divine discontent'" with the *Atlantic* prevailing in New York City and hoped the magazine would be a good competitor in order to improve the nation's literary output.[5] Socially and politically, the magazine developed a reputation of directness and unconventionality when compared to the staidness of Josiah Holland's *Scribner*'s or the high-culture aims of Howells's *Atlantic*. For Clemens, publishing in this new venue reflected his awareness of the relationship between quality magazines and literary reputation. As he wrote to Elisha Bliss, his book publisher: "I consider the magazine because it will give an opening for higher-class writing—stuff which I hate to shovel into a daily newspaper."[6] Mark Twain's presence in the quality magazine testified to his increasing acceptance into the realm of literary periodicals, as well as the increasing importance of humor in marketing such periodicals.

By the time the "Memoranda" column began in the *Galaxy*, the magazine was viewed by most as a prime competitor in prestige with the *Atlantic*, with one regional magazine claiming: "The *Galaxy* occupies the very highest place in magazine literature of the day." With the help of Mark Twain's column, the *Galaxy* reached its peak circulation of 23,000 in 1871.[7] The *Galaxy* department followed the common newspaper practice of printing a column of humorous squibs, jokes, and tales under a name like "Jottings," "Scraps," or "Miscellaneous." Various pieces from the *Galaxy* column became staples of newspaper circuits shortly after being published in the magazine, including some of his better-known early sketches, such as "The Facts in the Case of the Great Beef Contract," "How I Edited an Agricultural Paper

Once," and "My Watch—An Instructive Little Tale." Material from the column was freely pirated and published in newspapers and magazines across the country and in England. For instance, "The Facts Concerning the Great Beef Contract" was reprinted in the *Saturday Evening Post* on May 14, 1870, the same month that it was published in the *Galaxy*, and it was reprinted in a wide range of periodicals, from the Hartford *Courant* to the *Daily Central City Register*, the newspaper of a small Colorado mining town, and upwards of at least a dozen more.[8] Numerous *Galaxy* pieces showed up in pirated humor collections, such as *The Fun Library: An Illustrated Magazine of General Wit and Humor*, an undated compendium made up of humorous sketches, paragraphs, and jokes by both established humorists and ephemeral quipsters printed on cheap paper.

Along with his successes on the lyceum circuit, his *Galaxy* writings in many ways finished the task of making Mark Twain a national, and international, celebrity—America's foremost, or at least most popular, humorist. Mark Twain was well known when he began his columns—through his sketches and first book, through his lecture tours, and through the success of *The Innocents Abroad*. The *Galaxy* sketches boosted Mark Twain's brand within the wider print culture through the success of the magazine itself and through the wide reprinting of these sketches in newspapers and humor collections. For example, the *Chicago Tribune* had first noticed Mark Twain in 1866 in five articles, including a two-part printing of the "Jumping Frog" story. The number of pieces the paper reprinted increased greatly to fourteen in 1869, mostly consisting of excerpts from *The Innocents Abroad*. In both 1870 and 1871, the paper published approximately thirty articles per year on Mark Twain, mostly taken from or commenting upon his *Galaxy* articles. In this sense, the circulation of the *Galaxy* pieces in the magazine and in newspapers had "sold" Mark Twain to the public by keeping him in the public eye for a sustained period. Of note in this regard was a portrait of Mark Twain, published in August 1870 in lieu of his column, which was the first magazine portrait of Mark Twain. The *Aldine*, an illustrated magazine, followed with a portrait and short biography the next year.[9]

While Mark Twain's *Galaxy* contributions may not cohere as quality literature, the material provides insight into his concerns about reputation and his distrust of works intended to shape the beliefs, thoughts, and actions of readers. Throughout these pieces, Mark Twain's humor is based on the burlesque of the goals of print culture, showing how the various high-toned aims of reading—education, moral edification, information, public opinion, etc.—were susceptible to being undermined by

MARK TWAIN.

FIGURE 4.1: Mark Twain in the *Galaxy*, August 1870.
Courtesy of Kevin Mac Donnell, Austin, Texas

misreading or were misleading from the start. Mark Twain consistently made fun of the failure of writing to satisfy its aims: editors print nonsense, sham sentiment causes laughter rather than tears, life fails to conform to genre expectations, and readers misread, often with comic and grotesque outcomes. While much of the humor is found in the incongruity between intention and effect, one particular thread of articles—a hoax review of *The Innocents Abroad* and its aftermath—illustrates how Mark Twain was

SAMUEL L. CLEMENS—(MARK TWAIN).

FIGURE 4.2: Mark Twain in the *Aldine*, April 1871.
Courtesy of Kevin Mac Donnell, Austin, Texas

unable to fully control the circulation of his own reputation, which caused him to lose his sense of humor.

In his *Galaxy* columns, Mark Twain consistently blurred the line between the serious and the humorous, not so much to have the reader take his humor seriously, but to have the reader take the serious humorously. In framing the purpose of his column, Mark Twain burlesqued the purpose of his being hired by a high-toned literary magazine by pointing out that such magazines "lacked stability, solidity, weight" because they gave "too much space . . . to poetry and romance, and not enough to statistics and agriculture."[10] The contrast between the lightness of literature, of which humor surely would have been viewed as the lightest, and the solidity of facts, statistics, and other serious discourses runs throughout his column, as it had in his travel writing and lyceum lectures. In further framing his aims, he averred:

> These MEMORANDA are not a "humorous" department. I would not conduct an exclusively and professedly humorous department for anyone. I would always prefer to have the privilege of printing a serious and sensible remark, in case one occurred to me, without the reader's feeling obliged to consider himself outraged. We cannot keep the same mood day after day. I am liable, some day, to want to print my opinion on jurisprudence, or Homeric poetry, or international law, and I shall do it. It will be of small consequence to me whether the reader survive or not (May 1870).

Mark Twain framed his role with the *Galaxy* as an editor—collecting pieces of humor and the occasional "serious" piece into a mélange that combined the newspaper ephemera column with the magazine's columns of editorial musings. Viewing the "Memoranda" column as a creation of an editor, rather than as a collection of individual pieces by "Mark Twain," allows us to read the column as an index of Samuel Clemens's ambivalent feelings about his role as an author and the circulation of Mark Twain's works within a print culture beset with false sentiment and rife with poor readers.

The July 1870 issue contained a commentary on the role of the editor. In "How I Edited an Agricultural Paper Once," Mark Twain narrates his stint as guest editor of a farming magazine, despite his utter lack of agricultural knowledge. His paper was a sensation—sales boomed and men came from miles to look at the editor. One man, unloosed from reason, forces the editor to read from the paper. To wit:

> Concerning the Pumpkin — This berry is a favorite with the natives of the interior of New England, who prefer it to the gooseberry for the making of fruit cake, and who likewise give it the preference over the raspberry for feeding cows, as being more filling and fully as satisfying. The pumpkin is the

only esculent of the orange family that will thrive in the North, except the gourd and one or two varieties of the squash. But the custom of planting it in the front yard with the shrubbery is fast going out of vogue, for it is now generally conceded that the pumpkin, as a shade tree, is a failure.

Upon his return, the paper's editor is perplexed at both the large sales of the magazine and the fact that he would consent to edit with no knowledge of the job. To which, Mark Twain replies, "It's the first time I ever heard such a remark. I tell you I have been in the editorial business going on fourteen years, and it is the first time I ever heard of a man's having to know anything in order to edit a newspaper. You turnip! Who write the dramatic critiques for the second-rate papers? Why, a parcel of promoted shoemakers and apprentice apothecaries . . . Who review the books? People who never wrote one." As editor of both the "Memoranda" column and the Buffalo *Express*, Mark Twain's humorous jabs may be seen as self-referential, but they also point to a larger joke on the foundations of periodical culture—ignorance and sensation.

Mark Twain's pieces in the *Galaxy* comment on the burgeoning of ephemeral printed material available to the reading public, which seemed to call into question the value and uses of reading more generally. As editor of the "Memoranda," Mark Twain printed a consistent stream of commentaries on the moral, sentimental, or intellectual aims of literary products. Many of the monthly columns contain examples of what he called "hogwash"—"the sickliest specimen[s] of sham sentimentality" in the form of obituary and memorial poems. The column created a loop in which products of sentiment from local newspapers were republished as examples of humorously bad writing. Mark Twain turned real examples of maudlin sentiment into objects of laughter, and his readers seem to have taken to the joke, as they sent in their own clippings, which Mark Twain then reprinted in his column.

In addition to this example of deliberately misreading the sentiment of supposedly serious works, the "Memoranda" column also contained several important examples in which readers, especially children, misread printed material, with dire and violent consequences. For instance, the piece "Disgraceful Persecution of a Boy" (May 1870) strongly satirized the mistreatment of the Chinese through the mock indignation of the author at the arrest of a "well-dressed boy" for stoning a "Chinaman" on his way to Sunday school. The boy, Mark Twain writes, had been trained through the "daily items" in the San Francisco press to cheat, rob, scapegoat, or otherwise mistreat the Chinese and that "individuals, communities, the majesty of the state itself, joined in hating, abusing, and persecuting these humble strangers." Therefore, it was "more than natural" for the boy to stone the man, thinking to himself: "Ah, there goes a Chinaman! God will not love me if I do not stone him." The satire forcefully critiques the power of the newspaper, expressing a common community prejudice, to warp the moral perspective of a naive reading public.

Immediately following this piece was a similar satire entitled "The Story of the Good Little Boy Who Did Not Prosper." Here, the young boy modeled himself on the heroes of Sunday-school books and hoped for the same rewards that the Sunday-school boys always received in the stories, including the honor of dying young but first getting to lecture the community on the moral way of life, as good boys always did in books. Instead, each moral trope is turned on its head—the blind man he helps up from the mud hits him with his cane instead of blessing him, the dog he befriends viciously attacks him rather than becoming a boon companion, etc. The boy consults "the authorities" at each turn, but "the very things the boys in the books got rewarded for turned out to be about the most unprofitable things he could invest in." Finally, the boy tries to lecture some boys who had tied nitroglycerin bottles to the tails of stray dogs, but he is blown into the sky "with the fragments of those fifteen dogs stringing after him like the tail of a kite" before he is even able to make a dying speech, despite the moral authorities who held that proper for the death of such a good boy.[11] These satires of the "authorities" who shape the minds of the young resonate with the print authorities of the fictional world of Tom Sawyer, who himself would fall prey to the dictates of "authorities." Mark Twain exposed the sham of anti-Chinese racism and simple-minded "Sunday School" morality through satires of the dangers of taking texts literally.

The reader who misreads the humor of the situation seems to have concerned Mark Twain as his writings, and thus his reputation, circulated further and further afield.[12] Clemens's evident anxiety about the circulation of his works permeates a hoax he perpetuated, beginning in the December 1870 column, in which he wrote an elaborate review of *The Innocents Abroad* attributed to the London *Saturday Review*. In the fake review, which Mark Twain claimed to have copied from an actual source, an English reviewer reads the book at face value and finds a work of "imposing insanity" full of "audacious and exasperating falsehoods," undoubtedly written by a "gentle idiot." The "reviewer" continues: ". . . the reader may seek out the author's exhibition of his uncultivation for himself. The book is absolutely dangerous, considering the magnitude and variety of its misstatements and the convincing confidence with which they are made. And yet it is a text-book in the schools of America!" Only when the book talks about America, the reviewer admits, does the information seem truly instructive, while Mark Twain footnotes this assertion to point out that the instructive facts the reviewer praises are his own inventions.

Adding another level to the hoax, Mark Twain prefaced this made-up review with a real newspaper article from the Boston *Advertiser* (dated October 22, 1870) talking about the real London *Saturday Review* criticism, which had appeared on October 8. This article begins: "Perhaps the most successful flights of the humor of Mark Twain have been descriptions of the persons who did not appreciate his humor at all. . . . Mark Twain may now add a much more glorious instance to his string of trophies. . . . We can imagine the delight of the humorist in reading this tribute to his power; and indeed it is so amusing in itself that he can hardly do better than reproduce the article in full in his next monthly Memoranda." Mark Twain used this note as a pretense to write the burlesque review, which he then presented to the reader as the real review. He comments that initially he did want to reprint the review, "for I cannot write anything half so delicious myself. If I had a cast-iron dog that could read this English criticism and preserve its austerity, I would drive him off the door-step." His deadpan delivery, in print as in person, might make his humor read as misinformation and ignorance, if one missed the joke.

Mark Twain's literary hoax worked on numerous levels: piling burlesque on real and then treating both with a deadpan earnestness that should have been a warning to those familiar with Mark Twain. As a humorist, Mark Twain had developed enough of a reputation for hoaxes, and for distorting the truth in various ways, that whatever he wrote should have been viewed through a prism of suspicion, not necessarily for being false, but for being humorous. His early periodical writings are filled with literary hoaxes, deadpan jokes portrayed as news items that required the reader to realize the joke, or risk having the joke be on them.[13] In such cases, detecting deception was the difference between laughing *with* the humorist and being laughed *at* by those who got the joke. Mark Twain's hoaxes were not meant to be passed off as "real," in the sense of being read as genuine stories. Rather, the point was in the detection, the realization that Mark Twain was trying to put one over on his readers. The pleasure of this kind of hoax was in the puzzling over what was real and what was fake, not in being fooled into believing the humbug was real. The context of Mark

Twain's "Memoranda" column, with its focus on the troubled status of text, would have made the false review suspect as well.

As a hoax, Mark Twain's review was part of an urban, largely middle-class tradition of frauds that tested the boundary between authentic and fake. As James Cook has argued, in the "Age of Barnum," hoaxes (what he calls "artful deceptions" and Barnum called "humbugs") were not about duping innocent suckers but instead reflected the new middle class's concern with authenticity and fraud. Hoaxes provided entertaining perceptual puzzles that highlighted these concerns through a form of mostly harmless play in which audiences explored the line between real and illusion. This middle class, Cook points out, was beset by anxieties about deception—how to determine respectability over fraud, self-made men over confidence-men, fraud in the spirit world and the business world. As P. T. Barnum made clear, the "humbug" was based on a mixture of hyperbolic claims about a product's value—whether that product was commercial or an amuse-ment—and a product of high enough quality to satisfy the customer. The "Feejee Mermaid," for example, was realistic enough to convince custom-ers that a half-monkey, half-fish creature could exist, but the pleasure of the humbug was derived from the act of detection—from the puzzling through the possibilities and detecting what one thought was the truth. Mark Twain had been absorbed by Barnum's autobiography, *Life of P.T. Barnum, Written by Himself* (and published by subscription only), shortly after his marriage, to the confusion of his new wife.[14] But he had not yet met the showman.

Mark Twain's *Saturday Review* hoax divided his audience into those who got the joke and those who did not, allowing those who got it to laugh at the thought of taking Mark Twain's book seriously and at those who took the review seriously. The burlesque review reads humor straight and thus blurs the lines between fake and real, funny and serious, information and entertainment. These lines created central tensions for much of Mark Twain's humor, dividing his audience into those who enjoyed the conceptual play of his humor and those who preferred that the serious remain free from the taint of the humorous.

Since the humor of the humbug was predicated on frustrating, or at least tweaking, audience expectations, the failure of a reader to laugh at this disruption pointed to a deeper issue—the function of humor as a form of communication that could either expose certain truths or question the very existence of truth. Bruce Michelson has applied the concept of the "put-on" to the literary hoaxes Mark Twain undertook in his early career.

The concept, so named by Jacob Brackman in the 1960s, describes a form of humor distinct from satire and parody and with a different aim than irony. The put-on is a type of "miniature hoax" aimed not at passing a fake as real but at mixing up the categories of false and real for humorous effect. "The put-on," Brackman writes, "at once elevates the fraudulent and debases the true, rendering the entire proceedings questionable."[15] Unlike satire, which aims to convey truthful content below or behind its humor, the focus of the "put-on" is formal—the focus is on the act of communication, its difficulties, and its failures.

As Michelson argues, the put-on raises the possibility that humor might not have a clear and easy message to be interpreted (i.e., to be transposed back into the realm of the serious). Instead, such humor is defined as the anarchic function of humor or, in Michelson's definition, "humor as a subversion of seriousness."[16] Instead of the moralistic or humanistic sense that many readers and critics seek from Mark Twain's humor—the deeper meaning behind so-called quality humor that critics from Howells on have sought—this definition raises the possibility that humor might escape sense, rather than exposing (or at least hinting at) a deeper level of truth. Mark Twain's consistent put-ons of newspaper and other periodical "truths" called into question, or more precisely "made fun of," the idea that either individuals or societies could be adequately formed by a print culture that circulates beyond the control of its participants. In this way, the *Galaxy* column may be seen as a put-on of the goals of the so-called quality magazines, such as the *Atlantic Monthly*, *Scribner's Monthly*, and the *Galaxy* itself, all of which aimed to shape American culture through a periodical literature that should have a positive effect on both individual readers and society writ large.

But as Brackman points out, the put-on may in fact be more than mere play, as it often "brings the submerged antagonisms of a relationship perilously close to the surface—*without actually allowing them to come into the open*."[17] Mark Twain's antagonism toward print culture, and his anxiety at the circulation of his humor and his reputation that the "Memoranda" column raised, were based on the relationship between the humorist and his audience. Mark Twain's humbug review allowed him to laugh at those who missed the joke, as well as those who were not sold to laugh with him, while at the same time highlighting the underlying slipperiness that humor required to function. The hoax highlighted the difficulty of controlling the reception and interpretation of print culture, which escaped the author's control when it was sold.

Mark Twain's review attempted to reassert a relationship between humorist and audience that had already been violated by the supposedly serious review in the *Saturday Review*, and his response to those who misunderstood his humor, or his role as a humorist, tipped into anger when his own humor escaped his control in the very print culture he was laughing at. The question of who was sold, of whom the joke was on, became part of the circuit of commentary that Mark Twain's *Galaxy* column had created. The Boston *Advertiser*, whose notice had set off the original story, followed up by praising the hoax for fooling a number of readers, writing: "Some persons, indeed, may read the whole without perceiving the joke; and we have before us a paragraph from a perplexed paper which speaks of Mark Twain's having 'reproduced the Saturday Review's notice,' but denies that it can have been intended for a 'serious criticism' and inquires: 'Who is sold,—Mark Twain, the London Saturday Review, or the Boston Advertiser?'" The report goes on to point out that the person sold was to be found, by the confused reviewer, in the mirror. The *Advertiser* commented one week later, pointing out the continued correspondence of people willing to expose their "credulity" by the "gay deceiver." These people are deceived "only because they will be cheated in spite of every opportunity for escape, and we presume none will be more surprised and none more amused than the joker, who made his jest so broad that it seemed no one could fail to see the real point."[18] Presuming that he could control the meaning of his hoax, Mark Twain would have been the one to laugh easiest at the readers who misread his work by taking him too seriously.

The shift toward antagonism arose as Mark Twain's humbug review of his own work spiraled into the world of print and out of his own control, raising a third possibility that seems to have disturbed him—that it was Mark Twain himself who had missed the joke. In the January *Galaxy*, under the title "A Sad, Sad Business," Mark Twain took ownership of the hoax, claiming to have written the burlesque review based on the *Advertiser* paragraph before seeing the actual review. Reprinting a number of responses to the hoax, Mark Twain takes the confusion as praise. The Cincinnati *Enquirer*, for instance, wrote: "So it is with humor. The finer it is in quality, the more danger of its not being recognized at all. Even Mark Twain has been taken in by an English review of his 'Innocents Abroad.' Mark Twain is by no means a coarse humorist, but the Englishman's humor is so much finer than his, that he mistakes it for solid earnest, and 'larfs most consumedly.'" While amused at the failure of others to get the fineness of his joke, Mark Twain's response conveys a sense of anger, or at least consternation, with those who thought the joke on him, writing, "Bless me, some people thought that I was the 'sold' person!" To these persons, he offers a solution: "If any man doubts my word now, I will kill him. No, I will not kill him; I will win his money. I will bet him twenty to one . . . that the statements above made as to the authorship of the article in question are entirely true." His put-on seems to have brought his own anxieties perilously close to the surface of his column.

As the layers of the hoax multiplied, Mark Twain's vexation at any of the laughter being directed at him grew. In a letter, he wrote to Francis P. Church, the *Galaxy*'s editor: "I've got these *Enquirer* idiots just where I wanted *somebody*—don't you see why? Because half of the people don't know now whether to believe I wrote that thing or not, or whether it *was* from the *Review*, or whether it is all a sell, & no criticism ever *was* in the London paper. Now, over the shoulders of this Cincinnati fool, I'll make the whole thing straight."[19] The desire to make his hoax straight, to correct the impression that he was not in control of his humor, was frustrated by readers who failed to take his claim of authorship seriously.

The Cincinnati *Enquirer* seems to have been the main culprit in goading Mark Twain. In the February issue of the *Galaxy*, Mark Twain published a further response to the issue under the title "A Falsehood," in which any good humor on his part had been replaced by petulance. The article starts with the reprinting of an *Enquirer* article of December 17, 1870, which claimed that he had indeed been sold and only claimed authorship to save face, concluding, "The best thing for Mark to do will be to admit that he was sold, and say no more about it."[20] The paper offered to prove it. Mark Twain's response railed against this version of events, offering to pay the *Enquirer* $1,000 if they could, in fact, prove him wrong and ending with the appraisal, "I think the Cincinnati 'Enquirer' must be edited by children" (February 1870). For their part, the *Enquirer* shot back at Mark Twain for taking things too seriously or, in their words, for being "as matter-of-fact as last-year's bird nest." Whereas Mark Twain had predicated the whole situation on a lie, the newspaper claimed to find no harm in lying some more by claiming he had not written the piece. The article continues: "Now we have MR. TWAIN in the *Galaxy* copying our article, and crying in a loud voice. . . . Now, this is all bosh. As MARK TWAIN never told the truth in his life, how are we to know that he is not lying about his inordinate desire to gamble? . . . We are not to be 'bluffed.' . . . As for Mr. TWAIN'S threat of exposure, we care nothing. . . . Upon the whole, we have about concluded that the "Memoranda" of the *Galaxy* is edited by a lunatic." The refusal of this paper to take Mark Twain at his word, to "make fun" of him, did indeed seem to drive Mark Twain crazy, or at least it made him lose his sense of humor. If his put-on review had raised Mark Twain's anxieties of losing control of the meaning of his humor, his failure to maintain the deadpan role of the humorist when the put-on spiraled out of his control caused him to be the one "sold" after all.

One magazine article picked up on Mark Twain's use of the fake controversy, and the whole of his magazine writing, as one elaborate piece of advertising for Mark Twain and his writings. "How a Humorist uses Humor," from *The Phrenological Journal of Science and Health* (January 1871), praised the "advertising genius" of Mark Twain for knowing how to sell his books through a monthly advertising column.[21] Readers of the *Galaxy*, the article continued, "have swallowed with an astonishing relish, constantly asking for more, regular doses of sugar-coated advertisements of the wonderful book, thereby securing for the *Galaxy* publishers a *regular* contributor, and helping the enterprising author to cultivate a new crop of 'Innocents' for future use." The *Saturday Review* hoax, the piece claimed, was a further "advertising ruse," although they took Mark Twain's version to be a real review, but one written as a burlesque by someone else and used to stir up conversation, controversy, and sales.

Mark Twain's time at the *Galaxy* did stir up conversation, helping to make him a household name, but it did not cement his name as a quality humorist. If anything, it raised questions about what role Mark Twain could and should play as a humorist. Mark Twain had already decided as early as October 1870 that he would end his column in April 1871, and the illness of his wife that spring caused him to skip the March issue and issue a short valedictory in the April number. No further mention was made of his humbug review or his feud with the Cincinnati *Enquirer*. In his final column for the *Galaxy*, he wrote of his frustration at being forced to live up to his reputation as a humorist:

> I have written for THE GALAXY a year. For the last eight months, with hardly an interval, I have had for my fellows and comrades, night and day, doctors and watchers of the sick! During these eight months death has taken two members of my home circle and malignantly threatened two others. All this I have experienced, yet all the time been under contract to furnish "humorous" matter once a month for this magazine. I am speaking the exact truth in the above details. Please to put yourself in my place and contemplate the grisly grotesqueness of the situation. I think that some of

*the "humor" I have written during this period could have been injected into
a funeral sermon without disturbing the solemnity of the occasion.*

*The MEMORANDA will cease permanently with this issue of the mag-
azine. To be a pirate, on a low salary, and with no share in the profits of
the business, used to be my idea of an uncomfortable occupation, but I have
other views now. To be a monthly humorist in a cheerless time is drearier.*

Life in Buffalo was not to his liking, and the chore of periodical writing—both for the *Galaxy* and the *Express*—was not rewarding personally
or professionally. Similarly, the monthly humor column proved to be less
rewarding than expected, especially in the midst of his wife's recurring
illnesses and the deaths of his father-in-law, Jervis Langdon, and of a close
family friend. To his brother Orion in March, he wrote that "There isn't
money enough between Hell & Hartford to hire me to write once a month
for *any* periodical. . . . Haven't I risked cheapening myself sufficiently by a
year's periodical dancing before the public but must *continue* it?"[22] In the
same letter, he wrote that too much exposure had hurt his reputation,
which he wanted to improve in order to overtake the reputation of Harte,
which was at that point at its highest tide. He wrote—"I will 'top' Bret
Harte again or bust. But I can't do it by dangling eternally in the public
view." Mark Twain was discovering different types of fame.

Despite finding the task of writing a column frustrating, Mark Twain
found that his periodical work and the continued success of *The Innocents Abroad* placed him squarely in the public eye, and he attempted
to capitalize on this position by contracting with the publishers of the
Galaxy to release a book of his writings under the title *Mark Twain's Annual—1871*. Such a comic annual would have competed with *Josh Billings
Farmer's Allminax*, which had sold between 80,000 and 90,000 copies in
1870 and had better prospects for 1871. Collections of humor were a
booming business, ranging from cheap collections of pirated humor to
those connected to well-known humorists like Billings in America and
Tom Hood in England. Elisha Bliss, his subscription publisher, refused
to allow the *Galaxy* to publish the book, implying that such a book would
hurt the sale of *The Innocents Abroad* and seeming to hint that the *Galaxy*
column was already doing so. Clemens replied that the magazine "is a
good advertisement for me" but that he would quit all periodical writing
if Bliss or he decided it was hurting his reputation.[23]

Samuel Clemens's decision to quit the magazine seems to have had less
to do with that fear than with the difficulty of writing a monthly column.

He also gave up the idea of a comic annual, although he did publish the "Burlesque Autobiography" in 1871, which did not qualify as a "book" according to his contract, as well as contributing to Thomas Nast's new annual for 1872 (including "The Facts in the Case of the Great Beef Contract" from the *Galaxy*). He contracted with Bliss to publish a collection of sketches, including many of his periodical pieces, which would come out in 1875 as *Sketches, New and Old*. Clemens's commitment to subscription publishing prevented him from taking advantage of what he saw as public demand for his work. Since subscription books required advanced planning and proper spacing between releases, Mark Twain's works came out slower than he wished, a fact he believed hurt his commercial prospects and led to his eventual split with the American Publishing Company in 1880.

At the end of a year running a humor column in the *Galaxy*, and a year and a half editing the Buffalo *Express*, Samuel Clemens gave up both and moved from Buffalo to Hartford, Connecticut, where he took up residence in Nook Farm, a suburb populated by literary, religious, and political figures—large numbers of Beechers and Hookers, as well as Charles Dudley Warner, a fellow humorist and future collaborator, and the local Congregational minister, Joseph Twichell, who would become a lifelong friend. Mark Twain's withdrawal from regular periodical writing—in newspapers and magazines—as well as his move from Buffalo to Hartford, further helped shift his reputation away from the model of the literary humorist to that of quality humorist. At Nook Farm, Clemens began a new stage of his life as a professional writer freed from the obligations of the periodical press. In March he wrote: "I quit the *Galaxy* with the current number, & shall write no more for any periodical. Am offered great prices, but it's no go. Shall simply write books."[24] Mark Twain would begin occasional periodical publishing in the *Atlantic Monthly* in 1874, but this work was that of an author, not an editor or regular humorist, marking a shift in his role as a humorist

Clemens sold his interest in the *Express* and moved the family to Hartford, Connecticut, to pursue a life of a man of letters free from the encumbrances of daily obligations. The financial loss from the sale of the *Express*, along with the declining sales of *The Innocents Abroad*, forced him to undertake a lyceum tour after taking the 1870–1871 season off. Throughout this period, business matters greatly impacted Samuel Clemens's career as Mark Twain, as he sought to balance his newfound respectability with the necessity of making money to support his new family. His positions at the *Galaxy* and the *Express* were experiments in the different ways a humorist could make his circulation pay. And as a means to promote the reputation of Mark Twain as the most famous of American humorists, the periodical work sold. But it was not sustainable.

FUN FOR THE MILLION, DISGUST FOR THE FEW
MARK WARD ON ARTEMUS TWAIN

In October 1871, roughly six months after ending his column in the *Galaxy*, Mark Twain undertook a third lyceum lecture tour. During the summer, Samuel Clemens wrote and discarded two lectures before settling on the subject of "Reminiscences of some Uncommonplace Characters I have chanced to meet"—a lecture featuring stories on Artemus Ward, the Czar of Russia, and others. The review of the first night, in Bethlehem, Pennsylvania, saw the lecture as a distinct failure, estimating that the majority of the audience attended the lecture not to *hear* Mark Twain speak but to *see* the famous humorist (which might be for the best, the reviewer noted, since his low tone of voice made him hard to hear). It read:

> But everybody wanted to see "Mark Twain," and they saw him; . . . and with that sight most of them were satisfied—ourselves included. We had never seen Mr. Clemens; we wanted to see him; we knew that good writers seldom make good lecturers; we were willing to pay the price of admission to see him, even if it had been announced that he would mount the platform to be looked at, and would not open his mouth to speak. So we were all satisfied, but not instructed nor exactly entertained.[25]

Mark Twain was now a "celebrated," "popular," and "famous" humorist, to be seen for certain, but as for entertainment or edification, reviewers reported a wide range of audience responses—from uproarious laughter to angry disgust. The Philadelphia *Inquirer* review stated that the audience's "continuous roar of laughter" demonstrated his ability to create "fun for the million." But "fun," defined as the creation of laughter, was not sufficient to satisfy the expectations of all lyceum audiences, some of whom found such laughter to be out of place in the lecture hall. This ambivalent reception repeated throughout the tour, highlighting an increasing tension in the cultural reception of Mark Twain as a humorist.

In his new circumstances in Hartford, Samuel Clemens found himself in need of income and set out on October 16, 1871, for 76 performances in 15 states, excluding churches, Buffalo, and Jamestown, New York, all places he disliked because he thought they stifled laughter. In addition to the hardships of traveling and being separated from his family, which he always disliked when lecturing, Mark Twain's lectures on this tour were met with consistent and rankling criticisms of his humor and of his place on the lyceum stage. He would later refer to this lecture tour as "the most detestable lecture campaign that ever was," due to the fatigue of writing new lectures on the road and the fact that he ended the tour with only $1,500 in profit after "squandering" much of his profits.[26]

Making this tour worse, Clemens discarded his lecture on interesting characters after three nights and quickly revised the lecture to focus on Artemus Ward, stringing together humorous pieces by Artemus Ward and himself on a thin biography of the departed humorist.[27] Mark Twain's new lecture necessitated memorization and experimentation on the road. He wrote to Livy that "the same old practising on audiences still goes on—the same old feeling of pulses & altering manner & matter to suit the symptoms. The very same lecture that *convulsed* Great Barrington was received with the gentlest & most well-bred smiles & rippling comfort by Milford."[28] Looking ahead to Boston, he predicted that "as Boston goes, so goes New England," but he found that the "uproarious" Boston crowd was followed by a staid, puritanical audience in Worcester. This pulsing and alternating relationship between Mark Twain and his audiences, and Mark Twain and his subject matter, continued for almost six weeks of performances, when he jettisoned the Artemus Ward lecture in favor of "Roughing It on the Silver Frontier," based on his second book of travel, which he was in the process of revising. This lecture, again memorized and refined in the middle of a tour, was met with similar reactions: a mix of praise and disappointment.

Only a portion of the interest in the detestable campaign lies in Mark Twain's difficulties finding a lecture that would play. The expectations of the audience when they slogged through the snow and cold, packed into the halls or the occasional church, and settled in to listen to the well-known humorist present a unique index of the relationship between audience and humorist. Reviews of Mark Twain's lecture do not present audience reaction directly, but rather convey a mediated interpretation of the transaction between performer and audience. These expectations, whether explicitly stated or implicitly hinted, shape the basic interpretive possibilities for judging Mark Twain's lecture as a form of leisure. According to reviewers, some audiences expected to be instructed and edified by Mark Twain's performances, while others simply wanted to be entertained, to laugh, and to be distracted from the cares of the world. Others simply wanted to see the celebrity humorist who had made a name for himself through his writings. But based on the expectations portrayed in the newspaper reports, Mark Twain's lyceum audiences held too many contradictory views of the meanings of the lecture platform for him to be entirely successful with the large audiences he drew.[29]

Although the newspaper reports vary in length, tone, and subject matter, the form of these reviews usually falls into a set pattern: a description of the crowd and the performer, a description of the manner of Mark Twain as a speaker, a discussion or recitation of the subject matter of his talk, and an evaluation of the success or failure of the performance based on a set of expectations, often in terms of the meanings of the audience's laughter.

Many of the articles begin with a description of the size and quality of the audience who assembled to hear the humorist. In Washington, D.C., it was "the largest audience ever assembled, with all standing-room space filled and hundreds turned away." Audiences were "eagerly expectant," "one of the largest and most critical audiences ever assembled," "an enormous multitude."[30] In both Boston and Portland, the audience numbered over 2,000 people. In Philadelphia, bad weather did not prevent an audience "densely crammed; in fact, it contained the largest audience ever assembled within its walls to listen to a lecture." Clearly, the fame of Mark Twain as a humorist led to large audiences eager to see and hear him. In Brooklyn, the audience "from the first manifested that they had come with the determination of being amused, and . . . at the close went away with the happy consciousness of having effected their object satisfactorily." Very few reviews mention anything other than a full house; the notable exception being the Newark *Daily Advertiser*, which claimed not to be surprised that Mark Twain lectured to many empty seats, since "those who heard him once, did not care to suffer the infliction the second time." On the whole, the audiences were described as large and expectant to see Mark Twain perform.

Understanding the expectations of Mark Twain's audiences is complicated by the fact that much of his success as a lecturer came from reversing, or otherwise tweaking, the normal conventions of the lecture. For instance, on almost every stop of the tour, Mark Twain dispensed with the custom of being introduced by a local dignitary in favor of a self-introduction. He would come on stage and stand quietly, rubbing his hands together and gazing out into the audience until "titters" started to be heard; then he would say, in his low drawl, something along the lines of:

LADIES AND GENTLEMEN: I ask leave to introduce to you the lecturer of the evening, Mr. Samuel B. Clements [sic], otherwise known as "Mark Twain," a gentleman, I may say, whose devotion to science, aptness in philosophy, historical accuracy, and love of — truth [laughter] are in perfect harmony with his majestic and imposing presence. I — ah — refer — ah — indirectly to — to myself! [Shouts of laughter and applause.] It is not, I know, customary to introduce a lecturer after having the amount of advertising that I have had; but as the management desired that the introduction should be made, I preferred making it myself, being sure by this means of getting in all the — facts! [Laughter.][31]

This introduction cast humorous doubt on the speaker's learning and signaled that humor would be the keynote of the evening. The Exeter, New Hampshire, *News-Letter* enjoyed the introduction, which "led us to anticipate an enjoyable hour in the presence of the 'prince of American humorists;' but we were to be sadly numbered among the victims of disappointed expectations."[32] The vast majority of audiences expected a humorous performance, but the reviews show that audiences did not always get what they anticipated.

For all but a few who saw no place for the humorous in the lyceum, the problem with Mark Twain's lecture was not the intent but the delivery—in the manner of performance and the subject matter. The physical performance of Mark Twain—both in voice and body—also violated the expectations of the lyceum audience. His slow drawl, often monotonous in tone, was not of the level of oratorical polish that distinguished most successful lecturers. His physical deportment, frequently commented upon, confounded platform conventions—to either the enjoyment or disappointment of his audience. The Chicago *Evening Post* took great relish in describing Mark Twain's stage presence:

He dipped into pathos, rose into eloquence, kept sledding right along in a fascinating nasal snarl, looking and speaking like an embarrassed deacon telling his experience, and punctuating his tardy fun with the most complicated awkwardness of gesture. Now he snapped his fingers; now he rubbed his hands softly, like the catcher of the champion nine; now he caressed his left palm with his dexterous fingers, like the end minstrel-man propounding a conundrum; now he put his arms akimbo, like a disgusted auctioneer; and now he churned the air in the vicinity of his imperiled head with his outspread hands, as if he was fighting mosquitoes at Rye Beach. Once he

got his arms tangled so badly, that three surgeons were seen to edge their
way quietly toward the stage, expecting to be summoned; but he unwound
himself during the next anecdote.[33]

The *Daily Morning Chronicle* of Washington, D.C., took a less charitable
view of the manner of the humorist, writing, "Unfit habits of manner and
speech, all the inevitable eccentricities of bearing which are the outward
form of the inner peculiarity, serve to distract from force in speaking. . . .
Even the promise of his humor-stamped face seems to fail."[34] Mark Twain's
manner of performance, the physical manifestations of his presence as
humorist, divided audiences and reviewers separately from the actual
content of the performance.

Mark Twain may have intended to burlesque the lyceum genre of the
memorial lecture, which he had written of in the September 1870 *Galaxy*
following the death of Charles Dickens. The death of such an author,
he wrote, doomed the country to be "lectured to death" by anyone who
had heard the man read, had spoken with him, or who had seen him in
a barbershop from afar. A burlesque of the memorial lecture did not mix
particularly well with the need to pay actual tribute to Artemus Ward's
memory, all while also being funny. Clemens seems to have been aware
of this issue, writing to Livy that he was "trying to weed Artemus out of
it & work myself *in*. What *I* say, *fetches* 'em—but what *he* says, *don't*."[35]

Many reviews focused on the content of Mark Twain's lecture as
the source of either enjoyment or dissatisfaction. The "Artemus Ward"
lecture consisted of a series of humorous stories hung on the thread of
the biography of the Great Showman, with several digressions unique to
Mark Twain, ending on a sentimental note with a discussion of Artemus
Ward's early death, often accompanied by a sentimental poem from an
English newspaper. The topic seems to have confused his audience. In
a joking tone, the Washington *Evening Star* pointed out the conceptual
problem with the lecture under the title "Mark Ward on Artemus Twain,"
a review which was subsequently cited by other newspapers: "when they
come to study it all out to-day they have A. Twain's jokes so mixed up with
M. Ward's—no, M. Twain's with A. Ward's—and get so confused trying
to separate Clements [*sic*] from Browne that their mental condition is
pitiable. No lecturer has a right to trifle with his audience in that kind
of style."[36] While this reporter appears to have had his tongue in cheek,
other newspapers quoted Mark Twain's trifling with his audiences in less
charitable terms.

That Mark Twain chose to lecture on Artemus Ward only heightened the audience's focus on the humorist on the stage—specifically in the figure of Mark Twain and the role of humor more generally. In so doing, he tipped the balance between humorous anecdotes, eloquent descriptions, and instructive facts that had so impressed most reviewers during his earlier lecture tours. Clemens recognized this problem, writing:

> *Livy darling, good house, but they laughed too much. A great fault with this lecture is, that I have no way of turning it into a serious & instructive vein at will. Any lecture of mine ought to be a running narrative-plank, with square holes in it, six inches apart, all the length of it; & then in my mental shop I ought to have plugs (half marked "serious" & the others marked "humorous") to select from & jam into these holes according to the temper of the audience. . . .* [37]

The imbalance between "serious" and "humorous" plugs may help explain Mark Twain's own view that his Artemus Ward lecture never worked to his satisfaction. At the beginning of the lecture, Mark Twain joked that he would not "load you down with historic fact to such an extent that you will be unable to get home." Nor would he, to his personal dismay, share his philosophical deductions, which he admired but audiences reacted to with "intense and utter exasperation! [Laughter.]" [38] These jokes disguised, or possibly highlighted, the fact that the lecture gave little actual information on Artemus Ward, or on the subject of humor itself, nor did it contain notable passages of artistic description or "word painting"—a key factor in the positive reviews of previous lectures, leavening the laughter with instruction and beauty.

By defining Artemus Ward as America's greatest humorist, Mark Twain called into question the meanings of humor and the humorist in ways that did not reflect well on his own cultural position. In at least one version of the lecture, he further delineated a hierarchy of humorists by noting that while Artemus Ward was a great humorist, he "must not be compared with Holmes or Lowell. These men have refinement that he did not possess; but this does not detract from the great showman's ability to create fun for the million." [39] Mark Twain's lecture allowed his audience an opening to compare his humor to both Artemus Ward's highly popular works and to the quality expressions of the Boston greats, implicitly placing himself below all three in a hierarchy of humor.

The reactions of reviewers to his lecture ranged from disappointment to glowing praise. Positive reviews of the performances focused on laughter and merriment as positive social goods in terms of relaxation, distraction, or entertainment. Negative reviews saw the lyceum as a social institution of education, edification, and social uplift, with the humorist as a perversion of the institution's goals. Laughter did satisfy many audiences. Some audiences were described as "ready to laugh at anything and came here for that purpose." Various descriptions of audience reaction speak to laughter as a measure of success: "[T]he immense audience was kept in one continued roar of laughter," "rippling into continual merriment and bursting often into hearty laughter," and "his audience were highly entertained if frequent bursts of laughter are to be taken as indications of pleasure." Lecturing in Henry Ward Beecher's church in Brooklyn for "the usual Beecher people," Mark Twain's success "heartily pleased the audience, who frequently testified, by their applause and laughter, the satisfaction he had occasioned." The reviewer averred that "the man who went empty and rueful away must have had a very diminutive sense of the ridiculous."[40] In many of the reviews, laughter is simply pleasurable, and since Mark Twain was a humorist, his entertainment succeeded when the audience laughed, no matter other considerations.

One major meaning of humor in nineteenth-century America framed laughter as a healthy activity to be enjoyed without reference to moral or ethical concerns. As Jennifer Hughes has illustrated, laughter was viewed in America as a panacea, a medicine that cured whether it came in quality forms or in the low genres of the comic almanac, the minstrel show, or the laughing gas exhibition. This view found that laughter "could generally be assumed to serve the purposes of the body, no matter the root cause of the laughter."[41] While other uses of laughter, from carnivalesque transgression to repressive mockery, were undoubtedly operative during the nineteenth century, Hughes argues that the major trend of antebellum humor focused on its palliative effect on the body. This historical trend helps explain the positive reviews of Mark Twain's lectures, which tended to frame laughter using references to the relief of cares. Mark Twain's new hometown newspaper, the Hartford *Daily Courant*, featured an almost wholly positive review, possibly written by its editor and Clemens's neighbor Charles Dudley Warner, that summed up Mark Twain's success by stating that "the man who can give such an audience as that last evening an hour of innocent laughter is a public benefactor, and this we consider Mr. Clemens."[42] Such laughter served a social purpose through the physical pleasure of laughing and its ability to momentarily erase the problems of the "serious" world.

As he would throughout each period of his career, Mark Twain sought to clarify the terms of his successes and to control the reception of his humorous products. He held that the response of the Boston audience would predict the success of his tour: "Boston must sit up & behave, & do right by me. As Boston goes, so goes New England." Writing the next night after his Boston performance, Clemens reveled in the "perfectly uproarious" audience he had stirred up. His performances seem to have consistently caused audiences to laugh, sometimes too much, as he had pointed out to Mrs. Clemens. On the other hand, rousing laughter was not the only gauge by which all audiences measured his success. The review in the Boston *Daily Evening Journal* clearly delineated two central meanings of audience laughter—enjoyable and begrudging. The review concludes:

> *It was enough that Mr. Clemens made his hearers laugh, and laugh heartily and often, and that was what he came there for. Even the man who is not in the habit of laughing, and who thinks such things silly and undignified, was caught laughing several times, but stopped it when discovered.*
>
> *Taken as a whole the lecture served its purpose admirably. It afforded a pleasant evening to two thousand people, some of whom might otherwise have had a touch of the blues, and it served to keep green the memory of one to whom were are all indebted for quaint sayings without number, which have often driven away dull care and made us light-hearted and cheery for the time.* [43]

The major note here argues that Mark Twain's lecture served its purpose: enjoyable laughter that drove out the blues by providing a "cheery" time. On the other hand, a subset of the audience only laughed unwillingly and strained to regain their "dignity" by not laughing. The image of the "serious" man who found laughter, and by extension humor, beneath his dignity and the dignity of the lyceum was reflected in the numerous reviews that found Mark Twain's lecture to be no laughing matter.

Samuel Clemens enjoyed a momentary respite from the doubts caused by his Artemus Ward lecture after his success in Boston. The day after his lecture he attended the "dream" lunch with Howells and Harte described at the end of the previous chapter, marking one of his first personal forays into the Boston literary world. But his success in Boston did not, as he hoped, set the tone of reactions in New England. Under the title "Mark

Ward on Artemus Twain," the Exeter (N.H.) *News-Letter* excoriated Mark
Twain's "plagiaristic lecture" as a fraud. While the review praised Mark
Twain's writings as among the "first humorists of his age," it claimed to
express the popular verdict by censuring Mark Twain for his lectures, which
show that "he lacks almost every element of humor, and is lamentably
deficient in originality; and it passes our comprehension how any man
with such a reputation as he has acquired should barter it away on the
lecture platform for, comparatively, a mere pittance." The Manchester *Daily
Union* chided Mark Twain for including "some very silly jokes of his own
which were beneath the dignity of a clown in the circus." The Worcester
Gazette summarized what might have been a common audience reaction
by stating: ". . . the audience dispersed, the greater number sadly in doubt
whether they liked it or not. They thought it was rather thin, but then, it
would not have been funny if it had been thick, and on the whole, calling
to mind one after another the bright points which had bound a lodgment
in their memories they concluded that they did like it."[44] Boston's imprimatur had not cemented Mark Twain's success. It never would have that
power, despite his hope that it might. Despite his move into respectable
venues that might reframe his humor as high quality, some of his audience
would continue to see him in the realm of the clown.

The ambivalent audience reactions, and the varied expectations that
shaped them, illustrate the complexity of Mark Twain's reputation in
venues where the meaning of respectable performance reflected deeper
cultural fissures within mass culture. Mark Twain's cultural freight as
a lecturer cast him as, according to a review, one of a new "peripatetic
celebrities" who gained fame through violating all norms of an "acceptable speaker."[45] Seeing a "literary lion"—whether Mark Twain, Petroleum
Nasby, or Josh Billings—was the draw, and "the lack of grace and finish
is regarded as a proof of genius, and awkward gesticulation as the more
natural method of impressing an audience." Mark Twain's lecture kept
the audience in "good humor," but the ultimate goal was to "see and hear
Mark Twain." One review placed Mark Twain below Petroleum Nasby
and Josh Billings as a lecturer and pronounced that, had he not gained
a deserved reputation as a humorist through his writings, he would be
"considered as unfit to present to the enlightened and fastidious audiences
of New England." Mark Twain's increased celebrity made him a target
of both those who wished to maintain a moral social purpose of leisure
activities and those who wished to sell tickets, magazines, newspaper,
comic almanacs, and books.

Mark Twain's circulation as an author and a performer was increasingly fraught with conflicting interpretations of humor that he could not entirely control nor see as a laughing matter. In early December, he abandoned his Artemus Ward lecture in favor of one based on his forthcoming book, *Roughing It*. Returning to the form of the burlesque travel lecture, Mark Twain continued to meet with ambivalent reviews. Audiences laughed, but not all critics enjoyed the lecture. On his second visit to New York City, this time performing the "Roughing It" lecture, "the enjoyment of the audience was intemperate," and the *Tribune* judged Mark Twain as "a true humorist, endowed with that indefinable power to make men laugh which is worth, in current funds, more than the highest genius or the greatest learning."[46] On the other hand, the *Sun* of Logansport, Indiana, noted that the audience in that town came to be entertained and laughed heartily at the start of the lecture. But, soon, only "the boys" were laughing at the stale, clownish jokes. The review ended by asking if Mark Twain fit with the aims of the local lyceum:

> *The object and aim, we believe, of the two Christian Associations of this city, is to improve and elevate the moral and intellectual tone of society, and not merely money-making. In all candor we would ask if such lectures tend to thus elevate and refine? Does his picturing of Jack Harris, with his coarse allusions, and his buffoonery benefit the people? If not, then, in the name of society, let us have no more such performances under the auspices of the Christian Associations.*[47]

The continued vacillation of reviews—from quality humor to buffoonish clowning—illustrates Mark Twain's continued platform role as an index of a continued debate about the role of the humorist as a purveyor of both fungible fun and upright elevation in the Gilded Age.

Mark Twain's lectures for the 1870–1871 season were consistently advertised as being the final of his career, and he kept his word by retiring from the lyceum stage for more than a decade.[48] The detestable campaign marked a further transition point in Samuel Clemens's career as "Mark Twain, the humorist," as he gave up another major source of income and publicity and settled into his life at Nook Farm. But the end of his lyceum tour, and his purported retirement, did not end the question of his role on the lyceum stage. In February 1872, Dr. Josiah Gilbert Holland, the editor of *Scribner's Monthly*, printed an editorial column attacking "triflers" on the platform stage that was clearly aimed at Mark Twain and his ilk.

Clemens's vituperative response, a never-published article, illustrates the way in which Mark Twain took attacks on his professional life as a humorist with something less than good humor.

THE LITERARY BUFFOON AND THE INTELLECTUAL CHOLERA: JOSIAH HOLLAND AND MARK TWAIN

In July 1872, Mark Twain wrote a draft of an article, entitled "An Appeal from One That Is Persecuted," defending himself against the attacks of Josiah Gilbert Holland, who had recently published two editorials on the danger of "literary buffoons and drollerists" on the lyceum stage. Although Holland had not mentioned anyone by name, Clemens thought the description fit "like my own skin," and he proceeded to defend himself against Holland's charges that he and his ilk were bankrupting the lyceum system. In a withering manner, he attacked back:

> The real truth is that the doctor & his people go about the country massacreing [sic] lecture associations, & the buffoons follow after and resurrect them. It sounds strangely enough to hear Dr Holland, accusing us of killing the lecture business; it comes curiously enough from him—a man who has hung crape on more lyceum door-knobs than any other man in America—a man whose lecture route is a funeral procession, & his discourses an obituary under the low disguises of a moral "lecture." He moves through the lecture field a remorseless intellectual cholera; & wherever he goes—figuratively speaking—"death & hell follow after."[49]

Clemens was reacting to two articles from *Scribner's Monthly*, written by Holland but published anonymously in the editor's "Topics of the Times" column, from the February and July 1872 issues.

In the February article, titled "Triflers on the Platform," Holland railed against the imitators of Artemus Ward, the "literary buffoon" who had opened the lyceum stage to "triflers" and "mountebanks" and had done incalculable damage to the form. Clemens excerpted this portion of the article into his retort:

> The better class that once attended the lecture courses have been driven away in disgust, and among the remainder such a greed for inferior entertainments has been excited that lecture managers have become afraid to offer a first-class, old-fashioned course of lectures to the public patronage.

Accordingly, one will find upon nearly every list . . . the names of triflers and
buffoons who are a constant disgrace to the lecturing guild, and a constantly
degrading influence upon the public taste.[50]

Holland's solution was for the "triflers" to be banished by the lecture
bureaus and lyceum committees, which would elevate public taste and
bring back the audience who had fled due to the degrading effects of the
buffoons. In July, Holland wrote on "The Literary Bureaus Again," decrying
the negative effects of money and celebrity in the management of an institution that should serve the public good, one that was, indeed, "one of the
most powerful civilizing influences of our time." Again, Holland referred
to the negative impact of the "mountebank" and "trifler" in degrading the
public taste. Clemens seems to have reached the limit of his patience.[51]

Because Clemens's angry article went unpublished, or because Holland
has faded from literary and cultural history, the feud has received little
attention in scholarship on Mark Twain or Gilded Age literary culture.[52]
Holland's oblique attack on Mark Twain and other buffoons was not a
solitary incident but part of his consistent warnings about the decline
of popular and literary culture and the danger posed to the nation by
profane entertainment. As a popular lyceum lecturer, best-selling author,
and influential editor, Josiah Holland consistently complained about the
increasing irreverence of popular culture—from the lyceum to the novel
to the pulpit—and positioned himself as a representative of an uplifting,
Christian alternative to an increasingly debased mass culture. Holland's
critical view excluded Mark Twain from a vision of quality American Culture
that made a distinction between edifying leisure—based on instruction,
reverence, and Christian morality—and dangerous amusement, which
degraded the public taste. Sternly religious, reverent of tradition, and
skeptical of changes ranging from women's rights to public amusements,
Holland bridged the religious culture of antebellum New England with
the increasingly conservative culture of a postbellum cultural elite who
viewed Culture as a bulwark against the social changes of the Gilded Age.

Holland's jeremiads on the decline of the popular lecture and other
forms of culture were circulated primarily through his role as contributing editor of *Scribner's Monthly*, founded in 1870, one of the raft of New
York-based magazines that sought to compete with the *Atlantic Monthly*
for intellectual prestige and subscribers by publishing prominent American
authors—notably Edward Everett Hale, Henry James, Bret Harte, Harriet Prescott Spofford, Helen Hunt, Charles Dudley Warner, and George

Washington Cable. By paying contributors at a higher rate than the *Atlantic Monthly*, and lavishly illustrating its issues, *Scribner's* attracted authors who had published previously with the *Atlantic*, as well as a hefty share of the reading public, with a subscription list that began at approximately 40,000 and had surpassed 100,000 by 1880.[53]

A significant part of this popularity must be attributed to the editor, who contributed a monthly column called "Topics of the Times" that established the dominant critical ethos of the magazine.[54] Encompassing moral, religious, cultural, political, and literary questions, Holland's criticism constructed a relationship between cultural production and a religious vision of American culture. His position on "literary triflers" and their impact on American society form part of a larger viewpoint that both provided a counterweight to the *Atlantic's* culture of letters and offers a more complex picture of the larger literary culture of the Gilded Age, in which conceptions of the humorist circulated along with the concepts of morality, authorship, taste, culture, and literature.

Josiah Holland's contributions to the cultural conversation are crucial to recover, despite his previous consignment to literary oblivion due to his ponderous writings and heavily moralistic positions. It is his moral position, in fact, that makes him important for understanding Gilded Age literary cultures and Mark Twain's place within them. Placing (or re-placing) Josiah Holland into the literary history of postbellum American letters expands the question of Mark Twain's relationship to the literary culture of New England beyond the *Atlantic Monthly*, which too often stands in for all of the so-called "quality magazines" of the era. If the *Atlantic Monthly* is often stereotyped as the voice of a religious and social orthodoxy of New England, then that magazine's relative cultural and artistic liberalism is more clearly seen through the more conservative views of Holland and *Scribner's Monthly*.

Trained as a medical doctor, Holland moved to a literary career as editor and author in the late 1840s, becoming an editor and then part owner of the Springfield *Republican*, a paper that had established a reputation, to quote his biographer Harry Peckham, as "the most influential small-city newspaper in the United States."[55] Holland expanded the newspaper's influence by increasing coverage of literary, ethical, religious, and other cultural subjects. He left the newspaper in 1857, although he continued as a regular contributor until 1864. During these years, he published a wide variety of books—occasional and narrative poems, moral letters and essays, a biography of Lincoln, and several novels—and he began a successful

career as a lyceum lecturer. He continued to lecture and publish after being hired as the founding editor of *Scribner's* in 1870. His books had sold
just under 500,000 copies at his death in 1881, including the book-length
poem "Kathrina" (1868), which sold more than 90,000 copies, making it
the most successful poem of the era behind Longfellow's "Hiawatha."[56]

Holland was a nationally famous author, lecturer, and intellectual figure
whose death prompted the New York *Times* to eulogize him as "one of the
most celebrated writers . . . this country has produced." In summing up
his career shortly after his death, Edward Eggleston wrote that Holland
"has a worthy fame that is quite beyond the reach of literary oblivion."[57]
Nonetheless, Holland's clear relegation to that oblivion clarifies important
aspects about shifting forms of literary production and changing views
about the relationship of literature to American society. Holland's view of
culture consisted of sentimental and religious approaches to writing, both
literary and critical, that placed him in the tradition of Harriet Beecher
Stowe and others who relied on an appeal to Christian sentiment in order
to improve society. In the postwar period, this literary field was increasingly
being relegated to noncanonical status, devalued as an artistic approach
and gendered as feminine.

Josiah Holland spoke to, and to some degree for, a reading public envisioned as largely rural, ethically Christian, and dedicated to a vision of
American culture based on reverence to Christian morality and American
nationalism. Peckham defined Holland as "the Apostle of the Naïve" in
order to explain his greater popularity, which was perceived to be more
widespread in small towns than in larger cities. Holland rarely lectured in
larger cities, as he thought the competition of the opera and other public
entertainments competed for the best audiences.[58] In response to a friend's
suggestion that he travel to Europe to bring himself into contact with new
ideas, Holland responded that he was afraid to lose his main strength,
which he viewed as "his New England blood, and his familiarity with the
convictions and manners and faith of his own people. These he regarded
as his capital." Writing in *Century Magazine* shortly after Holland's death,
the poet John Greenleaf Whittier summarized his cultural status: "The
common heart of the people always kept time to his music. And his wide
influence was on the right side. Practical wisdom, broad Christian charity,
earnest patriotism, and crystal purity marked his writings."[59]

If Josiah Holland was the Apostle of the Naïve, then Mark Twain's heresy of trifling entertainment and literary dandyism made him the jester
of the urbane—making fun of the pieties Holland held in reverence and

questioning his theories of popular entertainment by delinking respectable pleasure and moral outlook. Despite a wide gulf between their works and their cultural views, the cultural positions of Holland and Mark Twain have intriguing overlaps—both came from modest beginnings and came to fame through work in newspapers, both were popular lecturers and authors whose works sold well, and both existed in an ambivalent position with the New England literary elite, some of whom questioned the value of their work in relation to the established literary models, although in vastly different terms. Even the first works of each author to gain notice contained intriguing surface similarities; each was originally published via a pseudonym in a newspaper, from which each circulated widely through exchanges. The main difference was genre: moralistic advice versus humor. Under the pseudonym of "Timothy Titcomb," Holland published a series of moral advice letters addressed to young people that helped establish his reputation as a genial moralist. One example, touching on the subject of humor, will suffice: "Genuine Wit in a man is almost always genial; wit in a woman, however genial it may be at first, almost always gets into personalities, sooner or later, which makes it very dangerous and very hateful. . . . I have known not a few women whose personal witticisms were enjoyed by the gossip-loving crowd around her, every man of whom would as soon think of marrying a tigress as the one he was flattering by the applause of his laugh."[60] Holland's discourses tended to be highly religious, highly gendered, and highly moralistic. And even though his writings circulated in similar ways to Samuel Clemens's writings as Mark Twain, the content and meaning of each was vastly different.

By attacking the triflers and buffoons, Holland was not attacking humor per se—of which he stated, "wit and humor are always good as condiments, but never as food"—but the professional humorist as a harbinger of the intrusion of a degrading mass culture into the realm of the lyceum. A well-established lecturer, Holland viewed the lyceum as an agent of "the elevation and purification of the public taste," especially taste in literary matters for the young. He viewed the "professional jesters" who had gained a place on the lyceum platform as low drollerists no different from "negro minstrels," except that the minstrels did not claim to be "respectable."[61] Whereas Howells was arguing for Mark Twain's respectable position in a hierarchy of humor, Holland placed him squarely at the bottom, among the minstrels.

Writing on "The Popular Lecture" in the *Atlantic Monthly* in 1865, Holland had argued that the lecture represented a central, yet unappreciated,

institution in shaping the popular taste in America. Working within the
Atlantic's ethos of social uplift, the article highlighted the moral dimensions of the lecture, which aimed to provide men with ideas on how to
understand life. The lecturer "takes the facts with which the popular
life has come into contact and association, and draws from them their
nutritive and motive power, and points out their relations to individual
and universal good, and organizes around them the popular thought."[62]
And this popular thought, Holland argued, has been organized around
a number of common goods inspired by the lecturer: a generous tolera-
tion of men and ideas, the education of public tastes, the improvements
of sermons by example, and the promotion of "universal liberty." By
educating the public taste, the lecture would destroy "the desire for all
amusements of a lower grade," thus uplifting the entire community to
wholesome endeavors and the patronage of uplifting speakers.[63] But he
noted that the lyceum had been sullied by the presence of "triflers" on the
platform, stating that humorous lecturers had "no better motive and no
higher mission than the stage-clown and the negro-minstrel." Holland's
attempts at correcting the institution were thus well developed before
Mark Twain had ever lectured.

The continued popularity of humorous lecturers and their inclusion
on the lists of lyceum programs clearly galled Holland, and the elevation
of Mark Twain to the foremost ranks of these performers made him Holland's clearest target, especially after the death of Artemus Ward. From
his new perch at *Scribner's,* Holland was able to continue his crusade in
favor of the uplifting lecture and against humorous triflers. For instance,
in an essay called "Lecture-Brokers and Lecture-Breakers" (March 1871),
Holland traced the financial decline of the lyceum to the formation of
lecture bureaus, which increased prices and foisted untested or otherwise
poor speakers onto lyceum societies. Not surprisingly, this includes certain
"literary jesters and mountebanks," whose popularity took away from
men of serious purpose who had "shaped opinion, developed sentiment,
agitated great public questions, denounced wrongs, taught, exhorted,
stirred the people." The current lyceum system was degrading into mere
entertainment that failed to minister to "manly and womanly want." The
articles that incensed Clemens appeared in 1872, followed by a piece
called "Star-Lecturing" in May 1874, again decrying the influence of the
lecture bureaus in promoting star performers who bankrupt lyceums by
cheapening them to mere entertainment and driving off quality speakers
and quality audiences. Throughout these articles, Holland consistently

defended the moral purpose he saw at the center of the lecture course, which he described as "one of the most powerful civilizing influences of our time," from the intrusions of mass culture and the specter of mere entertainment.[64] The changing face of the lyceum course clearly disturbed Holland, as he was losing in popularity to other lecturers. Figure 4.3 shows "The Lyceum Committeeman's Dream," an illustration from 1873 of prominent lecturers, including Mark Twain as a jester and including three humorous lecturers—Thomas Nast, Petroleum Nasby, and Josh Billings. Holland is nowhere to be found.

In his own defense, Mark Twain addressed the financial boon that his own performances had provided for lyceum societies that had been damaged by Holland's failure to draw an audience. Interestingly, in three separate places in his manuscript, Clemens crossed out the first-person "I" and replaced it with "one or two 'literary buffoons'" when giving examples of how he had earned large amounts of money for a lyceum by drawing an audience "who were willing to have their taste 'degraded' but did not need any threadbare 'instruction.'" He mocked Holland's insistence on "instruction" by pointing out that in the "old ignorant times" people only had crops and weather to talk about and could use "a little tedious miscellaneous 'instruction.'" But he added that in the days when newspapers and libraries provide a surfeit of such instruction (Mark Twain uses the phrase "cram everybody to suffocation"), what people look for in the lyceum is entertainment: "[T]he thing their overburdened heads pine for is wholesome relief in the shape of amusement, entertainment, care-banishing laughter—not a further stuffing at the hands of a blessed perambulating sack of chloroform." Following this brief flare of temper, Clemens seems to have dropped Holland out of his mind, apart from a brief correspondence between the two, but Holland's continued criticism in *Scribner's* at times targeted Mark Twain, as well as William Dean Howells.[65]

Samuel Clemens's brief burst of antagonism toward this "perambulating sack of chloroform" highlights his anxiety over the humorist's role in American culture and of the possibility of his being thought a mere buffoon. Holland's antagonism toward Mark Twain, on the other hand, represents one facet of a long-term attempt to shape American culture through literary work, one that cannot be dismissed because of his questionable artistic worth or ponderous moral sentiment. The popularity of Holland's views, and their widespread circulation, makes his Christian-critical perspective of crucial importance for understanding the literary and cultural world of the Gilded Age. As the contested field of literary culture is expanded to

FIGURE 4.3: The Lyceum Committeeman's Dream—Some Popular Lecturers in Costume from *Harper's Weekly*, November 15, 1873. **Collection of the Author**

include Josiah Holland's criticism, Mark Twain's critical reputation takes on new religious, literary, and popular dynamics.

Holland continued to use his editorial column at *Scribner's*, and two books of collected essays, to argue for his vision of American culture and the role of arts and literature in its development. His literary criticism was less about literature as a subject than about literary activities, including the lyceum, reading circles, and reading in general, as a response to what he perceived as a changing reading public and the threats to the "popular taste" by increasingly debased forms of entertainment. Holland never reviewed single books, and he only occasionally discussed individual authors. Instead, he favored broad pronouncements on broad subjects.

Holland's critical writings in *Scribner's*—on topics ranging from religion to art to literature to the popular lecture—point to the key idea that he promoted: the centrality of a moral purpose of artistic endeavors as a reflection of a Christian view of American culture. Holland's essay, "The Faults of Culture" (January 1872), chastised those who pursue culture for its own sake, rather than for the sake of Christian benevolence. "A culture which does not serve God," he wrote, "by direct purpose, and with loving and reverent devotion, is the purest type of practical infidelity." Literature, in this critical view, played the role of "artistic ministry": "literature has no uses save it ministers to the comfort, the pure pleasure, the strength, the elevation and the spiritual culture of the race" ("Literary Hindrances," March 1874). Holland's views framed American culture as moving teleologically toward a more perfect social system, one in which literary activities played a small but important role in shaping a Christian culture. The main reward of literary labor, then, was spiritual and manifested itself in a widespread social regard that gathers around those whom the public considered to be good in both literary output and in character. In surveying Holland's comments on literary figures, Peckham finds that Holland judged literary figures based on a combination of their popular appeal, moral quality, and personal character. Not surprisingly, Holland praised Stowe, Longfellow, and Whittier among American authors, while disapproving of the works and character of Poe, Whitman, and Thoreau.[66]

The relationship between criticism, religious taste, and literary popularity is central to understanding Holland's view of Mark Twain. The competent critic, he wrote in "The Indecencies of Criticism" (April 1872), plays an important role—"to assist the public in arriving at a just judgment of the various productions of literature and art, and the enlightenment and correction of their producers." The vast majority of critics, he wrote, do none of this and had therefore lost the ability to influence the public or accurately judge a book. He humorously (although it is hard to tell if the humor is intentional) catalogs the types of "indecent critics" by their faults, including the man of theory, who "assumes to be a sort of inspector-general of literary and artistic wares, and sorts them, as they come along, by their defects." As with Mark Twain and the "literary trifler" of the lecture hall, it is not hard to see here a reference to Howells and his position as editor at the *Atlantic Monthly*. Holland may also have had Howells in mind when criticizing an unnamed critic who seemed to hold that no poem could be good that sprang from moral, rather than artistic, aims. Holland argued that such a heretic criticism would hold that "the poetic muse is never to be either teacher or preacher; and a poem with a moral is a work of art with that one fatal blot, or taint, or weakness, or unseemly superfluity which destroys its genuineness" ("A Heresy of Art," April 1872). Whereas Howells wished for the author to explore morality through the portrayal of realistic characters, Holland subsumed artistic considerations to the moral aim of all artistic and cultural production.

For Holland, most criticism reflected the critic, not the true value of the book under consideration. In a January 1873 article, "Criticism as a Fine Art," Holland excoriated almost all literary criticism, which he saw as accomplishing nothing more than revealing the prejudices and views of the men who produced it. Critics, he argued, were powerless to determine public opinion about the value of books, which was determined elsewhere: "Though a thousand critics determine that a book ought not to live, if it is a real book it lives, without the slightest reference to their opinions and pro-tests." Of course, Holland was not immune to his own theory that criticism largely functions to reveal the man behind the criticism. Throughout his writings on literary subjects, Holland repeatedly complained of the critics who savaged a writer and his works, despite the fact that the public buys the books and finds value in them. In "Conscience and Courtesy in Criticism," for example, Holland bemoaned the animus of literary critics from which there is no escape or defense for writers: "they have published a book, in which they have incorporated the results of a life of labor and thought and suffering, with the hope of doing good, and of adding something to the literary wealth of their country; and they have in so doing committed a sin which places them at the mercy of every man who holds a periodical press at his command."[67] It is not hard here to see the man behind the critic who had been stung by the harsh criticisms of the press despite the popularity of his work.

And, indeed, Holland's work was rather consistently critically derided. Holland's biographer notes that Longfellow, Lowell, Whitman, Aldrich, Howells, and Harte all had negative things to say about Holland's writing.[68] Before coming to the *Atlantic*, Howells wrote an article "Concerning Timothy Titcomb," in which he noted that the popularity of Holland proved that reputation, unlike butter or eggs, were still "to be had cheap among us."[69] Reviewing the book-length poem, *Kathrina*, in the *Atlantic*, Howells professed to hold "reverence" for the high purpose Holland had for his writing. Howells then argued that the religious motive took a writer of high skill in order to make the characters of a parable "true to life," but that Holland fails to make his characters real. Holland's book would "doubtless find readers enough to agree with him, if he should not care to accept our estimate of his whole poem. Nevertheless, we must confess that it appears to us puerile in conception, destitute of due motive, and crude and inartistic in treatment." Howells's critiques of Holland's poem reflected his critical promotion of realistic writing, even in the form of a professedly didactic poem. Howells's early writings picture a young author and editor working through ideas about the relationship between realistic art and cultural production, whereas Holland's writings portrayed a coherent view of a moral universe where good literature ministered to the needs of its readers and was rewarded by reverence for the author and his or her popular, if not critical, standing in the popular imagination.[70]

Holland's own popularity bore out his theory that moral entertainment would find favor with the public: his magazine increased its circulation year by year, he remained popular on the lyceum circuit, and his works sold well throughout the era.

The distinction between moral instruction and edification, on one side, and degrading amusement and entertainment, on the other, was a central question when critics and editors created their versions of American culture and the role of the humorist within popular culture. In "The Legitimate Novel" (August 1880), Holland again took up the question of morality and the criticism of the novel, complaining of the critics who held that the only artistic novel was focused on society, rather than looking at the larger point of fiction—which he argued was both to amuse and to instruct. Holland's view of literature's ministerial function pertains to directly moral and religious works, as well as to the more general good of recreation. In an earlier piece, he wrote that readers, not critics, determined the value of fiction: "Life is humdrum, or fatiguing, and they come to the novel only for forgetfulness, or the pleasant excitement that a contemplation of new

scenes and new characters affords. To such as these, a good novel is a ben-
ediction, for it relieves them of their burdens, clothes the commonplace
with romance, and gives new meaning to human action and human life
("The Interest of Fiction," December 1876)."

The common reader, then, looked to literature not as an art form to be
perfected, the way Howells looked at it (although that name goes unspo-
ken), but for "fun." But he makes the further point that fun, amusement,
and joy are derived from works that eschew, or punish, vulgarity, vice,
crime, and scandal as the source of those pleasures.[71]

But Mark Twain's continued and growing popularity would have certainly not fit into this model of Christian popular culture, and Holland's writings
coalesced around a moral view of a culture that forcibly excluded Mark
Twain and other buffoons from the realm of respectable amusement. In his
essays, Holland tended to link the word "trifler" with the words "dilettanti"
and "dandy," as opposed to authors and critics who are "earnest" and who
demonstrate "virility" and "reverence." While he gives many examples of
earnest and virile authors, he largely eschewed referring to the triflers by
name, apart from a lengthy critique of Whitman and a brusque dismissal
of Poe and Thoreau ("Literary Virility," March 1876).[72] But in "Dandyism"
(September 1880), Holland extended his critique to Artemus Ward and
Mark Twain through the distinction between earnestness and "literary
dandies"—who focus on the surface, on the manner of saying something
rather than the matter, and who "perform literary gymnastics in order to
attract attention." Holland went on to speak of the one "eminent literary
dandy" in American literary history, presumably Artemus Ward. Holland
writes that instead of teaching or inspiring, this dandy was "content to
play with his pen, and seek for their applause," and, thus:

> People read his clever verses and clapped their hands, but those verses did
> not voice any man's or woman's aspirations, or sooth any man's or woman's
> sorrows. They helped nobody. They were not the earnest outpourings of a
> nature consecrated either to God or song, and the response that they met
> in the public heart was not one of grateful appropriation, though that heart
> was not slow to offer the incense of its admiration to the clever and graceful,
> even if supremely selfish, artist.

He brings this to the reader's attention, he continued, because figures
still living and writing are following the spirit of this work by producing literature that sought attention rather than to elevate and purify the culture.

For Holland, Mark Twain and his ilk were firmly on one side of a divide between good and bad forms of popular culture. The buffoon eroded public sentiment and "no thoughtful or sensible man can devote a whole evening to the poorest kind of nonsense without losing a little of his self-respect, and feeling that he has spent his money for that which does not satisfy." The trifler, in aiming only to elicit laughter, was degraded and made "unfit to be a teacher of anything."[73] Holland's persecution of triflers over the course of the 1870s demonstrates that Mark Twain's literary reputation was not settled through Howells's approval nor was Mark Twain fully accepted within the more general realm of "quality magazine." *Scribner's* imagined American culture and literature differently than the *Atlantic Monthly*. Mark Twain's exclusion from Holland's canon would have affected the ways in which readers perceived the value of the humorist as an author and a performer—pointing to important schisms in audience reception between rural and urban, by region, and by philosophical or cultural outlook.

THE HUMORIST ABROAD IN THE LAND

In order to defend Mark Twain from those who would, like Holland, group him with the mere trifling jester, William Dean Howells needed to convince his readers to adopt a critical view that linked Mark Twain to the quality humorist and severed the ties from the newspaper humorists who circulated in the larger mass culture. In his review of *Roughing It*, from the June 1872 *Atlantic*, Howells framed Mark Twain's humor positively, if not fully defending its literary quality, saying that as it is "the work of a human being, it is not unbrokenly nor infallibly funny; nor is it to be always praised for all the literary virtues; but it is singularly entertaining, and its humor is always amiable, manly, and generous."[74] These three adjectives were, for Howells, indicators of quality, especially in terms of humor. Clemens, of course, was not so sure, and Howells's review inspired his comment on the mixed paternity of his humorous child discussed earlier in this chapter. In the context of his then-red-hot antipathy toward Holland, as well as the anxiety exhibited through his writings for the *Galaxy* and performed in his detestable lyceum campaign, Clemens's anxiety over his role as a humorist takes on added resonance.

Clemens's burst of antagonism toward Holland in July of 1872 was part of a challenging personal period. His father-in-law Jervis Langdon had died in August 1870, followed by the premature birth of his first child, Langdon

Clemens, in November. Both mother and child were sick for much of the following year. After having quit both the Buffalo *Express* and the *Galaxy*, the Clemens family moved to Hartford in the summer of 1871. Later in the year, he had left his family, including a pregnant Livy, for the detestable lecture tour. In March 1872, the couple's first daughter, called Susy, was born, but on June 2, Langdon, the only son Samuel Clemens would ever have, died of diphtheria. The reaction of Mark Twain to the reviews of *Roughing It* by Howells and Louise Moulton, in which he references his books as children, takes on a level of pathos considering their relation to his personal life. But to the public, Mark Twain continued to be the successful humorist, most recently the author of *Roughing It*.[75]

For Mark Twain, the humorist and aspiring man of letters, the move to Hartford represented a new professional role. Having given up editing and retired for the foreseeable future from lecturing, Mark Twain was moving away from the model of professional humorist who relied on widespread circulation and constant work to make a living. In its place, Clemens settled into a select community of the genteel elite that included two authors who managed largely to earn a living from their works—Harriet Beecher Stowe and Charles Dudley Warner. As the center of subscription publishing, Hartford allowed Clemens more control over his publishing concerns, much to the consternation of Elisha Bliss.

The move to Nook Farm involved him in an intense social and intellectual community given over to constant visiting, intellectual conversation, and a stream of famous and nonfamous visitors. The Clemenses began construction on their expensive and stately, if eccentric, house in 1871, which became a topic of newspaper gossip as columns discussed its grand design and equally grand cost. Justin Kaplan notes the importance of Nook Farm's views of political and social issuing, arguing that "he shared the group's faith in a dynamic aristocracy, their high responsibility, their earnest idealism, and their intellectual dedication."[76] He was invited to join the Monday Evening Club, an elite group of men that included the governor, who discussed the issues of the day. It may be better to say that "Samuel Clemens" participated in this club by reading papers on organized labor, universal suffrage, and the press. But it was under the name "Mark Twain" that he published a letter to the editor in the New York *Tribune* in 1873 critiquing the jury system in relation to a recent murder case, writing, "The humorist who invented trial by jury played a colossal, practical joke upon the world."[77] This piece of satire dripped with sarcasm at the logic of those who defended the temperance and gentility of a man convicted of drunkenly beating a man to death. The following day a letter condemned the propriety of Mark Twain injecting satire into a sad and serious situation. The writer's logic is worth quoting:

> *We all of us enjoy a fair measure of good humor, and caricature, and we bless the fates for a goodly quota of satirical writers, whose calling it is to impart a healthful degree of zest and good feeling to an otherwise dull and staid existence. We, moreover, are disposed to attach to this class a respectful amount of consideration as successful and deserving members of society. But I venture to assert that the thinking community are not prepared to give precedence to the opinions, savoring of satire, of this class—those who, with actors and clowns, make it a business to cater to our amusement in jest and burlesque—when a subject like the Foster case is under discussion, with all its grave issues and painful bearings.*[78]

The author argues that Mark Twain's "ghastly flippancy" was out of place in such serious discussions, even while allowing that Mark Twain and other clowns and actors might have a deserving place in society. Satire, though, is consigned to the goal of "zest" and "good feeling" rather than serious laughter and humorous critique. One further letter to the *Tribune* addressed the question of satire by praising Mark Twain as "the very proper person to make himself heard at this juncture." The point of satire, this writer held, was to point out incongruity, which is exactly what Mark Twain had done.[79] The role of the humorist in American culture was far from settled.

Mark Twain's next book, *The Gilded Age*, which he would write in 1873 with his neighbor and fellow humorist, Charles Dudley Warner, would take a satirical eye toward large swaths of American culture—political corruption, rampant speculation, and the jury system, among other things. First, Clemens left Hartford for England in August 1872, partially to secure copyright on his books and partly to gather material for a new travel book. During visits to England in 1872 and 1873, Mark Twain became a central figure in British criticism of American letters, which had viewed "American Humour" as the primary fruit of a developing national literature of America. Mark Twain was celebrated in England as the next in a line of "Great American Humorists" that included both Lowell and the departed Artemus Ward, who had gained a higher reputation in England than in

America. The British reception of Mark Twain, although mixed critically, helped solidify his position in America, where critics and readers looked to England for approval of their writers.

CHAPTER FIVE

Transatlantic Twain

The Lion in London and Other
"Great American Humorists"

Shortly after his dismal lyceum campaign and move to Hartford, Mark Twain sailed for England—staying from August to November 1872 and returning with his wife the next year for a stay of almost six months, capped by a successful stint lecturing on the platform in London. The visit was ostensibly undertaken to gather material for a new travel book and to secure copyright on his works, which in the absence of international copyright laws, had circulated freely in England without any monetary gain for Clemens. In coming to England, Mark Twain surely felt some trepidation at what his reception would be. His *Saturday Review* hoax in the *Galaxy* displayed an anxiety that British critics might be humorless, even if it did also contain a certain irreverence toward British criticism as a standard.

Recounting his arrival in England in his autobiography, Mark Twain told a story that surely resonates on a mythical level in conveying his anxiety at how he would be read by the English. After spending an hour of "delight, rapture, ecstasy" viewing the English countryside from his seat on the train from Liverpool to London, he was distracted by a man seemingly engrossed in a book. Upon closer inspection, he discovered that the man was reading *The Innocents Abroad*, and to Mark Twain's dismay, the man had not smiled once. He continued in his reminiscence: "I could not take my eyes from the reader and his book. I tried to get a sort of comfort out of the fact that he was evidently deeply interested in the book and manifestly never skipped a line, but the comfort was only moderate and was quite unsatisfying. I hoped he would smile once—only just once—and I kept on hoping and hoping, but it never happened."[1] As the man finished the book, Mark Twain felt the relief "a condemned man must feel who is pardoned upon the scaffold with the noose hanging over him"—that is, until the man pulled out the second volume of the book and continued to read, without a smile ever crossing his face—or the face of Mark Twain, his eager watcher. The reminiscence of his "bad beginning" in England, real or apocryphal, displays a distinct concern over how he and his humor would be interpreted by the English.

Samuel Clemens, as the creator and promoter of his literary identity, was surely aware that literary success in England would improve "Mark Twain's" position in America, where British criticism of American letters, and "American humour," helped determine critical standards. To his evident surprise and delight, he experienced an unprecedented level of literary celebrity in London. He wrote to Livy of his shock at being the unexpected toast of a banquet honoring the new lord mayor of London:

> In accordance with ancient custom, a man got up & called the names of all that immense mass of guests, beginning with the new Sheriff (a tremendous office in London) & called a horde of great names, one after another, which were received in respectful silence—but when he came to my name along with the rest, there was such a storm of applause as you never heard. The applause continued, & they could not go on with the list. I was never so taken aback in my in life—never stricken so speechless—for it was totally unlocked-for [sic] on my part. I thought I was the humblest in that great titled assemblage—& behold, mine was the only name in the long list that called forth this splendid compliment.[2]

Mark Twain continued: "Imagine my situation, before that great audience, without a single word of preparation—for I had expected nothing of this kind—I did not know I was a lion." Greeted as a celebrity and feted by the literary and social elite of London, Mark Twain took his English success as a gratifying tribute, one quite different than the ambivalent cultural position he had experienced in America.

His successes in London soon dispelled this notion, proving instead that the English accepted the humorist as an American literary celebrity. But the ways in which the English "read" Mark Twain—as an American humorist—illustrate important distinctions between American and British cultures of letters central to understanding Mark Twain and his connection to his times.[3]

Mark Twain's English reception reflected the relatively higher social position of popular humorists in England, where humorists like Tom Hood and Charles Lamb, as well as humorous publications such as *Punch* and *Fun*, were well respected and widely circulated. Humor in England was hierarchical as in the United States, just differently delineated and valued. While Mark Twain enjoyed his reception as a celebrity by literary London, his literary reputation in England did not mean the same things that a similar reception in Boston would have meant. As chapter 1 discussed, English letters, as a broad but distinct culture of letters, held *humour*, and the concept of *American Humour*, in a different relation to the larger ideas of *Literature* and *American Literature* than American readers, authors, and critics.

Mark Twain entered into this critical discussion after the main contours of a critical hierarchy of American humorists were largely set. As American humor grew in popularity during the 1860s and 1870s, British critics responded to new productions of American humor with critical evaluations—quite often in articles entitled "American Humour"—of the meanings and major figures of that humor while making hierarchical distinctions between quality humor, popular humor, and low humor. In this critical milieu, James Russell Lowell was generally placed at the top of the hierarchy of American national humor, while figures such as Irving, Hawthorne, Stowe, and Holmes were praised for aspects of their humor but not viewed as distinctly American. In the 1860s, Artemus Ward became a commercial favorite, forcing critics to account for the advent of the professional humorist into England. Artemus Ward's reputation improved after his visit to, and subsequent death in, England, when some placed him as a unique genius while others judged him the proprietor of an entertaining humor below the level of literary quality.

Following Charles Farrar Browne's death in 1867, a number of "Great American Humorists" were imported to fill the popular British taste for American humor, and critics again reevaluated the hierarchy of American humor to include Bret Harte, Charles Leland, Josh Billings, and Mark Twain. Mark Twain was largely classed among the popular humorists who followed Artemus Ward into the robust British market for American humor, but he was largely viewed as not having attained the level of Lowell nor, indeed, the level of Bret Harte or Artemus Ward himself. For his part, Mark Twain seems to have not known or to have cared little for such critical distinctions, instead enjoying the critical status his successes in England provided him.

Mark Twain's popularity in England led to his wider circulation in continental Europe and beyond. While Mark Twain was lionized in England, his introduction to French letters through a critical appraisal and translation of "The Jumping Frog" in 1872 was less flattering and, I argue, less important—if amusing. Clemens kept a scrapbook of the reactions to his lectures in England in 1873 and crowed to Livy about his reception by the English elite. Faced with French criticism of his humor, Mark Twain responded by making fun of French ideas of civilization through his retranslation of "La Grenouille Sauteuse du Comté de Calaveras" back into the "civilized" language of English. This brief encounter with French criticism illustrates the different weight he put into British views than into French opinions. His success socially in England helped improve his literary standing, but such relationships were never evenly dialectical with his critical reputation because they took place within a larger context of Anglo-American literary relations in which national meanings of literature circulated differently and in which humor had different meanings.

While Mark Twain's visits to London certainly improved his literary status, Mark Twain as a subject remained ambiguously placed in the British critical discussion of the development of an American national literature. The mass circulation of American humor, both in print and in performance, continually caused British critics to reevaluate the meanings of American humor, especially after the rise of Artemus Ward and Mark Twain as celebrity humorists—what one critic jokingly referred to as a string of "Great American Humourists" imported for an insatiable British public. Critics still relied on a hierarchy of humor to evaluate American humor, but the distinction between quality humor and the merely popular was increasingly used as a way to dismiss the popular humorist, although the contours of the argument—who and what constituted a "quality" humor—were increasingly contested. Mark Twain's critical reputation was more ambivalently positioned in England than his popular reception and celebrity status suggest and, into the mid-1870s, British critics disagreed on whether Mark Twain would contribute to an American canon or whether he would be (or actively should be) consigned to literary irrelevance.

TRANSATLANTIC FROGS: MARK TWAIN AND OTHER AMERICAN EXPORTS

As was often the case, Artemus Ward set the stage for new developments in Mark Twain's career. In this case, Artemus Ward's reception as a celebrated American humorist in England expanded the demand for, and appreciation of, popular American humor. His untimely death both cemented a long-term English fondness for the Yankee Showman and left a void in the British market. Mark Twain did much to fill the market demand for a

popular humorist of the droll, exaggerative school, although he was sometimes compared unfavorably to Artemus Ward. As for the possibility of an
American humorist rising to the level of Lowell, as a truly national fruit
of the soil, Mark Twain was taken less seriously by critics. As in America,
this role was generally assigned to Bret Harte.

Artemus Ward rose to the position of preeminent American humorist
in England, largely through his presence in the country from June 1866
until his death from consumption in May 1867. British newspapers had
published his works starting as early as 1860, with his piece "Artemus Ward
and the Prince of Wales," and had published excerpts and other squibs
consistently through the 1860s.[4] Artemus Ward followed a general pattern
of the humorist growing as a celebrity, which was similar in England and in
America: pieces by the humorist started to appear in papers, either whole
works under their own heading or squibs in a column named something
like "Variety," "Scraps," or simply "Miscellaneous"—often to be picked up
and reprinted by two or three other newspapers and sometimes reprinted
over the course of several years. Eventually, phrases or sayings were quoted
in stories on other topics, as when a newspaper states "to use the phrase
of Artemus Ward" in an otherwise unrelated story. Finally, Artemus Ward
became the subject of general gossip, as when a report of an illness was
reported as news in 1864. With enough interest, publishers would then
publish books—either direct copies of American books or pirated com-
pilations—usually without permission or payment. By 1865, an English
version of *Artemus Ward: His Book* was the featured work in a series of
"Yankee Fun and Frolic Books" alongside Major Jack Downing, Petroleum
Nasby, *The Biglow Papers*, *The Autocrat of the Breakfast Table*, John Phoenix,
and J. Godfrey Saxe, and reviewed in various British papers.[5]

Artemus Ward was a new type of American humorist—one who performed his status both on stage and through his personal friendships. His
works and reputation had widely circulated in England before his arrival
in 1866. Reading Artemus Ward's writings, critics noted that "the drollery
would be better spoken than written," and his physical presence seems
to have shifted his reputation in England, where his embodiment as the
American humorist led to a vastly increased popular standing and almost
immediate literary celebrity—the original lion of London. Charles Farrar
Browne was quickly made a member of the Savage Club, a prestigious
literary and social club, and feted at dinners, receptions, and other social
occasions. By August of that year, he was publishing in the prestigious
British comedic periodical *Punch*, which had sought out his services and

published eight letters under the title "Artemus Ward in London," abandoning its tradition of pseudonymous publication.[6] (See Figure 5.1 for an illustration of his arrival.)

Artemus Ward brought his character of the Yankee Showman to the stage in November 1866 at London's Egyptian Hall. *Punch* advertised the show with a puff piece, and reviews were almost uniformly positive. The London *Spectator* wrote a lengthy review that focused on how the "personal influence" of Artemus Ward's performance combined incongruity and exaggeration with a deadpan delivery that was "as a true humorist should be, even better than his books." The American expatriate, and friend to both Browne and Clemens, Moncure Conway later recalled the effect of Artemus Ward's performances: "The refined, delicate, intellectual countenance, the sweet, grave mouth, from which one might have expected philosophical lectures, retained their seriousness while listeners were convulsed with laughter. There was something magical about it. Every sentence was a surprise. He played on his audience as Liszt did on a piano—most easily when most effectively."[7] Artemus Ward's performances in England continued for almost seven weeks, when he was forced to cancel his performances due to ill health. He died in England on March 6, 1867, the same day Mark Twain premiered as a lecturer in New York City. At the age of 32, Charles Farrar Browne—"Artemus Ward"—was only a year and a half older than Samuel Clemens.

Mark Twain largely followed the same path to widespread English celebrity as Artemus Ward—starting with brief notices in periodicals followed by the increased reprinting of short pieces, then books and critical attention, followed by a triumphant visit to London, although Clemens avoided the final step of Browne's model of lasting British fame. Mark Twain gained notice in the British press in 1867 with a short squib, probably taken from an American newspaper exchange: "Mark Twain, lecturing on the Sandwich Islands, offered to show how the cannibals eat their food if some lady would hand him a baby. The lecture was not illustrated." This squib was published at least fourteen times between 1867 and 1895 in British newspapers. Mark Twain's periodical presence increased with various squibs, extracts from his travel writings or speeches, and, starting in 1869, periodical pieces from his Buffalo *Express* and *Galaxy* writings. At this time, Mark Twain first appeared as an author in an English periodical, *The Broadway*, with "Cannibalism in the Cars."[8]

As in America, Mark Twain was introduced to a widespread English audience through the popularity of the jumping frog story, which was

Artemus Ward arrives in London—Introduces himself to Mr.
Punch—*Frontispiece.*

FIGURE 5.1: Artemus Ward arrives in London—Introduces himself
to Mr. Punch. Frontispiece of *Artemus Ward in London* (London:
G.W. Carleton & Co., 1867). **Collection of the Author**

published in a pirated edition of his first book of sketches (1867), which
was reviewed in the October 19, 1867, issue of *Fun* as "one of the funniest
books we have met with for a long time. . . . There are no misspellings, no

contortions of words in Mark Swain [sic]; his fun is entirely dependent upon the inherent humour in his writings. And although many jokers have sent us *brochures* like the present from the other side of the Atlantic, we have had no book fuller of more genuine and genial fun." Whereas the American edition of the Jumping Frog book had fizzled, selling roughly 4,000 copies, the English edition was popular enough that another British publisher released an edition that issued 16,000 copies between 1870 and 1873. Increasing demand for American humor in general, and Mark Twain in particular, led to at least two English publishing houses competing in the early 1870s to issue Mark Twain's works, most often in pirated editions, in order to capitalize on his growing popularity.[9]

Published in two volumes by John Camden Hotten in 1870, *The Innocents Abroad* further promoted Mark Twain's fame through an increased circulation of his writings and his reputation. Between 1870 and 1873, Hotten issued 48,000 copies of the first volume and 44,700 copies of the second. The volumes elicited two major critical reactions. When the reviewer took the book as mainly a humorous travel account, and Mark Twain as a "writer of light and entertaining literature," then the reviews followed *The Examiner* of London in praising the "freshness" and "racy humour" of the two volumes. In reviewing the second volume, the same paper discussed the national dimension of Mark Twain's writing: "The work abounds in fun and satire of the true American sort. No Englishman could have written it; perhaps no Englishman can hardly appreciate it. It is not always easy to tell when the author is laughing and when he is serious. Every page of it, however, is very amusing."[10] So long as reviewers approached Mark Twain as a humorist, and the book as amusing, then the reviews were generally favorable, although reviews sometimes betrayed a fear that the English would miss the full extent of American joking.

On the other hand, reviews in two major weekly journals conflated the humorist with his narrative persona, creating confusion about the genre and meaning of the book. The *Athenaeum*, one of the main literary magazines of the era, was confused by the book's introduction. Written by Artemus Ward's former lecture agent E. P. Hingston, the introduction portrayed Mark Twain as simply an editor from Nevada traveling in Europe, which caused the reviewer to read exaggerations as mistakes and deadpan as ignorance. The reviewer remained confused as to whether or not the narrator was "such a fool as he tried to look." The review in the *Saturday Review* of London, which was the article that started the chain of events leading to Mark Twain's put-on review in the *Galaxy*, takes Mark Twain less seriously than the *Athenaeum* review but still evinces confusion as to Mark Twain's objects of satire. While claiming to guard against "the imputation of taking a professional jester seriously," the reviewer admits to confusion on how to read the "dry joke" of the American: "We are sometimes left in doubt whether he is speaking in all sincerity or whether he is having a sly laugh at himself and his readers. To do him justice, however, we must observe that he has a strong tinge of the peculiar National humor; and though not equal to the best performers on the same instrument, manages to be an amusing representative of his class."[11] The review positioned Mark Twain as indistinguishable from the narrative voice—a vulgar traveler, whose "fun, if not very refined, is often tolerable in its way." Both of these reviews misread the humor by taking the author as narrator, thus missing the satire of American travelers and taking offense at the irreverence toward European high culture—for instance, each review mentions an incident where the Americans are unimpressed by the quality of Columbus's handwriting and the impertinence of continually asking of Michael Angelo: "Is he dead?"

The failure of these reviews to grasp the irony of Mark Twain's narrative position points to several crucial areas of Mark Twain's shifting role in English criticism. First, the idea of reading Mark Twain "seriously," apart from the exact details of the case, inspired him to write his own hoax British review, as discussed in the previous chapter. The reverberations of this put-on spread through several American newspapers but seemed to have made no waves in England.[12] Second, the reviews show that not all English readers understood, or appreciated, Mark Twain's form of American humor, whether it be too deadpan or too racy for quality British readers. The reviews generally split between mass-circulation newspapers and literary periodicals aimed at a higher class of readers. The split between popular and "quality," as a way to distinguish between hierarchical levels, often operated both in American and English letters to make distinctions in reading, most often on class lines. Finally, all the reviews of Mark Twain at this stage show that his critical position was far from settled. The reviews describe him as a journalist in San Francisco, the editor of a Nevada paper, or "a California humorist after the fashion of Artemus Ward," little known outside of the story of the Jumping Frog.[13] Clearly, English critics were not yet decided on what Mark Twain was, exactly where he was from, or how he fit into their understanding of American letters.

In the 1870s, Mark Twain's writings were more widely published in book form in England than in America, largely due to the absence of international copyright laws. In 1870, Hotten published four of Mark Twain's

"Memoranda" pieces in *The Piccadilly Annual of Entertaining Literature* along with pieces by Longfellow, Lowell, Harte, Orpheus C. Kerr, Dickens, Thackeray, and an assortment of others. Routledge published *Mark Twain's (Burlesque) Autobiography and First Romance*, possibly in cooperation with Clemens, in 1871.[14] Quick to measure public sentiment and publish works that would sell, Hotten published two collections of Mark Twain's sketches in 1871—entitled *Eye-Openers* and *Screamers*—which collected fifty-nine sketches attributed to Mark Twain, largely from the *Galaxy*, but with five pieces falsely attributed to him. Hotten issued 21,000 copies of *Eye-Openers* and 19,000 copies of *Screamers* in 1871 and 1872, along with 5,000 copies of the burlesque autobiography and 17,000 copies of the ponderously titled *Practical Jokes with Artemus Ward, including the Story of the Man Who Fought Cats*, attributed to "Mark Twain and Other Humourists" (1872). A collected edition, *The Choice Humorous Works of Mark Twain*, was published in 1873—a copy of which Clemens used to cull selections for his later *Library of Humor*.[15]

These collections of sketches received scant, but positive, reviews in the English newspaper press. The *Reader* noted that American humor had flooded the market. "Personally," the review began "we have had almost enough of books of American humour; still there would seem to be a popular demand for them, and there is not more indefatigable caterer for the public taste in that line than Mr. Hotten." Still, the reviewer found Mark Twain's brand of humor to be among "the best of its kind."[16] The *Spectator*, a weekly literary periodical, reviewed *Screamers* in May 1872, noting that "the United States are taking a lead in humorous literature of the day." The review placed Mark Twain as less subtle than Bret Harte, John Hay, and Artemus Ward because he was less political or social in character. On the other hand, the review found that Mark Twain's writing was more likely to be widely appreciated, possibly because it was less tied to strictly American topics. The review praised a number of sketches as "excellent nonsense"—including "The Good Little Boy Who Did Not Prosper" and "My Watch"—while pointing out the unequal merit of others, whether because the satire was pointless (the hoax review of *The Innocents Abroad*) or vulgar ("About Barbers," "Dan Murphy," "True Story of Chicago," and "Vengeance," the latter two being falsely attributed).[17] According to this review, two stories—"Baker's Cat" and "The Undertaker's Story"—went beyond the merely humorous to the level of pathos the reviewer associated with Bret Harte, showing "in a very droll, grotesque garb, it is true—as we have said, a more serious and cultivated humor, a deeper meaning, and a kindlier feeling than the others." The reviewer ended by hoping Mark Twain would cease with "vulgar papers, and the extravaganzas, and the no-sense as distinguished from the nonsense."

While the circulation of Mark Twain's work in American periodicals, especially the "Memoranda" of the *Galaxy* and subsequent newspaper reprintings, showed a market for his writings in America, his subscription publisher prevented him from releasing an American version of collected sketches until 1875. Subscription publishing required advance time to sell books, and Bliss was reluctant to have multiple new titles by a single author. British sales, on the other hand, showed that a large market existed for his works that "seems to have been insatiable."[18] One of Clemens's reasons for traveling to England in 1872 was to secure copyright on *Roughing It* and to make arrangements with the publisher Routledge to issue authorized editions of his works. Part of this process was to engage in a very public verbal war with Hotten, whom he accused of piracy. In 1872, Routledge issued five volumes of Mark Twain's work: *Roughing It*, *A Curious Dream and Other Sketches*, *Sketches Selected and Revised*, and *The Innocents Abroad* (in two volumes). The growth in popularity of Mark Twain's works was also accompanied by a shift in quality—from the "catch-penny" editions pushed by Hotten to higher quality editions by Routledge, as well as those later issued by the firm of Chatto & Windus, indicating an improved reputation and higher quality audience.

Mark Twain's increased presence in the British book market inspired a further reconsideration of American humor in the British periodical press in an 1871 article in the *Graphic*, with the always popular title of "American Humour." Tracing the demand for American jokes from Charles Matthews, an Englishman who had imported minstrel songs and the Yankee character to England in the 1820s, to Artemus Ward, whose "name had become inseparable with pleasure and laughter," the article frames American humor in hierarchical terms that would have been familiar to readers of British or American periodicals.[19] Matthews's introduction of minstrel songs is decried for introducing "the shower of blacks from which we have since suffered so severely," while Hawthorne's humor is subsumed into his position as the first, and possibly only, American writer of literary excellence. According to this article, the main thread of American humor, starting with Sam Slick and Washington Irving, took root in England with Artemus Ward and came from "the wilder and less civilised states" full of "'Injuns,' pigs, alligators, and Irishmen" leading to a humor of "naïve defiance of all truth, and a daring exaggeration." For British critics, American humor reflected what they perceived to be America's "uncivilized" national character, symbolized by the rather absurd list of its primary features.

The article argued that Artemus Ward had exported this hybrid, generically "frontier" American humor to England most successfully and performed it to wide acclaim. The importance of his manner of humor, especially in his performances as the Genial Showman, was key in presenting the surprise of the humor.[20] Mark Twain was viewed as an unlikely candidate to replace Artemus Ward as the figure of American humor in England. In discussing the humorists who might follow the genial showman, the author praises Charles Leland's "Hans Brietmann" poems as a new vein of American humor. Mark Twain was unfavorably compared to Bret Harte and to his fellow humorists "Josh Billings" and "Orpheus C. Kerr," especially in the "rather forced vein of humor" of his travel writing, which "laughs at our old-world conventions and shams, pretended cognoscenti, and all forms of feigned enthusiasm, with all the reckless defiant shrewdness of the newest part of the nation." Instead, the critic prefers the "Jumping Frog" and those times when Mark Twain is "serious," as well as "earnest and poetical," subtler traits of his writing that few critics at this point recognized in him. Echoing the praise of the *Atlantic Monthly*, and American letters more generally, the author viewed Bret Harte as less of a humorist than Mark Twain but more of a genius, summarizing his place at the forefront of American humor: "Weariness and sorrows of the world come as you will here is another humorist sent to cheer stray hours with what will both beguile the toil, and make us better fit to bear it."

Writing in the same year, the critic Margaret Oliphant praised Harte as an author who was creating a "lighter literature" that expressed the nationality of American life rather than mere imitation.[21] Harte's "native force" showed "better promise of a true original influence in literature" than any other American author. If he were to build on the foundation of his short stories, she argued, he "might be such a national bard as has not yet arisen in America,—a true exponent of her chaotic youth, her wild vigour of adolescence—the qualities that will ripen, not those which must die." While Harte's work was, for Oliphant, a product of America's youth and, as such, tended toward humor, it also showed a higher development in connecting humor with pathos: "The reader laughs, but it is with a tear in his eye, which is one of the highest luxuries of feeling." Oliphant clearly established Harte as being the primary hope for the development of an American literature that was racy yet distinct from the popular humor of vulgar doggerel that the "music-hall public" had made popular. Here, her example is Charles Leland, whose works were a "vulgar travesty of nature" equated, as was often the case, with the humor of "Ethiopian minstrels" and not worthy of critical attention, except to account for their popularity and to show how they are different from true art, like that of Bret Harte.[22] Oliphant did not mention Mark Twain, whose reputation at this point was still in the early stages of critical consideration in England.

Before his personal arrival in England, "Mark Twain's" persona had circulated in the country, gaining in popularity, but of unclear critical quality. As in America, Mark Twain's humor was seen as both a promise and a problem—challenging critical hierarchies and forcing critics to account for his popularity either by dismissing his value or by elevating him into the realm of quality American literature.

THE NEXT GREAT AMERICAN HUMOURIST
MARK TWAIN IN ENGLAND

As had been the case with Artemus Ward, the advent of Mark Twain in England as a living, breathing, joking humorist greatly improved his social and literary standing. The "lion" in London, as he had dubbed himself for Livy, enjoyed a major aspect of British literary life: hospitality for visitors through a highly active social life, especially in a variety of clubs and banquets. Clemens greatly enjoyed this busy social life, which had both elevated Artemus Ward and exhausted Charles Farrar Browne, so much so that Clemens appears to have forgotten his aim of collecting material for a book on England. He found an enthusiastic reception personally among men of letters and elite society and professionally among quality audiences when he performed on the lecture stage near the end of his second visit. Writing to Livy, he expressed satisfaction upon receiving invitations to lecture from "committees of *gentlemen*," writing "When *gentlemen* condescend in this way in England, it means a very great deal. An English gentleman never does a thing that may in the slightest degree detract from his dignity."[23] Mark Twain's reception in England placed him on a new level of respectable literary reputation, even if this reputation was not as clearly attached to the quality of his writings as it was to the English practice of celebrating American celebrities upon their visits.

While accepted as a celebrity in England and praised as a humorist, Mark Twain did not immediately rise to the level of quality humorist whose work would be placed in a national canon. James Russell Lowell continued to hold a place of critical eminence as the highest quality American humorist, racy of the soil and of national birth. The English reading public, on the other hand, eagerly consumed the works of new American humorists imported and sold as truly American products. The popularity of the new American humorist again raised the question of the link between humour and literature as critics attempted to clarify a hierarchy of humor and to promote new contenders for the American humorist who might augur a coming American literature.

Mark Twain's introduction to British literary society must be read in connection with the larger question of the reception and construction of "American Literature" as a critical subject. The *Atlantic Monthly* promoted a national literature worthy of consideration in the company of European traditions, but the majority of British critics viewed most American literature as imitative of, and often inferior to, European models. Such a reframing of the terms of a truly national literature by English critics was a significant factor in the founding of the *Atlantic Monthly* and its defense and promotion of American literature, as signified in the transatlantic bias of its name and the cultural nationalism of its editorial policies. At the same time, British critics, especially Leslie Stephen and Gerald Massey, valued American humour as the harbinger of a truly national literature, one that "smacked of the soil" and expressed the first stages of a national character.

American editors and authors faced the double bind of creating a uniquely national literature separate from European literature yet simultaneously modeled on European critical standards and looking to European critics for validation. This "Anglo-American struggle," as the literary scholar Robert Weisbruch has termed it, forced American authors to defend "American Literature" as a subject from its perceived shortcomings by looking for other bases of literary endeavor—shifting from the rich ground of history that British critics argued to be the foundation of literature to the "individual as a microcosm of America and America as the completion in secular reality of God's design for humanity."[24] Weisbruch argues that the perceived British dominance of letters, made very real by a consistent critical stance and by the dominance of European novels in the American market, provided a useful opposition against which Americans could redefine the meanings of literature by encouraging "a creative anger in America that in turn helped to create the very native literature whose absence was its own starting point."[25] This reasoning provided an excuse for a lack of American literature, allowing some American critics to argue that Americans as a people had been preoccupied with founding and expanding the country, personifying America as a hearty frontiersman too busy conquering a nation to write literature. British influence led to the critical call for such a national literature on some new basis, most famously in Emerson's "The American Scholar" (1837).

According to Weisbruch, American reactions to English influence tended to be directed toward Victorian contemporaries, rather than a shared heritage of Chaucer, Milton, Shakespeare, and the British Romantics. American authors dealt with their anxieties of influence via attacks on specific authors who become representatives of English letters writ large, usually in relation to what individual American authors perceived as their own analogues in English letters. This anxiety persisted past the Civil War, Weisbruch argues, notably in Mark Twain's own ambivalent relationship with Charles Dickens.[26] Clemens had read Dickens, and some of his works were clearly influenced by Dickens's. But Mark Twain publicly and repeatedly denied Dickens's influence, which Joseph Gardner has attributed to the intellectual insecurities of a self-taught man, but also fits Weisbruch's larger thesis on the reaction of American authors to British influence. The private man, Samuel Clemens, read Dickens, but the public figure of Mark Twain routinely denied the influence and saw, according to Gardner, "such comparisons as a kind of a threat and felt called upon to dissociate himself from Dickens as much as possible."[27]

Following the pattern of American authors attacking their British analogues by demystifying them, Clemens described his first and only encounter with Dickens in highly negative terms. In 1868, he had attended a Dickens reading with Olivia Langdon, a first date of sorts, and reported being "a great deal disappointed": "This was Dickens—Dickens. There was no question about that, and yet it was not right easy to realize it. Somehow, this puissant god seemed to be only a man, after all. How the great do tumble in common flesh, and know that they eat pork and cabbage and act like other men!"[28] Dickens, rather than a literary god, is merely a man with faults—here related to his questionable abilities as a performer, an area in which Mark Twain could compete with Dickens at that time. Mark Twain's humanizing of Dickens—merely a man who eats pork and cabbage—might have been seen as a form of high irreverence by the genteel readers of the East, if they had read his report. The incongruity between authors as men and authors as abstract ideals would be both a source of humor for Mark Twain—although not always a comfortable sort of humor—and a source of controversy. During the late 1860s through the 1870s, Mark Twain as a person developed personal relations with well-known authors, both American and English, at the same time that his literary personae circulated in wider circles and became more abstract.

During his 1872 visit to England, Mark Twain's time was filled with social occasions: banquets, visits, touring, and a number of after-dinner speeches. Mark Twain was now "the celebrated humorist" who was the guest of the well-known English humorist Tom Hood at a banquet also attended by Herbert Spencer and Ambrose Bierce ("himself a well-known American humorist").[29] American newspapers covered the visit, reprinting his after-dinner speeches and widely reporting on his trip. The London correspondent of the Cincinnati *Commercial* joked that the preferred English method of torture was the banquet, and that Mark Twain was growing thinner and paler each evening he was celebrated.[30] Moncure Conway wrote a long report for the same paper of Mark Twain's speech at the Savage Club, where Artemus Ward had cemented his English popularity with the literary elite. Mark Twain's speech, focusing on his pleasure sightseeing in London (but seeing and praising the least impressive parts of the city), was heartily received and represented the recognition of Mark Twain as "the successor to Artemus Ward."[31] Mark Twain ended with a stirring moment of sentiment in thanking the Club for "the kindly interest and the friendly offices which you lavished upon an old friend of mine who came among you a stranger, and you opened your English hearts to him and gave him a welcome and a home." The homage to Artemus Ward showed a keen insight into his audience and the importance of a positive English reception in promoting his place as an American humorist in England.

One London paper noted that Twain's visit would give new impulse to the sale of the authorized versions of his books, and that upon buying, the reader "cannot fail to be highly entertained by the truly comical style of Mark Twain." Another paper ended a sketch of Twain's life with the following: "As a humorist, Mr. Clemens shows the same quaint exaggerative spirit as the late Artemus Ward, though less dependent on bad spelling for his fun. Judging by the wide circulation of his works, he is highly popular both here and in his native country."[32] The newspaper included portraits of Mark Twain and Hans Breitmann.

Despite many offers to lecture, Clemens returned to America in early November 1872, promising in an oft-quoted squib to return to lecture "upon such scientific topics as I know least about, and may consequently feel least trammelled [sic] in dilating upon."[33] In a sign of his increasing fame, Mark Twain's joke was soon detached from its context and applied to other lecturers. Mark Twain's sayings could now circulate as similes

SAMUEL LANGHORNE CLEMENS ("MARK TWAIN")

FIGURE 5.2: "Mark Twain" from the *Graphic* (London), October 5, 1872.
Courtesy of Kevin Mac Donnell, Austin, Texas

outside of their context, demonstrating that the English public would understand the joke when a newspaper remarked: "as Mark Twain says . . ."

Commenting on Mark Twain's departure, a commenter from the London *Figaro* took a subtle jab at the craze for American humor Mark Twain had stoked in England. The article stated:

I am sorry he leaves us, mostly because, as he is one of the greatest of the "Great American Humourists" we have on hand, I think it likely Mr. Hotten will be importing at least six other G.A.H.'s to take his place. The importation of American humourists by Mr. Hotten, and a few other firms of his persuasion, has, for some time past, averaged exactly three humourists and a quarter per week; and I really think that, in our present state of civilisation, we cannot, honestly, do with more.[34]

The article was one of several probably written by Ambrose Bierce under the pseudonym "the Town Crier," mocking the predominant trend of American humor then popular in England.[35] Despite the mocking tone, Mark Twain had indeed become a leading candidate for the next G.A.H. in England.

Mark Twain's growing popularity, circulated through widely published works and galvanized by his embodiment of the American humorist, led to a reevaluation of his place in American letters. In between his visits, the literary magazine *Once a Week* published a short biography testifying to his newfound status, while introducing the author to a new class of readers who might not be familiar with the popular humorist. It read, in part:

The name by which the American humourist who wrote "The Jumping Frog" is known by the readers of his works is a nom de plume. Mr. Samuel L. Clemens has only lately left England, and has promised to come and see us "Britishers" again before long.

California has developed a literature of its own, and its proudest boast is the possession of Mark Twain. "The Jumping Frog," pronounced by the Saturday Review "an inimitably funny book," soon made its author famous, and gained for him readers wherever English is spoken. "The Jumping Frog" is a story of the California gold mines; it is very humorous, and very well told. "Eye-openers," "Screamers," "A Burlesque Autobiography," "The Innocents Abroad," and "The New Pilgrim's Progress," are all of them works of the peculiar humor invented by our American cousins, from the pen of the author of "The Jumping Frog." . . .

The author of these books is possessed of remarkable talent. His works are widely read, and very generally popular. Mark Twain is altogether the best living exponent of American humour, and he may be sure of receiving a hearty welcome whenever he revisits the Old Country.[36]

AMERICAN HUMOUR.

FIGURE 5.3: "American Humour" from *Once a Week*, 259 (December 14, 1872), 521. **Courtesy of Kevin Mac Donnell, Austin, Texas**

The article was illustrated with a caricature of Mark Twain riding a frog as an Englishman would a horse, showing him to be a uniquely American sort of humorist.

Further complicating the critical place of Mark Twain in American literature, the *Temple Bar* magazine published a lengthy evaluation of

"America and her Literature" by John C. Dent in March 1873. Restating the general critical sentiment as earlier framed by Massey and Stephen, Dent wrote that both the general public and men of letters hold as a doctrine that America has not developed a distinctive national literature to express its distinct, if not enviable, national character. While quality writers existed, they could very well be English, as "They do not smack of the soil. They are not redolent of the wild western breeze. They do not photograph for us the mighty river, the lone ranch, and the boundless prairie." Some authors had taken on American subjects—Longfellow, Holmes, Cooper, and Lowell—but Dent noted that the critic searching for "a production which is exclusively American, in spirit and tone, . . . will prove as helpless as was that of the blind Ethiopian who, with an extinguished candle, in a dark cellar, hunted for a black cat that was not there."[37]

Dent's article framed American literature in highly conventional critical terms, with two important differences. First, he found the writings of established American authors, who generally conform to a list of "Atlantic authors," almost as good as British writing (specifically, 9/10ths "might have been written by Englishmen"). Second, humor per se is not the mark of a new American literature; rather, the new "labourers" of American "mental culture" have in common a number of attributes that previous critics generally attributed to American humor: peace and prosperity, "manly self-assertion," and a democratic spirit. Like many critics on both sides of the Atlantic, the future of American literature was imagined to be the territory of white male authors. Female authors were discussed separately, usually without reference to nationality, while black writers were rarely discussed in the periodical writing of the 1860s and 1870s as literature.

Dent argued that American authors were beginning to cast off British models of literature, while still claiming the intellectual heritage of the English language, writing: "Their intellectual seed is beginning to germinate, and the first upshots already give out unmistakable indications of a prolific harvest."[38] Specifically, he praised Walt Whitman ("the very incarnation of American democracy: fresh, hopeful, and above all things self-reliant"), Joaquin Miller, Bret Harte, and Mark Twain. Each author is praised and critiqued, with Mark Twain being found *too thin* in his constant drollery. Still, Dent wrote that "his humour . . . is always *good* humour, and is never cynical. It is thoroughly American." Dent praised Mark Twain over the "false spelling and barbarous grammar" of Artemus Ward and Josh Billings, ending with a higher measure of praise than Mark

Twain had yet garnered in England: "All things considered, we believe that when the history of American literature comes to be written, the name of Samuel Langhorne Clemens will be mentioned among its founders."[39] If he read the article, which is highly possible, William Dean Howells would surely have been pleased with Dent's critical view of American literature and Twain's place within it, which went further in canonizing Twain than Howells had to this point (or even would before the 1880s).

"THE ART OF PUTTING THINGS": RECEPTION POPULARITY, AND PERFORMANCE

Shortly before sailing on his second visit to England in June 1873, Mark Twain made the news in a somewhat novel manner—a lawsuit. Clemens had been visited some months before by a publisher wishing to purchase a sketch to use in a humorous periodical. He demurred but allowed the publisher to print one sketch from the collections that had been published in England—largely made up of pieces from the *Galaxy*. By chance, the resulting book was for sale (price 10 cents) on his train ride from Hartford to New York as he prepared to return to England. The enjoyment at finding himself in *Fun, Fact and Fancy. A Collection of Original Comic Sketches and Choice Selections of Wit and Humor* was short-lived as he discovered that the publisher had published all the sketches without permission, as well as one sketch credited to him "although he emphatically declines to father it."[40] Mark Twain's lawyer requested an injunction and sought $25,000 in damages, claiming the collection had damaged negotiations for a collection of sketches. In his affidavit, he wrote: "I consider a volume of them worth (to me) not less than $25,000, & certainly would not publish a volume of them unless I felt sure of getting that much for it—one of my reasons being that I consider that an author cannot bunch a mass of disconnected humorous sketches together & publish the same without sickening the public stomach & damaging his own reputation." Another symptom of his anxiety with his lack of control over his works, the suit was his only successful use of a lawsuit against piracy, although Mark Twain's victory consisted of a permanent injunction, $10 in costs, and an injunction for the publisher to use only one story and not use Mark Twain's name in advertising. In referencing the incident in a later notebook entry, Clemens crowed that he "won a suit on uncopyrighted matter by pleading my *nom de plume* as trade mark."[41] Samuel Clemens would remain keen on protecting his *nom de plume*, expanding his copyright, and controlling his brand, but the suit did not stop publishers of other humor collections in this era from pirating his works for commercial gain.

Clemens returned to England with his wife and daughter. One paper referred to him as "one of the greatest living humourists" whose "irrepressible humour ... has made him famous." The Clemenses settled in London, toured Ireland and Scotland, and visited Paris. Mark Twain's reputation continued to develop through both personal and professional associations. Unlike in Boston, where he had been met with a certain level of social restraint by the literary elite, Mark Twain was welcomed by many British authors, including Trollope, Charles Kingsley, Charles Reade, and Harrison Ainsworth. He was invited to an exclusive social gathering featuring scholars, statesmen, and other prominent figures, including Robert Browning, one of his favorite authors. As Paine states: "It was the height of the season now, and being free to do so, he threw himself into the whirl of it, and for two months, beyond doubt, was the most talked-of figure in London. The Athenaeum Club made him a visiting member (an honor considered next to knighthood); Punch quoted him; societies banqueted him; his apartments, as before, were besieged by callers."[42]

Mark Twain lectured from October 13 to 18, accompanied his family back to America, and then returned alone after six days. He then lectured in December before returning to the United States in early January. During this time, he delivered his "Our Fellow Savages of the Sandwich Islands" for fourteen performances over thirteen days and the "Roughing It on the Silver Frontier" lecture sixteen times in twelve days. Each lecture was an established piece from a previous lecture tour, and each was certainly calculated to arouse public interest.[43] Mark Twain chose not to lecture about Artemus Ward, whose status in England may have made the lecture an easier sell than in America. Interestingly, he removed the offer to illustrate cannibalism for the crowd if someone would provide a baby, a joke that had been widely circulated in British papers. Mark Twain perceived the British audience to be more civilized than American audiences, but evidence of his reception shows that the London audiences focused on the entertainment value of the lectures without the American lyceum audience's expectations of instruction or edification.

Certainly, Mark Twain was eager to impress the London audience, as he had been eager to impress the Boston and New York audiences as a new lecturer.[44] With the help of Charles Dickens's lecture manager, Clemens booked the fashionable Queen's Concert Rooms and promoted the lecture with a letter to the London *Standard* promising to paralyze the recent public frenzy on the subject, "for I can allay any kind of an excitement by lecturing upon it."[45] Livy agreed to his lecturing in London, despite her desire to return with him to America, because it would give him a "larger" and "more enviable reputation." Moncure Conway argued that the choice of the fashionable hall, rather than the Egyptian Hall where Artemus Ward and other Americans performed, raised the status of his audience. Rather than the "popular" hall, he chose the "most fashionable hall in London" and charged higher admission than previous American lecturers. As a result, Conway noted that "the hall was crowded with fashionable people in evening dress, of whom few if any had ever seen Mark," and the audience was kept "in an ecstasy of delight and laughter from first to last." Fred Lorch, in summing up Mark Twain's decision to lecture in London, argues that "if there was a reputation to be won in England he wanted to win it from its leading citizens."[46]

While in London, Clemens wrote Livy of enjoying performing for the elegant and "heartily responsive" audiences, although he disliked the tedium of waiting and the dreary fog of London.[47] Charles Warren Stoddard later reminisced about their stay, noting their daily routines, Mark Twain's impatience to get his lecture started, the dreadful fog, and, most interestingly, the variable laughter of the audiences. His description is worth quoting at some length for what it says about Mark Twain's performances:

> *I found that a joke which took the house by storm one evening was not sure of a like success the following night. Some jokes took immediate effect and convulsed the house. The hearty laughter was as the laughter of one man with a thousand mouths. On another occasion the same joke caught feebly in one corner of the room, ran diagonally across the hall, followed by a trail of laughter, and exploded on the last bench. . . . Again a joke which never aspired to anything more than a genteel smile might on one occasion create a panic and ever after hold its peace; or the audience would be divided against itself, the one half regarding with indignation the levity of the other. . . .*[48]

This variability of the audience, both in relation to individual jokes and to audiences as a whole, seems to have both fascinated and frustrated Mark Twain.

The reviews clearly positioned Mark Twain as an "American humorist"—prefaced at times with the adjectives "well-known," "celebrated," and "popular."[49] His popularity worked against his reputation, at times, in articles that found his work inferior to Artemus Ward, Harte, or Lowell. One review noted that a "crowd of imitators have copied the mannerisms of 'A. Ward,' without his delicate pungency," continuing on to evoke the critical stance that equates popularity with lower quality humor prone to irreverence:

> America is rich in humourists, if not in humour; but there is a jerky irreverence about their fun which somewhat bars it from ready acceptance in this old-fashioned country. America has clearly a right to be eccentric in this as in other matters of taste. The scholarly wit of the "Autocrat" comes nearest to the flavour of the original English tap. Yet for strong thick drinks we sometimes draw upon Petroleum V. Nasby, Josh Billings, Mark Twain, and others of the screaming jokers.[50]

Mark Twain's lectures evoked hearty laughter, even if "his jokes are laboriously ambushed to provoke the sudden roar but will not bear repeated listenings." Still, the paper concluded that Mark Twain would take with him "a grateful recollection of his successful *debut* in this country."

As with Artemus Ward, Mark Twain's performances as a humorist added a new level to his persona through his embodiment of American humor. The London *Evening Echo* noted that "since the days of Artemus Ward, there has been no one to animate, so to speak, American drollery until Mark Twain."[51] Upon finishing the final lecture of his first run, Mark Twain appeared on stage, noticeably moved, and thanked the audience, stating: "I do not wish to appear pathetic, but it is something magnificent for a stranger to come to the metropolis of the world and be received so handsomely as I have been. I simply thank you."[52] His genuine appreciation at his reception is notable as a rare moment of emotion showing through his exterior as a deadpan humorist. But the applause of the crowds and the hospitality of literary gentlemen did not settle the question of the meanings of Mark Twain in England—or in America. As with other successes (and failures) in his career, Mark Twain's status as the "lion of London" raised contrasting opinions about his role as a humorist and about the import of American humor more generally.

Clemens viewed the positive reaction to Mark Twain's lectures in England as raising his status as a humorist in both England and America.

He paid Charles Warren Stoddard to clip articles about Mark Twain's performances in London into a scrapbook. Clemens kept many scrapbooks, collecting news reports, articles, and other information of interest. Often disorganized and disheveled, these collections are a unique and puzzling archive of Clemens/Mark Twain. Although many of these scrapbooks are in Mark Twain's own patented self-pasting scrapbook, his English visit was collected in a scrapbook called *Literary Scraps* produced by his publishing nemesis John Camden Hotten. Pencil markings in the articles show that Clemens probably read the articles as part of his keen interest in his London reception.[53] Figure 5.4 shows one such article from Mark Twain's scrapbook, with an image of him combined with one of his most popular characters.

The newspaper response to Mark Twain's performances was almost uniformly positive. As with previous reviews of Mark Twain's lecturing, reviewers focused on a number of consistent subjects: the quality of the audience, the manner of Mark Twain's speaking, the matter of his subject, and the audience responses. A review clipped into Mark Twain's scrapbook noted that "the audience were intellectually of the *elite*" who "were well pleased with him, and warmly testified it."[54] Newspapers noted the quality of the audiences and the number of celebrities, including the presence of P. T. Barnum on the first night, with the consistent view that the lectures were "repeatedly and loudly applauded." The

FIGURE 5.4: Mark Twain as Jumping Frog from the *Hornet*, December 13, 1873 as found in Mark Twain's Scrapbook. **Courtesy of the Mark Twain Papers and Project, University of California at Berkeley**

London *Cosmopolitan* noted that he was "cordially greeted by a large and select assembly, embracing many of the wits, the journalists, the authors, the celebrities, and, last not least, the beauties of London."[55] Stoddard described the scene: "Extra seats were introduced; the stage was thronged; Mark stood in the centre of the British public and held his own against the infinite attractions of the city. Saturday *matinee* and evening saw disappointed people turned from the door; for there was not even standing room in the hall."[56] The London *Observer* noted that the demand for tickets testified to the public appetite for Mark Twain's performances. A description of the room being packed to overflowing is marked in the scrapbook with pencil, presumably by Clemens himself as he considered extending his lectures beyond an original run of two weeks.

As in America, reviews often focused on Mark Twain's stage presence as an "admirable colloquial lecturer," not a skilled orator or rhetorician. Reviewers commented upon stylistic qualities—the "dry manner" of his remarks, his "curious accent," and the "grave countenance" of his face—as more notable than the subject of the lecture, although some reviewers noted that the lectures contained more information and artistic "word painting" than had been expected.[57] One paper noted that his amusing lecture was notable because of Mark Twain's "California dialect," stating, "Possibly for this very reason his witticisms were the more racy." While Mark Twain's dialect was only arguably "Californian," for reviewers his unique delivery increased the enjoyment of the jokes by making them seem more American. The *Sportsman* summarized: "If his books are humorous, his lectures are ten times more so, and if his printed jokes are laughable they possess the inestimable advantage of increased raciness when heard from his own lips."[58] In England, more so than in America where his accent was distinctly regional, Mark Twain spoke like an "American," or what the English might have imagined as the sound of the soil. The New York *Graphic* from November 5 featured an illustration of Mark Twain performing "Amongst the Britishers," with an interesting array of responses visible in the audience. One report summed up the lecture as "an odd and amusing mixture of solid fact and humorous extravagance"; another noted that Mark Twain "evidently has 'the art of putting things.'"[59]

As with his writings and other aspects of his reputation, Mark Twain's performances in England were judged in relation to Artemus Ward. One paper referred to the lecture as "of the Artemus-Ward type," while another called it the "freshest and most amusing entertainment" London had

FIGURE 5.5: "Amongst the Britishers" from the *New York Graphic*, November 5, 1873. **Courtesy of Dave Thomson Collection**

experienced since the showman's lectures. His deadpan manner and the gravity of his face, techniques borrowed from Artemus Ward, heighten the effect of the jokes and helped keep the audience "thoroughly under subjection."[60] The *Spectator*, a weekly literary magazine, found Mark Twain's lecture similar to Artemus Ward's but distinctly inferior, as it relied more on "commonplace fun" and extravagance, which combined moral coherence with intellectual incoherence. The reviewer linked the lower quality of Mark Twain's humor to a higher level of popularity, in a manner common to certain critics of humor, by stating: "His higher humour is not sustained, but it is eked out with so much skill of anecdote, so much command of American idiom, and such powers of mimicry, as to furnish an entertainment perhaps ever more generally popular than Artemus Ward's inimitable lectures themselves." Mark Twain's widespread popularity, even when it extended to the elite and literary classes, was viewed by some critics as a barrier to literary status—as racy but not the right quality of American humor. Still, by the end of his two stints lecturing, Mark Twain seems to have distinguished himself from Artemus Ward. One paper summarized by describing his delivery as a "singularly enjoyable strain of elegance which may be classified as peculiarly Mark-Twainian."[61]

Mark Twain's lecture also distinguished itself by actually being about the stated subject, unlike Artemus Ward's style of using the announced topic as an excuse for a series of digressions. Reviews praised the information provided by Mark Twain's discourse:

> A more genuine intellectual treat has not been presented to the public for years. Those of us who remember Artemus Ward's style would not have been surprised to find the Sandwich Islands made a jocose excuse for a dissertation on all other subjects but that. This was, however, not the case—Real information was pleasantly conveyed. Mark Twain, like all the best humourists, has that vein of pure gold—that appreciation of the seriousness of things—which makes its outcroppings of quaintness so valuable. What you pick up and laugh heartily at, as a quip, has on examination the true metal in it, to be laid aside for use. In a word his is the humour of an observant and reflective mind; though as a natural consequence there is at times a bubbling over of real rollicking fun in which an abundant good humour asserts itself against graver qualities.[62]

This review and others praised Mark Twain's "word paintings" and the mixture of this eloquence with information and humor. Twain had learned through the difficulties of the Artemus Ward lecture that a balance of serious and humorous was key to positive reviews.

While the descriptions of such reviewers are not an exact mirror of reception, it is clear from the London reviews that Mark Twain's lecture was received almost entirely positively. Reviews note the reaction of audiences: "applause was long and reiterated," "greeted with unanimous shouts of approbation," "often excite hearty laughter," and "it is seldom an audience laughs more heartily."[63] The London *Standard* ended their review by noting that "scores of anecdotes followed, each one more amusing and amusingly recounted than its predecessor, till at last the audience almost wished the lecture at an end, so that they might be relieved from the labour of laughing." A Liverpool paper noted than in addition to "uproarious laughter," Mark Twain had earned "unbounded admiration."[64] Unlike America, where laughter was sometimes frowned upon in lecture halls, London audiences seem to have shown no compunction against laughter and the enjoyment of a public lecture. As an urban amusement separate from any moral purpose, Mark Twain's lecture seems to have been received as highly enjoyable and highly popular.

"EH BIEN! JE NE VOIS PAS QUE CETTE GRENOUILLE AIT RIEN DE MIEUX QU'AUCUNE GRENOUILLE": L'HUMOUR AMÉRICAIN ET MARK TWAIN

Mark Twain's second and third European visits focused largely on his experience in England and the increase in literary status that his celebrity reception engendered. England loomed larger in the American literary imagination than France or Germany, and Mark Twain's focus on literary London demonstrates his continuity with his fellow American authors. Mark Twain's stories were not widely available on the continent until after 1872, when he secured a German representative and first gained critical attention in France. His interactions with German readers and critics did not occur until later, especially after his stay in Germany in the late 1870s and his subsequent travel book, *A Tramp Abroad* (1880).[65] Mark Twain encountered French views of his work sometime shortly after his English sojourns. Unlike British criticism, which he took seriously as an indication of his critical status, the French criticism of his works was transformed into an opportunity for humor, and French disapproval of his "uncivilized" humor was literally translated into mockery of French ideas of civilization.

In France, Mark Twain's works were introduced through the work of Thérèse Bentzon, the pen-name of Marie-Thérèse Blanc, the main French critic of American literature in the late nineteenth century. Publishing under the sobriquet Th. Bentzon (and sometimes "Theodore Bentzon"), Bentzon introduced Mark Twain and the subject of American humor to French readers through a two-part article published in the *Revue des deux mondes* in July and August 1872, shortly after Clemens had first arrived in London. In "Les Humoristes Américains," Bentzon introduced French readers to the new vogue of American humorists, who were then causing *"roars of laughter"* [English in the original] in Australia, India, New York, and London.[66] Bentzon attempted to make sense of American humor by examining Mark Twain (in the July issue), and then Artemus Ward, Josh Billings, and Hans Breitmann (in the August issue). Her definition of humor, grounded in a privileging of French wit, provides another transatlantic critical definition of American humor—"l'humour Américain"—that positioned Mark Twain as a lower type of American humorist, unique to his nation but not worthy of literary status.

Th. Bentzon's article begins from a familiar nationalistic argument. French wit, she states, does not envy the wit of other countries. Reversing the relationship between humor and wit found in American and English definitions, she argued that wit is the truest and highest form of the comic, but that "*humour*, while it comes from wit, whose home country is France, remains so foreign to us that up to now we have not been able either to translate or define a word of it." With wit as the fount of the risible, she defined humor as a "disease of stormy climates": England, Germany, and the "*uncivilized*" New World. Wit is the highest "fine art of banter," while humor is "a reflection of human life, rich in unexpected and rough contrasts." As such, humor tends to wear out French nerves, which are "refined, demanding, lined with good taste, hostile to dissonances."[67] The hierarchy of "comedy," as the French tended to distinguish the forms of funniness, privileged verbal wit over physical humor, although without the same evolutionary frames that English critics tended to apply. This hierarchy framed the ways in which Bentzon introduced American humor—not as a new type of national literary expression, as English critics and readers largely held it, but as an indicator of an unenviable and uncivilized American national character.

Unlike British critics, who praised American humor because it represented a national product not reliant on European models, Bentzon faulted American humorists precisely because she found them to be too racy of the soil. Bentzon classified Bryant, Emerson, Longfellow, Hawthorne, and Irving as serious authors indebted to European literature, while the writers who "amuse the masses" are "absolutely American."[68] Rather than being "literary," the humor of Mark Twain, Artemus Ward, Josh Billings, and Hans Breitmann were "a measure of the popular taste of a people who think themselves very superior to the Old Europeans." She writes: "There is in the American spirit an inclination to gross mirth, to pranks, which reveals that in certain respects this great people is still a childish people. To gain its favor, in the West especially, one must be willing to sacrifice to buffoonery."[69] Instead of the first fruits of a new literature, American humor was an indicator of an American character not to be envied. As Mark Wilson has shown, Bentzon's promotion of American literature tended to reflect a preference for established New England authors (Emerson, Hawthorne, Longfellow, Holmes, et al.) and their perceived heirs (Howells, James, Aldrich, and Warner), as well as local color writers from all sections (Cable, Page, Harte, Wilkins, and Jewett, among others).[70]

She argued that the American type of humor was "barbaric," if sometimes enjoyable, but caused more curiosity than admiration for the French critics and readers confronted with American exuberance. Bentzon made a clear mistake in assessing American humor—she confounded character for author. James C. Austin argues that Bentzon confused "Artemus Ward" the character with his author and Western humor with Down East, making her judgments confused and confusing.[71] She praised the Hans Brietmann character above the others, showcasing a common French prejudice against the German "hordes" peacefully invading America. Interestingly, Bentzon did not mention James Russell Lowell or Oliver Wendell Holmes as humorists. The former seems to have garnered little attention in France, at least for *The Biglow Papers*, while Holmes was more widely translated and discussed, probably due to his use of sophisticated wit and the difficulties of translating Lowell's dialect. Importantly, Bentzon published an article the month before her evaluation of Mark Twain praising Bret Harte, whom she consistently ranked as the best American author.[72]

Bentzon clearly viewed Mark Twain's humor and his personality as of a distinctly lower quality, important largely as a reflection of the American character. She described Mark Twain, both in person and his writings, as follows:

> There is . . . nothing refined or delicate, complete ignorance of tact, good taste, and all the qualities that sprout only in the soil of an advanced civilization. . . . Mark Twain possesses to the nth degree the temperament that his compatriots describe as jolly, bluffy, telling, queer [English in original], all quite untranslatable terms; droll, comic, clownish—such words give only a feeble idea of them. Such unquenchable verve often lacks lightness—you can't expect ale to have the froth of champagne. . . .[73]

While a jolly and bluffy temperament may have sounded positive to those who valued the exuberance of American humor, it is clear that Bentzon was not praising such humor in presenting it to a French audience. In explaining the "energetic" "bold" and "ingenious" new language of America, she cited California as the logical location for this "new Babel," while privileging Bret Harte's "audacity" over Mark Twain's "vulgar temerities."[74] She concluded: ". . . soon we will grow accustomed to an American language whose savory spiciness should not be sneezed at, even as we await the more delicate and revealing qualities which time will surely bring it."[75] Mark Twain's language, while instructive, lacked the refinement necessary for the perceived French reader. Interestingly, Bentzon also praised American humor for its "profound respect for modesty" and says that young women could read them without inconvenience, a distinct critical difference from the English critics who chastised American humorists for their profanity.[76]

Her lack of appreciation for American humor is demonstrated in her discussion of *The Innocents Abroad*. Taking Mark Twain's judgments to be serious, Bentzon found fault in the author gauging the glories of Europe through the cultural prejudices of America. She writes that "it is not enough to have wit or even a natural sense of taste to appreciate works of art and to form a proper aesthetic opinion; nothing replaces experience." Bentzon's inability to read the narrator as a character, and the narrative as a satire of both American travelers and European pretensions, opened her critique of the book up to a burlesque similar to Mark Twain's hoax review of the *Saturday Press*.[77]

Instead, Mark Twain responded to Bentzon's criticism by attacking the area where she most acknowledged her difficulties and praised Mark Twain: the difficulty of translating the "savage charm and moving simplicity" of his language. Not attacking per se, but making fun of her translation for his own humorous purposes. In order to demonstrate the "habits of mind" that humor demonstrates, Bentzon had translated "The Jumping Frog" as the most popular and, indeed, classic example of American humor. In April 1873, Clemens wrote to Livy that he had discovered the French version of the Jumping Frog story and that "fun is no name for it." He planned to translate it literally without hinting that he was not, in fact, quite the scholar of French. He would publish it in the *Atlantic Monthly* where it would make "toothsome reading." Indeed, while it is unclear in what form or when Clemens encountered Bentzon's article, his scrapbook did contain an article with selections translated into English from an American or English newspaper, which noted that the French critic had been tricked into that ". . . fatal misapprehension of our 'humor' which has fastened so many critics before him."[78] Th. Bentzon, neé Marie-Thérèse Blanc, had been "sold."

Mark Twain found the situation laughable. He published "The 'Jumping Frog.' In English. Then in French. Then Clawed Back into a Civilized Language once more by Patient, Unremunerated Toil," in *Sketches, New and Old* (1875). He does not object to the critic's evaluations, writing: "It is a very good article, and the writer says all manner of kind and complementary things about me—for which I am sure I thank him with all my heart."[79] Instead, he comically faults Bentzon for the translation of the Jumping Frog story, stating that "he has simply mixed all up; it is no more like the Jumping Frog when he gets through than I am like a meridian of longitude." Mark Twain then presents the original version of the Jumping Frog, Bentzon's translation, then his own re-translation of Bentzon, with occasional comments on the French, such as "[If that isn't grammar gone to seed, then I count myself no judge.—M.T.]" He concludes by asking, "And what has a poor foreigner like me done, to be abused and misrepresented like this?" He especially balks at the translation of the nub of the story:

"Well, I don't see no p'ints about that frog that's any better'n any other frog."

In French, the line is:

"Eh bien! je ne vois pas que cette grenouille ait rien de mieux qu'aucune grenouille."

The line ends up, after its recovery from the French, as:

"Eh bien! I no saw that that frog had nothing of the better than each frog."

As a reader with a basic knowledge of French should be aware, Mark Twain's translations are not to be trusted. From the very first paragraph, where he poorly translates the name of the journal (as "Review of Some Two Worlds") and the article (as "These Humorists Americans"), he gives himself away as untrustworthy.

Mark Twain's mock offense at the poor translation is clearly a dig at the pretensions of the French language and, by extension, the French critic, which both claim to be more refined and civilized than the American. The basis of the joke is Mark Twain's inability to unriddle French grammar, of which he says, "I think it is the worst I ever saw, and yet the French are called a polished nation." By clawing his story back into a "civilized" language, Mark Twain reverses, however jokingly, the relationship between French and American literary language, effectively tweaking the French critic at the tenderest point. As Mark Wilson notes, no matter how bad Mark Twain's actual understanding of French was at this point (and it was surely better than his translation would have one believe), he could hardly have failed to recognize the "cultural condescension" of Bentzon's article.[80]

His positioning of the French language as unpolished and uncivilized surely would have answered Bentzon's criticism—recalling that Bentzon argued that French wit—as a phenomenon of language—was the height of proper and quality humor.

After meeting Samuel Clemens in Paris in 1879, Bentzon corrected her impression that Samuel Clemens the person was the "Mark Twain" of the books, admiring his "correct manners" and admitting his retranslation had been a "witty revenge." Clemens took further revenge during a dinner party Bentzon gave in honor of Mark Twain and Thomas Bailey Aldrich. Unable to attend, Livy had asked Aldrich's wife Lilian to make sure he minded his manners. Mrs. Aldrich, whom Clemens had disliked from their first meeting in Boston, was a good friend of Mme. Blanc, and she reported that, during dinner, Clemens/Mark Twain sprang from his chair without warning and promenaded around the table waving his napkin as an "Admiral might his flag." Just as suddenly, he regained composure and furtively sat down. Mark Wilson interprets this as a performative moment in which Mark Twain tweaked both his Boston and his French antagonists through an absurd deadpan performance.[81]

Mark Twain was aware of, and resentful toward, Bentzon's criticism for many years following these incidents, and they became part of his lifelong antipathy toward the French. When he republished the Jumping Frog story in the early 1890s, along with some new materials, Bentzon's good friend Grace King, the southern writer, complained that the French critic had taken offense. Mark Twain replied in full force, stating: "You see, the whole trouble lies in the French character. It hasn't a shred of humor in it, consequently there is no depth to it. . . . When you have hurt a Frenchman, you have hurt a child; you can't reason with him, you can only kiss him & pet him & flatter him."[82] Mark Twain's view of French criticism, via Th. Bentzon, was not terribly serious, from this first encounter through much of his life. Unlike the English opinion of him, which he carefully studied while in England and triumphed over for years, Mark Twain's snub by the French was merely to be laughed at—to be made fun of.

"EVEN AT ITS WORST, IT IS POPULAR": THE GREAT AMERICAN HUMORISTS AND THE QUESTION OF "AMERICAN HUMOUR"

Samuel Clemens returned to America from England with his scrapbook filled with almost uniformly positive reviews of his performances. He would return to Europe in 1878, following the debacle of his speech at the Whittier birthday dinner, which is explored in chapter 7. While his relationship with British society and letters would be more fraught later, especially following his encounters (both personally and critically) with Matthew Arnold, Mark Twain in the early 1870s exhibited what one critic has called a case of "Anglophile euphoria" that led him to promote a system to award extra votes within a democracy in order to control the influence of the masses.[83]

Mark Twain's reception in England highlights an important facet of his developing reputation that was increasingly operative for Mark Twain: the distinctions between personal acceptance, celebrity status, and critical reputation. Mark Twain as a literary figure—in person and as a performer—was accepted into London society to a broader degree than he had been accepted into the New England culture of letters centered in Boston, but the place of Mark Twain as an abstract figure of American letters was not equally canonized within British criticism. Mark Twain's banquets with Robert Browning and other British literary figures did not make him a *critical* equal so much as a *social* equal. Mark Twain's "fashionable" audiences and lecture successes did not raise him to the critical level of Lowell, Bret Harte, or even Artemus Ward, whose status was somewhat unique because of the pathos attached to his early death in the country. Regardless of the laughter and applause of the "fashionable" crowd, Mark Twain's reputation was still a matter of debate, despite and possibly due to his popularity—for some critics, he remained confined to the "screaming humorists" of America.

As often happened, the public attention brought about by a new humorous sensation led to critical reevaluation of American humor more generally. Clearly standing out among the reviews of his lectures pasted into the scrapbook is an article from the *Daily News*, acquainting readers with a "new and odd school of American humour, which has made a way for itself among certain portions of the English public." The article compared Mark Twain as "mirth-maker" to the eternal humor of Lowell and Bret Harte.[84] Sniffing with snobbery, the critic hints that Mark Twain's humor did not elevate the British comic taste, nor would it be considered by the "educated American" to be "typical of the best wit and satire and mirth of his country's literature." One would not class Lowell with such company, he writes:

Mr. LOWELL, whatever his degree in the class, belongs decidedly to the brotherhood of the great humourists whose works are among the ornaments of literature and the reforming agencies of society. He is of kin to the genuine poets who were satirists as well; his humour is always refined by high culture, intensified by its tinge of pathos, and strengthened by manly purpose. Nor should we rank Mr. BRET HARTE with the general crowd of American mirth-makers.

Such mirth-makers focused on fun for its own sake, with the major "professors" of this art being well known in American and England: Artemus Ward, Mark Twain, Petroleum V. Nasby, Josh Billings, Orpheus C. Kerr, and, in a slightly different style, Charles Leland.

But it was Mark Twain who was the leading professor of this school, which overflowed American newspapers and had become popular in England. This type of humor, the critic continued, relies on surprises of incongruity and irreverence, often resorting to jokes of violence, drunkenness, and death, which "does not often add much to enduring literature." And while this style of humor was peculiarly American, the subject matter did little to reflect the actual national character of Americans, which this critic held not to be cruel or particularly given to drink. The article concluded with an evaluation that linked popularity with short-lived fame: "Fresh, original, and amusing this new kind of literature is; at its best, it is irresistible; even at its worst, it is popular. Its success here, as well as across the ocean, is beyond dispute. But we doubt whether it is destined to amuse the world for long; or whether anything more than ashes will be left when its fire goes out." Despite his successful visit to England, Mark Twain's critical position in British periodicals was far from settled.

In "Artemus Ward and the Humorists of America" (1876), Matthew Freke Turner argued that Artemus Ward should be viewed as the height of American humor in the post–Civil War period. Turner made a novel argument that Artemus Ward, alone among American authors, deserved a place in "the famous line which begins with Rabelais and ends with Charles Dickens."[85] Whereas earlier American authors had introduced a unique humor into the "scanty field of American letters," Turner did not acknowledge these men—Irving, Lowell, Holmes, or Hawthorne—as original enough to be classed highly in the world of letters, at least not for their humor. The school of writers that sprang up during the Civil War, on the other hand, were "redolent of American soil and racy of American manner." He then attempted to recover and defend this humor, especially in the figure of Artemus Ward, from critical evaluations that would hold them to be merely popular and ephemeral.

First, Turner explained the circulation of this humor—in newspapers and lectures—as a necessity for American authors who wished to reach wide audiences, as the American book market was hard for American writers to compete in due to the prevalence of British piracies (which helps explain, in the opposite case, the widespread circulation of American humorists in England). Artemus Ward's widespread newspaper circulation won him a wider audience than most writers but did not pay, forcing him to the lecture stage, where his character of the Showman was able to come to life as a dramatic figure almost equal to those produced by Dickens. He writes: "Setting aside the conceptions of Dickens . . . we greatly doubt if this century has produced any character of greater comic power, any that will float longer down the stream of time, than the Artemus Ward of Mr. Charles Brown." The cultural circumstances of these humorists, and Artemus Ward as "the head, the founder, and still incomparably the foremost of the new school of writers," help explain and justify their often ephemeral products and their popularity.[86]

Second, Turner justified the writings of Artemus Ward as "quite inimitable art," dismissing the criticism of his misspellings and his low vulgarity as an issue of improper reading. Apologizing to "persons of elevated literary tastes" who might read his extensive samples of Artemus Ward's work with "sickly disgust," Turner also hinted that these people may lack a full sense of humor—and he began his article by philosophizing that people who lack a sense of humor lack full wisdom and are condemned to both melancholy and stupidity.[87] He wrote:

> The humour is broad—too broad, perhaps, for some refined readers. There is absolutely no "culture" at all, or pretence to it, about Artemus Ward's "perlite literatoor." . . . It is perhaps because Mr. Brown somewhat disregarded the voices of such people that his reputation is not so high with ordinary readers as with those whose critical judgment has ceased to be on trial, and need not fear to pass a bold opinion. It takes more than a commonplace critic to see genius in a literary work where every ordinary rule of grammar and orthography and style is disregarded. The mass of common-place readers laugh at Mr. Brown's jests, but fail to see the art that underlies them.
>
> In this country it was, among the higher classes of literary men, that the young American was first recognized as a true genius.

Turner's defense of Artemus Ward's humor—as dramatic performance and literary art—was a bold critical opinion, an attempt to redefine the canon of American humor and "literatoor" to include a figure who refined readers do not appreciate and common readers merely find amusing. [88]

This defense of his artistic and cultural importance is unique in its strident elevation of Artemus Ward into a humorous canon. Turner attempted to reclassify "American humour" with the works of Artemus Ward at the top, with Harte at times reaching the level of genius, and with Mark Twain as a failure whose popularity was unwarranted. To Turner, only Mark Twain and Bret Harte, among the American humorists aspiring to Artemus Ward's model, had "shown any distinctive manner as well as original power in their mode of exposing the follies and absurdities of the public."[89] Despite some exasperating failures, Bret Harte was one of "the very few men of real comic genius whom this generation has produced." But Mark Twain, on the other hand, had failed to rise above the level of "professional jester." He was of a lower order and his "fun does not appeal to one as does that of Artemus Ward; it is drier, harder, less to the point, and not nearly so fresh and racy." Given to profanity and irreverence, Mark Twain lacked the genial quality that made Artemus Ward's humor successful but instead appealed to "well-dressed rowdies," not decent readers. While Mark Twain's popularity in England was probably greater than Artemus Ward's, Turner found him "a jester, and very little more"; the difference between them is "the difference between a breaker of jests and a true humorist; between our Dickenses and Thackerays, our Sternes and Goldsmiths, and such men as Hook and the younger Coleman."

Not all British critics, however, remained steadfast in the view that "American Humour" represented the first fruits of a racy and original American literature. *Lloyd's Weekly Newspaper* of London made a point in 1874 of questioning American humor as a true representative of American culture. While Mark Twain and Artemus Ward were the most popular of this school, the reviewer pointed to the importance of a "serious and distinct clique of writers who are bringing about a revolution of our literary tastes." For this review, the serious representatives of American literature were a book of Henry Ward Beecher's religious sayings and Josiah Holland's *Arthur Bonnicastle*. Another article in the same paper questioned the tendency to elevate humorists and denigrate serious American poets, worrying that this has led to the "gradually falling [of literature and poetry] to the level which France has reached, without the redeeming wit and sparkle of that unhappy land."[90] The article defended Longfellow as a poet of value above Mark Twain, Harte, and other humorists by arguing that there is serious work of value under the "frothy, evanescent" writings then so generally popular in both countries.

The critic most strenuously arguing against the humorous—or at least in favor of tempering the popularity of humor—was Leslie Stephen, the influential editor of the *Cornhill* magazine. In an article entitled "Humour" (1876), he revised his praise of humor from his article from 1866 (as discussed in chapter 1), taking several opportunities to praise genuine, vigorous humor against the "wretched caricature" of "what is called American humour." The fact that readers laugh at Artemus Ward and Mark Twain was conclusive proof, for Stephen, "that we have very little notion of what true humour means." In a telling critical move, he argued that humor and philosophy are opposed systems of thought, stating: "As philosophers have not succeeded in defining the quality, we need not seek to supply their place." As often follows such a definitional denial, Stephen spent several pages defining humor and its operations, often contradicting himself, but at times making for highly entertaining reading, vis.: "The humorist is the man who laughs through tears. . . . He laughs in the midst of prayer and is yet not consciously irreverent; in the very innermost mental recesses, consecrated to his deepest emotions, there are quaint grotesques and images due to the freaks of the wildest fancy; the temple in which he worships is partly an old-curiosity shop; he belongs to the sect which keeps monkeys in its sacred places."[91] Humor is a "morbid secretion," given naturally to the base instincts of profanity, brutality, and inhumanity, but also bound to fade in power over time.

After four full pages of not defining humor by giving an extensive, if confusing, series of distinctions between true humor and the merely amusing, Stephen ended by admitting that there is a time for jesting: "Shakspeare [*sic*] was a good writer; and one or two of his successors deserve some of the things that have been said about them." He then spent the rest of the article attacking, first, Jane Austen (coining the term "Austenolatry" to describe those who defend the author by accusing critics of having no sense of humor) and, second, American humour, which he saw as a bloodless caricature of the "savage" humor that takes delight in "revolting against the world, of outraging its decencies, flying in the face of its conventionalities, and pouring ridicule on its holiest creeds."[92] Stephen's view of the declension of true humor clearly differentiated between James Russell Lowell and his popular imitators—Artemus Ward and Mark Twain.

Writing on Lowell in 1875, he further distinguished between humor of "genuine literary force" and the vulgar humor of recent humorists. In

The Biglow Papers especially, he argued, Lowell achieved the finest kind of humor, which combines "a deep and generous sympathy with a keen perception of the ludicrous" that transformed his satire into "strains of genuine poetry." Artemus Ward and Mark Twain, on the other hand, merely traffic in cynical and violent "Yankee Humor": "The man must be straitlaced beyond all reasonable limits who would refuse to laugh at some of the 'goaks' of Artemus Ward or even of Mark Twain. But we laugh and have done with it. The fun of such writers is rapidly becoming a mere trick, and, to say the truth, a very offensive trick. The essence . . . is a simply cynicism which holds that there is something funny in brutality and irreverence." He argued that the humor of a young nation, which relies on vernacular, was soon to be replaced by vulgar humor as that civilization progressed—"for a genuine *patois* we have a barbarous slang, and the penny-a-liner is the chosen interpreter of popular feeling."[93] The early stages of quality, "racy" humour appears to have been short-lived as the nation outgrew—at least in Stephen's view—its "hobbledy-hoy" phase in favor of a more mature vintage of literature.

Mark Twain's personal success and professional celebrity in England may have had a greater critical impact in America, where the success was viewed more generally because from a greater distance. Most immediately, Clemens and Howells viewed the British reception as notable. In *My Mark Twain*, Howells acknowledged that the British were the first to recognize Mark Twain at his "transatlantic value":

> But it must be acknowledged that for a much longer time here than in England polite learning hesitated his praise. In England rank, fashion, and culture rejoiced in him. Lord mayors, lord chief justices, and magnates of many kinds were his hosts; he was desired in country houses, and his bold genius captivated the favor of periodicals which spurned the rest of our nation. But in his own country it was different. In proportion as people thought themselves refined they questioned that quality which all recognize in him now, but which was then the inspired knowledge of the simple-hearted multitude.[94]

As his most prominent and consistent critical promoter, Howells would have undoubtedly enjoyed Mark Twain's British reception. But he ignored his highly ambivalent position in British periodicals, which were as likely to dismiss Mark Twain as a merely popular import destined to be forgotten as they were to place him in a developing American canon.

The question of whether Mark Twain was a founding figure of a truly national American literature or merely a "penny-a-liner" selling cruel and irreverent tricks was not settled as a critical question in England (or America) in the 1870s. The contours of the critical landscape and the hierarchies of American literature and "American humour" point to a shared transatlantic question: did Mark Twain's humor represent something essential in the American character, and if so, was it of high enough quality to be promoted as "American Literature"? From the time of his introduction to the British reading public via the Jumping Frog through his two triumphal visits, Mark Twain's reputation rarely saw him classed above Artemus Ward, his fellow popular humorist, or Bret Harte, his fellow Californian (of sorts), comparisons that may have rankled his ego were he aware of the scope and slant of the British criticism. Instead, Clemens, along with Livy and Howells, focused on the celebrity status of the "Lion of London." Scholars of Mark Twain and his fellow humorists should not similarly see his British reputation only through the pleasure of his celebratory visits. Instead, the ambivalent critical position of Mark Twain—possibly among the founders of an American literature, possibly a merely popular jester bound to fade—strikes the keynote of Mark Twain's early critical reputation, both at home and abroad.

CHAPTER SIX

"There's Millions In It!"

Mark Twain and the Business of Satire in the Gilded Age

In March 1873, the *Galaxy* published a review of *The Gilded Age*, Mark Twain's first novel, cowritten with his Hartford neighbor, Charles Dudley Warner. The novel produced something of a sensation both before and after its publication due to the unique conjunction of two well-known humorists. As Mark Twain's first novel, *The Gilded Age* marks an important development in his career as a writer, and its topic—the current state of American life, or in the words of its subtitle, "A Tale of To-Day"—was Mark Twain's first attempt at a sustained satire of American life. Mark Twain and Warner's book was the first novel to be marketed by subscription, and its initial success relied on the reputation of its authors as humorists.

The review highlighted two major themes that criticism of the book would focus on: the reputation of the authors in selling the book and the role of criticism in shaping reactions to a text. The two themes were on Clemens's mind as he prepared the novel—which represented both a critical and financial risk—for publication. The review quotes from the book's preface at length, which was a burlesque of the common prefatorial tendency to apologize for a book and to shape the reader's expectations. Addressing the critic, the preface reads: "We do not object to criticism; and we do not expect that the critic will read the book before writing a notice of it: We do not even expect the reviewer of the book will say that he has not read it. No, we have no anticipations of anything unusual in this age of criticism. But if the critic, who passes his opinion on the novel, ever happens to peruse it in some weary moment of his subsequent life, we hope that he will not be the victim of a remorse bitter but too late."[1] The *Galaxy*'s critic took this as an opening to joke back, declaring that to take such a production seriously enough to actually read it would be to miss the joke. Instead, the critic pointed out that people would buy the book based on the authors' reputations as funny men: "Nevertheless we have looked into it, and can say that it is a work which no library should be without; for it is the production of two humorists whose names are well known throughout the United States, and who, if they seldom succeed in being funny, have at least the reputation of always being so—which come to very much the same thing." The jocular tone of this review thinly disguised a certain antagonism toward the authors, and some critics held that they had traded on their reputations as funny men in order to circumvent criticism that might find the book to be less than entertaining.

Examined outside of its historical milieu, *The Gilded Age* holds up poorly as a literary work. But as a literary event in the context of Mark Twain's evolving public and private development, the substantial attention the book garnered, and its promotion, reception, and transformations, illuminate important facets of literary production in the era that it named.[2] Specifically, the book's focus on speculation and commerce was both satire and symptom of its time—simultaneously making fun of and attempting to profit from the boom-and-bust cycle of the postbellum economy. As such, the book's importance lies not in the realm of literary quality but in the realm of literary business. As a case study, the book's unique place—both at its time and within Mark Twain scholarship—highlights central critical tendencies that marginalize questions of literary business in favor of an idealized artistic purity. The novel's satire of business speculation, while itself being a speculation in the literary marketplace, created friction between artistic and business aims, between text-as-product and text-as-idea, and between authors and critics who envisioned art as a realm outside of culture and those same individuals' necessity of supporting themselves. Clemens and Warner's book—on the contrary—showed just how much art and commerce were intertwined in the Gilded Age.

The novel originated in the winter of 1873, after Clemens had returned from his first trip to England. After they had complained about the state of current novels, Clemens and Warner were encouraged by their wives to write a novel.[3] The conventions of novel writing and expectations of novel readers were a vexed subject both for authors and for critics, and the pages of the *Atlantic Monthly* and other magazines in the United States and Europe commonly featured discussions on the present and the future of the novel. For the two authors, a first foray into novel writing was fraught with conflicting ideas about how to create a success for their production. Both men had come to writing as a career later in their lives and had both recently settled in the Nook Farm section of Hartford to undertake careers as authors. Warner was less well known than Mark Twain, although his books of essays had been favorably reviewed in the *Atlantic Monthly*, where Howells had written: "His book is light and easy to be read, and it is imbued with a humor which, if not very subtile [*sic*], is nearly always pleasant."[4] Both men wrote portions of their joint novel, revised the other's work, and shared the results with their wives.

That Susan Warner and Olivia Clemens had inspired the book, and acted as auditors and judges throughout its composition, is of central importance. In a later essay on the business of letters, Howells noted that women made up the largest class of readers of both "light literature" and "soft literature" and often determined a book's fate:

> The man of letters must make up his mind that in the United States the fate of a book is in the hands of the women. It is the women with us who have the most leisure, and they read the most books. They are far better educated, for the most part, than our men, and their tastes, if not their minds, are more cultivated. Our men read the newspapers, but our women read the books; the more refined among them read the magazines. If they do not always know what is good, they do know what pleases them, and it is useless to quarrel with their decisions, for there is no appeal from them.[5]

Only humorists, Howells argued, had gained a place in American literature without the help of this "largest reading-class," since the humorists had developed through newspapers, which he imagines having a primarily male readership. Clemens and Warner's attempt to market to the perceived female readership by including romantic subplots largely failed because the authors did not fully burlesque the literary conventions of the genre or adopt the conventions of domestic humor.[6]

Far from a genteel novel, despite the romantic plotlines, the book's main feature was social satire of a range of American locales and institutions, well beyond what either had produced previously. Writing to Bliss in February 1873, as he was in the process of writing the book, Clemens informed his publisher that his proposed book of collected sketches could wait: "Can get sketches ready any time, but shall wait awhile, as I have good hopes of finishing a book which I am working like a dog on—a book which ought to outsell the sketches, & doubtless will. It will make a pretty lively sensation I bet you."[7] The combination of two humorists' contributions to a novel was a speculative investment that might boom or bust, but Clemens's bet was that it would succeed, at least financially, and he worked with his publisher and coauthor to help assure its success. But the authors were also writing for a subscription audience, one that expected handsome and lengthy books, but one that did not expect fiction as a product that would be canvassed door-to-door.

Mark Twain's first novel is largely elided in Twain scholarship as a failed production, sitting between his early travel books and his turn to the subject of the river with "Old Times on the Mississippi" (1874) and *The Adventures of Tom Sawyer* (1876). Everett Emerson wrote that the book "is unduly long (subscription-book length), badly plotted, and uneven. Perhaps the best thing about the book is its title. . . ." In 1965, Charles Neider went so far as to pull Mark Twain's portion of the novel out, as if by literary cesarean, and publish it separately as *The Adventures of Colonel Sellers*. He argued that the book "lived" because of Mark Twain's share and despite Warner's.[8] But if the focus of Twain scholarship is shifted from primarily literary questions to cultural meanings, *The Gilded Age* becomes one of the central books in Mark Twain's oeuvre.

The relationship between literature and commerce in Mark Twain's career is a central question as he shifted from professional funny man to humorous author. The book was announced and prefaced by a considerable amount of press, making it "*the* event of the coming season."[9] Published with the subscription house that had published Mark Twain's two previous bestsellers, *The Gilded Age* was nonetheless a risk as a publishing venture. No novel had been published by a subscription firm, which tended to publish travel books, memoirs, and histories. Additionally, the book was in press when the Panic of 1873 struck. Spurred by the failure of Jay Cooke and Company and the subsequent closing of the stock market for ten days, due largely to unregulated speculation on railroad expansion, the Panic represented the first national crisis of industrial and financial capitalism in the United States following the consolidation and incorporation of industry in Civil War–era America. The Panic lasted until 1878, contributing to high unemployment, the rise of labor tension, and widespread dissatisfaction with Grant's administration. The failure of railroad speculation, along with numerous corruption scandals in the Grant administration, truly made the novel, in the words of its subtitle, "a Tale of To-Day." By 1876, the phrase "The Gilded Age" was in use as a name for the era of political corruption.[10]

As a satire, the timing of *The Gilded Age* was perfect, yet these same factors caused sales of the book to suffer. Healthy book sales were necessary for the Clemens family to recoup financial losses from investing with Jay Cooke and Company, which created a cycle of literary satire, real financial considerations, and literary speculation that magnified the tensions between art and commerce inherent in the book. Clemens wrote his friend Dr. John Brown in February 1874 and discussed the sales of the book:

The fearful financial panic hit the book heavily, for we published in the midst of it. But nevertheless in the 8 weeks that have now elapsed since the day we published, we have sold 40,000 copies—which gives £3,000 royalty to be divided between the authors. This is really the largest two-months' sale which any American book has ever achieved (unless one excepts the cheap edition of Uncle Tom's Cabin). The average price of our book is 16 shillings a copy—Uncle Tom was 2 shillings a copy. But for the panic our sale would have been doubled, I verily believe. I do not believe the sale will ultimately go over 100,000 copies.[11]

By the end of 1874, after a year in print, the American Publishing Company had printed just over 50,000 copies, a large sale by general standards, but a distinct drop in sales after the initial publication and canvassing. In a one-year span, the book had sold 15,000 fewer copies than *Roughing It* and 20,000 fewer copies than *The Innocents Abroad*, each of which outsold the book yearly after this point. In 1879, when the publisher's records end, only 56,484 copies of the book had been printed, the steepest drop-off of Mark Twain's early books in terms of continued sales year after year. Nevertheless, the *Sun* of Baltimore noted that, by March, Mark Twain and Warner had each received $15,000 in profits from their "racy literary work," a significant amount.[12]

The promotion, circulation, and reception of *The Gilded Age* illustrates the close connection between literary works and literary business, as well as the discomfort caused when that link was too directly dramatized. Clemens closely monitored both the sales of the book and the critical responses to the novel—and his reactions show that he connected critical reception with sales prospects. Before the novel's publication, Mark Twain and Warner attempted to control the promotion and the critical reception by soliciting notices and fretting over the impression those notices would leave for the reading (and buying) public. The authors managed to gain notice for a subscription book far beyond what was normal for the time, in which subscription publishing was viewed with distrust by critics, publishers, and authors. The reviews split between three main reactions: praise of the book's satire, despite notable faults in the book as a novel; consternation, if not censure, of the humorists, who left some critics feeling "sold" by the book; and amazement by foreign critics, who marveled at the book's condemnation of American politics. Mark Twain blamed negative critical reviews for the drop-off in book sales that he saw as a sign of the book's ultimate failure. Shortly thereafter, Mark Twain's dramatization of the book, under the title of *Colonel Sellers*, became one of the most successful productions of the American theater, making the title character an American symbol and the author a significant amount of money. As Colonel Sellers was fond of saying, the history of *The Gilded Age* showed that "There's millions in it!"—even if the financial and artistic meanings of the book are more complicated than the initial speculations proposed.

ACT ONE—BUSINESS AND LETTERS

Samuel Clemens and his brother Orion had a passion for invention—from board games to railroad brakes to flying machines to his disastrous entanglement with the Paige Typesetting Machine, a technological marvel, when functional, that helped bankrupt Clemens in 1895. Clemens's passion for inventions, and his investments in them, made him the most famous man of letters who also functioned as a man of business.

On August 11, 1872, shortly before sailing on his first journey to England, Clemens informed Orion of a new book project—"Mark Twain's Self-Pasting Scrap-book." He described a practical invention for preserving newspaper clippings using pre-gummed columns that customers could wet as needed, solving some of the messy nuisances of scrapbooking. In a characteristic moment of hucksterism and business acumen, Clemens advised Orion to keep the letter and the envelope as evidence of "the date of this great humanizing & civilizing invention." He was granted a patent the next June, his second patent following one for the "Improvement in Adjustable and Detachable Straps for Garments." Production began several years later, in 1876 or 1877.[13]

Mark Twain's Patent Self-Pasting Scrap-Book went by many names and eventually came in over fifty versions, with specially designed books for newspaper clippings and for photographs, for druggists, and for children. The *Scrap-Book* may have been Clemens's most profitable business venture, apparently making him a steady income. Business records are sparse, but the first extant statement lists 26,310 scrapbooks sold in the first half of 1877, with Clemens earning $1,071.57.[14] He renewed the patent in 1892, and the *Scrap-Book* was still for sale after his death. The manufacturer/publisher of the book was Dan Slote & Co., run by one of Mark Twain's fellow "pilgrims" from the *Quaker City* excursion. Mark Twain participated both as creator of scrapbooks and as inventor of his own brand. Through the *Scrap-Book*, Mark Twain's name and image circulated to new audiences, many of whom may not have been among his readers. Mark Twain's new "book" was commented upon and advertised in venues where he had received little attention, such as the *Christian Secretary*, a Hartford-based weekly that only began to notice Mark Twain in 1876 and first reviewed one of his books the following year—the *Scrap-Book*.[15]

The company published a number of promotional pamphlets that included an illustration of Mark Twain, testimonials from newspapers and other sources, and a humorous letter from Mark Twain, in which he puffed the book as "a sound moral work." He offered testimonials "of the best sort, and from the best people" and testified to his nonmercenary purpose, which was "not to make money out of it, but to economise the profanity of this country." One version of the pamphlet offered testimonials from newspapers and government officials from all sections—North, South, West, and East, such as:

Appleton's Journal: "It is everything that can be desired; neat, convenient and simple. We recommend it to all."

Norristown Herald: "No library is complete without a copy of the Bible, Shakespeare, and Mark Twain's Scrap Book."

New Orleans Picayune: "A decided convenience"

Danbury News: "It is a valuable book for purifying the domestic atmosphere, and, being self-acting, saves the employment of an assistant. It contains nothing that the most fastidious person could object to, and is, to be frank and manly, the best thing of any age—mucilage particularly."

The advertisement linked semiserious salesmanship with the slightly irreverent, but largely relied on Mark Twain's name to sell a decidedly practical product.

An enterprising collector wanting to gather the newspaper and magazine ephemera discussing Mark Twain and his works would have needed a shelf of scrapbooks during the 1870s, when his fame exploded into national and international markets and his doings became fodder for editors looking to fill rapidly expanding periodical space. Mark Twain's words were found

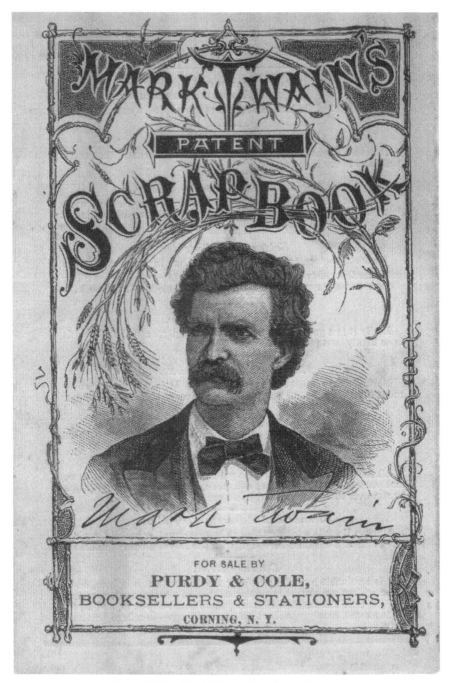

FIGURE 6.1: Mark Twain Scrapbook Cover.
Courtesy of Kevin Mac Donnell, Austin, Texas.

in newspapers in letters to the editor, excerpts from books, reprintings of previous periodical pieces, one-line squibs, and eventually interviews.[16] News about Mark Twain appeared in literary and personal gossip columns on a regular basis. Unauthorized advertisements, and flesh-and-blood imposters, spread his image into new commercial realms. As Louis Budd notes, Mark Twain's persona shifted dizzyingly in the 1870s: "More than at any other stage of Twain's career, even a well-wisher could reasonably feel free to pick from a gallery of images during the 1870s." Budd's description of Mark Twain's popular images spars between the commercial huckster and the literary author. He writes: "As 'Mark Twain,' selling out his dignity was still part of his business, but for nineteenth-century humor an effective 'sell' cast glory for shrewdness."[17] This tension between commercial shrewdness and respectable literary production helped frame Mark Twain's reputation, in his own time and throughout the history of Twain scholarship.

The critical tendency has been to look for the "real" Mark Twain lurking behind the "sell," to focus on the works that have emerged from the commercial tumult of this period as lasting literature—especially *The Adventures of Tom Sawyer* and "Old Times on the Mississippi," as well as parts of the travel books and a number of sketches. But the commercial and the artistic were intimately connected for Samuel Clemens/Mark Twain, as well as for other authors, navigating the shifting literary marketplace of postbellum America, even if some critics at his time and since would like to divorce art from commerce. That he married these two more frequently and publically than many authors did, that he sold occasional works of inferior quality or padded his books for subscription sale, and that he lived an often lavish life as a literary celebrity has opened his entire career to criticism that his artistic abilities were perverted by the marketplace. The founding works of Twain scholarship focused on the meanings of the divide between artistic quality and inferior popularity. Van Wyck Brooks argued, in his seminal work of Twain scholarship, that a religious veneration of material prosperity after the Civil War created "a vast unconscious conspiracy actuated all America against the creative spirit," which perverted Mark Twain's entire career.[18] Bernard DeVoto's spirited repudiation of Brooks sought to redeem certain works from the taint of commercialism. Both views took the line between art and the market as a natural division—not as a critical distinction used to separate the work from its context, a historical development in criticism beginning in Mark Twain's time and ranging forward to ours.

As with many critical questions on the meanings of Mark Twain, the links between commerce and art were first scouted by William Dean Howells, most thoroughly in his 1893 essay, "The Man of Letters as a Man of Business." In this essay, Howells looked back at the commercial situation of American letters stretching back to the age of Emerson, focusing on three levels: the ideals of artistic production, the challenges of artistic realities, and a solution that attempted to reframe the question.

Howells's argument attempted to separate ideal literary production from the marketplace by arguing that, in an ideal world, man would not have to live by art but would be able to produce literature separate from earning a living. Howells notes that people rightly feel that there is something profane or impious in taking money for a picture, poem, or statue, leading to his maxim that "Business is the opprobrium of Literature." But since business is "the only human solidarity," the man of letters was forced to operate in a "huckstering civilization" that violates the pure realm of art.[19] Whether Howells truly aspired to his ideal, or used it as a rhetorical device, the article attempted to create a new synthesis between business and letters in which the man of letters could reinvigorate his reputation through reframing literature as an occupation that "is allied to the great mass of wage-workers who are paid for the labor they have put into the thing done or the thing made." By grouping authors with workers, Howells attempted to move writing out of a classification as "leisure" to one of "labor" and to ally it with "the masses" rather than "the classes." As the scholar Michael Davitt Bell has argued, Howells's criticism framed literary production as masculine in order to distinguish his version of literary production from earlier cultural definitions that saw authors as feminine.[20] The focus in this essay on the *man* of letters in relation to the *man* of business is not only conventional gendered pronoun usage but also an attempt to create a masculine form of letters by recasting literary production's relation to business.

Despite the idealism of its framing, the majority of the essay dealt with practical observations about the business of letters. Howells's survey of the landscape of publication found a hierarchy in which certain authors—whom he names "literary artists"—earn both enough money to live and a form of cultural capital that raises them above the second-class authors who might earn more money but whose reputation does not benefit. Howells noted that authors before the Civil War could not live upon the earnings from their writing but relied upon their other occupations, whereas postbellum authors could make a living through the sale of their work due to an increase in magazine, newspaper, and book publication.[21] He distinguished between types of authors based on the type of publication through which they reached their readers. Magazines published the highest quality of literature; authors of literary quality earned their money by selling to a magazine editor and then publishing their work in book form, which may or may not have sold. Authors who chose to publish a book first, or aimed for the higher pay of newspapers, tended to produce inferior quality work that might pay financially but catered to a public with crude taste and thus degraded the artistic quality of the work. The reward of the literary artist for publishing in a magazine was financial and intellectual capital, defined as access to a better class of readers. Howells writes that magazine readers, "if we may judge from the quality of literature they get, are more refined than the book readers in our community; and their taste has no doubt been cultivated by that of the disciplined and experienced editors."[22]

Howells's essay reorganized the relationships between popularity, as measured by sales; fame, as an abstract literary quality; and taste, as a property of different classes of readers. This was precisely the vision of American literary culture that allowed him to dismiss the popularity of Josiah Gilbert Holland by divorcing the relationship between popularity and quality. The *Atlantic Monthly,* under Howells, sought an influential, educated readership that excused, or even trumpeted, a smaller circulation as a sign of distinction. The popularity of books that circulated on a mass scale, in this view, mitigated against their literary quality. It was in magazines, what Howells called "the regime of the great literary periodicals," that an author would make a true success: "Many factitious and fallacious literary reputations have been made through books, but very few have been made through magazines, which are not only the best means of living, but of outliving, with the author; they are both bread and fame to him."[23] Fame, as opposed to popularity, "pays" the first-rate author longer dividends.

Here are the practical shoals upon which Howells's idealistic ship foundered, and Mark Twain's example is the largest snag to be avoided. Much as his success had conflicted with Josiah Holland's link between mass success and moral quality, Mark Twain's commercial success challenged Howells's view of literature's proper relation to commerce. Unlike Holland, whose criticism throughout the 1870s sought to dismiss Mark Twain's popularity, Howells was dedicated to the promotion of his friend as a part of his canon of American literature. Several times in his essay, the counterexample of Mark Twain's success bubbled to the surface, such as when the distinctions between book success and magazine fame might seem to exclude the humorist. Howells at once made Mark Twain an exception and reintegrated him into the rule: "The most monumental example of literature, at once light and good, which has first reached the public in book form is in the different publications of Mark Twain; but Mr. Clemens has of late turned to the magazines too, and now takes their mint mark before he passes into general circulation." What Howells does not admit here is that he was the editor who first recognized Mark Twain as both light and good and provided the "mint mark" of the *Atlantic*, first through reviews and then through publication of his works in the magazine.[24]

Mark Twain again rises to the surface when Howells discussed low-quality books published only for popularity with a mass "public" uninterested in edification. His description of the qualities of such a book resonate with other critics' descriptions of Mark Twain:

> [I]f a book is vulgar enough in sentiment, and crude enough in taste, and flashy enough in incident, or, better or worse still, if it is a bit hot in the mouth, and promises impropriety if not indecency, there is a very fair chance of its success; I do not mean success with a self-respecting publisher, but with the public, which does not personally put its name to it, and is not openly smirched by it.[25]

Here, again, Howells used Mark Twain as the exception to prove the rule, arguing that Mark Twain was the only author to succeed in this form and that almost by accident. He wrote:

> No book of literary quality was made to go by subscription except Mr. Clemens's books, and I think these went because the subscription public never knew what good literature they were. This sort of readers, or buyers, were so used to getting something worthless for their money, that they would not spend it for artistic fiction, or indeed for any fiction all, except Mr. Clemens's, which they probably supposed to be bad.[26]

Howells's assertion that the readers, or "buyers," wanted to purchase something of poor quality and accidentally received good literature dismissed any serious thought into what the culture of reading of subscription books actually meant for readers—as does his condescending note that "Mr. Clemens himself no longer offers his books to the public in that way."

Critics in the 1870s often focused on the negative aspects of subscription publishing. The *Literary World*, a magazine devoted to news and gossip on the business of publishing, attacked subscription books in 1874 following Charles Dudley Warner's decision to publish by subscription, without mentioning Mark Twain. The article noted that subscription books did indeed earn more pecuniary rewards for their authors, but that other considerations should mitigate against these considerations:

> *Subscription books are in bad odor, and cannot possibly circulate among the best classes of readers, owing to the general and not unfounded prejudice against them as a class.*
>
> *Consequently an author of established reputation, who resorts to the subscription plan for the sake of making more money, descends to a constituency of a lower grade and inevitably loses caste. . . . For this loss no money could compensate.*[27]

The article argued that a book should sell based on its merit, not the "arts of importunity and trickery." The magazine largely ignored subscription publishing until it drew from "our best writers," when it was dismissed as damaging to the literary capital of the author, however beneficial it may be to that author's monetary capital.

Like many magazines, the *Literary World* largely ignored subscription books. The magazine also largely ignored Mark Twain, apart from a few mentions of his lecturing and miscellaneous comments. Pointedly, the magazine mentioned neither of Mark Twain's first two travel books. In 1871, the magazine reviewed *Mark Twain's (Burlesque) Autobiography*, which they held could only be a "money-catching scheme" with the literary quality of a "quack medicine almanac."[28] This is precisely the time in which Clemens had hoped to follow Josh Billings's lead in publishing a comic almanac, which had made his fellow humorist a significant income. The spectacle of an author, no matter how peripheral to the literary establishment in 1871, shilling for a quick buck violated the rule later expressed by Howells—authors should appear uninterested in pecuniary returns no matter how interested the author and the public actually were in the subject. Paradoxically, notices in the *Literary World* and in other magazines and newspapers consistently discussed the financial success of various books, betraying a strong connection between financial and artistic concerns that many critics tried to deny.

Mark Twain's business concerns—both literary and nonliterary—shifted in the early 1870s as he transitioned from the model of popular humorist to that of a literary author. Moving from Buffalo to Hartford, and from periodical author and editor to almost full-time author, marked a transition to the third major stage of Clemens's reputation, although Clemens's continued investment in subscription publishing, as well as his lingering status as a popular humorist, mitigated against his full acceptance into literary respectability. His new life in Hartford—a growing family and the construction of his mansion—necessitated financial capital, while his growing relationship with Howells and the prospect of publishing in the *Atlantic Monthly* highlights an increased literary capital. The English praise for Mark Twain as an author, as a lecturer, and as an American celebrity further shifted his reputation, and his decision not to lecture after 1873 shifted his financial base further away from popular venues toward publishing and invention. The decision to write a novel in which the character of "Mark Twain," central to the success of the travel books, was relegated to the role of author was both an artistic risk and a financial gamble. Thus, the publication of *The Gilded Age* reframed Mark Twain as a product, and Samuel Clemens as his creator put much stock into making the book a success—critically and financially. As Howells and other critics showed, the conjunction of these two forms of success was fraught with ideological and practical difficulties as Clemens and Warner's book entered into a literary marketplace in which such a book was a novel speculation.

ACT TWO—PUFFING THE PRODUCTIONS

While Howells and other critics pictured a realm of pure art separate from commerce, in reality, the business of letters was a pressing concern for most authors, editors, and publishers, especially as the market for writing expanded after the Civil War. The *Atlantic Monthly* undoubtedly paid more in social capital than any magazine in the 1870s, but its New York–based competitors, such as the *Galaxy* and *Scribner's Monthly*, managed to lure *Atlantic* contributors with higher pay of the more fungible sort. Even William Dean Howells was fascinated with the lavish life that subscription publishing and lecturing allowed Clemens in Hartford, and their correspondence is shot through with as much talk of business as with letters. The comfortable façade of life in Hartford tempted Howells and other *Atlantic* authors to consider subscription publishing, with Warner and Harte eventually publishing books with the American Publishing Company, of which Clemens was now part owner.

Clemens's life as a business speculator—as Mark Twain in books and articles, in publishing and bookmaking, in machines and contraptions—

placed him squarely within the cultural milieu of the era, in which the boom-and-bust cycles of capitalism based on speculation and expansion were central factors of American life. *The Gilded Age* took part in the cycle of financial boom, followed by a crash, and then a recovery, encapsulating the era, satirizing it, and ultimately providing one of its most apt names.

The Gilded Age was marketed to readers through three main methods: newspaper announcements, the subscription prospectus, and newspaper reviews. The advertising for the novel, in the prospectus and in the newspaper campaign leading up to publication, pitched the novel as a literary curiosity that should tempt readers to discover the results of an unprecedented experiment. The audience imagined for *The Gilded Age* was less clearly defined than it had been for Mark Twain's first two subscription books. As a novel, *The Gilded Age* was a new venture in subscription publishing, and it erased the "character" of Mark Twain and Warner, each of whom had relied on their narrative presence as the center of their humor. Mark Twain's earlier books had sought to ease reader concerns about irreverence by reframing the relationship between humor and information and by focusing on the central narrative presence of Mark Twain the traveler, whose "characteristic" and "unique" way of seeing things was highly amusing, with a cheerful mirth that was sold as nonthreatening. *The Gilded Age* presented a new marketing challenge.

In April 1873, as work on the novel progressed, Mark Twain and Warner began a publicity campaign for a planned fall release, although the publication was delayed until late December. To the newly created New York *Daily Graphic*, Mark Twain wrote a letter to the editor announcing the book, claiming that Warner provided the fiction and he "hurled in the facts." In a fit of parodic self-puffery, he wrote that "I consider it one of the most astonishing novels that ever was written. Night after night I sit up reading it over & over again and crying."[29] He ended by asking if his letter was advertising, and if so, would the paper charge a friend and orphan?

At the same time, he solicited a notice from Whitelaw Reid in the New York *Tribune*, where he published occasionally and whose influence Clemens had noted in worrying over its review of *Roughing It*. An initial notice appeared on April 19. Written by the humorist and political figure John Hay, the review's tone was flippant, ending with the lines: "It is no holiday work. It deals with every aspect of modern society, and we are authorized to announce that the paper on which it is written cost eleven dollars."[30] Clemens complained to Reid that by noticing the book facetiously rather than seriously, the *Tribune* would give the other newspapers the wrong impression, writing:

> *And now you give us a notice which carries the impression to the minds of other editors that we are people of small consequence in the literary world, & indeed only triflers; that a novel by us is in no sense a literary event. Half the papers in America will not see that you were meaning to say a pleasant word for us & simply chose an unfortunate way of doing it: they will merely see that you give us a stickful of pleasantry down in a corner—& every man of them will take his cue from you, (as they all do) & will act accordingly.*[31]

Clemens had held that Reid's paper helped set the tone of reviews, much like the *Atlantic Monthly* in the magazine world, and took offense at being publicized as a "trifler"—a word, it will be remembered, that was highly galling when it came from Josiah Holland one year before. He went on to argue that the novel would in fact be a literary event, even though he acknowledged that such a statement makes him sound egotistical. His ego overflows in a half-joking invective at his friend and occasional editor. Clemens notes that the "*voluntary*" subscriptions to his next book are in the thousands before it is announced, that his books continue to sell well, and that *The Innocents Abroad* had "entered permanently into the literature of the country." "These things all mean this:" he thundered (or possibly whined, depending on how you read his tone), "that I have a good reliable audience in this country—& it is the biggest one in America, too, if I do say it myself. So a novel from me alone would be a good deal in the nature of a literary event, & the *Tribune*, to be just, should have made it so I appear, I think."[32] Samuel Clemens appears to have equated literary reputation with popularity and sales without considering other factors that determined critical reputation.

Clemens's evident concern over the course and thrust of the publicity generated by notice is readily apparent. He consistently referenced the ability of the *Tribune* to set the tone of literary discussion and to advance the prospects of the book in terms of sales, ironically echoing the cloying speculations of Colonel Sellers in the book. Reid responded by writing another notice, a few days after the first, announcing for the first time in print the book's name and praising its authors:

> *It is an unusual and a courageous enterprise for two gentlemen who have already won honorable distinction in other walks of literature, to venture*

upon untrodden paths with a work so ambitious and so important as this
is likely to be. In one sense there is nothing to fear. An immense audience
is already assured beforehand; and it is fair to conclude that writers who
have displayed so much wit, insight, and delicate and fanciful observation,
in former works, will not be unprovided with the equipment which is nec-
essary to successful fiction. The new novel will be eagerly looked for and
enormously read, and we hazard little in predicting that it will contain as
much food for thought as for laughter.[33]

Clemens responded that the notice was "bully!" and averred that if
the notice deceived the public, they would be deceived in "the happy direction."[34] He seems to have not noticed, or ignored, the ambivalence of
Reid's notice, which raised the question of whether the humorists could
succeed in fiction and then dismissed this concern by pointing out that it
would sell either way.

The notices in the *Daily Graphic* and the *Tribune* did get literary gossip
stirring. In a letter dated April 22, Clemens enclosed to Reid a notice of
the book from the Springfield *Republican* from that day announcing the
book, which was drawn directly from the *Tribune*'s first notice. He noted
on the scrap: "Brief, but mighty good."[35] The Auburn, N.Y., *Daily News* cited the *Tribune* in discussing the "literary Siamese twins": "The parties are
Mark Twain and Charles Dudley Warner. The former is—well, everybody
knows Twain; the latter is the fresh, quaint, witty author of . . ." Notices
appeared in papers such as the Chicago *Tribune,* which recopied the New
York notices, throughout the summer and fall, testifying to the interest
in the book.[36]

The second stage of publicity was to stir the interest into action—specifically, the purchase of the book from the roaming agents who were soon
spreading across the country. The sales prospectus was the physical artifact
that presented "Mark Twain," along with his less well known coauthor, to
a public stretching across the country. The dummy illustrated the goals of
book buying and reading, the expanding bounds of Mark Twain's fame,
and the shifting goals of the humorist and his product. In September 1873,
Bliss printed one additional layer of advertising in the *American Monthly*,
seeking canvassers to peddle the book door-to-door, which read in part:

This novelty in the way of books will draw the attention of the public more
than anything printed for years. The great popularity of the authors, and the
desire to see how two so different in style can write upon the same subject

upon the same pages, will makes its sale sure and easy. This book will be fully illustrated and will, we are sure add to the fame of its authors, and put money in the pockets of agents.[37]

In trying to sell the sellers, Bliss pointed to the book's major selling point—its novelty—and teased its major sticking point: the contents of the novel, which were unlike anything either author had written before.

Comparing the prospectus for *The Gilded Age* with that of Mark Twain's earlier books presents an evolving picture of the humorist and his relation to his audience. The sales dummy for *The Innocents Abroad*, as discussed in chapter 2, presented Mark Twain to a subscription audience as a commodity—the author of "The Most Unique and Spicy Volume in Existence"—but promised a book filled with both information and beautiful descriptions, as well as "with 234 BEAUTIFUL, SPIRITED, AND APPROPRIATE DRAWINGS." The prospectus traded on the reputation and presence of Mark Twain as author and character as a central feature of the book. Most significantly, the second version of the prospectus included five pages of notices from the press, selected to portray Mark Twain as a suitable humorist for wide public consumption, balancing humor with information while downplaying the threat of irreverence.

The subsequent dummy for *Roughing It* highlighted similar themes and featured a similar construction, with a focus on illustrations over text and framed by written and visual images that illustrated Mark Twain's role as a humorous author fit for one's center table. The prospectus for *Roughing It* contained roughly sixty pages, focusing on the major topics of the book: western life, mining, the Mormons, the Sandwich Islands, and Mark Twain as a lecturer. Both the book and prospectus began with the "Prefatory" statement by Mark Twain that framed the relationship between the author and the reader: "This book is merely a personal narrative, and not a pretentious history or a philosophical dissertation. It is a record of several years of variegated vagabondizing, and its object is rather to help the resting reader while away and idle hour than afflict him with metaphysics, or goad him with science." In a move typical of Mark Twain, the preface jokingly framed his humorous discourse as different from, and more entertaining than, seemingly serious discourses of science and philosophy, by stating: "Yes, take it all around, there is quite a good deal of information in the book. I regret this very much; but really it could not be helped: information appears to stew out of me naturally, like the precious ottar of roses out of the otter. . . . Therefore, I can only claim indulgence at the hands of the reader, not justification."[38] Unlike the Preface of *The Innocents Abroad*, here Mark Twain burlesqued the expected connection between humor and information, which can be read as a sign of his growing comfort with his audience and their expectations.

Confined to the end of the dummy of *Roughing It*, the advertising section was notable for its lack of newspaper notices. It includes two single-page advertising posters, one with an illustration of a stagecoach and one featuring the illustration of Mark Twain's first lecture. As in the *Innocents* dummy, the illustration of the author exhibits the generic marks of the caricature of Mark Twain—a moustache, wild hair, and caricatured features.[39]

Each poster links humor to information, with one noting that the reader would find the book to contain "not only matter of an amusing character, but to be a valuable and correct history of an intensely interesting period, with ludicrous descriptions of scenes never before written up." The other, in a more ornamental sales style, trumpeted that the book was "Particularly adapted to Family Reading" and "Designed to Amuse and Instruct." As a companion volume to *The Innocents Abroad*, the ad promised: "It is suited to the wants of the old, the young, the rich, the poor, the sad, and the gay. 'There is a time to laugh,' and those who buy this book, will clearly see that the time has arrived." In a distinct sales patter closer to Barnum's productions than the dignified (and lengthy) justification of humor and dialect that had prefaced the second series of James Russell Lowell's *Biglow Papers*, the prospectus sought readers who would use the product for entertainment and is thus irreverent about the link between literature and business that concerned Howells and others.

Potential purchasers were being sold a known product—Mark Twain. The "Publisher's Announcement" framed the reader's interest in and knowledge of Mark Twain as stemming from the phenomenal success of *The Innocents Abroad*. The personality of Mark Twain as a travel narrator who sees the world with unique eyes sells the book, which is:

Brimful of characteristic humor, running over with smile-persuading and laughter-forcing incidents and ideas, those who seek amusement for idle moments, will find in this book an inexhaustible vein to work, full of the purest ore. . . .

This book is a characteristic one, full of those peculiarities which have made its author's writings so popular, a prominent one being a cheerfulness which pervades every line.

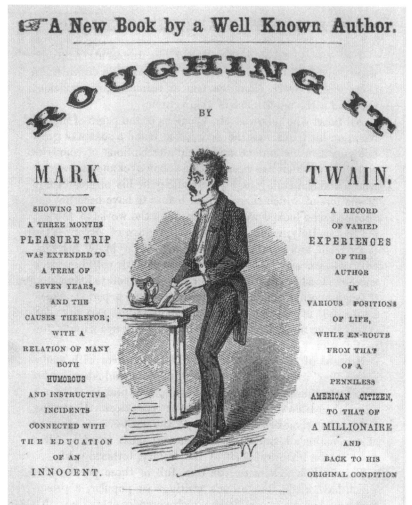

FIGURE 6.2: Advertising Poster from *Roughing It*.
Courtesy of Kevin Mac Donnell, Austin, Texas

The repetition of "characteristic" to describe the book indicates that the reader knows what to expect from Mark Twain's humor, and, to reinforce the point, the notice ends by promising that the reader would find on every page "warmth, light, cheerfulness, and innocent mirth." The prospectus also featured numerous illustrations, including several featuring visual representations of Mark Twain. A final page sets out the terms of sale, including promises of fine paper, beautiful and humorous illustrations, and over 600 pages for between $3.50 and $5.00, sold by subscription only.

The sales prospectus for *The Gilded Age* presented a different picture of the humorist, one that was neither "characteristic" nor entirely "cheerful." For the 1,362 sales prospectuses that went to canvassers, Bliss selected excerpts and illustrations from the book and wrote (or had written) an advertising puff about the book.[40] First, *The Gilded Age* was the first novel sold by subscription and, as a jointly written novel, was itself a unique production. Second, the combination of two humorous authors, of different styles and reputations, was both a selling point and a possible cause for concern for readers who appreciated one or the other of the authors. The very first page of the sales dummy contained the sales pitch for the novel as "A Literary Curiosity," which framed the production in terms that seek to both sell and reassure the reader:

> *The announcement some months since that such a book was to appear, created a marked sensation in literary circles and called forth much comment from the press; great expectations have been raised regarding it, and an unparalleled eagerness exists in the minds of the people to see and read it.*
>
> *The book will be found to be unique and original in all things, and while ostensibly still a novel, will differ from books generally known as such: the peculiar and opposite styles of its authors, being so interwoven and blended on every page, as to produce the most charming effect. The readers of Mark Twain's "INNOCENTS ABROAD," and "ROUGHING IT," and of Warner's "MY SUMMER GARDEN," and "BACK LOG STUDIES," will find in this volume, pages, on which will seem to be concentrated the force and humor of all those books, and its satire, although directed against prominent persons and things, will be found not to be misplaced.*

If the experiment was preceded both with eagerness and a touch of anxiety, the prospective reader is here reassured that the combination of the two humorists had produced "the most charming effect" and that the book's satire, not entirely characteristic of any of the books named, will "not be misplaced." Still, the dummy promised something for everyone, noting that "the superficial reader will find abundant entertainment in this volume, the careful studious one an ample supply of material for afterthought, while the scholar will discover something upon which to exercise his ingenuity." Now that Mark Twain's name and reputation were more established, the dummies were less concerned with respectability than salability.

The remainder of the dummy is similar to Mark Twain's previous prospectuses—with illustrations interspersed with fifty pages of text made up almost entirely of Mark Twain's material, including the description of a steamboat race, which was widely excerpted in newspapers. Warner's material made up only four of the fifty pages. It is unclear who made the selections, but Hamlin Hill speculates that the material was selected to highlight the voice of Mark Twain, which the publisher knew would be the selling point of the book.[41] The reader of the prospectus would have understood little of the plot of the book, but a careful reader would have learned several important plot points before their time.

The end of the prospectus does not contain a sales pitch, illustrated advertisement, or other puffery of the book, but it does contain a one-page defense of subscription publishing. Addressing the concerns that subscription books are priced much higher than comparable trade books, the article mounts a defense by pointing out that the illustrations and paper are of a higher quality than trade books, which can be tested by the buyer who will find that subscription books are equal to "any book equal in *weight*, *size*, and *popularity*." The notice also defends the reputation of the canvassing agents and notes that subscription books only end up in bookstores through fraud. The audience for this defense of subscription sales may have been double—both the readers/buyers considering a purchase, fearful about getting value for their money, and the agents themselves, who were afraid of competition from bookstores. Indeed, Elisha Bliss "dumped" a large number of copies of the novel into bookstores in December 1873 in order to capitalize on the holiday market, manufacturing a fake title page to make it appear that the edition was pirated.[42] The defense of subscription publishing might also speak to a new class of readers who may not have encountered subscription books before but would now wish to buy the unique production by two well-known authors.

Clemens and Warner's third stage of publicity was less successful. Their aim was to send review copies to as many as 60 leading periodicals and up to 500 newspapers, as stipulated by the authors' contract with the American Publishing Company. Clemens's friend Edward H. House proposed reviewing the novel for the New York *Tribune* but was rebuked by Reid. Clemens took House's side and wrote Warner not to have any more to do with Reid: "He is a contemptible cur, and I want nothing more to do with him. I don't want the *Tribune* to have the book at all. Please tell Bliss *not to send a copy there under any circumstances*."[43] In his impetuous manner, he turned his back on an influential, and largely friendly, outlet due to a perceived slight, which turned out to be exaggerated. In the realm of periodicals, Warner asked his friend E. C. Stedman to review the book for *Scribner's*, and Clemens solicited a review from William Dean Howells. Both critics were unable to write a review praising their friends' work, so they declined, and the book was not reviewed in any of the major American literary periodicals of the day, apart from the *Galaxy*.[44] While the book was widely noticed and reviewed by newspapers and some smaller magazines, the lack of attention by the quality magazines reflected the difficulty that critics had in making sense of the joint production.

It is a telling omission that the *Atlantic* failed to mention a novel written by Warner and Mark Twain. The book met with private critique from Howells, who wrote to Clemens:

> Up to the time old Hawkins dies your novel is of the greatest promise—I read it with joy—but after that it fails to assimilate the crude material with which it is fed, and it becomes a confirmed dyspeptic at last. Still it is always entertaining; and it kept me up till twelve last night, though I needed sleep. I was particularly sorry to have Sellers degenerate as he did, and none of the characters quite fulfill their early promise.[45]

He then offered to withhold his public opinion. Howells's response here is illustrative for two reasons: first, it shows in action the "realistic" criteria he used to judge a book's value (assimilation of material, character development) that matter despite a book's entertainment value, and second, it shows that he was willing to forgo his critical role in shaping the reading public in favor of his role as supporter and friend. Howells had visited Hartford in January and March of 1873, staying with Warner and visiting with Clemens. Howells and Mark Twain even went so far as to have characters in their respective books reading a book by the other.[46]

The critical reception of *The Gilded Age* is a point where Mark Twain's memory is illustrative, even when his relationship to the facts is not so solid. Holding the theory that all reviews would repeat the praise or censure of the first review, Clemens had solicited favorable early reviews to set the tone for the book's reception. In his *Autobiography*, Mark Twain claimed that he sent his books to Howells to shape critical reception:

> *Therefore, more than once I took the precaution of sending my book in manuscript, to Mr. Howells, when he was editor of the "Atlantic Monthly," so that he could prepare a review of it at leisure. I know he would way* [sic] *the truth about the book—I also know that he would find more merit than demerit in it, because I already knew that that was the condition of the book. I allowed no copy of it to go out to the press until after Mr. Howells's notice of it had appeared. That book was always safe. There wasn't a man behind a pen in all America that had the courage to find anything in the book which Mr. Howells had not found—there wasn't a man behind a pen in America that had spirit enough to say a brave and original thing about the book on his own responsibility.*[47]

Mark Twain defined the trade of critic as "the most degraded of all trades," based on the average man's lack of independent thought: "He is not interested in contriving an opinion of his own, by study and reflection, but is only anxious to find out what his neighbor's opinion is and slavishly adopt it."

As an example of the influence of critics, he tells the story of the reception of *The Gilded Age*. He remembered—incorrectly, thirty or so years later—that he had sent a copy of the book to Howells to review, but that the New York *Daily Graphic*, the illustrated paper in which he had first announced the book the previous April, issued a negative review that soured the press against the novel before Howells had a chance to review it. He claims to have given the editor an advance copy with the request that he wait to review the book until after the *Atlantic Monthly* review. In his recollection, the *Graphic* had published a review accusing Mark Twain of dishonesty in his "moral attitude toward the public" and charging him with swindling the public. The newspaper had, as he remembered, asserted that "I had used my name to float it [*The Gilded Age*] and give it currency; a currency—so the critic averred—which it could not have acquired without my name, and that this conduct was a grave fraud upon the people."[48] Mark Twain's facts are skewed, but his frustration with critical power, and his anxiety with the "currency" of his reputation, is clear. He ends his reminiscence with the swipe at humorists and critics that serves as this book's epigram:

> However, let it go. It is the will of God that we must have critics, and missionaries, and Congressmen, and humorists, and we must bear the burden. Meantime, I seem to have been drifting into criticism myself. But that is nothing. At the worst, criticism is nothing more than a crime, and I am not unused to that.
>
> —*MARK TWAIN'S AUTOBIOGRAPHY*[49]

ACT THREE—SATIRE OR FRAUD?

As a "literary event," *The Gilded Age* was both widely publicized and the cause of considerable critical confusion. The book inspired expectant curiosity to see the result of the unprecedented combination of two well-known American authors. The actual publication in December 1873, after a delay of several months, brought a product to the reading public that seemed to meet few expectations of style, tone, and subject while inspiring opposing views of the book's value. Without the influence of Howells's *Atlantic* or Reid's *Tribune*, newspaper reviews varied widely in their reviews of *The Gilded Age*, which was more widely reviewed than *Roughing It* but significantly less than *The Innocents Abroad*.[50] Reviews largely agreed that the book was far different than what had been expected from the two humorists, but reviewers largely split on whether the resulting production was a valuable satire on American life or whether the authors had "sold" the public a poor product.

Early reviews of the book indeed set the tone for the reviews that followed—but critics followed two different trends of thought on the value of the book. The *Graphic*'s review appeared on December 23, the official release date, and did not accuse the authors of fraud, as Mark Twain later remembered. Instead, the review noted that the book had disappointed the high anticipation of its creation, calling it an "incoherent series of sketches" lacking Mark Twain's "characteristic fun" and Warner's subtle humor. The review speculates that each author wrote separate parts, then edited them together, then each struck out what was characteristic of each other's humor, concluding, "And so it has come to pass that the two most brilliant humorists in America . . . have written a book in which we look almost in vain for the traces of either's pen."[51] The paper also hinted that the incoherence might have been a joke on Mark Twain's part, a trope that would appear in later criticism.

Reviews in the New York *Herald* and the Boston *Transcript*, from December 22 and 23, respectively, both praised the satirical thrust of the book, with the *Herald* calling it "a clever though rude satire upon certain customs and institutions, many of which deserve contempt and reprobation, it will scarcely be too highly praised."[52] The Hartford *Courant*, of which Warner was co-editor, reviewed the book on December 23, noting the main thrust of critical contention:

> *Perhaps the first thing to strike the attention of the reader will be that The Gilded Age is by no means a comic work. There is an abundance of dry humor and quiet wit, and caustic satire, but underneath it all, and perceptible to everyone is a serious purpose, an evident desire to hold up the mirror of truth to the eyes of a nation which greatly needs to recognize the truth. There is great enjoyment in the book, in its wit, its unexpected flashes of humor, its droll fancies, its occasional incongruous conceits and its frequently brilliant word pictures. . . .*[53]

Mark Twain's recollection, then, was largely mistaken in its salient points, although it demonstrates a distinct and long-lasting concern on his part about the power of critical reviews in shaping audience reaction. In the case of *The Gilded Age*, this anxiety was pronounced due to the novel's collaborative nature, its place as the first novel by both authors, and the financial risks it entailed.

The satire of ungrounded speculation in the book would surely have resonated with readers, and the character of Colonel Sellers was praised by reviewers as being one of the few lifelike characters in the book. Sellers observes:

> *Beautiful credit! The foundation of modern society. Who shall say that this is not the golden age of mutual trust, of unlimited reliance upon human promises? That is a peculiar condition of society which enables a whole nation to instantly recognize point and meaning in the familiar newspaper anecdote, which puts into the mouth of a distinguished speculator in lands and mines this remark:—"I wasn't worth a cent two years ago, and now I owe two millions of dollars."*[54]

Immediately following, Colonel Seller reassures his wife, who is worried by their constant indebtedness, by "drawing" her a map of the railroad line he was sure would make a fortune for their town—and his own fortune—using household objects to represent the towns sure to be along the new line. He ends with:

> ... and then away you go to Corruptionville, the gaudiest country for early carrots and cauliflowers that ever—good missionary field, too. There ain't such another missionary field outside the jungles of Central Africa. And patriotic?—why they named it after Congress itself. Oh, I warn you, my dear, there's a good time coming, and it'll be right along before you know what you're about, too. That railroad's fetching it. You see what it is as far as I've got, and if I had enough bottles and soap and boot-jacks and such things to carry it along to where it joins onto the Union Pacific, fourteen hundred miles from here, I should exhibit to you in that little internal improvement a spectacle of inconceivable sublimity. So, don't you see? We've got the railroad to fall back on. . . .[55]

The rollicking satire of Col. Seller's speculation seems to have been central to the authors—who used an illustration of the scene as a frontispiece. But the book was filled with passages of satire that were more disjointed, less fun, and only thinly disguised caricatures of current events.

Critical responses focused largely on the questions of satire and literary reputations—with one major thread valuing the book's satire, despite the fact that the novel was of questionable quality as fiction, and one major thread holding that the satire was poor and that the book was a failed speculation that banked on reader expectations of the authors. Reviews that praised the book, for the most part, focused on the quality of the satire rather than the book's worth as fiction. The Boston *Globe*, in a Christmas day review, opined that the book was amusing but lacked the "characteristic raciness" of both authors and was crude in artistic construction. Nevertheless, the review praised the book's satire, holding that "the moral taught by the book is excellent. That it is exceedingly entertaining the mere names on the title-page are sufficient assurance." The Springfield *Republican* framed the issue as a critical puzzle, writing that "to apply the usual canons of criticism to such a book would, of course, be absurd."[56] And while the story as such did not amount to much, they found the book to be one of the best satires of current life that had been printed. Numerous newspapers commented on the power of the satire from the early reviews in December through March, as commentary spread.

This critical thread was summed up in a column printed in two separate San Francisco newspapers in March 1874. The column was prefaced by a note claiming that the book had experienced unprecedented sales and had been attacked by politicians and the press. The excerpts provided, on the other hand, are uniformly positive, and the reviews from religiously inclined newspapers may be the most interesting:

> *The satire of the book is pungent enough to have grown on a red pepper plant, and the accuracy of aim with which it is delivered is not excelled.—[Hearth and Home, N.Y.*

> *A careful reading of the book from beginning to end; and [t]hat we undertook as a duty we finished with no little zest. WE WISH SOME TRACT SOCIETY WOULD SEE THAT IT IS WIDELY CIRCULATED AT WASH-INGTON.—[Boston Congregationalist.*

> *The way in which this work is done is simply admirable. Better satires upon the distinguishing features of our recent national life have never been put before the public, and done with a crispness of style that renders the work wonderfully attractive and readable.—[Springfield, Mass, Republican.*

> *. . . It is plain that the book must do good. Dickens did more than any other man to purify English politics, and it would seem that Mark Twain and Warner have a like mission to perform in the United States.—[Faribault, Minn., Democrat.*[57]

Hamlin Hill points out that Clemens's publisher collected a number of these positive reviews into an advertising broadside, presumably to help canvassers with sales and reviewers with public sentiment.[58]

Many reviews focused on the effects of the book as satire, not on the book as humor or as a novel. As Linda Morris notes, while satire as a literary form "relies upon humor to expose both human and institutional failure," its relationship to humor is not a constant.[59] In *The Gilded Age*, the character of Colonel Sellers was singled out by critics as characteristic of the exaggerative humor of the American school. On the other hand, the book's satire of political corruption lacked the humorous thrust of Sellers, and the whole of the book lacked an important element of satire—a clear alternative or solution to what was being critiqued.[60] Almost every critic failed to notice, or at least mention, Mark Twain and Warner's satire of sensation fiction, instead reading the poor plotting and hackneyed instances as poor novel writing, not as a satire thereof.

The discussion of satire posited a range of satirical aims and modes, which could be more humorous or more serious, shading into straight cultural critique. The seriousness of the satire was the basis for most of the positive critical attention received in magazines. The Unitarian magazine, *Old and New*, reviewed the work in March 1874, responding to those critics who found the satire too veiled or too serious. Instead, the review argued that the satire is of a type with the deadpan humor of both men, who never smile at their own jokes. "The result is," the review notes, "*that you see it yourself; and that* is what makes men laugh." The satire of the book, then, was marked by the absence of both humorists' personalities and from their judgment of the corruption portrayed. The reader must see the satire, and like deadpan humor, respond properly, although the result for this satire is not a laugh, but action to "PURIFY THE SUFFRAGE."[61] The praise of the book's "serious" satirical purpose—divorced from artistic quality—points to the possibility that satire could be divorced from humor and laughter.

The question of whether the book's satire was accurate, properly aimed, or appropriate was raised in numerous reviews, as in the review from the *Independent*, a leading religious newspaper that held that the book represented corruption and venality as the realities of American life. "Unfortunately," the reviewer notes, "the reader does not get the idea of strained and grotesque unreality which characterizes Mark Twain's other books; but that this is intended for a fair representation of congressional life; and he will learn from it that it is a disgrace to be a congressman and will learn to despise his country."[62] Reader response to the book was central to the question of interpretation. If critics thought that readers would see the satire as corrective of social ills, then the book was largely praised as satire, but if critics thought that the satire was too deadpan, or "serious," then the book was largely thought to be a failure.

The Boston *Daily Advertiser* argued that the book augured poorly for each author's future as novelists, and that as satirists their success was only partial. In trying to make the satire humorous, the authors had failed, and "the dreadful realism of the satire does not consort agreeably with the humor." Instead, the picture was "grave and gross," filled with "exasperating levity," but lacking sufficient scorn of its pictures of corruption to be corrective. The critic writes: "But there is great power here, and it is exerted strangely. The picture drawn is revolting to the last degree."[63] Harking back to Mark Twain's metaphor of the successful lecture, the balance between serious and humorous "plugs" inserted into the narrative seems to have been of out of balance, partially due to the collaborative nature of the book, but it can also be ascribed to critical expectations of the link between humor and satire, the reputations of the authors, and ways that readers approached the text.

The review in *Appleton's* took a different tack on the book by questioning whether it was wise to categorize Mark Twain as merely a humorist. The review praised the satire, the humor, and even the realistic description, but faulted the combination of the parts—like a salad poorly tossed. Most importantly, the review expresses a critical statement of the underlying power of Mark Twain's writings and the "painful penalty" that makes his audience look for a laugh. Thoughtful people, the critic insisted, are not blind to Mark Twain's "quaint and peculiar originality, acuteness, we will even say genius, of this author's mind; to its real power and subtilty, the keenness of its observation, and its perpetual and consistent hatred of feebleness and sham. There is always something in Mark Twain's writings . . . which makes us feel that it would do one positive good, and be a pleasure of no ordinary kind, to hear his talk or read his works when—if such a time ever could come—he was not funny."[64] This statement is one of the earliest versions of a trope that would counter the "buffoon narrative" of Holland and others: the "penalty of humor" that obscures Mark Twain's underlying power.

One review, from the Utica, New York *Morning Herald*, praised the book as both satire and as fiction, stating, "It is wonderfully varied and vivacious." The review notes that the reader will rush through the book without noticing its power, only to have "the thought that very much more than appears upon the surface of the page runs beneath it." Not only is the book's satire worthwhile—"a broadside discharge of heavy guns at everything hollow in modern society"—but the story and characters are praised: "The prevailing characteristic of the book is life; life thoughtout." Whereas other critics searched for the distinctive voices of its authors, this reviewer found the book "characteristic of both its authors": "It has Mark Twain's startling mixtures and situations, and Mr. Warner's quieter, subtiler plays of thoughts and words. . . . The book is so novel, so bold, and so entertaining that an immense sale must follow its publication." This review is noteworthy as the only to praise the book so highly in terms of its composition and its satire.[65]

Insofar as reviewers evaluated the book as satire, reviews were largely positive, with the exceptions noted above. The negative reviews, for the most part, focused on the reputation of the authors—to their detriment. The *Literary World* argued that the "buffoon" could not lead to reform, but saved most of its criticism for the commercial aspects of the project, writing: "The book has a strong savor of lucre; it was evidently written to sell, and in the hope of gaining a liberal heap of that money, whose worship it purports to ridicule."[66] This view was in holding with the magazine's consistent dislike of subscription publishing and its previous critique of Mark Twain as too interested in money. The *Literary World* wondered that a man with Charles Dudley Warner's literary reputation would "lend his name to such cheap and feeble stuff."

The "savor of lucre" that critics discerned about the book threatened to damage the reputation of both authors, and reviews showed that those reputations were a form of property to be guarded. The San Francisco *Daily Evening Bulletin* noted that authors and publishers had as much right to the "tricks of the trade" of publicity as patent-medicine sellers in order to attract attention, and that the production clearly demonstrates the power of "Printing-house Square" to bank on the reputations of authors rather than the quality of work. It reads: "Literary reputation in these days is as merchantable as any other copy-righted manufacture; suffers damage, has its protection in law, rises and falls with the changes of fashion, may be bequeathed for the support of a family."[67] Mark Twain, Warner, and their publisher had taken advantage of the curious circumstances of the book to circulate the novel, which would sink or float under its own merits (which were, according to this review, rather thin).

Clemens certainly remembered the negative press and ascribed the supposed failure of the book to the negative review of the *Daily Graphic*, although scholars assume that the negative review he referred to in his autobiography was actually from the Chicago *Tribune*.[68] This review, more than any other, excoriated the authors for perpetrating a fraud on the reading public by circulating inferior goods based on their reputations. If the authors hadn't been well known, with a reputation for quality entertainment, then the book would have found an audience based on its merits and would not require "severest censure": "[W]hen the two have condescended to trifle with their honorable reputation and with the confidence of the public, indignation is justly excited and outspoken." The review recited the reputations of the authors—Warner as purveyor of "refined and delicate beauty," and Mark Twain's humor as "quaint and fertile," deserving "even a trans-Atlantic popularity." The indignation is palpable and repeated:

> When, therefore, a book so utterly bald, so peurile, so vicious even . . . appears with the signatures of Mark Twain and Charles Dudley Warner to give it passport among respectable readers, wrath and disgust may rightfully inspire the critic to chastise them with mercy.
> . . . Their names had become a sort of certificate to high character. It is a fraud to the reading public to append them to a trashy book like the mongrel before us. Stupidity can be forgiven, but deliberate deceit—never.[69]

The review also points out that book reviews could not warn customers in far-flung places who would buy the book from a canvasser and would be defrauded by the authors without warning.

This review appeared in a paper that had staunchly defended Grant, and other negative reviews appeared in Republican-leaning papers.[70] The growing scandals of the administration, especially the exposure of the Credit Mobilier scandal the year before, which had mixed railroad speculation and Congressional corruption, would surely have resonated with the book's satire. The political dimensions of the book's interpretation adds to the complexity of evaluating its reception by pointing out the possibility that critics (and readers) approached the book with both literary and political prejudices in mind. As a political satire, the book raised the fraught subject of representing American society as an object of ridicule and correction.

The politics of national representation were the key aspect of the book's international reception. In discussing the book on its merits, the *Independent* had included the remark: "We should blush to see this book republished in Europe."[71] In the half-year leading up to the book's publication, Mark Twain was in England, enjoying his status as "Lion," performing his lectures, and securing copyright for English and Canadian editions of *The Gilded Age*. The vogue for Mark Twain described in the previous chapter did not translate into either sales or critical success of his new book. Clemens's English publisher, Routledge, printed only 8,500 copies in the first year, and it was not reprinted until 1877.[72] Critical reception in England was fairly consistent in damning the book as both literature and as satire. Reviews noted that *The Gilded Age* was far more critical of America than the works of British authors who had been criticized by Americans for speaking ill of their country. The London *Graphic*'s review is both illustrative and colorful: "Messrs. Twain and Warner are both American citizens, and so can hardly be suspected of any wish wantonly to foul their own nest for the amusement of foreigners; but we are confident that if any Englishmen had ventured on a picture of American manners and institutions half as highly coloured, he would have at once been loudly accused of the most rancorous spite and the grossest misinterpretation." Dennis Welland points out that British views of humor clearly separated humor from serious intention, with the notable exception of Dickens, and that Mark Twain's reputation to this point was almost wholly as a humorous author and lecturer. Serious social satire from American authors was largely unknown in England until the next decade.[73]

British criticism, and much of the American, seemed to have missed Mark Twain's (and Werner's) ostensible moral, which was spelled out in a preface to the English edition: "But I have a great strong faith in a noble future for my country. A vast majority of the people are straightforward and honest; and this late state of things is stirring them to action."[74] English reviews discussed in America showed that this point was largely glossed over. In a moment of transatlantic circulation, the Syracuse *Daily Courier* printed a notice in the "Current Topics" section reporting on the negative review of the *Athenaeum* of London and the "washing of so much of the dirty linen of American speculative politics in the face of the public."[75] The Hartford *Daily Courant* similarly printed a European assessment of the book, a translation of Th. Bentzon's "L'Age Dore En Amerique" from the *Revue des Deux Mondes* (i.e., "The Review of Some Two Worlds"). Here, the French critic praised Mark Twain and Warner for showing that the Golden Age of America had devolved into gilding covered with "plague spots and dirt." Coming from two Americans, this truth was more powerful than all the Europeans who had similarly pointed out American faults. As a novel, it is a "coarse daguerreotype" and a "mixture of good sense and of folly," but Bentzon notes that one should not expect quality from Mark Twain but only frank and buffoonish caricatures that "drown the truth in exciting a laugh."[76] The French critic was more than happy to accept the poor picture as portraying a truth about America's lack of civilization.

ACT FOUR—*COLONEL SELLERS* AS SPECULATIVE INVESTMENT

The timing of *The Gilded Age* was perfect, in a cultural—if not a business—sense, as it was published in the midst of the Panic of 1873. Healthy book sales were necessary for the Clemens family to recoup financial losses from investing with Jay Cooke and Company, the bank whose collapse due to railroad speculations had initiated the Panic, which created a circle of literary satire, real financial considerations, and literary speculation that made the success of the book distinctly important. The book initially sold well, possibly outselling Mark Twain's two previous travel books in the first two months. But sales faded quickly.

For reasons that remain unclear, the sales of *The Gilded Age* dropped precipitously in the spring of 1874, the time when the Chicago *Tribune* and other newspapers were debating whether the book was indeed a fraud. In a pattern that would repeat in newspaper comments on other controversies, such as the discussion of the Whittier birthday dinner discussed in the next chapter, the later newspaper comments took a perverse pleasure in mocking the failure. An early April article in the St. Louis *Democrat* argued that the book was actually a hoax played by the authors, claiming:

> It utterly lacks Twain's quaintness and Warner's breezy freshness of style. But the secret is out. It is confidently asserted that the "Gilded Age" is a gigantic practical joke. It is declared that, wishing to test the credulity of the public, these two notorious wits had the book prepared by several obscure newspaper local reporters. . . . [T]he whole story is probably a canard, but any one who, out of respect for the alleged authors, will read the book, will feel that the account is extremely probable.[77]

This story could be a humorous reverberation of the Chicago *Tribune*'s not-so-funny accusation of fraud, or it could be an April Fool's Day joke on the reputation of the authors. Writing to Howells in 1880, Clemens rehearsed the effect of reviews on the sales of the book by claiming that he had long since forbade review copies from going to anyone but Howells, David Gray, and Warner. He wrote:

> You were the three men whom I could trust to say the good thing if it could be honestly said; or be & remain charitably silent. I am justified in being afraid of the general press, because it killed the "Gilded Age" before you had a chance to point out that there were merits in that book. The sale ceased almost utterly until the adverse criticisms were forgotten—then began again, & has kept smoothly on. During the past 12 months (to Jan. 1) it has sold a trifle over 1500 copies—not greatly behind Innocents & Tom Sawyer, each of which sold a fraction under 2200 copies—& hardly any behind Roughing It, which sold 1800.[78]

Despite some selective memory of the circumstances, Clemens's evident concern with the damaging effects of critical approbation upon sales illustrates his belief that the public measure of literary worth was intimately linked to the business of letters.[79]

By late spring 1874, the boom-and-bust cycle of literary speculation had largely relegated *The Gilded Age*, as a book, to a failed speculation, despite the rather large sums it had earned both authors. At the same time, Mark Twain turned his portion of the literary property into one of the most popular stage plays of the age, which would become one of the most financially lucrative productions of his career. The stage version of *The Gilded Age*, renamed *Colonel Sellers* soon after its run began, was a hit—it played in New York for 119 nights, from September 1874 to January 1875. It then toured around the country, playing in Chicago, Boston, and New Orleans, and was revived almost yearly from 1876 to 1888. The play made Clemens as much as $70,000, the equivalent of $1.7 million in 2013.[80] Finally, and unexpectedly, there were in fact riches to be found in Mark Twain's speculations.

Relatively little scholarly attention has been paid to the role of the play in Mark Twain's career, possibly since it is of questionable quality or because its monetary importance might cast a shadow on his artistic value. Phillip Walker notes that the unexpected success of *Colonel Sellers* inspired for Clemens "more than twenty-five years of unsuccessful intermittent endeavor in the theater."[81] More exactly, the unexpected success of the play led Samuel Clemens to try to replicate his stage success with a series of failed plays.

Clemens and Warner had copyrighted the dramatic rights to the book in 1873 but seem to have had no plans to dramatize the book until Clemens learned of an unauthorized production staged in San Francisco. Written by the theater critic for the San Francisco *Golden Era*, the play had proven a success with the comedian John T. Raymond in the role of Colonel Sellers. The San Francisco *Figaro* noted that Raymond "presented one of the best hits of character acting ever seen. If he does not make 'The Gilded Age' his star piece, he will miss the tide which, taken at the flood, leads on to fortune." Clemens protested the production and soon purchased the rights to the play for $200 (later giving the author $200 more).[82] He also convinced Warner to relinquish dramatic rights to each other's characters, cutting Warner out of any profits from the play, a situation that may have lead to their falling out.[83] Clemens wanted the prominent actor Edwin Booth to play the role of Seller, but settled for Raymond.

As a play, *Colonel Sellers* was mainly a vehicle for the title character, helping to solidify Sellers's place as an iconic American character type. The character had been the most highly (and often the only) character praised in reviews of the novel. Clemens had based the character of Sellers on his mother's cousin, James Lampton, and he felt a lifelong fondness for both the man and the character, writing in his autobiography: "The real Sellers, as I knew him in James Lampton, was a pathetic and beautiful spirit, a manly man, a man with a big foolish, unselfish heart in his bosom, a man to be loved." He viewed the character's mixture of humor and pathos to be key, and he feuded with Raymond over aspects of the portrayal he found clownish. Comparing Raymond's version of Sellers to its model, Clemens later fumed, "The real Colonel Sellers was never on the stage. Only half of him was there. Raymond could not play the other half of him; it was above his level." The half Raymond lacked was the character's heart, and since Clemens thought Raymond had no heart, he failed to capture his vision.[84] This reaction to the play may also be traced to his jealousy that Raymond received credit for the character's success. Clemens acknowledged the play's faults and strengths to Howells shortly after its opening: "I believe it will go. The newspapers have been complimentary. It is simply a *Setting* for the one character, Col. Sellers—as a *play* I guess it will not bear a critical assault in force."[85]

The play and its successes received nearly as much critical attention as the book. The newspaper reviews from New York City are instructive, considering the play's debut there and that city's prominence in American theater. The New York *Tribune*, which had not reviewed the book due to Mark Twain's feud with its editor, reviewed the play, saying that "Mark Twain's play goes a great way to solve the problem of the possibility of the American drama, resting not on the piles driven into the mud and slime of French sensationalism, but founded on American society and manners. It is to a certain extent a success."[86] The play's success rested not on the story but on the character of Sellers and the acting of Raymond, which "shed a bright light of humor over the whole." The reviewer's conclusion highlights the general thrust of reviews, which the *Tribune* may have, in fact, helped set the tone for: "Mr. Raymond has won a genuine success, and certainly Mr. Clemens's drama is not a failure." Subsequent reviews noted three major points: that the play as such was not as well constructed as it could be, that Raymond's portrayal of Sellers was the high point and a marked success, and that the play might augur something new for American drama.

FIGURE 6.3: The Jumping Frog from the New York *Daily Graphic*, September 21, 1874. **Image courtesy of Tom Tryniski, Old Fulton N.Y. Postcards**

Clemens's hometown newspaper printed selections from the reviews in the New York papers, most of which focused on Raymond's success as "a valuable and unique" contribution to the American stage.[87] The New York *Times* was disappointed in the piece, apart from Raymond's portrayal of Sellers, while the New York *Herald* congratulated Mark Twain on filling a void in the theater for dramas of American life. The New York *Times*, in a later editorial, extended the praise of his contribution to the theater, writing:

> . . . "*Mark Twain,*" *has made a long stride toward the American drama. For the first time, we believe, truly national characteristics have been brought out on stage in high relief, and without offensive coarseness or extravagance. . . . Here, then, we recognize a truly American work. It is of native authorship, color, motive, flavor, and humor. It is worth while that we should go out of our way, as it might appear, to speak of an achievement that is so unusual and that deserves so well of an American public.*[88]

And after criticizing much American theater as "French nastiness" unrecognizable to Americans, the reviewer praises Colonel Sellers (along with jury trials, newspaper "boys," land speculation, and southern chivalry) as "native-born. . . . They are all national. They may be foibles and weaknesses, but they have the too rare merit of being honest and lifelike." Mark Twain's humor, embodied however imperfectly in his eyes through Raymond, had been renewed or elevated to its native raciness.

In the context of the novel's quick decline in sales, the play's success was truly remarkable. Howells later remembered Clemens's reaction to his nightly reports of profits, which came in the form of a postcard from an agent whom he had hired to travel with the play: "The postals used to come about dinner-time, and Clemens would read them aloud to us in wild triumph. One hundred and fifty dollars—two hundred dollars—three hundred dollars were the gay figures which they bore, and which he flaunted in the air before he sat down at table, or rose from it to brandish, and then, flinging his napkin into his chair, walked up and down to exult in."[89] Howells's desire to separate art from commerce surely would have been tested as he saw the financial windfall Clemens reaped—and the comfort it provided him in Hartford.

The enhanced quality of *The Gilded Age*, transformed into *Colonel Sellers*, was widely noted, including by Howells in the *Atlantic Monthly*. Howells dedicated the entirety of the "Drama" section in June 1875 to the play, praising both Raymond—who takes his place with other masters of his art as one of the "realistic actors"—and Mark Twain, for creating "character-material [that] is simple, natural, and good."[90] In his increasingly conventional way of elevating a cultural production, Howells framed both the acting and the play as "realistic" in their own ways. The play, he argued, is only a sketch for its characters, which is the necessity of good "acting-plays" in a way wholly unlike good novels, a slight nod to the failures of the novel. But as a play, the judgment must be different: "Yet any one who should judge it from the literary standpoint, and not with an artistic sense greater and more literary, would misjudge it. The play is true, in its broad way, to American conditions, and is a fair and just satire upon our generally recognized social and political corruptions."[91] Extending his critical perspective to the drama, Howells focused on the portrayal of character as central to the play's realistic thrust. He praised both Mark Twain and Raymond for allowing the audience to feel "the worth of his worthlessness," a type of pathos intermixed with the humor that was key to the character of Sellers. Possibly in deference to his friend, Howells criticized a few moments when Raymond went beyond the author's intention and cheapened the character with melodrama or cheap jokes.

The continued success of *Colonel Sellers*, as it toured the country sending (relative) millions back to Sam Clemens, and as it was revived over the following years, helped the Clemens family recover from the Panic of 1873, which had proven the satire of both book and play prescient. Clemens often could not resist the lure of speculative endeavors, and the financial success of the play led him to try to repeat his boom times as a playwright for decades, always unsuccessfully. On another level, the play was a unique success as a production of the American theater that, like American Literature, was seen as in need of a uniquely American style. In a widely reprinted piece from the Cincinnati *Commercial* from late 1875, a reporter noted the impact of the play: "But the book as a novel, though eminently successful, has been fairly eclipsed by its career in dramatized form. It has even been said by critics that our national drama consists of this single play. None other, perhaps, smacks so thoroughly of the soil of America, the 'Land of the free.'"[92]

ACT FIVE—"THE BUSIEST WHITE MAN IN AMERICA"

The success of *Colonel Sellers* as a play, much like the success of *The Innocents Abroad* as a subscription book, set Samuel Clemens up with financial expectations for subsequent productions that were almost uniformly disappointing in financial terms. Clemens's/Mark Twain's shift from the western vagabond of *Roughing It* to the semisettled author of Hartford did not change his focus on the business aspects of his career. As Hamlin Hill writes, a continued focus on business "cluttered up his life and energy during the 1870's and 1880's with so many projects for making himself a stereotype Horatio Alger that his work suffered."[93] It might be more fitting, considering the circumstances, to compare Mark Twain to his own speculative creation, for in the business of letters there was no busier speculator than Mark Twain. Unlike Colonel Sellers, some of Clemens's speculations had paid, and handsomely, but following the unprecedented successes of his travel books and of *The Gilded Age* as novel and play, Mark Twain's commercial success declined. Clemens responded with a frenzy of activity—plays, novels, sketches, inventions, and newspaper letters—although he resisted the financial lure of lecturing for more than a decade after his English lectures.

On February 25, 1874, he wrote his friend and confidante "Mother" Mary Fairbanks of his activities. He was writing two books—one on England and another he had begun in 1872. He had written two plays, neither of which ever appeared. He was also revising a selection of sketches for publication. He was, he wrote, "the busiest white man in America—& much the happiest." His many schemes—literary and otherwise—kept him in a Sellers-like whirl of spending, writing, and speculation. In June, the Clemens's second daughter, Clara, was born. Writing to John Brown in the fall of 1874, he described the scope of his summer's work. He had been consumed that summer with a new novel, writing fifty pages of manuscript per day of what would become *The Adventures of Tom Sawyer*. He had reached an impasse, so had taken up one of his favorite occupations—billiards. In two days, he wrote, he was heading to Buffalo to oversee previews of *The Gilded Age* performed, although he held that he "would about as soon spend a night in the Spanish Inquisition as sit there & be tortured with all the adverse criticisms I can contrive to imagine the audience is indulging in."[94] Clemens also mentions his self-pasting scrapbook, although he had decided to put off production as he only wanted publicity for one production at a time. After previews in Buffalo, the family would be in New York for five days to buy furniture for their new house in Hartford, the eccentric mansion that was (and still is) a monument to Mark Twain's grand vision. The letter goes on to describe his octagonal study in Elmira, New York, where he had spent the summer writing, and to describe an enclosed picture of the summer occupants of Quarry Farm. Parenthetically, he noted that "Auntie Cord" is in the picture and that he had just sent a "fragment of whose history" to a magazine, which would be "A True Story," Mark Twain's first publication in the *Atlantic Monthly*.

In his memoir of Mark Twain, Howells recalls a visit in 1874 to Hartford that he undertook with Thomas Bailey Aldrich, a similarly situated author and editor, and their wives. Clemens bragged of the "army" of agents across the country selling his books, with *The Innocents Abroad* selling along "just like the Bible." Howells writes:

> *The vividest impression which Clemens gave us two ravenous young Boston authors was of the satisfying, the surfeiting nature of subscription publication. . . . But he lectured Aldrich and me on the folly of that mode of publication in the trade which we had thought it the highest success to achieve a chance in. "Anything but subscription publication is printing for private circulation," he maintained, and he so won upon our greed and hope that on the way back to Boston we planned the joint authorship of a volume adapted to subscription publication. We got a very good name for it, as we believed, in Memorable Murders, and we never got farther with it, but by the time we reached Boston we were rolling in wealth so deep that we could hardly walk home in the frugal fashion by which we still thought it best to spare car fare; carriage fare we did not dream of even in that opulence.*[95]

Clemens wrote Howells encouraging him, or Aldrich or both, to move to Nook Farm. To Elisha Bliss, he wrote encouraging him to negotiate with Howells on a history of Venice, in addition to the books by his friends Harte, Miller, and DeQuille: "I would like to see them *all* quit the 'trade'—still, if they prefer to stick to the 'trade,' nobody is much damaged but themselves. I hope you will sell a pile of Howells's book when it comes out—& Harte's. The effect will be good."[96] Through the years, Clemens would propose moneymaking literary schemes to Howells, such as a further play based on Colonel Sellers or a reading tour with Howells, Aldrich, Cable, and Mark Twain to be called a "Literary Menagerie." Usually, Howells resisted Clemens's personal magnetism, and he never published by subscription, taking his extra pay in literary prestige in his growing role as "Dean of American Letters." Despite his idealism, Howells was clearly focused on the implications of literary production as a business, which during the 1870s may have been connected with his own financial difficulties and the declining sales of the *Atlantic Monthly*.

By 1874, Mark Twain had become one of the most famous men of letters and one of the most successful in the business of letters. Up to this point, critical attention had largely been confined to reviews of his books and lectures, but in 1874 Mark Twain began to be more widely discussed in magazines, lectures, and books that discussed humor as a phenomenon.

Mark Twain had become a central player in a cultural drama. His increasing circulation—in person and in print—more and more found Mark Twain in higher quality venues in which the presence of a popular humorist was considered a novelty. Articles or lectures that discussed Mark Twain's critical reputation during this time illustrate a continued critical confusion over the place of humor in American culture and the meanings of the humorist as a cultural actor.

In 1874–1875, Bret Harte performed a lecture entitled "American Humor," in which he discussed the history and meanings of the cultural phenomenon of humor. The lyceum tour was conducted under the impetus of mounting debts that had caused him to rush a number of pieces into print for monetary reasons. He was writing a novel for the American Publishing Company, Mark Twain's publisher, on whom he drew at least $3,600 in advances. Where Harte had received the most generous contract that the *Atlantic Monthly* had offered to any writer in 1871, by 1874 he was shopping his works to the highest bidder, and Howells was so unimpressed with one story that he only offered $150, well less than the $400 it sold for and the $500 that Harte had requested. To Howells, Harte wrote that he wished the editor "lived out of a literary atmosphere which seems to exclude any vision of the broader literary world beyond,—its methods, profits and emoluments."[97] Harte never submitted to the *Atlantic* again, and the role of the rising American humorist in the pages of the magazine shifted to Mark Twain.

For many people at the time, Bret Harte himself had promised to become the great American humorist of post–Civil War America.[98] Harte was the writer whose fiction had most captured the balance of pathos and humor that critics in America and England viewed as characteristic of the best quality humor—that of James Russell Lowell, not that of Mark Twain, Artemus Ward, or their ilk. But Harte, like Lowell and many American authors before him, had a difficult time balancing the aims of literary production with the needs of pecuniary support. While the literary marketplace had expanded following the Civil War, it was still difficult for authors to make a living on the fruits of their literary production. The raft of new magazines, the opportunities of the lyceum circuit, and increased book sales extended the circulation of American authors, but many still required jobs as editors, publishers, or professors to support their writing. Harte tried or considered all of these professions.

Bret Harte's speech on American Humor was a general failure, and Harte abandoned the lecture after five performances. As Clemens's success in subscription publishing and in adapting his first novel for the stage had shown, the job of managing the role of a successful literary figure was one that included not only artistic work but promotional and business savvy. Mark Twain possessed these skills; Bret Harte did not. While both Clemens and Harte often spent beyond their means, Clemens was able to support his lavish life more successfully than Harte, whose financial and critical successes were behind him.

The "American Humor" lecture came at a time when Harte's role as a lecturer was ending. Harte had gone to the lyceum stage in 1872 under the management of James Redpath and had done well, financially and critically, with his lecture on "The Argonauts of '49: California's Golden Age." But his pedantic lecture style and conservative dress failed to satisfy audiences for long. As one scholar has noted, Harte's lectures failed because he *analyzed* his subjects but failed to *vivify* them like Mark Twain or Joaquin Miller, who played both the role of humorist and westerner in order to meet the expectations of the audience.[99]

Harte argued that what was called "American Humor" was not a "nationally distinct intellectual quality" but rather a type of "modern extravagance" that had taken hold that was "sufficiently characteristic of our people to be called national, as the true, genuine humor."[100] Against the tide of criticism from both sides of the Atlantic that held that humor was a reflection of national character, Harte held instead that humor was a reflection of its time. So-called "American humorists" were not so much uniquely American as they were uniquely modern. American humor was not geographically unique, but temporally so. It was the "form or method of to-day . . . an epoch of curt speech, and magnetic telegraphs and independent thought." For Harte, the humorist was simply an observer of his time, to the degree that an English humorist transplanted to nineteenth-century America would have become an American humorist and an American would in turn have developed a characteristic British humor if born in eighteenth-century England.

In delineating the history of what is considered to be American humor, he followed the conventional view that it had evolved from the Yankee character, but that the works of "Sam Slick," Washington Irving, and James Russell Lowell had not been distinctively American because they were too exclusively regional or relied on European models.[101] Instead of the humor of the Old Southwest, which some had credited as a native American form of humor, Harte looked first to the humor of African slaves, stating, "It was in the South, and among conditions of servitude and the habits of an inferior race, that there sprang up a humor and pathos as distinct and original, as perfect and rare as any that ever flowered under the most beneficent circumstances of race and culture." As largely oral humor, he noted that this tradition had been lost except for the songs of Stephen C. Foster. He does not note any direct influence of black humor on white humorists.

But it was a second tradition of regional humor that had come to stand for American humor. Harte spent the majority of the lecture discussing this humor and ranking the humorists who represented this tradition. While British critics praised Artemus Ward, Harte found "a want of purpose in him" that the British ignored due to a habitual "condescending patronage."[102] Harte praised Orpheus C. Kerr, Petroleum V. Nasby, Josh Billings, and the "Dansbury Newsman," but he reserves his highest praise for Mark Twain, stating, "Mark Twain stands alone as the most original humorist that America has yet produced. He alone is inimitable."[103] Yet Mark Twain was a little too much fun, in Harte's view, reflecting the American tendency to laugh no matter how serious or grave the circumstance. He noted that "laughter makes us doubly serious afterward, and we do not want to be humorists always, turning up like a prize-fighter at each round, still smiling."

Summing up, Harte stated that he looked forward to the looming figure of the future American humorist who would perfect the form. This future humorist was a critical trope that appeared on occasion in discussions of American humor to highlight the flaws of current humor in light of a more perfect humor that would combine humor and pathos into lasting American art. Harte concluded: "Perhaps our true humorist is yet to come: when he does come he will show that a nation which laughs so easily has still a great capacity for deep feeling, and he will, I think, be a little more serious than our present day humorists."[104] For many critics and readers, Mark Twain is this true American humorist, who combined laughter with deep feeling in his masterpieces of American literature. In late 1874, this outcome was neither preordained, nor may it have seemed very likely, as Mark Twain had produced little humor that delved into the depths of pathos, a common criticism of his work that, like Artemus Ward's poorly regarded cacography, relegated Mark Twain to the status of mere humorist for most readers and critics at the time.

Despite his improving reputation as he moved into the company of a more respectable literary ilk, Mark Twain's reputation as a humorist was still located below Harte's, and well below that of Lowell and Holmes. In July 1874, the first critical article dedicated to Mark Twain as a subject appeared in *Appleton's Journal*. The article was part biography, part critical evaluation, and part theory of American humor. Written by George T. Ferris, who had made a reputation writing biographies of famous figures, the article begins with a critical trope that defines humor as coming "the nearest to being the one complete revelation" of national character. He writes: "For humor is a direct product from the life-blood. It sucks its ingredients from each hidden taint and essential virtue; from intellectual perversity and moral insight; from external environment and from internal fact."[105] This true American humor had been spread throughout the country, mostly by "a legion of quacks," but Mark Twain and Bret Harte had come to be the most pronouncedly American humorists. Lowell and Holmes, he quickly noted, might appear national but are too cosmopolitan and "Anglo-Saxon" to be considered uniquely and peculiarly American.

Ferris took pains to distinguish Mark Twain's success from that of Harte, with Harte possessing a "subtile feeling for the truth that good and evil are facts that melt and glide into each other imperceptibly, a recognition of which in painting life is the tap-root of the soundest philosophy and the deepest humor." Mark Twain, on the other hand, "rarely touches the latent springs of human sentiment, nor is his style more than narrative and descriptive. He strolls in the open, breezy sunshine, happy-go-lucky fashion, yet with a keenness of vision that allows nothing in his horizon to escape him." Returning later in the article to his point that Harte is better than Mark Twain, Ferris notes: "Of humor in its highest phase, perhaps Bret Harte may be accounted the most puissant among our contemporary American writers. . . . Mark Twain, while lacking the subtilty and pathos of the other, has more breadth, variety, and ease." Mark Twain's success as a humorist, then, was not in its literary power but in its capturing of the native American penchant for exaggerative humor. In this way, Ferris argued, Mark Twain is a reflection of the native journalism of his country, from which he evolved and from which he still possesses "rudimentary organs and limbs." In summary, Ferris maintains that Mark Twain's value lies in his humor's charm and geniality despite its faults of origin.[106]

The article also provides a detailed description of Clemens's life and Mark Twain's progress as an author, lecturer, and celebrity, along with an illustration of Mark Twain. Noting that Mark Twain "rose of a flood-tide of popularity," Ferris provided a summary of his success:

> During the five years which have elapsed since the issue of "The Innocents Abroad," the aggregate sale of our author's works has reached two hundred

ries, the gloomy cañons, and the grand forests of the far West. There in mining-camp or squatter settlement we see the figures of Mark Twain, Bret Harte, or John Hay, casting long shadows before them. In the tedious *entr'actes* between fiery whiskey, coffee, and buckwheat "slapjacks," we can hear them make merry over adventures and fancies, which, vitalized by the breath of genius, were soon to ripple the world's face with laughter.

Such whimsical caprices never cease to haunt the students of the humorous in books with a sense of nearness and intimacy in their favorites. We are impertinently curious about them, make them mental bedfellows, as it were, because we love them. The laugh in literature is the "one touch of Nature" (above all others) "which makes the whole world akin."

America has of late years bristled with humorous writers, as does the porcupine with quills. But few of these quills have been pungent in point or well feathered for flight. Yet what persistent jokers! They have sought to offset failures at the lawyer's brief, the doctor's pill-box, the counter-jumper's measuring-tape, the carpenter's plane, or what not. Still, amid a legion of quacks, there are some who have been crowned and anointed with the true "laying-on of hands."

In surveying the distinctive and peculiar American humor, it becomes necessary to banish two highly-gifted men, Holmes and Lowell. The "Hosea Biglow Papers" have all the pungent wit of Pope, the meaty and athletic vigor of Swift. The genial front of the "autocrat" shines like a fixed star. But their passports are not properly *viséd* by the home stamp. In spite of the use of dialect and other forged ear-marks, with which they would cunningly hoodwink us, we say to these magnificent impostors: "Get you gone, you belong to the world, not to America; you are giants truly, but your national angles, prejudices, and crudities, have been so ground down in the social mill, so polished away in

the intellectual workshop, that your humor is that of the cosmopolite. It self-registers as much for any other Anglo-Saxon as for the American."

Mark Twain and Bret Harte may, on the whole, be pronounced our most marked types of humorists. Each one has a noble constituency, but in many respects they are at the antipodes from each other. The latter is impelled to create and idealize, even when most faithful to externals. His plummet feels for the deep heart of hidden mysteries, and finds love, sweetness, and self-sacrifice, beneath what is odd, grotesque, and barbaric. True, he deals largely with suffering, crime, and misery, in his most vigorous and characteristic sketches, yet is it with that sunny charity, which is the moral equivalent of searching insight. He has learned a lesson of the mining-camp, and knows where to look for gold in unsightly places. The essentially dramatic spirit, to which his instincts of form in art lead him, is no doubt partly responsible for the vividness of light and shade which intensifies his stories both in prose and rhyme. Yet, underlying form and method, seems to

be a subtile feeling for the truth that good and evil are facts that melt and glide into each other imperceptibly, a recognition of which in painting human life is the tap-root of the soundest philosophy and the deepest humor.

Mark Twain, on the other hand, rarely touches the latent springs of human sentiment, nor is his style more than narrative and descriptive. He strolls in the open, breezy sunshine, happy-go-lucky fashion, yet with a keenness of vision that allows nothing in his horizon to escape him. But, before any further study of the author, let us briefly sketch the man, who was generally known to his little circle as SAMUEL L. CLEMENS, before the world coddled and petted him as Mark Twain.

He was born in Missouri in 1835, and got but scanty gleanings of early education. He became a printer's apprentice when his father died, and found that setting type at the case was by no means a bad school. After a few years, most of which were spent in itinerating from one country newspaper to another, young Clemens became a pilot on a Mississippi steamboat running between St. Louis and New Orleans. The picturesque life which he saw in this new business seems to have stimulated his literary faculties, for we soon find him writing for the newspapers. One day while he was pondering as to what *nom de plume* he should attach to his articles, he heard a sailor, who was taking soundings of the river, call out, "Mark twain!" The phrase tickled the fancy of our young literary pilot, and he adopted it for his own.

After seven years of this river-life, in which Mark Twain sedulously cultivated the art of writing, he went to Nevada Territory as private secretary of his brother, who had been appointed Secretary of the Territory. The chance was peculiarly grateful to one who had a keen thirst for adventure, and a vivid appreciation of the ludicrous. Nevada was just then beginning to swarm with

MARK TWAIN.

FIGURE 6.4: Illustration of Mark Twain from George T. Ferris, "Mark Twain," *Appleton's Journal* 12, no. 276 (July 4, 1874), 15. **Collection of the Author**

and forty-one thousand copies, representing money-value of nine hundred and fifty thousand dollars. Though a large sale is by no means the only or even the best measure of literary excellence, the above-mentioned fact is so remarkable as to be almost unparalleled.[107]

While these figures are surely distorted, as sales figures of his works often were by his publisher and by the press, Mark Twain's sales were clearly remarkable, and newspapers commented on his financial successes frequently. The tension between mass popularity and literary respectability runs throughout the article, placing Mark Twain squarely on the side of the popular while excusing his lack of quality literary polish.

As the first extended critical evaluation of Mark Twain to appear in a national magazine, Ferris's piece neatly summed up one thread of criticism on his reputation. Mark Twain might have become the best example of the exaggerative school of American humor, but the quality of his writing was rarely viewed as moving beyond the surface of American life to the deeper roots in which humor connected with pathos, sentiment, or satire to become something beyond the merely funny. Ferris put Mark Twain's humor in the context of a common metaphor: "Its tap-root takes no deep hold in the subsoil, and we may not always find a subtle and penetrating fragrance in its blooms. But these are so lavish, bright, and variegated that we should be ungrateful indeed not to appreciate our author's striking gifts at their full worth."[108] Only at the end of this article, when discussing portions of *The Gilded Age*, did Ferris gesture toward the possibility of Mark Twain becoming something more than representative humorist.

Knowing the course of Mark Twain's career, many readers have argued that Mark Twain's tap-root in fact penetrates deeper into the subsoil of American life than most, if not all, American writers of his age, or even since. Mark Twain's quality as an American author is the keynote of one thread of Twain scholarship leading back to Howells. But at this point, the question of Mark Twain's quality was dominated by the thread that saw his writing as that of the popular humorist—lavish and bright but not of a higher literary quality. More important than determining which of these threads are more accurate, the critical debate over Mark Twain's role as a humorist in American humor highlights significant contours of American humor and American literature as subjects both bound together and bound to specific times. In 1874, following the literary speculations of *The Gilded Age*, Mark Twain continued his shift away from the roles of the popular humorist and toward a new model of respectable humor—different than Lowell and Holmes and distinct from Harte. What this model would be, and its success in integrating into the respectable cultures of letters in New England, is the subject for the next chapter.

Assessing the proliferation of American humorists that same year, the *Phrenological Journal of Science and Health* gave a unique explanation for the humor of America's chief Humorists, of whom the journal printed a group of portraits with Mark Twain at the center. These portraits exhibited the primary development of the humorist: "Mirthfulness is the organ chiefly related to the appreciation and production of wit and humor, and is located two inches above the eyebrows, at the outer part of the forehead, or at the angles formed by the junction of the frontal and temporal regions."[109] A brief biography of each man followed, with Mark Twain described as "the author of 'Innocents Abroad,' is a resident of Hartford, Conn. He has been a resident of the Sandwich Islands and of California, where his 'Jumping Frog' first attracted attention to him. He married a lady with a fine estate." The illustration was taken from the New York *Daily Graphic* of October 9, 1873, which also published Mark Twain "amongst the Britishers" from the previous chapter. New printing technologies, and the popularity of illustrated periodicals, meant the public was beginning to see more representations of Mark Twain. Increasingly, Mark Twain was visible to the public in magazine and newspaper illustrations, as well as in other ephemera, like an author card game produced by the West and Lee Game company in 1873.[110]

Mark Twain's challenges integrating himself and his work into the literary community of respectable Boston was dramatized by his continued fraught relationship with Lilian Aldrich. During the visit of the Howellses and the Aldriches to Nook Farm in March 1874, Clemens began to enact a form of payment for Mrs. Aldrich's cold reception of him in 1872. The morning after an almost magical evening of dinner and talk, Clemens knocked on the room where the Aldriches were staying. In her memoir, Lilian Aldrich recounts the story of how she listened as Clemens berated her husband for the noise they had made during the night, which had caused Livy a great headache in the room below. "For heaven's sake, Aldrich," Mrs. Aldrich quotes him as saying, "what are you doing? Are you emulating the Kangaroos, with hob-nails in your shoes, or trying the jumping-frog business?" In their embarrassment, the couple went down to breakfast and found Livy, who informed them that she had no headache and that her room was in another wing of the house. Clemens, looking as guileless as "a combination of cherubim and seraphim," drawled out for Aldrich to stop talking and eat his breakfast.[111]

In his lifelong dislike of Mrs. Aldrich, Clemens took this and several other opportunities to perform his eccentricity for the woman he came to

FIGURE 6.5: American Humorists, from the New York *Daily Graphic*, October 9, 1873. **Collection of the Author**

consider a representative of the disapproving faction of polite New England. In his autobiographical dictations, he memorialized her as:

> *a strange and vanity-devoured, detestable woman! I do not believe I could ever learn to like her except on a raft at sea with no other provisions in sight. . . . I conceived an aversion for her the first time I ever saw her, which was thirty-nine years ago, and that aversion has remained with me ever*

since. She is one of those people who are profusely affectionate, and whose demonstrations disorder your stomach. You never believe in them; you always regard them as fictions, artificialities, with a selfish motive back of them. Aldrich was delightful company, but we never saw a great deal of him because we couldn't have him by himself.[112]

In their dueling memoirs, Lilian Aldrich became a symbol of New England orthodoxy, and Mark Twain became for Aldrich a symbol of the wildness of the frontier, whose years on the Mississippi and in California "lacked the refining influence of a different civilization." The coarseness and profanity of his influences was only partially mediated by the calming influence of Livy. For Aldrich, the physical presence of Mark Twain embodied a "nature so untrained and undisciplined, so filled with wild and savage impulses," which had only been partially tamed by Livy's angelic nature. But for Aldrich, "in despite of Mr. Clemens's desire for better things, he was still a man untrained and unpolished; the customs of the frontier still held him fast."[113]

On one level, this relationship was personal, between Sam and Lilian, Livy and "Aldrich," between friends and relations. As Samuel Clemens entered the literary world, he got to know the personages of New England letters, although it is unclear whether he referred to James Russell Lowell and Oliver Wendell Holmes as "James" and "Wendell." Still, as Mark Twain would later learn at the Whittier birthday dinner, the authors and public figures with whom he rubbed shoulders were both men and ideas. If the line between Samuel Langhorne Clemens and Mark Twain had remained clearer, it may have provided a convenient example of the distinction between private self and public author. But such a clear line does not exist, and the line between author-as-person and author-as-personality was not clear for Mark Twain, nor was it for William Dean Howells and other literary figures of the era—if it ever was or is.

In this case, the string of interactions between Clemens and Lilian Aldrich—from their first interaction in 1872 to the visit of 1874 to his odd outburst in Paris in 1879 for Mrs. Aldrich and Mme. Bentzon—might be viewed as performances of the eccentricity of Mark Twain. While these interactions were ostensibly private, and only became public in memoirs much later, the semiritualized activities of visiting and banqueting into which Samuel Clemens, often in his public role as "Mark Twain," was being initiated can also be examined as symbolic performances. The final evening of the 1874 visit to Hartford is especially evocative in this light. The night made a clear impact on Howells and Mrs. Aldrich, each of whom included it in their memoirs. For Aldrich, the night was still as clear as if those present "lived still sentient with life and happiness." The group planned to drink wassail at midnight, but finding they were out of ale, Clemens donned "his historic sealskin coat and cap" and ventured into the night. Aldrich writes: "In an incredibly short time he reappeared, excited and hilarious, with his rapid walk in the frosty air—very wet shoes, and no cap." Justin Kaplan, in his biography, speculates that Clemens had sampled the whiskey at a saloon and returned "excited, hilarious, distinctly over-heated."[114] After sending the butler to search for the cap and changing into cow-skin slippers, with the fur on the outside, he performed what Kaplan calls "a crowning act of confident alienation from his guests": he danced.

In Howells's recollection, Clemens, shorn in fur shoes, danced "a crippled colored uncle to the joy of all beholders. Or, I must not say all, for I remember also the dismay of Mrs. Clemens, and her low, despairing cry of, "Oh, Youth!" Mrs. Aldrich remembered the same slippers and the same dance: "[W]ith most sober and smileless face, he twisted his angular body into all the strange contortions known to the dancing darkies of the South. In this wise the last day of the joyous, jubilant visit came to the close. Untroubled by the flight of time I still can hear a soft and gentle tone, 'Youth, O Youth!' for so she always called him." Shelley Fisher Fishkin reads this story as one instance of several in which African American dancing appeared in the works or life of Mark Twain, evidence of the influence of black forms of culture on Mark Twain's works.[115] The pleasure of the assembled company, including Lilian Aldrich's apparent enjoyment of "the strange contortions known to the dancing darkies of the South," complicates the scene, which may not have been a performance of alienation from genteel norms so much as a performance of a humorous personae influence by minstrel conventions. Or it may have been a performance of displaced anxiety, in which the outsider performed an even more excluded, although "authentic," form of American humor—the humor of African Americans being one of the native forms of American humor, separate from the bastardization of minstrel performers.

As a performance, the moment does not, and cannot, settle into a definitive interpretation. Sources are too sparse, and the moment exists as a type of put-on whose meaning remains evocative of a range of interpretations too slippery to be pinned down. This performance, like many, plays with the comic possibilities of Mark Twain's relationship with the polite literary culture of New England—symbolized not only by Lilian Aldrich, but her husband, by Howells, and by Livy, with her gentle remonstrances. The next chapter examines the developing relationship between Mark Twain and the quality world of New England letters as Mark Twain increasingly showed up in print and in person in those literary cultures.

Several days later, Sam Clemens/Mark Twain mailed Mrs. Aldrich a picture with a short note on the back:

> To Mrs. T. B. Aldrich
>   With regards not to be expressed in their full strength because of the overlooking eye of T. B.
>
>   Sam. L. Clemens
>   Mark Twain.
>   Hartford, Mch. 9, 1874. [116]

FIGURE 6.6: Mark Twain photograph sent to Lilian Aldrich, front and back
Autograph File (Samuel Clemens portrait, 1874).
Houghton Library, Harvard University

To Mrs. T. B. Aldrich

With regards not to
be expressed in their
full strength because

ROGERS & NELSON.
ART PHOTOGRAPHERS.
AND PORTRAIT PAINTERS,
215. REGENT ST
LONDON, W.

of the overlooking
eye of T. B.

Saml L. Clemens
Mark Twain.

Hartford Mch. 9, 1874.

CHAPTER SEVEN

The Stripèd Humorist

Mark Twain Makes Waves in the *Atlantic*'s Ocean

Beginning in 1874, William Dean Howells began publishing articles by Mark Twain in the *Atlantic Monthly*, paying at a higher rate than for any previous author. Mark Twain published some of his highest quality work of the decade in the magazine, including the sketch "A True Story" and the series "Old Times on the Mississippi." But other pieces conveyed a barely hidden anxiety about the relationship between the humorist and the respectable literary culture for which he was now writing. In these years, Mark Twain published a collection of sketches and his first solo novel, *The Adventures of Tom Sawyer* (1876), which Howells helped him edit and praised highly in a review as a new development in his realistic writing. Howells played a central role in encouraging Clemens to submit pieces and in providing editorial suggestions. Clemens increasingly relied on Howells's literary opinion, both as published in the pages of the *Atlantic* and in their personal friendship, which had blossomed through letters and visits between Howells's Boston and Mark Twain's Hartford.

As William Dean Howells increasingly brought Samuel Clemens, as a person, and Mark Twain, as a literary figure, into the realm of the *Atlantic Monthly*, Clemens's anxiety with Mark Twain's cultural position became increasingly focused on his role as a literary humorist. In 1874, as Clemens was writing the series "Old Times on the Mississippi" for the *Atlantic*, Howells attempted to ease his fears about the audience he was writing for, stating in a letter, "Don't write *at* any supposed *Atlantic* audience, but yarn it off as into my sympathetic ear." Clemens responded with a line that reflects a sense of relief at this new professional opportunity: "It isn't the *Atlantic* audience that distresses me; for *it* is the only audience that I sit down before in perfect serenity (for the simple reason that it don't require a 'humorist' to paint himself stripèd & stand on his head every fifteen minutes.)"[1] The possibility of earning a living, or at least a reputation, as a new type of humorist—one who didn't have to curry public favor or risk buffoonery—seems to have appealed to Clemens.

The appreciation of the *Atlantic*'s audience not requiring him to paint himself striped and stand on his head implies a style of performance that the magazine allowed him to overcome—the humorist was allowed to lay aside the jester's clothes to write in "perfect serenity" to his imagined audience without anxiety. Unlike Clemens's earlier letter to Howells, in which he had used the metaphor of a mother worried about miscegenation to convey his anxiety, the image of Mark Twain as a clown allowed to shed his paint conveyed different anxieties about his role in literary culture. As mother to his works, his metaphor imagined the author plagued by the fear that it might not meet public approval, either through a stranger's disapproving glance or, much more powerfully for the time, from the taint of a disapproved (and racialized) paternity. His fear was of the low-humor paternity of the mere buffoon, one which his wife Livy most consistently expressed, and which bound them both to Howells in gratitude for his reviews.

The unpainted clown, on the other hand, implies a relief from anxiety. Freed from the audience demand for antic performance, Mark Twain rose above the figure of the clown, which had been used by critics, along with the minstrel, as the generic humorists at the bottom of the cultural hierarchy. These two metaphors—the worried mother and the unpainted clown—place Clemens in different bodily positions in relation to his persona, his books, and his audience. He is either the guilty mother, hiding the possible low paternity of his creations, or the clown, allowed to shed his paint and entertain the public without buffoonish acts. These two possibilities can be found in Howells's reviews of Mark Twain, which act as a testimony to the patrimony of his humor and a defense of quality that he saw behind the merely humorous ornament of Twain's humor. Remember that Howells had framed Artemus Ward and Petroleum V. Nasby as the bastard children of Thackeray rather than the legitimate heirs of Lowell—a role that was filled in his reviews by Bret Harte, Charles Dudley Warner, and Mark Twain.

In addition to his entrance into the *Atlantic*'s culture of letters as a contributor, Mark Twain also entered the magazine's orbit through a series of performances at formal banquets celebrating the role of the magazine and its contributors in shaping American culture. These lavish banquets featured multicourse meals and hours of speeches and poems, and they were part of a wider trend of celebratory banquets in which writers, politicians, and other public figures praised some aspect of American culture or other in an orgy of rhetoric and heavy food. Mark Twain gave after-dinner speeches at three of these banquets—at an 1874 dinner celebrating the sale of the magazine, at the Whittier birthday dinner in 1877, and at the Holmes Breakfast in 1879. While two of these speeches made hardly a ripple and have been largely ignored in Twain scholarship, the Whittier birthday speech became a highly symbolic dramatization of Mark Twain's relation to respectable literary culture—both at the time and in Twain scholarship.

At each of these occasions, Mark Twain gave a speech that dramatized his relationship to the idea of the literary culture being celebrated. But at the Whittier birthday dinner, his speech tweaked the main sentiment of the evening—the reverence for Whittier and his fellow, august contributors to the *Atlantic*—by telling a tall tale that featured Emerson, Longfellow, and Holmes as characters. The speech told of an incident that took place in California twenty years earlier, when the newly minted Mark Twain sought hospitality from a solitary miner by attempting to trade on his new literary reputation. The miner groans when finding out he was a "littery man" and then narrates the story of the visit the previous night by Emerson, Holmes, and Longfellow, who had berated him with snippets of verse while eating his beans, drinking his whiskey, threatening him with violence, and stealing his boots. Upon being informed by the narrator (the young "Mark Twain") that these men were impostors, the miner asks, "Ah—impostors were they? are *you*?"[2]

The Whittier birthday speech created a locus around which the discussion of Mark Twain's cultural meanings were debated publicly. As a highly symbolic event, the Whittier birthday dinner highlighted the rhetoric of reverence on which the *Atlantic* was founded and maintained; Mark Twain's role as "impostor" or "jester" dramatized questions about his literary status that Howells had been unable to argue away. While scant evidence exists to show that these literary figures, or any of the other guests, were offended, Howells and Clemens felt that he had made a "hideous mistake"—one that haunted each of them for the remainder of their lives. Instead of a conscious or unconscious attack on the New England literary elite, as most critics have held, I argue that Mark Twain's speech, and the vociferous criticism that emanated from certain quarters of the press after the fact, dramatizes the distinction between public persona and private person. By "trifling" with the personalities of the *Atlantic* greats, Mark Twain had offended critics and readers who held such authors in reverence, while not seeming to disturb the actual men. This distinction between an author and his or her reputation helps clarify the circulation of literary reputation as both an ideality and commodity.

On the other hand, Mark Twain's performances at these three banquets—along with a banquet given in honor of Ulysses S. Grant—reflect his anxiety at being included as a quality humorist in the presence of revered cultural figures rather than his antipathy toward those figures or what they represented. Indeed, Clemens's responses to his banquet performances—both well received and not—shows the high regard he felt toward the culture of the *Atlantic Monthly* and his shame at having been perceived to have given offense. Rather than Mark Twain as a western rowdy thumbing his nose at polite Boston culture, reading these speeches together points to Samuel Clemens as an author eager to make his *nom de plume* part of the *Atlantic*'s literary atmosphere, as well as the existence of those who continued to view him as an impostor. As he transitioned to new roles as a humorist, Clemens experienced tension over the proper aims and uses of humor in quality venues, leading him to retreat to Europe and the form of the travel narrative until his return to public life with successful banquet speeches at celebrations of Grant and of Oliver Wendell Holmes.

"A GREAT SURPRISE AND A STRONG EMOTION IN STORE FOR HIM": MARK TWAIN IN THE *ATLANTIC* AND ON THE MISSISSIPPI

Mark Twain's s first piece in the *Atlantic Monthly* appeared in November 1874—"A True Story, Repeated Word for Word as I Heard It."[3] In the story, the narrator—"Misto C——," sits on a porch with his family on a summer's evening, teasing their African American servant, "Aunt Rachel." Beginning using the conventional frame tale of much American humor, the story takes a dramatic turn when the narrator asks how Rachel seems to have had no trouble in her life, whereupon Rachel takes over the narrative to tell the story of her life as a slave, the sale of her children, and her reunion with one of her sons. Reversing the racial politics of the Southern Frontier tradition of Old Southwest Humor, as I have argued elsewhere, this story brought the traditional humorous forms of the frame tale and vernacular speaker into the pages of the *Atlantic* not as humorous tale but as a form of critique of racial attitudes of its mostly Northern readers.[4] The story represented both a new audience and a new subject—a beginning of Mark Twain's discussion of slavery and its aftermaths both North and South—through a humor that increasingly relied less on Mark Twain as a character and more on clearly drawn characters aimed at quality audiences.

Mark Twain's writing was so clearly connected to both humorous sketches and travel writing—with the notable and ambivalently received example of *The Gilded Age*—that the appearance of the sketch, as Howells recalled, "resulted, we remember, in some confusion of the average critical mind, when it was first published. . . ."[5] "A True Story" is the centerpiece of the Howells's review of *Sketches, New and Old* (1875), which came out the next year. Attuned to the general critical world, and often concerned about Mark Twain's reception, Howells's discussion of the story might reflect more of his anxieties (and possibly Clemens's) than critical realities, but either way, his view is illustrative of the story's central importance in shifting Mark Twain's role as a humorist. In the review, he claimed that critics, viewing Mark Twain as a humorist, were confused by the story and classified it as a humorous piece, fearing "a lurking joke." For Howells, the piece was something much more:

> *Not above two or three notices out of hundreds recognized A True Story for what it was, namely, a study of character as true to life itself, strong, tender, and most movingly pathetic in its perfect fidelity to the tragic fact. We beg the reader to turn to it again in this book. We can assure him that he has a great surprise and a strong emotion in store for him. The rugged truth of the sketch leaves all other stories of slave life infinitely far behind and reveals a gift in the author for the simple dramatic report of reality which we have seen equaled in no other American writer.*[6]

Here we have the critical inception in the *Atlantic Monthly* of Mark Twain not only as a realist-humorist but also as an author capable of realist works of great power. Mark Twain's humor, Howells wrote, "seems such plain and simple fun at first, doubling and turning upon itself till you wonder why Mr. Clemens has ever been left out of the list of our *subtile* humorists." Howells praised Mark Twain's "growing seriousness of meaning in the apparently unmoralized drolling, which must result from the humorist's second thought of political and social absurdities." The moral quality of Mark Twain's humor would be increasingly important in Howells's promotion of the humorist's works as a permanent part of the American canon.

While the review would have been the public word on Mark Twain's book, readers would have not known the personal discussions behind the review. Howells sent the review to Clemens in advance, referring to it in a mocking tone as "awful rot" and asking him to return his objections.[7] Clemens replied with gratitude; in a tone that would have undoubtedly flattered Howells, he wrote: "Yours is the recognized critical Court of Last Resort in this country; from its decision there is no appeal; & so, to have gained this decree of yours before I am forty years old, I regard as a thing to be right down proud of. Mrs. Clemens says 'Tell him *I* am just as grateful to him as I can be.'" While his puffing of Howells's critical stature reflects their jovial relationship, Livy's gratitude at Howells's critical reframing of Mark Twain reads as genuine, even through the humorous tone. He continues: "(It *sounds* as if she were grateful to you for heroically trampling the truth under foot in order to praise me—but in reality it means that she is grateful to you for being bold to utter a truth which she fully believes all competent people know, but which none has heretofore been brave enough to utter.) You see, the thing that gravels her is that I am so persistently glorified as a mere buffoon, as if that entirely covers my case—which she denies with venom."[8] Like Olivia Clemens, Howells saw the serious artist behind the humorist, but Howells had the critical platform to help transform Mark Twain's reputation.

"A True Story" had seemed to cause confusion for Sam Clemens, who sent it to Howells along with another piece that he seemed to have considered to be better, writing: "I enclose also a 'True Story' which has no humor in it. You can pay as lightly as you choose for that, if you want it, for it is rather out of my line." Howells, on the contrary, found the piece to be of such interest that he rushed it into print, having it set in proof and to Clemens within two weeks, stating: "I've kept the True Story which I think is extremely good and touching with the best and reallest kind of black talk in it," and "[t]his little story delights me more and more: I wish I had about forty of 'em!"[9] Howells later wrote that the magazine paid 20 dollars per page for the story, "a rate unexampled in our modest history," and that this monetary value reflected a sense of literary value: "I myself felt that we were throwing in the highest recognition of his writing as literature, along with a sum we could ill afford; but the late Mr. Houghton, who had then become owner and paymaster, had no such reflection to please him in the headlong outlay. He had always believed that Mark Twain was literature, and it was his zeal and courage which justified me in asking for more and more contributions from him, though at a lower rate."[10] The success of

"A True Story" led Howells and Houghton to solicit more work from "Mark Twain," leading to the serial publication of "Old Times on the Mississippi" from January to June 1875.

"Old Times on the Mississippi" not only brought Mark Twain into the company of the literary elite in the pages of the *Atlantic Monthly*, it also set him on a new path as a humorist. The first installation of "Old Times" begins with an evocative passage that previews some of Mark Twain's most enduring subjects: the imaginative days of youth—in which the dream was to become a steamboat pilot, if not a circus performer, traveling minstrel, or pirate—and the drowsy life of the Mississippi River town brought to booming life by the arrival of a steamboat. This "white town drowsing in the sunshine of a summer's morning" set in motion the subject of his Missouri past—which would become the St. Petersburg of Tom Sawyer and Huck Finn and the Dawson's Landing of David Wilson and Roxy.[11] The first journey on the river also inspired a new identity that was key in the development of his reputation: "I was a traveler! A word never had tasted so good in my mouth before. I had an exultant sense of being bound for mysterious lands and distant climes which I never have felt in so uplifting a degree since."[12]

Clemens would continue to publish shorter pieces in the magazine for much of the 1870s while Howells was editor, but the business of letters was still a keen consideration. The financial issues that had inspired his whirl of activity that had included lectures in England, *The Gilded Age* and *Colonel Sellers*, as well as business investments in published subscription books and scrapbooks, had continued as the family moved into their stately and eccentric mansion in Hartford in September 1874. He tried to sell his friends the vision of making a good living from subscription publishing. Howells and Aldrich declined, and the subscription books published by his friends Dan DeQuille and Bret Harte sold poorly.[13] The preparation and promotion of these books took time and resources away from Mark Twain's own books.

The market for Mark Twain's sketches was less lucrative than Clemens had hoped by the time *Sketches, New and Old* appeared in 1875. Collections of shorter pieces were an unproven commodity for subscription publishers, and Clemens added only seven new sketches to go with fifty-six previously published pieces, including three sketches on England, "A True Story," and the retranslated Jumping Frog. At 320 pages with only 150 illustrations, the book was shorter than the standard subscription book, and books of sketches tended to sell fewer copies than other genres. The financial repercussions of the Panic of 1873 were still resonating as well, and the entire book industry had yet to recover.[14]

The sales dummy of Mark Twain's book of *Sketches* repeated many of the same techniques of earlier books, including a focus on the illustrations and a page of puffery. Mark Twain appeared at the beginning as his initials on a piece of paper, surrounded by figures presumably from the sketches or a representation of his varied audiences.[15] The salesmanship rings of a certain uncertainty, first trumpeting Mark Twain's humor, then the illustrations, then the quality of the paper and the binding, and ending with a lengthy argument about the quality of Mark Twain's humor. Unable to link humor to information, as with Twain's travel books, or with novelty, as with *The Gilded Age*, the prospectus makes two unique arguments about Mark Twain's writings that are worth quoting at length:

> *That the pen of our author is not a useless one is proven by the fact that his readers are largely men and women of a highly cultivated class. Scarcely a greater favorite of the Clergy can be named, and Lawyers, Scholars, Merchants, Mechanics, and Farmers all read him with undisguised pleasure. While graver men are making war upon the vices or weaknesses of a community with heavy guns and by slow approaches, our author by a bold sally and sudden onslaught, under cover of some ridiculous, laughable story, overwhelms the enemy and ends his career; or what is oftener the case, his ready pen by some sharp and cutting satire arouses the public to a sense of wrong existing in their midst, heretofore undiscerned. His most extravagant tales have an application and a moral.*

The first argument, that Mark Twain's books were a favorite of the cultivated class, is hard to classify but was a common argument of book canvassers, who were instructed to secure the subscriptions of prominent members of a community first (or to save room for their names at the front of the subscription blanks) in order to impress prospective customers. One canvassing guide, reprinted by Hamlin Hill, argues "It is a *fact, philosophy,* UNIVERSAL EXPERIENCE. Society everywhere follows its leaders. The great majority of people are afraid to trust their own unaided judgment about buying a book. . . ."[16]

The second argument of the quoted passage was that Mark Twain's works attacked "the vices and weaknesses of a community" with a "ridiculous, laughable story" or exposed an unexposed wrong to public scrutiny through satire. While this was a critical trope occasionally employed to argue for a deeper meaning to Mark Twain's humor, in this context it reads more like an argument meant to assuage the worries of those same community leaders who might think that humor was of questionable taste. Thus, the assertion, "His most extravagant tales have an application and a moral," reads more as commercial puffery than critical insight. Very few of Mark Twain's sketches contained any useful application or ready moral, unless it was to be wary of trusting what you read—a moral that the publisher and canvassers might have been wary of selling to their class of cultivated readers.

Released in September 1875, *Sketches* sold just over 27,000 copies in its first year, and it had not reached the 50,000 mark by 1893, when the publisher renegotiated Clemens's contract to avoid paying an extra 2.5% royalty on all sales.[17] In the Gilded Age, such a sale (and the royalties earned thereupon) would have been regarded as a solid success for most authors. For Samuel Clemens, it was a financial declension that could be traced partially to the economic depression of the 1870s and partially to the lack of critical attention paid to the book. Unlike *The Gilded Age*, Mark Twain was quite present as a character in *Sketches*—both in the text and visually through the illustration of some of his best-known stories, such as the Jumping Frog (including the French translation). He also appeared as a lecturer for one illustration.

Following his plan, Clemens sent Howells one of the first copies for review, writing that "Have told Bliss to send my volume of *Sketches* to you before any one else (it is in press now). I think it is an exceedingly handsome book."[18] Unlike the promotional onslaught that he and Warner had undertaken for *The Gilded Age*, Clemens and Bliss spent relatively little time promoting the book in periodicals. Howells was one of the few reviewers to take notice, especially in the magazine world. Louis Budd lists only eight reviews of the book, of which most are only brief notices, with little critical discussion. The New York *Tribune* briefly noted that "'Mark Twain' was to be honored by a complete edition of his sketches, new and old." The Hartford *Courant* noted that the book "will be a better antidote for dyspepsia than the drug store can offer." As Hamlin Hill summarizes, "In this case, Howells was not only the court of last resort; he was the only court before which *Sketches* was tried."[19] This was not entirely true. The San Francisco *Evening Bulletin* used the book as an occasion to discuss the relative place of humorists in America, writing:

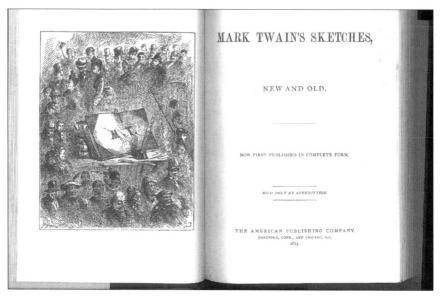

FIGURE 7.1: Frontispiece from *Sketches, New and Old.*
Courtesy of Kevin Mac Donnell, Austin, Texas

Our country enjoys the distinction of having produced an entirely unique
school of humorists—a school of which "John Phoenix" was the founder,
and Mark Twain the present acknowledged head. We do not include in this
school such men as Holmes, Saxe and Harte, who belong to a higher order
of creative workers, in whom genius is tempered and disciplined by art. Nor
does Mark Twain himself aspire to a place among the first rank of authors.

Still, the reviewer argues that Mark Twain is "something more than a
mere 'funny writer,'" and his writing contains a vein of quality that had
grown stronger over time.[20]

The poor timing of the book—as an investment both in business and
in literary reputation—may have been Clemens's reason for doing little to
promote it. The lack of critical attention to his book of sketches does not
mean that Mark Twain was fading from public view—quite the contrary.
Critical discussion of Mark Twain in other venues continued to focus on
his place as a humorist in American culture, ranging from those who would
dismiss Mark Twain and his ilk from the first rank to those who argued
for Mark Twain's value beyond mere humor.[21]

Mark Twain's continued presence in the *Atlantic*, and his turn to the
Mississippi River as a subject, raised new questions of literary reputation
and raised new anxieties for both Clemens and Howells. Howells did not

comment publicly on "Old Times on the Mississippi," but in letters he complimented it as "capital—it almost made the water in our ice-pitcher muddy as I read it."[22] Writing about his life on the Mississippi inspired Clemens to new subjects and new approaches, and he began writing the story that would become *The Adventures of Tom Sawyer* in the summer of 1874. Writing without a definite plan, Clemens worked on the novel through the summer, until running into a block, the description of which contains echoes of Howells's criticism. He wrote to a friend: "But night before last I discovered that that day's chapter was a failure, in conception, moral, truth to nature & execution—enough blemishes to impair the excellence of almost any chapter—& so, I must burn up the day's work & do it all over again. It was plain that I had worked myself out, pumped myself dry. So I knocked off, & went to playing billiards for a change." Finishing the novel the next summer, he turned to Howells as both critic and editor. Clemens seemed clear on his expected audience, writing, "It is *not* a boy's book, at all. It will only be read by adults. It is only written for adults."[23] He expressed a desire for the book to appear in the pages of the *Atlantic*, although he was not sure it would "pay" for him or his publisher, adding in apology: "You see I take a vile, mercenary view of things—but then my household expenses are something almost ghastly." Finally, Clemens asked Howells to read the manuscript of the book, stating, "I don't know any other person whose judgment I could venture to take fully & entirely." Howells was becoming the court of last appeal for both the public and for Clemens as an author.

Howells responded in glowing terms and encouraged Clemens to treat it as a boy's book. By a "boy's book," Howells meant framing the book as being from a boy's point of view, rather than the adult, which would please both young and adult readers—and make it more realistic. While he demurred from publishing the book serially in the *Atlantic*, Howells did ask for an early review copy in order to "start the sheep jumping in the right places." Clemens seems to have been relieved by Howells's approval of the manuscript: "It is glorious news that you like Tom Sawyer so well. I mean to see to it that your review of it shall have plenty of time to appear before the other notices. Mrs. Clemens decides with you that the book should issue as a book for boys, pure & simple—& so do I. It is surely the correct idea."[24] Howells had become friend, editor, advisor, occasional publisher, and reviewer for Clemens, and the roles overlapped with Mark Twain's first solo novel, as Howells read the manuscript, advised Clemens on content and publishing, and then reviewed the book in the *Atlantic*. Relying on

Howells as advisor, Clemens sought acceptance in the *Atlantic*—one of the most prestigious of cultural standards, which sought to promote and shape a national literature worthy of canonical status.

The Adventures of Tom Sawyer came at an important time for Clemens. Still struggling with the financial drain of living a respectable literary life in Hartford, he was looking for financial capital to float his new life, especially after the disappointing sales of *Sketches, New and Old*. On the other hand, Mark Twain was beginning to move away from work calculated to produce immediate financial gains—possibly due to the rocky experience of *The Gilded Age*—instead seeking through his work in the *Atlantic Monthly* to bank some of the literary capital of prestige. Although he would later write to Andrew Lang that he had always aimed for the "masses" and not "the classes" and their "culture-standard," he was, in the 1870s, pulled between the desire to appeal to the classes and the necessity of selling to the masses.

The promotion and reception of *Tom Sawyer* should be seen within this contested realm of literary production, in which Clemens hoped for both financial and literary credit for a novel. The failure of the book as a business venture, in this case, was tempered by its critical acceptance by Howells, as well as the seemingly permanent move of Mark Twain into the ranks of *Atlantic* authors. Howells reviewed *The Adventures of Tom Sawyer* in May 1876, grouping it with Thomas Bailey Aldrich's *Story of a Bad Boy* (1870), which he had praised as a signal advancement in the American novel.[25] Mark Twain's realism, for Howells, was found in the portrayal of boyhood in the West. The character of Tom is portrayed "with a fidelity to circumstance which loses no charm by being realistic in the highest degree, and which gives incomparably the best picture of life in that region as yet known to fiction." For Howells, the excellence of the character was a reflection of Mark Twain's growth as a writer. He writes: "The local material and the incidents with which his career is worked up are excellent, and through-out there is scrupulous regard for the boy's point of view in reference to his surroundings and himself, which shows how rapidly Mr. Clemens has grown as an artist. We do not remember anything in which this propriety is violated, and its preservation adds immensely to the grown-up reader's satisfaction in the amusing and exciting story." The reader, whether young or old, sees a picture in this review of Mark Twain as an author capable of "entertaining character, and of the greatest artistic sincerity," not a mere humorist. Praising the book's realistic handling of its subject, Howells focused on the special nature of the "boy-mind" and "boy-nature," which have a reality separate from the physical world of adults and which Mark

Twain had captured through his young characters. In line with Howells's critical ethos at the *Atlantic*, Mark Twain was classed as a realist author due to the honest portrayal of his characters, not the subject or plot.

The release of the English version of *Tom Sawyer* in June 1876 was overseen by Clemens's friend Moncure Conway, who then reviewed the book in both the London *Examiner* and the Cincinnati *Commercial* in June 1876. Conway's reviews noted that the book made it increasingly difficult to assign the author a "literary *habitat*." "'American humorist,' he continues, "has for some time been recognised as too vague a label" in light of his descriptive skills and a depth of meaning. Adopting a Howellsian view of Mark Twain's writing, Conway argued that "without being pathetic he is sympathetic, and there is also an innate refinement in his genius felt in every subject it selects and in his treatment of it." Of his skill in fiction, the review notes that "everything is alive, and every face physiognomical," and claims it is impossible to pick a passage to convey the spirit of "a novel so replete with good things, and one so full of significance, as it brings before us what we can feel is the real spirit of home life in the far West."[26] In the American paper, Conway also noted the difficulty of classifying Mark Twain, stating: "There are some respects in which Mark Twain excels any living humorist—if we can still so describe a writer who has shown such various powers (which is doubtful)—and one is his innate refinement and self-restraint."[27] In these reviews, Mark Twain's literary reputation moved further away from that of mere humorist.

Unfortunately, the attempts of Howells and Conway to jump-start the critical sheep came more than six months too early due to problems with the American Publishing Company. Delays pushed the American version later than planned, with the prospectuses ready on November 14, and the first copies in early December.[28] The book was mentioned as being in print by the Chicago *Tribune* and the Hartford *Tribune* in April, and newspapers began printing excerpts—of the whitewashing scene and "The Beetle, The Boy, and the Dog"—in late June, and the fence scene was reprinted more than a dozen times before the American publication.[29] By June, Clemens was demanding of the Board of Directors that the firm reduce its size so as to focus on its main form of profit-making: "Mark Twain." American sales of *Tom Sawyer* numbered just over 23,000 in the first year—and only 4,000 in England—and the book made him much less money than his travel books or *The Gilded Age*.[30]

Attempting to ease the concerns of customers who might not be sure of buying another novel from Mark Twain, the sales prospectus for *The*

Adventures of Tom Sawyer featured a variety of scenes from the book, along with a large number of illustrations, including the first illustrations of Tom Sawyer and Huck Finn. The advertising material contained short snippets from the London reviews from the *Examiner* and the *Athenaeum*, as well as a blurb from the *Daily Enquirer* of Cincinnati and a lengthy excerpt from the review in the *Atlantic Monthly*.[31] On the following page, the advertising copy trumpeted the success of the book, claiming: "PRONOUNCED BY ALL WHO HAVE SEEN IT TO BE THE MOST HUMOROUS AND WONDERFUL PRODUCTION OF THE AUTHOR'S PEN." The subtext of the advertisement seems to be the goal of reassuring readers that this was, in fact, a MARK TWAIN book worth buying. The genius of the author is vouched for by "the burst of enthusiastic praise with which the publication of "TOM SAWYER" in England, has been received." It continues: "No words have seemed too strong to express the pleasure felt at this fresh exhibition of the author's powers, exerted in a direction least expected. In entering the new field here introduced, Mr. Clemens by no means abandons his old style of writing, as will be realized at once in the perusal of the book. From the beginning to the end, the pages of 'TOM SAWYER' are replete with lively sallies, humorous ideas, and scathing hits." The vaguely defensive tone might reflect the difficulty in selling a novel via subscription, especially one half the size of most subscription books, to the public who purchased such books—even if it was by Mark Twain. *The Gilded Age*, *Sketches, New and Old*, and *Tom Sawyer* were experiments in subscription publishing, and their relative failures signified a decline in Clemens's business prospects, even if the book's critical successes augured new possibilities for his fiction critically.

Tom Sawyer was not widely reviewed upon its American publication, although the publisher sent the book to major periodicals for review. The Hartford *Courant* echoed many of the points Howells had made in his earlier review, arguing that the book represented an advance for "Mr. Clemens"—"an advance we mean as a piece of literary work, careful in finish, and thought out more maturely."[32] Noting a "spark of genius," the reviewer heaped high praise on Mark Twain's humor, his style, and his use of language, claiming that "there is no one writing to day who has a finer intuitive sense of the right word in the right place." At one point, the reviewer's praise directly echoes Howells's in the discussion of the universality of "boy nature" and its "local coloring."

British reviews of the book show an improvement of Mark Twain's reputation in England. The mass-circulation papers, such as the *Graphic*, the *Penny Illustrated*, and the *Pall Mall Gazette*, praised the book as an entertaining read, largely focusing on a plot review.[33] More respectable periodicals, as was often the case, grappled with the meanings and appreciation of Mark Twain's humor. The London *Times* framed the book in terms of class and the ability to appreciate entertaining drollery. After a lengthy review of the book, the unsigned critic states:

> *But we should say that a perusal of* Tom Sawyer *is as fair a test as one could suggest of anybody's appreciation of the humorous. The drollery is often grotesque and extravagant, and there is at least as much in the queer Americanizing of the language as in the ideas it expresses. Practical people who pride themselves on strong common sense will have no patience with such vulgar trifling. But those who are alive to the pleasure of relaxing from serious thought and grave occupation will catch themselves smiling over every page and exploding outright over some of the choicer passages.*[34]

An unsigned review in the *Athenaeum* notes that the book escapes the normal literary milieu of Mark Twain: the railway station, where he is associated with a "library" of Artemus Ward, sporting newspapers, "the *Racing Calendar*, and *Diseases of Dogs*," along with ads for Brown & Polson's Corn Flour and other commercial products. The reviewer states that the book was not read in a railway station, yet the reviewer laughed anyway, which is a compliment that can be read as a class-based assessment. Mark Twain's humor had improved and "is not always uproarious, but it is always genuine and sometimes almost pathetic, and it is only now and then that the heartiness of a laugh is spoilt by one of those pieces of self-consciousness which are common blots on Mark Twain's other books." The reviewer also notes the presence of "slang words and racy expressions," but excuses most of them as natural to the book's subject.[35] These reviews rehearse major critical themes of Mark Twain's reputation: the emerging genius, the entertaining drollerist, the care-banishing humorist, and the low-class entertainer possibly worthy of attention.

Having written a novel that Howells could review without reservation, Mark Twain continued to navigate the *Atlantic*'s culture of letters as a contributor and author. He would publish eleven pieces in the *Atlantic* while Howells was editor, ranging from powerful satires of morality ("The Facts Concerning the Recent Carnival of Crime," June 1876) to burlesques of sentimental literature ("About Magnanimous-Incident Literature," May 1878). And while his ascension into the realm of belles lettres may have

seemed settled to the many readers of the magazine, Howells's promotion
was not accepted without question in the *Atlantic*'s circle of contributors.
Mark Twain himself—or Samuel Clemens as his creator—was one to always
question the terms and meanings of the successes and failures of Mark
Twain. In his first article to be published after the successful run of the
"Old Times" series, he wrote an extended comic sketch on the hypnotic,
yet meaningless, power of humorous writing to infect one's mind like a
virus. Entitled "A Literary Nightmare" (February 1876), the piece starts
with a verse of poetry:

> Conductor, when you receive a fare,
>   Punch in the presence of the passenjare!
> A blue trip slip for an eight-cent fare,
>   A buff trip slip for a six-cent fare,
> A pink trip slip for a three-cent fare,
>   Punch in the presence of the passenjare

> CHORUS
>   Punch, brothers punch with care!
>   Punch in the presence of the passenjare![36]

These lines, the narrator "Mark" writes, "took instant and entire possession of me." For days, the only thing on his mind are the lines of verse—
they keep him from his work, wreck his sleep, and turn him into a raving
lunatic singing "punch brothers punch. . . ." After several days of torture,
he sets out on a walk with his friend, a Rev. Mr. ————- (presumably his
good friend Rev. Joe Twichell). After hours of silence, the Reverend asks
the narrator what the trouble is, and Mark tells him the story, teaching
him the lines of the jingle. Instantly, the narrator puts the verse out of
his mind. The Reverend, on the other hand, has "got it" now. Several days
later, the Reverend returns—drawn, weak, and pale—and tells the story
of his inability to shed the "nightmare," even when performing a funeral
service for a dear friend. The words of homily fell into the rhythm of the
jingle so that by the end "the entire assemblage were placidly bobbing their
heads in solemn unison, mourners, undertaker, and all."[37]
    In order to save his friend from the asylum, the narrator takes the
Reverend to a local university to teach the jingle to the "poor, unthinking
students," with a sad result he refuses to detail. Then, addressing the reader,
the narrator explains why he wrote the article: "It was for a worthy, even a

noble, purpose. It was to warn you, reader, if you should come across those merciless rhymes, to avoid them—avoid them as you would a pestilence." Of course, that warning comes too late. We have already been exposed to the nonsense jingle and will be repeating it in our heads until we can figure out how to dislodge it (and if it is not in your head, I warn you don't go back now to see how something so silly could get lodged therein . . . the jingle still works).[38]

On the surface, the sketch is rather light and entertaining, if effective at its joke of infecting the reader with its jocular jingle. Still, coming when it did in Mark Twain's career and in the pages of the *Atlantic Monthly*, the story seems to contain a seed of anxiety with the place of such humor in the august realm of American high culture. If the mere jingle of entertaining words can infect not only the novelist but the minister, the student, and the reader of the *Atlantic*, then the role of the popular entertainment that the poem represents can be seen as a danger to both the literary and religious realms of culture, which were viewed as protectors of cultural values. The roots of New England's literary culture certainly sunk into a soil that linked reform to Christian values and viewed the author's function in moral terms. And while Howells had made steps to move the *Atlantic*'s vision of American literature beyond the magazine's focus, many of the major contributors and, presumably, many of the readers still linked literature with social reform, often in religious terms.

The ability of an ephemeral scrap of popular culture to infect the interconnected realms of literary and religious culture represented a danger to the serious moral purpose of the very magazine that Mark Twain was writing for. His mock serious purpose, to warn readers to avoid the very poem to which he had just exposed them, comments on his own position as a humorist. In order to fulfill the moral function of the humorist, he warned them against the infection of the merely humorous entertainment that had flooded popular culture, of which Mark Twain was often seen as a primary example. The warning could be read as a defense, although highly paradoxical, of his own moral purpose, and his subsequent piece in the *Atlantic*—"The Facts Concerning the Recent Carnival of Crime"—is still read as one of his central explorations of morality. On the other hand, one could read "A Literary Nightmare" as a statement of anxiety over the perceived disruptive or anarchic power of nonsense—in which the merely fun overtakes the serious realms of cultural meaning.[39] That tension exploded into view shortly thereafter in a highly public manner.

REMEMBER THE DINNER-BELL
THE ANXIETY OF REVERENCE IN
MARK TWAIN'S AFTER-DINNER SPEECHES

Mark Twain's burlesques of nonsense points to an alternate reading of his presence in the literary culture of the *Atlantic*—one in which his acceptance by Howells is taken by critics and authors that the realm of serious, artistic culture that the *Atlantic Monthly* promoted had been lowered by the presence of a mere buffoon. These possible meanings echoed through Samuel Clemens's/Mark Twain's other major connection to the culture of the *Atlantic Monthly*—his presence at celebratory banquets and his "hideous mistake" at the Whittier birthday banquet.

Mark Twain continued to appear on the pages of the *Atlantic Monthly* as a contributor through the mid-1870s, in shorter sketches and in travel narratives, such as "Some Rambling Notes of an Idle Excursion," a four-part account of his trip to Bermuda with Joseph Twichell. The final installation of this piece appeared in the January 1878 issue, the same time as the publisher of the magazine held a lavish banquet to celebrate the magazine and its contributors. While the anxieties about Mark Twain's inclusion in the *Atlantic*'s canon can be seen, however implicitly, in the ways that Howells framed his critical readings of Twain's books, and more distinctly in Clemens's private responses and some of his periodical pieces, they exploded into public view in an after-dinner speech he performed for a grand banquet given by the publisher of the *Atlantic Monthly* on December 17, 1877, to celebrate both the anniversary of the magazine and the birthday of one of its grandfathers—John Greenleaf Whittier. The "Whittier Birthday Speech," as it came to be known, has become a key scholarly touchstone in discussing Mark Twain's relationships to literary culture, that of Boston and more generally, and his role as a humorist in a culture of letters that held certain ideas and authors in reverence.

In an age of celebratory banquets, Mark Twain was one of the most famous after-dinner speakers in America. He had been elevated to the role of star of the celebratory banquet during his trips to England, where his name brought storms of applause for "the lion of London" and his successful speeches, especially his toast "To Woman," were reprinted in England and in the United States. To the cultural historian T. J. Jackson Lears, the banquet is a preeminent symbol of Gilded Age American culture: "Affluent Americans devoured heavy meals at huge banquets. They accepted the congratulations of after dinner orators. The speaker announced the marriage of material and spiritual progress. His audience nodded approval. There was no limit to American abundance. There was no impediment to the partnership of Protestantism and science. The audience applauded. They rose stiffly to leave. It was an age of confidence."[40]

In order to understand the culture of America in this period, Lears argues, it is necessary to "listen . . . to what was being said at the banquets."[41] At such dinners, guests would dine sumptuously, sometimes drink spirits, smoke fine cigars, and listen to tributes that took part in the larger cultural ritual of banquets celebrating some aspect of culture or another. As part of these quasi-religious celebratory banquets, the humorist was in a tricky position. Tasked with lightening the mood and entertaining the crowd, the humorist had to make fun of the evening's subject without making fun of the sentiment of the evening, in a negative sense. Wit aimed at oneself or one's position, or a burlesque of the verbose rhetoric of such occasions, were common, usually framed by praise for the evening's main figure or sentiment. Satire, which separated the humorist from his subject by deflating rhetoric or mocking the target, was more likely to cause offense.

The Whittier birthday dinner was not Mark Twain's introduction to celebratory banquets, to dining with the *Atlantic* greats, or to flirting with the line between humorous tribute and possible offense in his speeches. In December 1874, Howells implored Clemens to come to "meet Emerson, Aldrich, and all 'those boys'" at a banquet held to celebrate the January issue of the *Atlantic Monthly* and the purchase of the magazine by Houghton & Co. Twenty-eight guests were present, including Howells, Aldrich, Whipple, Holmes, Longfellow, James, and T. S. Perry, while many notables sent letters of regret, the reading of which was part of the ceremony of the evening. The presence of a reporter for the New York *Evening Post* made the event a semipublic ritual.[42]

Meanwhile, Mark Twain's presence at this "Dinner on Parnassus" reflected his new presence in the magazine, which was marked by the first installment of "Old Times on the Mississippi" in the January 1875 issue, alongside the initial chapter of Henry James's first novel and works by Longfellow, Holmes, Aldrich, and Bayard Taylor. Writing for the New York *Tribune*, Louise Chandler Moulton wrote that the January issue was of the highest quality and that the magazine's "uniform standard of excellence is higher than that of any of the English monthlies." Of Mark Twain's contribution, she wrote that it was "in the best vein of the best of American humorists," and she quotes approvingly of the description of his ambition to be a steamboatman—a passage that was printed at length in the New York *Times* and other newspapers.[43]

While the *Atlantic* had been founded over a dinner of notables, and many a meal had been eaten in its name, this banquet marked an institutionalization of the occasion by the new publisher. The evening celebrated the *Atlantic Monthly* as an institution, dramatizing its culture and the centrality of its pages and its contributors in shaping American literature and culture. This sentiment may have been best expressed in the occasional poem Oliver Wendell Holmes penned for the event, which began by joking about the terrors of being called upon to memorialize such an occasion and ended with "a hope that the magazine would help humanize the world and that people would worship the true and the pure and the beautiful":

> And preying no longer as tiger and vulture do,
>   All read the *Atlantic*, as persons of culture do.[44]

According to one newspaper report, "the brotherhood of authorship cemented at the early dinners has been renewed in a new generation, and its fruits promise to be broad and lasting."[45]

Mark Twain gave two speeches at the banquet. These were not preserved, but newspaper reports give a sense of his speech in response to the toast: "The President of the United States, and the Women who write for *The Atlantic*," which the New York *Tribune* referred to as an "inimitable and utterly reportable speech." In the style of Artemus Ward, he claimed that he could talk for weeks on the two proposed subjects but instead wandered among unrelated subjects. He then told a story of trying to pass himself off as a poet when "sailing on the blue Mediterranean." None of his fellow passengers believed him, and he wagered that he could get a poem (forwarded by cable from Gibraltar) published in the *Atlantic*, which resulted in Mark Twain arriving home with only $3 in his pocket. In a second joint speech with James R. Osgood, the two joked that Mark Twain knew cards better than poetry and warned that it was not safe to play cards—with Mark Twain.[46]

Mark Twain's introduction to the *Atlantic* social circle through the ritualized banquet saw no public reaction to his joking in the presence of giants. Howells had a grand time sitting near Clemens, Aldrich, and James, and he talked with Aldrich and Clemens until late at night.[47] Mark Twain's presence, and the laughter his speeches seem to have inspired, caused no discernible waves in the *Atlantic*'s surface, public or private. Even the end of Mark Twain's speech, which jokingly tweaked the relationship between author and publisher, seems to have been taken in good cheer:

> He then passed to other matters, and alluding to the dinner, confessed that he had had doubts, when first asked, as to whether he had better come to a publishers' dinner. But he was agreeably surprised: he found that the publishers treated their contributors as if they were persons whom they really wanted to conciliate. He had had a nice dinner. [Laughter.] He was willing to call it a good dinner. [More laughter.] An admirable dinner! It was as good as he should have got at home.[48]

Even if the final nub tweaked the vanity of the publishers by indicating that their lavish fare was as good as his usual, Mark Twain's speeches fulfilled their function as humor fit to the occasion.

By all accounts, the Whittier birthday banquet three years later was as convivial as the previous occasion, although it was both larger and more freighted with symbolic meaning. Instead of celebrating the *Atlantic* and its contributors in general, the banquet celebrated the seventieth birthday of John Greenleaf Whittier and the twentieth anniversary of the magazine. The banquet was an elaborate occasion—gastronomically, rhetorically, symbolically. The majority of consistent contributors to the *Atlantic* were invited to the Hotel Brunswick in Boston for an extravagant, multicourse meal starting with *Oysters on Shell* and featuring numerous courses intermingled with wine, smoking, and talk. The Boston *Daily Advertiser* rhapsodized the next day that "the company was without doubt the most notable that has ever been seen to this country within four walls" and claimed that "if a painter could have caught for his canvas the picture presented when the hosts and guests were all seated, the scene would, as reality, have rivaled the imaginary one of Shakespeare and his friends."[49] The assembled company was of impressive stature. At the head table sat Charles Dudley Warner, Howells, Holmes, H. O. Houghton, publisher of the *Atlantic*, Whittier, Emerson, and Longfellow. Approximately fifty guests lined two tables stretching away from the head table. The main notables missing were Lowell, who was the U.S. Minister to Spain at the time, James T. Fields, who was on a lecture tour, as well as the female contributors to the magazine, who were not invited to dinner but were invited to join the party for the speeches.

In a separate article, the *Daily Advertiser* made clear the public symbolism of the evening lay not only in the honor paid to Whittier but to the fact that Whittier represented the central place of the *Atlantic* in the American national mind: "Mr. Whittier's peculiar place in our literature is what we take this Boston magazine to hold,—an exponent of the New England idea, provincial, so far as local color and the choice of home and homely topics go; national, in a catholic spirit and a fervid patriotism." The central cultural role of the *Atlantic Monthly*—"to represent the highest elements of pure literature, and that distinctly American"—made the evening more than a dinner to a public that held the poet and magazine in high esteem. "There is," the article claimed "probably, no man in this country, excepting, perhaps, Mr. Longfellow, whose name is so widely known as Mr. Whittier's, and who has an established and honored place in so many families."[50] Whittier's reputation was wide enough and strong enough for the publishers of the magazine to offer a life-size portrait of the "beloved and honored Quaker poet" as an inducement to subscribers. Paying a four-dollar annual subscription, the *Atlantic* subscriber could purchase a portrait of Whittier (or of Longfellow or Bryant) for only $1.00 and receive, at no additional charge, the November and December numbers from 1877. This offer was published, as an ad or an article, in locales ranging from the *Weekly Arizona Miner* of Prescott, Arizona, to the Macon *Telegraph and Register* of Georgia to the *American Socialist* of Oneida, New York, testifying to the wide reach of the *Atlantic*, its contributors, and the reputation of both.

The night's speeches followed a similar pattern, with one notable exception—Mark Twain. Each speech contained a paean to the great Quaker poet and a discussion of the importance of the *Atlantic* to American letters and culture. Henry Nash Smith points out that the keyword for the evening was "reverence" and argues that Mark Twain's mistake was a failure to pay proper respect as perceived by some listeners and later readers.[51] Smith cites the letter of regret sent by Josiah Holland as evidence of the tone of reverence that permeated the night. Holland argued that reverence for high art represented a boon to American life:

> *I wonder if these old poets of ours—Mr. Dana, Mr. Bryant, Mr. Emerson, Mr. Longfellow and Mr. Whittier—appreciate the benefit they confer upon their fellow-citizens by simply consenting to live among them as old men? Do they know how they help to save the American nation from the total wreck and destruction of the sentiment of reverence? Why, if they will only*

live and move and have their being among us, from seventy years of age
to a hundred, and consent to be loved and venerated and worshipped and
petted, they will be the most useful men we have in the development of the
better elements of the American character.[52]

The praise of the poet (specifically Whittier, but also as a concept) and
of the culture of letters found in Boston (especially in the *Atlantic Monthly*)
ran through almost all the speeches. The poets being praised that night
were certainly, in Smith's phrase, "custodians of culture," but we must be
careful of viewing that culture as a "monolithic Brahmin culture," as Smith
defines it.[53] From a close view, the "Brahmin" culture of Boston and its
surroundings were not unified socially, politically, or even intellectually,
a fact that had been represented in the *Atlantic*'s pages for two decades.

While reverence was certainly the keynote of the evening, especially
in the comments regarding Whittier, not enough attention has been paid
to the presence of humor in certain speeches. For instance, Houghton
opened the speechmaking by praising Whittier and then the goals and
contributors of his magazine, stating:

We are glad to welcome here tonight those who, in the vigor of manhood,
were its founders and constant contributors, and who still give it the
influence of their great names and well-earned reputation, as well as the
matured product of a genius enriched by a lifetime of labor. May the day
be far distant when we shall lose the light of their example, or miss their
genial presence! We also welcome here tonight the younger contributors,
who are pressing on, with no unequal steps, to scale those loftier heights of
fame and usefulness, which the vastly broadening area of human thought
and endeavor makes possible.[54]

Houghton placed the *Atlantic* in its assumed cultural position, as "exponent of the Highest American culture in literature," as well as in art,
science, and politics. However, his speech was not confined to this reverent
praise, but ended with an extended, presumably humorous defense of
publishers against literary men as a class. Houghton's joke relied on the
conceit that books had been, and still were in many locations, mainly sold
in drugstores, so that

pills and poetry, essences and essays, drugs and dramas, were disbursed over
the same counter and by the same hands. In the process of natural selection

it was perhaps logical that a decoction of poetry should be followed by a
purgative of pills. The publisher of the first collected edition of the works of
our revered poet was also the vender of Brandreth pills. He made a fortune,
and I leave you to infer whether it was from the pills or the poetry.[55]

There is no indication in the record whether the assembled authors found
the joke funny or not.

Mr. Whittier, a shy man who had only decided to attend at the last
moment, spoke briefly and had Longfellow read a poem composed for
the occasion. Howells, as toastmaster for the night, followed, starting off
with a somewhat labored joke equating after-dinner speeches with Aztec
sacrifices and exempting from "extorted eloquence" any man who so chose,
especially those planning reprisals on the person or work of Howells. Following hearty but subdued praise of Whittier, Howells then launched into
an extended description of the place of the *Atlantic Monthly* in American
letters, which is worth quoting at length:

> *For twenty years it has represented, and may be almost said to have em-*
> *bodied, American letters. With scarcely an exception every name known in*
> *our literature has won fame from its pages, or has added lustre to them, and*
> *an intellectual movement, full of a generous life and of a high ideal, finds*
> *its record there in vastly greater measure than in any or all other places.*
> *Its career is not only distinguished among American periodicals, but upon*
> *the whole is unique. It would not be possible, I think, to point to any other*
> *publication of its sort which so long retained the allegiance of its great*
> *founders, and has added so constantly so many names of growing repute*
> *to its list of writers. . . . All young writers are eager to ally their names with*
> *the great memories and presences on its roll of fame; its stamp gives a new*
> *contributor immediate currency; it introduces him into the best public, the*
> *best company, the company of those Boston authors who first inspired it*
> *with the life so vigorous yet. It was not given us all to be born in Boston, but*
> *when we find ourselves in the Atlantic we all seem to suffer a sea-change,*
> *and aesthetic renaissance; a livelier literary conscience stirs in us; we have*
> *its fame at heart; we must do our best for Maga's name as well as for our*
> *own hope; we are naturalized Bostonians in the finest and highest sense.*
> *With greater reverence and affection than we can express, we younger and*
> *youngest writers for the Atlantic regard the early contributors whom we*
> *are so proud and glad to meet here, and it is with a peculiar sense of my*

own unworthiness that I salute them, and join the publishers in welcoming
them to this board.[56]

Howells's reverence is clearly directed toward the magazine, its elder luminaries, its Bostonian center, and its role in conferring literary and cultural status on younger writers who join its culture, however unworthy they may feel. The night was truly, to use an earlier phrase of Howells's, "the company of the best." With Howells, as with Houghton and other guests who would speak later, the keynote of reverence was modulated with a humorous note of self-deprecation, often as a joke about not being worthy (or even wanting) to speak about such lofty subjects.[57]

Howells introduced Mark Twain, making it clear that he was, indeed, a humorist while at the same time framing the purpose of humor for this occasion. Mark Twain, he stated, was

a humorist, whose name is known wherever our tongue is spoken, and who
has perhaps, done more kindness to our race, lifted from it more crushing
care, rescued it from more gloom, and banished from it more wretchedness
than all professional philanthropists that have live[d]; a humorist who
never makes you blush to have enjoyed his joke; whose generous wit has no
meanness in it, whose fun is never at the cost of anything honestly high or
good, but comes from the soundest of hearts and the clearest of heads.[58]

This statement has two points of interest. First, it applies a modified version of the *Atlantic*'s social utility—the artistic and social uplift of American culture—to humor. Here, humor functions to lift gloom and banish wretchedness through light entertainment. This aim reflects Howells's propensity toward avoiding conflict, which would have been a fitting aim for humor in the reverential context of after-dinner speaking. Second, Howells frames the ethical dimension of Mark Twain's humor as being nothing to blush at and never being aimed at what was high or good.

It is in light of the symbolic and rhetorical expectations of the evening's proceedings that Mark Twain's speech can be better understood as both a rhetorical event and a cultural drama. Clearly, the speech, no matter its reception by the assembled crowd, violated the central rhetorical expectations of the night. Mark Twain did not praise, or even mention, Whittier or the *Atlantic*, and the humor was only ambivalently self-deprecating, opening up the interpretation that Mark Twain was, in fact, making fun at the expense of the very living, breathing embodiments of the good and high seated at the front of the banquet hall.

The crux of the speech and its reception is whether the humor was aimed at the figures named in the speech—Emerson, Longfellow, and Holmes—or at Mark Twain himself. Without the ritual invocation of the evening's purpose, the speech lacks a reverent framing, instead dropping right into colloquial language:

> *Mr. Chairman—This is an occasion peculiarly meet for the digging up of pleasant reminiscences concerning literary folk; therefore I will drop lightly into history myself. Standing here on the Atlantic & contemplating certain of its biggest literary billows, I am reminded of a thing which happened to me fifteen years ago, when I had just succeeded in stirring up a little Nevadian literary ocean-puddle myself, whose spume-flakes were beginning to blow thinly California-wards.*

Resolving to test the merit of his *nom de plume*, "Mark Twain" stopped at a miner's cabin for hospitality. The sullen miner sighs and states that he is going to have to move, as Mark Twain was the fourth "littery man" to visit in the last day. The narrative voice then shifts to the miner's story, as he tells of a visit the previous day by "Emerson," "Holmes," and "Longfellow." It would have been clear to the assembled company that the "littery men" described were not the men sitting at the head of the table, even before hearing the physical descriptions given by the miner, which in no way matched the literary greats. Nevertheless, the miner does not suspect the veracity of the men, even as they drunkenly berate him with lines of their poetry. For instance, after dinner the miner sets out a jug of whiskey for his guests, to which Holmes "yells" a line from one of his poems:

> Flash out a stream of blood-red wine!—
> For I would drink to other days.[59]

Saying that he "didn't want to sass such famous littery people," the miner tells "Mr. Holmes" that he will drink whiskey or nothing. The men then move on to cards, fighting, and arguing, including an argument over which poet has the best poem, in which they claim poems by Whittier,

Lowell, and Bryant as their own. Upon leaving, the littery men steal the tormented miner's boots. The miner ends his narrative with the line: "As I said, Mr. Twain, you are the fourth in twenty-four hours—and I'm going to move; I ain't suited to a littery atmosphere."

At this point, "Mark Twain" comes back into the narrative to inform the miner of his mistake: "'Why my dear sir, *these* were not the gracious singers to whom we & the world pay loving reverence & homage: these were imposters.' The miner investigated me with a calm eye for awhile, then said he, 'Ah—imposters, were they? are *you*?'" He ended the speech with a further caveat, excusing himself from exaggerating any details since "I believe it is the first time I have ever deflected from perpendicular fact on an occasion like this."

Rhetorically, the humor of Mark Twain's speech is based on a comparison of the history of the "literary billows" of the *Atlantic* with the "ocean-puddle" of Nevada. The miner knows the *nom de plume*'s of the authors but does not know enough to know that his reverence is misplaced by allowing the miscreants to abuse his trust. Their use of the poets' words for base purposes inverts the rhetoric of the banquet, which held that the poems, indeed, the very presence of the old poets, as Holland had argued, was a boon to the cultural life of America. The end of the story attempts to correct the inversion of high and low by returning the poets to "loving reverence & homage" and the putative trio to the status of con men, which the auditors would have known all along. But the sentiment of reverence is again destabilized by the necessary punch line—the miner's question of "imposters were they? are *you*?"

While Mark Twain's "Whittier Birthday" speech lacked a certain amount of reverence, in the conventional manner of praising Whittier and the *Atlantic* authors, it does exhibit an odd form of reverence in which the western miner alone in the California wilds would attempt to perform all duties he perceived to be owed to the famous "littery men." Indeed, the poet's names carry so much capital that the miner goes so far as to decide to move, since he is not "suited to a littery atmosphere." The biggest question about Mark Twain's speech was not whether it was funny or not, but whether it was suited to the "littery atmosphere" in which it was presented. While the reactions of his audience seem to have been pleasant, or even positive, the aftermath of the Whittier birthday speech found some groups questioning whether Mark Twain was, in fact, an imposter out of place in the culture of the *Atlantic*.

A CALIFORNIA BULL IN THE *ATLANTIC*'S COURT
RESPONSES TO THE WHITTIER BIRTHDAY SPEECH

> *Mark Twain's speech at the Whittier Birthday banquet was, perhaps,*
> *very funny—to them that like such things; but what will the historian*
> *of American literature a hundred years from now make of it, when he*
> *shall dig it out of the rubbish of musty newspapers?*
>   —THE ADVANCE 12, NO. 539 (JANUARY 3, 1879), 11.

Mark Twain's speech at the Whittier birthday dinner appears to have been well received—whether because the attendees actually found it funny or because they were polite. Newspaper reports from Boston showed little evidence that either Mark Twain or any of his audience found the speech to be in poor taste or out of place. Only later discussions of the evening—coming from newspapers outside of Boston, as well as from Samuel Clemens and William Dean Howells—discussed the evening in terms of Mark Twain's failure. For instance, the Chicago *Tribune* summarized one major thread of later criticism by stating: "Boston does not take it kindly, and is as cold as its sharpest winter day, because of the irreverence of the mad wag. Even a King's jester should know when it will do to shake his cap and bells in the royal presence."[60] Some responses to the speech thus demonstrated the view of those who questioned the inclusion of Mark Twain in the company of *Atlantic* authors. For both Clemens and Howells, the speech functioned as a focal point for anxiety about Mark Twain's inclusion in a canon of American letters, as will be discussed in the next section.

The newspaper response to the event was extensive, testifying to the importance of both Whittier and the *Atlantic Monthly* as cultural symbols. Reactions to Mark Twain's speech fall in four rough categories: silence; value-free or positive descriptions; negative reactions originating later outside of Boston; and reactions making fun of the incident. Many newspapers either did not report on the event, or reported on the evening in straightforward ways, either ignoring Mark Twain's speech or listing him as a speaker without expounding on his speech. The Boston *Globe* of December 18, for instance, printed the speech with the gloss: "This eccentric story was told in Mr. Clemens's characteristic drawling, stammering way, and produced the most violent bursts of hilarity. Mr. Emerson seemed a little puzzled about it, but Mr. Longfellow laughed and shook, and Mr. Whittier seemed to enjoy it keenly."

The immediate reaction of the Boston press framed Mark Twain's speech as a humorous highlight, reprinting it in whole while only briefly mentioning Charles Dudley Warner's humorous contribution. The Boston *Evening Transcript* acknowledged some difference of opinion regarding the taste of the speech, but stated: "There was no mistaking the hearty fun elicited by the droll attitude in which these literary lights were represented. They appreciated the joke, as will the public who read, and laugh while they read." The newspaper did reconsider their view the next day, stating "The general verdict seems to be that Mark Twain's speech, though witty and well worked-up, was in bad taste and entirely out of place. As one critic puts it, 'if the three gentlemen named in his remarks had been entertained in New York, and a speaker had said what Twain did, Boston would have felt insulted.'"[61] Other papers, in New England and further afield, reported the Whittier banquet in positive terms. The speech was described as "in a characteristic vein" and "one of his most humorous of speeches," and the speech was reprinted, often as a stand-alone piece, in numerous papers. In fact, any controversy over Mark Twain's speech was initially overshadowed by two more immediate outrages: a letter from the Women's Christian Temperance Union protesting wine being served at a dinner for a well-known teetotaler and protests at the exclusion of women from the event as full participants.[62]

As time went on, newspaper reports began to argue that Mark Twain had insulted "Boston" and its literary giants. Outsiders perceived an outsized offense.[63] Criticism of the speech seems to have spread from New England to the midwest to the West Coast as newspapers reprinted editorial comments or weighed in with their own. The most immediate negative reaction to the speech was from the December 18 Worcester *Gazette*, which opined:

> *Mark Twain made a speech at the* Atlantic *dinner, last night, which was in bad taste. We refer to it, because Mark's sense of propriety needs development, and it is not his first offence. . . . It was, of course, meant to be a piece of incongruous absurdity, and although the idea was not at all original, it might have seemed funny in some circles, when told with Mark's drawl, but men who have attained the years and fame of Longfellow and Emerson are entitled to some degree of respect amongst a company of their friends. The offence is easier to feel than describe, but it is one which if repeated would*

cost Mark Twain his place among the contributors to the Atlantic Monthly, where indeed his appearance was in the beginning considered an innovation.[64]

The New Orleans *Times Picayune* complained that the *Atlantic* had degraded Whittier to "a circus of himself" by using the dinner, as well as the advertising portrait, to promote the magazine. The paper printed the speech under the heading, "Mark Twain's Funny Speech. How the Hartford Humorist Stirred Them Up At the Whittier Dinner."[65]

Mark Twain had certainly stirred something up. The Springfield (Mass.) *Republican* was highly critical, publishing two articles and an unsigned letter to the editor excoriating the humorist as "vulgar." The letter to the editor echoed the attitudes of Josiah Holland who had been the assistant editor and part owner of the paper from the 1840s to the mid-1860s. The unsigned letter decried the words of "Mark Twain" intruding into a reverent scene, which is described in detail, beginning: "Imagine the scene, the really brilliant company, bright in the best sense of that suggestive word. . . . Fit combination of events, the celebration of the progress of a life, which has had for its object the making of to-morrow better than today; and the speeding of an enterprise, which having passed its teens, looks forward to an earnest, ever broadening life."[66] This attitude toward Whittier and the *Atlantic* are extended, in this letter, to each of the authors Mark Twain spoke about in similar effusions of reverent rhetoric. The author's attack is so rich in cultural meaning that it is worth quoting at length:

> *Into this China shop bursts a wild Californian bull. True gentlemen bear insult in silence, and let such things dash on to their own destruction. But there is food for reflection in the incident. The songs, literature, the wit and humor of a land tell tales, and when a bright and clever man, who does possess genuine humor, and has really discovered a new and curious vein, instead of fitting it into something that will amuse and relax the mind, without polluting it, finds his greatest glory in embellishing with his gift the low, poor, weak parts of nature, and dressing in the garb of bar-room habitués the men who stand at the other end of life,—is it not well to inquire whether the popularity of this man ought not to have already reached a climax?*

The author closed with a clear explanation of why such humor, which aimed for the "gutter," was out of place for literary men. "American social life," the letter reads, "upon which, by God's aid, must be built to mighty fabric of the future state, is in the formative period, and, jealous as we might have been of our political honor, a thousand times more jealous must we be of that most precious possession—reverence for that which is truly high." If not written by Josiah Holland, the letter was clearly written by someone well versed in his views of literature and society.

These negative reactions show that Mark Twain's speech was, indeed, controversial in some circles, but also that the controversy went beyond whether it was in good taste to whether he belonged in the company of the *Atlantic*'s authors in the first place.[67] Public reactions to Mark Twain's appearance as a regular contributor to the *Atlantic Monthly* had been muted up to this point, but the reaction to the Whittier birthday speech demonstrates a strong undercurrent of disapproval in the presence of the "stripèd clown" in midst of the American cultural elite. Several newspaper columns clearly demonstrate a widespread anxiety at Mark Twain's cultural position in relation to Boston and its magazine. For instance, the *Daily Rocky Mountain News* of Denver printed a column in January that cobbled together reactions from a variety of sources. Stating that "this literary lion has roared once too often in the classic shades of Boston, and his name is now tabooed in the best literary circles of the modern Athens," the story prints snippets from at least four sources. A quote from the *Woman's Journal* nicely links the main controversies of the evening, stating that the female contributors to the *Atlantic*, as well as Mr. Whittier, would not have liked the presence of wine and cigar smoke, and that, in this masculine environment, the "essay" of Mark Twain "fitly furnished the key-note for this kind of entertainment relished by these masculine scribblers."[68] The article also focused on Mark Twain's relationship to Boston literary culture: "It is well known that Beacon street never received Mr. Clemens. Mrs. Julia Ward Howe said some time ago that the *Atlantic* was losing caste and lowering its tone by admitting the Twain papers to its pages, and perhaps Mark considers that he owes nothing to Boston in the way of courtesy or consideration." Finally, the paper concluded that the objection to his speech was not that it offended Boston, but that it offended "every intelligent reader."

More than just one speech, the Whittier birthday issue had raised the issue of Mark Twain's place in the culture of the *Atlantic,* which can be seen as a proxy argument about the changing state of American letters. An article entitled "A Thundering Row about That Whittier Dinner" took all the criticisms of the evening—wine, women, advertising, and Mark Twain—and addressed them in a dialogue between an unnamed author and unnamed editor on the subject. Addressing Mark Twain's speech, the author stated that it strikes one in a "very ludicrous manner" but that "one wants to kick the fellow who is making us laugh by such a connection." Most importantly, the author highlighted the connection between Mark Twain's breach of taste and William Dean Howells as his promoter, writing:

> But to me the funniest thing is in the way this is all reacting on Howells. Howells, you know, thinks Twain is immense; took him up from the first, rushed him into the Atlantic, floated him in Atlantic society. Howells, you know, who is rigorously refined . . . is suddenly obliged to sit and swallow all this bilge water from his favorite contributor, in the presence of such fine company, too; has to see the man he has endorsed degrade himself to the rank of a buffoon. It must have been tough for Howells.[69]

The speech obviously stirred up a strong reaction that ultimately went beyond questioning the humor of the speech and its appropriateness for the circumstance to the issue of Mark Twain's literary reputation within the literary ocean of the *Atlantic*.[70]

That any negative response was muted among the evening's guests and the Boston papers may indicate a tendency to ignore or forgive offenses. The cultural symbol of "the *Atlantic Monthly*"—the publisher of the American Olympians—that was feted and toasted in Boston that night was also a loose group of friends, acquaintances, and occasional enemies, who referred to each other as "Wendell," "William," and "Mark." The reaction to Mark Twain's speech highlighted the difference between Emerson, Holmes, and Longfellow as ideas, as *noms de plume*, whose fame spread across the country as cultural ideas, and the three "littery" men as people. The distance between the author in person and the author as text—the very distinction on which the humor of the speech rested—might explain the numerous reactions that stated that the speech may have been funny in person, but in print it was of poor taste. For instance, the Chicago *Tribune* printed a dialogue report between the paper's Boston correspondent and one of the attendees, who states of the three literary greats:

> "But they liked it; they laughed as much as anybody."
> "Perhaps they did laugh. I don't believe they enjoyed it. If they would confess the truth,—Longfellow and Emerson, I mean,—I believe they would say that they were embarrassed. Of course they had to laugh."
> "Stuff! Longfellow and Emerson are not such milksops. They've had so much tall talk bestowed upon them that they must have been relieved to be treated to a joke like other men."[71]

In this view, the praise heaped on the authors is "tall talk" that Mark Twain's joke attempted to relieve by treating the authors like men, which might help explain the distance between the actuality of the event and the symbolic readings.

The final response to the Whittier birthday speech in the press was of jovial gossip. Mark Twain's speech, like many things that Mark Twain did or said, was fodder for humor columns. The jokes seem to be roughly evenly aimed at those who took the speech too seriously and at Mark Twain. For instance, the New York *Times* commented that the only funnier thing than Twain's speech was the "plaint" of a Boston paper that it was in bad taste. *Puck*, quoting the St. Louis *Journal*, similarly made light of those who took offense: "The speech Mark Twain made concerning the Yankee poets has caused those concerned no concern at all, but those whom the concern did not concern appear to be unduly concerned about the concern." Other responses joked about Twain's failure, aiming the commentary at him: "Mr. Mark Twain will think twice or thrice before he makes another such a speech as he did at the Whittier Dinner. When Boston spanks, she spanks hard and long."[72] Interestingly, the New Orleans *Times Picayune* took great relish in making a series of jokes at Twain's expense in late January and February:

> . . . *He is sorry for it, and will not go to the next* Atlantic Monthly *dinner; that is if Mr. Houghton has control of the invitations. (1/24/1878)*

> *Mark Twain's late speeches hardly come up to the mark. (2/2/1878)*

> *Mark Twain feels like a banquet hall deserted. He will be invited to no more brain dinners. (2/11/1878)*

> *Instead of talking, Mark Twain says that at all future banquets he intends to eat. (2/15/1878)*

"WITH HIS JOKE DEAD ON HIS HANDS": MARK TWAIN'S "HIDEOUS" MISTAKE AND THE ANXIETY OF MEMORY

The newspaper responses to the Whittier Banquet demonstrate a clear undercurrent of anxiety at Howells's insistence on Mark Twain's value in the literary realm of the *Atlantic*. The other major response to the speech was from Clemens and Howells, for whom the speech created an immediate horror and assumed a lasting, mythic resonance. In describing the importance of the speech, and the vivid yet largely apocryphal memory of the event held by Clemens and Howells, Henry Nash Smith argued that "the vivid scene described by Mark Twain and Howells embodies the kind of truth appropriate to fiction or even to mythology."[73] Mark Twain recollected the evening most vividly in his autobiographical musings published in the *North American Review*, where the December 1907 installment featured a lengthy review of the incident. Standing before "that row of venerable and still active volcanoes," Mark Twain expected his speech to be "the gem of the evening" until he started to speak of Emerson and the other tramps. This gained the "*attention*" of the guests, but each face "turned to a sort of black frost," and he writes that he slowly gave up hoping that "somebody would laugh, or that somebody would smile, but nobody did." Wanting to give up, but unable to, he writes that he struggled through to the end, always aware of the stony faces confronting him. He writes: "It was the sort of expression their faces would have worn if I had been making these remarks about the Deity and the rest of the Trinity; there is not milder way in which to describe the petrified condition and the ghastly expression of those people. When I sat down it was with a heart which had long ceased to beat. I shall never be as dead again as I was then. I shall never be as miserable again as I was then."[74] Howells, he remembered, understood "the size of the disaster" and tried to say something but "couldn't get beyond a gasp."

For his part, Howells remembered the Whittier fiasco in *My Mark Twain* (1910) in similar terms of horror and embarrassment. While the speech may have been funny to some listeners, Howells noted, Mark Twain underestimated the "species of religious veneration" in which his subjects were held. Howells writes of the incident:

> *Here, I said, in sum, was a humorist who never left you hanging your head for having enjoyed his joke; and then the amazing mistake, the bewildering blunder, the cruel catastrophe was upon us. I believe that after the scope of the burlesque made itself clear, there was no one there, including the burlesquer himself, who was not smitten with a desolating dismay. There fell a silence, weighing many tons to the square inch, which deepened from moment to moment, and was broken only by the hysterical and blood-curdling laughter of a single guest, whose name shall not be handed down to infamy. Nobody knew whether to look at the speaker or down at his plate. I chose my plate as the least affliction, and so I do not know how Clemens looked,*

except when I stole a glance at him, and saw him standing solitary amid his appalled and appalling listeners, with his joke dead on his hands.[75]

Writing more than thirty years after the fact, Howells remembered nothing of the dinner after the speech until he was with Clemens and Charles Dudley Warner in a hotel room, with Warner saying to Twain: "Well, Mark, you're a funny fellow." Mark Twain recalled that his speech halted the evening's proceedings, causing the young novelist who followed him to fail after a few lines and slump "down in a limp and mushy pile."[76] In his memory, the program ended there—the scheduled speakers were dazed, stupefied, none could speak, and the evening ended with Howells "mournfully, and without words" pulling him into another room and telling him that "there was no help for this calamity, this shipwreck, this cataclysm; that this was the most disastrous thing that had ever happened in anybody's history. . . ." Clearly, there exists an important gap between reports of the evening and the memories of Clemens and Howells.

The overstated horror of the two men's responses are not accurate in their details—the speech was met with laughter (by more than the one blood-curdling guest), not silence, and the speeches went on after Mark Twain spoke, but the stories reveal a truth of the event as it seems to have been experienced by the two men. Almost immediately after the banquet, both men expressed their horror. In a letter to Charles Eliot Norton, Howells wrote that Clemens had felt the "awfulness" of what he was doing as he went but that he was helpless to stop, and Howells was unable to figure out any way to save him. "He was completely crushed by it," Howells wrote, "and though it killed the joy of the time for me, I pitied him; for he *has* a good and reverent nature for good things, and his performance was like an effect of demoniacal possession." Joseph Twichell, his minister and close friend, wrote in his diary that Clemens knew he was making a mistake as he spoke, although he had thought the speech "the best thing he had ever done." Twichell then noted that the "irreverence" of the speech would have been plain to others: "Anybody could have told him that before, that had the chance, for he was shockingly out of taste, but he didn't know it."[77] It appears that neither Howells nor Olivia Clemens read the speech, for they would have almost certainly recognized its problems.

In turn, Mark Twain's first biographer and a generation of subsequent scholars accepted the mythic version of events without looking at the details. Bernard DeVoto, in his foundational work of criticism, *Mark Twain's*

America (1932), saw the speech as "a distillation of essences" of Mark Twain's relationship to the literary culture of New England. For DeVoto, New England was the "village," a genteel province sheltered from the vastness of the frontier and controlled by "refined womanhood . . . by means of the tyranny of congealment, the righteousness of offended purity." With a fine flair for flattening entire social orders into tropes, as was allowed in DeVoto's era, he summarized the villagers in this way: "They were children of an immense provincialism, immutably virginal. They had studied, they had traveled, they had philosophized—wrapped forever in the swaddlings of Yankee morality." Mark Twain entered the village of New England as an outsider—the embodiment of the Frontier, who "spoke more directly of the bastards of the devil," who had seen men die, and whose "very hair and mustache announced anarchy." The Whittier birthday speech symbolized the intrusion into the village of a frontier world in which reverence for great figures was not automatic. In short, DeVoto summarized that "The village, in simple fact, witnessed blasphemy."[78] This flattening of Mark Twain's attack on "the village" (i.e., Boston) demonstrates one of the major thematic approaches to the Whittier birthday speech: a psychological and cultural interpretation that sees Mark Twain as an outsider whose speech attacked, or at least confronted, the almost religious reverence of New England toward its own literary icons.

And while this reading is intriguing in its evocative images, it is largely based on a reading of the mythical resonances of the event, not on the existing evidence. There is little or no evidence that Mark Twain meant his speech as an attack on New England literary culture, whether consciously or unconsciously, apart from circumstantial readings that hint that he *must* have known what he was doing. Samuel Clemens's reaction, on the other hand, shows a keen horror on his part on his own failure of reverence more than a reaction to the actual events of the dinner. The psychological insight into Clemens and Howells and their relations with literary culture that the event dramatized, which is in fact the reason the event has so much resonance in Twain scholarship and literary history, must remain a matter of speculation informed by a close reading of the rhetorical and historical contexts of the evening. Most scholars in writing about this event have focused on the personal dramas of the evening, spurred on by the mythic memories of Clemens and Howells, largely focusing on Mark Twain's motivations for the speech, most often in terms of a more or less conscious aggression towards belles lettres. Henry Nash Smith's "That Hideous Mistake of Poor Clemens's (1955)" revised the historiographical understanding of the event by showing that Howells's and Clemens's memory varied from the reports of the evening. As James Caron has argued, many of the scholarly readings of the event focus on the personal dimensions of Samuel Clemens's authorial identity rather than the drama at the "symbolic cultural level."[79] It was at this symbolic level, rather than at the personal level of the assembled men of letters, that the speech caused offense, but only to groups or individuals who had some investment in the ideality—namely, the press, Howells, and Mark Twain.

Richard Lowery argues that the speech represented an ongoing negotiation between Mark Twain and his audience in regards to new developments of authorship. He writes: "The result is neither an affirmation of reverent distinction nor an oppositional critique of it, but rather a narrative of posture and imposture generated by parody and held together by humor. What emerges is not so much an expression of cultural conflict as a tale that lays claims to being the site of that struggle."[80] In other words, Mark Twain's speech unintentionally dramatized the cultural conflicts already present in his attendance of the banquet without resolving or denying them. And while Lowery focuses this drama on the idea of "authorship" in intriguing ways, the cultural conflicts of the evening apply equally to the distinction between humorous irreverence and reverent Culture that was central to understanding the shifting role of Mark Twain as a popular humorist entering the culture of quality letters symbolized by the *Atlantic*.

Reactions to the speech might also be understood as a highly symbolic instance of larger literary trends that the authors in attendance were facing: the fragmentation and expansion of the literary marketplace, including the declining centrality of the *Atlantic Monthly*; the continued popularity and sales of "lesser" forms of literature, including those of popular humorists; and the generational transformation from the literary centrality of the New England greats to a largely undefined literary future. Both Clemens and Howells, in their own and in linked ways, were central to the cultural conversation about such issues. The rhetoric of reverence that underwrote the banquet's symbolism was linked to an anxiety of authorship that went beyond the question of Mark Twain's inclusion in the canon to larger issues of cultural production and meaning. The *Atlantic Monthly* and its associated authors viewed the role of the magazine and the literary culture it attempted to represent in terms of a cultural mission that went far beyond aesthetic questions. The sentiment of reverence envisioned a moral purpose to art that would guide the nation toward a fulfillment of its ideals. Mark Twain's presence in the *Atlantic* and at the

Whittier Dinner challenged some of those who promoted that sentiment of reverence, which was undergoing an intensification during this period as certain cultural actors attempted to "sacralize"—to use Lawrence Levine's apt term—certain areas and forms of cultural production in the face of a growing mass culture in need of uplift.[81]

The exchange of letters that followed the event clearly demonstrates the anxieties that Clemens and Howells seemed to have held regarding Mark Twain's position in American literary culture. The first response was sent by Howells on the night of the 18th, sometime after midnight following the speech, which simply reads: "All right, you poor soul!"[82] Three days later, Howells sent Clemens a short letter, along with proofs of an article and several books, seemingly ignoring the speech and its aftermath, but Clemens, writing on the 23rd, delved deeply into the aftermath:

> My Dear Howells:
>
> My sense of disgrace does not abate. It grows. I see that it is going to add itself to my list of permanencies—a list of humiliations that extends back to when I was seven years old, & which keep on persecuting me regardless of my repentancies.[83]

As his focus on the incident for decades after shows, the speech was indeed added to the list. Clemens further stated that Livy and he had decided that it would be best to withdraw a story slated for the *Atlantic*, since the "misfortune has injured me all over the country; therefore it will be best that I retire from before the public at present." His sense of shame is clear. "It seems I must have been insane when I wrote that speech," he wrote, "& saw no harm in it, no disrespect toward those men whom I reverenced so much. And what shame I brought upon *you*, after what you said in introducing me! It burns me like fire to think of it." In spite of numerous critical readings that see in the speech Mark Twain's adversarial position to New England literary culture, this response indicates Clemens's awareness of his mistake, his reverence for the authors involved, and his knowledge of Howells's role in the creation of his public persona.

Howells responded by first squelching talk of Mark Twain not writing for the *Atlantic*, stating: "You are going to help and not hurt us many a year yet, if you will."[84] But he did not ignore the speech. Saying that everyone he had spoken to regarded it as a "fatality"—"one of those sorrows into which a man walks with his eyes wide open, no one knows why"—he then writes that members of the *Atlantic* circle would understand the circumstance. He continued: "But I don't pretend to not agree with you about it. All I want you to do is not to exaggerate the damage. You are not going to be floored by it; there is more justice than that even in *this* world. And especially as regards *me*, just call the sore spot well. I could say more and with better heart in praise of your good-feeling (which was what I always liked in you) since this thing happened than I could before." Howells then approved of Clemens's plan to apologize to the literary figures he had offended. The apology would help smooth over hard feelings on a personal level with the men involved and would also be seen as an instance of Clemens being educated into the proper relationship between reverence and humor.

The identical letters of apology Clemens mailed to Emerson, Longfellow, and Holmes on December 27 offered "repentance" for his offense and an illuminating perspective of how he viewed "Mark Twain," or wanted others to view him, in relation to polite literary culture. His offense, he explains, would be inexcusable in a man of "fine nature," but that he said that he undertook the speech "innocently & unwarned."[85] His rhetoric of innocence continues, calling upon Howells as a witness: "You will think it is incredible; but it is true, & Mr. Howells will confirm my words. He does not know how it *can* be true, & neither does any one who is incapable of trespassing as I did; yet he knows it *is* true." When he realized his guilt, he writes, his suffering was acute and was not tempered by his innocent intent, but his guilt was more keenly felt by his barometer of propriety: "As to my wife's distress, it is not to be measured; for she is of finer stuff than I; & yours were sacred names to her. We do not talk about this misfortune—it *scorches*, so we only think—and think." Clemens did not ask for forgiveness but merely for understanding, for the men to believe that "I am only heedlessly a savage, not premeditatedly."

Clemens's invocation of his wife and of Howells as witnesses to both his essential innocence and his intense guilt at his trespass rhetorically created "Mark Twain" as a character—the innocent humorist who did not realize his joke was out of taste. To Howells, the next day, he wrote: "Ah, well, I am a great and sublime fool. But then I am God's fool, & all His works must be contemplated with respect." The response to the incident reveals a profound and sincere horror at his trespass, one that would influence him for years. Writing in his autobiography, Mark Twain finished the story by stating that the episode "pretty nearly killed me with shame during that first year or two whenever it forced its way into my mind."[86]

Clemens's apology eased any resentments the greats may have had and reframed the reactions of the press. Emerson's daughter Ellen wrote

to Mrs. Clemens on behalf of her family, expressing a mix of pity, amusement, and reprobation. Some in the family, she wrote, thought the speech
funny, others were disappointed, but Clemens's letter had restored their
enjoyment of "Mark Twain," whom "we have liked almost everything we
have ever seen over Mark Twain's signature." Emerson, for his part, seems
to have looked puzzled at the dinner because he could not hear, and while
the speech amused him when it was read to him, Ellen Emerson wrote
that it hardly registered: "To my Father it is as if it had not been, he never
quite heard, never quite understood it, and he forgets easily and entirely."
Longfellow responded by declaring that he was only troubled that Clemens seemed so troubled about an insignificant matter stirred up by the
newspapers. The evening was pleasant for everyone, Longfellow insisted,
and the problem was that after-dinner speeches did not translate well into
newspapers, for "one needs the lamp-light, and the scenery. These failing,
what was meant in jest, assumes a serious aspect."[87]

Holmes, perhaps unsurprisingly, evinced sympathy for a fellow humorist, and his letter evoked interesting insights into the question of humor.
Like Longfellow, Holmes expressed dismay that Clemens was troubled at
a "trifling" matter.[88] He did admit to hearing some debate about the good
taste of the speech, but he cites two friends, "gentlemen of education and
the highest social standing"—who found the speech "infinitely amusing"
and defended it—as well as "one of the cleverest and best known ladies
we have among us," who was "highly delighted" with the speech. Holmes's
response indicates his awareness at the difficulty of the position of the
humorist:

> The idea was a very amusing one and with a little less of broad farce about
> it might have pleased everybody as it did so many. Any man who knows
> your bonhomie and evident kindness of disposition would never think of
> supposing you meant to strike anything with the heat-lightning of your
> wit and humour.
>   . . . The world owes you too large a debt for the infinite pleasure and
> amusement you have furnished to both hemispheres to quarrel with you
> because your invention has for once led you a little farther than what some
> would consider the proper limit of its excursions.

The responses of the "targets" of Mark Twain's humor demonstrate
some combination of their lack of offense, their senses of humor, their tact
with a fellow writer, and their hearing infirmities, as well as the impression

that Mark Twain's offense against the reverent authors increased as one's distance from the actual men increased.

Samuel Clemens's apology—transformed into "Mark Twain's" for the public—was reported in the press on at least a few occasions in January. In a story from the Boston *Herald*, reprinted elsewhere as well, under the title "Mark Twain Apologizes," the apology is described as "characteristic" and "utterly abject and forlorn," so much so that "all will forgive Mark from the bottom of their hearts."[89] The story states that Mark Twain referred to himself as "God's fool"—a phrase contained in his letter to Howells—hinting that Howells, or someone whom Howells had told of Clemens's sentiments, was the source of the news of the apology, rather than Emerson, Holmes, or Longfellow.

The Whittier incident added several rich metaphors for contemplating Mark Twain's relation to the elite literary culture of his time: the heedless savage, the embarrassed supplicant, the California bull, God's fool, the literary lion roaring at the Boston elite. It also made it clear that portions of the *Atlantic*'s audience viewed Mark Twain as an innovation to be wary of—that even an unstripèd, right-side-up clown might still be a clown or that Twain's literary offspring were not pure enough to escape suspicion.

"I THOUGHT THAT HUMOR WAS PLAYED OUT IN AMERICA": MARK TWAIN ABROAD, AGAIN

Following the failure of the Whittier birthday speech, however imagined or overexaggerated it may have been, Samuel Clemens's productivity declined. For two years, between 1877 and 1879, only two books of Mark Twain's were published—the *Scrap-Book* and *Punch, Brothers, Punch!* (1878)—both published by Slote, Woodman, and Company. The second book was largely an advertisement for the first, reprinting "A Literary Nightmare" renamed, along with a range of previously published pieces.[90] In April 1878, Samuel Clemens, his family, and three companions (a friend, a nursemaid, and a valet) sailed for Europe, where they would stay for over sixteen months. He left America partially to escape his own success, which left him hounded by the public and paying for his lavish house, and partially to escape the failures of the Whittier Dinner, of *Tom Sawyer*, and of the play *Ah Sin*.[91] While in Europe, Clemens returned to the genre of travel writing, working on what would become *A Tramp Abroad*.

While Clemens was physically absent from the United States, his *nom de plume* remained a presence in American periodicals. Four sketches appeared in the *Atlantic Monthly*, which were reprinted and/or commented upon in newspapers. An anonymous review in the *Atlantic* of the Paris Exposition of 1879 noted that the "American youths, corrupted to the marrow by Mark Twain, pass through seeking humorous solutions to things."[92] In newspapers, Mark Twain was the subject of gossip about his doings in Europe. His works were also frequently republished. During his absence, newspapers reprinted older works, including "The Jumping Frog," works from the *Galaxy*, miscellaneous sketches, and extracts from his most recent works in the *Atlantic Monthly*. Certain pieces reverberated through multiple newspapers, such as an interview in which Mark Twain explained why he couldn't write a book about the English (because there was nothing funny in England) and his announcement of running for president.[93]

"Mark Twain," as a public idea, circulated in newspapers, often beyond Samuel Clemens's intentions or control. For instance, the New York *Sun* published at least five spurious interviews with Mark Twain between 1876 and 1881. In January 1878, the *Sun* ran two purported interviews—the first regarding Mark Twain's new position as the editor of the Hartford *Courant* and the second exposing the first story as a hoax he had perpetrated on the reporter. In the second false interview, in which Mark Twain explained why he perpetrated the hoax on the reporter, he explained that he had put out the story as a test to see if the press still had a sense of humor. The false Twain explains:

> "Latterly," he continued, "I have been down in the mouth. I began to think my luck was down on me. My speech at the Whittier dinner didn't exactly take. I meant it merely as a cheerful conceit, and yet people wouldn't laugh. My article in the Atlantic containing the joke about the two dying soldiers quarreling for the first choice of coffins, seemed to fall flat. A good many well-meaning people refused to see it in the spirit intended. I got gloomy. I smoked all day and almost all night. I thought that humor was played out in America."[94]

This fake Twain article was reprinted or reported in Wisconsin, Georgia, Colorado, Arkansas, and Colorado, although the major papers in New York, Boston, and Chicago did not bite on the "news."[95] Clemens wrote to his friend Rollin Daggett denying the report, and his letter was reprinted in the Virginia City *Territorial Enterprise*, where his position as editor had been mentioned as fact. Most of the interviews Mark Twain gave to the press occurred after 1880. Of the 258 authenticated interviews collected in *Mark Twain: The Complete Interviews*, only eight of them occurred before he left America in the spring of 1878.[96]

Returning from abroad on September 3, 1879, Mark Twain soon returned to the public stage. On November 13, he delivered an oratorical masterpiece at a banquet for Ulysses S. Grant at the Palmer House in Chicago during a reunion of the Army of the Tennessee. Mark Twain was the final of fifteen speakers, following a phalanx of generals and politicians, and several hours of speeches, music, food, cigars, and alcohol. His speech—"The Babies, As they Comfort us in Our Sorrows, Let Us Not Forget Them in Our Festivities"—compared the discipline of army life and the terror of battle to the discipline and terror of the baby, and found the baby to be the task that could best a general. Praising the future leaders of America, just then rocking in cribs all over the land, Mark Twain ended by imagining the future president of the United States. In a snippet of autobiography from 1885, he remembered the conclusion of the speech:

> "And now in his cradle somewhere under the flag is the future illustrious Commander-in-Chief of the American armies is so little burdened with his approaching grandeur and responsibilities as to be giving his whole strategic mind at this moment to trying to find out some way to get his big toe into his mouth—something, meaning no disrespect to the illustrious guest of this evening, which he turned his entire attention to some fifty-six years ago"—
>
> And here, as I had expected, the laughter ceased and a sort of shuddering silence took its place—for this was apparently carrying the matter too far.
>
> I waited a moment or two to let this silence sink well home.
>
> Then, turning toward the General I added:
>
> "And if the child is but the father of the man there are mighty few who will doubt that he succeeded."
>
> Which relieved the house: for when they saw the General break up in good-sized pieces they followed suit with great enthusiasm.[97]

His success with "The Babies" reflects back on the failure of the Whittier speech, each of which was given at banquets honoring American icons, replete with nationalistic and moralistic reverence, and each featuring a moment of awful silence in which Mark Twain's humor—perhaps going too far—required a release of tension for the speech to be a success.

Writing to Olivia at 5 A.M. following the speech, Clemens described the evening as a "great night, a memorable night, a marvelous night" and rapturously described the speeches that had preceded him: "Lord, what an organ is human speech when it is played by a master! All these speeches may look dull in print, but how the lightnings glared around them when they were uttered, & how the crowd roared in response!" Only the speech preceding his had fallen flat, ending in "funereal silence" that echoed what he remembered from his own speech for Whittier. Clemens told Livy how the taciturn and quiet audience (it was well after 2 A.M.) soon "burst forth like a hurricane & I saw that I *had* them! From that time on, I stopped at the end of each sentence, & let the tornado of applause & laughter sweep around me." The ultimate success of the speech, though, lay in Grant's reaction, which gave sanction for the audience to laugh: "And do you know, Gen. Grant sat through fourteen speeches like a graven image, but I fetched him! I broke him up, utterly! He told me he laughed till the tears came & every bone in his body ached. (And do you know, the biggest part of the success of the speech lay in the fact that the audience *saw* that for once in his life he had been knocked out of his iron serenity.)"[98]

Writing to Howells several days later, he still spoke of his success with rapture, framing his success in military terms:

> Grand times, my boy, grand times. Gen. Grant sat at the banquet like a statue of iron & listened without the faintest suggestion of emotion to fourteen speeches which tore other people all to shreds, but when I lit in with the fifteenth & last, his time was come! I shook him up like dynamite & he sat there fifteen minutes & laughed & cried like the mortalest of mortals. But bless you I had measured this unconquerable conqueror, & went at my work with the confidence of conviction, for I knew I could lick him.[99]

Mark Twain's success, then, came in making Grant mortal, by showing him human through his laughter. Celebrating the grand hero of the Republic, the banquet framed Grant as a symbol of military and national success, one who might as well have been a statue. Mark Twain succeeded in making him human through the laughter engendered by the universal experience of babyhood. Contrasted with the Whittier birthday speech, during which the targets of the speech (the "immortals": Emerson, Longfellow, and Holmes) listened without laughter, the Grant speech marks a counterexample in which an immortal symbol was shown human. The success of the speech shows that the humor of a banquet could, indeed, make the revered guest human, and without offense.

One scrap of ephemera from this period pictured Mark Twain as a baby, as part of a ten-card series of advertising cards of famous Americans pictured as different types of infants. Mark Twain was "funny baby," and General Grant was the "contented baby."

Mark Twain's next speech put him back in the company of the *Atlantic Monthly* greats. Howells wrote Clemens after his return in September asking if he had any "Atlanticable papers" to contribute. He replied that he had no manuscript for Howells at present due to his work on *A Tramp Abroad*, although he attempted to again entice Howells into a collaboration on a play featuring Orion Clemens or Captain Wakeman as the central character.[100] Shortly thereafter, he enclosed his profane sketch, "1601. Conversation, as It Was by the Social Fireside, in the Time of the Tudors," to Howells, claiming in jest that he was offering it to the *Atlantic* before he sent it to Beecher's *Christian Union*. In October, Clemens invited Howells to Chicago for the Grant banquet, and Howells invited Clemens to Boston for the Holmes Breakfast, a sequel to the Whittier Dinner in honor of the Autocrat's 70th birthday. He vacillated on the invitation, first replying "Will I come? O *hell*-yes!—as the energetic Arkansaw [*sic*] student said to Rev. Joe Twichell in the Black Forest when Joe asked him if he was homesick. O *hell*-yes!" Writing to Howells after the Grant banquet, Clemens claimed he was too busy with his book to attend the Holmes event, but Howells and Warner convinced him it was better to attend. Clemens agreed, writing to Howells: "If anybody talks, there, I shall claim the right to say a word myself, & be heard among the very *earliest*—else it would be confoundedly awkward for me—& for the rest, too."[101] Mark Twain's return to the social banquet of the *Atlantic Monthly* was fraught with tension and viewed by Clemens and Howells as an opportunity to make amends and restore whatever was damaged at the Whittier Dinner.

The Holmes Breakfast began at noon, with dinner at one, speeches at four, and the gathering breaking up around six. The New York *Times* focused on the lavish setting of the banquet, especially the elaborate flower arrangements and the framed pictures of Holmes, Longfellow, Whittier, and others. The report also noted the presence of the "lady contributors" to the magazine, who partook in both the social aspect and the formal speeches and poems. After the multicourse meal, the diners were called to celebrate, in the words of the *Atlantic*'s full report of the event, "one whose aim and achievement in literature, as recorded in The *Atlantic*, had been so high and so conspicuous."[102] H. O. Houghton, the magazine's publisher, spoke first, praising the assembled company and their contributions to American life. He claimed that it was always the intention to invite women to such dinners, but that publishers were "bashful," like suitors asking the hand of a young lady (there is no record if the women present laughed at this joke). Houghton praised Holmes at length:

> It is our thoughts which he speaks; it is our humor to which he gives expres-
> sion; it is the pictures of our own fancy that he clothes in words, and shows
> us what we ourselves thought, and only lacked the means of expressing. We
> never realized, until he taught us by his magic power over us, how much
> each of us had of genius, and invention, and expression. And it is especially
> fitting that we should honor, even in his own country, a prophet who has
> revealed to us what wonderful people we all are.[103]

Whether due to the presence of ladies, the absence of alcohol, or the more convivial and less imposing grandeur of the guest of honor, the Holmes Breakfast featured a lighter tone of oratory and a different sort of reverence—and none of the controversy.

The guest list was impressive—at least one hundred guests sat at six tables—with speeches or poems by Holmes (who read a poem and had a speech read for him), Whittier (read by James T. Fields), Howells, Julia Ward Howe, Charles Dudley Warner, Helen Hunt Jackson, President Eliot of Harvard (where Holmes lectured on anatomy four days per week), J. W. Harper (of Harper's publishing), E. C. Stedman, Thomas Bailey Aldrich, William Winter, J. T. Trowbridge, Col. T. W. Higginson, and Mark Twain. Of the *Atlantic* immortals, Emerson, Stowe, and Whittier were in attendance. Numerous others sent letters of regret and praise, including President Hayes, Josiah Holland, and Frederick Douglass, who praised Holmes as "one of the most brilliant American authors and scholars, a poet and philosopher; one whose genial wit has often brushed away clouds of care and sadness from the thoughtful brow of Boston, and mantled our land generally with smiles of joy and gladness." The surprise hit of the banquet, according to several newspaper reports, was Mary Sprague, whose novel *An Earnest Trifler* (published anonymously) was the sensation of the season in Boston.[104] The *Atlantic's* review, published in the most recent issue, had praised both the humor of the author and the reality of the characters, but nowhere does discussion of her work connect her humor with that of

Mark Twain or American Humor as a subject, although *Scribner's* compared her with Henry James.[105]

The peculiar nature of the banquet was delineated by the lengthy report in the Boston *Daily Advertiser* the following day. The report began by noting that such events often gain brief notice by the press but were then forgotten. But the guests at the Holmes banquet were undoubtedly aware of the historical significance, and each imagined the scene as "a real event in the literary history of our country" that symbolized the lasting praise of a prophet, poet, and wit—or so the reporter imagined. On the first hand, the event was framed as highly symbolic of "American Literature" and of the place of the Autocrat within a pantheon of immortal greats. But on the second, the paper noted that the assemblage of literary figures in one place had an opposite effect:

> *There was a wonderful clearing up of mysteries. Names that have been so long a household word that the reading public has almost ceased to remember that the men and women who bear them are a reality; names of later fame which carry with them no picture of a personality that agrees with the author; young names sounded just long enough to stir the curiosity—all these found their owners, or rather their owners found them at the tables in the dining-hall.*[106]

This passage shows the split between the author-in-person and the author-as-idea that the Whittier Speech had played with and to which its failures can be attributed. Such banquets made authors real to each other through dining, talk, and speeches, while the sentiments expressed functioned largely on the symbolic level of imagined communities of readers.

As with the Whittier Banquet, the Holmes Breakfast was dedicated to praising the guest of honor in tones of reverence, although humor was a constant presence in speech and song. Both Houghton's and Howells's speeches commented humorously on the relationships between publisher, editor, and contributors, with Houghton introducing Howells as the assistant editor, with the real editor—a gothic monster with cadaverous features and a sharp knife used to cut contributions to pieces—safely locked in his attic, from which he was seldom released.[107] By all accounts, the festivities and the oratory of the event were a grand success, unmarred by any controversy apart from the hurt feelings of those who wished to be invited but were not. Two newspapers, frequently critical of Mark Twain, commented on his improved behavior. The *Christian Union* noted that the speeches demonstrated "a greater evenness of sympathy and good feeling" than the Whittier Speech, having been "spared the rough buffoonery of Mark Twain (he made a very good and proper speech on this occasion)."[108] *The Literary World* echoed the evaluation, noting:

> *If none of the poetry or the speaking reached so high a pitch of excellence as at the Whittier dinner, there was a greater evenness of good quality, and there was no rude break of good taste such as marked the former occasion. Mark Twain's speech this time, indeed, was so far suitable and funny that we give it below, with Dr. Holmes's poem. These two performances, and Mr. Houghton's remarks, fairly divided the honors of the evening.*[109]

Clearly, the speech had redeemed Mark Twain in the eyes of the more reverent press, which had played a large role in castigating him following the Whittier dinner.

Before he rose to speak, Howells introduced him with the brief, but telling, remark: "We will now listen to a few words of truth and soberness from Mark Twain." In the *Atlantic* report of the evening, the description remarks that Mark Twain rose "diffidently" to deliver his speech, which began with a statement of praise for Holmes, framing his remarks as in line with the banquet's purpose.[110] He then told of how the first letter he received from a great man was from Holmes. Following the publication of *The Innocents Abroad*, a friend had pointed out that he had stolen the dedication to the book from one of Dr. Holmes's books. Mark Twain traced the "unconscious plagiarism" to having read the book numerous times while idle with illness in the Sandwich Islands. Having written the Autocrat to apologize, Mark Twain told of receiving a letter back exculpating him for the offense and noting that all writers occasionally thought an idea original that they had read or heard. At several points, Mark Twain infused his remarks with humor, but humor clearly aimed at himself. He noted that he offered Holmes the use of any ideas the Autocrat might find "good protoplasm for poetry." He argued that any man with a teaspoon full of brains had too much pride to steal another man's words, and that "admirers had often told me I had nearly a basketful, though they were rather reserved as to the size of the basket."

Mark Twain ended with a slight feint toward his tendency toward digression, which had been the whole basis for his Whittier Speech. He stated: "I have met Dr. Holmes many times since; and lately he said—However, I am wandering wildly away from the one thing which I got on my feet to do, that is, to make my compliments to you, my fellow teachers of the great public, and likewise to say I am right glad to see that Dr. Holmes is still in his prime and full of generous life. . . ." That one moment of threatened digression may have been calculated to alarm Howells, or to worry the assembled company about the direction the humorist was taking, but the ending returns to the keynote of the evening, showing that Mark Twain had learned from the failure of the Whittier speech and the success of the Babies. Symbolically, Mark Twain had kept his speech well within the bounds of propriety, while still managing to humanize Holmes, without mocking him, by portraying his personal response to Mark Twain in a manner in keeping with the public image of the man.

Mark Twain's speech was well received, by all accounts, with the New York *Tribune* noting that Mark Twain's "witty remarks were frequently checked by ebullitions of mirth."[111] This laughter symbolized the return of the jester into the good graces of the literary public, as represented by both the assembled company and the public who read about the historic gathering. Mark Twain's first biographer argues that the Holmes speech repaired whatever damage Twain had done with the Whittier speech. Interestingly, Mark Twain's return to literary respectability, in this one symbolic space, has been much less examined by literary scholars who focus heavily on the Whittier incident. Henry Nash Smith, who set the groundwork for later scholarship, does not mention the Holmes speech in his article on the Whittier Dinner, possibly because it challenges his thesis that the Whittier speech showed "unconscious antagonism" toward the Boston elites and that his humor, despite Howells's assertions, was "basically irreverent." While scholars have read Mark Twain's Whittier speech in relation to other speeches or works that border on irreverent, few have directly compared two occasions linked by location, guest, patron, and symbolic connection.[112] If the Whittier birthday speech marks a "primal scene" of Mark Twain's disjuncture from New England literary culture, then the Holmes Breakfast must mark a détente with that culture. For, on its surface, the breakfast speech contains as much reverence for that culture as the Whittier dinner speech contained of irreverence, whether unconscious or not.

It is unclear whether this reverence was for the personal friendships with Howells and Holmes, along with the others assembled, or for the abstract idea of respectable American letters. Or both. Mark Twain's move into the culture of letters of the *Atlantic Monthly* demonstrates a clear desire to join the ranks of quality literary humorists, as well as outbreaks of anxiety about his place in that culture. Samuel Clemens's attempt to cast off the stripes of the popular humorist for his persona signifies a crucial transition toward literary respectability, although it was a transition that continued to face opposition from certain quarters. After the Holmes breakfast, few incidents of cultural approbation are to be found, although Josiah Holland continued his editorial crusade against debased literary culture. For his part, Samuel Clemens took up a prominent role in another literary question—copyright. Canadian piracy of his books was incentive for Mark Twain to support international copyright protection, a cause in which he proposed to circulate a petition first signed by Longfellow and Lowell, and then Howells, Whittier, and Holmes—"men whom the country cannot venture to laugh at."[113]

CONCLUSION

"The Most Popular Humorist Who Ever Lived"

The Transformations of Mark Twain

Dear David:

The only notices of the Tramp which I have seen are yours & How-ells's—the deep & pleasurable surprise which these have given me, is a thing which cannot be expressed in words. You will remember, maybe, how I felt about "Roughing It"—that it would be considered pretty poor stuff, & that therefore I had better not let the press get a chance at it; well, I felt the same way about this one; so I sent copies to only you & Howells, & to no other journalists, knowing I could depend upon you both for what I fully expected of you, viz., the most profound & generous **silence** *regarding the work. When Howells came out with two pages of* **compliment,** *the surprise of it took my breath away—& now you have surprised me, too, & in the same delightful way. Bless me, what an effect other people's opinions do have upon us!*

—LETTER TO DAVID GRAY, JUNE 10, 1880[1]

ABROAD AGAIN: MARK TWAIN'S SHIFTING REPUTATION

In the aftermath of the Whittier birthday speech, Clemens's time in Europe, and his repatriation into the culture of respectable letters, the literary reputation of Mark Twain as an author and cultural figure was still a contested matter, nor was Samuel Clemens ever able to escape the tensions that had helped to shape Mark Twain's early reputation—between literary respectability and mass success, between humorous anarchy and deeper seriousness, between the popularity of the mere buffoon and the role of respectable man of letters. Mark Twain's cultural position was never settled, and his meanings remained slippery as he set about finishing his book of travel in late 1879, a decade after the publication of his first travel

355

book had catapulted him to fame and raised the question of his place in American letters. Almost ten years exactly after their first meeting in Boston, Clemens began sending William Dean Howells advanced chapter proofs of *A Tramp Abroad* to allow Howells time to prepare a review for the *Atlantic* and set the tone for the critical reception of the latest subscription book from the American humorist.

A Tramp Abroad can be taken as a symbolic transition point to a fourth stage of Mark Twain's reputation. The first stage had been characterized by his appearance as a newspaper reporter, magazinist, and lecturer in California—"the Wild Humorist of the Pacific Slope," which culminated in the success of his jumping frog. The second was marked by his ascension to national and international fame as an "American Humorist" and his transition from peripheral figure to central exponent of the unique and peculiar school of a distinctly national humor—"the best of our second-rate humorists." The third stage focused on the tension between mass success and literary respectability as Mark Twain moved into new venues in which he might be considered, in the words of his most important promoter—"quite worthy of the company of the best." The critical reactions to Mark Twain's next two works—*A Tramp Abroad* and *The Prince and the Pauper*—indicated a shift to a new stage in which Mark Twain's work was discussed largely in relation to his earlier work, rather than in relation to other humorists. Mark Twain's central role as an American humorist—whom Howells called, in 1882, "the most popular humorist who ever lived"—placed him at the center of the debate over the value and role of humor in American culture. In these new contexts, critics framed the question of Mark Twain's literary reputation in novel ways, recasting previous debates and language to suit new questions and new works.

For Clemens, *A Tramp Abroad* marked a return to travel writing and financial success. Mark Twain's reputation had transformed in the decade since *The Innocents Abroad* had made him "the best of our second-rate humorists." In reviewing the book, critics pointed out few connections between Mark Twain and other American humorists, especially those of the so-called school of "American humor," with whom he had been characterized since the release of his first book. The *Spectator* of London noted that the book contained "those quaint, happy drolleries of expression which are characteristic of American humour." However, the Chicago *Tribune* argued that the book contained only two or three instances "of that genuine American humor of which Mr. Clemens has been so conspicuous a producer."[2] Apart from these two references, and the arguments of William Dean Howells, which will be examined separately below, there is no mention of other popular humorists, of Bret Harte, or of the subject of the peculiar American humor through which critics had classified Mark Twain. Instead, Mark Twain was compared with Mark Twain—and found wanting.

Critically, the book was not widely reviewed. Louis Budd lists thirteen American reviews, nine British, and three from continental Europe. Reviews put forward familiar critical tropes, eliminate others, and raise new ways of contextualizing Mark Twain as a subject of literary and critical consideration. Many of the reviews compare the book to *The Innocents Abroad* and *Roughing It*. The *Graphic* found it "a worthy sequel," while the *Spectator* found it "in nearly every respect inferior." The Utica *Herald* held *The Innocents Abroad* in relation to *A Tramp Abroad* as the "sparkling, iridescent champagne" that a host serves his friends was to the "flat, sour stuff" the servant pours out the next day.[3] Still, the sparkling products to which Mark Twain is being compared are his own writings. Much of the book's failure was attributed to his tendency to attempt to be funny at all times, even when he was trying to be serious. Such criticisms extended the critical trope that Mark Twain's humor either hid or undercut his ability to produce beautiful or artistic writing—the so-called "penalty of humor." The Chicago *Tribune* wrote that: "The author is unfortunate in one respect. Every time he opens his mouth or puts his pen to paper he is credited with the intention of making you laugh. That is his avowed object in life. For that he exists. That is his profession. When he fails to make laughter—no matter how much useful information he may convey or whatever else he may accomplish—his work is apt to be regarded as a failure." A notice in the *British Quarterly Review* praised Mark Twain for being pleasing to "the cultured and uncultured alike" but criticized his tendency "to practice his trick too often." He was contrasted with the German author Heinrich Heine, who best balanced "the grave and the gay," a trope used to distinguish quality humor from the merely entertaining. Still, the review concluded that Mark Twain's book was "delightful."[4]

A Tramp Abroad was reviewed almost as extensively in England as it was in America, and the reviews taken as a whole were more positive. British critics certainly found fault, but most deemed it a success as long as one did not try to read too much of the book at once. The *Literary World* found the book "eminently racy" and said many readers would find value in it, even if the humor was overdone at many points. The *Observer* praised the book, in small doses, noting that American humor reflected the general American view that there was "nothing sacred or worthy of reverence."[5] Whereas earlier critics, especially Gerald Massey and Leslie Stephen, had criticized the tendency toward irreverence, for this critic, it was this incongruity between the profane and sacred that is the basis of Mark Twain's entertaining humor, which the reviewer repeatedly noted is "fun" in moderation, even if it might prove too "ephemeral." Whether Mark Twain's humor was merely temporary fun or of lasting quality was a major critical theme in the 1870s and would continue to be through the remainder of his life, and beyond. A review in the *Athenaeum* argued for Mark Twain's quality as a literary artist whose works would last as literature—a distinct change in tone from earlier reviews. The reviewer joined Mark Twain with Walt Whitman as "the most strictly American writer of what is called American literature." Unlike American writers who relied on English models, Mark Twain was "as distinctly national as the fourth of July itself." The "peculiarity" of his work—that of a professional humorist who somehow intoxicated his readers and his reviewers—meant that British critics continued to pay attention to him even when other humorists, such as Josh Billings and Petroleum Nasby, had faded from critical consciousness.[6]

While the book was widely excerpted, American critics reviewed the book much less extensively than previous or subsequent books by Mark Twain. The *Atlantic*'s review was alone among magazines. The two most negative reviews, both from papers in San Francisco, framed the book as a critical failure. The *Evening Bulletin*, which had commented on the financial meanings of both *The Gilded Age* and *Sketches*—began its review with a statement that set up a critical paradox: "Mark Twain has obtained—and justly—that measure of literary renown which will insure a host of eager readers for whatever he writes, whether it be good, bad, or indifferent. It matters little, therefore, what the critics say about his last book . . . so far as concerns its success as a commercial venture. Everybody will read it, everybody will talk about it, and the great majority will take the flattering unction to their souls that they have got their money's worth." Despite this review's conceit that criticism would have no effect, the critic ranked the book "immeasurably behind *The Innocents Abroad*." Despite it being readable and "in parts exceedingly amusing," the book "lacks the freedom and lawless abandon, the sublime audacity, the unctuous and spontaneous humor, the irresistible drollery" of Mark Twain's first European travel book. According to the San Francisco *Chronicle*, the book was largely filled with "absolutely dull and stupid" passages, despite the occasional quality chapter. Ironically, the review faults Mark Twain for relying on other guidebooks (even though he provides attribution) and then plagiarizes from the *Evening Bulletin*'s review, with important differences, by concluding "It does not matter much, however, so far as the sale of the book is concerned, whether it is good, bad or indifferent. Mark Twain's established reputation will cause it to sell, and people will read it and be disappointed."[7]

These reviewers may have had a point. *A Tramp Abroad* helped rees-tablish Mark Twain's financial standing as a subscription author after the relatively poor sales of *Sketches, New and Old* and the *Adventures of Tom Sawyer*. The book was made available for sale by the American Publishing Company in March 1880, after a delay of several months as Clemens fin-ished portions of the manuscript. The book was issued as "a companion volume to Innocents Abroad," just as *Roughing It* had been billed. The book contained, for the first time for Mark Twain's books, an engraving of the author and featured numerous illustrations of the author.[8]

While the text contains some quality humorous sketches and fine passages of description, Mark Twain's third book of travel writing is the least examined out of his five books of travel—to be followed later by *Life on the Mississippi* (1883) and *Following the Equator* (1897). Financially, the book marked a return to previous sales, with 47,563 copies sold in the first three months and approximately 62,000 copies sold during its first year.[9] While not quite to the standards of his other travel books, these sales outperformed his previous book of sketches and two novels considerably.

Learning lessons (right or wrong) from his previous publishing expe-rience, Clemens attempted to limit the amount of reviews of the book, instead relying on excerpts and a few well-placed reviews. As Hamlin Hill notes, selections from the book were printed widely in newspapers, pre-sumably circulated by the publishers after a first prospectus was issued in November 1879.[10] For his part, Clemens discouraged Frank Bliss from courting newspaper attention, writing shortly after the book's release in March that he liked the book "exceedingly well" but that he was concerned with Canadian pirates and newspapers. He wrote:

> I am ~~relieved~~ glad no big newspaper has had a chance to give it a black eye with a left-handed notice—for in your accompanying statement I see distinct evidence that if the Gilded Age *had been kept away from the newspapers, it would have given excellent satisfaction & its early sale would not have been "knocked." It now sells nearly up to Roughing It—& there never was*

FIGURE 8.1: Frontispiece of *A Tramp Abroad*.
Courtesy of Kevin Mac Donnell, Austin, Texas

THE AUTHOR'S MEMORIES.

FIGURE 8.2: "The Author's Memories" from *A Tramp Abroad*.
Courtesy of Kevin Mac Donnell, Austin, Texas

any reason why it shouldn't—except the newspapers. You keep my books strictly out *of the newspapers & we'll find our profit in it.* ~~I never want a book mentioned in anything but the Atlantic.~~[11]

Though Clemens crossed out the line about his desire to have the *Atlantic* be the only review, to Howells he wrote that he had forbidden press copies being sent to anyone but him, David Gray, and Charles Dudley Warner:

You were the three men whom I could trust to say the good thing if it could be honestly said; or be & remain charitably silent. I am justified in being afraid of the general press, because it killed the "Gilded Age" before you had a chance to point out that there were merits in that book. The sale ceased almost utterly *until the adverse criticisms were forgotten—then began again, & has kept smoothly on. During the past 12 months (to Jan. 1) it has sold a trifle over 1500 copies—not greatly behind Innocents & Tom Sawyer, each of which sold a fraction . . . under 2200 copies—& hardly* any *behind Roughing It, which sold 1800.*[12]

Fearing the effects of other reviews on the financial and critical prospects of his work, Clemens had come to rely on Howells's literary opinion in the years since he had visited the offices of the *Atlantic Monthly* to thank the editors for their kind review of *The Innocents Abroad*. To Joseph Twichell, he wrote, quoting Howells:

Howells replied that he was composing the Atlantic *review praising the book:*
    I have been feebly trying to give the Atlantic readers some notion of the charm and the solid delightfulness of your book; and now I must tell you privately what a joy it has been to Mrs. Howells *and me. . . . Mrs. Howells declares it the wittiest book she ever read, and I say there is* sense *enough in it for ten books. That is the idea which my review will try to fracture the average numbscull* [sic] *with.—Well, you are a blessing. You ought to believe in God's goodness, since he has bestowed upon the world such a delightful genius as yours to lighten its troubles.*[13]

For his part, Clemens responded that the letter had brightened his and Mrs. Clemens's view of the book, and that "[a] check for untold cash could not have made our hearts sing as your letter has done." At this time, Clemens was closely watching the returns on his book, fretting about Canadian pirates, and angered at the failure of his English publisher to secure timely copyright. To Moncure Conway, acting as his British agent, he wrote an angry letter about this failure but also noting the success of the book in America, writing "No book of mine has made so much talk here, since Innocents Abroad—and to my infinite surprise and delight, it is strongly *complimentary* talk. Howells's "Atlantic" notice has just arrived and pleases me exceedingly. I enclose it."[14]

Howells's review from May 1880 is framed as a response to "serious-minded people" who worry that America was "in danger of degenerating into a nation of wits." This is due, he argued, to "copyists" who seem to have cheapened the original humor of Mark Twain, which was "racy of the original soil." In his defense, Howells described a serious undercurrent of Mark Twain's humor as springing from "a certain intensity of common sense, a passionate love of justice, and a generous scorn of what is petty and mean." Howells noted that other humorists of Mark Twain's "school" lacked these "earnest" qualities. As a means to repair Mark Twain's relationship to quality humor, Howells argued that his humor sprang from a deeper purpose: "Its wildest extravagance is the break and fling from a deep feeling, a wrath with some folly which disquiets him worse than other men, a personal hatred for some humbug or pretension that embitters him beyond anything but laughter."[15]

Unlike his earlier reviews of Mark Twain's travel books, which focused on the entertainment stemming from their "realistic" humor, Howells here makes his most strenuous argument for the moral quality of Mark Twain's humor, in which laughter is a weapon against humbug and folly. He writes: "At the bottom of his heart he has often the grimness of a reformer: his wit is turned by preference not upon human nature, not upon droll situations and things abstractly ludicrous, but upon matters that are out of joint, that are unfair or unnecessarily ignoble, and cry out to his love of justice for discipline." Increasingly, Howells focused on the ethical aspects of Mark Twain's humor, implying that humor was the outer ornament of the serious, artistic value of the work and framing him as the heir to James Russell Lowell's morally serious humor. For Howells, the serious value in *A Tramp Abroad* was not only in its laughter at sham but in its particular representation of the impressions of the "Western American" encountering Europe for a second time, after having reflected on the meaning of the contact of Americans with Europe. Howells argued that the danger was not that the reader would not laugh enough over the book, but that "there is a possibility that they may not think enough over it." And what the "average American" should experience is "much to comfort and stay him in such

Americanism as is worth having, and nothing to flatter him in a mistaken national vanity or a stupid national prejudice." Unlike many of Howells's reviews of Mark Twain and others while he was editing the *Atlantic*, this review focused less on ideas of "realistic" literature than on the relation of literature to the nation. In the late 1870s, and into the1880s, the quality American humorist for William Dean Howells was increasingly embodied by one figure—"Mark Twain."

"TO MAKE HUMOR ALL HUMOROUS"
MARK TWAIN'S NEW DEPARTURES

The year 1881 saw a number of changes for both Clemens/Mark Twain and Howells. Howells departed from the *Atlantic* on March 1, subsequently publishing his novel *A Modern Instance* in the *Century* in 1882. Mark Twain published *The Prince and the Pauper* in December 1881. He had been working on this book since 1876 but finished it after writing *A Tramp Abroad*. Clemens left the American Publishing Company and issued the book, by subscription, with James R. Osgood, the one-time owner of the *Atlantic Monthly,* who also published Howells's novel as a trade publication. Mark Twain would also issue *Life on the Mississippi* (1883) with James R. Osgood & Co. before setting up his own subscription firm, Charles L. Webster and Company, an investment that would follow the boom-and-bust cycle he had both experienced and satirized.[16]

The review of Mark Twain's new novel in the *Atlantic Monthly*, written by Hjalamar Hjorth Boyesen under the title "Mark Twain's New Departure," praised him for writing a book that no critic would ascribe to him without knowing it was his—one that seems to be "by Clemens; it does not seem to be by Twain."[17] Rather than "the most heterogeneous accumulations of ill-assorted material that ever defied the laws of literature," Boyesen held that critics and the reading public would welcome Mark Twain's new guise as "the author of a tale ingenious in conception, pure and humane in purpose, artistic in method, and, with barely a flaw, refined in execution."

Howells reviewed the book anonymously in the New York *Tribune*, the influential newspaper Clemens had earlier cut off from reviews. He praised the book more highly than he had Mark Twain's previous works, seeing "an interesting evidence of growth in a man who ought still to have his best work before him." In two separate places in the review, Howells makes the case for both Mark Twain's artistic and moral quality to a degree that would "surprise those who have found nothing but drollery in Mark

Twain's book, and have not perceived the artistic sense and the strain of deep earnestness underlying his humor." After having discussed the work in some detail, Howells again made his case:

> . . . [W]e have indicated its power in this direction rather than in its humorous side, because this has struck us as peculiarly interesting in the work of a man who has hitherto been known only as a humorist—a mere <u>farceur</u>—to most people. The romance is imagined with poetic delicacy; it has scenes and episodes touched with the tenderest, sweetest feeling. It is full of action, and the interest holds to the end; and on its artistic side nothing is more remarkable than the conscientious realism of its treatment.[18]

Not only did Howells raise Mark Twain's work above the merely humorous by finding poetical, artistic, and ethical aspects to praise apart from the humor, he also made a new and unique argument in finding the humor of the book "Cervantean"—but with a modern "pitying tenderness" Cervantes could not have known but that was "oftener characteristic of our chief humorist's fun than has been generally recognized." Mark Twain's new departure had gained both the seal of the *Atlantic* and of Howells separately.

As with *Tom Sawyer*, Howells was both editing page proofs of the novel and reviewing it at the same time. Responding to the review, Clemens wrote that he and Livy were delighted: "What you have said, there, will convince anybody that reads it; a body cannot help it. That is the kind of a review to have; a doubtful man, even the prejudiced man, is persuaded, & succumbs."[19] He then tells of meeting a friend on the street who raved about the review and notes that it should take "care of the opinions of the general press pretty effectually," which was his main concern. And while the press continued to be divided about Mark Twain's general value, and the specific value of each book that came out, Howells's efforts to elevate Mark Twain are more and more in evidence in reviews.

As both Clemens and Howells had each been concerned with what Boston thought of Mark Twain, the change in tone of the reviews from that city's papers is worth noting. The *Herald* review began with a long discussion of the shifting reputation of Mark Twain from one who made "the world merry with sketches" to "a true artist." While his early work had shown skill and caused many to simply, the paper held that some readers "who perceived that their sympathies were touched as well as their laugh muscles." And while Mark Twain's humor inspired others to enter his field—and readers to grow "weary of laughing . . . and sated with 'humor'"—Mark Twain's work remained above theirs in artistry: "He was more than a caricaturist or humorist draughtsman, and so he took his sunny gifts to a congenial field and a true artist was ripened therefrom." The *Transcript* held Mark Twain's "new departure" in high esteem, above the after-dinner speeches and travel books, and free from "farce or mockery." Finally, the *Evening Transcript* held that the key element of the book was humor, but not the "broad exaggerated, newspaper humor, with which the name of the author has become so strongly associated, but of a quality so refined and yet so searching as to excite wonder that it should flow from the same pen as that which wrote *The Innocents Abroad* and 'The Jumping Frog of Calaveras.'"[20] Clearly, Mark Twain's reputation was shifting, and many newspapers borrowed Boyeson's phrasing of the book being "a new departure."

While Mark Twain's new path would seem to have placed him squarely within the tradition of quality humor that the *Atlantic* had long promoted, and continued to promote under the editorship of Clemens's friend Thomas Bailey Aldrich, the magazine did not publish Mark Twain's works again and barely commented on him or his books until the 1890s. Only *Life on the Mississippi* (1883) was reviewed, and a only brief mention was made of *Adventures of Huckleberry Finn* (1885).[21] The magazine made no mention of *A Connecticut Yankee in King Arthur's Court* (1889) or of *Mark Twain's Library of Humor* (1888), a collection he edited with Howells. For his part, Mark Twain followed Howells to the *Century* to publish portions of *Adventures of Huckleberry Finn*, after which he would only publish sporadically in a variety of magazines.

Each of these books, as well as his "Twins of Genius" reading tour with George Washington Cable in 1884–1885, would require an in-depth reading in order to understand the ways in which Mark Twain's reputation was discussed and transformed in the 1880s. This reading is out of the purview of this book, but the critical debates about Mark Twain's roles as a humorist on the American and European stages during his ascension to fame in the 1860s and 1870s set many of the terms of discussion for his reception in the 1880s and beyond. The shift in Mark Twain's reputation might be best seen as more a matter of focus and tone rather than the shift to new debates altogether. The meanings of the humorist in American culture, the tension between popular success (along with the money attached to it) and literary respectability, and the meaning of "American" culture reflected by these debates continued to frame Mark

Twain's reputation and the meaning of American humor—subjects that were now inextricably intertwined.

One critical evaluation from the early 1880s will serve as a capstone of this book's history of Mark Twain's cultural reputation. Whereas William Dean Howells had discussed authors and literature in the pages of the *Atlantic*, he had written only one extended critical evaluation in that magazine, of Thomas Bailey Aldrich, in the November 1880 issue. In the fall of 1882, Howells published extended critical evaluations of two American authors—Mark Twain and Henry James. In the September issue of the *Century*, Howells wrote a profile entitled "Mark Twain," which marked a key moment in the transformation of Mark Twain's critical reputation to "the most popular humorist who ever lived."[22] The article extended the arguments that Howells had made in his earlier reviews and highlighted three of the main tropes that were central to discussions of Mark Twain's work: the distinction between cruel and humane humor, the American nature of his humor, and the moral and artistic quality of his writing, which should ultimately be viewed as serious literature. The issue contained a frontispiece of Mark Twain.

The piece begins with a biography of Clemens's early life and literary career. Howells claims that his Southern upbringing did not cripple his moral sense: "If the boy's sense of justice suffered anything of that perversion which so curiously and pitiably maimed the reason of the whole South, it does not appear in his books, where there is not an ungenerous line, but always, on the contrary, a burning resentment of all manner of cruelty and wrong."[23] Getting to the matter of Mark Twain's humor, Howells began with his tendency to be autobiographical, which distinguished him, in Howells's mind, from the disguises used by other humor writers such as Artemus Ward, Petroleum Vesuvius Nasby, and Josh Billings. For Howells, Mark Twain's success was attributable to the "humane spirit" that had begun to characterize American humor, replacing "the stupid and monkeyish cruelty of motive and intention" that had previously characterized the nation's humor. Howells writes that Mark Twain was the first American humorist to be true and moral: "Except the political humorists, like Mr. Lowell . . . the American humorists formerly chose the wrong in public matters; they were on the side of slavery, of drunkenness, and of irreligion; the friends of civilization were their prey; their spirit was thoroughly vulgar and base." Mark Twain, on the other hand, did not offend Howells's vision of "self-respect" in a humorist:

FIGURE 8.3: Mark Twain. Frontispiece to the *Century* 24, no. 5
(September 1882). **Collection of the Author**

I cannot remember that in Mr. Clemens's books I have ever been asked to join him in laughing at any good or really fine thing. But I do not mean to leave him with this negative praise; I mean to say of him that as Shakespeare, according to Mr. Lowell's saying, was the first to make poetry all poetical, Mark Twain was the first to make humor all humorous. He has not only added more in bulk to the style of harmless pleasures than any other humorist; but more in that spirit that is easily and wholly enjoyable.[24]

This distinction delineates between cruelty and humanity, which placed Mark Twain as a humorous writer who reflected Howells's views of American character and American literature.

For Howells, Mark Twain's humor was great not only because it was humane—which is a keyword in his early form of realistic writing—but because it was "purely and wholly American." America was a homogenous nation, according to Howells, and Mark Twain's humor appealed to the whole of the American people. Howells writes:

In another generation or two, perhaps, it will be wholly different; but as yet the average American is the man who has risen; he has known poverty, and privation, and low conditions; he has very often known squalor; and now, in his prosperity, he regards the past with a sort of large, pitying amusement; he is not the least ashamed of it; he does not feel that it characterizes him any more than the future does. Our humor springs from this multiform experience of life, and securely addresses itself . . . to the intelligence bred of like experience. It is not of a class for a class; . . . its conventions, if it has any, are all new, and of American make.[25]

This vision of humor as uniquely American rests on a dream of a classless society in which the American people, or American men more exactly, enjoy a degree of self-sufficiency that allowed them to deny the class, race, ethnicity, and gender inequalities that threatened a vision of "America" embodied in certain American characters. Howells's vision of humor was based on an ideal view of American character founded on the exclusion of problematic Americans—in a sense, laughter eased the tensions of the Gilded Age, at least for Howells.

But Howells could not just accept the view of Mark Twain being merely a humorous writer, even if he "transcends all other American humorists in the universal qualities." The final move that Howells made was to transform Mark Twain into a serious writer—a reclassification that Howells tried in several different ways. First, he attempted to redefine the importance of humor in Mark Twain's work. "Elsewhere, I have tried to persuade the reader that his humor is at best the foamy break of a strong tide of earnestness in him," Howells writes. But he argued that defining him as a humorist was limiting, although Mark Twain had hurt his case as a moralist by making people laugh too much. "This" he concluded "is the penalty . . . of making one's first success as a humorist." The possibility that Mark Twain's humor was not his main importance, but the outward manifestation or ornament of some deeper power, allowed Howells to redefine Mark Twain's moral and artistic worth. The second tack Howells took in his reclassification was to define his writing as moral. He writes: "I shall not insist here upon Mark Twain as a moralist; though I warn the reader that if he leaves out of the account an indignant sense of right and wrong, a scorn of all affectation and pretense, an ardent hate of meanness and injustice, he will come indefinitely short of knowing Mark Twain." This moral sense in Mark Twain's work, Howells writes, is often obscured by his humor, as his readers do "not believe him serious; they think some joke is always intended."

Howells thus sets up a dichotomy between the humorous and the serious that operated in both moral and artistic terms. Howells found Mark Twain's works to be artistically serious, a fact that he casts as the foundation of his worth as a writer. Howells writes that he would "prefer to speak of Mr. Clemens's artistic qualities because it is to these that his humor will owe its perpetuity. All fashions change, and nothing more wholly and quickly than the fashion of fun." He continued:

> . . . and Mark Twain would pass with the conditions that have made him intelligible, if he were not an artist of uncommon power as well as a humorist. He portrays and interprets real types, not only with exquisite appreciation and sympathy, but with a force and truth of drawing that makes them permanent. . . . There is no drawing from casts; in his work evidently the life has everywhere been studied: and it is his apparent unconsciousness of any other way of saying a thing except the natural way that makes his books so restful and refreshing.[26]

The drafting of Mark Twain into the realist camp is accomplished by making his humor representative of American life (however ideally imagined) and by valuing his writing as true to life. For Howells, the question of Mark Twain's humor should be separate from the question of his value as a literary writer, and the devaluation of his humor is a necessary step that allows for his ascension to literary worth. This article created the model for a critical stance that values Mark Twain's writing as uniquely American in order to devalue the humor as a shell of the serious writer beneath—a model that allows for Mark Twain to be elevated out of the discourse of humor without the necessity of examining his cultural role as a humorist (always remembering that the term "humorist" has no inherent meanings but multiple meanings that must be sussed out in historical contexts). Howells cemented the devaluation of humor at the close of his article by saying that while the reader may expect an analysis of Mark Twain's humor, he "prefers" not to because "analyses of humor are apt to leave one rather serious, and to result in an entire volatilization of humor."[27]

Over the next decade, other critics followed Howells's lead in defining Mark Twain as a serious literary artist, while certain critics questioned the place of a buffoon in the quality literature of the nation. Most prominently, the English critic Matthew Arnold attacked Mark Twain's humor as representative of a vulgar and primitive literature typical of American character in an essay from May 1882, "A Word About America."[28] When Arnold visited America the next year, he called on Howells, only to learn he was in Hartford visiting Mark Twain. Arnold replied, according to Howells's *My Mark Twain*, "Oh, but he doesn't like *that* sort of thing, does he?" To which, Mrs. Howells replied, "He likes Mr. Clemens very much . . . and he thinks him one of the greatest men he ever knew." Later, at a reception in Hartford, Arnold and Clemens met at a reception. Howells's description is telling:

> While his hand laxly held mine in greeting, I saw his eyes fixed intensely on the other side of the room. "Who—who in the world is that?" I looked and said, "Oh, that is Mark Twain." I do not remember just how their instant encounter was contrived by Arnold's wish, but I have the impression that they were not parted for long during the evening, and the next night Arnold, as if still under the glamour of that potent presence, was at Clemens's house. I cannot say how they got on, or what they made of each other; if Clemens ever spoke of Arnold, I do not recall what he said, but Arnold had shown a sense of him from which the incredulous sniff of the polite world, now so universally exploded, had already perished.[29]

At that time, the polite world had not yet perished, and the feud between Mark Twain and Arnold was yet to come. Unfortunately, this fascinating meeting seems to have left little impression on the historical record. Only one anecdote of the dinner has been preserved. The Reverend Edwin Parker, who joined the dinner, left with Arnold after a night in which Mark Twain had kept his guests in a gale of laughter. Arnold repeated some of the lines, then asked Parker, "And is he never serious?" to which the minister replied, "Mr. Arnold, he is the most serious man in the world."[30]

Increasingly, the Arnoldian view of "Culture" based on "the power . . . of intellect and knowledge, the power of beauty, the power of social life and manners" was used to dismiss Mark Twain, and humor in general, from a sacralized version of the high culture in America.[31] At the same time, the Howellsian view of Mark Twain as more than a humorist attempted to rescue his works from the critical oblivion commonly predicted of humorous works that fade along with their historical context. While these two views might be dominant in Twain scholarship, a third option persisted from earlier evaluations of Mark Twain and humor—that humor might have its own unique values separate from the critical stringency of quality that so often hinged on the idea of the serious. As one reviewer in the *Saturday Evening Review* had held of *The Innocents Abroad*, there was value in a work that was "good for the blues, lively for dyspepsia, a damper on melancholy, a solace for many woes, an enlivener for anybody who has been lately dabbling in gold stocks."[32] Humor—in all of its humorousness—continued to hold value in the works of Mark Twain and in American humor more generally.

Mark Twain, the American humorist, contained all of these potential meanings, and the critical attempts to pin him down in his time and ours have only led to further volatilization of the meanings of his humor. One thing is clear: when critics discussed the role of humor in American life and letters in the Gilded Age, it was most often the figure of Mark Twain who was the example of the nation's humor—not Artemus Ward, not Bret Harte, not James Russell Lowell. As the criticism of *A Tramp Abroad* had intimated, Mark Twain was no longer one of the more prominent of a school of American humor. He had become the icon of American Humor. And while the particular manifestations of these arguments varied according to the circumstance and author, Mark Twain—American humorist—now loomed as the central figure of what American humor had been and what it might become.

Notes

Introduction

1. Mark Twain, "Letter from Carson City," Virginia City *Territorial Enterprise*, February 3, 1863. Quoted in *The Works of Mark Twain: Early Tales & Sketches,* vol. 1, *1851–1864* (University of California Press, 1979), 194–98. James Cox, *Mark Twain: The Fate of Humor* (Princeton: Princeton University Press, 1966), 19.

2. Lawrence Levine, *Highbrow/Lowbrow: The Emergence of Cultural Hierarchy in America* (Berkeley: University of California Press. 1989).

3. John Bird is especially insightful on the rich meanings of "Mark Twain" as a pseudonym that was both a metonym for Clemens and as a rich site of metaphor (of both "Mark" and "Twain"). See Bird, *Mark Twain and Metaphor* (Columbia: University of Missouri Press, 2007), 33–40. See also Leland Krauth, *Proper Mark Twain* (Athens: University of Georgia Press, 1999), 7–9, and James Caron, *Mark Twain: Unsanctified Newspaper Reporter* (Columbia: University of Missouri Press, 2008), 2–3. For the different origins of the name, see Paul Fatout, "Mark Twain's Nom de Plume," *American Literature* 34, no. 1 (March 1962): 1–7. For a discussion of usage, see Guy Cardwell, "Samuel Clemens' Magical Pseudonym," *The New England Quarterly*, 48, no. 2 (January 1875): 175–93. See also Louis J. Budd, *Our Mark Twain: The Making of His Public Personality* (Philadelphia: University of Pennsylvania Press, 1983), 20. For a text-based theory on the pseudonym, see Kevin MacDonnell, "How Samuel Clemens Found 'Mark Twain' in Carson City, Nevada," *Mark Twain Journal* 50, nos. 1 & 2 (Spring/Fall 2012): 9–47.

4. This book does not go into individual reader responses, which tend to be idiosyncratic, beyond the judgment of professional critics. Mark Twain received much fan mail in his career, but less in the years under consideration than later. See Kent Rasmussen, ed., *Dear Mark Twain: Letters from His Readers* (Berkeley: University of California Press, 2013).

5. Nancy Glazener, *Reading for Realism: The History of a U.S. Literary Institution, 1850–1910* (Durham: Duke University Press, 1997), 5, 6.

6. Frank Luther Mott, *American Journalism: A History of Newspapers in the United States through 260 years: 1690 to 1950*, rev. ed. (New York: The MacMillan Company, 1950). Mott notes that the number of newspapers almost doubled in the 1870s, to roughly seven thousand, including an increasing number that were independent of political party influence (411–12). See also 392–94 and 483–86 on humor in newspapers. Three dissertations on Mark Twain's reputation and

presence in contemporary periodicals were consulted: Arthur Vogelback, "The Literary Reputation of Mark Twain in America, 1869–1885" (Ph.D. diss., University of Chicago, 1938); Robert Rodney, "Mark Twain in England: A Study of English Criticism of and Attitude toward Mark Twain: 1867–1940" (Ph.D. diss., University of Wisconsin, 1945); and Durant Da Ponte, "American Periodical Criticism of Mark Twain, 1869–1917" (Ph.D. diss., University of Maryland, 1953). Rodney's work will be discussed in chapter 4. Both Vogelback and Da Ponte start from the assumption that Mark Twain was a canonical author and his reputation suffered by "the sub-literary position held by humor," to quote Da Ponte (16), as well as Samuel Clemens's decision to publish by the subscription method. While these were factors in shaping his reputation, I depart from their conclusions by historicizing the meaning of the "humorist," as well as in not assuming Mark Twain's deeper significance as a "literary artist" as a given.

7. Scholarship on subscription publishing is limited and incomplete, as Amy Thomas lays out in "'There Is Nothing So Effective as a Personal Canvass': Revaluing Nineteenth-Century American Subscription Books," *Book History* 1 (1998): 141–52. See James Hart, *The Popular Book* (Berkeley: University of California Press, 1950), 150–52, and John Tebbel, *A History of Book Publishing in the United States* (New York: R. R. Bowker, 1972), 2:511–34. Mark Twain's experience with subscription has received the most attention. Discussions of individual books will be cited in further notes. See also Stephen Railton, "The Subscription System," http://etext.virginia.edu/railton/marketin/soldxsub.html.

8. Individual comic lecturers, such as Artemus Ward, often billed their lectures as "lyceum" lectures, even when not part of a lyceum program, either to add respectability to the event or to burlesque audience expectations, or both.

9. On the illustration process for Mark Twain's books, see Beverly David, *Mark Twain and His Illustrators*, vol. 1, *1869–1875* (Troy, N.Y.: The Whitson Publishing Company, 1986).

10. Draft of a letter to Andrew Lang, 1890. Reprinted in Frederick Anderson, *Mark Twain: The Critical Heritage* (London: Routledge and K. Paul, 1971), 336.

11. Clemens sought the approval of specific members of the cultured classes throughout the 1870s, especially through his friendships with Howells and others in the *Atlantic* circle and through his move to the elite enclave of Nook Farm in Hartford, Connecticut, in 1871, where he was neighbors with Harriet Beecher Stowe and Charles Dudley Warner, whose success as a genteel humorist illustrated a different model for the humorist in polite letters. His aim at the "members" is even more false, as he consistently cut sexual references from his books. Justin Kaplan notes Clemens's Victorian prudishness when it came to public works and his fascination with sexuality, especially that of the French, in *Mr. Clemens and Mark Twain: A Biography* (New York: Touchstone, 1966).

12. Judith Yaross Lee, *Twain's Brand: Humor in Contemporary American Culture* (Jackson: University Press of Mississippi, 2012), 6–8, 23–25.

13. Daniel Wickberg, *The Senses of Humor: Self and Laughter in Modern America* (Ithaca: Cornell University Press, 1998), 124, 29.

14. The starting place for the twentieth-century memory and memorialization of Mark Twain is Shelley Fisher Fishkin's *Lighting Out for the Territory: Reflections on Mark Twain and American Culture* (New York: Oxford University Press, 1997).

15. See Joseph Csicsila, *Canons by Consensus: Critical Trends and American Literature Anthologies* (Tuscaloosa: University of Alabama Press, 2004), 87–106, on Mark Twain's canonization in college textbooks.

16. Richard Brodhead, Cultures of Letters: Scenes of Reading and Writing in Nineteenth-Century America (Chicago: University of Chicago Press, 1993), 8. The history of the book views literature as a historical and material subject rather than as a collection of timeless classics. Works that discuss literature and reading as fields of study with their own history are Jane Tompkins, Sensational Designs: The Cultural Work of American Fiction, 1790–1860 (New York: Oxford University Press, 1985), esp. the introduction, "The Cultural Work of American Fiction," and Cathy N. Davidson, ed., Reading in America: Literature and Social History (Baltimore: Johns Hopkins University Press, 1987).

17. Bruce Michelson, *Mark Twain on the Loose: A Comic Writer and the American Self* (Amherst: University of Massachusetts Press, 1995), 3, 3–4. Instead, Michelson discusses Mark Twain in terms of anarchy of self and signification, framing the denial of coherence and a "delight in disorder" as a way to read Mark Twain. Of course, Michelson runs the risk of turning anarchy into a grand organizing principle of Twain studies and thus paradoxically stabilizing Mark Twain's writing and personality as inherently unstable. The risk is stumbling into what Stanley Fish has called "postmodern theory-hope," which he defines as the tendency of postmodern scholars to use their discussion of the contingency of knowledge and the slipperiness of signification to claim a privileged position, as if by pointing out the muddy footing of a pathway somehow made one immune to falling. To his credit, I think Michelson avoids falling. Such a keyword approach draws on Raymond Williams's analyses of "significant, binding words" in activity, interpretation, and thought. See Raymond Williams, *Keywords: A Vocabulary of Culture and Society* (London: Oxford University Press, 1976. Rev. ed., 1985), 15. Williams focuses on the different meanings of "Culture" as a keyword, focusing on the split experienced in the nineteenth century between "culture" as a "central formation of values" often found in the literature of a people (an Arnoldian sense) and "culture" as a word used to define a social group, often in relation to the keyword "society." American culture can thus mean a general field of life in a changing and contested geographical area called "the United States of America" and selected artistic representations of that entity that define something central about it—often, in the time of the present study, in terms of the "character" of the American people.

18. Van Wyck Brooks, *The Ordeal of Mark Twain* (New York: E. P. Dutton & Company, 1920), 218. Bernard DeVoto, *Mark Twain's America* (Boston: Houghton Mifflin Company, 1932), 240. See chapter 9 for DeVoto's refutation of Brooks. The other important literary figures of this era, according to DeVoto, were William Dean Howells and Henry James, and that is all. For instance, DeVoto writes: "For the future in America he is the author of 'Roughing It,' 'The Gilded Age,' 'Life on the Mississippi,' 'The Man Who Corrupted Hadleyburg,' 'Pudd'nhead Wilson,' 'The Adventures of Tom Sawyer,' and 'The Adventures of Huckleberry Finn'" (240).

19. Brooks, *The Ordeal of Mark Twain*, 218. DeVoto, *Mark Twain's America*, 265, 206.

20. For instance, Gladys Carmen Bellamy argued in *Mark Twain as a Literary Artist* (Norman: University of Oklahoma Press: 1950) that Mark Twain's humor evidenced clear literary artistry, which implies that popular humor springs forth from its time. Bellamy thus recreates the distinction between the "genuine humorist"—whose work belongs to the literary realm—and the popular humorists, who influenced Samuel Clemens but whom he superseded. She argues that "Mark Twain" was a "born humorist"; that is, he was born of a humorous temperament that influenced his personal and professional life. See chapter 5, "A 'Born Humorist' and 'Born Reformer.'" For her discussions of Mark Twain's roles as a humorist more generally, see 51, 58–59, 115, and 136. The 1960s also saw a sort of rebirth of Mark Twain with the popularity of Hal Holbrook's *Mark Twain Tonight!* as stage show and television special. Holbrook helped cement a vision of Mark Twain as the old sage philosopher, clad in white suit, which has greatly influenced public memory of Mark Twain. Holbrook has now performed as "Mark Twain" longer than Samuel Clemens.

21. Henry Nash Smith, *Mark Twain: The Development of a Writer* (Cambridge: Belknap Press, 1962), 110. See also Smith, "Mark Twain 'Funniest Man in the World'," in *The Mythologizing of Mark Twain*, edited by Sara deSaussure Davis and Philip D. Beidler, 56–60 (Tuscaloosa: University of Alabama Press, 1984). Taking another tack, Pascal Covici argued in *Mark Twain's Humor: The Image of a World* (Dallas: Southern Methodist University Press, 1962) for the artistic quality of Mark Twain's humor, while using the term "humorist" sparingly and without specified meaning. Covici's view that Mark Twain's humor was an artistic tool, not merely an end to itself, was highly influential in how humor has been framed in Twain studies, even while reflecting a lack of attention to the meaning of humorist as a cultural position. Joseph Csicsila shows in *Canons by Consensus: Critical Trends in American Literature Anthologies* (Tuscaloosa: University of Alabama Press, 2004) how critical focus on different authors and meanings reshaped the canon within academic anthologies over time. In the 1920s through the 1950s, this meant a focus on modernist impulses and a reshaping of the mid-nineteenth-century canon to privilege certain figures (Emerson, Whitman, Melville, Hawthorne, and Thoreau) over others.

22. Cox, *Mark Twain: The Fate of Humor*, xvii, 20, 60–62.

23. MTEB, 70. Peter Messent has framed the issues in this manner: "In the moves between identification with 'genteel culture' and with populist entertainment, between instruction and amusement, between a reliance on and burlesque of popular forms, there lies a series of ongoing and irreconcilable tensions at the very roots of Twain's artistic identity." Peter Messent, *The Short Works of Mark Twain: A Critical Study* (Philadelphia: University of Pennsylvania Press, 2001), 118.

24. Budd, *Our Mark Twain*, xiii. As a "culture-hero," in Budd's terms, Mark Twain's eminence was largely a masterful performance created and maintained by Samuel Clemens. Budd is reluctant to refer to Mark Twain as a "celebrity." If one starts Daniel Boorstin's famous definition of a celebrity as "someone who is well-known for his well-knowness," then Mark Twain certainly must be discussed in terms of celebrity. On the rise of celebrity in the later nineteenth century, see Charles Ponce de Leon, *Self-Exposure: Human-Interest Journalism and the Emergence of Celebrity in America, 1890–1940* (Chapel Hill: University of North Carolina Press, 2002). Budd also created several key archives central to this project, especially *Mark Twain: The Contemporary Reviews* and *Critical Essays on Mark Twain, 1867–1910* (Boston: G. K. Hall, 1982). Budd, *Our Mark Twain*, xiv–xv. Budd notes that one of the major methodological difficulties in writing about Mark Twain as a public figure is the distinction between critics representing various elite views, who used their access to print culture to shape the image of Mark Twain (and literary culture in general), and the various groups that made up the general public, who formed their own opinions of Twain's value. *Our Mark Twain* focuses on the public persona created by Clemens, but it largely brackets the question of audience reception, which I aim to undertake, in part, by examining critical reception. Budd, *Our Mark Twain*, 20–22.

25. Leland Krauth, *Proper Mark Twain* (Athens: University of Georgia Press, 1999), 3.

26. In other terms, this approach to Mark Twain is not based on "symptomatic reading," which has been the dominant form of literary interpretation in English departments. Stephen Best and Sharon Marcus define symptomatic reading as "an interpretive method that argues that the most interesting aspect of a text is what it represses, and that, as Frederic Jameson argued, interpretation should therefore seek 'a latent meaning behind a manifest one.'" They instead offer a range of interpretive practices called "surface reading" that value the material, linguistic, and affective meanings of texts. Steven Best and Sharon Marcus, "Surface Reading: An Introduction," *Representations* 108, no. 1 (Fall 2008), 3.

27. Caron, *Mark Twain: Unsanctified Newspaper Reporter*, 1–3. Using the concept of the "unsanctified reporter," Caron traces Mark Twain's career from his role as a Western newsman to a national author of the best-selling *The Innocents Abroad* and examines his influences and styles of humor in the changing circumstances of his writing and publishing.

28. Critics most often referenced clowns and minstrels as generic cultural categories without distinguishing between individual performers and without acknowledging the efforts of Barnum, in the circus, and the San Francisco Minstrels, on the minstrel stage, to make their performances more respectable for a higher class of audience. On the changing meanings of the circus in Gilded Age America, see Janet Davis, *The Circus Age: Culture & Society under the American Big Top* (Chapel Hill: University of North Carolina Press, 2002) and Bluford Adams, *E pluribus Barnum: The Great Showman and the Making of U.S. Popular Culture* (Minneapolis: University of Minnesota Press, 1997). On minstrelsy and Twain, see Sharon McCoy, "'The Trouble Begins at Eight': Mark Twain, the San Francisco Minstrels, and the Unsettling Legacy of Blackface Minstrelsy," *American Literary Realism* 41, no. 3 (Spring 2009): 232–48.

Chapter One

1. SLC to Orion and Mary E. (Mollie) Clemens, 19 and 20 Oct 1865, San Francisco, Calif. (*UCCL 00092*). Letters 1:322–25.

2. Caron, *Mark Twain: Unsanctified Newspaper Reporter*, 267–77. See the section "Periodicals and the Professional Comic Writer" (169–77) for how the idea of hierarchy divided and shaped the era's periodicals.

3. This view is based on an increase in number and length of periodical discussion in British periodicals, as found in Arnella Turner, *Victorian Criticism of American Writers* (San Bernardino, Calif.: The Borgo Press, 1991). Beginning in the 1820s, American authors began to gain notice in British periodical criticism, particularly Washington Irving and James Fenimore Cooper. While these periodicals featured twelve to seventeen articles on American literature per decade before 1850, the following decades saw a boom in articles on American writers, with forty-eight articles in the 1850s, thirty-one in the 1860s, and sixty in the 1870s. From 1820 to 1849, the British periodicals examined discussed Irving in approximately ten articles and Cooper in seven. Other authors discussed were Benjamin Franklin, Charles Brockden Brown, William Ellery Channing, William Cullen Bryant, Nathaniel Parker Willis, J. C. Early, Catherine Maria Sedgwick, and Lydia Sigourney. These calculations are my own based on Turner's data, which is divided by periodical and does not specifically trace general patterns over time. In the 1850s, both Stowe and Longfellow appeared in a dozen articles each, while numerous articles also appeared on Edgar Allen Poe (seven), Nathaniel Hawthorne (six), Ralph Waldo Emerson (four), Herman Melville (four), as well as continued discussion of Irving and Cooper and initial interest in James Russell Lowell and Oliver Wendell Holmes. Additional figures gaining notice in the 1850s included: Bryant (two), Margaret Fuller, Richard Henry Dana, Alice Carey, and John Greenleaf Whittier. In the 1860s, a total of thirty-one articles on literary subjects discussed the following figures: Hawthorne (nine), Lowell (five), Holmes (five), Longfellow (four), Emerson (four), Stowe (three), Bryant

(three), Whittier (two), Irving (two), Artemus Ward, and Poe (one). Turner notes that British critics saw a need for a distinctly American literature that expressed the national character without being derivative. Especially in poetry, American authors showed talent but remained largely limited by their reliance on European models. Only Poe, and later Whitman, showed true American originality to British eyes, yet each remained controversial because of the idiosyncrasies of their verse and their personal lives. In fiction, Cooper and Irving gained early notice as original writers, followed by Harriet Beecher Stowe, especially *Uncle Tom's Cabin*, and the fiction of Nathaniel Hawthorne. Critical variations existed across periodicals, and across time, but Turner argues that the general consensus of British periodical writing was that American authors had failed to develop a national literature. Turner, *Victorian Criticism of American Writiers*, 10–11.

4. John Robertson, "Yankeeana," *The Westminster Review* (December 1838). Quoted in *The Museum of Foreign Literature, Science, and Art*, vol. 7—New Series (Philadelphia: E. Littell & Co., 1839), 75–76.

5. Ibid., 76.

6. Gerald Massey, "American Humour," *The North British Review* 33, no. 66 (November 1860), 484.

7. Lowell's description of humor's value as a weapon, in the preface to the second series of *The Biglow Papers* (Boston: Ticknor and Fields, 1867), demonstrates the humorist's goal of creating a lasting artistic accomplishment beyond the immediate aims of humor:

> If I put on the cap and bells and made myself one of the court-fools of King Demos, it was less to make his majesty laugh than to win a passage into his royal ears for certain serious things which I had deeply at heart. I say this because there is no imputation that could be more galling to any man's self-respect than that of being a mere jester. I endeavored, by generalizing my satire, to give it what value I could beyond the passing moment and the immediate application (viii–ix).

8. Massey, "American Humour," 471. For his lack of American soil, see ibid., 121.

9. Ibid., 479.

10. For a discussion of literary wit, see Bruce Michelson, *Literary Wit* (Amherst: University of Massachusetts Press, 2000). Massey, "American Humour," 464.

11. Ibid., 477.

12. Ibid., 471–76, 475.

13. Mimosa Stephenson, "Humor in *Uncle Tom's Cabin*," *Studies in American Humor* 3, no. 20 (2009), 4, 9–10. See also Richard Yarborough, "Strategies of Black Characterization in *Uncle Tom's Cabin* and the Early Afro-American Novel," in *New Essays on Uncle Tom's Cabin*, edited by Eric Sundquist, 47–48 (Cambridge: Cambridge University Press, 1986).

14. Shelley Fisher Fishkin, *Was Huck Black? Mark Twain and African-American Voices* (New York: Oxford University Press, 1994), 4. A starting point for these studies are Nancy A. Walker and Zita Dressner, eds. *Redressing the Balance: American Women's Literary Humor from Colonial Times to the 1980s* (Jackson: University Press of Mississippi, 1988); Nancy A. Walker, *A Very Serious Thing: Women's Humor and American Culture* (Minneapolis: University of Minnesota Press, 1988); Linda Morris, *Women Vernacular Humorists in Nineteenth-Century America: Ann Stephens, Francis Whitcher, and Marrietta Holley* (New York: Garland Publishing, Inc., 1988); and Mel Watkins, *On the Real Side: A History of African American Comedy* (Chicago: Lawrence Hill Books, 1994).

15. Morris, *Women Vernacular Humorists*, 149. *Critic* magazine quoted in ibid., 146.

16. Leslie Stephen, "American Humour," *The Cornhill Magazine* 13 (January 1866), 28–29, 30, 30–31. Stephen, characteristically, undertakes the definitional denial, of saying he won't define humor then doing so, writing that "it would be necessary, if it were desirable, to explain what we mean by humour—a task which we may at once decline as hopelessly impracticable" and then defining humor as a relationship between wit and sentiment that the English alone had mastered: "the happy combination where the feelings are at the right distance from the intellect, so that the sparks struck out by wit fall instantly on our sentiment" (30–31).

17. Stephen, "American Humour," 32, 35. Gerald Massey, "Yankee Humour," *London Quarterly Review,* 122 (January 1867), 112, 118. Printed in British and American editions, with slight variations. Quotes are from the American edition. Also published in *Living Age* 4 (March 1867): 673–85. The *Round Table* cited this article as evidence of the declining influence of quarterly magazines and critiqued Massey for discussing only a portion of the books he purports to review and for selecting poor examples from the books he does. See "Literariana," *Round Table* 5:115 (April 6, 1876), 221. Massey does make the argument that the distortion of language for humor was a well-known African American trait that had been made grotesque by imitators of the form of "sham Ethiopian and other serenaders." Goodman and Dawson point out that Howells clipped and carried English reviews of his first book that he memorized; see Susan Goodman and Carl Dawson, *William Dean Howells: A Writer's Life* (Berkeley: University of California Press, 2005), 115. After leaving the editorship of the *Atlantic* in 1882, Howells and family undertook their own London sojourn, being met there by a reception of figures that could have been a table of contents of the *Atlantic*: J. R. Osgood (publisher of the magazine), Henry James, Thomas Bailey Aldrich, Bret Harte, John Hay, Moncure Conway, Charles Dudley Warner, and Clarence King (Goodman and Dawson, *William Dean Howells,* 224). This testifies to the transatlantic circulation of American authors, not only through books and periodicals, but also in person.

18. Stephen, "American Humour," 42, 39, 33. Meiosis is the opposite of hyperbole, rhetorically. Whereas hyperbole exaggerates for effect, meiosis "represents a thing as less than it is." See William S. Walsh, *Handy-Book of Literary Curiosities* (Philadelphia: J. B. Lippincott Company, 1893), 696–97. Walsh points out that the technique is a popular trick of American humor, as opposed to English comedians who constantly underscore the joke, and uses the "risin' ground" example, attributing it as a Yankee "chestnut." Stephen, "American Humour," 35; Massey talks about "high-falutin'" humor in *Handy-Book of Literary Curiosities* in "Yankee Humour," 114. Massey, "Yankee Humour," 118, 117. See also Stephen, "American Humour," 35.

19. Stephen, "American Humour," 35, 41. Massey, "Yankee Humour," 123, 122.

20. *The Nation* 11 (December 29, 1870), 434. Quoted in Da Ponte, "American Periodical Criticism of Mark Twain," 25.

21. The most important work on this category is David E. E. Sloane's *Mark Twain as a Literary Comedian* (Baton Rouge: Louisiana State University Press, 1979). For a revision of the label, see James Caron, "Why 'Literary Comedians' Mislabels Two Comic Writers, George Derby ('John Phoenix') and Sam Clemens ('Mark Twin')," *Studies in American Humor* 3, no. 22 (2010), 44.

22. Walter Blair, "The Popularity of Nineteenth-Century American Humorists," *American Literature* 3, no. 2 (May 1931), 178–79. Walter Blair, "The Popularity of Nineteenth-Century American Humorists," 185. Sales figures are estimates, as they are often based on publisher boasts. "Q.K. Philander Doesticks, P.B." stands for "Queer Kritter Philander Doesticks, Perfect Brick." James Caron traces the major influences of Mark Twain in *Mark Twain: Unsanctified Newspaper Reporter*, "Act One—The Comic Lineage of Mark Twain," 25–81. John Phoenix, *Phoenixiana; or, Sketches and Burlesques by John Phoenix* (New York: D. Appleton, 1856; London: Beeton, 1865). For information on the Phoenix-Twain connection, see Gladys Carmen Bellamy, "Mark Twain's Indebtedness to John Phoenix," *American Literature* 13, no. 1 (March 1941): 29–43.

23. See especially Caron, *Mark Twain: Unsanctified Newspaper Reporter*, "Act One—The Comic Lineage of Washoe Mark Twain," and David E. E. Sloane, *Mark Twain as a Literary Comedian* (Baton Rouge: Louisiana State University Press, 1979), chapters 1–3.

24. Daniel Wickberg has argued that that only in "the mid- to late-nineteenth century did the term 'humorist' come to refer to the self-conscious creator of a product called 'humor.'" Wickberg, *The Senses of Humor*, 123–24.

25. Kenneth Schuyler Lynn, *Mark Twain and Southwestern Humor* (Boston: Little, Brown, 1959). See also the introduction to anthologies of the genre: Hennig Cohen and William B. Dillingham, eds., *Humor of the Old Southwest* (Boston: Houghton and Mifflin, 1964), ix, and M. Thomas Inge and Edward J. Piacentino, eds. *The Humor of the Old South* (Lexington: University Press of Kentucky,

2001), xi. This argument can be traced to DeVoto, *Mark Twain's America*, esp. 240–41, and Walter Blair, *Native American Humor* (New York: Harper Collins College Division, 1960), 157. The best review of this argument is Caron's section in *Mark Twain: Unsanctified Newspaper Reporter*, "Act One—The Comic Lineage of Washoe Mark Twain," especially the first chapter, "Washoe Mark Twain and the Old Southwest Writers" (25–32). See also my argument in "'I wa' n't bawn in de mash to be fool' by trash!': Mark Twain's 'A True Story' and the Culmination of Southern Frontier Humor," *Southern Frontier Humor: New Directions,* edited by Ed Piacentino, 131–53 (Oxford: University Press of Mississippi, 2013). David E. E. Sloane, *Mark Twain as a Literary Comedian* (Baton Rouge: Louisiana State University, 1979); see especially the first chapter, 1–12. Sloane also notes the importance of British and Irish humorists on Twain; see 4–7. I have, to date, discovered only one contemporary account that links the humor of Samuel Clemens to any Southern Frontier humorist—Sut Luvingood. In fact, most accounts either frame Mark Twain as a product of the West or as a reformed Southerner.

26. Don Seitz, *Artemus Ward (Charles Farrar Browne): A Biography and Bibliography* (New York: Harper & Brothers, 1919), 319. See also John Raymond Pascal, *Artemus Ward: The Gentle Humorist* (Master's Thesis, Montclair State University, 2008), 12.

27. *Territorial Enterprise,* c. November 27, 1863. Effie Mona Mack, *Mark Twain in Nevada* (New York: F. C. Scribner's Sons, 1947), 289–90; See also Barbara Schmidt, "Virginia City Territorial Enterprise," an archival collection at http://www.twainquotes.com/teindex.html, specifically http://www.twainquotes.com/18631127t.html

28. For an account of this evening from Joe Goodman, see "Artemus Ward: His Visit to the Comstock Lode," San Francisco *Chronicle*, January 10, 1864?, 1. SLC to Jane Lampton Clemens, 2? Jan 1864, Carson City, Nev. In Letters 1:268. See notes 5–8 on Mark Twain's night with Artemus Ward and Ludlow's praise. Fitz Hugh Ludlow, "A Good-bye Article," *The Golden Era*, November 22, 1863.

29. Harte's comments appeared in *The Golden Era*, December 27, 1863. Quoted in Seitz, *Artemus Ward,* 146–47.

30. On humor during the Civil War, see Cameron Nickels, *Civil War Humor* (Oxford: University Press of Mississippi, 2010).

31. The issue also featured a serialization of Charles Dickens's *Our Mutual Friend* and introduced Josh Billings to the magazine with a selection of "Sayings of Josh Billings," such as: "Most ennyboddy kan write poor sense, but thare aint but few that kan write good nonsense—and it almos takes an eddykated man tew appreciate it after it iz writ" (242).

32. Caron, *Mark Twain: Unsanctified Newspaper Reporter,* 257–59. Caron also argues that the sketch owes as much to the influence of Artemus Ward as it does to the Humor of the Old Southwest, to which early generations of humor

scholars traced Mark Twain's reputation. See also Paul Rogers, "Artemus Ward and Mark Twain's 'Jumping Frog,'" *Nineteenth-Century Fiction* 28, no. 3 (December 1973): 273–86. Caron, *Mark Twain: Unsanctified Newspaper Reporter,* 261.

33. Frank Luther Mott, *A History of American Magazines,* vol. 3, *1865–1885* (Cambridge: Belknap Press of Harvard University Press, 1938), 319–24. "American Humor and Humorists," *Round Table,* September 9, 1865, 2. Arnold died a short time after this article was published, and his works published under the names "Mc Arone" and "Allen Grahame" have been largely forgotten. David Crockett, the piece notes, could be considered the father of this type of American humor, despite the fact that most of the pieces attributed to him were probably apocryphal. All subsequent quotes are from this page.

34. "Library Table," *Round Table,* December 7, 1867, 376.

35. In a letter to his family, Clemens wrote: "The book will issue the 25th. James Russell Lowell ('Hosea Biglow,') says the Jumping Frog is the finest piece of humorous writing ever produced in America." SLC to Jane Lampton Clemens and Family, 19 Apr 1867, New York, N.Y. (*UCCL 00123*). Letters 2:27–28. See note 3 on Lowell's remark, which has never been verified. October 7, 1865, 69. The reviewer was disappointed in "Mr. Brown's" use of plain English in the travel portion of the book, not because of the value of cacography, but because the misspelled parts of the book were better than those in plain English. The value of the showman is said to be in making his characters real, despite their starting as impossible characters who might not exist in the real world.

36. *Round Table,* September 1, 1866, 69; March 9, 1867, 154; July 7, 1866, 426.

37. See Caron, *Mark Twain: Unsanctified Newspaper Reporter*, "Act Four—Correspondent on Assignment," 283–349.

38. John Paul [Charles Henry Webb], "Advertisement," *The Celebrated Jumping Frog of Calaveras County, And other Sketches* (New York: C. H. Webb, 1867), v–vi.

39. SLC to Jane Lampton Clemens and Family, 7 June 1867, New York, N.Y. (*UCCL 00134*). Letters 2:57–9. See note 1 for sales figures. Budd lists twenty-two reviews or notices of the book in *Mark Twain: The Contemporary Reviews,* 25–31. Lee, *Twain's Brand,* 11–15.

40. "New Publications/Miscellaneous," New York *Times,* May 1, 1867, in Budd, 25. New York *Citizen,* May 4, 1867, in ibid., 26. "Gossip about Publishers and Books," New York *Evening Post,* May 8, 1867, in ibid., 28.

41. "The Citizen's Book Table," May 4, 1867, in Budd, 26.

42. "Mark Twain's New Book," June 1, 1867, in Budd, 29.

43. *Round Table,* May 25, 1867, 332, an epigraph of "Peter Pindar," an English satirist.

44. "Notes on New Books," New York *Herald,* May 12, 1867, in Budd, 28. Sacramento *Union,* June 6, 1867, in ibid., 30. "Western Humor," Chicago *Sunday Times,* May 5, 1867. From Louis J. Budd Archive at Elmira College. The article

mentions Richard Grant White and Sut Luvingwood [sic], two humorists in relation to whom Clemens was rarely, if ever, discussed.

45. "Mark Twain's Lecture," *Wilkes Spirit of the Times*, May 18, 1867, 193.
From Louis J. Budd Archive at Elmira College.

46. "Library Table," *Round Table* 5 (May 25, 1867): 332. Chicago *Sunday Times*,
May 5, 1867, 2. The piece notes, "it required the life, climate and habits of California to bring him out."

47. "Mark Twain's Book," *Californian* 7 (June 1, 1867), 9. New York *Citizen*
quoted in "A Fair Hit," *Californian* 7 (August 24, 1867), 8. From Louis J. Budd
Archive at Elmira College.

48. "California Humour," *London Review of Politics, Society, Literature, Art &
Science*, 15 (September 21, 1867): 330–31. From Louis J. Budd Archive at Elmira
College. "Our Library Table," *Fun* 6 (October 19, 1867), 65, in Budd, 30–31.

49. The "Sandwich Islands" was the colonial colloquialism rather than the native name for the Hawaiian Islands. Both names were in common use in the
nineteenth century, as illustrated by the title of a travel book published shortly
before the baseball tour called *Scenes of Hawai'i: or, Life in the Sandwich Islands*. I
will use the term "Sandwich Islands" when referring to Mark Twain's usage and
"the Kingdom of Hawaii" when referring to the actual place. For more information on Mark Twain's writings and views on Hawaii, see James Caron, "The
Blessings of Civilization: Mark Twain's Anti-Imperialism and the Annexation
of the Hawai'ian Islands," *The Mark Twain Annual* 6, no. 1 (November 2008):
51–63; Walter Francis Frear, *Mark Twain and Hawaii* (Chicago: The Lakeside
Press, 1947); Stephen Sumida, *And the View from the Shore: Literary Traditions
of Hawai'i* (Seattle: University of Washington Press, 1991), 38–56; Jim Zwick,
"Mark Twain's Hawaii," in *Confronting Imperialism: Essays on Mark Twain and the
Anti-Imperialist League* (Infinity Publishing, 2007); and Amy Kaplan, "Imperial
Triangles: Mark Twain's Foreign Affairs," *Modern Fiction Studies* 43, no. 1 (1997):
237–48.

50. Mark Twain, *Roughing It* (1872) (New York: Oxford University Press,
1997), 560–63. Jim Caron notes that the details of this story are to be doubted as representations of fact in *Mark Twain: Unsanctified Newspaper Reporter*,
373–77.

51. Frear, *Mark Twain and Hawaii*, 167, 169. See also Caron, *Mark Twain: Unsanctified Newspaper Reporter*, 373–92. Paine quoted in Frear, *Mark Twain and
Hawaii*, 168.

52. The major sources on Mark Twain as a lecturer are Paul Fatout, *Mark Twain
on the Lecture Circuit* (Bloomington: Indiana University Press, 1960); Mark
Twain, *Mark Twain Speaking*, edited by Paul Fatout (Iowa City: University of Iowa
Press, 1976); and Fred Lorch, *The Trouble Begins at Eight: Mark Twain's Lecture
Tours* (Ames: Iowa State University Press, 1968). See also Louis J. Budd, "Hiding
Out in Public: Mark Twain as Speaker," *Studies in American Fiction* 13 (Autumn

1985): 129–4, and Hal Holbrook, "Introduction" to Mark Twain, *Speeches* (New York: Oxford University Press, 1996). Marlene Vallin's *Mark Twain: Protagonist for the Popular Culture* (Westport, CT: Greenwood Press, 1992) provides a rhetorical reading of Twain's humor, focusing on his platform lectures and occasional speeches. Randall Knoper's *Acting Naturally: Mark Twain in the Culture of Performance* (Berkeley: University of California Press, 1995) focuses on the idea of "performativity" in Mark Twain's written works.

53. Brander Matthews, "Mark Twain as Speech Maker and Story Teller," *The Mentor*, May 1924, 24. Frear, *Mark Twain and Hawaii*, 180.

54. San Francisco *Evening Bulletin*, October 3, 1866. Stephen Railton has created invaluable archives on Mark Twain's lecture tours at "Mark Twain in His Times" that will be used when discussing his lectures. Railton compiles reviews, but does not provide page numbers for newspaper articles. For his Western debut, see: http://etext.virginia.edu/railton/onstage/sandwest.html.

55. Sacramento *Bee*, October 12, 1866. "Mark Twain's Lecture," San Francisco *Dramatic Chronicle*, as quoted in Caron, *Mark Twain: Unsanctified Newspaper Reporter*, 284.

56. *Daily Bulletin*, October 3, 1866. *Alta California,* October 3, 1866. *Alta California*, October 7, 1866.

57. "Mark Twain's Lecture," New York *Tribune*, http://etext.virginia.edu/railton/onstage/67lect2.jpg New York *Times*, May 6, 1867, 7. The lecture was also listed under a separate heading of "Amusements this Evening" as a "Humorous Lecture on the Sandwich Islands," 4.

58. Mark Twain, *Mark Twain's Autobiography,* 2 vols., edited by Albert Bigelow Paine (New York: Harper and Brothers, 1924), 1:353–54.

59. Frear, *Mark Twain and Hawaii*, 188, and Appendix D6, 454–55. See also http://etext.virginia.edu/railton/onstage/cooperad.html

60. New York *Times,* May 8, 1867. For reviews, see http://etext.virginia.edu/railton/onstage/mtlect67.html.

61. "Mark Twain as Lecturer," New York *Tribune*, May 11, 1867. Later attributed to Edward H. House.

62. Several scholars have written about Mark Twain's relationship with the Kingdom of Hawaii, but few have addressed the importance of the Sandwich Islands speeches in the development of his thought. I attempt to do so in relation to the question of imperialism and with reference to baseball in "'Interrupting a Funeral with a Circus': Mark Twain, Imperial Ambivalence, and Baseball in the Sandwich Islands," in *Mark Twain's Geographical Imagination*, edited by Joseph A. Alvarez, 131–47 (Newcastle upon Tyne: Cambridge Scholars Publishing, 2009).

63. "Mark Twain on the Sandwich Islands," Brooklyn *Eagle*, May 11, 1867, 3. House quoted in Kaplan, *Mr. Clemens and Mark Twain*, 34. The New York *Tribune*'s review was unique in claiming that it is the opposite of Artemus Ward's nervous quickness and deadpan delivery; most critics tended to find Artemus

Ward and Mark Twain's style quite similar, especially its use of a deadpan delivery that did not acknowledge the jokes.

64. "Eastern," San Francisco *Daily Dramatic Chronicle*, May 11, 1867, 3.

Chapter Two

1. *The Independent*, May 2, 1867, 4, provided a list of passengers, including Gen. Sherman and "Samuel Clemens ("Mark Twain"), of California." The New York *Tribune*, discussing the impending departure on June 8, listed "Mark Twain" as first in the list of celebrities taking the trip, along with the actress Maggie Mitchell, the journalist Moses Beach, and "several others." The New York *Times* noted that "after the withdrawal of these two leading names [Beecher and Sherman] from the bill of attractions, the passenger list gradually diminished. . . . Nevertheless the party will doubtlessly be equally jolly, if not quite so select as first contemplated. . . ." Mark Twain was listed as "S. (Mark Twain) Clemens" in the passenger list. June 9, 1867, 8.

2. Kaplan, *Mr. Clemens and Mark Twain*, 55. New York *Harold*, quoted in ibid., 56. Elisha Bliss, November 21, 1867. Reproduced in Albert Bigelow Paine, ed., *Mark Twain's Letters*, 2 vols (New York: Harper and Brothers, 1917), 1:140.

3. SLC to Elisha Bliss, Jr., 2 Dec 1867, Washington, D.C. (*UCCL 00165*). Letters, 2:31. Letter dated 27 Jan 1868, quoted in MTEB, 13–14. Letter dated 22 July [1869] details Mark Twain's anger in the delay of publication (22–24). Mark Twain also asked Bliss for an advance to focus on finishing the manuscript (14–15), inquired about publishing representation on the West Coast and in Japan and China (16), and tried out different names for the book (19).

4. Jeffrey Steinbrink, *Getting to Be Mark Twain* (Berkeley: University of California Press, 1991), xvi–xvii, 5. On revisions of the *Quaker City* material for publication, see ibid., chapter 1, n. 4, as well as Leon T. Dickinson, "Mark Twain's Revisions in Writing *The Innocents Abroad*," *American Literature* 19 (1947): 139–57; Robert H. Hirst, "The Making of *The Innocents Abroad*" (Ph.D. diss., University of California, Berkeley, 1975); and Robert Regan, "The Reprobate Elect in *The Innocents Abroad*," *American Literature* 54 (May 1982): 240–57.

5. SLC to Mary Mason Fairbanks, 2 Dec 1867, Washington, D.C. (*UCCL 00166*). Letters 2:121–24. A full recounting of this relationship is beyond the scope of this chapter, and as it occurred largely in private letters, only portions bear direct connection to the question of Mark Twain's reputation, but the question of reverence and its opposite were key in the responses to Mark Twain's book and to many subsequent items that Mark Twain published, as well as those that Mark Twain decided not to publish. In a letter from 1869, Mark Twain addressed this topic directly, if playfully, in responding to Fairbanks's criticism of one of his stories. He wrote:

> Me "getting cross over your talk?" No—bang away—I li [*sic*] enjoy it.
> No, I don't mean that—I mean I don't mind it—or rather, I mean that

I *like* [it. Now]I have got it. I like your criticisms, because they nearly
always convince me—always, I guess, is nearer the truth. And because
I love you, I would like the criticisms, even if they *didn't* convince me.

Well, I'll let Death alone. I will, mother—honest—if I won't bother
him if he don't bother me. No, but really, I *will* be more reverential, if
you want me to, though I tell you it don't jibe with my principles. There
is a fascination about meddling with forbidden things."

SLC to Mary Mason Fairbanks, 26 and 27 Sept 1869, Buffalo, N.Y. (*UCCL
00359*). Letters 3:358–61.

6. As the reviewer for the Reese River *Revielle* in Austin, Nevada, stated after
laboring through a long, decidedly unfunny paraphrasing of the lecture: "It is
not easy to give a correct report of this lecture; to be properly appreciated it
must be heard, and the distinguished lecturer himself . . . must deliver it." "Mark
Twain's Lecture," April 23, 1868. Lorch, *The Trouble Begins at Eight*, 106.

7. "Mark Twain's Lecture," San Francisco *Daily Morning Call,* April 16, 1868.
See http://etext.virginia.edu/railton/onstage/68rev04a.html

8. "Mark Twain's Lecture," Sacramento *Daily Union,* April 18, 1867, http://
etext.virginia.edu/railton/onstage/68rev06.html

9. MTEB, 28–29. See Fred Lorch, "Mark Twain's Lecture Tour of 1868–1869:
'The American Vandal Abroad,'" *American Literature* 26, no. 4 (January 1955):
515–27.

10. Sources on the lyceum and public speaking, in general, are Melville Landon,
Kings of the Platform and Pulpit (Chicago: The Werner Company, 1895); Charles
Horner, *The Life of James Redpath and the Development of the Modern Lyceum* (New
York: Barse & Hopkins, 1926); Carl Bode, *The American Lyceum* (Oxford: Oxford
University Press, 1956); and Angela Ray, *The Lyceum and Public Culture in the
Nineteenth-Century United States* (Ann Arbor: Michigan State University Press,
2005). Robert Tarbell Oliver, *History of Public Speaking in America* (Boston: Allyn
and Bacon, 1965), 434–36. As Mark Twain stated to Charles Warren Stoddard in
1869, "About lecturing. The *only* way to do it is to get into 'the field'—the regular
lyceum field. Individual enterprise cannot but fail—even Nasby cannot lecture
on his own hook, as I do in California." SLC to Charles Warren Stoddard, 25 Aug
1869, Buffalo, N.Y. (*UCCL 00340*). Letters 3:320–21. Billings quoted in Oliver,
History of Public Speaking in America, 436. From Josh Billings, *Josh Billings, His
Works, Complete* (New York: G. W. Carleton, 1876), 373. Oliver, *History of Public
Speaking in America*, 467

11. SLC to Mary Mason Fairbanks, 24 Sept 1868, St. Louis, Mo. (*UCCL 02752*).
Letters 2:258. In a letter to Livy from early October, Clemens noted that he had
"teased" Fairbanks with a letter meant to provoke her wrath through an "absurd synopsis" of the lecture. Letters 2:274. Letter from SLC to Mary Mason
Fairbanks, 12 Oct 1868, Hartford, Conn. (*UCCL 02758*). Letters 2:264. SLC to
Mary Mason Fairbanks, 31 Oct 1868, New York, N.Y. (*UCCL 02761*). Letters
2:27

12. Lorch, *The Trouble Begins at Eight*, 285. Lorch notes that Mark Twain preferred male audiences to female, as he felt that men laughed more easily while women were less inclined to laugh in public. During these early tours, the audiences were apparently of mixed gender, with more women attending matinees than evening shows (240–41).

13. Ibid., 294. Mark Twain continued: "We saw no ladies anywhere that dressed with such excellent taste as do our ladies at home here. I am not a married man, but—but—I would like to be. I only mention it in the most casual way, though, &—do not mean anything—anything personal by it." It is unclear whether this portion of the lecture was given in Elmira, N.Y., when Olivia Langdon was present. Letter from SLC to Mary Mason Fairbanks, 12 Oct 1868, Hartford, Conn. (*UCCL 02758*). Letters 2:263–64.

14. Lorch, *The Trouble Begins at Eight*, 297.

15. "Mark Twain," Chicago *Tribune*, January 8, 1869. Interspersed with these observations were comments on his reputation and performance style: "Mark Twain (Samuel G. Clemens [*sic*]), is a gentleman of some notoriety, and his effusions are constantly making the rounds of the press. As a humorous lecturer, he is a success." The review continued:

> There is nothing in his lectures, for he very properly sacrifices everything to make his audience roar, and they do it. . . . He would laugh at his own jokes, but that his doing so would detract from the fun of his hearers, so he contents himself by refusing to explode, and swallowing his risibility until the lecture is over, when he feels easier, and blows off steam. . . . During the evening, as if to prove that there was something besides humor in him, he branched out into quite eloquent passages, which were applauded. The lecture was good and the attendance large.

16. SLC to Olivia L. Langdon, 30, 31 Oct, 1 Nov 1869, Pittsburgh, Penn. (*UCCL 00365*). Letters 3:379.

17. *Herald*, November 18, 1868. See http://etext.virginia.edu/railton/innocent/vandrev1.html Mark Twain's interest in his reviews is evidenced by a letter he wrote to Mother Fairbanks on January 12, 1869, which included three reviews from papers in Michigan that Mark Twain wanted Fairbanks to print to keep up interest. One of these reviews clearly links Mark Twain to his fellow humorists, ending:

> As a humorous lecturer we have no hesitation in giving Mark Twain a decided preference over the renowned and lamented Artemus Ward. If Nasby, by the will of Lowell, becomes his successor as a humorist, we think Mark Twain is destined to more than make good the place formerly filled by Ward. He is sure to provoke the hearty laugh that shakes the cobwebs from the brain and the hypochondria from the ribs. And as laughter is no sin, if it takes the proper time to come

in, we hope Mark Twain will make his calling and election sure, and continue to amuse as well as instruct the grave, austere, American nation.

SLC to Mary Mason Fairbanks, 12 Jan 1869, El Paso, Ill. (*UCCL 00229*). Letters 3:28.

18. "The First Lecture," Iowa City *Republican*, January 13, 1869.

19. "The Vandal in Iowa City," Iowa City *Republican*, January 22, 1869. See http://etext.virginia.edu/railton/innocent/vandrev8.html

The review continues to discuss behavior the next morning, in which he abused the landlord of the boarding house. The review notes that "the Y.M.C.A. were wretchedly imposed upon by Mark Twain, and so of course were the audience." They noted Mark Twain was the only lecturer in the series whose personal character was not known and that the next speaker, Oliver O. Howard, was of impeccable character. Mark Twain wrote a letter of apology.

20. Lorch, *The Trouble Begins at Eight*, 293.

21. Henry Nash Smith notes that Livy and Mrs. Fairbanks were "spokesmen for the dominant culture" who embodied what Mark Twain already knew about the views of his increasing audience. See Henry Nash Smith, *Mark Twain: The Development of a Writer*, 25–26. Susan Harris has convincingly argued that scholars have largely flattened Olivia Langdon Clemens into a caricature of a nineteenth-century womanhood they saw (and attacked) as antithetical to modernist values, ignoring both Mark Twain's affinities to the middle-class society she was a part of and Langdon's intellectual vivacity and the importance of her influence on Mark Twain. See Susan K. Harris, *The Courtship of Olivia Langdon and Mark Twain* (Cambridge: Cambridge University Press, 1997), 8–11.

22. SLC to Thomas Bailey Aldrich, 27 Jan 1871, Buffalo, N.Y. (*UCCL 00567*). Letters 4:316.

23. George Ade, "Mark Twain and the Old Time Subscription Book," *The American Review of Reviews*, June 1910. Quoted in Stephen Railton, "Ade on MT as a Subscription Author," http://etext.virginia.edu/railton/marketin/geoade.html

24. MTEB, 159–62.

25. Nancy Cook, "Finding his Mark: Mark Twain's *The Innocents Abroad* as a Subscription Book," in *Reading Books*, edited by Michele Moylan and Lane Stiles, 151–78 (Amherst: University of Massachusetts Press, 1996). See especially 151–54.

26. MTEB, 3. As Hill notes further, "Although the most feverish portion of the author's energies went into the composing, publishing, and marketing of his books, the most vitriolic of his hatreds were reserved for the very men who helped guide his literary work through its production and presentation to an audience." MTEB, 2.

27. MTEB 37, 38. Leon T. Dickinson, "Marketing a Best Seller: Mark Twain's *Innocents Abroad*." *Papers of the Bibliographical Society of America* 41 (1947):

107–22. There were 1,231 prospectuses delivered with the first copies of the book in July and roughly 800 of the second version. MTEB, 39–40.

28. See Stephen Railton, "Selling *Innocents*," http://etext.virginia.edu/railton/innocent/dummyhom.html

29. Undated, copy in the Mark Twain Papers. See Letters 3:492–95. The poster lists Mark Twain as "The Popular Correspondent and Humorist" on the right side of the page, unlike the above version.

30. MTEB, 36.

31. SLC to Elisha Bliss, Jr., 2 Sept 1869, Buffalo, N.Y. (*UCCL 00342*). Letters 3:327–8. "Advertising Supplement," Buffalo *Express*, October 9, 1869, 1–2. Printed between July 28 and August 31, approximately. Of the twenty-eight reviews, several are not listed in Budd, but of the ones that are, the New York *Herald*'s review from the end of August is the latest. American Publishing Company, "Paragraphs from Notices of this Book" (Hartford: American Publishing Company, 1869).

32. "Well, I believe I haven't anything more to say, except that I like the circulars, I like the book, I like you and your style and your business vim, and believe the chebang will be a success" (12 August 1869) in MTEB, 26; "I think the book is making more stir than other people's books, and I guess you are pushing it for all it is worth." (postscript to 27 Sept 1869) in MTEB, 29.

33. SLC to Elisha Bliss, Jr., 28 Jan 1870, Elmira, N.Y. (*UCCL 00418*). Letters 4:40.

34. Robert H. Hirst, *The Making of The Innocents Abroad: 1867–1872* (Ph.D. diss., University of California, Berkeley, 1975), 314, 316. See MTEB, 39-40, for further monetary figures. Sales are estimates based on the bindery records kept by the American Publishing Company, compiled in Hamlin Hill, *Mark Twain's Book Sales, 1869–1879* (New York: New York Public Library, 1961).

35. Budd, 35–89. Some quotes from the review found in Louis J. Budd Archive, Center for Mark Twain Studies, Elmira College. The Syracuse *Standard* made an interesting distinction in calling Mark Twain "the first of American humorists, as James Russell Lowell is undoubtedly the first of American wits," Budd, 68. "Book Notices," Elmira *Saturday Evening Review*, October 2, 1869, in Budd, 67, and Toledo *Commercial*, "Literary Matters," September 3, 1869, in Budd, 55. "New Publications, *Flags of Our Father* 25 (January 8, 1870): 24, in Budd, 76

36. "A Jolly Record of Travels," Albany *Journal*, September 14, 1869, in Budd, 57. "Literary," Cleveland *Leader*, September 29, 1869, in Budd, 64.

37. For instance, Arthur Vogelback argues that Mark Twain's decision to publish via subscription led to the book being the least reviewed of Mark Twain's books, which was determined by Vogelback's limited sample of three major newspapers and the prestigious periodicals. Arthur Vogelback, "The Literary Reputation of Mark Twain in America, 1869–1885" (Ph.D. diss., University of Chicago, 1938).

38. "New Books," Buffalo *Express*, August 16, 1869, in Budd, 41–42. "Recent Publications," Paterson *Guardian*, August 23, 1869, in Budd, 48–49.

39. "Mark Twain's New Book," New York *Sun*, August 16, 1869, in Budd, 42. "Mark Twain's New Book," Newark *Morning Register,* August 12, 1869. From Louis J. Budd Archive, Center for Mark Twain Studies, Elmira College.

40. "New Publications," Cleveland *Plain Dealer*, September 24, 1869, in Budd, 62–63. "Literary," Cleveland *Leader*, September 29, 1869, in Budd, 65. "Mark Twain's Book," Virginia City *Territorial Enterprise*, October 7, 1689, in Budd, 70–71. "Book Notices," *Saturday Evening Review*, October 2, 1869, in Budd, 67. Pittsburgh *Gazette*, September 4, 1869, 8. From Louis J. Budd Archive, Center for Mark Twain Studies, Elmira College.

41. Jennifer Hughes, "Telling Laughter: A Cultural History of American Humor, 1830–1890." (Ph.D. diss., Emory University, 2009), chapter 1, "Selling Humor," esp. 25–42. For a history of theories of laughter, see Wickberg, *The Senses of Humor*, 46–68, 173–86.

42. "Book Notices," *Saturday Evening Review*, October 2, 1869, in Budd, 67.

43. "Literary," Newark *Advertiser*, August 14, 1869, in Budd, 41. In an undated excerpt from the Norwich *Bulletin* printed in the prospectus, a new danger is detected: "If people don't stop laughing so immoderately in the dead hours of the night as to keep their neighbors awake, there will probably be trouble, that's all. The cause is said to be Mark Twain's new book, which everybody is reading. But that is no excuse."

44. "Mark Twain's New Book," Fort Plain (N.Y.) *Mohawk Valley Register*, August 20 1869, 2. From Louis J. Budd Archive, Center for Mark Twain Studies, Elmira College.

45. "New Publications," *Saturday Evening Post*, October 9, 1869, 3. From Louis J. Budd Archive, Center for Mark Twain Studies, Elmira College.

46. "The New Pilgrims' Progress/Mark Twain on His Travels," Hartford *Courant*, July 31, 1869, in Budd, 36. "*The Innocents Abroad*," Cleveland *Herald*, September 23, 1869, in Budd, 61–62.

47. "Ishmael's Corner," Elmira *Saturday Evening Review*, August 21, 1869, in Budd, 46. "Ishmael" was the pseudonym of Ausburn Trower, who had angered Mark Twain with his criticisms of American humor. After this review appeared, Mark Twain wrote but did not send Trower a letter clearly stating his opinion: "My Dear Insect: With more than the solicitude of a mother I have watched your little ambitions develop, one by one, & with more than the grief of such a parent have seen them, one by one take their places among the world's unnoticed failures." SLC to Ausburn Towner (Ishmael), 17 Sept 1869, Elmira, N.Y. (*UCCL* 08697). Letters 3:352. For a history of their feud, see SLC to Elisha Bliss, Jr., 15 Aug 1869, Buffalo, N.Y. (*UCCL 00333*). Letters 3:301–2.

48. "Mark Twain's Pilgrimage," San Francisco *Evening Bulletin*, August 7, 1869, in Budd, 37.

49. SLC to Whitelaw Reid, 15 Aug 1869, Buffalo, N.Y. (*UCCL 00334*). Letters 3:303.

50. "Mark Twain's Book," New York *Tribune*, August 27, 1869, in Budd, 49.

51. American Publishing Company, 1869, "Paragraphs from Notices of this Book." Advertising supplement in the prospectus for *The Innocents Abroad*. A lengthy excerpt from the Hartford *Courant* was similarly edited to exclude critiques of his writing, while shorter excerpts focused on the positive (and saleable) aspects of the book.

52. SLC to Whitelaw Reid, 7 Sept 1869, Buffalo, N.Y. (*UCCL 00350*). Letters 3:342–43.

53. SLC to Elisha Bliss, Jr., 3 Sept 1869, Buffalo, N.Y. (*UCCL 00344*). Letters 3:329–30.

54. Unsigned review, October 16, 1869. Buffalo *Express* article quoted in Anderson, *Mark Twain: The Critical Heritage*, 26.

55. "The Innocents Abroad," Elmira *Advertiser*, September 17, 1869, in Budd, 59. "The Innocents Abroad," Cleveland *Herald*, September 23, 1869, in Budd, 61. Another recognized a disposition that is almost but not quite irreverence toward sacred scenes: "Yet he is far from sneering at what is recognized as essentially holy, and in frequent passages shows that, amid all his sportiveness, he cherishes earnest and heartfelt sympathies for what is venerable and good." "New Publications," Cincinnati *Gazette*, August 31, 1869, in Budd, 51.

56. "Literature," New York *Herald*, August 31, 1869, in Budd, 52–53.

57. "The Innocents Abroad," Syracuse (N.Y.) *Standard*, October 5, 1869, in Budd, 68-70.

58. "Mark Twain's New Book," New York *Leader*, August 14, 1869, in Budd, 39. "The Innocents Abroad," Philadelphia *Inquirer*, October 5, 1869. From Louis J. Budd Archive, Center for Mark Twain Studies, Elmira College. "New Publications," Springfield *New England Homestead*, September 4, 1869. From Louis J. Budd Archive, Center for Mark Twain Studies, Elmira College. "Book Table," *Independent*, 21 (September 30, 1869), 6. From Louis J. Budd Archive, Center for Mark Twain Studies, Elmira College.

59. "Mark Twain's Pilgrimage," San Francisco *Evening Bulletin*, August 7, 1869, in Budd, 38.

60. One reviewer made a metaphorical connection between Mark Twain's humor and wine: "There is more fun in this volume than any other book we have ever read. The humor is that dry and crusted sort, like an old cobwebby bottle of Madeira, before they started making Madeira in New Jersey." This reviewer's critiques are undercut by the admission, at the end, that he or she has not yet read the book! "A Critical Review" *Ohio State Journal*, October 22, 1869, 2. From Louis J. Budd Archive, Center for Mark Twain Studies, Elmira College.

61. Albany *Journal*, September 14, 1869, in Budd, 57.

62. *Packard's Monthly* [unsigned], ii, October, 1869, 318–19.

63. "Literary," Cleveland *Leader*, September 29, 1869, in Budd, 65. "Mark Twain's Book," New York *Tribune*, August 27, 1869, in Budd, 50.

64. "Literary Matters," Toledo *Commercial*, September 3, 1869, in Budd, 55. "A Jolly Record of Travesl," Albany *Journal*, September 14, 1869, in Budd, 57. The Cleveland *Plain Dealer* argued that they would rank Mark Twain as the "greatest" humorist of the past decade, although they then reconsidered and place Artemus Ward at the head since he "was the pioneer in a field that had been imperfectly tilled before him, and gave impetus to the latent humor of the country." As the first Artemus Ward letters had been published in this paper, it came as no surprise that they held him in high regard, making the elevation of Mark Twain to his status a larger compliment than the *Tribune*'s ambivalent support.

65. "*The Innocents Abroad*," *Liberal Christian*, August 21, 1869, in Budd, 45. The *Missionary Herald* used the book as "testimony" in favor of missionary work through the story of "Dr. B," who followed the model of Jesus—"He healed the sick." *Missionary Herald* 66, no. 2 (February 1870), 63.

66. SLC to Olivia L. Langdon, 10 and 11 Nov 1869, Boston, Mass. (*UCCL 00367*). Letters 3:393.

67. "Mark Twain on 'The Sandwich Islands,'" Boston *Daily Advertiser*, November 11, 1869. SLC to Pamela A. Moffett, 9 Nov 1869, Boston, Mass. (*UCCL 00371*). Letters 3:387. Thirty years later, Mark Twain misremembered in telling ways:

> We had to bring out a new lecture every season, now, ⌃(Nasby with the rest,)⌃ & expose it in the "Star Course," Boston, for a first verdict, before an audience of 2500 in the old Music Hall; for it was by that verdict that all the lyceums in the country determined the lecture's commercial value. The campaign did not really *begin* in Boston, but in the towns around; we did not appear in Boston until we had rehearsed about a month in those towns, & made & all the necessary corrections & revisings.

SLC (Samuel Langhorne Clemens). "Old Lecture Days in Boston." Untitled autobiographical reminiscence. MS of sixteen pages. Published in part as "Old Lecture Days in Boston" in *MTA* 1:147–53, and, untitled, in AMT, 166–69. Boston was the third stop on the tour. SLC to Olivia L. Langdon, 10 Nov 1869, Boston, Mass. (*UCCL 00366*). Letters 3:390–91.

68. SLC to Olivia L. Langdon, 10 and 11 Nov 1869, Boston, Mass. (*UCCL 00367*). Letters 3:392.

69. Mark Twain, *Speeches* (1910) (New York: Oxford University Press, 1996), vii.

70. Originally published in *Youth's Companion,* October 3, 1895. Reprinted in Mark Twain, *How to Tell a Story and Others* (1897) (New York: Oxford University Press, 1996), 7–8.

71. Boston *Advertiser,* November 11, 1869.

72. SLC to Olivia L. Langdon, 14 Dec 1869, Springfield, Mass. (*UCCL 00387*). Letters 3:423. He continued:

> Last night I got to one particular point in it 3 different times before I could get by it & go on. Every time I lifted my hand aloft & took up the thread of the narrative in the same old place the audience exploded again & so did I. But I got through at last, & it was very funny. This teaches me that a man might tell that Jumping Frog story fifty times without learning *how* to tell it—but between you & I, privately, Livy dear, it is the best humorous sketch America has produced, yet, & I must read it in public some day, in order that people may know what there is in it.

Philadelphia *Press*, December 8, 1869, and *The Cohoes Cataract*, January 15, 1870.

73. Philadelphia *Daily Evening Bulletin*, December 8, 1869. Hartford *Courant* quoted in the Oswego *Commercial Advertiser and Times*, January 14, 1870.

74. Fred Lorch pointed out negative reviews in Holyoke, Mass.; Hornellsville (now Hornell), N.Y.; and Norwich, Conn., in "Mark Twain's 'Sandwich Islands' Lecture and the Failure at Jamestown, New York, in 1869," *American Literature* 25, no.3 (November 1953), 322. New Haven *Daily Palladium*, December 29, 1869.

75. Lorch, "Mark Twain's 'Sandwich Islands' Lecture," 319.

76. Ibid., 315. Mark Twain wrote a letter to the author, whom he learned of through Nasby, but the letter was never sent and was published in Clara Clemens, *My Father Mark Twain* (New York, 1931), 69–70. Mark Twain wrote that "the article had not a merit in the world, except that it was well written and true." He acknowledged that the lecture was poor and he was tired, making the criticism an ungenerous truth that should have been kept silent. *Journal*, January 28, 1870. Emphasis in the original. The letter is reprinted in full in Lorch, "Mark Twain's 'Sandwich Islands' Lecture," 316–18.

77. Twain, *Mark Twain Speaking*, 6.

78. "Mark Twain on the 'Sandwich Islands,'" Boston *Daily Advertiser*, November 11, 1869.

79. Lorch, "Mark Twain's 'Sandwich Islands' Lecture," 316.

80. Ibid., 317. Lorch argued that the Mark Twain lecture was one instance of a local battle in Jamestown between the editor of the *Journal* and a faction opposed to the inclusion of comic lecturers in the lyceum program—a skirmish in a larger battle about the content of such programs. See Lorch, "Mark Twain's 'Sandwich Islands' Lecture," 320–23.

81. SLC to Orion and Mary E. (Mollie) Clemens, 19 and 20 Oct 1865, San Francisco, Calif. (*UCCL 00092*). Letters 1:322.

82. Albert Bigelow Paine, *Mark Twain, a Biography; the Personal and Literary Life of Samuel Langhorne Clemens*, 2 vols. (New York: Harper & Brothers, 1912),

1:427. For more on Ward, see Franklin Riley, ed., *Publications of the Mississippi Historical Society* (Oxford: Mississippi Historical Society, 1902), 262.

83. William Ward, "American Humorists," Macon *Beacon*, May 14, 1870, 2. Quoted in Paine 1:427. See also Anderson, *Mark Twain: The Critical Heritage*, 44–45.

84. Despite the practice of extensive copying in newspaper exchanges, I have found no evidence that the piece was reprinted or that Mark Twain was aware of it.

85. "Editorial Items," *The Phrenological Journal of Science and Health* 51, no. 2 (August 1870), 142.

86. Ibid., 143. "There is also a wholesomeness in his fun which is commendable. His humor is a moral tonic without cant or affectation."

87. "Sum Biographical—Mark Twain," New York *Weekly*, October 6, 1870.

88. Mark Twain's Autobiography and First Romance (New York: Sheldon, 1871).

89. See SLC to Mary Mason Fairbanks, 26 April 1871, Elmira, N.Y. (*UCCL 00606*). Letters 4:381.

Chapter Three

1. [William Dean Howells], "A Poetical Lot," 24, no. 143 (September, 1869): 387. [William Dean Howells], "*The Innocents Abroad*," 24, no. 146 (December 1869), 766.

2. *The Nation*, September 2, 1869, 195.

3. [Henry Giles], "Thomas Hood," 6, no. 37 (November 1860): 516. The very first book review in the *Atlantic*—of a collection of epistolary philosophy—critiques the author's skill as a humorist, which is placed in the same category as "reasoner" and "writer" (*Atlantic* 1, no. 1 [November 1857]: 122). Throughout the book reviews and articles in the early volumes, "humorist" is used in this way as a category of description in conjunction or contrast with terms like "critic," "poet," "dramatist," and "moralist."

4. Quoted in Frank Luther Mott, *A History of American Magazines*, vol. 2, *1850–1865* (Cambridge: Belknap Press of Harvard University Press, 1938), 499–500 and n. 22. Unfortunately, the copies archived in the online database "The Making of America" at Cornell and in the University of Texas library have cut the end pages out of their copies, deleting this statement.

5. The magazine was founded by a group of New England authors, among them Emerson, Holmes, Lowell, Stowe, and Longfellow, and by the publishing firm of Phillips, Sampson and Company. The magazine combined Stowe and Phillips's experience that antislavery literature could sell with the longstanding desire of New England writers to found and sustain an intellectual and antislavery magazine out of Boston. The magazine followed the failed efforts to

create and sustain a journal based in Boston that could sustain its existence on a national level: for instance, the New England Magazine (1831–1835), The Dial (1840–1844), and the Pioneer (1843). All suffered from low circulation. Two journals, the North American Review (founded in 1815 as a scholarly journal) and the Liberator (1831–1865), succeeded within their specific audiences—scholars and antislavery readers, respectively—but did not publish literary work. Emerson, who had edited the short-lived magazine The Dial, wrote that among Boston intellectuals "the measles, the influenza, and the magazine appear to be periodic distempers." Letter to Samuel Ward, 24 February 1850, quoted in Edward Emerson, Early Years of the Saturday Club, 1855–1870 (Boston: Houghton-Mifflin, 1918), 10.

6. Van Wyck Brooks, The Flowering of New England (New York: E. P. Dutton & Company., 1936), 483, quoted in Ellery Sedgwick, The "Atlantic Monthly," 1857–1909: Yankee Humanism at High Tide and Ebb (Amherst: University of Massachusetts Press, 1994), 21.

7. Brooks, Flowering of New England, 24.

8. On Parrington, see Sedgwick, The "Atlantic Monthly," 7, 26. Vernon Louis Parrington, Main Currents in American Thought, vol. 2, 1800–1860, The Romantic Revolution in America (New York: Harcourt, Brace & World, Inc., 1927).

9. On the cultural and intellectual backgrounds of the era, see Sedgwick, The "Atlantic Monthly," chapter 1, "The Founding of the Atlantic (1857): Boston's High Tide," esp. 21–24:

> From a modern or postmodern perspective, Lowell's tastes and editorial judgment were clearly circumscribed by certain moral and aesthetic standards specific to the mid-nineteenth century. But if his judgment lacked the sophisticated irony, the pure aestheticism, and the ethical relativism on which modern taste has congratulated itself, he did more than any contemporary editor to hold the line against the prevailing literary sins of the time: excessive sentimentality and moral didacticism. (53)

On the other hand, the rehabilitation of literary figures or publications to something of a "liberal" status should not be the goal of literary history—the Atlantic Monthly is important within literary history not because of its politics in relation to ours, but because it was influential in shaping key ideas of American literature and culture during the Gilded Age.

10. As Richard Brodhead points out, the Atlantic, along with other "quality" magazines, existed in the same high cultural realm as did the museum and the symphony orchestra. Brodhead, Cultures of Letters, 124. The Century, the Atlantic Monthly, and Harper's Monthly Magazine, Brodhead and others have argued, were the literary manifestations of a cultural trend that solidified hierarchical distinctions between high culture and popular culture.

11. Sedgwick, *The "Atlantic Monthly,"* 6–7. This is not to say that the magazine was purely, or even predominantly, egalitarian in its views. Many of the intellectual elite associated with the magazine shared a longstanding distrust of the democratic masses that was expressed in terms of a larger view of the intellectual as an active agent in the training of the reading public. Sedgwick argues that the *Atlantic* moved more toward this latter view of culture after Howells's departure in 1881. But for his part, Howells became in many ways more democratic and liberal while others, his mentor Lowell included, became more culturally conservative in the face of the social problems attendant with urbanization, immigration, and the social divisions of the later 1900s.

12. Sedgwick, *The "Atlantic Monthly,"* 41.

13. Ibid., 52.

14. In the pre–Civil War era, the average book sold 2,000 copies, rarely reaching 30,000. Monthly magazines, on the other hand, averaged 12,000 copies, with *Harper's* sometimes reaching 100,000. Ibid., 27. John Tebbel notes that *The Scarlet Letter* was a success, selling out a first printing of 2,500 and requiring another printing of that size, in *A History of Book Publishing in the United States*, 1:397. For magazine sales, see Frank Luther Mott, *A History of American Magazines*, 2:9–12 in general and 2:505–6 for the *Atlantic*. For a detailed examination of book sales of Ticknor and Fields before the Civil War, see Michael Winship, *American Literary Publishing in the Mid-Nineteenth Century: The Business of Ticknor and Fields* (Cambridge: Cambridge University Press, 1995).

15. In an 1849 article in the *North American Review*, Lowell had argued:

> That Art in America will be modified by circumstances, we have no doubt, though it is impossible to predict the precise form of the moulds into which it will run. . . . In the meantime we may fairly demand of our literature that it should be national to the extent of being as free from outworn conventionalities, and as thoroughly impregnated with humane and manly sentiment, as the ideas on which our political fabric rests.

Thus, a great literature would be a national literature that looked to the conditions of its social life, rather than being costumed in "a foreign or antique fashion." National literature demands that "authors should use their own eyes and ears, and not those of other people. We ask of them human nature as it appears in man, not in books. . . ." (130) James Russell Lowell, "Nationality in Literature." *North American Review* 69 (July 1849): 196–211. Reprinted in *Literary Criticism of James Russell Lowell*, edited by Herbert F. Smith (Lincoln: University of Nebraska Press, 1969), 128–29. But Lowell distinguishes between a nationality of ideas that connect to universal ideas of the human race and a nationality that was merely provincial—"a sublimer sort of clownishness and ill-manners. It deals in jokes, anecdotes, and allusions of such purely local character that a majority of the company are shut out from all approach to an understanding of them" (127).

16. "The Origin of Didactic Poetry," 1, no. 1 (November 1857): 112.

17. These were: *The Autocrat of the Breakfast-Table* (1858), *The Professor of the Breakfast-Table* (1859), *The Poet at the Breakfast-Table* (1872), and *Over the Teacups* (1890).

18. [Oliver Wendell Holmes], "A Visit to an Asylum for Aged and Decayed Punsters," 7:39 (January 1861), 113–17. The asylum is for men only, for as it is pointed out: "THERE IS NO SUCH THING AS A FEMALE PUNSTER."

19. [Howard Malcom Ticknor], "Vanity Fair," 10, no. 58 (August 1862): 254.

20. For instance, in dismissing a book of "Yankee humor," an early example of its genre, the reviewer distinguishes between Yankee dialect and bad spelling, writing that "this shows that he mistakes means for ends,—just as one who supposes Mr. Merryman, in the circus, must, of necessity, be funny, because he wears the motley and his nose is painted red." [Unknown reviewer], "High Life in New York," 4, no. 23 (September 1859): 386.

21. [Henry Giles], "Thomas Hood," 6, no. 37 (November 1860): 521. [Josiah Holland], "The Popular Lecture," 15, no. 89 (March 1865): 366.

22. Martin Duberman, *James Russell Lowell* (Boston: Houghton Mifflin Company, 1966), 95–96. The reaction to the new *Biglow Papers*, which appeared in January 1862, was poor—the tone of the piece was too jocular for the serious mood of the country and the magazine's readers. Charles Eliot Norton, with whom Lowell would soon be the co-editor of the *North American Review*, advised him to focus his satire, which had been too diffuse in the first paper, and the second paper's satire of England's position was both well-received and pointed out Lowell's strengths as a humorist (208–14).

23. [James Russell Lowell], "Birdofredum Sawin, Esq. to Mr. Hosea Biglow," 9, no. 51 (January 1862): 131–32. James Russell Lowell, *The Biglow Papers*, vii.

24. Ibid., xiii–ix.

25. [James Russell Lowell], "*Elsie Venner*," 7, no. 42 (April 1861): 510. Published serially in the *Atlantic Monthly* as "The Professor's Story" in 1860. Subsequent quotes from this page.

26. Lowell, *The Biglow Papers*, xviii, xii. This dialect exists, he argues, "Between the lifeless dictionary of 'the Universal Schoolmaster' and the 'stretching and swelling' of language by the newspaperman."

27. Ibid., lii. Lowell's introduction to the *Second Series* is an extended philological essay that traces pronunciation, Americanisms, and other sources of dialect to their sources in English, French, and prominent literatures, arguing in effect that dialect, defined as a type of linguistic flexibility, was the source of literary advance. In this sense, a focus on the standard English of manuals retarded the true source of artistic development—the living language of a place, which Lowell viewed as a nationally based phenomenon.

28. Lowell, *The Biglow Papers*, lxii. Lowell did praise Petroleum V. Nasby as a satirist, but Howells, in his review of the book, placed Nasby on the side of humorists who rely on tricks of spelling.

29. Parrington, *Main Currents in American Thought*, 2:443. F. O. Matthiessen, *American Renaissance: Art and Expression in the Age of Emerson and Whitman* (London: Oxford University Press, 1941. All three mentions are almost parenthetical; see 18n, 208, 375.

30. The combination of metered poetry, prose, wit, and drama in his table-talk books makes him difficult to fit into the preferred genres of modernist criticism—the novel or the free-verse poem. On the other hand, his three so-called "medicated novels," which explored psychological themes that anticipated Freud, have received very little scholarly attention. See Michael A. Weinstein, "The Power of Silence and Limits of Discourse at Oliver Wendell Holmes's Breakfast-Table," *The Review of Politics* 67, no. 1 (January 1, 2005): 113–33.

31. Parrington, *Main Currents in American Thought*, 2:446.

32. Sedgwick, *The "Atlantic Monthly," 1857–1909*, 59. Lowell, as editor and close friend, defended Holmes from the religious press, which he called "a true sour-cider press with bellyache privileges attached" (ibid.).

33. Walter Blair and Hamlin Hill, *America's Humour* (Oxford University Press, 1978), 172–73.

34. Howells, *Literary Friends*, 2–3.

35. Ibid., 12–13.

36. Ibid., 39, 55. Howells's visits to Thoreau and Emerson were less successful, with the young author failing to find encouragement in the abstractions of the literary greats. He convinced himself that he had, in some way, offended Emerson during the visit, an imagined offense that tortured him until he unburdened himself to Fields, who saw the humor in the young pilgrim's imagined offenses. This reaction, the imagined insult given the New England giants by the Western upstart, would be echoed almost twenty years later in the mortification Howells and Clemens felt in the aftermath of Mark Twain's Whittier birthday speech, to be discussed in chapter 7.

37. Ibid., 37.

38. Howells, *Literary Friends*, 70. The *Saturday Press* folded again in June 1866. While Howells viewed the *Press* as the *Atlantic*'s main literary comparison, he found the group's "bitterness" toward both Boston and respectability to be untoward. He admired individual writers associated with New York, but he preferred the "neighborhood" feeling of Boston, which involved "the sense of responsibility, which cannot be too constant or too keen. If it narrows, it deepens; and this may be the secret of Boston."

39. William Dean Howells, "Literary Boston Thirty Years Ago," *Harper's New Monthly Magazine* 91, no. 546 (November 1895): 865.

40. Howells, "Literary Boston," 867. Ibid.

41. Publishing semiannual indexes with author names started in 1862, and printing names in the magazine began in 1870. Additionally, Fields began to accept advertisements even before he took over the editorship. Along with advertising the catalog of Ticknor and Fields, a portion of the ads featured medicinal

and professional products and services. James C. Austin, *Fields of the Atlantic Monthly* (San Marino: The Huntington Library, 1953), 143.

42. Following a number of business and personal issues, Fields began leaving the bulk of the duties to Howells, especially after 1868. In 1868, Fields bought out (or deposed) William Ticknor's son Howard, who had been his assistant for a number of years and who had taken over for his father after the elder Ticknor's death in 1864, ostensibly for being discovered kissing a secretary of the company. During Fields's frequent trips, sometimes up to six months in duration, Howells was left in charge of many of the duties of editor (Sedgwick, The *"Atlantic Monthly," 1857–1909*, 108–9).

43. Austin, *Fields of the Atlantic Monthly*, 356.

44. On reviewing during this period, see Mott, *A History of American Magazines*, 3:233, and Sedgwick, *The "Atlantic Monthly,"* 72, 87–88. W. S. Tryon, *Parnassus Corner: A Life of James T. Fields, Publisher to the Victorians* (Boston: Houghton Mifflin Company, 1963), 85.

45. However, he refused works by important authors—such as Whitman and Sarah Orne Jewett—because they didn't fit his image of writing. Sedgwick, *The "Atlantic Monthly,"* 136–37.

46. Howells wrote between a third and a half of the reviews as assistant editor, sending the remainder out to other reviewers, especially T. W. Higginson, T. S. Perry, and E. W. Whipple. While Howells wrote only a portion of the reviews, and the reviews were published anonymously, the whole of the section was Howells's responsibility. Sedgwick argues that Howells was able to develop his views of criticism through his position as reviewer during the late 1860s, despite the pressure from his position as assistant to Fields (88). When Howells began, the magazine featured between two and eight reviews, although tending toward five per issue. Initially, each review was separate, or of several related books under one heading, but in 1872, the newly minted editor combined all reviews into joint essays with no separation between the reviews, which were written by different reviewers and grouped into "Recent Literature," which began with American and English writing, a separate "French and German" section, and separate "Art," "Music," "Science," and "Politics" sections. Sedgwick argues that this increased focus on literary subjects had a negative effect on the magazine, which faced a decrease in subscriptions from a high of approximately 50,000 in 1865 to 35,000 in 1871 when Fields retired from publishing altogether and sold his interest to James R. Osgood (110–11, 120). While the subscriptions continued to fall, to 20,000 in 1874 and 12,000 in 1881 when Howells left, the major factor seems to be the increased competition from other magazines, for both subscribers and contributors. The *Atlantic's* continued decision to not employ new technologies of illustration may have been the largest factor. The conventional story was that editorial decisions had offended longtime subscribers, causing a decrease in circulation. In 1869, Howells accepted a piece by Harriet Beecher Stowe excoriating the recently deceased Lord

Byron and defending his wife, in part by strongly insinuating an incestuous relationship on Byron's part. Meant to save America's youth from the "brilliant, seductive genius," the article was a sensation, leading first to increased sales of the single issue and then a spate of subscription cancelations from offended readers.

Many of Howells's reviews did focus on poetry and travel writing, the two genres in which he had written most. Portions of these reviews will be highlighted in the coming sections, but I will not offer a reading of his overall views on these subjects as constructed from his reviews, as they are less germane to the topic at hand. While it may seem that travel writing would be key to understanding Howells's review of the *Innocents Abroad*, his review of that book is much more in terms of humor than travel writing.

47. *Round Table*, January 27, 1866. Reprinted in W. D. Howells, *Selected Literary Criticism,* vol. 1, *1859–1885,* edited by Ulrich Halfmann (Bloomington: Indiana University Press, 1993), 60–62.

48. Howells concludes his *Round Table* article by addressing the reasons critics tend to focus on faults rather than weaknesses. What is good in a book, he explains, is bound to be discovered by the public, but negatives might not be discovered: "[T]he only fear is lest faults shall be deliberately concealed and errors in thought, fact, style, or language passed by which will impede the progress of American literature" (Howells, *Selected Literary Criticism*, 62).

49. [William Dean Howells], 26, no. 154 (August 1870): 255.

50. [William Dean Howells], "Higginson's *Atlantic Essays,*" 28, no. 169 (November 1871): 639. Howells rarely took the time to dismiss a book outright as trash. In the review that directly preceded his first review of Mark Twain, Howells did savage William Hepworth Dixon's historical novel, *Her Majesty's Tower,* "as a model of nearly everything that is to be shunned in literature" and commended it to young writers as a guide of how not to write. 24, no. 146 (December 1869): 764.

51. [William Dean Howells], "Charles Reade's *Griffith Gaunt,*" 18, no. 110 (December 1866): 767–69.

52. [Albert Stuart Evans], "Reviews and Literary Notices," 18, no. 110 (December 1866): 770–71. The majority of the review is not about the poetical works but about the quality of the printing and illustrations of the editions.

53. Evans's other output seems to have been several travel books and articles, including *A la California. Sketches of Life in the Golden State* (San Francisco, 1873), possibly capitalizing on the market for travel accounts of California influenced by the success of Mark Twain's work, specifically *Roughing It* (1872).

54. [William Dean Howells], "A Poetical Lot," 24, no. 143 (September, 1869): 382.

55. Ibid., 386.

56. Sedgwick, *The "Atlantic Monthly,"* 120. Howells himself wrote only one essay in the magazine that can be classified as criticism, although it focused on the Boston theater season and the unfortunate, to his mind, advent of burlesque

theater. "The New Taste in Theatricals," 23, no. 139 (May 1869): 635–44. Higginson feuded with Howells in the early 1870s and subsequently published with other magazines, predicting Howells would fail due to "the lowering of the literary standard of the [*Atlantic*] (to meet a supposed popular demand) which has been so conspicuous under Mr. Howells." *Women's Journal*, February 14, 1874. Quoted in Sedgwick, The *"Atlantic Monthly,"* 134.

57. Helen McMahon, *Criticism of Fiction: A Study of Trends in the "Atlantic Monthly,"* 1857–1898 (New York: Bookman Associates, 1952), 11–14. McMahon focuses her study on thematic categories, collapsing chronology in a way that misses, in my view, the development of ideas over time.

58. For instance, consider Lowell's review of Josiah Holland's poem "Bitter-Sweet," in which he praised an approach that linked the "remoteness from ordinary life . . . essential in poetry" with an American subject, rather than foreign in time or place. "It is only here and there that a man is found," writes Lowell, "like Hawthorne, Judd, and Mr. Holland, who discovers or instinctively feels that this remoteness is attained, and attainable only, by lifting up and transfiguring the ordinary and familiar with the *mirage* of the ideal." 3, no. 19 (May 1859): 652.

59. Letter dated February 4, 1859. Quoted in Harriet Beecher Stowe, *Life of Harriet Beecher Stowe* (Houghton, Mifflin and Co., 1891), 333–34.

60. [James Russell Lowell], *"The Marble Faun,"* 5, no. 30 (April 1860): 509. Hawthorne is lacking this quality for Lowell, although his peculiar genius allows him to create "a so thorough conception of the world of moral realities that Art becomes the interpreter of something profounder than herself." But Hawthorne's genius is not put forward as a model of authorship.

61. Howells, *Literary Friends*, 118. As late as 1871, Howells praised the reprint of Sylvester Judd's 1845 romance, *Margaret. A Tale of Blight and Bloom*, as a masterpiece comparable to Hawthorne, Shakespeare, and Goethe, stating "it is not nature, but the love of nature; it is not reality, but truth." 27, no. 159 (January 1871): 144. Louis Budd makes this same point, largely in reference to Howells's later criticism, in "W.D. Howells' Defense of Romance," *PMLA* 67, no. 2 (March 1952): 32–42. Even the genre of memoir could be more or less realistic, as with Ralph Keeler's collection *Vagabond Adventures*, which Howells praised for its "truth of local color and the integrity of the hero's character," as well as for showing the true colors of poverty in order to "disenchant youth with adventure." 26, no. 158 (December 1870): 759. He does predict that the "truly American novel" would be a story of personal adventure.

62. [William Dean Howells], *"Pink and White Tyranny,"* 28, no. 167 (September 1871): 377.

63. Howells, *Literary Friends*, 117.

64. [William Dean Howells], *"Literature and its Professors,"* 20, no. 118 (August 1867): 254–55. Howells does agree with Purnell on what later came to be called "the intentional fallacy," stating that the critic should judge the author solely by his work, not by anything known about him. How well Howells was able to

follow this dictum, when reviewing close friends and mentors, is a matter of opinion.

65. Louis Budd only briefly mentions the years before 1875 in his article on the Howells-Twain friendship, speculating that Mark Twain "helped Howells resist the local push and pull of elitism." In "W. D. Howells and Mark Twain Judge Each Other 'Aright,'" *American Literary Realism* 38, no. 2 (January 1, 2006), 101. See also Edwin Cady, *The Road to Realism: The Early Years 1837–1885 of William Dean Howells* (Syracuse University Press, 1956), 162–69; Kenneth Eugene Eble, *Old Clemens and W. D. H.: The Story of a Remarkable Friendship* (Baton Rouge: Louisiana State University Press, 1985), 17–19; Leland Krauth, *Mark Twain & Company: Six Literary Relations* (Athens: University of Georgia Press, 2003), 51–55; and Susan Goodman and Carl Dawson, *William Dean Howells: A Writer's Life* (Berkeley: University of California Press, 2005), chapter 7, "His Mark Twain."-Peter Messent, *Mark Twain and Male Friendship: The Twichell, Howells, and Rogers Friendships* (New York: Oxford University Press, 2009), 108–10, recounts the divided opinions on whether Mark Twain was a realist or not, but ignores Mark Twain and Howells's writings before the 1880s.

66. For instance, Michael Davitt Bell focuses largely on Howells's views from the 1880s on defining his view of realism in *The Problem of American Realism: Studies in the Cultural History of a Literary Idea* (Chicago: University Of Chicago Press, 1993).

67. From June 1866–June 1871, Howells was mainly responsible for the review section of the magazine, writing approximately half of the reviews and selecting the reviewers for the remainder. He wrote 116 total reviews of 134 books. The reviews can be broken down into literary subjects (poems, prose, translations, travel, humor, criticism, literary memoir)—66 reviews of 85 books—and nonfiction (history, memoir, biography, current events, philosophy, religion, etc.): 50 reviews. As Jeffrey Alan Melton argues in regard to Mark Twain's early works, travel writing was viewed as a literary genre at this time, with literary figures writing much of the best-known travel writing: Bayard Taylor, Howells, Dickens, and Mark Twain himself. *Mark Twain, Travel Books, and Tourism: The Tide of a Great Popular Movement* (Tuscaloosa: University Alabama Press, 2002), 16–17.

68. Howells reviewed eleven books that can be classified as humor during his years as assistant editor, ranging from poetry to sketches to travel. These categories are imprecise, as distinctions between genres are not often precise. Most of the books were by frequent *Atlantic* contributors—Lowell, Edward E. Hale, Ralph Keeler. Charles Dudley Warner—and many of their pieces had appeared in the magazine. Two English humorists—Thackeray (a combined review of a novel and a five-volume collected works) and Leigh Hunt—were reviewed, along with two books of German-American dialect poetry by Charles Leland and Mark Twain's *The Innocents Abroad.*

69. [William Dean Howells], "*The Biglow Papers.* Second Series," 19, no. 111 (January 1867): 124 (subsequent quotes in this paragraph are from this page).

70. The attacks on Howells began as early as 1887, with Hjalamar Hjorth Boy-esen's essay, "Why We Have No Great Novelists?" *The Forum* 2 (February 1877): 615–22. Laurel T. Goldman states that this article initiated a line of attack that argued that Howells thwarted great art by censoring works to appeal to his readers, who were often imagined to be women. "A Different View of the Iron Madonna: William Dean Howells and His Magazine Readers," *The New England Quarterly* 50, no. 4 (December 1977), 563–86.

71. "Our novelists, therefore, concern themselves with the more smiling as-pects of life, which are the more American, and seek the universal in the individ-ual rather than the social interests." From "Dostoyevsky and the More Smiling Aspects of Life." *Harper's* 73 (1886): 641–42. While Howells's formulation comes from a later date, it is fair to categorize his view of satire in his years at the *Atlan-tic* as a type of "smiling satire."

72. [William Dean Howells], "*The Biglow Papers*. Second Series," 124.

73. Howells, *The Biglow Papers*, 123. (Further references to this review in the paragraph are from this page). In a February 1870 review of Thackeray's five-volume *Miscellanies,* Howells claims that Thackeray "set up many smaller wits in that sort of humor," but that even his second-rate work was better than most humorist's first rate (25, no. 148, 247).

74. [William Dean Howells], review of *Hans Breitmann's Ballads* in "A Poetical Lot," 24, no. 143 (September 1869): 387. One of Howells's funniest reviews, the review of five books of "poetastry" (as opposed to poetry) begins by considering an older school of "inhuman" criticism that would have, necessarily but horribly, leapt on such a "succulent heap" of "rhymesters . . . whose bones were crunched and whose struggles were derided before a sickened and brutalized audience!" Instead, the reader may hear a "blow perhaps, and a faint cry," before the "critic will immediately come forward again with a pleasant, reassuring smile, and go on with his general remarks upon the science of aesthetics" (382). This is one of the few reviews by Howells written in a humorous voice.

75. Ibid., 388. He answers: "We have reserved till now, in reply to this ques-tion, a confession for which the reader will have been prepared by the foregoing observations:—*We don't know.*"

76. [William Dean Howells], "*If, Yes, and Perhaps: Four Possibilities and Six Ex-aggerations, with some Bits of Fact,*" 22, no. 133 (November 1868): 634.

77. Howells, "A Poetical Lot," 387. [William Dean Howells], "*The Biglow Papers.* Second Series," 125.

78. [William Dean Howells], "*The Innocents Abroad*," 24, no. 146 (December 1869): 764. Kamatschatka (now Kamatchka) is a peninsula in eastern Russia, which had a port prominent in Alaska's exploration. Howells, "*The Innocents Abroad,*" 765.

79. Howells writes: "As Mr. Clements [*sic*] writes of his experiences, we imag-ine he would talk of them; and very amusing talk it would be: often not at all

fine in matter or manner, but full of touches of humor,—which if not delicate are nearly always easy,—and having a base of excellent sense and good feeling." Ibid., 765-66

80. Ibid., 766.

81. [William Dean Howells], "*Roughing It*," *Atlantic Monthly* 29, no. 176 (June 1872), 754–55. Here Howells spells "Clemens" correctly in the review, referring to the author as such, although the citation lists the author as "Mark Twain (Samuel T. Clemens)." The book is reviewed in a composite review of eight books: a book of verse and a book of tales by Bayard Taylor, three books of poetry, a history of missionaries in the western U.S., and a biography of the politician John J. Crittendon. In his review of Holmes's third book of "Table-Talk," Howells wrote of Holmes's approach in terms of a unique individual voice that reflected the lives of others through knowing himself keenly. Holmes's creation of a central character, often humorous but also philosophical and poetic, was similar to the character of "Mark Twain" in his books of travel/memoir, although Howells's critique of Mark Twain was more critical than his unstinting praise of Holmes, not surprisingly. See "Recent Literature," 30, no. 82 (December 1872): 745–46.

82. [William Dean Howells], "Saunterings," 30, no. 178 (August 1872): 242. [William Dean Howells], "*Backlog Studies*," 31, no. 186 (April 1873): 495. [William Dean Howells], "Warner's *Baddeck*," 33, no. 200 (June 1874): 748. Howells was occasionally referred to as a humorist in the instrumental sense, as in a review of his first travel book in the January 1868 *North American Review*: "[H]e takes them as a man of the world, who is not a little a moralist,—a gentle moralist, a good deal a humorist, and most of all a poet," 106 (January 1868): 316.

83. [William Dean Howells?], "*South Sea Idylls*," 32, no. 194 (December 1873): 740–46. No author was listed for this review in the *Atlantic Index* published in 1889. See "Making of America: Atlantic Index," http://digital.library.cornell.edu/cgi/t/text/pageviewer-idx?c=atla;cc=atla;rgn=full%20text;idno=atla0ind-1;didno=atla0ind1;view=image;seq=00011;node=atla0ind-1%3A1 "*South Sea Idylls*," 740. Subsequent quotes on this page from this source.

84. The "Californians of occasion" were Clemens (then in Hartford), Harte and Charles Webb (then in New York), and Stoddard and Prentice Mulford (then in England). None of these, Howells points out, were "sons of the red soil and blue sky," which allowed them to be "conscious of their California, and view it objectively" as what it truly is: "a stupendous joke, of which he is an amusing part," "*South Sea Idylls*," 740. Webb published *The Californian* and Mark Twain's first book of sketches, *The Celebrated Jumping of Calaveras County* (1867). Mulford was a New Yorker who lived in California from 1856–1872. He then returned to New York to work as a humorist.

85. See especially Bell, *The Problem of American Realism*, esp. Part One.

86. "Little" in both senses, it seems. James rarely mentioned Mark Twain and vice versa. In a review of a book on Luther, Milton, and Goethe, James

offhandedly swiped at Mark Twain, writing: "In the day of Mark Twain there is no harm in being reminded that the absence of drollery may, at a stretch, be compensated by the presence of sublimity." From *The Nation*, February 18, 1875, quoted in Harold Bloom, *Mark Twain* (New York: Chelsea House Publications, 2008), 112. Clemens only mentioned James occasionally, as when he tried to get Howells to help with a scheme to write a round-robin novel with Howells, Aldrich, Lowell, Holmes, Trobridge, Warner, and James in 1876. The scheme was never consummated. SLC to William Dean Howells, 12 Oct 1876, Hartford, Conn. MTHL 1:160. In a letter from July 21, 1885, Clemens dismissed three of Howells's favorite authors—Eliot, Hawthorne, and James—writing of James: "And as for the Bostonians, I would rather be damned to John Bunyan's heaven than read that." SLC to William D. Howells, 21 July 1885, Elmira, N.Y.

87. Sedgwick, *The "Atlantic Monthly,"* 139. [William Dean Howells], "James's *Passionate Pilgrim*," 35, no. 210 (April 1875): 490, 493–94. While Howells would consistently promote James, he wrote only this one review of his fiction.

88. Howells, *Literary Friends*, 292. See also Kaplan, *Mr. Clemens and Mark Twain*, 130. SLC to John Henry Riley, 3 March 1871, Buffalo, N.Y. (*UCCL 00582*), n. 6. 1995, 2007. Letters 4:337–40. See editorial note #6 for more on Harte's reputation and journey east.

89. For his lavish pay, Harte produced little of note in the *Atlantic*, and his reputation in America declined, even though his reputation in Europe was maintained during his career and his established place in American letters continued well after his death. Gary Scharnhorst's "Whatever Happened to Bret Harte?" in Quirk and Scharnhorst, eds., *American Realism and the Canon* (Newark: University of Delaware Press, 1994) takes up the question of Harte's reputation and canonization. Even though his early stories and poems marked the height of his reputation, he continued to write until his death in 1902. Through the first half of the twentieth century, Harte's works were highly anthologized. Scharnhorst traces his decline to two factors—New Critics who attacked his writing as sentimental, and Twain scholars who attacked the writer in comparison to Mark Twain, who continually and savagely attacked him following their falling out in 1877. Harte had thus fallen out of favor so much so as to be excluded from all the major anthologies of literature, which Scharnhorst attributes to his position as a white male, despite the fact of his immense popularity, his progressive politics, and the general rehabilitation of sentimental fiction as part of the canon.

90. [William Dean Howells], "Harte's *Luck of Roaring Camp*," 25, no. 151 (May 1870): 633–635.

91. William Dean Howells, *My Mark Twain: Reminiscences and Criticisms* (New York: Harper and Brothers, 1910), 6–7. Clemens's letter to Livy sets the date of the lunch, and the commentary provides more details: SLC to OLC, 1 Nov 1871, Boston, Mass. (*UCCL 00669*), n. 1. 1995, 2007. Letters 4:484–86. The feud seems to have stemmed from the circumstances of Harte's review of

The Innocents Abroad for the *Overland Monthly* (January 1870). Harte had had to purchase a copy, as Mark Twain's West Coast representative—Hubert H. Bancroft—had failed to deliver a copy to Harte, causing a rift. Clemens did not seem to find Harte's criticism of the book offensive, as far as existing evidence shows. In a letter to Charles Henry Webb, Clemens explained that he was glad to see Harte's career soaring, despite their being "off," and explained that the book snafu had caused Harte to send "the most daintily contemptuous & insulting letter you ever read—& what I want to know, is, where I was to blame? How's that?" Unfortunately, Harte's letter has not been found. See letter and notes at SLC to Charles Henry Webb, 26 Nov 1870, Buffalo, N.Y. (*UCCL 00544*). Letters 4:247–50.

92. Howells, *My Mark Twain*, 46.

93. Kaplan, *Mr. Clemens and Mark Twain*, 91. SLC to Olivia L. Langdon, 14 Jan 1869, Davenport, Iowa (*UCCL 00232*), n. 8. Letters 3:42. Fairbanks's letter does not survive.

94. Mrs. Thomas Bailey (Lilian) Aldrich, *Crowding Memories: Autobiography* (Boston: Houghton Mifflin, 1920), 128–29.

95. Ibid., 131–32.

96. Mary Thacher Higginson, *Thomas Wentworth Higginson: The Story of His Life* (Boston: Houghton Mifflin Co., 1914), 259–60. The memoir continues: "But he had no wine at his table and that seemed to make the grace a genuine thing. This hasty estimate of the popular humorist was a passing one, and the acquaintance developed into a cordial friendship."

Chapter Four

1. SLC to William Dean Howells, 22–29? May 1872, Elmira, N.Y. (*UCCL 00754*). Letters 5:95–96.

2. Fishkin, *Was Huck Black?* Howells, *My Mark Twain*, 3. Howells remembered this letter as being in response to his review of *The Innocents Abroad*. But Howells's modesty was not prudish, at least in retrospect, but almost awestruck by Mark Twain's power of language:

> Throughout my long acquaintance with him his graphic touch was always allowing itself a freedom which I cannot bring my fainter pencil to illustrate. He had the Southwestern, the Lincolnian, the Elizabethan breadth of parlance, which I suppose one ought not to call coarse without calling one's self prudish; and I was often hiding away in discreet holes and corners the letters in which he had loosed his bold fancy to stoop on rank suggestion; I could not bear to burn them, and I could not, after the first reading, quite bear to look at them. I shall best give my feeling on this point by saying that in it he was Shakespearian, or if his ghost will not suffer me the word, then he was Baconian. (3–4)

3. New York *Tribune*, June 10, 1872.

4. SLC to Louise Chandler Moulton, 18 June 1872, Hartford, Conn. (*UCCL 00757*), Letters 5:108–9.

5. Frank Luther Mott, "'The Galaxy': An Important American Magazine," *The Sewanee Review* 36, no. 1 (January 1928): 86–103. *Nation*, April 26, 1866, 534–35. Robert Scholnick, "'The Galaxy' and American Democratic Culture, 1866–1878," *Journal of American Studies* 16, no. 1 (April, 1982): 75.

6. SLC to Elisha Bliss, Jr., 11 March 1870, Buffalo, N.Y. (*UCCL 00443*). Letters 4:90–91. Not all reviewers found Mark Twain's work to be of the high quality of the magazine. One magazine wrote: "The Galaxy continues its brilliancy. . . . Whether Mark Twain is a star of a nebula, is doubtful. His 'Memoranda' shine with a sort of diffused light, sometimes a little obscure, and then again with the star-like sparkle" (*Massachusetts Teacher and Journal of Home and School Education* 23, no. 12 [December 1870]: 455).

7. "Editor's Table" *Maine Farmer* 39 (December 17, 1870): 2. Circulation figures are from Mott, *A History of American Magazines,* 3:101. The circulation of the *Atlantic* was approximately 35,000 at this time. By 1878, when the magazine was subsumed into the *Atlantic Monthly*, the circulation had decreased to approximately 7,000. Although Mott does not address the reasons for this decline, the magazine's abandonment of illustration in 1872 reflects Mott's argument about the decline in circulation of the *Atlantic* at the same time.

8. Other newspapers and magazines that published "The Facts Concerning the Great Beef Contract" include *Southern Planter and Farmer* (1867–1881) 4, no. 9 (September 1870): 556; Auburn (N.Y.) *Bulletin*, May 9, 1870; (Central City, Colo.) *City Register*, May 11, 1870; Chicago *Tribune*, April 24, 1870; Hartford *Courant*, Apr 23, 1870; Huntingdon (Penn.) *Globe*, June 28, 1870; Boston *Daily Evening Transcript*, April 16, 1870.

9. *The Aldine: A Typographic Art Journal* 4 (April 1871), 52. The biography read, in part: "I was born November 30th, 1935. I continue to live just the same. Thus narrow, confined, and trivial, is the history of the common human life!—that part of it, at least, which it is proper to thrust in the face of the public. And thus little and insignificant, in print, becomes this life of mine, which to me has always seemed so filled with vast personal events and tremendous consequences. . . ."

10. Mark Twain's pieces in the *Galaxy* ran from May 1870 (9, no. 5) to April 1871 (11, no. 4). Citations will be given to month and year.

11. As an illustration of the ways Mark Twain's column circulated in a larger periodical realm, the next month's column contains Mark Twain's explanation of how he had borrowed the conclusion of the story, been accused of plagiarism in a Philadelphia paper, and then accuses the party of being a known literary plagiarist. He chooses not to name the party so as to not provide him enough fame to start up a career:

> I do not print this party's name, because, knowing as I do upon what
> an exceedingly slender capital of merit, fame, or public invitation, two

or three of the most widely popular lecturers of the day, of both sexes, got a foothold upon the rostrum, I might thus help to pave the way for him to transfer the report of somebody's speech from the papers to his portfolio, and step into the lecture arena upon a sudden and comfortable income of ten or fifteen thousand dollars a season. I cannot take this person's evidence. Will the party from whom he pilfered the nitro-glycerine idea please send me a copy of the paper in which it first appeared, and with the date of the paper intact? I shall now soon find out who really invented the exploded boy.

"A LITERARY 'OLD OFFENDER' IN COURT WITH SUSPICIOUS PROPERTY IN HIS POSSESSION," June 1870.

12. For instance, in December 1870, Mark Twain commented on a joke sent to him from a New York reporter, who tells of a subscription canvasser who attempted to sell *The Innocents Abroad* to a New England clergyman. The reverend found the idea of Mark Twain weeping at the Tomb of Adam too absurd to bear, calling him "the great sniveling, overgrown calf!"

13. Such as the petrified man discovered in the Sierra Nevadas who is literally thumbing his nose at the reader, from the Virginia City *Territorial Enterprise*, October 4, 1862. Michelson discusses this hoax in *Mark Twain on the Loose*, 14–18. See also Cox, *Mark Twain: The Fate of Humor*, 14–16.

14. James Cook, *The Arts of Deception: Playing with Fraud in the Age of Barnum* (Cambridge: Harvard University Press, 2001), 26. Paine, *Mark Twain, a Biography*, 410.

15. Jacob Brackman, *The Put-on: Modern Fooling and Modern Mistrust* (Chicago: Henry Regnery and Company, 1967), 48.

16. Michelson, *Mark Twain on the Loose*, 9.

17. Brackman, *The Put-on*, 89.

18. Boston *Advertiser*, Thursday, November 17, 1870. Ibid., Thursday, November 24, 1870.

19. SLC to Francis P. Church, 23 Dec 1870, Buffalo, N.Y. (*UCCL 02786*). Letters 4:283–5.

20. Quoted in Letters 4:284.

21. "How a Humorist Uses Humor," *The Phrenological Journal of Science and Health* 52, no. 60 (January 1871): 60. The quote continues, ". . . not always, it is true, for their humor, but for their entertaining and instructive qualities."

22. On Mark Twain's career at the Buffalo *Express*, see Mark Twain, *Mark Twain at the Buffalo Express*, edited by Joseph B. McCullough and Janice McIntire-Strasburg (DeKalb: Northern Illinois University Press, 1999), esp. xxxiii–xiv. Eighteen pieces appeared in both the *Galaxy* and the *Express*. SLC to Orion Clemens, 11 and 13 March 1871, Buffalo, N.Y. (*UCCL 00587*). Letters 4:349.

23. SLC to Elisha Bliss, Jr., 13 Oct 1870, Buffalo, N.Y. (*UCCL 00511*). 1995, 2007. Letters 4:209–10. See n. 3 for information on Josh Billings. The 1871

almanac received a single order of 100,000 copies, which was the largest single order of a book in American history. SLC to Elisha Bliss, Jr., 26 Oct 1870, Buffalo, N.Y. (*UCCL 00514*). Letters 4:212–4.

24. SLC to John Henry Riley, 3 March 1871, Buffalo, N.Y. (*UCCL 00582*). Letters 4:338.

25. *The Bethelehem Daily Times*, October 17, 1871. This and subsequent reviews are from Stephen Railton, "*Roughing It* on the Road," http://etext.lib.virginia.edu/railton/roughingit/lecture/7172tourhp.html

26. Lorch, *The Trouble Begins at Eight*, 115. Clemens requested a number of conditions from his agent, James Redpath: lectures on main rail lines, quality hotel accommodations, no church venues, and no lectures in Buffalo or Jamestown, New York. He believed that people did not like to laugh in church, and both Buffalo and Jamestown were places where he had conflicts with the lyceum committees. He was booked into several churches. SLC to Mary Mason Fairbanks, 13 Feb 1872, Hartford, Conn. (*UCCL 00725*). Letters 5:43–5. While scholars have argued that Clemens undertook lecture tours for financial reasons, Paul Fatout argues that he made relatively little on his lecture tours and instead toured because he enjoyed performing and the attention it brought him. Paul Fatout, *Mark Twain on the Lecture Circuit* (Bloomington: Indiana University Press, 1960), 149–50.

27. It is unclear how he settled on Artemus Ward as a topic. Writing to Livy after the third night, he wrote of his predicament: "Bless your dear heart, I shall reach Washington tomorrow night, & then for two days & nights I shall work like a beaver on my new lecture. How I ever came to get up such a mess of rubbish as this & imagine it *good*, is too many for me." SLC to OLC, 18 Oct 1871, Wilkes-Barre, Pa. (*UCCL 00664*). Letters 4:475–76.

28. SLC to OLC, 31 Oct 1871, Milford, Mass. (*UCCL 00668*). Letters 4:483–84.

29. In larger cities, Mark Twain's financial and popular success was clear. But when he ventured into towns, especially smaller towns, where the purpose of the local lyceum was based on older models, he faced the prospect of a prejudged failure for people who disliked the presence of humorists and other "mere" entertainers on the platform.

30. In some instances, I have selected quotes from numerous newspaper sources from Stephen Railton's archive without individual attribution. Where a significant amount is quoted, the individual paper is cited.

31. *The Press* (Philadelphia), November 21, 1871.

32. Exeter (N.H.) *News-Letter*, November 13, 1871.

33. Chicago *Evening Post*, December 19, 1871.

34. "Mark Twain's Lecture at Lincoln Hall," *The Daily Morning Chronicle*, October 24, 1871.

35. SLC to OLC, 15 Nov 1871, Haverhill, Mass. (*UCCL 00674*). Letters 4:491–92.

36. Washington *Evening Star*, October 24, 1871.

37. SLC to OLC, 27 Nov 1871, Bennington, Vt. (*UCCL 00680*). Letters 4:498–500.

38. "Mark Twain," *The Press* (Philadelphia), November 21, 1871. The only note of seriousness was Mark Twain's description of Artemus Ward's death, along with his occasional inclusion of a poem on Artemus Ward, at the end of the lecture, which ended the lecture on a somber note and did little to balance its overall tone. See Appendix B for a copy of the poem.

39. "Mark Twain." Philadelphia *Inquirer*, November 21, 1871.

40. "Mark Twain," Brooklyn *Eagle*, November 22, 1871.

41. Hughes, "Telling Laughter," 49. The value of laughter was not necessarily cross-cultural. See Paul Johnson, *Humorists: From Hogarth to Noel Coward* (New York: Harper, 2010), xv–xvii. Johson largely ignores American humor in the nineteenth century.

42. "Mark Twain's Lecture," Hartford *Daily Courant*, November 9, 1871. SLC to OLC, 1 Nov 1871, Boston, Mass. (*UCCL 00669*). Letters 4:484–6.

43. "Artemus Ward, The Humorist," Boston *Daily Evening Journal*, November 2, 1871. Echoing the Boston paper, *The Daily Eastern* of Portland noted that "even the man who is not in the habit of laughing, and who thinks such things silly and undignified, was caught laughing several times, but stopped it when discovered." "Artemus Ward," November 17, 1871.

44. "Mark Ward on Artemus Twain," Exeter (N.H.) *News-Letter*, November 13, 1871. "Mark Twain's Lecture," Manchester *Daily Union*, November 15, 1871. "The Lecture Season. Mark Twain in the Lyceum Course," Worcester *Gazette*, November 10, 1871.

45. "Mark Twain's Lecture," Malden (N.H.) *Messenger*, November 11, 1871.

46. "Mark Twain at Steinway Hall," New York *Tribune*, January 25, 1872.

47. Logansport, Indiana, *Sun*, January 4, 1872. While exceptions exist, generally, lyceum courses in smaller towns continued to maintain their original purpose—instruction and uplift—while larger cities judged the performances more in terms of entertainment.

48. This did not keep James Redpath and lyceum committees from asking Mark Twain to perform, nor did it keep Mark Twain from public speaking. The venue largely switched to the after-dinner speech, a genre of which Mark Twain was an acknowledged master and will be examined in more detail in chapter 7.

49. SLC (Samuel Langhorne Clemens). 1872. "An Appeal from One That Is Persecuted," MS of nineteen pages, written ca. 18 July 1872. W. T. H. Howe Collection. Manuscript at NYPL. Quoted in Letters 5:123–24. For unknown reasons, Mark Twain never published "An Appeal from One That Is Persecuted," although the withering attack on Holland would probably never have made it past Olivia Clemens, Howells, or any respectable editor, personal or professional.

50. Pasted into "An Appeal from One That Is Persecuted," from *Scribner's Monthly* (February 1872).

51. It might be worth noting that the following article in Holland's column points to his much broader view of social development. In "Our President," Holland speaks of a coming "golden age" that all Christian people expect to occur, a time in which the president of the United States will rule wisely over a nation in which "the brain and heart of Christendom will be Christianized. There will be reverence for worth in the popular heart, and an Christian nation will have none but a Christian ruler." Clearly, times have changed.

52. See Lorch, *The Trouble Begins at Eight*, 232; Fatout, *Mark Twain on the Lecture Circuit*, 100, 102, 142–43.

53. Mott, *A History of American Magazines,* 3:466–67. Holland promoted the importance of illustration from the beginning, and the magazine pioneered several printing techniques and gained a reputation as the best printed magazine. Mott attributes much of *Scribner's* popularity, as well as the decline of the *Atlantic*, to the illustrations or lack thereof.

54. Many of these essays were collected into two versions of a book, *Every-Day Topics: A Book of Briefs*, 1st ed. (New York: Scribner, Armstrong and Company, 1876), and *Every-Day Topics, A Book of Briefs,* 2nd ed. (New York: Charles Scribner's Sons, 1882).

55. Harry Houston Peckham, *Josiah Gilbert Holland in Relation to His Times* (Philadelphia: University of Pennsylvania Press, 1940), 37.

56. Edward Eggleston, "Josiah Gilbert Holland." *The Century Magazine* 23, no. 2 (December 1881): 165.

57. Quoted in Peckham, *Josiah Gilbert Holland in Relation to His Times*, v. To attest to his popularity, Peckham notes that Holland's 1872 lyceum speech in Columbus, Ohio, received twice the newspaper coverage as Mark Twain's speech six nights earlier had (52–53). *The Century Magazine* 23, no. 1 (Winter, 2002): 1-53. Eggleston, "Josiah Gilbert Holland," 167. Despite his apparent popularity, Holland has been forgotten. The only scholarly article found on him after 1940 is on his biography of Lincoln. See Allen C. Guelzo, "Holland's Informants: The Construction of Josiah Holland's 'Life of Abraham Lincoln'," *Journal of the Abraham Lincoln Association*.

58. Peckham, *Josiah Gilbert Holland*, 56. Holland's explanation of his lyceum schedule is from Josiah Gilbert Holland, *Plain Talks on Familiar Subjects: A Series of Popular Lectures* (New York: Charles Scribner's Sons, 1865), 12.

59. Mrs. H. M. Plunkett, *Josiah Gilbert Holland* (New York: Charles Scribner's Sons, 1894), 101. "Communications," *Century Magazine*, October 24, 1881.

60. Timothy Titcomb, esq. [Josiah Holland], *Titcomb's Letters to Young People, Single and Married.* (New York: C. Scribner, 1866), 135.

61. [Josiah Gilbert Holland], "Triflers on the Platform." *Scribner's Monthly* (February 1872), 489. Subsequent references to Holland's *Scribner's* columns will be given parenthetically with date and year.

62. [Josiah Holland], "The Popular Lecture." 15, no. 89 (March 1865): 367. As one of the most popular lyceum speakers of the era, Holland's economic interest in maintaining his type of lecturing as *the* type of lyceum style might be apparent. More importantly, Holland consistently framed the lyceum as a key component of moral literary culture.

63. Ibid., 369–70, 366. The cultural import of the earnest lecturer is summarized at the end of the article in clearly hyperbolic Christian rhetoric:

> When the cloud which now envelops the country shall gather up its sulphurous folds and roll away, tinted in its retiring by the smile of God beaming from a calm sky upon a nation redeemed to freedom and justice, and the historian, in the light of that smile, shall trace home to their fountains the streams of influence and power which will then join to form the river of the national life, he will find one, starting far inland among the mountains, longer than the rest and mightier than most, and will recognize it as the confluent outpouring of living, Christian speech, from ten thousand lecture-platforms, on which free men stood and vindicated the right of man to freedom. (370)

64. By December 1875, Holland seemed resigned that the popular lecture had succumbed to amusement over culture, and he recommended that young people form reading clubs "with culture in view as the great ultimate end." Again, he belabors the "literary trifler" who had degraded the platform to "meet the tastes of the vulgar crowd" ("Winter Amusements" *Scribner's Monthly*, 273–75).

65. SLC (Samuel Langhorne Clemens). 1872. "An Appeal from One That Is Persecuted," W. T. H. Howe Collection. Manuscript at NYPL. Quoted in Letters 5:123–24. Holland wrote Mark Twain on April 28, 1875, asking him to contribute an article to *Scribner's* on Hartford, writing, "It is not often that a writer is invited into our magazine, with his place of residence. But a jewel in its appropriate setting is so much more desirable!" (UCLC 31933). He responded: "I thank you very much for the compliment of the offer, but I am not a capable person for the work, even if I had the time. There is probably not another man in Connecticut who is so besottedly ignorant of Hartford as I am. I have lived here 3 or 4 years (in the fringe of the city) & I only go down town when it is necessary to abuse my publisher." SLC to Josiah G. Holland, 29 Apr 1875, Hartford, Conn. (*UCCL 01266*). Letters 6:470–71.

66. See *Every-Day Topics*, 19, 32, 40. Holland does not ignore the economics of reward, ending "The Rewards of Literary Labor" with the concession that authors do, in fact, need monetary as well as spiritual rewards for their labor, which would be accomplished by the creation of an international copyright, a point that Mark Twain and Holland would have agreed upon (33–34). Peckham, *Josiah Gilbert Holland in Relation to His Times*, 69–81, for the reputation of American and British authors in Holland's eyes.

67. Holland, *Every-Day Topics,* 1st. ed., 71–72. This article did not appear in *Scribner's*.

68. Peckham, *Josiah Gilbert Holland in Relation to His Times*, 62, 108. Some critics lightly mocked his moralistic versifying and speechifying by referring to Holland as "the American Tupper," referring undoubtedly to the British moralist whose verse was popular but of poor quality, although the other meanings of "tupper" may have added another layer of obscene fun to the nickname. Hjalamar Hjorth Boyesen later wrote that this nickname "rankled his gentle mind." See "American Literary Criticism and Its Value," 462. Reprinted in Charles Wells Moulton, ed. *Library of Literary Criticism of English and American Authors: 1875–1890* (New York: Henry Malkan, Publisher, 1910), 333. Lowell's review was less patronizing than Peckham seems to think in its praise of Holland's use of the ordinary and familiar as his theme. *Atlantic Monthly* 3, no. 19 (May 1859): 651–52. Peckham notes that most magazines of the era "poked fun" at the works of Holland (82).

69. [William Dean Howells], "Concerning Timothy Titcomb," *Nation* (November 23, 1865), in *Selected Literary Criticism,* 1:52–54. The review ends with a statement on popularity that is worth considering:

> "It may be objected to the censure of such writers as Mr. Holland that, granting their popularity to be factitious, they do a great deal of good to commonplace people; that they reach a large class of hearers and readers who could not be reached by men of genius; that they act as smoked glasses for the weak vision that would else turn away from thought, or, regarding her, would be dazzled to death by her aspect. We desire to give Mr. Holland's admirers and apologists the benefit of this doubt" (54).

70. [William Dean Howells], "*Kathrina,*' *Atlantic Monthly* 20, no. 122 (December 1867): 763–64. A review of *Every-Day Topics* in the *Atlantic Monthly* faulted Holland for his lack of style and taste, despite his evident desire to do good, concluding: "To our thinking, he has qualities better than taste alone, but they are warped and injured by the absence of taste. And his mistakes, though serious, might be passed over but for his influence with the thousands of readers who, he reminds us, are familiar with his editorials." [George Lathrop], 38, no. 229 (November 1876): 632.

71. In "Fiction" (March 1878), Holland again took aim at critics who focus on "fiction for the sake of art" and defines "the supreme uses of fiction, viz., the organization into attractive, artistic forms of the most valuable truths as they relate to the characters and lives and histories of men." "Vulgarity in Fiction and On the Stage," May 1879. Holland did not argue that only pure or good characters should be portrayed in literature. In fact, he acknowledged that the "bad" character is often far more interesting than the good. An artistically good novel, he argues, must end with the reader horrified and disgusted with vice, rather than in love with it. Thus, vice, vulgarity, and other depravity is material for the novel, being part of reality, but the novelist is bound to portray it "not as a

moralist, but as a literary man . . . in its proper relation to the scheme of things which he finds established, as it concerns the happiness and well-being of the individual and society." "Literary Materials and Tools," December 1878.

72. Shakespeare, Scott, Thackeray, and Dickens are his examples of virile authors. He dismisses the work of Poe, Thoreau, and Whitman in "Our Garnered Names" (October 1878) and Whitman in detail in "Is It Poetry?" (May 1876).

73. "Triflers on the Platform," February 1872. Holland's views were echoed in certain portions of the religious press, such as the article "The Religious Newspaper as an Evangelizing Agency" by the Rev. C. D. Helmer, who wrote of the need for Christian editors to provide something "that may satisfy the natural craving which otherwise, in its greediness will swallow the indigestible diet of Josh Billings or Mark Twain." Chicago *Advance* 8 (June 3, 1875): 682. Quoted in Durant Da Ponte, "American Periodical Criticism of Mark Twain, 1869–1917" (Ph.D. diss., University of Maryland, 1953), 12. Criticism of Mark Twain in religious periodicals varied in similar degrees as in the secular press.

74. [William Dean Howells], *"Roughing It,"* 29, no. 176 (June 1872): 755.

75. Newspapers of the time gossiped about the sales of the book, but I have found no reference to his children at this time.

76. Kaplan, *Mr. Clemens and Mark Twain*, 141.

77. New York *Tribune*, March 10, 1873.

78. Ibid., March 11, 1873.

79. Ibid., March 12, 1873.

Chapter Five

1. Aaron Watson, *The Savage Club: A Medley of History, Anecdote, and Reminiscence. With a Chapter by Mark Twain* (London: T. Fisher Unwin, 1907), 131–33.

2. SLC to OLC, 28 Sept 1872, London, England (*UCCL 00815*). Letters 5:183.

3. See Rodney, "Mark Twain in England," 39; Howard Baetzhold, *Mark Twain and John Bull: The British Connection* (Bloomington: Indiana University Press, 1970), 10; and Dennis Welland, *Mark Twain in England* (Atlantic Highlands, N.J.: Humanities Press, 1978), chapter 2, "Establishing a Reputation," 30–46.

4. The piece "Artemus Ward Sees the Prince of Wales" was published in the London *Daily News* in October 1860 and appeared in at least two other papers that year. For example, see *Freeman's Journal and Daily Commercial Advertiser*, Dublin, Ireland, Thursday, December 24, 1863.

5. On his illness, see London *Daily News*, February 26, 1864, and *Birmingham Daily Post*, June 13, 1864. *Penny Illustrated Paper*, October 28, 1865. Artemus Ward's book warranted its own ad and got top billing in a separate ad with the listed authors. The publisher, S. O. Beeton, sanctimoniously declaimed its piracy: "NOTICE—All these books are published without the authority of the several

American authors. They are printed without their leave or sanction, precisely as Mr. Beeton's books and Englishmen's works generally are reprinted in America without their leave or sanction. "*Artemus Ward. His Book,*" *Birmingham Daily Post*, Monday, June 13, 1864.

6. Artemus Ward's name was posted in large letters over the magazine's office door. In response, he wrote to a friend:

> This is the proudest moment of my life. To have been as well appreciated here as at home; to have written for the oldest comic journal in the English language, received mention with Hook, Jerrold and Hood, and to have my picture and my pseudonym as common in London as in New York, is enough for
>
> —Yours Truly, A. Ward."

Quoted in Seitz, *Artemus Ward (Charles Farrar Browne)*, 190.

7. London *Spectator*, November 24, 1866. Quoted in Seitz, *Artemus Ward (Charles Farrar Browne)*, 198–99. Conway quoted in ibid., 210.

8. Newspaper pieces started with "Mark Twain's 'Day at Niagra'" in Liverpool *Mercury*, October 16, 1869, from the Buffalo *Express* and the "Map of Paris" in *The Derby Mercury*, October 19, 1870. "Cannibalism in the Cars," *The Broadway: A London Magazine* 1 (Sept. 1868): 138. The *Broadway* was published by Routledge, who had brought out the first edition of Mark Twain's Jumping Frog sketches. Clemens later recalled being paid $12.50 per magazine page, and Welland speculates that this was the start of his formal link to Routledge as publisher (*Mark Twain in England*, 16). The magazine aimed to capitalize on the popularity in England (as in America) of monthly literary magazines in the 1860s, while specifically aiming for a transatlantic audience. An ad in the *Athenaeum* trumpeted: "It is our earnest desire that Britannia should shake hands with Columbia intellectually, and that both should shake hands with us financially" (August 10, 1867, 189). The magazine featured at this time an article by Moncure Conway reflecting the critical consensus that American literature had been largely imitative but that "the first results have already appeared in the raising of a distinctively American standard of literature" ("Three American Poets," 240). He cites the poets John A. Dorgan, Myron Benton, and William Dean Howells.

9. *Fun* quoted in Welland, *Mark Twain in England*, 16. For sales figures, see ibid., 15–16, 232. Clemens admitted in December 1870 that when he published the *Jumping Frog* book in 1867, he "fully expected" it to "sell 50,000 copies & it only sold 4,000," the latter being an accurate approximation of its actual sale in the United States by that time. SLC to Francis S. Drake, 26 Dec 70, Letters 4:287–88. The publishing details are not essential. Each house—Routledge and Hotten (later Chatto & Windus)—both pirated and claimed to work with Mark Twain, although he worked directly with Routledge for a time and then published later with Chatto & Windus, after the death of Hotten, with whom he had a public feud. See Welland, *Mark Twain in England*, 15–32.

10. Figures from Welland, *Mark Twain in England*, Appendix 1, 231. *The Examiner* (London), September 10, 1870. For the review of the second volume, see ibid., September 18, 1870.

11. *Athenaeum*, September 24, 1870, 395–96. Reprinted under the title "An English Estimate of American Humor" in the Chicago *Tribune*, October 16, 1870, with the comment that the reviewer, "in his puzzled condition of mind arrives at conclusions which are almost as good as if Mark Twain himself had written them." *The Saturday Review* (London), October 8, 1870. Reprinted as "Mark Twain and the Saturday Review" in the Chicago *Tribune*, December 18, 1870.

12. I have found no newspaper mention of the incident at the time. Mark Twain's review from the *Galaxy* was pirated into a collection of sketches in 1871. *The Era* (London), in reviewing the book, states that readers may be pleased at "an article in which some of his comicalities are treated seriously by an English journal of high standing." May 19, 1872.

13. *The Examiner*, September 10, 1870; *Lloyd's Weekly Newspaper*, September 18, 1870; *The Era* (London), November 6, 1870; and the reviews from the *Athenaeum* and *Saturday Review* cited above.

14. *The Piccadilly Annual of Entertaining Literature: Retrospective and Contemporary* (London: John Camden Hotten, [1870]). Mark Twain's pieces were "The Story of the Good Little Boy," "Wit-Inspirations of Two Year Olds," "The Late Benjamin Franklin," and "Higgins." Harte was represented by "That Heathen Chinee" and "Dickens in Camp." James Camden Hotten soon thereafter pirated that collection, printing 5,000 copies (Welland, *Mark Twain in England*, 233). On Hotten, see Welland, *Mark Twain in England*, 16–18.

15. *Eye-Openers: Good Things, Immensely Funny Sayings & Stories that will bring a smile upon the gruffest countenance* and *Screamers: A Gathering of Scraps of Humour, Delicious Bits, and Short Stories. Practical Jokes with Artemus Ward* included six more pieces from the *Galaxy*, as well as "Mark Twain's First Interview with Artemus Ward" and an introductory piece on Mark Twain's introduction to *Artemus Ward in Virginia City*. All thirty-eight pieces in the collection are unattributed, except where the title refers to Mark Twain or Artemus Ward. Copy of *The Choice Humorous Works of Mark Twain* held in the Elmira College Mark Twain Archive. Clemens marked page xxxii of the introductory sketch in which Hotten discussed the positive reception of *The Innocents Abroad* in England and xxxvii, which discussed the positive reception of Mark Twain in England for his lectures.

16. March 30, 1872. Also reviewed positively in *The Era* (London), May 19, 1872.

17. *The Spectator*, May 18, 1872, 633–34. The reviewer also praises "The Bad Little Boy who did not come to Grief" and "The late Benjamin Franklin." They find the satire on the *Saturday Review* to be pointless "because the *Saturday Review* cannot be charged with stupidity," although they quote at length from the

piece. The review also calls "How I edited a Paper" and "An Enigma" "extravagant rubbish," while saying the only piece that truly fails is the first essay on nursery rhymes, which was attributed to "Carl Byng"—a pseudonym Hotten believed to belong to Clemens.

18. Welland, *Mark Twain in England*, 30–31.

19. "American Humour," *The Graphic* (London), Saturday, April 1, 1871.

20. The paper describes it as "A Quaker suddenly flinging a cracker at you— that was the character of the surprise, and it always startled and delighted one."

21. Only in the works of Hawthorne, and in *Uncle Tom's Cabin*, are found the beginning of a national, rather than local, literature, according to Margaret Oliphant, "American Books," *Blackwood's Edinburgh Magazine* 110 (October 1871): 422, 430, 427.

22. Ibid. Oliphant, as much if not more than Howells at this point, seems to have an editorial ethos based on a type of realism, praising Harte: "Nothing can be more rude or less lovely than the life here portrayed—nothing can be more simply true than the narrative. Here nothing is hidden, nothing excluded, no false gloss put on; and yet the heart is touched, the mind elevated by the strange tale" (427). Later, she praises both the "true human nature" of the characters (427) and lines "full of truth and nature" (429). For "music-hall public," see 435. For another article praising Harte, see "A New Transatlantic Genius," *Chamber's Journal*. Reprinted in *Transatlantic Magazine, containing Choice Selections from Current Foreign Literature* 4 (July–December 1871), 103–9.

23. Welland, *Mark Twain in England*, 51-52. SLC to OLC, 25 Oct 1872, London, England (*UCCL 00823*). Letters 5:201.

24. Robert Weisbruch, *Atlantic Double-Cross: American Literature and British Influence in the Age of Emerson* (Chicago: University of Chicago Press, 1986), xv–xvii, 12.

25. Ibid.

26. Weisbruch argues that the reaction was one-sided, with Americans being much more focused on British influence than vice versa. The responses tended to be virulent, consisting "in angry refutation, destructive undoing by parody, deliberately wild misreading, and outright competition" (Ibid., 20).

27. Ibid., 32. Gardner argues that Mark Twain's aggressive denial of Dickens is more a reaction to the cult of Boz he experienced through his brother Orion, through Bret Harte in San Francisco, and through Livy and her genteel circle on the East Coast (97). I am arguing, through Weisbruch, that it might also be a matter of his own version of the Transatlantic literary struggle to establish an American humor not indebted to Dickens. Joseph H. Gardner, "Mark Twain and Dickens," *PMLA* 84, no. 1 (January 1969): 94–95.

28. Quoted in Weisbruch, *Atlantic Double-Cross*, 32, from a letter to the *Alta California*, February 5, 1868.

29. "Mark Twain at the Whitefriar's Club," Birmingham *Daily Post*, September 9, 1872. A notice of this speech appeared in numerous American newspapers,

including the *Little Rock Daily Republican,* September 25, 1872; the *Boston Daily Advertiser*, September 25, 1872; the *Yankton Press* (Yankton, S.D.), October 9, 1872; the *Cleveland Herald*, October 15, 1872; and the *Owyhee Avalanche* (Ruby City, Idaho), November 2, 1872.

30. "Dined into Dyspepsia. Mark Twain's Sad Experience in England—Too Many Dinners." Copied by the Milwaukie *Sentinel*, December 10, 1872. The joke that "British hospitality has always had something deadly about it" might not be terribly funny to Artemus Ward.

31. Conway notes that Artemus Ward's English success was untainted by his unpopular views on slavery, which had hurt his reputation in America, and "his exuberant genius to flowered in its fulness [*sic*]." "Mark Twain." Copied by the Cleveland *Herald*, October 19, 1872. Some version of this report was printed by the Boston *Daily Advertiser*, October 19, 1872, the *Daily Central City Register* (Colo.), October 30, 1872.

32. "Mark Twain, one of America's best humorists," *The Penny Illustrated Paper and Illustrated Times,* September 28, 1872. "Two American Humorists—Hans Brietmann and Mark Twain," *The Graphic*, October 5, 1872.

33. Letter to *Daily News*, quoted in Hampshire *Telegraph and Sussex Chronicle*, November 9, 1872; see also Welland, *Mark Twain in England*, 53. Somewhat surprisingly, this line became a "circulating simile," being quoted in newspaper stories unrelated to Mark Twain, as in the Belfast *Newsletter* of February 6, 1873: "A degree of accuracy is required, which, as Mark Twain would say, trammels the lecturer." See also *The Examiner* of November 30, 1872, which considers a critic's lack of knowledge on a subject to be "like the opinions of Mr. Mark Twain's proposed lectures. . . ."

34. London *Figaro*, May 16, (1872). This article is clipped into Mark Twain's scrapbook from his 1873 trip and dated 1873 (Scrapbook #12, page 1, article 6).

35. Roy Morris notes that Mark Twain and Bierce had a somewhat adversarial relationship, stemming in part from a banquet at the Whitefriars Club at which Bierce was the guest of honor but was upstaged by Mark Twain, whose deadpan response to Bierce's speech caused the audience to stay quiet, disturbing Bierce to the extent that he never again spoke in public (not to mention Joaquin Miller—dressed in buckskin and sombrero, he ate a live goldfish whole and announced "a wonderful appetizer!" before storming out). See Morris, *Ambrose Bierce: Alone in Bad Company* (New York: Crown Publishers, Inc. 1995), 142–43.

36. "Mark Twain," *Once a Week* 259 (December 14, 1872): 521.

37. John C. Dent, "America and her Literature," *Temple Bar* 37 (March 1873), 396-97.

38. Ibid., 399–404. Whitman is praised above the others, and although not a humorist per se, Dent notes that a correspondent declared Whitman "to be more absurd than Artemus Ward, without any self-consciousness of his buffoonery." Dent also cites Leland (who is not truly national in his scope), John Hay (who

relies on "too much irreverence"), and Dan DeQuille as writers who may join the ranks of truly American authors with time (404).

39. Ibid., 402–3.

40. New York *Tribune*, June 11, 1873.

41. Affidavit reprinted in *The Publisher's Weekly*, June 7, 1873, 554–55. Mark Twain, *Mark Twain's Notebooks & Journals, 1877–1883*, vol. 2 of *The Mark Twain Papers*, edited by Frederick Anderson (Berkeley: University of California Press, 1975), 271.

42. *The Ipswich Journal*, April 29, 1873. Paine, *Mark Twain, a Biography*, 1:496.

43. Following the death of King Kamehameha in December 1872, interest in the Hawai'ian Islands was renewed in both countries, both of which were vying for political and commercial interest in the islands. Clemens claimed to be "unspeakable sick" of the Sandwich Islands lecture. He may also have had an eye toward increasing sales of *Roughing It*. SLC to OLC, 6 Dec 1873, London, England (*UCCL 00992*), n. 1. Letters 5:494–95.

44. Fred Lorch, "Mark Twain's Public Lectures in England in 1873," *American Literature* 29, no. 3 (November 1857): 298–99. Lorch writes that the English knew Mark Twain through *The Innocents Abroad* and one book of humorous tales, whereas the bibliographic record shows the English public knew far more about him than that.

45. London *Standard*, October 9, 1873.

46. Paine, *Mark Twain, a Biography*, 1:489. Undated letter cited in SLC to Charles Warren Stoddard, 19 Oct 1873, London, England (*UCCL 00976*). Letters 5:458. Moncure Conway, *Autobiography and Reminiscences* (Boston: Houghton, Mifflin, and Company, 1904), 142–43. Conway recalls that Clemens stated he would lecture on the Sandwich Islands but, in the style of Artemus Ward, instead went through a series of digressions on his Western travels—thus conflating the two lectures Mark Twain delivered in England. Lorch, *The Trouble Begins at Eight*, 139.

47. SLC to OLC, 13 and 15 Dec 1873, London, England (*UCCL 01004*). Letters 5:512–17. Despite his successes, Clemens still held a dislike for lecturing, again stating that he would retire from the "scaffold" permanently. SLC to George H. Fitzgibbon, 30 Dec 1873, London, England (*UCCL 01020*). Letters 5:539–41.

48. Charles Warren Stoddard, *Exits and Entrances: A Book of Essays and Sketches* (Freeport, N.Y.: Books for Libraries Press, 1963; orig., 1903), 67–68.

49. "'Mark Twain' as a Lecturer," *The Times of London*, October 14, 1873; "Mr. Mark Twain," *The Times of London*, December 12, 1873; "Mark Twain's Lecture," *The Era*, December 14, 1873.

50. "Mark Twain in Liverpool," unknown paper, October 21, 1873. Scrapbook #12, page 29, article 33. The Scrapbooks are found in the Mark Twain Papers at the University of California-Berkeley.

51. "Mark Twain's Lecture," October 14, 1873. Scrapbook #12, page 13, article 19.

52. "Mark Twain's Lecture, London *Observer*, October 19, 1873. Scrapbook #12, page 11, article 17.

53. There are eight scrapbooks from Mark Twain's second visit to England. The first (Notebook 11) was probably kept by Clemens and features fourteen pages of clippings, most notably an obituary of John Camden Hotten. Based on the pasting style, this was probably Sam Clemens's scrapbooking. Notebook #12 (MTP) is the collection of reviews of Mark Twain's lectures. Notebooks #13–18 are articles related to the Tichborne trial, then ongoing in London, in which an Australian imposter claimed to be the lost heir to a baronacy. He later used material from the case in *Following the Equator*.

54. Unknown source, no date. Scrapbook #12, page 1, article 8.

55. "'Mark Twain' as a Lecturer," *The Times of London*, October 14, 1873. Scrapbook #12, page 7, article 13. *London Cosmopolitan*, "Mark Twain as Lecturer," October 16, 1873, Scrapbook #12, page 19, article 25 (MTP).

56. Charles Warren Stoddard, "A Humorist Abroad," in *Exits and Entrances*, 63.

57. "'Mark Twain' as a Lecturer" *The Times of London*, October 14, 1873. *The Examiner*, October 18, 1873. Liverpool *Mercury*, October 21, 1873. Lorch notes that critics varied in their appreciation of Mark Twain's dialect ("Mark Twain's Public Lectures in England in 1873," 301).

58. "Mark Twain as Lecturer," London *Cosmopolitan*, October 16, 1873. Scrapbook #12, page 19, article 25. "Mark Twain on the Sandwich Islands," London *Standard*, October 14, 1873. Scrapbook #12, page 14, article 21. "Mark Twain's Lecture," London *Sportsman*, October 18, 1873. Scrapbook #12, page 15, article 22.

59. "Mark Twain on the Sandwich Islands," *The Illustrated Police News* (from *Daily News*), October 18, 1873. *The Graphic*, October 1873.

60. *The Graphic*, October 18, 1873. "Mark Twain on the Sandwichers," *The Penny Illustrated Paper and Illustrated Times*, October 18, 1873. *Lloyd's Weekly Newspaper*, in an article called "Mark Twain on Savages" (October 19, 1873), noted that Mark Twain's lectures differed from Artemus Ward's in sticking to the subject announced, unlike Artemus Ward's lectures, which relied on digressions as a main source of entertainment. This review also uses the phrase "mirth-moving" to describe Mark Twain's anecdotes—a phrase occasionally used in the reviews. "Mark Twain," unknown source. Scrapbook #12, page 1, article 7. "Mark Twain," *The Spectator*, October 18, 1873, 1302–3. London *Observer*, December 14, 1873.

61. Scrapbook #12, page 48, article 58.

62. "Mark Twain," London *Fun*, n.d. Scrapbook #12, page 10, article 14. Reprinted in Elmira *Times* according to pencil note in scrapbook.

63. All from Scrapbook #12: articles 19, 22, 60, and 33.

64. "Mark Twain on the Sandwich Islands," October 14, 1873. Scrapbook #12, page 15, article 21. "Mark Twain's Lecture on the Sandwich Islands," Liverpool *Journal*, October 23, 1873. Scrapbook #12, page 29, article 30.

65. German versions of *The Celebrated Jumping Frog of Calaveras County* and *Roughing It* appeared in 1874 and the first German criticism in 1875. J. C. B. Kinch notes that early German critics focused on Mark Twain's role as a humorist and author of children's books, often focusing on his coarseness. *Mark Twain's German Critical Reception, 1875–1986: An Annotated Bibliography* (Westport, Conn.: Greenwood Press, 1989), ix. See also Robert Rodney, *Mark Twain International: A Bibliography and Interpretation of His Worldwide Popularity* (Westport, Conn.: Greenwood Press, 1982).

66. Th. Bentzon, "Les Humoristes Américains: Mark Twain." Translated by Greg Robinson in Shelley Fisher Fishkin, ed., *The Mark Twain Anthology: Great Writers on His Life and Works* (New York: The Library of American, 2010), 25.

67. Ibid., 25.

68. James C. Austin, *American Humor in France: Two Centuries of French Criticism of the Comic Spirit in American Literature* (Ames: Iowa State University Press, 1978), 69–70. This is from the second part of the essay, published in August 1872.

69. Bentzon translated in Austin, *American Humor in France*, 70–71.

70. Mark K. Wilson, "Mr. Clemens and Madame Blanc: Mark Twain's First French Critic," *American Literature* 45, no. 4 (January 1974), 544.

71. Th. Bentzon, "Les Humoristes Américains: I. Mark Twain," *Revue des deux mondes,* 100 (July 15, 1872), 313. My translation of a portion not printed in *The Mark Twain Anthology*. Austin, *American Humor in France*, 70. He notes that this was written less than two years after the Prussian occupation of Paris.

72. Ibid. on Holmes. Lowell merits little attention in Austin. The implications of these facts—i.e., the translation of dialect vs. wit—is my supposition, not Austin's. Wilson, "Mr. Clemens and Madame Blan," 544. See also Austin, *American Humor in France*, 72–73.

73. Bentzon, "Les Humoristes Américains" (trans. Robinson), 26.

74. Bentzon "Les Humoristes Américains: I. Mark Twain," 335. My translation of a portion not printed in *The Mark Twain Anthology*, except for her appraisal of Mark Twain, which is from page 29. Bentzon cites the American style, language, and "often picturesque mixture of neologism, dialect and what the Americans often call *slang*." [English in original, trans. Robinson], 28.

75. Bentzon, "Les Humoristes Américains" (trans. Robinson), 29.

76. Bentzon, "Les Humoristes Américains: I. Mark Twain," 321. Again, my translation of a portion not printed in *The Mark Twain Anthology*.

77. Bentzon, "Les Humoristes Américains" (trans. Robinson), 27. Wilson notes the critic's consistent mistake in taking character for author, for reading "Mark Twain" as Samuel Clemens ("Mr. Clemens and Madame Blanc," 546), but he does not link Mark Twain's response to his pattern of satirizing critics who read him poorly. Instead, Wilson views the incident as one foundation of Mark Twain's long-term dislike of the French, which is undoubtedly also a factor. See 537–38 for this discussion.

78. SLC to OLC, 26 Apr 1873, Hartford, Conn. (*UCCL 00909*). Letters 5:357–59. "Mark Twain in the *Revue des Deux Mondes*," ns., nd. Scrapbook #9, Article 168. Pasted inside of back cover and unrelated to other contents.

79. Mark Twain, *Sketches, New and Old,* 1875 (New York: Oxford University Press, 1996), 29.

80. Wilson, "Mr. Clemens and Madame Blanc," 548.

81. Lilian Aldrich, *Crowding Memories: Autobiography.* (Boston: Houghton Mifflin, 1920), 230–31. Wilson, "Mr. Clemens and Madame Blanc," 555.

82. Quoted in ibid., 553.

83. Welland, *Mark Twain in England*, 50.

84. *Daily News*, October 17, 1873. Scrapbook #12, pages 3 & 5, article 9.

85. Turner was the penname of Oswald Crawfurd, a diplomat and minor author, who was the founder and editor of the *New Quarterly*. Matthew Freke Turner, "Artemus Ward and the Humorists of America." *The New Quarterly Magazine* 6 (April 1876), 199.

86. Ibid., 200.

87. Ibid., 205, 198.

88. Ibid., 205–6. He does argue that Artemus Ward's deserved place in American letters (in his eyes) is easier for British audiences, who enjoyed the "freshness and originality" of his work during his visit, than for Americans, who view him as a "low writer," largely due to his jarring joking about the Civil War. He summarizes: "So it is, I believe, that a people gifted with a very strong sense of humor, and possessing a very true literary judgment, have failed to appreciate a writer who in breadth, in insight, in perception and in expression is pre-eminent, and who is a true master of all that goes to make a great humorist" (206–7).

89. Turner, 208 (on Harte), 212 (on Mark Twain). Subsequent quotes in this paragraph are from these pages.

90. *Lloyd's Weekly Newspaper*, April 26, 1874, and June 14, 1874. The comments on American poets was in reference to a review of the *Transatlantic Magazine* (published in Philadelphia). This issue republished a lecture called "The Poet Longfellow" by James T. Fields, former editor of the *Atlantic Monthly*, which was originally given at the Girl's High Dchool in Boston, published in the New York *Tribune*, presumably republished in a British magazine, and then re-republished in the *Transatlantic*. This was probably the London-based *Transatlantic*, not the Philadelphia version, which reprinted articles from British magazines for an American audience, much like the magazine *Every Saturday*, which Fields had published along with the *Atlantic*. I have been unable to find the British magazine with Field's lecture.

91. Stephen, "Humour," 326, 319, 320.

92. Ibid., 324, 326.

93. [Leslie Stephen,], "Mr. Lowell's Poems," *Cornhill Magazine* 31 (January 1875), 66, 67, 69.

94. Howells, *My Mark Twain*, 46.

Chapter Six

1. Mark Twain and Charles Dudley Warner, *The Gilded Age*, 1873 (New York: Oxford University Press, 1996). Excerpted in: "Current Literature," *Galaxy* 17, no. 3 (March 1874), 428. Subsequent quotes are from this review.

2. Bryant Morey French argues that the book received more critical attention than any of his previous books, or any of the subsequent six books, in *Mark Twain and the Gilded Age: The Book That Named an Era* (Dallas: Southern Methodist University Press, 1965), 21.

3. Kaplan, *Mr. Clemens and Mark Twain*, 159.

4. [William Dean Howells], "Warner's *My Summer Garden*," *Atlantic Monthly* 27, no. 161 (March 1871), 397.

5. William Dean Howells, "The Man of Letters as a Man of Business," *Scribner's Magazine* 14, no. 4 (October 1893), 438.

6. The presence of the romantic subplots in the book may have been the authors' playing to a perceived audience, one made real every night as the authors read their day's work to their wives. Clemens wrote to Mrs. Fairbanks, another proxy for genteel and literate womanhood, of the process and its results, noting that the women "pleaded so long & vigorously for Warner's heroine, that yesterday Warner agreed to spare her life & let her marry—he meant to kill her. I killed my heroine as dead as mackerel yesterday (but Livy don't know it yet). . . ." SLC to Mary Mason Fairbanks, 16 Apr 1873, Hartford, Conn. (*UCCL 00900*). Letters 5:339–41.

7. SLC to Elisha Bliss, Jr., 26 Feb 1873, Hartford, Conn. (*UCCL 00876*). Letters 5:301.

8. Everett Emerson, *Mark Twain: A Literary Life* (Philadelphia: University of Pennsylvania Press, 2000), 83. Mark Twain, *The Adventures of Colonel Sellers*, edited by Charles Neider (New York: Doubleday & Company, Inc. 1965), xiii.

9. "Home and Foreign Notes," *Appleton's Journal of Literature, Science and Art* 9, no. 216 (May 10, 1873), 639.

10. Elmus Wicker, *Banking Panics of the Gilded Age* (New York: Cambridge University Press, 2000). For an example of the adoption of the term, see "The Gilded Age. Stripping Grantism of its Superficial Coating," the Galveston *Daily News*, March 8, 1876.

11. SLC to John Brown, 28 Feb 1874, Hartford, Conn. (*UCCL 01056*). Letters 6:53–57. The publisher had printed just over 35,000 copies at this point, sold for an average of $3.68 per book. This earned a royalty of $6,300, approximately $1,000 less than stated here.

12. "Literary Profits," Baltimore *Sun*, March 19, 1874. MTEB, 85. According to one inflation calculator, $15,000 would be just over $300,000 in 2013. http://www.westegg.com/inflation

13. SLC to Orion Clemens, 11 Aug 1872, New Saybrook, Conn. (*UCCL 00791*). Letters 5:143–46. On the importance of scrapbooks in American culture, see

Ellen Gruber Garvey, *Writing with Scissors: American Scrapbooks from the Civil War to the Harlem Renaissance* (New York: Oxford University Press, 2012).

14. See n. 4 of SLC to Orion Clemens, 11 Aug 1872, New Saybrook, Conn. (*UCCL 00791*). Letters 5:143–46.

15. The *Christian Secretary*'s first mention of Mark Twain was in the "Wit and Humor" column from July 20, 1876: "Mark Twain says: 'It is a blessed thing to live in a land of plenty when you have plenty of land.'" Their "review" of the *Scrap-book* notes: "The book opens well and preserves throughout the fresh crispness of the author's style. . . ." (May 31, 1877).

16. On Mark Twain interviews, see Gary Scharnhorst, ed., *Mark Twain: The Complete Interviews* (Tuscaloosa: University Alabama Press, 2006). On Mark Twain's letters to the editors, see Gary Scharnhorst, ed., *Mark Twain on Potholes and Politics: Letters to the Editor* (Columbia: University of Missouri Press, 2014).

17. Budd, *Our Mark Twain*, 73. Chapter 4—"The Mark Twain Mazurka"—is the key starting point for tackling the wide circulation of images, works, and meanings of Mark Twain. On the "sell," see Budd, 63.

18. Brooks, *The Ordeal of Mark Twain*, 45–46.

19. Howells, "The Man of Letters as a Man of Business," *Scribner's Magazine* 14, no. 4 (October 1893), 429–30. For Howells, post–Civil War America was a "nation of business men" and even the "high-cost man of letters" who had a national reputation had an income commensurate with a "rising young physician, known to a few people in a subordinate city" (431). Howells's insecurity is both palpable and humorous as he sums up the status of the man of letters:

> He must still have a low rank among practical people; and he will be regarded by the great mass of Americans as perhaps a little off, a little funny, a little soft!
>
> Perhaps not; and yet I would rather not have a consensus of public opinion on the question; I think I am more comfortable without it.

20. Ibid., 445. The re-inscribed idealism of the argument can be traced to Howells's increasingly socialist tendencies in the 1880s and 1890s. During the time Howells was at the *Atlantic*, it is fair to say that he was distinctly interested in the reading habits of the classes. Bell, *The Problem of American Realism*, 6.

21. He also notes that literary property lacked the same kind of protection from the law as other types of property, even with the current forty-two year term of copyright and new international copyright laws. He writes: "So long as this remains the case, we cannot expect the best business talent to go into literature, and the man of letters must keep his present low grade among business men" (Howells, "The Man of Letters as a Man of Business," 431).

22. Ibid., 432.

23. Ibid., 433.

24. Ibid., 433, 444.

25. In critiquing authors who come to popularity through book publishing, Howells makes a distinction between the cultural meaning of the two types of fiction and their audiences. For readers of low fiction (whom he calls "the masses"), books are a type of necessity, along with clothing, food, and shelter, but for "the classes," fiction is not a necessary commodity. He writes: "The sort of fiction which corresponds to the circus and the variety theatre in the show-business seems essential to the spiritual health of the masses, but the most cultivated of the classes can get on, from time to time, without an artistic novel." While he wishes to align the quality author with the masses, he acknowledges that the masses have little interest in "quality" fiction, and he cannot ultimately transcend the hierarchical definitions he sets up (Howells, "The Man of Letters as a Man of Business," 434).

26. Ibid., 434.

27. "Subscription Books," *Literary World* 5, no. 3 (August 1, 1874): 40.

28. "Mark Twain's Autobiography," *Literary World* 1, no. 11 (April 1, 1871): 165.

29. French, *Mark Twain and the Gilded Age*, 11. Twain signed off with the salutation: "Drooping now, under the solemn peacefulness, the general stagnation, the profound lethargy that broods over the land, I am Yrs truly, Sam'l L. Clemens (Mark Twain)." Twain, *Adventures of Colonel Sellers*, xxviii.

30. French, *Mark Twain and the Gilded Age*, 12.

31. SLC to Whitelaw Reid, 20 Apr 1873, Hartford, Conn. (*UCCL 00903*). Letters 5:346–50.

32. Clemens also included a clipping from Henry Ward Beecher's newspaper, the *Christian Union*, from April 16. The article was a puff of the latest book by Edward Eggleston, who was an editor on the paper. The article notes that Eggleston's literary reputation had increased greatly in the past year. The article reads, in part, "Their success is the success of genuineness. They smack of the soil of Hoosier Dom *as truly as the first "Biglow Papers" do of the soil of Yankeedom.*" (emphasis by Clemens). He also underlined the words *ten thousand copies* and *insatiable curiosity* and noted, "Lowell & Eggleston on the same level!" See n. 8 of SLC to Whitelaw Reid, 20 Apr 1873, Hartford, Conn. (*UCCL 00903*), Letters 5:346–50.

33. New York *Tribune*, April 23, 1873.

34. SLC to Whitelaw Reid, 22 Apr 1873, Hartford, Conn. (*UCCL 00906*). Letters 5:352–3. Reid apparently telegraphed the notice to Mark Twain, or the letter is misdated.

35. He writes: "Why of *course* the Tribune would make Hartford talk,—& the rest of the country, for that matter—else why would I be so solicitous about what the Tribune said? That is just the point—I want the Tribune to say it *right* & say it powerful—& then I will answer for the consequences."

36. Auburn *Daily News*, April 25, 1873. For more reactions, see French, *Mark Twain and the Gilded Age*, 13–14.

37. *American Monthly* 1 (September, 1873): 97. Quoted in MTEB, 84.

38. Stephen Railton notes that the American Publishing Company issued two versions of the prospectus, one in November 1871 and one in January 1872. The first was missing the "List of Illustrations" and the "Contents" listing. http://etext.virginia.edu/railton/roughingit/prospect/riproshp.html To his brother, Orion, he wrote: "I mean to make it a good one in spite of everything—then the illustrations will do the rest. When the prospectus is out I believe Bliss will sell 50,000 copies before the book need be actually issued." SLC to Orion and Mary E. (Mollie) Clemens, 21 June 1871, Elmira, N.Y. (*UCCL 00619*). Letters 4:411.

39. For information on the illustration of this book, specifically of Mark Twain's image within it, see David, *Mark Twain and His Illustrators*, Chapter 3, esp. 110–11, 114–18, and 120.

40. MTEB—*The Innocents Abroad* had 1,231 prospectuses printed (39) and *Roughing It*, 1,637 (63).

41. Ibid., 85.

42. Ibid., 82.

43. For sales figures, see ibid., 287, n. 93. SLC to Charles Dudley Warner, 17 May 1873, SS Batavia (*UCCL 00917*). Letters 5:367. This incident ended Clemens's relations with Reid and the *Tribune* for at least a dozen years and made Reid an object of his wrath. He later learned of Reid's version of their kerfuffle—that he disliked House and would not work with him—and took a different view of the situation. See French, *Mark Twain and the Gilded Age*, 15 n. 69. The same letter was filled with business matters, including notes on the dramatization of the book and Mark Twain's lawsuit against the publisher discussed in the previous chapter:

> "I shall probably write some letters for Herald & possibly for Advertiser.
>
> We saw Boucicault, who, in some minor respects, is an ass. If you describe the outside of your trunk to him he can tell you what it's got in it.
>
> I will not consent to his having more than one-third for dramatising the book.
>
> Yesterday I sued a New York fraud for $20,000 damages for violating my copyright."

44. French, *Mark Twain and the Gilded Age*, 14.

45. Letter from Howells to Warner, December 28, 1873. In William Dean Howells, *W. D. Howells, Selected Letters*, vol. 2, *1873–1881*, edited by George Arms and Christoph K. Lohmann (Boston: Twayne Publishers, 1979), 46.

46. MTHL 1:12–13. In the *Gilded Age*, for example, Laura Hawkins refuses such fare as *The Pirate's Doom, or the Last of the Buccaneers* in favor of Howells's *Venetian Life*. In *A Chance Acquaintance*, a character fond of Shakespeare and *Don Quixote* states that he had read one book of travel—the *Innocents Abroad*—and that "he need never read anything else about the countries of which it treated" (MHTL, 13).

47. *North American Review* 183, no. 601 (October 19, 1906), 705–16. Also in *Mark Twain's Own Autobiography: The Chapters from the "North American Review,"* edited by Michael J. Kiskis (Madison: The University of Wisconsin Press, 1990), 36–37.

48. Twain, *Autobiography* (February 7, 1906), 339–40, 339.

49. Ibid., 340.

50. French claims that the book was more widely reviewed than any other of Mark Twain's books during the timeframe of this book (*Mark Twain and the Gilded Age*, 21). Budd lists only fifty-one reviews, plus four papers that probably reviewed the book, but which haven't been found. This is approximately half the reviews of the *Innocents Abroad* but double that of *Roughing It*. See Budd.

51. New York *Daily Graphic*, December 23, 1873. Quoted in full in Twain, *Adventures of Colonel Sellers*, xxiv–xxv.

52. Quoted in French, *Mark Twain and the Gilded Age*, 20. Budd, 117–19. This statement is prefaced by a less flattering appraisal: "As an exposition of individual human character . . . and of the intertangle of passion, motive and external incident of which life is made up, *The Gilded Age* is entitled to no rank at all; but as a clever though rude. . . ." (Budd, 119).

53. "K. ," "The Gilded Age," Hartford *Courant*, December 23, 1873. The review ends: "Apparently after satirizing the shams of the age, they considered their work accomplished and decided to let their characters with a few exceptions take care of themselves. But there is enough consistency and interest to the plot taken in connection with its reality and humor, to make the book one which will be read, discussed, and remembered." From Louis J. Budd Archive at Elmira College.

54. Mark Twain and Charles Dudley Warner, *The Gilded Age* (1873) (New York: Oxford University Press, 1996), 243.

55. Ibid., 249.

56. "New Publications," Boston *Daily Globe*, December 25, 1873. Springfield *Republican*, "Literature and Music," December 24, 1873, in Budd, 123.

57. San Francisco *Daily Evening Bulletin*, March 21, 1874. San Francisco *Chronicle*, March 22, 1874. The *Democrat* also argues that the negative reviews are a symptom of the book "scalping" the friends and backers of certain prominent newspapers undertook. The *Christian Union* mentioned the book in an advice column from March 4, 1874, in which a questioner asked if the burlesque prayer in the book, intended to incite laughter, was pernicious. The commenter answered no, that genuine religion was not damaged by a "good-natured laugh" at its eccentric followers, and that "the very use of a sense of the ludicrous is to discriminate between what is outward, accidental, and discordant, and what is real and substantial" (9, no. 9, 172). The review from *Hearth and Home* is printed in French, *Mark Twain and the Gilded Age*, 20–21: "There is fun enough in the book to make the fortune of half a dozen novels, but clearly it was written not in fun but very much in earnest."

58. MTEB, 81, n. 26.

59. Linda Morris, "American Satire: Beginnings through Mark Twain," in *Companion to Satire*, edited by Ruben Quintero (Oxford: Wiley-Blackwell, 2007), 377.

60. Gregg Camfield, *The Oxford Companion to Mark Twain* (Oxford: Oxford University Press, 2003), 532–33.

61. "The Gilded Age," *Old and New* 3, no. 9 (March 1874): 387. *Old and New*, edited by frequent *Atlantic* contributor Edward Everett Hale, was folded into *Scribner's Monthly* in 1876.

62. *Independent*, January 1, 1874. Quoted in French, *Mark Twain and the Gilded Age*, 19.

63. Boston *Daily Advertiser*, January 10, 1874. The paper had published a notice on April 28, 1873, of the book, noting: "Their taste in some things are congenial; both have a fondness for humor, though not exactly of the same class; both *are* humorous, in different views, but if they are alike in anything it is in their dislike of sham."

64. "Literary," *Appleton's Journal of Literature, Science and Art* 11, no. 25 (January 10, 1874): 59.

65. New York *Morning Herald*, "Literary Matters," December 26, 1873. From Louis J. Budd Archive at Elmira College. The Philadelphia *Press* of January 13, 1874, referred to the book as "more of a true American novel than any story produced for a long time" and pronounced Warner "the most genuine humorist of the two." The Baltimore *Sun* praised the book as well: "The name of Mark Twain as a humorist is familiar to American ears. There is a mine of sparkling entertainment in this volume. It is filled with descriptions of people and things which he has seen with his own eyes, and relates in his own style." As if Warner did not exist, the review ends by claiming the book would "add new reputation to the author." From Louis J. Budd Archive at Elmira College.

66. "Literary News," *Literary World* 4, no. 8 (January 1, 1874), 126.

67. "New Publications," San Francisco *Daily Evening Bulletin*, March 7, 1874. On the other hand, the *Sun* of Baltimore held that the book would "add new reputation to the author." "Mark Twain's New Book," *Sun*, February 6, 1874. The review mentions Warner but acts as if Mark Twain were the only author.

68. Twain, *Autobiography of Mark Twain*, 339, note on 584–85. See also French, *Mark Twain and the Gilded Age*, 16–17.

69. "The Twain-Warner Novel," Chicago *Tribune*, February 1, 1874.

70. French, *Mark Twain and the Gilded Age*, 18–9.

71. Ibid., 19.

72. Welland, *Mark Twain in England*, 43.

73. London *Graphic*, February 28, 1874. Quoted in French, *Mark Twain and the Gilded Age*, 23. Welland, *Mark Twain in England*, 45–46. The book also circulated into English colonies, as it was advertised for sale in the *Times of India* (July 20, 1874) and reviewed in Australia, which noted that the book would have the positive effect of tempering adulation of America: "As a novel, we think the

Gilded Age is far from being a success, but as a picture, we fear too true a one, of American life, manners, and character, it is full of interest and value. . . . There is in these colonies a tendency to excessive admiration of American institutions and to an imitation of American ways. If the Gilded Age opens people's eyes to the dangers of any such tendency it will do a great deal of good." Melbourne *Evening Post*, August 19, 1874. The Otaga *Witness*, also from Australia, wondered if the book was not an elaborate jest, but deciding to take the book seriously, found it to be a statement that the American model is "hopelessly corrupt." February 6, 1875.

74. Quoted in Welland, *Mark Twain in England*, 42. This preface was reprinted in the Hartford *Daily Courant*, January 5, 1874. "Novels of the Week," 24, no. 11 (January 10, 1874): 53, in Budd, 131–32.

75. *Appleton's Journal* also reported a transatlantic review, from the *Saturday Review*, which advised those "who wish to retain their admiration of Mark Twain unalloyed, had better leave 'The Gilded Age' alone." 11, no. 261 (March 21, 1874): 379. The London *Spectator*, no. 2386 (March 21, 1874): 371–72, wrote a lengthy review, noting the national dimensions, praising certain aspects of the book, especially Col. Sellers, critiquing aspects such as the profanity of some of the humor, and ending with the assessment that "there is great talent—there is something almost like genius—in the book, but a better effect might have been produced by a more careful elaboration of half the materials." From Louis J. Budd Archive at Elmira College.

76. "L'Age Dore en Amerique. Translated for the Courant," Hartford *Daily Courant*, April 16, 1875.

77. Reprinted in the Chicago *Daily Tribune*, April 5, 1874, and Laramie *Sentinel*, April 4, 1874. Little else was said about the book, although the Chicago *Tribune* took one more swipe at the text in September, jokingly hoping that a reported Mark Twain impostor had written the *Gilded Age*, and suggesting the real Mark Twain find the villain and pin the "monstrous sketch" on him. Chicago *Daily Tribune*, September 11, 1874.

78. SLC to William Dean Howells, 24 March 1880, Hartford, Conn. MTHL 1: 294–95.

79. For his part, Howells was skeptical of the effect of reviews: "Advertising will not avail, and reviewing is notoriously futile. If the book does not strike the popular fancy, or deal with some universal interest . . . the drums and cymbals shall be beaten in vain." This statement may indicate Howells's artistic romanticism, just as much as his editorial skepticism, reflecting his view that commercial and artistic concerns were separate—or at least should be. Howells, "Man of Letters," 437.

80. The most recent year available. See http://www.westegg.com/inflation

81. Phillip Walker, "Mark Twain, Playwright," *Educational Theatre Journal* 8, no. 3 (October, 1956): 185. Mark Twain's plays include *Ah Sin* (co-written with

Bret Harte and produced in 1877), *Cap'n Simon Wheeler, The Amateur Detective* (written 1877, not produced), *Col. Sellers As A Scientist* (a collaboration with Howells in 1883), *The American Claimant* (Mark Twain's revision of the previous, produced in 1887), adaptations of *Tom Sawyer* and *The Prince and the Pauper* (not produced), and *Is He Dead?* (published in 2002 and produced in 2007). See Walker, "Mark Twain, Playwright," 185–93. See also Mark Twain, *Is He Dead? A Comedy in Three Acts*, edited by Shelley Fisher Fishkin (Berkeley: University of California Press, 2006).

82. San Francisco *Figaro* quoted in the New York *Daily Tribune*, August 5, 1874. This article was a preview of the upcoming New York version, which starred Raymond but was significantly different than the California version. See French, *Mark Twain and the Gilded Age*, 245.

83. Gregg Camfield holds that Clemens and Warner drifted apart due to Warner's discomfort with Howells's literary realism in the 1880s, as well as the possibility of Clemens's disapproval of Warner's alleged mistress, in whose house he died in 1900. Camfield, *The Oxford Companion to Mark Twain*, 640.

84. Twain, *Autobiography* (2010), 207. French, *Mark Twain and the Gilded Age*, 249, n. 60. This reminiscence took place after the two men had fallen out over business and Mark Twain had consigned him to the permanent status of enemy.

85. SLC to William Dean Howells, 20 Sept 1874, Hartford, Conn. MTHL 1: 26–7. To William C. Brownell, city editor of the New York *World*, he put it more bluntly: ". . . it isn't a good play. It's a bad play, a damned bad play. I couldn't write a good play. But it has a good character, and that character is the best I can do." Quoted in Walker, "Mark Twain, Playwright," 186.

86. While a full examination of the reviews of the play, both its first run and subsequent tours, is out of the scope of this chapter, it should be noted that the initial reviews seem to have established the major themes of subsequent reviews. The play had gone through previews in Buffalo, and the reviewer there had also hit the highpoints of subsequent criticism:

"As a production of Mark Twain, the humorist, the play will undoubtedly be received by the public with considerable favor. There are numerous good things in it, and the character of *Colonel Sellers* is particularly strong in a humorous sense. The language of the part indicates plainly the originality and wit of the famous humorist. Dramatically the play is weak and unsatisfactory." "The 'Gilded Age,'" The Buffalo *Express*, September 8, 1874, 1. New York *Tribune*, September 18, 1874.

87. "Mark Twain's New Play," Hartford *Daily Courant*, September 18, 1874. Echoing these reviews, but framing them within a previous dislike of the novel, the Chicago *Tribune* held that Raymond had redeemed the "hopelessly stupid" novel through his portrayal of the character, writing, "He is said to have contributed a very unique and valuable creation to the American stage, to have restrained the eccentricity of the character within possible limits, and kept the

audience in a continual state of boisterous merriment." "Mark Twain, The Playwright," Chicago *Daily Tribune*, September 27, 1874.

88. Quoted in Hartford *Daily Courant*, September 19, 1874.

89. Howells, *My Mark Twain*, 22–23.

90. [William Dean Howells], "Drama," *Atlantic Monthly* 35, no. 212 (June 1875): 749–51. Howells compares Raymond's performance to other great character actors, including Sothern (of "Lord Drundreary") and Jefferson (of "Rip Van Winkle"), as such "[l]ike them he does not merely represent; he becomes, he impersonates, the character he plays" (749).

91. Ibid., 750.

92. Reprinted in the *Constitution* (Atlanta), November 28, 1875, and *Inter Ocean* (Chicago), December 2, 1875.

93. MTEB, 71.

94. SLC to Mary Mason Fairbanks, 25 Feb 1874, Hartford, Conn. (*UCCL 01055*). Letters 6:46–50. SLC and OLC to John Brown, 4 Sept 1874, Elmira, N.Y. (*UCCL 01122*). Letters 6:221–27.

95. Howells, *My Mark Twain*, 8.

96. SLC to William Dean Howells, 20 March 1874, Hartford, Conn. (*UCCL 02468*). MTHL 1:15–6. SLC to Elisha Bliss, Jr., 21 Oct 1874, Hartford, Conn. (*UCCL 11532*). Letters 6:260.

97. Gary Scharnhorst, *Bret Harte: Opening the American Literary West* (Norman: University of Oklahoma Press, 2000), 106–7. Harte quoted in Scharnhorst, *Bret Harte*, 110.

98. One article in the *Atlantic Monthly*, of unknown authorship, asked, "[W]ho is a representative American? Is he an Adams, a Jefferson, a Lincoln, a Barnum, a Butler, or a Fisk? Are Longfellow and Lowell, Hawthorne and Emerson, our representative literary men, or Bret Harte and his followers?" Unattributed, "What Is an American?" *Atlantic Monthly* 35, no. 211 (May 1875), 562.

99. Patrick D. Morrow, *Bret Harte: Literary Critic* (Bowling Green: Bowling Green State University Popular Press, 1979), 95–96. Morrow notes that Harte's reputation led Redpath to drop Harte's lecture fee for 1874 and book him into more midwestern and southern towns (96).

100. Bret Francis Harte, "American Humor," in *The Lectures of Bret Harte*, compiled by Charles Meeker Kozlay (Brooklyn: Charles Meeker Kozlay, 1909), 19. Harte lost all copies of the speech, which was partially reconstructed by Kozlay from newspaper sources.

101. He notes that the first Yankee humorist was Judge Haliburton, an English officer in Canada who created Sam Slick of Slickville. On the other hand, American humorists such as Irving used British models or were distinctly regional, such as Lowell. Only in the South and West did two traditions of humor develop that are "characteristic of our lives and habits as a people" (Harte, "American Humor," 22).

102. Ibid., 25–26. Harte spoke further of Artemus Ward:

His success in England was a surprise to even his most ardent admirers. The personality of the man as a lecturer had much to do with his
reception in England. He captivated average Englishmen by his cool
disregard of them, his quiet audacity, and his complete ignoring of the
traditions of the lecture–room. . . . It was after the war. Englishmen
were inclined to be friendly, and their good feeling had taken the form
which their good feeling takes toward everything that is not British—
condescending patronage" (26).

103. Ibid., 27.

104. Ibid., 28.

105. George T. Ferris, "Mark Twain," *Appleton's Journal* 12, no. 276 (July 4, 1874), 15.

106. Ibid., 16, 17.

107. Ibid., 17.

108. Ibid., 17.

109. "American Humorists, With Portraits," *The Phrenological Journal of Science and Health* 59, no. 6 (December 1874), 45.

110. Mark Twain was one of the representatives of "Humorists" in the game, which also included cards for poets, journalists, historians, etc. James Russell Lowell was the example of poet, along with Whittier, Holmes, and Longfellow

111. Aldrich, *Crowding Memories*, 146, 147–48.

112. Mark Twain, *Mark Twain in Eruption*, edited by Bernard DeVoto (New York: Harper and Brothers, 1940), 293–95.

113. Aldrich, *Crowding Memories*, 156. Lillian Aldrich reads Livy's influence as positive, unlike many later scholars who viewed her as a censoring agent of genteel society. She writes: "But always to help and sustain her was the knowledge of his idolizing love for her. He soon learned to realize her rare literary perception, and always, as far as she was able, she encouraged him to give only his best to the world" (156). The second quote is from ibid., 151. Her description of Mark Twain (aged 31 or 32) is instructive: ". . . a sparely built man of medium height; a finely shaped, classical head, covered with thick, shaggy, red-colored hair; a mustache of the same tawny hue; eyes which glimmered, keen and twinkling, under overhanging, bushy eyebrows, each hair of which was ruffled itself, taking part with unwarrantable intrusion in Mr. Clemens's moods, were they grave or gray" (150).

114. Ibid., 174. Kaplan, *Mr. Clemens and Mark Twain*, 174. Howells, *My Mark Twain*, 5.

115. Aldrich, *Crowding Memories*, 160. Fishkin, *Was Huck Black*, 111–13.

116. SLC to Lilian Aldrich, 9 March 1874, Hartford, Conn. (*UCCL 10843*). Letters 6:63–4.

Chapter Seven

1. William D. Howells to SLC, 3 Dec 1874, (UCLC 32073) MTHL 1:49–50. SLC to William Dean Howells, 8 Dec 1874, Hartford, Conn. (*UCCL 0527*). Letters 6:305.

2. Kaplan, *Mr. Clemens and Mark Twain*, 209. Twain, *Mark Twain Speaking*, edited by Fatout, 110–15.

3. Mark Twain, "A True Story, Repeated Word for Word as I Heard It," *Atlantic Monthly* 34, no. 205 (November 1874): 591–94. Also published in *Once a Week*. 1, no. 12. (November 21, 1874): 155–56.

4. Wuster, ""I wa' n't bawn in de mash to be fool' by trash!," 131–53. The story was preceded shortly before by a short piece called "Sociable Jimmy" in the New York *Times*, November 29, 1874, which is also his first extended narration of a boy's voice. See Fishkin, *Was Huck Black?* "Part I—Jimmy."

5. [William Dean Howells], *Atlantic Monthly* 36, no. 218 (December 1875), 750. There is no critical discussion of this sketch within the pages of the *Atlantic* group. The novelist John W. De Forest, who was credited by Howells as being "realist before realism was named" ("Editor's Study" *Harper's Magazine* 74, no. 441 [February 1887]: 784), wrote to Howells: "By the way, tell Mark Twain to try pathos now & then. His 'True Story,' . . . was a really great thing, amazingly natural & humorous, & touching even to the drawing of tears." Quoted in MTHL 1:25. Howells sent this letter to Clemens with the passage above underlined. Searching has led to little critical discussion of the piece, apart from general notices in columns that noted magazine contents. *The Literary World*, usually critical of Mark Twain, either made a poor joke or took Mark Twain too literally when they noted that repeating a story word for word would be impossible "unless he took own the words in short-hand." 5, no. 6 (November 1, 1874), 94. The English magazine *Fun* found the piece amongst the best in the issue. November 28, 1874, 226. It is unclear whether Howells is referring to a general critical confusion, of which there is little textual evidence, or to his own confusion as an "average" critical figure. The most telling evaluation came from the *Western Christian Advocate*, which noted that the *Atlantic* "contains a faithful sketch of a Southern negro woman, by 'Mark Twain.' The humorist scarcely appears at all in his own person, but he puts the character he draws in a very clear light." 41, no. 42 (October 21, 1874), 333.

6. [William Dean Howells], *Atlantic Monthly* 36, no. 218 (December 1875): 750–51.

7. William Dean Howells to SLC, 19 Oct. 1875, Cambridge, Mass. (UCCL 32223) MTHL 1:94, (October 19, 1875), 106.

8. SLC to William Dean Howells, 19 Oct 1875, Hartford, Conn. (*UCCL 02495*). MTHL 1:95, (October 19, 1875), 107.

9. SLC to William Dean Howells, 2 Sept 1874, Elmira, N.Y. (*UCCL 02473*). MTHL 1:22–3. MTHL—the first quote ("I've kept . . . " is 1:17 (Sept 8, 1874), 22–23, and the second ("[t]his little. . ." from 1:18 (September 17, 1874), 24–25.

10. William Dean Howells, "Recollections of an Atlantic Editorship," *Atlantic Monthly* 100, no. 5 (November 1907): 601. Upon agreeing to write the pieces, Clemens wrote Howells: "All right—I'll presently sail in—but you must be sure to mention me in the advertisements or I shall be as uppish & airish as any third-rate actor whose name is not made loud enough in the bills." MTHL 1:24 (October 29 [1874]), 35. Howells later wrote that Mark Twain's presence in the *Atlantic* may not have increased sales as hoped, as the pieces were quickly plagiarized by newspapers around the country that had been sent advanced advertising copies. "Recollections of an Atlantic Authorship," 601. It is unclear how often pieces from magazines were reprinted in newspapers, which would both spread the influence of the writing and hurt profits.

11. "Old Times on the Mississippi" was serialized from January through August 1875 in six parts (skipping the July number). Mark Twain, "Old Times on the Mississippi. 1," *Atlantic Monthly* 35, no. 207 (January 1875), ibid., 69.

12. Mark Twain, "Old Times," 72. In addition to the importance of the themes of boyhood on the Mississippi and the romanticism of travel, the pieces also highlight two humorous themes that weave through Mark Twain's work: the sublimity of swearing, when done properly (as exemplified in the chief mate), and the romance of storytelling, even when it turns out to be romantic humbug (as with the night watchman who turns out not to be of English nobility). Although both Howells and Livy policed his writing for profanity, the mate is quoted as calling a crew member a "dash-dash-dash-*dashed* split between a tired mud-turtle and a crippled hearse-horse!" Followed by the line: "I wished I could talk like that" (73). This section was printed in the book-length *Life on the Mississippi* (James R. Osgood, 1883) as chapter 4—"The Boy's Ambition" and chapter 5—"I Want to be a Cub-pilot."

13. By the standards of subscription publishing, these books were a failure; DeQuille's book sold only 2,173 copies in its initial push, and Harte's book sold only 3,354 in its first year. MTEB, 92.

14. For the history of publication, see MTEB, 85–91. Hill notes that at least twelve pirated or authorized editions of Mark Twain's sketches had appeared in England between 1871 and 1875, thoroughly saturating the European market. Writing to Charles Henry Webb, the man he had sued to retrieve his copyright on his early pieces, Clemens noted that the sales of his first two books had dropped in 1874 due to "the prevailing business prostration." Webb had been disappointed in the subscription sales of his own collection of sketches, under the pseudonym "John Paul," published by Bliss. It was, Clemens wrote, "a mighty tough year for books," and he ended by noting he was releasing a new book into the market, which was "a thing I could not have been hired to do during any part of the past 12 months, for it would have been a sort of deliberate literary suicide." SLC to Charles Henry Webb, 8 Apr 1875, Hartford, Conn. (*UCCL 01219*). Letters 6:442.

15. For information on Mark Twain's image in *Sketches*, see David, *Mark Twain and His Illustrators*, 207–15.

16. MTEB, 172.

17. Ibid., 98–99.

18. SLC to William Dean Howells, 14 Sept 1875, Hartford, Conn. (*UCCL 01261*). MTHL 1:89 (September 14, 1875), 99. Clemens notes that he had "destroyed" a number of sketches (i.e., taken them out) and wishes he had destroyed more. He gives no hint as to which he desired cut. Beverly David notes that Clemens was largely disappointed with both the quality and the sales of the book (215). He did send an inscribed copy to Oliver Wendell Holmes reading: "The author of this book will take it as a real compliment if Mr Holmes will allow it to lumber one of his shelves." SLC to Oliver Wendell Holmes, 3? Nov 1875, Hartford, Conn. (*UCCL 12099*). Letters 6:580. Clemens also sent an inscribed copy to Mary Ann Cord, reading: "The author of this book offers it to Aunty Cord with his kindest regards, & refers her to page 202 for a well-meant but libelous portrait of herself & also the bit of personal history which she recounted to him once at 'Quarry Farm.'" SLC to Mary A. Cord, 18 Nov 1875, Hartford, Conn. (*UCCL 11342*), 593.

19. New York *Tribune* quoted in MTEB, 95. Hartford *Courant*, "Mark Twain's Sketches," September 9, 1875, in Budd, 149. Hill quote from MTEB, 96.

20. "Sketches by Mark Twain," San Francisco *Evening Bulletin*, October 23, 1875, in Budd 150. The reviewer argues further that "were he not a humorist we are not sure he might not have been a poet."

21. In the April and May 1875 *Harper's Magazine* article by Hon. S. S. Cox, entitled "American Humor," Mark Twain is but one of many examples Cox uses to demonstrate one or another types of American humor, specifically his talent for caricature and his use of exaggeration in the vein of Artemus Ward and Bret Harte. Hon. S. S. Cox, "American Humor," *Harper's Monthly* 50, no. 299 (April 1875), 698 and 50, no. 300 (May 1875). Discussing some general philosophy of humor (especially the difference between humor, wit, and farce) and questions of humorous temperament (are fat men really more humorous than skinny? for instance), Cox settles into the basic subject of his article—the varieties and importance of national humor. American humor, he argued, might seem to some to be burdened by the combined multitudes of the nation—a confused Babel of laughing tongues. Instead, he argued that this greater variety of peoples is in fact a source of the "golden veins" of the nation's humor:

> It is this absorption of characteristics of every clime and time which makes our society the most incongruous, grotesque, odd, angular, *outré*, and peculiar ever yet known to history. . . . If the power of man consists in the multitude of his affinities, in the fact that his life is intertwined more with his fellows of every caste, degree, and nation—if he thus become a more complete compend of all time, with all its tastes, affections, whims, and humors—then the American man ought to be more potent in his individuality than any other (697)

One further characteristic of American life was "Plenty," which created rush, excitement, and friction that Mark Twain had so successfully caricatured in Col. Sellers (698). Cox still classed Mark Twain with the popular humorists, and apart from literary humorists, while praising especially his passage on the Tomb of Adam from the *Innocents Abroad*: "This is the humorous sublime! It is the lachrymosely comic magnificent!"

22. MTHL 1:30 (November 23, 1874), 42–43.

23. SLC and OLC to John Brown, 4 Sept 1874, Elmira, N.Y. (*UCCL 01122*). Letters 6:221–27. SLC to William Dean Howells, 5 July 1875, Hartford, Conn. (*UCCL 01247*). MTHL 1:82 (July 5, [1875]), 91.

24. SLC to William Dean Howells, 23 Nov 1875, Hartford, Conn. MTHL 1:98 (November 21, 1875), 110–11. SLC to William Dean Howells, 23 Nov 1875, Hartford, Conn. MTHL 1:99 (November 23, 1875), 112.

25. [William Dean Howells], "*The Adventures of Tom Sawyer*" 37, no. 23 (May 1876), 621.

26. Moncure Conway, Unsigned review, London *Examiner*, June 17, 1876. Quoted in Anderson, *Mark Twain: The Critical Heritage*, 62–64. Hamlin Hill notes that the Boston *Transcript* quoted from the review in late April, as did a pirated Canadian edition, printed in the summer (MTEB, 117). The Hartford *Courant* noted the review in late April, alongside a spirited defense of Mark Twain's influence on travelers. "Current Comments on Mark Twain," April 22, 1876. By July 17 the book was advertised for sale in India, listed third in a list, after *The Atonement of Leam Dundes*, by Mrs. E. Lynn Linton, and *Gabriel Conroy*, by Harte. *The Times of India*, July 17, 1876.

27. M. D. C. "London Letter," Cincinnati *Commercial*, June 26, 1876. From Louis J. Budd Archive at Elmira College.

28. MTEB, 120. Sam Clemens was both an author under contract with the American Publishing Company and a stockholder, and he feuded with Bliss over the company's plans to publish up to ten books during the spring of 1876. This number included books by Warner, Harte, and DeQuille, whom he had brought to the company. See MTEB, 112–17 for details on the runup to publication of *Tom Sawyer*.

29. "Literary Notes," Chicago *Tribune*, April 15, 1876. "Mark Twain's 'Tom Sawyer,'" Hartford *Courant*, April 25, 1876. The *Courant* states that the delay was due to copyright issues in England. In a letter to William Dean Howells, Clemens noted that he planted the story in the *Courant* to explain the delay, which he was feuding with Bliss about, and that he would keep planting stories to explain the delay until autumn. (SLC to William Dean Howells, 26 Apr 1876, Hartford, Conn. MTHL 1:115, 131–33). *The Independent* printed a similar notice on May 11, 1876. On July 3, 1876, the Chicago *Tribune* printed a sketch by Moncure Conway that discussed the book's publication in England and printed several excerpts, including the fence-painting scene. The story was printed under the title

"Tom Sawyer and His Friends" in the Milwaukie *Daily Sentinel*, June 29, 1876, and on the same day in the Philadelphia *Sunday Republic* (according to MTEB, 119, n. 106). "How Tom Sawyer Got His Fence White-Washed" appeared in the Hartford *Courant* on June 30, 1876; in the Boston *Globe* (under the title "Shrewd Tommy Sawyer") on July 6, 1876; in the San Francisco *Daily Evening Bulletin* on July 8, 1876; in the *American Socialist* (under the title "New Story by Mark Twain") on July 13, 1876; in the Lowell *Daily Citizen* (as "Tom Sawyer's Contract") on July 15, 1876; in the *Independent Statesman* Concord, N.H. (as "Whitewash") on August 3, 1876; in the *Christian Union* on August 23, 1876; in the St. Louis *Globe-Democrat* (as "Tom Sawyer") on November 5, 1876; in the *Wisconsin State Register* (as "Tom Sawyer") on November 11, 1876; and in the *Maine Farmer* on December 9, 1876. "The Boy, The Beetle, and The Dog" appeared in the Boston *Globe* on July 11, 1876; in the Chicago *Tribune* and the *Wisconsin State Register* on July 15, 1876; in the Hartford *Courant* on July 26, 1876; and in the St. Louis *Globe-Democrat* on August 19, 1876. This search is not exhaustive of the extent of possibilities but is suggestive of the reach of the extracts.

30. To the Board of Directors, Clemens wrote: "I have a selfish interest at stake. Tom Sawyer is a new line of writing for me, & I would like to have every possible advantage in favor of that venture. When it issues, I would like it to have a clear field, & the *whole* energies of the company put upon it; & not only this, but I would like the canvassers to distinctly understand that no new book would issue till Tom Sawyer had run 6, or even 9 months. In that case I think we should all be better off." SLC to the Board of Directors of the American Publishing Co., 24 June 1876, Elmira, N.Y. (*UCCL 01346*). Mark Twain. *Microfilm Edition of Mark Twain's Previously Unpublished Letters*, prepared by Anh Quynh Bui, Victor Fischer, Michael B. Frank, Robert H. Hirst, Lin Salamo, and Harriet Elinor Smith (Berkeley: The Bancroft Library), Reel 1. Also available on the Mark Twain Project website. Hill estimates that Clemens made $58,000 from the *Innocents Abroad* and *Roughing It* but only $15,000 from *Sketches* and the *Adventures of Tom Sawyer* by 1879 (MTEB, 121). Sales were hurt by a pirated Canadian version, taken from the British edition printed in June, which flooded much of the marketplace for Mark Twain's book in America with 75 cent and one dollar versions. Welland, *Mark Twain in England*, 234. Between 1876 and 1907, approximately 76,000 copies were printed in England, making it one of his most enduring works in England. The profit is cited in n. 1 of SLC to Moncure D. Conway. 29 Dec 1876, Hartford, Conn. (*UCCL 01397*). Twain, *Microfilm Edition of Mark Twain's Previously Unpublished Letters,*Reel 1. In the fall of 1876, Clemens also struck an agreement with Christian Tauchnitz, a German publisher, to publish *Tom Sawyer*, despite the fact that the publisher was not required to pay American copyright. He paid 500 marks (approximately $119) in December.

31. The blurb from the *Athenaeum* was modified to eliminate the reference to the railway station. The blurb from the Ohio paper called the book Mark Twain's

most notable work, which would "signally add to his reputation for variety of powers." See Railton, "Selling Tom Sawyer," http://etext.virginia.edu/railton/tomsawye/tomdumhp.html

32. "Literary Notices," Hartford *Courant*, December 27, 1876. Possibly written by Charles Dudley Warner, the Hartford review was copied in a shortened version and printed as the review in the Boston *Globe* two days later. "Mark twain's Latest Book," Boston *Globe*, December 29, 1876. The review acknowledges its source. The New York *Tribune* did not review the book. The New York *Times* reviewed the book as a children's story and found the book to contain too much "ugly realism" for children, as well as faulting the book for encouraging children to become pirates, an all-too-common fault of recent books for children according to the reviewer (January 13, 1877, in Anderson, *Mark Twain: The Critical Heritage*, 69–71). The book was also reviewed in the San Francisco *Chronicle* (January 7, 1877) and the San Francisco *Daily Evening Bulletin* (January 20, 1877), which noted: "Whatever Mark Twain writes is pretty sure of an eager popular recognition. And it is due to him to say that he finds his readers and admirers among all classes here and in England. His humor has that eclectic quality that makes itself appreciated alike by the tutored and untutored, by the refined and course natured; for it appeals to the instinctive love of the ludicrous and the exaggerated, which dwells in all human souls."

33. *Pall Mall Gazette* Saturday, October 28, 1876; *Penny Illustrated Paper and Illustrated Times*, Saturday, June 24, 1876; *Graphic* (London, England), Saturday, July 1, 1876.

34. London *Times*, August 28, 1876, in Anderson, *Mark Twain: The Critical Heritage*, 68.

35. June 24, 1876, no. 2539, 851 in Anderson, *Mark Twain: The Critical Heritage*, 64–65. This review was partially reprinted in *The Independent* 28 (July 27, 1876), 1443, and the same excerpt in the San Francisco *Chronicle* on September 24, 1876. On the other hand, critics in the *Athanaeum* wrote that same year of their low opinion of "American humor" as it flooded the English market after Artemus Ward. The fan of such "dry humor" was likely to "rob a church," in their opinion. From Louis J. Budd Archive at Elmira College.

36. Mark Twain, "A Literary Nightmare," *Atlantic Monthly* 37, no. 220 (February 1876), 167.

37. Ibid., 169.

38. A discussion of the phenomenon of "horse-car poetry" inspired by Mark Twain's story was printed in *Record of the Year, A Reference Scrap Book: Being the Monthly Record of Important Events Worth Preserving* (G. W. Carleton and Company, 1876). The book relates a story from the Chicago *Tribune* of a woman reading the story in the *Atlantic* only to have her husband find the "elegant little lady waltzing around the room like one possessed." Her possession ends with them both on the floor—battered and exhausted—until she drives her husband out of

the room by setting the poem to music. He then writes the story to warn other husbands so they could avoid his fate. Clemens wrote Howells that he opposed any collection of horse-car poetry: "[T]o stack together *all* of it that has been written, & then add to it my article would be to enrage & disgust each & every reader & win the deathless enmity of the lot." SLC to William Dean Howells, 26 Apr 1876, Hartford, Conn. MTHL 1:131–3.

39. Mark Twain's other contribution to the *Atlantic* in 1876—"The Canvasser's Tale"—tells of the relentless onslaught of door-to-door salesmen selling useless products, specifically a canvasser with a collection of echoes (who is, literally, selling sound) who won't take no for an answer. The narrator, despite threatening violence to the salesman, ends up with two "double-barreled" echoes and an echo that only speaks German. While on the surface, the tale is a light satire on the consumer culture inundating Americans on their very doorsteps (of which Mark Twain's own army of subscription book salesmen were a part), the piece seems to be equally a joke about the ability of the mass culture to sell anything—even something that does not exist.

40. T. J. Jackson Lears, *No Place of Grace: Antimodernism and the Transformation of American Culture, 1880–1920* (New York: Pantheon, 1981), 4.

41. Ibid., 7.

42. The firm of James R. Osgood & Co. had failed, and H. O. Houghton & Co. had taken over. Osgood would later publish the book *Life on the Mississippi* in 1883. George P. Lathrop, an occasional *Atlantic* contributor, was the "historian of the evening and the chronicler of its events." Letters 6:319–20.

43. L. C. M., "Boston. Literary Notes." December 12, 1874. Mark Twain, "Western Life. Old Times on the Mississippi." December 16, 1874.

44. Arthur Gilman, "Atlantic Dinners and Diners," *Atlantic Monthly* 100, no. 5 (November 1907), 651.

45. "A Dinner on Parnassus," New York *Tribune*, December 18, 1874.

46. Ibid. Boston *Transcript*, December 16, 1874. Quoted in Twain, *Mark Twain Speaking*, edited by Fatout, 651.

47. Clemens had implored Howells to stay with him in an earlier letter: "I want you to ask Mrs. Howells to let you stay all night at the Parker House & tell lies & have an improving time, & take breakfast with me in the morning. I will have a good room for you, & a fire. Can't you tell her it always makes you sick to go home late at night, or something like that?" SLC to William Dean Howells, 13 Dec 1874, Hartford, Conn. MTHL 1:42, 53–4.

48. George Parsons Lathrop, "The Atlantic Dinner," New York *Evening Post*, December 17, 1874, 2.

49. December 18, 1877, 1.

50. "The Atlantic Dinner," December 18, 1877. Boston *Daily Advertiser*, reprinted in Lowell *Daily Citizen*, December 17, 1877.

51. Henry Nash Smith, "That Hideous Mistake of Poor Clemens's," *Harvard Library Bulletin* 9, no. 2 (1955): 169–70.

52. Quoted in the Boston *Daily Globe*, December 18, 1877.

53. Smith, "That Hideous Mistake of Poor Clemens's," 170, 153.

54. Boston *Daily Globe*, December 18, 1877, and Boston *Daily Advertiser*, same date. Subsequent quotes in this paragraph are from this source.

55. Remember Fields's comment about the magazine from chapter 3: "All is well, the pills are puffed, and pills thus puffed will sell." Tryon, *Parnassus Corner*, 85.

56. Boston *Daily Globe*, December 18, 1877.

57. Even Holmes, whom Howells introduced as not only naming the magazine but giving it its sense of purpose, began his occasional poem with such as statement:

> A doom like Scheherezade's falls upon me
> In a mandate as stern as the Sultan's decree:
> I'm a florist in verse, and what *would* people say
> If I came to a banquet without my bouquet?

58. All quotes will be taken from Henry Nash Smith's "That Hideous Mistake of Poor Clemens," which recreates the text based on Mark Twain's original manuscript and newspaper reports presumably based on that manuscript, rather than the version from the *North American Review* (1906) or Paine's version of *Speeches* (1923), which contain small but notable revisions. See 176–80.

59. Ibid., 178. From the poem, "Mare Rubrum." The other poems quoted are: Emerson's "Mithridates," "Concord Hymn," "Brahma," "Song of Nature," and "Monadnock"; Holmes's "Chambered Nautilus" and "A Voice of the Loyal North"; and Longfellow's "Hiawatha," "Evangaline," and "The Village Blacksmith." Only "Song of Nature" appeared in the *Atlantic Monthly*. All the phrases are correct except for the line from "Song of Nature," which is changed from "I tire of globes & races!—/Too long the game is played!" to "I tire of globes & aces . . ."

60. Chicago *Tribune*, December 26, 1877. Quoted in Smith, "That Hideous Mistake of Poor Clemens," 157–58.

61. Boston *Evening Transcript*, December 18, 1877. Quoted Smith, "That Hideous Mistake of Poor Clemens," 147–48. See ibid. for further immediate reactions of Boston papers. Boston *Evening Transcript*, December 27, 1877, cited in Smith, "That Hideous Mistake of Poor Clemens," 157.

62. The Chicago *Inter Ocean* reprinted this notice with the note that "Boston is 'mad and tickled too' about Mark Twain's speech. . . ." December 22, 1877, 4. *Inter Ocean*, December 18, 1877, 5. New York *Times* December 18, 1877, 1. The speech was printed in the New York *Times* by itself on December 20, 1877, 2, and on December 18 in numerous Boston papers (*Advertiser, Globe, Journal*, and *Transcript*). It was also published in the Galveston *Daily News* on December 30, 1877, the Chicago *Tribune* on December 22, and the Quincy (Ill.) *Whig*, January 3, 1878. For other controversies, see "The Atlantic-Whittier Dinner—A

Woman's Thoughts Thereof," in Boston *Daily Advertiser*, December 20, 1877. Written by a woman signed "A Few Among Many," the Boston *Daily Advertiser* article says that women expected an explanation, "But no: from generous publisher and genial editor to grotesque humorist, all combined, 'to let expressive silence muse their praise.'" See Smith, "That Hideous Mistake of Poor Clemens," n. 17, for details on the women and wine controversies.

63. Interestingly, the Whittier dinner and its aftermath were not a subject of discussion in the quality magazines of the era, with no mention made at all in the *Atlantic*. Smith also reports combing through the papers and letters of a large number of attendees and finding only one hint of consternation. Smith, "That Hideous Mistake of Poor Clemens," 152–53. He notes that John Fiske referred to Mark Twain's "ghastly mistake" but may have been influenced by newspaper reports, as the letter was not written until December 30.

64. Quoted in Smith, "That Hideous Mistake of Poor Clemens," 157.

65. New Orleans *Times Picayune*, December 29, 1877, 4, and December 30, 1877, 16.

66. "Mark Twain's Mistake at the Whittier Dinner," Springfield *Republican*, December 27, 1877. Quoted in Smith, "That Hideous Mistake of Poor Clemens," 159–60. Peckham, in *Josiah Gilbert Holland in Relation to his Times*, 44, writes that the *Republican* was well known for its moralistic stance, promoted by Holland. The paper did not publish a Sunday edition until 1878.

67. The Cincinnati *Commercial*, in an article reprinted in the Boston *Globe* and the San Francisco *Daily Evening Bulletin*, lectured Mark Twain on his "offense against good taste." Mark Twain, the paper argued, should have known better, and the "instincts of a gentleman" should have kept him from his coarse character sketch. He had failed to understand the type of quaint humor the night required and thus needed a harsh lesson on humor and propriety:

> Wit has been defined as the faculty of discovering new and surprising meanings in words and things and bringing them into such relations as excite to mirth. Mr. Twain may have postulated his speech on the definition, and thought that by bringing these poets and philosophers, whose lives have been passed amid books . . . and in refined society into intimate relations with whisky, cards, bowie knives and larceny, he was doing an irresistible funny thing, that would set the table in a roar and wrinkle a continent with laughter. It was a mistake, however.

San Francisco *Daily Evening Bulletin*, January 8, 1878.

68. Quoted in *Daily Rocky Mountain News*, January 5, 1878. Henry Nash Smith traced the reactions from Boston to the Midwest, but he notes with some surprise that the discussion of the speech did not reach the western United States. The speech was, in fact, discussed in both western and at least one southern newspaper, but later than the other newspapers.

69. "A Thundering Row about That Whittier Dinner," Chicago *Times*, dated December, 17, 1877, reprinted in San Francisco *Daily Evening Bulletin*, January

10, 1878. The editor, playing the voice of reason, responds: "Not a bit. Howells takes things easy. Catch him feeling responsible for any contributor who chooses to make a fool of himself."

70. One further response of note, from the writer Ambrose Bierce, with whom both Clemens and Howells had a difficult relationship. In the *Argonaut* on January 5, 1878, Bierce wrote that Mark Twain's speech had "so wrought upon the feelings of 'the best literary society' in that city that the daring joker is in danger of lynching. I hope they won't lynch him; it would be irregular and illegal, however roughly just and publicly beneficial. Besides, it would rob many a worthy sheriff of an honorable ambition by dispelling the most bright and beautiful hope of his life." Quoted in Morris, *Ambrose Bierce: Alone in Bad Company*, 169.

71. Chicago *Tribune*, December 23, 1877, 16. Quoted in Smith, "That Hideous Mistake of Poor Clemens," 154.

72. New York *Times*, December 21, 1877. *Puck* 2, no. 45 (January 10, 1878), 14. *Independent* 30, no. 1519 (January 10, 1878), 12.

73. Smith, "That Hideous Mistake of Poor Clemens," 146. This argument of the speech's "mythic resonance" is also forwarded by Harold Bush, "The Mythic Struggle between East and West: Mark Twain's Speech at Whittier's 70th Birthday Celebration and W. D. Howells' 'A Chance Acquaintance," *American Literary Realism, 1870–1910* 27, no. 2 (Winter 1995), 58.

74. Mark Twain, "Chapters from My Autobiography—XXV," *North American Review* 186, no. 625 (December 1907), 486-87.

75. Howells, *My Mark Twain*, 60.

76. Mark Twain, *Autobiography* (1907), 488.

77. Howells's letter to Norton quoted in Smith, "That Hideous Mistake of Poor Clemens," 162. Twichell's letter from Manuscript diary of the Rev. Joseph H. Twichell, Yale University Library, December 18–19, 1877, as quoted in Smith, "That Hideous Mistake of Poor Clemens," 162.

78. DeVoto, *Mark Twain's America*, 196, 194, 193, 205. DeVoto thus framed Mark Twain in terms of a clash between New England civilization and frontier irreverence—directly stating: "He was, that is, a savage" (193). And this savagery was expressed as a lack of reverence for key aspects of New England culture:

> He was anarchy. He had derided a culture which these people venerated: he had even derided the veneration. . . . He had guffawed at reverend traditions. He had denounced picturesqueness as poverty. He had mocked simple faith as superstition. He had laid hands of violation on literary and artistic traditions toward which these people had yearned from childhood. . . . The years brought a succession of plain statements from the backwoods pen. These were as distressing as his more personal incapacity for reverence. (195)

Mark Twain's "blasphemy" stemmed from his "unretouched" characters, who offended the village, which preferred to see humanity "through the pink mist of allegory."

79. James Caron, "The Satirist Who Clowns: Mark Twain's Performance at the Whittier Birthday Celebration" *Texas Studies in Literature and Language* 52, no. 4 (Winter 2010), 435–37. Caron argues that Mark Twain was playing the role of "Citizen Clown" whose performance admonished the community for transgressions (436).

80. Richard Lowry, *"Littery Man": Mark Twain and Modern Authorship* (New York: Oxford University Press, 1996), 35.

81. Lawrence Levine, *Highbrow/Lowbrow: The Emergence of Cultural Hierarchy in America* (Berkeley: University of California Press, 1989).

82. William D. Howells to SLC, 18 December 1877. MTHL 1:172.

83. SLC to William Dean Howells, 23 Dec 1877, Hartford, Conn. MTHL 1:174.

84. William D. Howells to SLC, 25 Dec 1877, Cambridge, Mass. MTHL 1:175.

85. Each letter seems to have been addressed to all three men. The only surviving copy is in the Emerson Papers in the Harvard College Library, reprinted in Smith, "That Hideous Mistake of Poor Clemens's," 164. All further references in this paragraph are from this source. He signed the letters as "Sam L. Clemens."

86. SLC to William Dean Howells, 28 Dec 1877, Hartford, Conn. MTHL 1:176. Mark Twain, "Chapters from My Autobiography—XXV" *North American Review* 186, no. 625 (December 1907), 489.

87. Ellen Emerson's letter dated December 31, 1877. Paine, *Mark Twain, a Biography*, 2:608–9, and in Smith, "That Hideous Mistake of Poor Clemens's," 166–67. Longfellow's letter dated January 6, 1878. Published in part in Paine, *Mark Twain, a Biography*, 2:607, and in Smith, "That Hideous Mistake of Poor Clemens's," 167.

88. Holmes's letter dated December 29, 1877. Published in part in Paine, *Mark Twain, a Biography*, 2:607–8, and in Smith, "That Hideous Mistake of Poor Clemens's," 166.

89. Reprinted in San Francisco *Bulletin*, January 28, 1878, and Milwaukee *Daily Sentinel*, January 18, 1878.

90. James R. Osgood also published a Pocket Vest version of "A True Story" and "A Recent Carnival of Crime in Connecticut" in 1877. The previously published pieces included "Map of Paris," from the *Galaxy*, "An Encounter with the Interviewer," two speeches, and several pieces from the *Atlantic Monthly*.

91. Powers, *Mark Twain: A Life*, 414–16. Kaplan, *Mr. Clemens and Mark Twain*, 213.

92. The sketches were "The Loves of Alonzo Fitz Clarence and Rosannah Ethelton" (March 1878), "About Magnanimous Incident Literature" (May 1878), "The Recent French Duel" (February 1879), and "The Great Revolution in Pitcairn" (March 1879). [W.H. Bishop], "Round the World at the Paris Exhibition," 43, no. 255 (January 1879), 46.

93. "Mark Twain Interviewed," from interview with New York *World*, May 11, 1879. Reprinted in Milwaukie *Daily Sentinel*, Lowell *Daily Citizen*, St. Louis *Globe-Democrat*, San Francisco *Evening Bulletin*. "Mark Twain as Candidate,"

New York *Evening Post*, June 9, 1879. Mark Twain's platform was to publicize the worst parts of his record so as to not give opponents ammunition, ending, "If my country don't want me I will go back again. But I recommend myself as a safe man—a man who starts from the basis of total depravity, and proposes to be fiendish to the last." Reprinted in the Galveston *Daily News*, St. Louis *Globe-Democrat*, San Francisco *Daily Bulletin*, *Inter Ocean* (Chicago), Galvesten *Daily News* (again), *The Globe* (Atchinson, Kans.)

94. "Mark Twain's Enterprise/The Celebrated Humorist Takes Editorial Charge of the Hartford COURANT," New York *Sun*, 7 Jan 1878, and "Not Quite an Editor/The Story of Mark Twain's Connection with the *HARTFORD COURANT*," New York *Sun*, 26 Jan 1878, p. 2.

95. Milwaukie *Daily Sentinel*, January 14, 1878; *Georgia Weekly Telegraph and Georgia Journal & Messenger* (Macon, Ga.), January 15, 1878; *Daily Rocky Mountain News* (Denver, Colo.) January 15, 1878; *Daily Arkansas Gazette* (Little Rock, Ark.) January 16, 1878; San Francisco *Daily Evening Bulletin*, January 17, 1878.

96. SLC to Rollin M. Daggett, 24 Jan 1878, Hartford, Conn. (*UCCL 01526*). The spurious interviews are discussed at: http://www.twainquotes.com/interviews/interviewindex.html One further interview reported the departure of Mark Twain's boat for Europe in 1878, one lengthy interview reported on Mark Twain from Paris (and is the source of the story on why Mark Twain didn't write about England), and four reported his return to America in September 1879. Scharnhorst, ed., *Mark Twain: The Complete Interviews*, 14–31.

97. Twain, *Autobiography of Mark Twain*, 70.

98. SLC to OLC, 14 Nov 1879, Chicago, Ill. (*UCCL 01715*). Albert Bigelow Paine, ed. *Mark Twain's Letters*, 370–73.

99. SLC to William Dean Howells, 17 Nov 1879, Hartford, Conn. *MTHL* 1:278–80.

100. MTHL 1: 201 and Clemens's reply: SLC to William Dean Howells, 15 Sept 1879, Elmira, N.Y. MTHL 1:202. Howells declined working on the play in fear of hurting Orion (MTHL 1:268–70).

101. SLC to William Dean Howells, 1? Oct 1879, Elmira, N.Y. MTHL 1:203. MTHL 1:208. Charles Dudley Warner to Howells, quoted in MTHL 1:211, n. 2. SLC to Howells, 29 Nov 1879, Hartford, Conn. MTHL 1:214.

102. "Honoring the Autocrat." December 4, 1879. Dinner included multiple courses, including Filet of Sole; Stuffed Saddle; Rock Oyster, Roasted; Omelette with Chicken Livers; Cutlets of Chicken; French Peas; Filet of Beef, larded with Mushrooms; Potato Croquettes; Tomatoes; Broiled Woodcock on Toast; Roast Quail, stuffed with Truffles; Dressed Celery; Creams and Ices—Cakes—Fruits, and Coffee. *The Atlantic Monthly Supplement. The Holmes Breakfast*, 45, no. 268 (February 1880), 1.

103. Ibid. Houghton ended his speech with the line, "O King! live forever!" In 1905, at Mark Twain's own 70th Birthday Banquet at Delmonico's in New York, Howells modified the sentiment, declaiming: "I will try not to be greedy on your

behalf in wishing the health of our honored and, in view of his great age, our revered guest. I will not say, 'Oh King, live forever!' but 'Oh King, live as long as you like!'"

104. A few letters, including that from President Hayes, were read at the banquet, while others were printed in the Holmes Breakfast supplement to the *Atlantic*, 16–17, 19–24. Some of the letters were destroyed before publication in a fire that destroyed the offices of the *Atlantic*. The success of Sprague's book was announced at the banquet when James Osgood reported a large order of the book. Osgood noted that "the phenomenal sale of which was surprising the publishers." New York *Tribune*, December 10, 1879. Gilman, "Atlantic Dinners and Diners," 654.

105. [H.W. Preston], "*Old Creole Days* and other Novels," *Atlantic Monthly* 45, no. 267 (January 1880). In *Scribner's*, an editorial, probably written by Richard Watson Gilder, noted the book "may be commended to young women between the ages of fifteen and twenty-five as a novel, pleasant to read, which is more instructive than moving." "Culture and Progress," *Scribner's Monthly* 19, no. 3 (January 1880), 472.

106. "The Holmes Breakfast," Boston *Daily Advertiser*, December 4, 1879.

107. *The Holmes Breakfast*, 6.

108. Ellery, "The Holmes Breakfast." *Christian Union*, December 10, 1879, 490.

109. "The Holmes Breakfast." *Literary World* 10, no. 26 (December 20, 1879), 435.

110. The *Atlantic Monthly Supplement*, "The Holmes Breakfast," 45, no. 268 (February 1880), 11-12. All subsequent quotes are from this source.

111. New York *Tribune*, December 10, 1879.

112. Paine, *Mark Twain, a Biography*, 2:660. Caron in "The Satirist Who Clowns" reads the Whittier speech in relation to "The Babies" and "A Recent Carnival of Crime in Connecticut." Lowry in *Littery* Man does not mention the Holmes speech, although he discusses the idea of "unconscious plagiarism" (65). Krauth reads the autobiographical remembrance of the Whittier speech in *Proper Mark Twain*, 247–49, but he does not review the Holmes speech, which supports his thesis of the ways in which Clemens sought the approval of establishment norms.

113. SLC to William Dean Howells, 18 Sept 1875, Hartford, Conn. MTHL 1:90, 99–101. For a history of copyright, including Mark Twain's views, see Siva Vaidhyanathan, *Copyrights and Copywrongs: The Rise of Intellectual Property and How It Threatens Creativity* (New York: NYU Press, 2001).

Conclusion

1. SLC to David Gray, 10 June 1880, Hartford, Conn. (*UCCL 11405*). He continues: "I am effectually barred from questioning the excellence of your & Howells's judgement by the unassailable logic of figures: up to now, we have printed

50,000 copies, & *they are sold.* This is a considerably bigger sale than I have made on any previous book in the same length of time. And the sales go briskly on." *Microfilm Edition of Mark Twain's Previously Unpublished Letters.*

2. "*A Tramp Abroad*," *Spectator* 53 (June 26, 1880), 820–21, in Budd, 193.

3. Reviews are mostly to be found in "Literature/*A Tramp Abroad*," Chicago *Tribune*, April 10, 1880, in Budd, 183. Budd, 183–95. "The Reader," *Graphic* 21 (May 1, 1880), 451, in Budd, 188–89, and "*A Tramp Abroad*," *Spectator* 53 (June 26, 1880), 820–21, in Budd, 193. "New Books," Utica *Observer*, May 17, 1880, 21, in Robert H. Woodward, "A Selection of Harold Frederic's Early Literary Criticism, 1877–1881," *American Literary Realism* 5, no. 1 (Winter 1872), 18. Frederic would become an important foreign correspondent and author in London, but his early criticism shows some flaws, such as misspelling "Clemmens" and holding that Mark Twain had not published anything but "fugitive sketches" since the failure of *The Gilded Age*. The review holds that other newspaper humorists—such as Lewis of the Detroit *Free Press*—had captured the "ear of the public . . . and have done such droll and jolly work that there is no room for a pretentious funny book which is not funny." This review shows how Mark Twain's work had outgrown its newspapers roots and become more "sober," in the reviewer's word.

4. "Literature/*A Tramp Abroad*," Chicago *Tribune*, April 10, 1880, in Budd, 183. "Belles Letters, Poetry, and Fiction," *British Quarterly Review* 72 (July 1880), 228–29, in Budd, 193. The reviewer notes that "the Sunday School Union and Mr. Matthew Arnold might both find . . . apt illustrations of culture become cynical and allied with wit!"

5. N.S. 21 (May 21, 1880), 326–28. From Louis J. Budd Archive at Elmira College. "A Tramp Abroad," *Observer*, October 3, 1880.

6. [William Earnest Henley], *Athenaeum* 2739 (April 1880), 529–30, in Anderson, *Mark Twain: The Critical Heritage*, 73–76. This review also faulted Mark Twain for trying to be too funny: "It is the peculiarity of Mark Twain that, while he is always bent on being funny—deliberately and determinedly funny—he almost always succeeds in his intent. He has a certain dry, imaginative extravagance of fun that is neither more nor less than a literary intoxicant, so irresistible is its operation and so overwhelming its effect."

7. "New Publications," *Evening Bulletin*, May 15, 1880, in Budd, 190. "Literature/Mark Twain's Latest Book," San Francisco *Chronicle*, May 23, 1880, in Budd, 190–91. The review concluded: "They will console themselves, though, with the reflection that he has done well enough in the past to warrant them in not passing a harsh judgment on his latest work."

8. Clemens briefly left the American Publishing Company to work with Frank Bliss, the son of Elisha Bliss, his longtime publisher. But Elisha's ill health, and the struggles of the American Publishing Company, of which Clemens was still a stockholder, led Frank Bliss to convince Clemens that the two should return to the company. On the illustrations of *A Tramp Abroad*, see Beverly R. David

and Ray Saperstein, "Reading the Illustrations in *A Tramp Abroad*," in *A Tramp Abroad*, edited by Shelley Fisher Fishkin, 20–25 (New York: Oxford University Press, 1996).

9. MTEB, 152.

10. Ibid., 148–49.

11. SLC to Elisha Bliss, Jr., 20 March 1880, Hartford, Conn. (*UCCL 02540*). MTEB, 121–22.

12. SLC to William Dean Howells, 24 March 1880, Hartford, Conn. MTHL 1:294–95. Clemens noted that he had not had the book sent to Warner, since he would have to send it to other papers in Hartford as well.

13. SLC to Joseph H. Twichell, 24 March 1880, Hartford, Conn. MTHL 1:293.

14. SLC to William Dean Howells, 24 March 1880, Hartford, Conn. MTHL 1:294–5. SLC to Moncure D. Conway, 20 and 21 Apr 1880, Hartford, Conn. Mark Twain. *Mark Twain's Letters to His Publishers, 1867–1894*, edited by Hamlin Hill (Berkeley: University of California Press, 1967), 123. Three days later, he wrote to Hjalamar Hjorth Boyesen, thanking him for his praises of the book trumpeting a printing of 35,000 and the presses still running at full speed. SLC to Hjalamar H. Boyesen, 23 Apr 1880, Hartford, Conn. Marc Ratner, "Two Letters of Mark Twain." *Mark Twain Journal* 12 (Spring), 9.

15. [William Dean Howells], "Mark Twain's New Book," *Atlantic Monthly* 45, no. 271 (May 1880), 686-687. Subsequent quotes are from 687.

16. The *Century* had come from the demise of *Scribner's Monthly* following the death of Josiah Gilbert Holland in 1881. Webster and Company operated from 1885-1894 and published books by Mark Twain, a variety of military and political leaders (Grant's autobiography, David Kalakaua, Custer's widow, etc.), as wells as books of humor, biography, cooking, philosophy, and literature, including works by Tolstoy and Whitman.

17. [Hjalamar Hjorth Boyesen], 48, no. 290 (December 1881), 843–45.

18. [William Dean Howells], "A Romance by Mark Twain," New York *Tribune*, October 25, 1881. From Louis J. Budd Archive at Elmira College. As with earlier works in a variety of genres, Howells was able to make romance conform to realistic standards, writing, "Like all other romances, it asks that the reader shall take its possibility for granted, but this once granted its events follow each other not only with probability but with realistic force."

19. SLC to William D. Howells, 26 October 1881, Hartford, Conn., Hartford, Conn. (UCCL 02553). MTHL 1:377.

20. "Mark Twain's Romance," Boston *Herald*, December 4, 1881. From Louis J. Budd Archive at Elmira College. While there is no author listed of this review, its tone and argument seem clearly indebted to Howells's review. "New Publications," Boston *Transcript*, December 19, 1881, in Budd, 202. "Literary Matters/ New Publications," Boston *Evening Transcript*, January 4, 1882, in Budd, 209.

21. In a list of recent books, it was noted that the book was a sequel to *Tom Sawyer*, but that each book was complete to itself, ending "Huckleberry Finn,

Tom Sawyer's old comrade, is not only the hero but the historian of his adventures, and certainly Mr. Clemens himself could not have related them more amusingly. The work is sold only by subscription." "Books of the Month," 55, no. 330 (April 1885), 576.

22. Although the Henry James piece ("Henry James Jr.," *Century* 25, no. 1 (November 1882), 24–29) is out of our scope here, it should be noted that this piece helped ignite the so-called "Realism War" that led to a reification and, I would argue, transformation of Howells's view of realism from his earlier, scattered use at the *Atlantic*. Mark Twain's role in this new skirmish would be worth exploring as his reputation developed in relation to a more fervent definition of Howellsian realism. William Dean Howells, "Mark Twain," *Century* 24, no. 5 (September 1882), 781.

23. Howells, "Mark Twain," 780.

24. Ibid., 781. Subsequent quotes taken from this page.

25. Ibid., 782. Subsequent quotes taken from this page.

26. Ibid., 783. Subsequent quotes taken from this page.

27. A word Howells seems to have made up for the occasion. He sent the manuscript to Clemens in the summer of 1882, and Clemens sent it on to the *Century* after he and Livy had read it. To Howells, he wrote: "*Of course* it pleases *me*—that goes without saying—& I hope the public will be willing to see me with your eyes. I shouldn't ask anything better than that. Well, I am mighty glad you had the time & disposition to write it." SLC to William D. Howells, 16 June 1882, Hartford, Conn. (*UCCL 02220*). MTHL 1:405.

28. Matthew Arnold, "A Word About America," *The Nineteenth Century* 11, no. 63 (May 1882), 689. Arnold wrote: "The Quinionian humor of Mr. Mark Twain, so attractive to the Philistine of the more gay and light type both here and in America, another French critic fixes upon as literature exactly expressing a people of this type and no higher." This "type" indicate—according to French critics quoted by Arnold— "intellectual mediocrity," "vulgarity of manners," "superficial spirit," and "lack of general intelligence." Quinion was a minor character from Dickens. See Krauth, *Mark Twain & Company*, 160, and chapter 4.

29. Howells, *My Mark Twain*, 28–29.

30. Paine, *Mark Twain, a Biography,* 2:758–59.

31. Arnold, "A Word About America," 686. These are the qualities, along with the "powers of industry and conduct," that are necessary to help establish a "national civilisation."

32. "Book Notices," *Saturday Evening Review*, October 2, 1869, in Budd, 67.

Bibliography

Archival Materials

Berg Collection, New York Public Library

Harry Ransom Center, University of Texas at Austin

Mark Twain Archives, Elmira College

Mark Twain Papers, University of California, Berkeley

W.T.H. Howe Collection, New York Public Library

Books and Articles

"American Humor and Humorists." *Round Table* (September 9, 1865): 2.

"American Humorists, With Portraits." *The Phrenological Journal of Science and Health* 59, no. 6 (December 1874): 44–46.

Cartoon Portraits and Biographical Sketches of Men of the Day, The Drawings by Frederick Waddy. London: Tinsley Brothers, 1873.

"Editorial Items." *The Phrenological Journal of Science and Health* 51, no. 2 (August 1870): 142.

"How a Humorist Uses Humor." *The Phrenological Journal of Science and Health* 52, no. 60 (January 1871): 60.

"Mark Twain." *Once a Week* 259 (December 14, 1872): 520–21.

The Museum of Foreign Literature, Science, and Art, vol. 7———New Series. Philadelphia: E. Littell & Co., 1839.

The Piccadilly Annual of Entertaining Literature: Retrospective and Contemporary. London: John Camden Hotten, [1870].

Adams, Bluford. *E pluribus Barnum: The Great Showman and the Making of U.S. Popular Culture*. Minneapolis: University of Minnesota Press, 1997.

Ade, George. "Mark Twain and the Old Time Subscription Book." *The American Review of Reviews* (June 1910).

Aldrich, Lilian. *Crowding Memories: Autobiography*. Boston: Houghton Mifflin, 1920.

Allen, Robert. *Horrible Prettiness: Burlesque and American Culture*. Chapel Hill: University of North Carolina Press, 1991.

Anderson, Frederick. *Mark Twain: The Critical Heritage*. London: Routledge and K. Paul, 1971.

Arnold, Matthew. "A Word about America." *The Nineteenth Century* 11, no. 63 (May 1882): 689.

Austin, James C. *American Humor in France: Two Centuries of French Criticism of the Comic Spirit in American Literature*. Ames: Iowa State University Press, 1978.

————. *Fields of the "Atlantic Monthly."* San Marino: The Huntington Library, 1953.

Baetzhold, Howard G. *Mark Twain and John Bull: The British Connection.* Bloomington: Indiana University Press, 1970.

Bakhtin, M. M. *The Dialogic Imagination: Four Essays.* University of Texas Press, 1981.

Bakhtin, Mikhail. *Rabelais and His World.* Bloomington: Indiana University Press, 2009 (1968).

Bentzon, Th. (Marie-Therese Blanc). "Les Humoristes Américains." *Revue des deux mondes* 100 (July 15, 1872): 313–55, and 102 (August 15, 1872): 837–62.

Bell, Michael Davitt. *The Problem of American Realism: Studies in the Cultural History of a Literary Idea.* Chicago: University Of Chicago Press, 1993.

Bellamy, Gladys Carmen. *Mark Twain as a Literary Artist.* Norman: University of Oklahoma Press, 1950.

————. "Mark Twains Indebtedness to John Phoenix." *American Literature* 13, no. 1 (March 1941): 29–43.

Bergson, Henri. *Laughter: An Essay on the Meaning of Comic.* Wildside Press, 2008 (1911).

Best, Steven and Sharon Marcus, "Surface Reading: An Introduction." *Representations* 108, no. 1 (Fall 2008): 1–21.

Billings, Josh. *Josh Billings, His Works, Complete.* New York: G. W. Carleton, 1876.

Bird, John. *Mark Twain and Metaphor.* Columbia: University of Missouri Press, 2007.

Blair, Walter. *Native American Humor.* New York: American Book Company, 1937.

————. "The Popularity of Nineteenth-Century American Humorists." *American Literature* 3, no. 2 (May 1931): 175–94.

Blair, Walter, and Hamlin Hill. *America's Humour.* Oxford University Press, 1978.

Bloom, Harold. *Mark Twain.* New York: Chelsea House Publications, 2008.

Bode, Carl. *The American Lyceum.* Oxford: Oxford University Press, 1956.

Brackman, Jacob. *The Put-on: Modern Fooling and Modern Mistrust.* Chicago: Henry Regnery and Company, 1967.

Brodhead, Richard. *Cultures of Letters: Scenes of Reading and Writing in Nineteenth-Century America.* Chicago: University of Chicago Press, 1993.

Brooks, Van Wyck. *The Flowering of New England.* New York: E. P. Dutton & Co., 1936.

————. *The Ordeal of Mark Twain.* New York: E. P. Dutton & Company, 1920.

Boyesen, Hjalamar Hjorth. "Why We Have No Great Novelists?" *The Forum* 2 (February 1877): 615–22.

Budd, Louis J. *Critical Essays on Mark Twain, 1867–1910.* Boston: G. K. Hall, 1982.

————. *Mark Twain: The Contemporary Reviews.* Cambridge: Cambridge University Press, 1999.

————. *Our Mark Twain: The Making of His Public Personality.* Philadelphia: University of Pennsylvania Press, 1983.

————. "Hiding Out in Public: Mark Twain as Speaker." *Studies in American Fiction* 13 (Autumn 1985): 129–41.

————. "Mark Twain's 'An Encounter with an Interviewer': The Height (or Depth) of Nonsense." *Nineteenth-Century Literature* 55, no. 2 (September 2000): 226–43.

————. "W. D. Howells and Mark Twain Judge Each Other 'Aright'." *American Literary Realism* 38, no. 2 (January 1, 2006): 97–114.

————. "W. D. Howells' Defense of Romance." *PMLA* 67, no. 2 (March 1952): 32–42.

Bush, Harold. "The Mythic Struggle between East and West: Mark Twain's Speech at Whittier's 70th Birthday Celebration and W. D. Howells' 'A Chance Acquaintance'." *American Literary Realism, 1870–1910* 27, no. 2 (Winter 1995): 53–73.

Cady, Edwin. *The Road to Realism: The Early Years 1837–1885 of William Dean Howells*. Syracuse: Syracuse University Press, 1956.

Camfield, Gregg. *The Oxford Companion to Mark Twain*. Oxford: Oxford University Press, 2003.

Cardwell, Guy. "Samuel Clemens' Magical Pseudonym." *The New England Quarterly* 48, no. 2 (January 1875): 175–93.

Caron, James. *Mark Twain: Unsanctified Newspaper Reporter*. Columbia: University of Missouri Press, 2008.

————. "The Blessings of Civilization: Mark Twain's Anti-Imperialism and the Annexation of the Hawai'ian Islands," *The Mark Twain Annual* 6, no. 1 (November 2008): 51–63

————. "The Satirist Who Clowns: Mark Twain's Performance at the Whittier Birthday Celebration." *Texas Studies in Literature and Language* 52, no. 4 (Winter 2010): 434–66.

————. "Why 'Literary Comedians' Mislabels Two Comic Writers, George Derby ('John Phoenix') and Sam Clemens ('Mark Twin')." *Studies in American Humor* 3, no. 22 (2010): 43–68.

Conway, Moncure. *Autobiography and Reminiscences*. Boston: Houghton, Mifflin, and Company, 1904.

Cook, James. *The Arts of Deception: Playing with Fraud in the Age of Barnum*. Cambridge: Harvard University Press. 2001.

Cook, Nancy. "Finding His Mark: Twain's *The Innocents Abroad* as a Subscription Book." In *Reading Books*, edited by Michele Moylan and Lane Stiles, 151–78. Amherst: University of Massachusetts Press, 1996.

Covici, Pascal. *Mark Twain's Humor: The Image of a World*. Dallas: Southern Methodist University Press, 1962.

Cox, James. *Mark Twain: The Fate of Humor*. Princeton: Princeton University Press, 1966.

Cox, S. S. "American Humor." *Harper's Monthly* 50, no. 299 (April 1875): 698, and 50, no. 300 (May 1875).

Csicsila, Joseph. *Canons by Consensus: Critical Trends and American Literature Anthologies*. Tuscaloosa: University of Alabama Press, 2004.

David, Beverly. *Mark Twain and His Illustrators*, Vol. 1, *1869–1875*. Troy, N.Y.: The Whitson Publishing Company, 1986.

David, Beverly R., and Ray Saperstein. "Reading the Illustrations in *A Tramp Abroad*." In *A Tramp Abroad*, edited by Shelley Fisher Fishkin, 20–25. New York: Oxford University Press, 1996.

Davidson, Cathy N., ed. *Reading in America: Literature and Social History*. Baltimore: Johns Hopkins University Press, 1989.

Davis, Janet. *The Circus Age: Culture & Society under the American Big Top*. Chapel Hill: University of North Carolina Press, 2002.

Dent, John C. "America and her Literature." *Temple Bar* 37 (March 1873): 396–406.

DeVoto, Bernard. *Mark Twain's America*. Boston: Houghton Mifflin Company, 1932.

Dickinson, Leon T. "Marketing a Best Seller: Mark Twain's *Innocents Abroad*." *Papers of the Bibliographical Society of America* 41 (1947): 107–22.

———. "Mark Twain's Revisions in Writing *The Innocents Abroad*." *American Literature* 19 (1947): 139–157.

Duberman, Martin. *James Russell Lowell*. Boston: Houghton Mifflin Company, 1966.

Eble, Kenneth Eugene. *Old Clemens and W. D. H.: The Story of a Remarkable Friendship*. Baton Rouge: Louisiana State University Press, 1985.

Eggleston, Edward. "Josiah Gilbert Holland." *The Century Magazine* 23, no. 2 (December 1881): 165.

Emerson, Edward. *Early Years of the Saturday Club, 1855–1870*. Boston: Houghton-Mifflin, 1918.

Emerson, Everett. *Mark Twain: A Literary Life*. Philadelphia: University of Pennsylvania Press, 2000.

Enkvist, N. E. "The Biglow Papers in Nineteenth-Century England." *The New England Quarterly* 26, no. 2 (June 1853): 219–36.

Erenberg, Lewis. *Steppin' Out: New York Nightlife and the Transformation of American Culture, 1890–1930*. Westport, Conn.: Greenwood Press. 1981.

Fatout, Paul. *Mark Twain on the Lecture Circuit*. Bloomington: Indiana University Press, 1960.

———. "Mark Twain's Nom de Plume." *American Literature* 34, no. 1 (March 1962): 1–7.

Ferris, George T. "Mark Twain." *Appleton's Journal* 12, no. 276 (July 4, 1874): 15–18.

Fields, James T. *Biographical Notes and Personal Sketches*. Boston: Houghton, Mifflin and Company, 1881.

Freud, Sigmund. *Jokes and Their Relation to the Unconscious*. The Standard Edition. Edited by James Strachey and Peter Gay. W. W. Norton & Company, 1990 (1905).

Fish, Stanley, "Consequences." In *Against Theory: Literary Studies and the New Pragmatisim*. Edited by W. J. T. Mitchell, 11–30. Chicago, University of Chicago Press, 1982.

Fishkin, Shelley Fisher. *Lighting Out for the Territory: Reflections on Mark Twain and American Culture*. New York: Oxford University Press, 1997.

————. *Was Huck Black? Mark Twain and African-American Voices*. New York: Oxford University Press, USA, 1994.

————, ed. *The Mark Twain Anthology: Great Writers on His Life and Works*. New York: The Library of American, 2010.

Frear, Walter Francis. *Mark Twain and Hawaii*. Chicago: The Lakeside Press, 1947.

French, Bryant Morey. *Mark Twain and the Gilded Age: The Book that Named an Era*. Dallas: Southern Methodist University Press, 1965.

Gardner, Joseph H. "Mark Twain and Dickens." *PMLA* 84, no. 1 (January 1969): 90–101.

Garvey, Ellen Gruber. *Writing with Scissors: American Scrapbooks from the Civil War to the Harlem Renaissance*. New York: Oxford University Press, 2012.

Gilman, Arthur. "Atlantic Dinners and Diners." *Atlantic Monthly* 100, no. 5 (November 1907): 647–57.

Glazener, Nancy. *Reading for Realism: The History of a U.S. Literary Institution, 1850–1910*. Durham: Duke University Press, 1997.

Goldman, Laurel T. "A Different View of the Iron Madonna: William Dean Howells and His Magazine Readers." *The New England Quarterly* 50, no. 4 (December 1, 1977): 563–86.

Goodman, Susan, and Carl Dawson. *William Dean Howells: A Writer's Life*. Berkeley: University of California Press, 2005.

Harris, Susan K. *The Courtship of Olivia Langdon and Mark Twain*. Cambridge: Cambridge University Press, 1997.

Hart, James. *The Popular Book: A History of America's Literary Taste*. Berkeley: University of California Press, 1950.

Harte, Bret Francis. *The Lectures of Bret Harte*. Compiled by Charles Meeker Kozlay. Brooklyn: Charles Meeker Kozlay, 1909.

Higginson, Mary Thacher. *Thomas Wentworth Higginson: The Story of His Life*. Boston: Houghton Mifflin Co., 1914.

Hill, Hamlin. *Mark Twain and Elisha Bliss*. Columbia: University of Missouri Press, 1964.

————. *Mark Twain's Book Sales, 1869–1879*. New York: New York Public Library, 1961.

Holland, Josiah Gilbert. *Every-Day Topics: A Book of Briefs*. 1st ed. New York: Scribner, Armstrong and Company, 1876.

————. *Every-Day Topics, A Book of Briefs*. 2nd ed. New York: Charles Scribner's Sons, 1882.

————. *Plain Talks on Familiar Subjects: A Series of Popular Lectures*. New York: Charles Scribner's Sons, 1865.

————. "The Popular Lecture." *Atlantic Monthly* 15, no. 89 (March 1865): 362–71.

Holmes, Oliver Wendell. "A Visit to an Asylum for Aged and Decayed Punsters" *Atlantic Monthly* 7, no. 39 (January 1861): 113–17.

Horner, Charles Francis. *The Life of James Redpath and the Development of the Modern Lyceum*. New York: Barse & Hopkins, 1926.

Howells, William Dean. *Literary Friends and Acquaintances*. New York: Harpers and Brothers, 1900, 1911.

―――. *My Mark Twain: Reminiscences and Criticisms*. New York: Harper and Brothers, 1910.

―――. *Selected Literary Criticism*. Vol. 1, *1859–1885*. Edited by Ulrich Halfmann. Bloomington: Indiana University Press, 1993.

―――. *W. D. Howells, Selected Letters*. Vol. 2, *1873–1881*. Edited by George Arms and Christoph K. Lohmann. Boston: Twayne Publishers, 1979.

―――. "Literary Boston Thirty Years Ago." *Harper's New Monthly Magazine* 91, no. 546 (November 1895): 865–79.

―――. "The Man of Letters as a Man of Business." *Scribner's Magazine* 14, no. 4 (October 1893): 429–46.

―――. "Mark Twain." *The Century* 24, no. 5 (September 1882): 780–84.

―――. "The New Taste in Theatricals," *Atlantic Monthly* 23, no. 139 (May 1869): 635–44.

―――. "Recollections of an Atlantic Editorship." *Atlantic Monthly* 100, no. 5 (November 1907): 594–606.

Johnson, Paul. *Humorists: From Hogarth to Noel Coward*. New York: Harper, 2010.

Kaplan, Amy. "Imperial Triangles: Mark Twain's Foreign Affairs." *Modern Fiction Studies* 43, no. 1 (1997): 237–48.

Kaplan, Justin. *Mr. Clemens and Mark Twain: A Biography*. New York: Touchstone, 1966.

Kasson, John. *Amusing the Million: Coney Island at the Turn of the Century*. New York: Hill and Wang, 1978.

Kasson, Joy. *Buffalo Bill's West: Celebrity, Memory, and Popular History*. New York: Hill and Wang, 2000.

Kibler, M. Allison. *Rank Ladies: Gender and Cultural Hierarchy in American Vaudeville*. Chapel Hill: University of North Carolina Press, 1999.

Kinch, J. C. B. *Mark Twain's German Critical Reception, 1875–1986: An Annotated Bibliography*. Westport, Conn.: Greenwood Press, 1989.

Knoper, Randall. *Acting Naturally: Mark Twain in the Culture of Performance*. Berkeley: University of California Press, 1995.

Krauth, Leland. *Mark Twain & Company: Six Literary Relations*. Athens: University of Georgia Press, 2003.

―――. *Proper Mark Twain*. Athens: University of Georgia Press, 1999.

Landon, Melville. *Kings of the Platform and Pulpit*. Chicago: The Werner Company, 1895.

Lang, Candace. *Irony/Humor: Critical Paradigms*. Baltimore: Johns Hopkins University Press, 1988.

Lears, T. J. Jackson. *No Place of Grace: Antimodernism and the Transformation of American Culture, 1880–1920*. New York: Pantheon, 1981.

Lee, Judith Yaross. *Twain's Brand: Humor in Contemporary American Culture*. Jackson: University Press of Mississippi, 2012.

Levine, Lawrence. *Highbrow/Lowbrow: The Emergence of Cultural Hierarchy in America*. Berkeley: University of California Press. 1989.

Lorch, Fred. *The Trouble Begins at Eight: Mark Twain's Lecture Tours*. Ames: Iowa State University Press, 1968.

———. "Mark Twain's Lecture Tour of 1868–1869: 'The American Vandal Abroad.'" *American Literature* 26, no. 4 (January 1955): 515–27.

———. "Mark Twain's Public Lectures in England in 1873." *American Literature* 29, no. 3 (November 1957): 297–304.

———. "Mark Twain's 'Sandwich Islands' Lecture and the Failure at Jamestown, New York, in 1869." *American Literature* 25, no. 3 (November 1953): 316–18.

Lowell, James Russell *The Biglow Papers. Second Series*. Boston: Ticknor and Fields, 1867.

———. *Literary Criticism of James Russell Lowell*. Edited by Herbert F. Smith. Lincoln: University of Nebraska Press, 1969.

———. "Nationality in Literature." *North American Review* 69 (July 1849): 196–211.

Lowry, Richard S. *"Littery Man": Mark Twain and Modern Authorship*. New York: Oxford University Press, 1996.

MacDonnell, Kevin. "How Samuel Clemens Found 'Mark Twain' in Carson City, Nevada." *Mark Twain Journal* 50, nos. 1 & 2 (Spring/Fall 2012): 9–47.

Mack, Effie Mona. *Mark Twain in Nevada*. New York: F. C. Schribner's Sons, 1947.

Massey, Gerald. "American Humour." *The North British Review* 33, no. 66 (November 1860): 461–85.

———. "Yankee Humour." *London Quarterly Review*, 122 (January 1867): 111–24.

McCoy, Sharon, "'The Trouble Begins at Eight': Mark Twain, the San Francisco Minstrels, and the Unsettling Legacy of Blackface Minstrelsy." *American Literary Realism* 41, no. 3 (Spring 2009): 232–48.

McMahon, Helen. *Criticism of Fiction: A Study of Trends in the "Atlantic Monthly," 1857–1898*. New York: Bookman Associates, 1952.

Melton, Jeffrey Alan. *Mark Twain, Travel Books, and Tourism: The Tide of a Great Popular Movement*. Tuscaloosa: University Alabama Press, 2002.

Messent, Peter. *Mark Twain and Male Friendship: The Twichell, Howells, and Rogers Friendships*. New York: Oxford University Press, 2009.

———. *The Short Works of Mark Twain: A Critical Study*. Philadelphia: University of Pennsylvania Press, 2001.

Michelson, Bruce. *Literary Wit*. Amherst: University of Massachusetts Press, 2000.

———. *Mark Twain on the Loose: A Comic Writer and the American Self*. Amherst: University of Massachusetts Press, 1995.

Morris, Linda. *Women Vernacular Humorists in Nineteenth-Century America: Ann Stephens, Francis Whitcher, and Marrietta Holley*. New York: Garland Publishing, Inc., 1988.

———. "American Satire: Beginnings through Mark Twain." In *Companion to Satire*. Edited by Ruben Quintero, 377–399. Oxford: Wiley-Blackwell, 2007.

Morris, Roy. *Ambrose Bierce: Alone in Bad Company*. New York: Crown Publishers, Inc. 1995.

Morrow, Patrick D. *Bret Harte: Literary Critic*. Bowling Green: Bowling Green State University Popular Press, 1979.

Mott, Frank Luther. *A History of American Magazines*. Vol. 2, *1850–1865*. Cambridge: Belknap Press of Harvard University Press, 1938.

———. *A History of American Magazines*. Vol. 3, *1865–1885*. Cambridge: Belknap Press of Harvard University Press, 1938.

———. *American Journalism: A History of Newspapers in the United States through 260 years: 1690 to 1950*. Revised. The MacMillan Company, 1950.

———. "'The Galaxy': An Important American Magazine." *The Sewanee Review* 36, no. 1 (January 1928): 86–103.

Moulton, Charles Wells, ed. *Library of Literary Criticism of English and American Authors: 1875–1890*. New York: Henry Malkan, Publisher, 1910.

Nasaw, David. *Going Out: The Rise and Fall of Public Amusements*. Cambridge: Harvard University Press. 1993.

Nickels, Cameron. *Civil War Humor*. Columbia: University of Missouri Press, 2010.

Oliphant, Margaret. "American Books." *Blackwood's Edinburgh Magazine* 110 (October 1871): 422–42.

Oliver, Robert Tarbell. *History of Public Speaking in America*. Boston: Allyn and Bacon, 1965.

Ownby, Ted. *Subduing Satan: Religion, Recreation, and Manhood in the Rural South, 1865–1920*. Chapel Hill: The University of North Carolina Press, 1990.

Paine, Albert Bigelow. *Mark Twain, a Biography; the Personal and Literary Life of Samuel Langhorne Clemens*. 2 Vols. New York: Harper & Brothers, 1912.

———, ed. *Mark Twain's Letters*. 2 vols. New York: Harper and Brothers, 1917.

Parrington, Vernon Louis. *Main Currents in American Thought*. Vol. 2, *1800–1860: The Romantic Revolution in America*. New York: Harcourt, Brace & World, Inc., 1927.

Peckham, Harry Houston. *Josiah Gilbert Holland in Relation to His Times*. Philadelphia: University of Pennsylvania Press, 1940.

Peiss, Kathy. *Cheap Amusements: Working Women and Leisure in Turn-of-the-Century New York*. Philadelphia: Temple University Press. 1986.

Phoenix, John. *Phoenixiana; or, Sketches and Burlesques by John Phoenix*. New York: D. Appleton, 1856; London: Beeton, 1865.

Ponce de Leon, Charles. *Self-Exposure: Human-Interest Journalism and the Emergence of Celebrity in America, 1890–1940*. Chapel Hill: University of North Carolina Press, 2002.

Powers, Ron. *Mark Twain: A Life*. New York: Free Press, 2005.

Plunkett, Mrs. H. M. *Josiah Gilbert Holland*. New York: Charles Scribner's Sons, 1894.

Quirk, Tom, and Gary Scharnhorst, eds. *American Realism and the Canon*. Newark: University of Delaware Press, 1994.

Rasmussen, Kent, ed. *Dear Mark Twain: Letters from His Readers*. Berkeley: University of California Press, 2013.

Ratner, Marc L. "Two Letters of Mark Twain." *Mark Twain Journal* 12 (Spring 1964): 9.

Ray, Angela G. *The Lyceum and Public Culture in the Nineteenth-Century United States*. Ann Arbor: Michigan State University Press, 2005.

Regan, Robert. "The Reprobate Elect in *The Innocents Abroad*." *American Literature* 54 (May 1982): 240–57.

Riley, Franklin, ed. *Publications of the Mississippi Historical Society*. Oxford: Mississippi Historical Society, 1902.

Robertson, John. "Yankeeana." *The Westminster Review* (December 1838).

Rodney, Robert. *Mark Twain International: A Bibliography and Interpretation of His Worldwide Popularity*. Westport, Conn.: Greenwood Press, 1982.

Rogers, Paul. "Artemus Ward and Mark Twain's 'Jumping Frog.'" *Nineteenth-Century Fiction* 28, no. 3 (December 1973): 273–86.

Rourke, Constance. *American Humor: A Study of the National Character*. Reprint, Doubleday Anchor Books, 1931.

Rydell, Robert, and Kroes, Rob. *Buffalo Bill in Bologna: The Americanization of the World, 1869–1922*. Chicago: University of Chicago Press, 2005.

Scharnhorst, Gary. *Bret Harte: Opening the American Literary West*. Norman: University of Oklahoma Press, 2000.

———, ed. *Mark Twain: The Complete Interviews*. Tuscaloosa: University of Alabama Press, 2006.

Seitz, Don C. *Artemus Ward (Charles Farrar Browne): A Biography and Bibliography*. New York: Harper & Brothers, 1919.

Scholnick, Robert. "'The Galaxy' and American Democratic Culture, 1866–1878." *Journal of American Studies* 16, no. 1 (April 1982): 69–80.

Sedgwick, Ellery. *The Atlantic Monthly, 1857–1909: Yankee Humanism at Hightide and Ebb*. Amherst: University of Massachusetts Press, 1994.

Sloane, David E. E. *Mark Twain as a Literary Comedian*. Baton Rouge: Louisiana State University Press, 1979.

Smith, Henry Nash. *Mark Twain: The Development of a Writer*. Cambridge: Belknap Press, 1962.

———. "Mark Twain 'Funniest Man in the World.'" In *The Mythologizing of Mark Twain*. Edited by Sara deSaussure Davis and Philip D. Beidler, 56–60. Tuscaloosa: University of Alabama Press, 1984.

———. "That Hideous Mistake of Poor Clemens's." *Harvard Library Bulletin* 9, no. 2 (1955): 145–80.

Steinbrink, Jeffrey. *Getting to Be Mark Twain*. Berkeley: University of California Press, 1991.

Stephen, Leslie. "American Humour." *The Cornhill Magazine* 13 (January 1866): 28–43.

———. "Humour." *Cornhill* 33 (March 1876): 318–26.

———. "Mr. Lowell's Poems." *Cornhill Magazine* 31 (January 1875): 65–78.

Stephenson, Mimosa. "Humor in *Uncle Tom's Cabin.*" *Studies in American Humor* 3, no. 20 (2009): 4–20.

Stoddard, Charles Warren. *Exits and Entrances: A Book of Essays and Sketches.* Freeport, N.Y.: Books for Libraries Press, 1963; orig., 1903.

Stowe, Harriet Beecher. *Life of Harriet Beecher Stowe.* Houghton, Mifflin and Co., 1891.

Sumida, Stephen. *And the View from the Shore: Literary Traditions of Hawai'i.* Seattle: University of Washington Press, 1991.

Tebbel, John. *A History of Book Publishing in the United States.* 2 vols. New York: R. R. Bowker, 1972.

Tenney, Thomas. "Mark Twain as 'Heathen Chinee.'" *Mark Twain Journal* 38, no. 1 (Spring 2000): 9.

Thomas, Amy M. "'There Is Nothing So Effective as a Personal Canvass'": Revaluing Nineteenth-Century American Subscription Books." *Book History* 1 (1998): 140–55.

Titcomb, Timothy, esq. [Josiah Holland]. *Titcomb's Letters to Young People, Single and Married.* New York: C. Scribner, 1866.

Tompkins, Jane. *Sensational Designs: The Cultural Work of American Fiction, 1790–1860.* New York: Oxford University Press, 1985.

Tryon, W. S. *Parnassus Corner: A Life of James T. Fields, Publisher to the Victorians.* Boston: Houghton Mifflin Company, 1963.

Turner, Arnella. *Victorian Criticism of American Writiers.* San Bernardino, Calif.: The Borgo Press, 1991.

Turner, Matthew Freke. "Artemus Ward and the Humorists of America." *The New Quarterly Magazine* 6 (April 1876): 198–220.

Twain, Mark. *The Adventures of Colonel Sellers.* Edited by Charles Neider. New York: Doubleday & Company, Inc. 1965.

———. *The Adventures of Tom Sawyer.* 1876. New York: Oxford University Press, 1996.

———. *A Tramp Abroad.* 1880. New York: Oxford University Press, 1996.

———. *Autobiography of Mark Twain.* Berkeley: University of California Press, 2010.

———. *The Celebrated Jumping Frog of Calaveras County, and Other Sketches.* New York: C. H. Webb, 1867.

———. *Eye-Openers: Good Things, Immensely Funny Sayings & Stories that will bring a smile upon the gruffest countenance.* London: Hotten, 1871.

———, and Charles Dudley Warner. *The Gilded Age.* 1873. New York: Oxford University Press, 1996.

———. *How to Tell a Story and Others.* 1897. New York: Oxford University Press, 1996.

———. *The Innocents Abroad.* [Publisher's Dummy]. Hartford: The American Publishing Company, 1869.

———. *Is He Dead? A Comedy in Three Acts*. Edited by Shelley Fisher Fiskin. Berkeley: University of California Press, 2006.

———. *Mark Twain at the Buffalo Express*, edited by Joseph B. McCullough and Janice McIntire-Strasburg. DeKalb: Northern Illinois University Press, 1999.

———. *Mark Twain in Eruption*. Edited by Bernard DeVoto. New York: Harper and Brothers, 1940.

———. *Mark Twain Speaking*. Edited by Paul Fatout. Iowa City: University of Iowa Press, 1976.

———. *Mark Twain's Autobiography*. 2 vols. Edited by Albert Bigelow Paine. New York: Harper and Brothers, 1924.

———. *Mark Twain's Autobiography and First Romance*. New York: Sheldon, 1871.

———. *Mark Twain's Letters*. Vol. 1, *1853–1866*. Edited by Kenneth M. Sanderson, Edgar M. Branch, and Michael B. Frank. Berkeley: University of California Press, 1987.

———. *Mark Twain's Letters*. Vol. 2, *1868–78*. ed. Harriet E. Smith, Richard Bucci, and Lin Salamo. Berkeley: University of California Press, 1990.

———. *Mark Twain's Letters*, Vol. 3, *1869*. Edited by Victor Fischer and Michael B. Frank. Berkeley: University of California Press, 1992.

———. *Mark Twain's Letters*. Vol. 4, *1870–1871*. Edited by Victor Fischer, Michael Frank, and Lin Salamo. Berkeley: University of California Press, 1995.

———. *Mark Twain's Letters*. Vol. 5, *1872–1873*. Edited by Lin Salamo and Harriet Elinor Smith. Berkeley: University of California Press, 1997.

———. *Mark Twain's Letters*. Volume 6: *1874–1875*. Edited by Michael B. Frank and Harriet Elinor Smith. Berkeley: University of California Press, 2002.

———. *Mark Twain's Letters to His Publishers, 1867–1894*. Edited by Hamlin Hill. Berkeley: University of California Press, 1967.

———. *Mark Twain's Notebooks & Journals, 1877–1883*. Vol. 2 of *The Mark Twain Papers*. Edited by Frederick Anderson. Berkeley: University of California Press, 1975.

———. *Mark Twain's Own Autobiography: The Chapters from the "North American Review."* Edited by Michael J. Kiskis. Madison: University of Wisconsin Press, 1990.

———. *Mark Twain's Sketches, New and Old*. [Publisher's Dummy]. Hartford: The American Publishing Company, 1875.

———. *Microfilm Edition of Mark Twain's Previously Unpublished Letters*. Prepared by Anh Quynh Bui, Victor Fischer, Michael B. Frank, Robert H. Hirst, Lin Salamo, and Harriet Elinor Smith. 8 vols. Berkeley: The Bancroft Library.

———. *Roughing It*. [Publisher's Dummy]. Hartford: The American Publishing Company, 1872.

———. *Roughing It*. 1872. New York: Oxford University Press, 1997.

———. *Screamers: A Gathering of Scraps of Humour, Delicious Bits, and Short Stories*. London: Hotten, 1871.

————. *Sketches, New and Old*. 1875. New York: Oxford University Press, 1996.

————. *Speeches*. 1910. New York: Oxford University Press, 1996.

————. *The Works of Mark Twain: Early Tales & Sketches*. Vol. 1, *1851–1864*. Berkeley: University of California Press, 1979.

————. "A Literary Nightmare." *Atlantic Monthly* 37, no. 220 (February 1876): 167–70.

————. "A True Story, Repeated Word for Word As I Heard It." *Atlantic Monthly* 34, no. 205 (November 1874): 591–94.

————. "Old Times on the Mississippi. 1." *Atlantic Monthly* 35, no. 207 (January 1875): 69–74.

————, and William Dean Howells. *Mark Twain-Howells Letters: The Correspondence of Samuel L. Clemens & William D. Howells, 1869–1910*. Edited by Henry Nash Smith and William Gibson. Cambridge: Belknap Press of Harvard University Press, 1960.

Vaidhyanathan, Siva. *Copyrights and Copywrongs: The Rise of Intellectual Property and How It Threatens Creativity*. New York: New York University Press, 2001.

Walker, Nancy A., and Zita Dressner, eds. *Redressing the Balance: American Women's Literary Humor from Colonial Times to the 1980s*. Jackson: University Press of Mississippi, 1988.

Walker, Nancy A. *A Very Serious Thing: Women's Humor and American Culture*. Minneapolis: University of Minnesota Press, 1988.

Walker, Phillip. "Mark Twain, Playwright." *Educational Theatre Journal* 8, no. 3 (October 1956): 185–93.

Walsh, William S. *Handy-Book of Literary Curiosities*. Philadelphia: J. B. Lippincott Company, 1893.

Watkins, Mel. *On the Real Side: A History of African American Comedy*. Chicago: Lawrence Hill Books, 1994.

Watson, Aaron. *The Savage Club: A Medley of History, Anecdote, and Remininscence. With a Chapter by Mark Twain*. London: T. Fisher Unwin, 1907.

Weinstein, Michael A. "The Power of Silence and Limits of Discourse at Oliver Wendell Holmes's Breakfast-Table." *The Review of Politics* 67, no. 1 (January 1, 2005): 113–33.

Weisbruch, Robert. *Atlantic Double-Cross: American Literature and British Influence in the Age of Emerson*. Chicago: University of Chicago Press, 1986.

Welland, Dennis. *Mark Twain in England*. Atlantic Highlands, N.J.: Humanities Press, 1978.

Wickberg, Daniel. *The Senses of Humor: Self and Laughter in Modern America*. Ithaca: Cornell University Press, 1998.

Wicker, Elmus. *Banking Panics of the Gilded Age*. New York: Cambridge University Press, 2000.

Williams, Raymond. *Keywords: A Vocabulary of Culture and Society*. London: Oxford University Press, 1976. Rev. ed., 1985.

Wilson, Mark K. "Mr. Clemens and Madame Blanc: Mark Twain's First French Critic." *American Literature* 45, no. 4 (January 1974): 537–66.

Winship, Michael. *American Literary Publishing in the Mid-Nineteenth Century: The Business of Ticknor and Fields*. Cambridge: Cambridge University Press, 1995.

Woodward, Robert H. "A Selection of Harold Frederic's Early Literary Criticism, 1877–1881." *American Literary Realism* 5, no. 1 (Winter 1872): 1–22.

Wuster, Tracy. "'Interrupting a Funeral with a Circus': Mark Twain, Imperial Ambivalence, and Baseball in the Sandwich Islands." In *Mark Twain's Geographical Imagination*, edited by Joseph A. Alvarez, 131–147. Newcastle upon Tyne: Cambridge Scholars Publishing, 2009.

———. "'I wa' n't bawn in de mash to be fool' by trash!': Mark Twain's 'A True Story' and the Culmination of Southern Frontier Humor." In *Southern Frontier Humor: New Approaches*, edited by Ed Piacentino, 131–53. Oxford: University Press of Mississippi, 2013,

Yarborough, Richard. "Strategies of Black Characterization in *Uncle Tom's Cabin* and the Early Afro-American Novel." In *New Essays on Uncle Tom's Cabin*, edited by Eric Sundquist, 47–48. Cambridge: Cambridge University Press, 1986.

Zwick, Jim. *Confronting Imperialism: Essays on Mark Twain and the Anti-Imperialist League* West Conshohocken, Penn.: Infinity Publishing, 2007.

Theses and Dissertations

Da Ponte, Durant. "American Periodical Criticism of Mark Twain, 1869–1917." Ph.D. diss., University of Maryland, 1953.

Hirst, Robert H. "The Making of *The Innocents Abroad: 1867–1872*." Ph.D. diss., University of California, Berkeley, 1975.

Hughes, Jennifer. "Telling Laughter: A Cultural History of American Humor, 1830–1890." Ph.D. diss., Emory University, 2009.

Pascal, John Raymond. *Artemus Ward: The Gentle Humorist*. Master's thesis, Montclair State University, 2008.

Rodney, Robert. "Mark Twain in England: A Study of English Criticism of and Attitude toward Mark Twain: 1867–1940." Ph.D. diss., University of Wisconsin, 1945.

Vogelback, Arthur. "The Literary Reputation of Mark Twain in America, 1869–1885." Ph.D. diss., University of Chicago, 1938.

Periodicals

The Advance
Albany *Evening Journal*
The Aldine
Alta California
American Monthly
The American Review of Reviews

American Socialist
Appleton's Journal
Athenaeum
Atlanta *Constitution*
Atlantic Monthly
Auburn (N.Y.) *Bulletin*
Auburn (N.Y.) *Daily News*
Baltimore *Sun*
Belfast *News-Letter*
Bethlehem (Penn.) *Daily Times*
Birmingham *Daily Post*
Blackwood's Edinburgh Magazine
Boston *Advertiser*
Boston *Evening Journal*
Boston *Evening Transcript*
Boston *Globe*
Boston *Times*
Boston *Transcript*
Broadway: A London Magazine
Brooklyn *Eagle*
Buffalo *Courier*
Buffalo *Express*
Central City (Colo.) *City Register*
The Century
Chamber's Journal
Chicago *Advance*
Chicago *Evening Post*
Chicago *Inter Ocean*
Chicago *Times*
Chicago *Tribune*
Christian Secretary
Christian Union
Cincinnati *Commercial*
Cincinnati *Enquirer*
Cincinnati *Gazette*
Cleveland *Herald*
Cleveland *Leader*
Cleveland *Plain Dealer*
Cornhill Magazine
Daily Arkansas Gazette
Derby (Ireland) *Mercury*
Elmira *Advertiser*

Elmira *Times*
The Era (London)
Exeter (N.H.) *News-Letter*
Flags of Our Union
The Forum
Freeman's Journal and Daily Commercial Advertiser (Dublin, Ireland)
Fun
Galveston *Daily News*
Georgia Weekly Telegraph and Georgia Journal and Messenger (Macon)
The Globe (Atchinson, Kans.)
The Golden Era (San Francisco, Calif.)
The Graphic (London)
The Graphic (New York)
Hampshire *Telegraph* and Sussex *Chronicle*
Harper's Monthly
Harper's Weekly
Hartford *Courant*
Hartford *Times*
Hearth and Home
Huntingdon (Penn.) *Globe*
Illustrated Police News (London)
The Independent
Independent Statesmen (Concord, N.H.)
Iowa City *Republican*
Ipswich *Journal*
Larimie *Sentinel*
Liberal Christian
The Literary World
Little Rock *Republican*
Liverpool *Journal*
Liverpool *Mercury*
Living Age
Lloyd's Illustrated Weekly
Logansport (Ind.) *Sun*
London *Cosmopolitan*
London *Daily News*
London *Era*
London *Evening Echo*
London *Examiner*
London *Figaro*
London *Observer*
London Quarterly Review (London and New York)

London *Spectator*

London *Sportsman*

London *Standard*

Lowell *Daily Citizen*

Macon (Mass.) *Beacon*

Macon (Ga.) *Telegraph and Register*

Maine Farmer

Malden (N.H.) *Messenger*

Manchester (N.H.) *Daily-Union*

Massachusetts Teacher and Journal of Home and School Education

Melbourne *Evening Post*

Milwaukie *Sentinel*

Moore's Rural New Yorker

The Nation

New Jersey *Journal*

New Orleans *Times Picayune (one more?)*

New Quarterly Magazine

New York *Citizen*

New York *Evening Post*

New York *Herald*

New York *Leader*

New York *Sun*

New York *Times*

New York *Tribune*

New York *Weekly*

New York *World*

The Nineteenth Century

North American Review

North British Review

Old and New

Once a Week

Otaga *Witness*

Owyhee *Avalanche* (Ruby City, Ind.)

Pall Mall Gazette (London)

Paterson (N.J.) *Guardian*

Penny Illustrated Paper (London)

Philadelphia *Enquirer*

Philadelphia *Sunday Republic*

The Phrenological Journal of Science and Health

Portland (Maine) *Daily Eastern*

The Press (Philadelphia)

Publisher's Weekly

Puck

Punch (London)

Quincy (Ill.) *Whig*

The Reader (London)

Record of the Year, A Reference Scrap Book

Reese River *Revielle* (Austin, Nev.)

Revue des deux Mondes

Rocky Mountain News

Round Table

Sacramento *Bee*

Sacramento *Daily Union*

San Francisco *Chronicle*

San Francisco *Daily Dramatic Chronicle*

San Francisco *Evening Bulletin*

San Francisco *Morning Call*

Saturday Evening Review (Elmira, N.Y.)

Saturday Review (London)

Scribner's Magazine

Scribner's Monthly

Southern Planter & Farmer

Springfield (Mass.) *Republican*

St. Louis *Globe-Democrat*

St. Louis *Journal*

Syracuse *Standard*

Temple Bar

Times of India

Times of London

Toledo *Commercial*

Transatlantic Magazine

Virginia City *Territorial Enterprise*

Washington (D.C.) *Evening Star*

Washington (D.C.) *Morning Chronicle*

Weekly Miner (Prescott, Ariz.)

Westminster Review

Wisconsin *State Register*

Worcester (Mass.) *Gazette*

Yankton (S.D.) *Press*

Websites

Making of America, Cornell University Library

Home Page: http://ebooks.library.cornell.edu/m/moa

Atlantic Monthly: http://ebooks.library.cornell.edu/a/atla/

Mark Twain Project

    Home Page: http://www.marktwainproject.org/homepage.html

    Letters: http://www.marktwainproject.org/xtf/search?category=letters;rmode
=landing_letters;style=mtp

**Stephen Railton, "Mark Twain in his Times," Department of English,
University of Virginia**

    Home Page: http://etext.virginia.edu/railton/index2.html

    "The Trouble Begins at 8:00": http://etext.virginia.edu/railton/onstage
/lectures.html

    "Marketing Twain": http://etext.virginia.edu/railton/marketin/mrkthp.html

    "The Subscription System": http://etext.virginia.edu/railton/marketin/soldxsub
.html

**Barbara Schmidt, "Mark Twain Quotations, Newspaper Collections, &
Related Resources"**

    Home Page: http://www.twainquotes.com

    "Virginia City Territorial Enterprise, 1862–1868": http://www.twainquotes
.com/teindex.html

    "The Galaxy, 1868–1871": http://www.twainquotes.com/Galaxy/gindex.html

**The Vault at Pfaff's, An Archive of Art and Literature by the Bohemians of
Antebellum New York, Lehigh University**

    Home Page: http://digital.lib.lehigh.edu/pfaffs/sat/press/

Index of Works

Books

Sketches

Lectures

Plays

Speeches

Index of Subjects

See Index of Works for individual entries on Mark Twain's writings and lectures.

African American humor, 26, 37, 43–44, 46, 163–64, 301–2

Alcott, Louisa May, 128

Aldine, The, 169

Aldrich, Lilian, 4, 161, 242, 298–304

Aldrich, Thomas Bailey, 4, 86, 141, 159, 161, 203, 238, 242, 290–91, 311, 323–24, 350, 366, 367

   Story of a Bad Boy (1870), 316

Alta California, 69, 75

American humor, 372

   as concept, 25–27, 104–5, 115, 134, 136, 150–51, 152, 153, 155, 238, 293–94, 297, 356–57, 366–69, 372

   as defined by English critics, 27, 30, 37, 39–41, 44–47, 152, 207, 211, 212, 219–20, 228, 242–48, 283, 357–58

   as specific grouping of humorists, 2–3, 17, 28, 36–37, 48, 50–51, 77, 104–5, 111, 115–18, 122, 149, 155–56, 157, 160, 207–8, 211, 226, 356, 364

American literature, 15, 18, 124, 297

   anxiety about, 28, 29, 31, 37, 129, 160, 164–65, 167–68, 199, 212, 266–67

   commerce and, 6, 12–15, 18–19, 21, 30–31, 88, 118–19, 252–53, 255–56, 259–64, 292, 310–11, 316

   as concept, 3, 6–7, 20, 32, 40–41, 115, 124–25, 126, 128–29, 134, 141–42, 149, 152, 201, 358, 369

   as defined by English critics, 39–41, 45–46, 50, 211, 220, 222–23, 228

studies and canon, 16–9, 20–24, 33, 39, 123–24, 129, 135, 144–45, 309

American Publishing Company, 45, 76, 77–78, 79, 92, 182, 255, 264, 273, 292, 317, 359, 364. *See also* Bliss, Elisha

American Renaissance, the (Vernon Parington), 135–36

Appleton's Journal, 257, 280, 293–97

Aristophanes, 123

Arnold, George, 56–57

Arnold, Matthew, 4

   feud with Clemens, 243, 371

   meeting with Samuel Clemens, 371

   views on humor, 372

   "Word about America, A" (1882), 371

"Artemus Ward" (pseudonym for Charles Farrar Browne), 2, 4, 13–14, 17, 18, 26, 27, 30, 36, 37, 39, 40, 45, 46, 48, 50, 51, 55, 56–57, 58, 59, 62, 64, 79, 103, 105, 111, 115, 150–51, 155, 156, 183, 184, 204, 207–8, 211, 215, 219–20, 234–36, 237, 238, 239, 244–45, 247–48, 249, 293, 306, 319, 367

   Artemus Ward: His Book (1865), 52–53, 54, 213

   "Babes in the Woods," 69

   death of, 63, 69, 105, 187, 198, 211, 214, 243

   as lecturer, 9, 50, 53–54, 68–69, 72–73, 193

   Mark Twain's lecture on, 29–30, 160

   as model for Clemens, 13–14, 17,